COUNTDOWN FOR TEST DAY

DAY 5	DAY 4	DAY 3
☐ Learn and re-learn vocabulary (Part 5)	☐ Work on mathematical weaknesses (Part 6)	☐ Review the test-taking strategies (Parts 3 and 4)

☐ DURING DAYS 5, 4, AND 3, TAKE A FULL-LENGTH PRACTICE EXAM OR TWO

DAY 2	DAY 1	TEST-DAY
☐ Review vocabulary ☐ Review math and verbal strategies ☐ Do timing drills	☐ Wind down—no need to cram ☐ Prepare items for tomorrow morning ☐ Know your test site ☐ Sleep!	☐ Review "Getting Ready: The Night Before and the Day of the Test," in Chapter 2. ☐ Relax—you've studied hard and you'll do well.

TOP 5 TEST-CONQUERING TIPS YOU MUST REMEMBER THE DAY OF THE TEST!

1. **SKIP THE DIRECTIONS AND SKIM THE SECTION.** You already know the directions from your practice in the book, so start the exam by skimming the first section to find the number and types of questions.

2. **ANSWER EASY QUESTIONS FIRST.** The easy questions are worth just as much as the hard ones. Answer the easy ones first, read your favorite passage first, and boost your score. *But be careful:* Skip to the right number on the answer sheet, and check your place on the sheet frequently.

3. **EXPECT THE TRICKIER QUESTIONS TO FALL NEAR THE END OF EACH GROUP.** In most sections of the SAT, the groups of questions are arranged in order of difficulty, with the most difficult and "distractor" questions appearing at the end.

4. **YOU DON'T NEED TO ANSWER EVERY QUESTION, BUT AN EDUCATED GUESS CAN IMPROVE YOUR SCORE.** You can earn a high score on the SAT by answering two-thirds to three-quarters of the questions right. *But remember:* There's no penalty for wrong answers. Eliminate answers or use the skills you've learned in this book to make educated guesses, and you may add points to your score.

5. **FIVE MINUTES BEFORE THE END OF THE TEST, STOP AND DO THE DRILL:** Finish the question you're looking at. Glance through the remaining questions in that section and answer the easy ones as quickly as possible. Skim reading passages for the main idea/point of view, and answer questions as you can (and remember, vocabulary may be easiest here). For math, sentence completion, or analogies, answer 3–5 questions near the beginning of the section.

CHECKLIST: WHAT YOU *MUST* BRING THE DAY OF THE TEST

You *must* bring:

☐ YOUR OFFICIAL ADMISSIONS TICKET
☐ PHOTO IDENTIFICATION
☐ 2 OR 3 SHARPENED #2 PENCILS WITH ERASERS

It's a good idea to *also* bring:

☐ A BATTERY-OPERATED CALCULATOR
☐ A SNACK FOR BREAK
☐ A SWEATER

If you bring this card, too, for last-minute coaching, you'll have to leave it with other checked items outside the test room. However, **don't forget to bring this card back home with you!**

COLLEGE ADMISSIONS/FINANCIAL AID COUNTDOWN
SENIOR YEAR

SEPTEMBER
- ☐ Continue honing list of target schools, on-campus interviews and alumni interviews.
- ☐ Get financial aid information from guidance counselors and give teacher recommendations to appropriate teachers.
- ☐ Register for October ACT, October SAT I, or November SAT I.
- ☐ Begin Early Action/Early Decision steps now. Check deadlines with appropriate schools.

OCTOBER
- ☐ Register for December ACT, December SAT I, or November SAT II.
- ☐ Take October ACT, October SAT I exam.
- ☐ Draw up a master schedule of application and financial aid due dates and mark them on your calendar.
- ☐ Continue working on college essays and personal statements. Follow up on teacher recommendations.
- ☐ Submit Early Decision and Early Action applications.

NOVEMBER
- ☐ Reduce college "long list" to "short list" where applications will be sent.
- ☐ Plan Thanksgiving-break visit to college campuses.
- ☐ Get someone to proofread your applications and essays.
- ☐ Take the November SAT I or SAT II; prepare for December ACT.
- ☐ Send first-quarter grades to colleges; send test scores (include ETS numbers) for ED/EA applications and regular admissions.

DECEMBER
- ☐ Pick up any additional financial aid forms you need and attend financial aid workshops, if possible. Follow up with guidance counselors and teachers on references letters and transcripts.
- ☐ Take ACT, SAT II subject tests this month.
- ☐ Submit all regular applications.
- ☐ If accepted on Early Decision, withdraw remaining applications. If deferred on Early Decision, send follow-up letter to college.

JANUARY
- ☐ Fill out financial aid forms. Finish and mail as soon as possible. NEVER BE LATE WITH THESE!
- ☐ Complete all applications regardless of later deadlines. Photocopy everything. If taking the SAT this month, are RUSH scores required? Ask target colleges if you're not sure. Register for February ACT now.

FEBRUARY
- ☐ ACT administered this month.
- ☐ Call those colleges that didn't confirm receipt of completed applications.

MARCH
- ☐ It's not too late to apply to more schools—get any remaining applications out this month.
- ☐ Actively seek and pursue scholarship opportunities and draw up your financial aid plan to pay for next year's expenses.

APRIL
- ☐ Prepare for May AP exams.
- ☐ Plan "crunch time" visits to campuses and compare financial aid decisions.
- ☐ Return "Wait List" cards as needed. Check admissions offices for Wait-List status.
- ☐ Make your decision! Send the deposit or your place won't be held; for most schools May 1 is the deadline, so do it now.
- ☐ Notify those schools you won't be attending.

MAY
- ☐ Take AP exams where appropriate.
- ☐ Check housing options: When will forms be mailed? Should you check alternative arrangements?
- ☐ Start thinking about summer employment—last chance to build up a "nest egg" for freshman year!

JUNE
- ☐ Write thank-you notes to anyone who helped you: guidance counselors, teachers, admissions counselors, etc.
- ☐ Make sure final high school transcripts are sent to the college you'll attend.

ARCO
master
the SAT*

2001 EDITION

Phil Pine

IDG Books Worldwide, Inc.
An International Data Group Company
Foster City, CA • Chicago, IL • Indianapolis, IN • New York, NY

*SAT is a registered trademark that is the exclusive property of the College Entrance Examination Board. ARCO is a division of IDG Books Worldwide, Inc., and is not affiliated with the College Entrance Examination Board. This book has been prepared by ARCO and the author, who bear sole responsibility for its contents.

REFUND POLICY

ARCO agrees to refund the purchase price of your book if, after using it, your test score shows no increase compared to your test score prior to using the book. To claim your refund, submit a copy of the score confirmation you received before using the book and a copy of the score confirmation after use. Both score confirmation receipts must be issued by the authorized testing service for the exam. You must also enclose your dated sales receipt for the book that indicates purchase between the dates noted on your test score confirmations. Send these three documents along with this book to ARCO REFUND, 10475 Crosspoint Blvd., Indianapolis, IN 46256. A check for the full purchase price of the book, as noted on the sales receipt, will be mailed to you. Please indicate the name to which the check should be made payable and the mailing address.

2001 Edition

IDG Books Worldwide, Inc.
An International Data Group Company
919 E. Hillsdale Boulevard
Suite 400
Foster City, CA 94404

Copyright © 2000 by IDG Books Worldwide, Inc.

All rights reserved including the right of reproduction in whole or in part in any form.

An Arco Book

ARCO and colophon is a registered trademark of IDG Books Worldwide, Inc.

For general information on IDG Books Worldwide's books in the U.S., please call our Consumer Customer Service department at 800-762-2974. For reseller information, including discounts and premium sales, please call our Reseller Customer Service department at 800-434-3422.

Library of Congress information available on request

ISBN: 0-7645-6120-0 (book only)
ISBN: 0-7645-6085-9 (book with CD-ROM)

Manufactured in the United States of America

10 9 8 7 6 5 4 3 2 1

CONTENTS

Introduction xiii
   How this Book Helps You Succeed on the Exam xiii
   How to Use this Book xiv
   You're on Your Way to Success xiv

PART 1   SAT BASICS   1

Chapter 1   Getting Started 3
   How the SAT Is Used for College Admission 3
   When You Should Take the SAT (and SAT II) 4
   How Many Times You Should Take the SAT 4
      Score Choice on the SAT II Subject Tests 5
   How to Register for the SAT 5
   Make an SAT Study Plan 6
      The Complete Course 6
      The Accelerated Course 7
   Working Through Your Study Plan 7
   Summary: What You Need to Know About SAT Preparation 9

Chapter 2   Inside the SAT 11
   Get to Know the SAT Format 11
   Get to Know the SAT Question Types 12
      The SAT Verbal Reasoning Question Types 12
      The SAT Math Questions 13
   The SAT Answer Sheet 13
   How the SAT Is Scored 15
   Some Test-Wise Strategies for SAT Success 15
      Pace Yourself 15
      Question Sets Usually Go from Easiest to Most Difficult—You Should, Too 15
      You Can Set Your Own Speed Limit 16
      It's Smart to Keep Moving 16
      The Easy Answer Isn't Always Best 16
      You Don't Have to Read the Directions 16
      You're Going to Need a Watch 16
   Educated Guessing Will Boost Your Score! 16
      How Educated Guessing Can Help 17
   Getting Ready: The Night Before and the Day of the Test 18
   Summary: Understand the SAT, Conquer Test Anxiety 20

Chapter 3   SAT Questions: A First Look 21
   How the SAT Tests Verbal Reasoning 21
   Understanding Analogies 21
   Understanding Sentence Completions 23
   Understanding Critical Reading 24
   How the SAT Tests Mathematical Reasoning 25

Understanding Multiple-Choice Math 25
Understanding Quantitative Comparisons 28
Understanding Grid-Ins 30
Summary: What You Need to Know About the SAT Question Types 31

PART 2   DIAGNOSING STRENGTHS AND WEAKNESSES   33

Chapter 4   Diagnostic Examination 35
The Exam 37
Answer Key 63
Explanatory Answers 65
Computing Your Scores on the Diagnostic Exam 76
Pinpointing Relative Strengths and Weaknesses on the Diagnostic Exam 77
    Verbal Question Types 77
    Math Question Types 78
    Math Subtopics 78
Measuring Your Progress 79
Conversion Scales for Diagnostic Examination 80
    Self-Evaluation Charts 80

PART 3   SAT VERBAL STRATEGIES   81

Chapter 5   SAT Analogies Strategies 83
A Closer Look at Analogies 83
    SAT Analogy Questions 83
    Question Format 83
Solving Analogies: Strategies That Really Work 84
    Build a Bridge 84
    Plug in the Answer Choices 84
    Get Narrow as Needed 85
    Look for the Test-Makers' Favorite Relationships 86
Solving Analogies: The Best Tips 88
    Use the Analogy Structure to Guess Words You Don't Know 88
    Don't Fear the Flip Flop 90
    When All Else Fails 90
Solving Analogies: The Most Important Warnings 90
    Ignore the Topics of the Word Pairs 90
    Be Prepared to Jump from the Concrete to the Abstract 91
Exercise: Identifying Possible Right Answers 92
    Exercise Answers 92
Summary: What You Need to Know About Analogies 93
Exercises: Analogies 94
    Exercise 1 94
    Exercise 2 97
    Answer Keys and Explanations 99

Chapter 6 SAT Sentence Completions Strategies 101
A Closer Look at Sentence Completions 101
Sentence Completion Questions and Their Format 101
Methods and Strategies for Solving Sentence Completions 102
The Best Strategies for Sentence Completion Questions 104
Summary: What You Need to Know About Sentence Completions 108
Exercises: Sentence Completions 108
Exercise 1 108
Exercise 2 112
Answer Keys and Explanations 114

Chapter 7 SAT Critical Reading Strategies 117
A Closer Look at Critical Reading 117
SAT Reading Passages 117
Question Format 118
Best Strategies for Answering Critical Reading Questions 118
Sample Critical Reading Passage 119
Sample Paired Critical Reading Passages 121
Learn the Most Important Critical Reading Tips 124
Do the Critical Reading Questions Last 124
Answer All of the Questions Before You Move On to the Next Passage 124
Remember that the Questions Follow the Order of the Passage 125
Do Double Passages One Passage at a Time 125
Don't Panic When You Read an Unfamiliar Passage 125
Remember that Everything You Need to Know
   Is Right There in Front of You 125
Start with the Passages that Interest You 125
Use Your Pencil to Highlight Important Information as You Read the Passage 126
Don't Get Bogged Down in the Details 126
Don't Confuse a "True" Answer with a "Correct" Answer 126
Strategies for Answering Specific Question Types 126
Remember that the Answer to a Main Idea Question
   Is Neither Too General nor Too Specific 128
Check the Introductory and Conclusion Paragraphs for the
   Main Idea of the Passage 128
Plug in Choices to Solve Vocabulary-in-Context Questions 128
Find the Right Restatement by First Restating an Author's Phrase
   in Your Own Words 129
Read Between the Lines to Draw Inferences from the Passage 129
Look for Descriptive Words to Clue You In to the
   Tone or Mood of the Passage 130
Summary: What You Need to Know About Critical Reading 130
Exercises: Critical Reading 131
Exercise 1 131
Exercise 2 136
Answer Keys and Explanations 141

PART 4 SAT MATH STRATEGIES .145

Chapter 8 SAT Multiple-Choice Math Strategies ... 147
Why Multiple-Choice Math Is Easier ... 147
    SAT Multiple-Choice Math Questions ... 147
    Question Format ... 148
Solving Multiple-Choice Math Questions ... 148
Know When to Use Your Calculator ... 150
Learn the Most Important Multiple-Choice Math Tips ... 150
    The Question Number Tells You How Hard the Question Is ... 150
    Easy Questions Have Easy Answers—Difficult Questions Don't ... 152
    When Guessing at Hard Questions, You Can Toss Out Easy Answers ... 153
    Questions of Average Difficulty Won't Have Trick Answers ... 153
    It's Smart to Work Backwards ... 153
    When Working Backwards, Always Start from the Middle ... 154
    It's Easier to Work with Numbers than with Letters ... 155
    It's OK to Write in Your Test Booklet, so Use It for Scratch Work ... 156
    Questions in the Three-Statement Format Can Be Solved
        by the Process of Elimination ... 156
    The Area of an Unusual Shape Is Really the Difference Between
        the Areas of Two Regular Figures ... 157
    Using the Measure of an Angle or a Side of Another Shape
        Can Help You Find a Measure You Need ... 158
    A Reality Check Can Help You Eliminate
        Answers that Can't Possibly Be Right ... 158
    Your Eye Is a Good Estimator ... 159
    If Some Questions Always Give You Trouble, Save Them for Last ... 160
Summary: What You Need to Know About SAT Multiple-Choice Math ... 160
Exercises: Multiple-Choice Math ... 161
    Exercise 1 ... 161
    Exercise 2 ... 165
    Answer Keys and Explanations ... 168

Chapter 9 SAT Quantitative Comparisons Strategies ... 171
Get to Know the Quantitative Comparison Format ... 171
    SAT Quantitative Comparison Questions ... 172
    Question Format ... 172
Solving Quantitative Comparisons ... 172
Learn the Most Important Quantitative Comparison Tips ... 175
    Make the Columns Look Alike ... 175
    Eliminate Whatever the Columns Share ... 176
    Plug in Values for X ... 179
The Best Tips ... 180
    Memorize the Answer System ... 180
    Look for Math Shortcuts ... 180
The Most Important Warnings ... 181
    Assume Nothing! ... 181

When There's No Unknown, Don't Guess (D)	183
Summary: What You Need to Know About Quantitative Comparisons	184
Exercises: Quantitative Comparisons	185
Exercise 1	185
Exercise 2	188
Answer Keys and Explanations	190

Chapter 10   SAT Grid-In Strategies   **193**

Why Grid-Ins Are Easier than You Think	193
SAT Grid-In Questions	193
Take a Look at a Grid	193
How to Record Your Answers	194
Guessing on Grid-Ins Can't Hurt You	197
Summary: What You Need to Know About Grid-Ins	197
Exercises: Grid-ins	198
Exercise 1	198
Exercise 2	200
Answer Explanations	202

PART 5   SAT VOCABULARY PREP COURSE   205

Chapter 11   How Word Parts Work   **207**

How Words Are Built	207
The Three Basic Word Parts and How They Work	208
List of Common Word Parts	208
Prefixes	208
Suffixes	212
Roots	214
Summary: What You Need to Know About Word Parts	225
Exercises: Word Parts	226
Exercise 1	226
Exercise 2	226
Exercise 3	227
Exercise 4	227
Exercise 5	227
Answer Keys	228

Chapter 12   The SAT "Top 500" Word List   **229**

The Best Ways to Learn New Words	229
1. Make Some Portable Lists	229
2. Make Flashcards	230
The Top 500 SAT Words	230
The SAT Word List	230
Summary: What You Need to Know About SAT Words	245
Exercises: SAT Words	246
Exercise 1	246
Exercise 2	250
Answer Keys	252

PART 6 SAT MATH REVIEW 253

Chapter 13 SAT Arithmetic Review 255
1. Operations with Integers and Decimals 255
2. Operations with Fractions 258
3. Verbal Problems Involving Fractions 263
4. Variation 267
5. Finding Percents 270
6. Verbal Problems Involving Percent 276
7. Averages 282

Chapter 14 SAT Algebra Review 287
1. Signed Numbers 287
2. Linear Equations 289
3. Exponents 293
4. Quadratic Equations 295
5. Literal Expressions 298
6. Roots and Radicals 300
7. Monomials and Polynomials 304
8. Problem-Solving in Algebra 307
9. Inequalities 312
10. Defined Operation Problems 315

Chapter 15 SAT Geometry Review 317
1. Areas 317
2. Perimeters 318
3. Circles 319
4. Volumes 320
5. Triangles 321
6. Right Triangles 322
7. Parallel Lines 323
8. Polygons 324
9. Similar Polygons 325
10. Coordinate Geometry 326

PART 7 PRACTICE EXAMINATIONS 333

Chapter 16 How to Effectively Use the Practice Examinations 335
How to Simulate Test-Taking Conditions 335
    Find Three Quiet Hours 335
    Work at a Desk and Wear a Watch 336
    Practice on a Weekend Morning 336
How Timing Drills Can Help When You Are Short on Time 336
    Math Timing Drills 336
    Verbal Timing Drills 337
    A Table of Timing Drills 337
Summary: What You Need to Know to Take Practice Tests
    and Do Timing Drills 338

Contents   ix

Chapter 17 Seven Practice Examinations **339**
  Practice Examination 1 .... **339**
    Answer Key 367
    Explanatory Answers 369
  Computing Your Scores on Practice Examination 1 377
  Conversion Scales for Practice Examination 1 378
    Self-Evaluation Charts 378
  Practice Examination 2 .... **379**
    Answer Key 407
    Explanatory Answers 409
  Computing Your Scores on Practice Examination 2 418
  Conversion Scales for Practice Examination 2 419
    Self-Evaluation Charts 419
  Practice Examination 3 .... **421**
    Answer Key 449
    Explanatory Answers 451
  Computing Your Scores on Practice Examination 3 460
  Conversion Scales for Practice Examination 3 461
    Self-Evaluation Charts 461
  Practice Examination 4 .... **463**
    Answer Key 493
    Explanatory Answers 495
  Computing Your Scores on Practice Examination 4 503
  Conversion Scales for Practice Examination 4 504
    Self-Evaluation Charts 504
  Practice Examination 5 .... **505**
    Answer Key 534
    Explanatory Answers 536
  Computing Your Scores on Practice Examination 5 544
  Conversion Scales for Practice Examination 5 545
    Self-Evaluation Charts 545
  Practice Examination 6 .... **547**
    Answer Key 576
    Explanatory Answers 577
  Computing Your Scores on Practice Examination 6 586
  Conversion Scales for Practice Examination 6 587
    Self-Evaluation Charts 587
  Final Practice Examination **589**
    Answer Key 618
    Explanatory Answers 620
  Computing Your Scores on Final Practice Examination 627
  Conversion Scales for Final Practice Examination 628
    Self-Evaluation Charts 628

PART 8 THE PSAT/NMSQT 629

Chapter 18 All About the PSAT/NMSQT 631
How to Register for the PSAT/NMSQT 631
Why the Student Search Survey Is Important 631
How the PSAT Differs from the SAT 632
Get to Know the PSAT Format 632
How to Interpret and Use Your PSAT Scores 633
How Your Selection Index Can Qualify You for National Merit 634
    Becoming a Commended Scholar 634
    Becoming a Semi-Finalist and Applying for Scholarships 635
Summary: What You Need to Know About the PSAT/NMSQT 635

Chapter 19 PSAT/NMSQT Diagnostic Examination 637
PSAT/NMSQT Diagnostic Examination 639
    Answer Key 662
    Explanatory Answers 663
Computing Your Scores on PSAT/NMSQT Diagnostic 670
Pinpointing Relative Strengths and Weaknesses on the PSAT/NMSQT 671
    Verbal Question Types 671
    Math Question Types 672
    Math Subtopics 673
    Writing Skills 674
Measuring Your Progress 675

PART 9 THE SAT AND BEYOND 677

Appendix A Choosing the Right College 679
Which College Is Right for You? 679
Tips on Visiting Campuses 681
Hanging Out with Other Students Online 682
    Usenet Newsgroups 682
    E-mail Mailing Lists 683
    Check Out College and Student Web Pages 683
College Search Sites on the Internet 684

Appendix B Applying to the College of Your Choice 689
When to Apply 689
    About the Early Action and Early Decision Options 689
How to Apply 690
    Filling Out the Application 691
    Other Materials to Submit 691
Applying Online 692
College Admissions Timeline 692

Appendix C Finding Financial Aid 699
Figuring Out Financial Aid 699
    What You Will Pay 699

What's Covered by Financial Aid 699
Sources of Financial Aid 700
    Federal Aid 700
    State Aid 703
    College Funds 703
    Employers 703
    Private Scholarships 703
Finding Financial Aid Online 704
    The Department of Education 704
    The College Board 704
    State Programs 705
    Sallie Mae and Other Lenders 705
    College Web Sites 706
    Third-Party Resources 706
    Scholarship Searches 707
A Step-by-Step Guide to Applying for Financial Aid 707
    Before You Apply: Assembling the Paperwork 707
    Getting and Filling Out Financial Aid Forms 708
    Keeping Track of Paperwork: What to Do with the Student Aid Report 709
    Receiving Your Award Letter 710
Putting It All Together: The Financial Aid Calendar 711

Appendix D   Using Other Study Aids **713**
Online Study Aids 713
Software Study Aids 714
Coaching Courses 715
    Individual Tutoring 715
    School-Based Programs 716
    Local Commercial Courses 716
    National Commercial Courses 717

INTRODUCTION

You hold in your hands the most powerful tool available to triumph over the dreaded SAT. Arco's *Master the SAT* has been designed to be the most comprehensive SAT book on the market. Unlike other sources, *Master the SAT* does far more than offer some practice tests or make a few suggestions. It was prepared by SAT experts who have spent thousands of hours researching the SAT and studying its patterns—and teaching people just like you to get the highest scores on the exam. In this book, they share the most **innovative test-taking techniques** available and give you an opportunity to apply them. The book also includes a review of all of the mathematical concepts ever tested on the SAT as well as a list of the **500 most popular SAT vocabulary words.** And this book won't just boost your test scores—it offers you valuable information and advice for life "after the SAT." You get real information on the college application process, how to search for and secure financial aid, and how to find the best online tools and information for both endeavors.

Master the SAT was not designed to offer "the easiest way" to improve your SAT scores. That's because there really is no "easy way out" when it comes to SAT preparation. But for students who take their preparation seriously, *Master the SAT* can help seriously improve their scores.

HOW THIS BOOK HELPS YOU SUCCEED ON THE EXAM

Whether you have 3 months or 4 weeks to prepare for the exam, *Master the SAT* helps each student **develop a study plan** that is catered to his or her individual needs and time table. These step-by-step plans are easy to follow and remarkably effective. No matter which plan you select, you begin the Arco program by taking a diagnostic exam. The diagnostic does more than give you a testing experience. Easy to use **diagnostic tables** help you track your performance, convert your scores, identify your strengths, and pinpoint your weaknesses. At the end of the diagnostic test, you will know whether you are weak in verbal topics such as analogies, sentence completions or critical reading. And you will know whether multiple choice math, quantitative comparisons, or grid-ins are giving you the most trouble. Moreover, you will receive deeper insight into your vocabulary, arithmetic, geometry, and algebra needs. No other book helps you identify your weaknesses as painlessly and completely. By understanding your testing profile, you can immediately address your weak areas by reading the relevant chapters, learning the relevant techniques, and doing additional **practice exercises.**

When you have completed most of your formal review, it's time to use the book's **7 sample examinations** to gain important practice. Because even if you understand the SAT, you need to practice applying the methods you have learned. *Master the SAT* teaches you how to take these exams under simulated test conditions. And because we made sure that our practice examinations perfectly mirror the content and format of the SAT, there will be no surprises for you on test day. At the end of each practice exam, you not only have access to the correct answers, but also to **comprehensive explanations** of every one of the book's 1,200+ test questions! In such a way, you can really learn from your mistakes. If you lack the time to take full-length practice tests, *Master the SAT* explains how to use **timing drills** to take shorter sections of exams to combat your weaknesses, work on your pacing, and increase your level of confidence.

You'll also find that *Master the SAT* discusses all of the **"big picture issues"** other books ignore. It addresses questions such as: How is the SAT really used for college admission? When should you take the test? How many times should you plan to take the SAT? How do the PSAT and SAT differ from one another? Do all PSAT, SAT, and SAT II scores "count" in the college admissions game? By addressing these questions, *Master the SAT* debunks prevailing myths and helps you put the SAT into its proper perspective. It also serves as your "college guidance counselor," giving you the expert advice you need to truly plan to apply to college. And when you think about it, that's our number one goal here. Our objective is to help you dramatically raise your scores so that you can maximize the likelihood of getting into the college of your choice. And if you use this book properly, we can help you reach that goal.

HOW TO USE THIS BOOK

Master the SAT was designed to be as user friendly as it is complete. Its design is contemporary and its voice is approachable. Each chapter begins with a **bulleted road map** that highlights what will be covered; and each chapter ends with a point-by-point summary that captures the essence of what was discussed. These **chapter summaries** reflect Arco's belief in the value of repetition and reinforcement. You can use these summaries to supplement your understanding of a chapter, and you can revisit them as an effective means of review.

Master the SAT includes several different features to make your preparation easier. **Sample questions** give you instant insight into the SAT question types, and our walk-through answer explanations let you know exactly how you can arrive at the right answers on test-day. In addition, look to the margins for these special test-prep tools:

NOTE
Notes highlight critical information about the SAT format—things you need to know, but that may be overlooked in other test-prep books and programs.

TIP
Tips draw your attention to valuable concepts, advice, and shortcuts for tackling the SAT and PSAT. By following the tips alone, you will learn how to approach different question types, use process of elimination techniques, pace yourself, and guess most effectively.

CAUTION
Where ever you need to be wary of a common pitfall or test-taker trap, you'll find a **Caution**. This information reveals and eliminates the misperceptions and wrong-turns so many people make on the exam.

By taking full advantage of all of the book's features, you will become much more comfortable with the SAT and considerably more confident about your ability to defeat it.

YOU'RE ON YOUR WAY TO SUCCESS

By providing you with the most comprehensive and usable SAT preparation guide, we at Arco hope that you can actually learn to enjoy the SAT process. After all, knowledge is power. And by reading this book, you will become extremely knowledgeable about the SAT. We look forward to helping you raise your SAT scores and improve your college prospects. GOOD LUCK!

Phil Pine
SAT Czar

ACKNOWLEDGMENTS

We would like to thank Judith Berg, Charlotte Klaar, and Andrew Bryan for their invaluable help, insight, and advice in creating this book. Their knowledge and experience provided us with critical feedback during all stages of this book's production, and ultimately helped us create a comprehensive yet concise test-prep resource.

PART 1

SAT Basics

PREVIEW

CHAPTER 1 *Getting Started*

CHAPTER 2 *Inside the SAT*

CHAPTER 3 *SAT Questions: A First Look*

Chapter

1

Getting Started

Getting started to study for the SAT can be intimidating. Our goal is to make that first step as easy as possible. In this chapter, you will learn that the SAT is not an unconquerable beast, but a very coachable test. You will receive expert advice about how the SAT is used for college admission, when you should take the test, and how many times you should take the exam to maximize your scores. Most importantly, this chapter will help you formulate a plan that takes into account how long you have until the SAT and how much time you can devote to SAT study. When you finish reading this chapter, you will know exactly how to prepare for the SAT.

HOW THE SAT IS USED FOR COLLEGE ADMISSION

One explicitly stated purpose of the SAT is to predict how students will perform academically as college freshmen. But the more practical purpose of the SAT is to help college admissions officers make acceptance decisions. When you think about it, admissions officers have a difficult job, particularly when they are asked to compare the academic records of students from different high schools in different parts of the country taking different classes. It's not easy to figure out how one student's GPA in New Mexico correlates with that of another student in Florida. Even though admissions officers can do a good deal of detective work to fairly evaluate candidates, they benefit a great deal from the SAT. The SAT provides a single, standardized means of comparison. After all, virtually every student takes the SAT, and the SAT is the same for everyone. It doesn't matter whether you hail from Maine, Maryland, or Montana.

So the SAT is an important test. But it is not the be-all, end-all. Keep it in perspective! It is only one of several important pieces of the college admissions puzzle. Other factors that weigh heavily into the admission process include GPA, difficulty of course load, level of extracurricular involvement, and the strength of the college application itself.

ROAD MAP

- *Learn how the SAT is used for college admission*
- *Decide when you should take the SAT (and SAT II)*
- *Understand how many times you should take the SAT (and SAT II)*
- *Learn how to register for the SAT*
- *Make an SAT study plan*
- *Measure your progress*

WHEN YOU SHOULD TAKE THE SAT (AND SAT II)

When you decide which schools you're going to apply to, find out if they require the SAT. Most do! Your next step is to determine when they need your SAT scores. Write that date down. That's the one you *really* don't want to miss.

You do have some leeway in choosing your test date. The SAT I (that's the basic test this book addresses) is offered on one Saturday morning in October, November, December, January, March, May, and June. Check the exact dates to see which ones meet your deadlines. To do this, count back six weeks from each deadline, because that's how long it takes ETS to score your test and send out the results.

What if you don't know which schools you want to apply to? Don't panic! Even if you take the exam in December or January of your senior year, you'll probably have plenty of time to send your scores to most schools.

When you plan to take the SAT, there is something even more important than the application deadlines of particular schools. You need to select a test date that works best with your schedule. Ideally, you should allow yourself at least two to three months to use this book to prepare. Many students like to take the test in March of their junior year. That way, they take the SAT several months before final exams, proms, and end of the year distractions. Taking the test in March also gives students early feedback as to how they are scoring. If they are dissatisfied with their scores, there is ample opportunity to take the test again in the spring or following fall. But your schedule might not easily accommodate a March testing. Maybe you're involved in a winter sport or school play that will take too much time away from SAT studying. Maybe you have a family reunion planned over spring break in March. Or maybe you simply prefer to prepare during a different time of year. If that's the case, just pick another date.

If the schools you've decided on also require SAT II (subject tests), here's one good piece of advice: Try to take SAT II tests immediately after you finish the subject(s) in school. For most of you, this means taking the SAT II exams in June. By taking the exam then, you'll save an awful lot of review work. Remember this, too: You have to register for the SAT II tests separately, and you can't take the subject tests on the same day as the SAT. So check the dates, think ahead, and plan it out. It's worth it in the end.

HOW MANY TIMES YOU SHOULD TAKE THE SAT

Different colleges evaluate the SAT I in different ways. Some will take your highest math and verbal scores, even if they were earned on different test days. So if you nailed the math portion in March and the verbal portion in

---

TIP

Are you starting to prepare a little later than you had planned? Don't get upset, it happens. Using the Accelerated Course, you should be able to cover most of the material within a month. You probably won't have much time to practice, but you'll get the most important facts about the test and be able to take a few sample exams. You'll find directions for the Accelerated Course at the end of this chapter.

October, they will combine those two numbers to maximize your overall score. Not bad, huh? But many other schools don't do that. Some pay most attention to your highest combined score on a particular day. Many others will average all of your scores or lend equal weight to all of them.

So what does this mean? It means that you should only take the SAT I when you are truly prepared. Because no matter what each school's individual policy tends to be, every single SAT I score you earn is part of your permanent transcript, so colleges see them all. Ideally, you should try to earn your "goal score" sooner rather than later. For example, a student who hits his objective of 1100 in one sitting certainly has an advantage over a student who needed 5 tries to squeeze out 1100.

There is nothing wrong with taking the SAT two or three times, so long as you are confident that your scores will improve substantially each time. Let's say that you scored a 1080 on your first SAT. If you would have been thrilled to have hit 1100, it's probably not worth taking again. Most colleges look at SAT scores in ranges and will not hold 20 points against you. They understand that scoring 1080 means that you were only one or two questions away from 1100; and no sane admissions officer would deny you admission based on one or two questions! But if you scored 1080 and expected to score closer to 1150 or 1200 based on practice testing, then you should probably retake the exam. In other words, it is of little value to take the SAT multiple times if you expect to earn roughly the same score. But it is worthwhile if you expect to score significantly higher on a second or third try. For more advice about this, see your high guidance counselor.

SCORE CHOICE ON THE SAT II SUBJECT TESTS

The SAT II subject tests work differently. When you register for SAT II exams, you have the option to withhold your scores from college reporting by indicating *score choice* on your registration form. Score choice means that your SAT II scores are sent only to you. So you have the option of deciding whether to send them to colleges. Good deal, huh? This means that if you have a bad day, no one has to know about it, and you can retake the exam at your leisure. Even with the luxury of score choice, you should only take the SAT II subject tests when you are reasonably prepared. To sit for the test before you are ready is a waste of time and money, even if it won't hurt your chances of admission to the college of your choice.

HOW TO REGISTER FOR THE SAT

You should register for the SAT at least six weeks before your testing date. That way you will avoid late registration fees and increase your chances of taking the exam at your first choice testing center. You can register through the mail by completing the SAT registration form found inside the annual SAT Bulletin. Your high school guidance office should have plenty of extra copies of the SAT Bulletin. If you'd like, you can also painlessly register online or by telephone. Mailing addresses, phone numbers, and Web addresses for both of the main SAT registration centers are shown in the following table.

College Board SAT Program Addresses

P.O. Box 6200	P.O. Box 1025
Princeton, NJ 08541-6200	Berkeley, CA 94701
(609) 771-7600	(415) 849-0950
(8:30am to 9:30pm Eastern Time)	(8:15am to 4:30pm Pacific Time)
www.collegeboard.org	www.collegeboard.org

NOTE

You may be wondering how you can possibly wade through all this information in time for the test. Don't be discouraged! We wrote this book knowing that some of you would be on very short schedules. The information in this section will help you construct a study plan that works for you—one that will help you boost your score no matter how short your timeline may be. Remember though, that practice and targeted study are essential elements of that score-boosting, so invest as much time as possible in your SAT preparation.

MAKE AN SAT STUDY PLAN

As with almost any form of learning, preparing for the SAT is an investment of time. The more you have, the better your chances of boosting your score significantly. Next, we'll walk you through two different study plans, each tailored to a specific amount of preparation time. Find the plan that fits your circumstances and adapt it to your needs.

Regardless of how much time you have before the actual exam, your first step should be to take the **Diagnostic Examination in Part 2** of this book. After you score it, compute your category percentages to assess your relative strengths and weaknesses. Hang on to the scoring sheet so you know where to get started.

If you are using this book to get early preparation for the PSAT, you should take the **PSAT Diagnostic Examination in Part 8.** This diagnostic serves a similar purpose to the diagnostic exam in Part 2. After you score it, compute your PSAT category percentages to assess your relative strengths and weaknesses.

THE COMPLETE COURSE

If you have three or more months to prepare, you should congratulate yourself! This will give you sufficient time to familiarize yourself with the test, learn critical strategies, review vocabulary and mathematical fundamentals, and take full-length practice tests.

You'll get the most out of your SAT preparation if you read this whole book from cover to cover. No, you can't do that in a weekend! But if you have two or three months, you'll have enough time to read and reread at your own pace and work through all of the examples, exercises, and practice exams without breaking a sweat.

THE ACCELERATED COURSE

If you have one month or less to prepare for the SAT, you shouldn't even attempt to read this book from cover to cover. Or if you have several months, but can't devote too much time to SAT study, you should opt for the Accelerated Course. Take the diagnostic exam. Read Chapter 2 to ensure that you understand the format, structure, and scoring of the SAT. Then visit the chapters that cover material that is most problematic for you.

WORKING THROUGH YOUR STUDY PLAN

It does seem like you're on a treadmill sometimes, doesn't it? Question after question after question—are you really getting anywhere? Is all of this studying really working?

The way to find out is to monitor your progress throughout the preparation period, whether it's three months or four weeks. By taking a diagnostic examination at the beginning, you'll establish your "home base" of skills, and you'll be able to craft the study plan that's right for you. Then, you can either start to read the entire book (if you are taking the Complete Course) or go directly to the chapters that address your weaknesses (if you are taking the Accelerated Course). At the end of each chapter, complete the exercises and compare your percentages to your original diagnostic percentages. How have you improved? Where do you still need work? Even if you haven't reached your ultimate performance goal, are you at least applying new test-taking methods?

When you are approximately one-third of the way through your course of study—this can be after 10 days or a month—it's time to take one of the practice examinations in Part 7. Compare your overall scores with your original diagnostic scores. Then compare subcategories. Hopefully you're doing better. But if you're not, don't panic. At this stage in the game, it's not unusual to score roughly the same as you did at the beginning. What's more important than *what* you score is *how* you take the test. Are you really using the test-taking strategies to which you've been introduced? If you aren't, it's time to go back and either reread chapters or their summaries. Then continue your review. Read more chapters, do exercises, and compare your percentages with your diagnostic percentages.

After you have reviewed the vast majority of the chapters (under the Complete Course) or all of your weaknesses (under the Accelerated Course), it's time to take another practice examination. By now you should be seeing some real score improvement. If your weaknesses continue to plague you, revisit problematic material. But for the most part, this last phase of study should involve *less learning* and *more practice*. Take more practice examinations! By now, you probably understand how to take the SAT. What you need is more practice actually taking the test under simulated test-day conditions.

TIP
Here's an important point: You don't have to go through the parts in order. You might want to start with the kind of question you find most difficult, such as critical reading or quantitative comparisons. Then you can move to the next most difficult and so on down the line, saving your best stuff for last. If you take the Accelerated Course, you should definitely take this approach.

TIP
Based on the results of your SAT Diagnostic Test, rank the six question types in order of priority, from the one on which you need the greatest improvement to the one on which you currently perform the best.

When you take additional practice exams, be sure you do so in a near-test environment (see the beginning of Part 7 for ways to do this). Keep analyzing your scores to ensure that all of this practice is working. Determine which areas need additional work. Now is probably the perfect time to take timing drills. (For more information about timing drills, see the beginning of Part 7.) Because you have already reviewed the chapters, work on your weaknesses by doing timing drills.

One last word of advice: No matter what study plan you select, you should probably take one full, timed SAT the week before the SAT. This will get you ready for the big day. But don't take that test the day before the SAT. That's a time when you should be relaxing, not cramming.

For more information about what to do the day before the SAT, see "Some Test-Wise Strategies for SAT Success," in Chapter 2.

Here's a list that highlights your goals for forming and following an SAT study plan:

Working Through Your Study Plan: The Key Points

- Get started by taking the diagnostic test in Part 2 (or PSAT Diagnostic in Part 8).
- Compute your category percentages to assess your relative strengths and weaknesses.
- If you have sufficient time and initiative, take the Complete Course. Do the book from cover to cover. You can read the book in order, or you can start with the kind of question you find most difficult. At the end of each chapter, do exercises and assess your performance.
- If you have one month or less, follow the Accelerated Course. Read Chapter 2 to familiarize yourself with the SAT. Then visit the chapters that cover material that is most problematic for you. At the end of each chapter, do exercises and assess your performance.
- When you are one-third of the way through your preparation, take a practice test. Compare your scores with your original results. Make sure you are applying new test-taking strategies.
- Revisit problematic chapters and chapter summaries. Then read additional chapters, do exercises, and compare your percentages with your original category percentages.
- After you have reviewed all of the chapters (the Complete Course) or all of your weaknesses (the Accelerated Course), take another practice examination.
- During the last phase of your review, take as many complete practice tests as possible under simulated test conditions. For more information about simulating test conditions, see Part 7.
- If you continue to have weak areas, take timing drills to pinpoint your study. For more information about timing drills, see Part 7.

- The week before the SAT: Take a full exam to make sure you're ready. Don't take this exam the night before when you should be relaxing!

Summary: What You Need to Know About SAT Preparation

- Don't be intimidated! The SAT is a coachable test that you can prepare for!
- Although the SAT is the most important test you'll take in high school, it is not the most important factor in getting into college. So study seriously, but keep it in perspective.
- You should only take the SAT when you are adequately prepared because every score you earn is part of your transcript.
- Most people take the SAT more than once. There is nothing wrong with taking the exam a couple of times, as long as you are confident that your scores will improve. To take the test multiple times and earn roughly the same score is a waste of time, money, and energy.
- Register for the SAT at least six weeks before the test date to ensure that you can take the test at a familiar test center.
- Make certain that you take the SAT early enough to fulfill the application requirements of the colleges you're interested in.
- Make an SAT study plan! Depending upon your time and initiative, select either the Complete Course or the Accelerated Course. For more information about these study plans, revisit the last section of this chapter.

TIP
Don't forget that the anxiety you feel is completely natural! If you are well prepared for the test, anxiety can be a great aid to you on test day! But too much anxiety can really hurt your performance. That's why you're smart to be using this book; the strategies you'll learn and the practice and in-depth reviews you'll work through will boost your confidence on test day. When you're prepared for the test, you have much less to feel anxious about.

Chapter

2

Inside the SAT

When you boil it down, the SAT is a standardized exam. You've been taking standardized exams for years. Why is the SAT different? SAT scores are used by many colleges and universities to help them make their admissions decisions. That's a big difference. Because the SAT is such an important test, you should be as familiar with the exam as possible. In this chapter, you will learn more about the SAT format, its question types, and how the exam is scored. You will also learn some pacing, guessing, and test-taking strategies that can really boost your confidence—and your score!

GET TO KNOW THE SAT FORMAT

The SAT has seven sections. This seems like a lot, but there are really just three math sections and three verbal sections, plus a "wild card" section. The wild card can be another math section or another verbal section. This is where ETS—the company that writes the SAT—tries out questions that might be used on future tests. Even though the wild card section doesn't count toward your score, you won't know which section it is. ETS does this on purpose. It knows that if you knew which section did not count, you probably wouldn't try your hardest on it! So you'll have to do your best on all seven SAT sections.

Each section is timed to take either 15 or 30 minutes. The whole test will take you three hours to complete. This chart will give you a good idea of what to expect. Note, though, that the order of the sections can vary. In other words, don't memorize the chart, just use it as a guide.

Format of a Typical SAT I

Section #/Content	# of Questions	Time
(1) Verbal Reasoning	30 or 31	30 min.
Sentence Completions	9	
Analogies	6	
Critical Reading	15	
(2) Mathematical Reasoning	25	30 min.
Standard Multiple-Choice Mathematics		

ROAD MAP

- *Get to know the SAT format*
- *Get to know the SAT question types*
- *Take a look at the SAT answer sheet*
- *Understand how the SAT is scored*
- *Educated guessing will boost your score!*
- *Get ready for test day*

TIP

The questions in a set usually go from easiest to hardest. Try to go through the easy ones quickly.

Format of a Typical SAT I (continued)

Section #/Content		# of Questions	Time
(3)	Verbal Reasoning	35 or 36	30 min.
	Sentence Completions	10	
	Analogies	13	
	Critical Reading	12	
(4)	Mathematical Reasoning	25	30 min.
	Quantitative Comparisons	15	
	Grid-Ins	10	
(5)	"Wild Card" Section	varies	30 min.
(6)	Verbal Reasoning	12 or 13	15 min.
	Critical Reading		
(7)	Mathematical Reasoning	10	15 min.
	Standard Multiple-Choice Mathematics		

TIP

On the SAT, all questions count the same. You won't get more points for answering a really difficult math question than you get for answering a very simple analogy. Remember that when you're moving through the test. The more time you spend wrestling with the answer to one "stumper," the less time you have to whip through several easier questions.

GET TO KNOW THE SAT QUESTION TYPES

The question types in the SAT don't cover a wide variety of topics. Actually, the field is pretty limited—no science, no foreign languages, no social studies. You'll just find questions testing verbal and math skills—skills you've been working on since you were six years old.

Most of the questions are multiple-choice questions. That's good; it means that you have four or five answers to choose from—and the right answer is always given to you! Only 10 questions in one of the math sections ask for "student-produced" answers. This means you need to do the calculations and then fill in bubbles to show your answers. (More about the bubbles later!) In this section of the chapter, we take a closer look at the individual question types you'll encounter in each of these two SAT subject areas.

The information in this chapter is just an overview of the SAT and its contents. In Chapter 3, "SAT Questions: A First Look," you'll see examples of the SAT question types and learn how to tackle them.

THE SAT VERBAL REASONING QUESTION TYPES

All right, so what exactly will you find in a "verbal reasoning" section? Well, this section has questions that test reasoning, vocabulary, and reading comprehension. The three types of questions are analogies, sentence completions, and critical reading. Briefly, here's what these question types involve:

- **Analogies** present a pair of words that have some logical relationship. Then the choices present other pairs of words. You have to choose the pair that has the same kind of relationship as the first pair.
- **Sentence completion** questions ask you to choose a word or words that fill in the blanks in a given sentence. They test how well you can use context clues and word meanings to complete a sentence.
- **Critical reading** questions relate to a passage that is provided for you to read. The passage can be about almost anything, and the questions after it test how well you understood the passage and the information in it.

THE SAT MATH QUESTIONS

Now, let's talk a minute about the math questions. The questions in this section are about problem solving in arithmetic, elementary algebra, and geometry. Here are some details about the three kinds of questions you'll find—standard multiple-choice, quantitative comparison, and grid-ins:

- **Standard multiple-choice questions** give you a problem in arithmetic, algebra, or geometry. Then you choose the correct answer from the five choices.
- **Quantitative comparison questions** test your skills in comparing information and in estimating. You'll see two quantities, one in Column A and one in Column B. Your job is to compare the two quantities and decide if one is greater than the other, if they are equal, or if no comparison is possible.
- **Grid-Ins** do not give you answer choices. You have to compute the answer and then use the bubbles on the answer sheet to fill in your solution.

THE SAT ANSWER SHEET

This is where we get to the bubbles. When you get the test booklet, you'll also get a separate sheet on which you'll mark your answers.

For each multiple-choice question, you'll see a corresponding set of answer ovals (these are the bubbles!). The ovals are labeled from A to D or E, depending on the number of answer choices given for the question. Here's the main point to remember: Answer sheets are read by machines—and machines can't think. That means it's up to you to make sure you're in the right place on the answer sheet every time you record an answer. The machine won't know if you really meant Question 25 when you marked the space for Question 26. Another thing to remember: Don't be a wimp with that pencil. Fill in your chosen answer ovals completely and boldly so there can be no mistake about which one you chose.

TIP

Make sure you're in the right place! Always check to see that the answer space you fill in corresponds to the question you are answering.

Take a look at this sample answer sheet. You can just imagine what the machine will do with it.

In the answer-sheet example we show you here, the only answers that will be registered correctly are 29 and 35. Question 30 isn't filled in completely, and Question 31 isn't dark enough, so the machine might miss them. Question 32 is a total mess—will the machine choose A, B, or C?

Since Question 33 has two ovals filled in, they cancel each other out and this is registered as an omitted question. There's no penalty, but there's no credit either. The same will happen with Question 34; no answer, no credit.

Let's move on to the student-produced responses. You'll still be filling in ovals, but they will look a little different from the multiple-choice ovals. Here's a sample of the special grid you will use.

TIP

You are allowed to use a four-function, battery-powered, scientific or graphing calculator for the math sections of the SAT. You may not use the following: hand-held mini-computers, laptop computers, pocket organizers, calculators that print or "talk," or calculators with letters on the keyboard.

← boxes to write your numerical answer
← fraction lines—use at most one per answer
← decimal points—use at most one per answer

At the top of the grid, you'll write in the actual numerical answer. The slashes are used for answers with fractions. If you need one of these fraction lines in your answer, darken one of the ovals. The ovals with the dots are for answers with decimal points—use these ovals just as you do the fraction line ovals. Then you use the number ovals to represent the actual numbers in your answer. Chapter 10 has more details about these special grids, and you'll be able to see some samples, too.

HOW THE SAT IS SCORED

OK, you've filled in all your ovals, the three hours are up (and not a moment too soon), and you turn in your answer sheet. What next? Off it goes to the machines at ETS. The machines scan the sheets in seconds (aren't you glad you were careful with those ovals?) and calculate a score. In this calculation, you get one point for each correct answer, and you lose one-quarter of a point for each incorrect answer to a standard five-choice question. (For incorrect answers to four-choice quantitative comparison questions, you lose one-third of a point; incorrect answers to grid-in questions have no effect on your score.) The result of these calculations is your raw score, which is then converted to a scaled score between 200 and 800. This is the score that is reported to you and to the schools you have designated.

> **NOTE**
> Because the SAT can vary in format, scaled scores allow the test-maker to account for differences from one version of the SAT to another. Using scaled scores ensures that a score of 500 on one SAT is equivalent to 500 on another.

SOME TEST-WISE STRATEGIES FOR SAT SUCCESS

What makes some people better test-takers than others? The secret isn't just knowing the subject, it's knowing specific test-taking strategies that can add up to extra points. This means psyching out the test, knowing how the test-makers think and what they're looking for, and using this knowledge to your advantage. Smart test-takers know how to use pacing and guessing to add points to their score.

PACE YOURSELF

As any comedian will tell you, it's all in the timing. For example, the scored sections of the SAT contain 78 verbal questions to be answered in 75 minutes. That means that you have nearly a minute to answer each question. But smart test-takers know that that's not the best way to use their time. If you use less than a minute to answer the easier questions, you'll have extra time to help you answer the more difficult ones. That's why learning to pace yourself is so important. Here are some pacing guidelines you need to remember:

QUESTION SETS USUALLY GO FROM EASIEST TO MOST DIFFICULT—YOU SHOULD, TOO

Except for the critical reading questions, SAT questions follow this pattern. So work your way through the earlier, easier questions as quickly as you can. That way you'll have more time for the later, more difficult ones.

YOU CAN SET YOUR OWN SPEED LIMIT

All right, how will you know what your speed limit is? Use the practice tests to check your timing and see how it affects your answers. If you've answered most of the questions in the time limit, but also have a lot of incorrect answers, better slow down. On the other hand, if you are very accurate in your answers but aren't answering every question in a section, you can probably pick up the pace a bit.

IT'S SMART TO KEEP MOVING

It's hard to let go, but sometimes you have to. Don't spend too much time on any one question before you've tried all the questions in a section. There may be questions later on in the test that you can answer easily, and you don't want to lose points just because you didn't get to them.

THE EASY ANSWER ISN'T ALWAYS BEST

Are you at the end of a section? Remember, that's where you'll find the hardest questions, which means that the answers are more complex. Look carefully at the choices and really think about what the question is asking.

YOU DON'T HAVE TO READ THE DIRECTIONS

What? Yes, you read it correctly the first time—you don't have to read the directions. Look, by the time you actually sit down to take the SAT, you've read this book, you've taken all the practice tests you could find, and you've read enough SAT directions to fill a library. So when the exam clock starts ticking, don't waste time rereading directions you already know. Instead, go directly to Question 1.

YOU'RE GOING TO NEED A WATCH

If you're going to pace yourself, you need to keep track of the time—and what if there is no clock in your room or if the only clock is out of your line of vision? That's why it's a good idea to bring a watch to the test. A word of warning: Don't use a watch alarm or your watch will end up on the proctor's desk.

EDUCATED GUESSING WILL BOOST YOUR SCORE!

The fractional deduction for wrong answers makes random guessing a wash—statistically speaking, you're unlikely to change your score. This means that if you come to a question that you have absolutely no idea how to answer, you're probably better off skipping it and moving on, rather than just choosing an answer at random.

Although random guessing won't help you, anything better than random guessing will. On most questions, you should be able to guess better than randomly by using common sense and process of elimination techniques that are developed throughout this book. Even if you aren't certain which answer is correct, you might be certain that one or more of the answer choices is definitely *wrong*. If you can knock out one choice out of five, you have a 25 percent chance of guessing correctly. If you can knock out two choices, the odds go up to $33\frac{1}{3}$ percent. If you can knock out three, you have a 50/50 chance of guessing the right answer. With odds like this, it makes sense to guess, especially when you realize that a single correct guess can raise your scaled score as much as 10 points.

HOW EDUCATED GUESSING CAN HELP

Let's take a sample situation to demonstrate the effectiveness of educated guessing. Let's say that on the entire SAT there were 40 questions you were unsure of. Now we know what you're thinking. Forty questions seems like an awful lot of questions with which to have difficulty. But think about it: If you answered every other one of the SAT's 138 questions correctly, you'd already be scoring over 1200! So to have trouble with 40 questions is not only possible, it's likely.

Now remember how the SAT is scored. Every question you answer correctly is worth one raw score point, which corresponds to roughly 10 scaled score points. For every question you leave blank, you gain nothing and lose nothing. And for every incorrect answer you mark down, you lose $\frac{1}{4}$ of a raw score point, which corresponds to approximately 2.5 scaled score points. When students first learn this, they usually get nervous about guessing. After all, who wants to lose points on questions they're unsure of? However, a more careful look demonstrates the exact opposite: Educated guessing can dramatically improve your score even if you make many incorrect guesses along the way.

Let's get back to those 40 difficult questions. You basically have three choices: You can leave them all blank in fear of losing points; you can guess randomly; or you can use process of elimination techniques to make educated guesses. Let's examine the outcome of each approach:

The Fearful Student takes the first approach and leaves all 40 questions blank. For his effort, he receives no points and loses no points. So he breaks even.

The Random Guesser picks answers for random reasons. Maybe he picks choice (C) for every one. Or maybe he fills in his answer sheet in such a way as to make a visually appealing pattern. What will happen to the Random Guesser? Well, statistically speaking, he will answer one out of every five questions correctly, since most questions have five answer choices. That means he will answer 8 questions correctly out of 40 ($\frac{1}{5}$ of 40). For his effort,

CAUTION
Don't spin your wheels. Don't spend too much time on any one question. Give it some thought, take your best shot, and move along.

the Random Guesser will pick up 80 points for the questions he got right (8 × 10pts) and lose 80 points for the 32 questions he got wrong (32 × 2.5pts). So the Random Guesser ends up in the exact same position as the Fearful Student.

The Smart Test-Taker will take advantage of what he does know to make educated guesses. You will become the Smart Test-Taker! You will use process of elimination techniques that we develop in this book. On virtually every question, you will eliminate one, two, or three poor choices. Let's say that you answer 16 questions correctly out of the 40 you're unsure of. Even though that's a pretty low percentage, you will do considerably better than the Fearful Student or the Random Guesser. For the 16 questions you answer correctly, you will receive 160 points (16 × 10pts), and for the 24 questions you answer incorrectly, you will lose 60 points (24 × 2.5pts). So by doing nothing more than answering questions you've already thought about, you pick up 100 scaled score points. Here's a table that might make more sense of these numbers:

Guessing on 40 Difficult Questions

	#Right	#Wrong	#Blank	Total Pts.
The Fearful Student	0	0	40	0 pts
The Random Guesser	8 (+80)	32 (–80)	0	0 pts
The Smart Test-Taker	16 (+160)	24 (–60)	0	100 pts

Obviously, the better you get at eliminating implausible choices, the more points you will pick up from educated guessing. But no matter what, if you have time to read through a question and eliminate at least one choice, it is always to your benefit to guess. Don't worry about the fact that you will probably get the question wrong, because you don't need to guess correctly on too many questions to gain points. As long as you are guessing better than randomly, you will do considerably better.

GETTING READY: THE NIGHT BEFORE AND THE DAY OF THE TEST

If you follow the guidelines in this book, you will be extremely well prepared for the SAT. You will know the format inside and out; you will know how to approach every type of question; you will have worked hard to strengthen your weak areas; and you will have taken multiple practice tests under simulated testing conditions. The last 24 hours before the SAT is not the time to cram—it's actually the time to relax. Remember that the SAT is primarily a test of how you think, not what you know. So last minute cramming can be more confusing than illuminating.

That having been said, there are plenty of steps you can take over the final 24 hours to get ready. For one thing, don't do anything too stressful. On the night before the big day, find a diversion to keep yourself from obsessing about the SAT. Maybe stay home and watch some of your favorite television shows. Or go out to an early movie. Or talk for hours and hours on the phone about a subject other than the SAT. Do whatever is best for you. Just make sure you get plenty of sleep.

You should also lay out the following items before you go to bed:

- **Registration ticket:** Unless you are taking the test as a "standby" tester, you should have received one of these in the mail.
- **Identification:** A driver's license is preferable, but anything with a picture will do.
- **Pencils:** Make sure you bring at least three #2 pencils; those are the only pencils that the machines can read.
- **Calculator:** Bring the calculator that you're most comfortable with. Don't pack a scientific or graphing calculator if you're unfamiliar with how it works. And don't take any calculator that beeps, produces a paper tape, makes any noise at all, or that is a part of a computer or other device. You won't be allowed to use such a calculator on the SAT.
- **Layered clothing:** You never know what the test-taking temperature will be. By dressing in layers, you can adapt to extreme heat or cold.
- **Wristwatch:** Your classroom should have an operational clock, but if it doesn't, you want to come prepared. Again, don't wear a watch that beeps, unless you can turn off the alarm function. You won't be allowed to wear a noise-making watch during the exam.
- **Snack:** You're not allowed to eat during the test administration in your test room, but you are given a 5- to 10-minute break after Section 2. So be armed with a fortifying snack that you can eat quickly out in the hallway.

When you awake on test day, make sure you allow enough time to comfortably arrive at the test site by 8:00 am. (If you're uncertain how long the trip from your home to the site will take, practice the drive ahead of time.) Take a shower to wake up and then eat a sensible breakfast. If you are a person who usually eats breakfast, you should probably eat your customary meal. If you don't usually eat breakfast, don't gorge yourself on test-day, because it will be a shock to your system. Eat something light (like a granola bar and a piece of fruit) and pack that snack.

Summary: Understand the SAT, Conquer Test Anxiety

- Familiarize yourself with the SAT's seven sections. Knowing the test format will relieve test anxiety because you will know exactly what to expect on test day.

- Within each question set (except critical reading), questions are arranged from easiest to most difficult. So where a question is placed provides an instant indication of how difficult it is.

- Remember that all SAT questions count the same, so you receive the same number of points for an easy question as for a more difficult one. So nail the easier questions—they're a good source of points!

- Make sure that you fill in the answer bubbles cleanly and completely. Otherwise, the machine won't give you credit for your answers.

- Remember that random guessing will have no effect on your score, but educated guessing will boost your score. So if you've had time to read through a question and eliminate at least one choice, guess!

- It pays to pace yourself and move through the test relatively quickly. But you can get a very good score even if you don't answer every question. As a matter of fact, a raw score of 36 out of 78 on verbal—or 27 out of 60 on math—is equivalent to a 500!

- Relax the day before the SAT. Before you go to bed the night before the exam, however, check through the list of things you need to take with you to the test site. Make sure your calculator has fresh batteries, eat breakfast, and head for the site.

- Remember—if you're working through this book, you're giving yourself the best preparation available for succeeding on the SAT. Let your preparation give you the confidence you need to be calm and focused during the exam.

Chapter 3

SAT Questions: A First Look

As you learned in Chapter 2, there are six primary types of questions that are used on the SAT exam. In this chapter, we will take an in-depth look at each of these question types. You will be able to take a few sample problems from each category to further familiarize yourself with the questions. This way, you will be fully prepared for all of the question types when you're taking the actual exam.

HOW THE SAT TESTS VERBAL REASONING

The SAT exam determines your verbal reasoning skills in three ways. You will be tested using the following types of questions:

1. analogies
2. sentence completions
3. critical reading

The scored sections of the test will contain a total of 19 analogies, 19 sentence completions, and 40 critical reading questions. Even if you're not a math whiz, you can see that critical reading accounts for more than half of your total verbal score. The following sections discuss each of the verbal reasoning question types, to give you a clear idea of what you can expect on the verbal sections of the SAT.

UNDERSTANDING ANALOGIES

SAT analogy questions ask you to match up pairs of words that are related in the same way. Each question starts with a word pair. You have to pick the pair of words from five answer choices that has the same logical relationship.

The directions for SAT analogy questions look like this:

> **Directions:** Each question below consists of a related pair of words or phrases, followed by five pairs of words or phrases labeled A through E. Select the pair that *best* expresses a relationship similar to that expressed in the original pair.

ROAD MAP

- *Learn how the SAT tests verbal reasoning*
- *Understand analogies*
- *Understand sentence completions*
- *Understand critical reading*
- *Learn how the SAT tests mathematical reasoning*
- *Understand multiple-choice math*
- *Understand quantitative comparisons*
- *Understand grid-ins*

NOTE

When you've finished this chapter, you can rest assured that you have learned about *every* type of SAT question. No need to worry what the test will "really" be like—this book will present everything as it appears on the test!

Here are three sample SAT analogy questions. Try each one on your own, then read the explanation that accompanies it.

1. HORSE : UNICORN : :
   (A) lizard : dragon
   (B) ram : stallion
   (C) sheep : lamb
   (D) reptile : scale
   (E) mare : mermaid

The correct answer is (A). A horse is a real animal and a unicorn is an imaginary horse-like animal, just as a lizard is a real animal and a dragon is an imaginary lizard-like animal. Let's look at the other answer choices to see why they are wrong. Answer (B) is wrong because the only relationship between ram and stallion is that they are both male animals. In answer (C), the relationship is that a sheep is an adult lamb. In answer (D), the relationship is that a reptile is covered with scales. Answer (E) is close. A mare is real and a mermaid is imaginary, but a mermaid bears no resemblance to a female horse. So, (E) is not the best answer.

2. SPOOL : THREAD : :
   (A) bale : hay
   (B) sack : potatoes
   (C) verse : song
   (D) coil : rope
   (E) reel : line

The correct answer is (E). Thread is wrapped around a spool, just as a fishing line is wrapped around a reel. Answer (A) is wrong because hay is bundled, not wrapped, in a bale. Answer (B) is wrong because potatoes are stored in, not wrapped around, a sack. In answer (C), the only relationship is that a verse is part of a song. And answer (D) is wrong because the relationship is only that rope can be shaped into a coil.

3. RICE : WEDDING : :
   (A) food : groom
   (B) celebration : ceremony
   (C) wheat : meal
   (D) bran : cereal
   (E) confetti : parade

The correct answer is (E). Rice is often thrown at a wedding, just as confetti is often thrown at a parade. Just try this sentence with the other choices and you'll see that none of them even comes close to working.

UNDERSTANDING SENTENCE COMPLETIONS

Just as the name implies, sentence completions are "fill-in-the-blank" questions. SAT sentence completion questions may have one or two blanks. Your job is to choose from among the answer choices the word or words that best fit each blank.

The directions for SAT sentence completion questions look like this:

> **Directions:** Each of the following sentences contains one or two blank spaces to be filled in by one of the five choices listed below each sentence. Select the word or words that best complete the meaning of the sentence.

NOTE
Note that these directions ask you to choose the *best* answer. That's why you should always read all the answer choices before you make your final selection.

Here are three sample SAT sentence completion questions. Try each one on your own, before you read the explanation that accompanies it.

1. Many hours of practice are required of a successful musician, so it is often not so much ---- as ---- which distinguishes the professional from the amateur.

    (A) genius..understanding
    (B) money..education
    (C) talent..discipline
    (D) fortitude..mediocrity
    (E) technique..pomposity

The correct answer is (C). How do you know this? The sentence gives you a clue. The "not so much... as..." lets you know that there is some kind of contrast here. Choices (B) and (C) both show a contrast, but (C) is the only one that makes sense in the sentence.

2. The sudden death of the world-renowned leader ---- his followers, but it ---- his former opponents.

    (A) saddened..devastated
    (B) shocked..encouraged
    (C) depressed..tempered
    (D) satisfied..aided
    (E) prostrated..depressed

The correct answer is (B). The word "but" is your clue that the word in the second blank will contrast with the word in the first blank. Only the words shocked and encouraged offer the logical contrast that is expected between the feelings of followers and opponents on the death of a leader.

3. Despite his valor on the football field, the star athlete ---- when forced to take a flu shot.

   (A) relaxed
   (B) trembled
   (C) hustled
   (D) sidled
   (E) embellished

The correct answer is (B). The word "despite" is your clue that the athlete will do something less than heroic when confronted with the flu shot. Trembled completes the sentence and continues the strong tone of irony.

UNDERSTANDING CRITICAL READING

SAT critical reading questions present a passage that you are to read and answer questions about. The questions follow the order in which information appears in the passage. The directions for critical reading questions look like this:

> **Directions:** The passage below is followed by a set of questions. Read the passage and answer the accompanying questions, basing your answers on what is stated or implied in the passage.

Here is a sample of what to expect. (Note that this passage is much shorter than a standard SAT passage.)

The following passage discusses the mythical island of Atlantis.

A legendary island in the Atlantic Ocean beyond the Pillars of Hercules was first mentioned by Plato in the Timaeus. Atlantis was a fabulously beautiful and prosperous land, the seat of an empire nine thousand years before Solon. Its inhabitants overran part of Europe and Africa, Athens alone being able to defy them.
(5) Because of the impiety of its people, the island was destroyed by an earthquake and inundation. The legend may have existed before Plato and may have sprung from the concept of Homer's Elysium. The possibility that such an island once existed has caused much speculation, resulting in a theory that pre-Columbian civilizations in America were established by colonists from the lost island.

NOTE
It's an open-book test. In SAT critical reading questions, the answers will always be directly stated or implied in the passage.

1. The main purpose of the passage is to discuss

   (A) the legend of Atlantis
   (B) Plato's description of Atlantis in the Timaeus
   (C) the conquests made by citizens of Atlantis
   (D) the possibility that the Americas were settled by colonists from Atlantis
   (E) the destruction of Atlantis

The correct answer is (A). The main purpose should be represented by an overall statement. While the details in (B), (C), (D), and (E) are all mentioned in the text, (A) is the only overall statement.

2. According to the passage, we may safely conclude that the inhabitants of Atlantis

    (A) were known personally to Homer
    (B) were a peace-loving people who stayed close to home
    (C) were a religious and superstitious people
    (D) used the name Columbus for America
    (E) were never visited by Plato

The correct answer is (E). At the time Plato mentioned Atlantis, it was already legendary. Therefore, Plato could not have visited the island.

3. According to the legend, Atlantis was destroyed because the inhabitants

    (A) failed to obtain an adequate food supply
    (B) failed to conquer Greece
    (C) failed to respect their gods
    (D) believed in Homer's Elysium
    (E) had become too prosperous

The correct answer is (C). The only cause that's mentioned in the passage is the "impiety" of the people of Atlantis.

HOW THE SAT TESTS MATHEMATICAL REASONING

The SAT tests your mathematical reasoning ability with these three question types:

- standard multiple-choice
- quantitative comparisons
- student-produced response

The scored sections of the test will contain a total of 35 standard multiple-choice questions, 15 quantitative comparisons, and 10 student-produced response questions.

UNDERSTANDING MULTIPLE-CHOICE MATH

SAT standard multiple-choice math questions look like all the other multiple-choice math questions you've ever faced, but they usually require some logical thinking to solve them. The directions for SAT math questions include many of the concepts you need to know. Here's what they look like:

26 Master the SAT

Directions: Solve the following problems using any available space on the page for scratchwork. On your answer sheet, fill in the choice which best corresponds to the correct answer.

Notes: The figures accompanying the problems are drawn as accurately as possible unless otherwise stated in specific problems. Again, unless otherwise stated, all figures lie in the same plane. All numbers used in these problems are real numbers. Calculators are permitted for this test.

Reference Information

Circle: $C = 2\pi r$, $A = \pi r^2$
Rectangle: $A = lw$
Rectangular Solid: $V = lwh$
Cylinder: $V = \pi r^2 h$
Triangle: $A = \frac{1}{2}bh$
$a^2 + b^2 = c^2$

45°-45°-90° triangle: sides x, x, $x\sqrt{2}$
30°-60°-90° triangle: sides x, $x\sqrt{3}$, $2x$

The number of degrees of arc in a circle is 360.
The measure in degrees of a straight angle is 180.
The sum of the measures in degrees of the angles of a triangle is 180.

Here are some sample multiple-choice math questions. Try them yourself before looking at the solutions that are given.

1. A certain triangle has sides that are, respectively, 6 inches, 8 inches, and 10 inches long. A rectangle with an area equal to that of the triangle has a width of 3 inches. What is the perimeter of the rectangle, in inches?

   (A) 11
   (B) 16
   (C) 22
   (D) 24
   (E) 30

Note: A 🖩 following a math answer explanation indicates that a calculator could be helpful in solving that particular problem.

The answer is (C). The area of the triangle is $\frac{1}{2}bh$, which in this case is $\frac{1}{2} \times 6 \times 8 = 24$. The area of a rectangle is $A = l \times w$. Since we know the width and area, $24 = l \times 3$; therefore, $l = 8$. The perimeter of the rectangle is $P = 2l + 2w$, which we find to be $(2 \times 8) + (2 \times 3) = 16 + 6 = 22$. 🖩

2. A room 27 feet by 32 feet is to be carpeted. The width of the carpet is 27 inches. What is the length, in yards, of the carpet needed for this floor? (1 yard = 3 feet = 36 inches)

   (A) 1188
   (B) 648
   (C) 384
   (D) 128
   (E) 96

The answer is (D). The length of one side of the room in inches is 27 ft. × 12 in. = 324 in. The width of the carpet is 27 in.; therefore, it takes 324 ÷ 27 = 12 lengths of carpet at 32 ft. per length, or 12 × 32 = 384 ft. The length needed in yards is 384 ft. ÷ 3 ft./yd. = 128 yards.

3. Given: Right ABC with $AB = 6$ and $AC = 7$. What does BC equal?

   (A) 1
   (B) $\sqrt{13}$
   (C) 6
   (D) $\sqrt{29}$
   (E) $\sqrt{98}$

The answer is (B). By the Pythagorean Theorem, $(AB)^2 + (BC)^2 = (AC)^2$, or $(BC)^2 = (AC)^2 - (AB)^2$. Substituting the values in this equation yields $(BC)^2 = (7)^2 - (6)^2 = 49 - 36 = 13$, and $BC = \sqrt{13}$.

4. The closest approximation to the correct answer for $5 - \sqrt{32.076} + 1.00017^3$ is

   (A) 9
   (B) 7
   (C) 5
   (D) 3
   (E) 0

The answer is (E). $\sqrt{32.076}$ is slightly more than halfway between 5 and 6, say 5.6. 1.00017^3 is very slightly over $1^3 = 1$. Therefore, $5 - 5.6 + 1 = 0.04$. The closest answer given is 0.

5. If the numerator and denominator of a proper fraction are increased by the same quantity, the resulting fraction is

   (A) always greater than the original fraction
   (B) always less than the original fraction
   (C) always equal to the original fraction
   (D) one-half the original fraction
   (E) not determinable

TIP

While a calculator may be helpful in solving some SAT math questions, it isn't *absolutely necessary* for any problem—and in some cases it won't help you at all. In this book, we show you where we think a calculator may be helpful. On test day, use your judgment in choosing if—and when—to use a calculator.

The correct answer is (A). If the numerator and denominator of the fraction $\frac{n}{d}$ are increased by a quantity q, the new fraction is $\frac{(n+q)}{(d+q)}$. Compare this to the old fraction by finding a common denominator $d(d+q)$. The old fraction is $\frac{n(d+q)}{d(d+q)} = \frac{(nd+nq)}{d(d+q)}$; the new fraction is $\frac{d(n+q)}{d(d+q)} = \frac{(nd+dq)}{d(d+q)}$. Comparing the old numerator $(nd + nq)$ with the new, the new fraction is larger, since $d > n$. The fraction in this example must be a proper fraction.

6. The total number of feet in x yards, y feet, and z inches is (1 yard = 3 feet = 36 inches)

    (A) $3x + y + \dfrac{z}{12}$

    (B) $12(x + y + z)$

    (C) $x + y + z$

    (D) $\dfrac{x}{36} + \dfrac{y}{12} + z$

    (E) $x + 3y + 36z$

The correct answer is (A). x yards = $3x$ feet; z inches = $\frac{z}{12}$ feet. Therefore, x yards + y feet + z inches = $3x$ feet + y feet + $\frac{z}{12}$ feet, or $3x + y + \frac{z}{12}$ feet.

UNDERSTANDING QUANTITATIVE COMPARISONS

SAT quantitative comparisons are probably not like any other math question you've ever seen. These questions present you with two quantities, one quantity is presented in Column A, and the other in Column B. Your job is to decide which quantity is greater, whether the two quantities are equal, or whether no comparison is possible. There are only four answer choices for this question type, and they are always the same. Here is what the directions look like:

Directions: For each of the following items, compare the quantity in Column A with the one in Column B and determine whether:

(A) the quantity is greater in Column A

(B) the quantity is greater in Column B

(C) both quantities are equal

(D) no comparison can be made with the information given

Notes:

(1) Information concerning one or both of the compared quantities will be centered between the two columns for some of the items.

(2) Symbols that appear in both columns represent the same thing in Column A as in Column B.

(3) Letters such as x, n, and k are symbols for real numbers.

(4) Do not mark choice (E), as there are only four choices.

CAUTION

Don't pick (E)! Quantitative comparisons have only answer choices (A) through (D). Marking (E) won't get you any credit.

SAT Questions: A First Look   29

Column A   Column B

$$a > 0$$
$$b > 0$$
$$m > 1$$

1. $(m^a)^b$ $m^a m^b$

(D) In Column A, $(m^a)^b = m^{ab}$, with $ab > 0$, since $a, b > 0$. In Column B, $m^a m^b = m^{a+b}$, with $a + b > 0$ since $a, b > 0$. Since we know nothing else about a and b, we cannot tell if $ab > a + b$ or vice versa.

2.   Area of smaller circle   Area of shaded portion

(D) The area of the larger circle is $\pi(r+2)^2$. The area of the smaller circle is πr^2. The area of the shaded region is

$$\pi(r+2)^2 - \pi r^2$$
$$= \pi(r^2 + 4r + 4) - \pi r^2$$
$$= \pi r^2 + 4\pi r + 4\pi - \pi r^2$$
$$= 4\pi r + 4\pi = 4\pi(r+1)$$

Since we know nothing about the radius r, we cannot tell which area is larger.

3.   39% of 87   87% of 39

(C) The trick to the problem is realizing that in both columns you will multiply 39×87 and move the decimal point two places to the left.

Column A	Column B

A(-3,6)   *B*(3,6)
C(0,0)

4. | Distance from A to B | Distance from B to C |

(B) The distance from A to B is

$$\sqrt{(3+3)^2 + (6-6)^2} = \sqrt{36} = 6.$$

The distance from *B* to *C* is

$$\sqrt{(0-3)^2 + (0-6)^2} = \sqrt{9+36} = \sqrt{45}$$

The square root of 45 is greater than 6. Therefore, the distance from *B* to *C* is greater than the distance from *A* to *B*.

UNDERSTANDING GRID-INS

SAT grid-in questions are the only SAT questions that don't give you the answers. That is your job. You do the calculations, you find the answer, and you write the information in on a special part of the answer sheet. You do this by filling in ovals that correspond to your answer. These examples and explanations will help prepare you for the questions to come.

TIP
Only the bubbles count. The machine that scores your test can only "read" the bubbles. Even if you write in the correct answer to a grid-in question, you'll get no credit for it unless you fill in the bubbles.

Directions: Solve each of the following problems and write the arithmetic value of your answer in the open spaces at the top of the correspondingly numbered grid on your answer sheet. Then grid your answer by blackening the ovals that correspond to the decimal point, fraction line, and numbers in your answer.

Notes: If a question has more than one correct answer, grid only one of them.

To grid $4\frac{1}{4}$, use 4.25 or $\frac{17}{4}$. Do not use $4\frac{1}{4}$ as it will be read as $\frac{41}{4}$. None of these answers requires a minus sign.

Answers may begin in any grid column.

Decimal answers should be entered with the greatest accuracy allowed by the grid.

1. The circumference of a circle is 20. If the area of the circle is a, what is the value of a?

   $C = 2\pi r = 20\pi$
   $r = 10$
   $A = \pi r^2 = \pi(10)^2 = 100\pi = a\pi$

   $\therefore a = 100$

2. If 35% of a number is 70, what is the number?

   $\dfrac{35}{100} \cdot x = 70$

   $\dfrac{35x}{100} = 70$

   $x = 200$

3. Find the mode of the following group of numbers: 8, 8, 9, 10, 11

   The mode is the number which occurs the most frequently. The mode = 8.

Summary: What You Need to Know About the SAT Question Types

This information is the foundation that you're going to build on as you prepare for the SAT.

- Learning the SAT question types is the best way to prepare for the SAT. Since the question types never change, you'll know exactly what to expect on test day.
- There are 19 analogies on the SAT. Each question asks you to find the answer choice that best express a relationship similar to the one expressed by the capitalized pair.
- There are 19 sentence completions on the SAT. Each question asks you to find the answer choice with the word or words that best fit into each blank.
- There are 40 critical reading questions on the SAT. Remember that the answers to every question will always be directly stated or implied in the passage. So find them!

- There are 35 multiple choice questions on the SAT. Remember to use the reference formulas at the beginning of each math section to help you with these questions.
- There are 15 quantitative comparison questions on the SAT. Each one asks you to compare two quantities and decide which is greater. Remember that there are only four answer choices for this question type!
- There are 10 grid-in questions on the SAT. Unlike other math questions, grid-ins require that you provide your own answer by filling in the ovals of a special grid. Remember that only the bubbles count, so make sure you fill them in correctly.
- You can use a calculator to tackle SAT math questions. While a calculator may be helpful on some problems, it isn't *absolutely necessary* for any of them. So use your calculator, but don't rely on it too much.

PART 2

Diagnosing Strengths and Weaknesses

CHAPTER 4

PREVIEW

Diagnostic Examination

DIAGNOSTIC EXAMINATION
Answer Sheet

If a section has fewer questions than answer ovals, leave the extra ovals blank.

Section 1

(Questions 1–40, answer ovals A B C D E)

Section 2

(Questions 1–40, answer ovals A B C D E)

Section 3

(Questions 1–40, answer ovals A B C D E)

Section 4

1. Ⓐ Ⓑ Ⓒ Ⓓ Ⓔ
2. Ⓐ Ⓑ Ⓒ Ⓓ Ⓔ
3. Ⓐ Ⓑ Ⓒ Ⓓ Ⓔ
4. Ⓐ Ⓑ Ⓒ Ⓓ Ⓔ
5. Ⓐ Ⓑ Ⓒ Ⓓ Ⓔ
6. Ⓐ Ⓑ Ⓒ Ⓓ Ⓔ
7. Ⓐ Ⓑ Ⓒ Ⓓ Ⓔ
8. Ⓐ Ⓑ Ⓒ Ⓓ Ⓔ
9. Ⓐ Ⓑ Ⓒ Ⓓ Ⓔ
10. Ⓐ Ⓑ Ⓒ Ⓓ Ⓔ
11. Ⓐ Ⓑ Ⓒ Ⓓ Ⓔ
12. Ⓐ Ⓑ Ⓒ Ⓓ Ⓔ
13. Ⓐ Ⓑ Ⓒ Ⓓ Ⓔ
14. Ⓐ Ⓑ Ⓒ Ⓓ Ⓔ
15. Ⓐ Ⓑ Ⓒ Ⓓ Ⓔ

Note: ONLY the answers entered on the grid are scored.

Handwritten answers at the top of the column are NOT scored.

16. [grid-in] 17. [grid-in] 18. [grid-in] 19. [grid-in] 20. [grid-in]

21. [grid-in] 22. [grid-in] 23. [grid-in] 24. [grid-in] 25. [grid-in]

Section 5

1. Ⓐ Ⓑ Ⓒ Ⓓ Ⓔ
2. Ⓐ Ⓑ Ⓒ Ⓓ Ⓔ
3. Ⓐ Ⓑ Ⓒ Ⓓ Ⓔ
4. Ⓐ Ⓑ Ⓒ Ⓓ Ⓔ
5. Ⓐ Ⓑ Ⓒ Ⓓ Ⓔ
6. Ⓐ Ⓑ Ⓒ Ⓓ Ⓔ
7. Ⓐ Ⓑ Ⓒ Ⓓ Ⓔ
8. Ⓐ Ⓑ Ⓒ Ⓓ Ⓔ
9. Ⓐ Ⓑ Ⓒ Ⓓ Ⓔ
10. Ⓐ Ⓑ Ⓒ Ⓓ Ⓔ
11. Ⓐ Ⓑ Ⓒ Ⓓ Ⓔ
12. Ⓐ Ⓑ Ⓒ Ⓓ Ⓔ
13. Ⓐ Ⓑ Ⓒ Ⓓ Ⓔ
14. Ⓐ Ⓑ Ⓒ Ⓓ Ⓔ
15. Ⓐ Ⓑ Ⓒ Ⓓ Ⓔ
16. Ⓐ Ⓑ Ⓒ Ⓓ Ⓔ
17. Ⓐ Ⓑ Ⓒ Ⓓ Ⓔ
18. Ⓐ Ⓑ Ⓒ Ⓓ Ⓔ
19. Ⓐ Ⓑ Ⓒ Ⓓ Ⓔ
20. Ⓐ Ⓑ Ⓒ Ⓓ Ⓔ

Section 6

1. Ⓐ Ⓑ Ⓒ Ⓓ Ⓔ
2. Ⓐ Ⓑ Ⓒ Ⓓ Ⓔ
3. Ⓐ Ⓑ Ⓒ Ⓓ Ⓔ
4. Ⓐ Ⓑ Ⓒ Ⓓ Ⓔ
5. Ⓐ Ⓑ Ⓒ Ⓓ Ⓔ
6. Ⓐ Ⓑ Ⓒ Ⓓ Ⓔ
7. Ⓐ Ⓑ Ⓒ Ⓓ Ⓔ
8. Ⓐ Ⓑ Ⓒ Ⓓ Ⓔ
9. Ⓐ Ⓑ Ⓒ Ⓓ Ⓔ
10. Ⓐ Ⓑ Ⓒ Ⓓ Ⓔ
11. Ⓐ Ⓑ Ⓒ Ⓓ Ⓔ
12. Ⓐ Ⓑ Ⓒ Ⓓ Ⓔ
13. Ⓐ Ⓑ Ⓒ Ⓓ Ⓔ
14. Ⓐ Ⓑ Ⓒ Ⓓ Ⓔ
15. Ⓐ Ⓑ Ⓒ Ⓓ Ⓔ

Diagnostic Examination

SECTION 1

31 Questions • Time—30 Minutes

Directions: Each of the following questions consists of an incomplete sentence followed by five words or pairs of words. Choose that word or pair of words which, when substituted for the blank space or spaces, *best* completes the meaning of the sentence and mark the letter of your choice on your answer sheet.

Example:

> In view of the extenuating circumstances and the defendant's youth, the judge recommended ----.
>
> (A) conviction
> (B) a defense
> (C) a mistrial
> (D) leniency
> (E) life imprisonment
>
> Ⓐ Ⓑ Ⓒ ● Ⓔ

1. Her position in the agency authorized her to award contracts and to ---- obligations for payment of expenses.
   (A) rescind
   (B) incur
   (C) procure
   (D) recur
   (E) resume

2. Despite all his courtroom experience, the attorney was able to pry very little information out of the ---- witness.
   (A) cooperative
   (B) recalcitrant
   (C) reactionary
   (D) presumptive
   (E) credulous

3. Although over the years ---- resources had been devoted to alleviating the problem, a satisfactory solution remained ----.
   (A) natural..costly
   (B) adequate..probable
   (C) substantial..elusive
   (D) capital..decisive
   (E) conventional..abstract

4. The team attributes its ---- season to a number of ---- factors.
   (A) losing..propitious
   (B) long..irrelevant
   (C) remarkable..derogatory
   (D) embarrassing..optimistic
   (E) winning..favorable

5. While fewer documents are being kept, the usefulness of those ---- is now ---- by an improved cataloging system.
   (A) printed..documented
   (B) discarded..concurred
   (C) read..emblazoned
   (D) retained..insured
   (E) received..negated

GO ON TO THE NEXT PAGE

6. The ---- with which the agent calmed the anxieties and soothed the tempers of the travelers ---- by the delay was a mark of frequent experience with similar crises.
   (A) evasiveness..angered
   (B) reverence..pleased
   (C) facility..inconvenienced
   (D) mannerism..destroyed
   (E) acuity..accommodated

7. The lover of democracy has an ---- toward totalitarianism.
   (A) antipathy
   (B) empathy
   (C) equanimity
   (D) idolatry
   (E) obstinacy

8. A ---- of employment opportunities ---- prospective employees entering the job market.
   (A) surfeit..impedes
   (B) paucity..discourages
   (C) plethora..deters
   (D) dearth..inspires
   (E) deluge..enervates

9. In truth, ---- has a cost; for every free person we pay with the ---- of fifty others.
   (A) liberty..subjection
   (B) liberalism..environmentalism
   (C) capitalism..punishment
   (D) independence..individualism
   (E) authority..autonomy

Directions: Each of the following questions consists of a capitalized pair of words followed by five pairs of words lettered A to E. The capitalized words bear some meaningful relationship to each other. Choose the lettered pair of words whose relationship is most similar to that expressed by the capitalized pair and mark its letter on your answer sheet.

Example:

DAY : SUN : :
(A) sunlight : daylight
(B) ray : sun
(C) night : moon
(D) heat : cold
(E) moon : star
Ⓐ Ⓑ ● Ⓓ Ⓔ

10. POWERFUL : MIGHTY : :
    (A) muscular : alert
    (B) mediocre : ordinary
    (C) tense : springy
    (D) weak : small
    (E) deep : murky

11. HAIR : HORSE : :
    (A) feather : bird
    (B) wool : sheep
    (C) down : pillow
    (D) fuzz : peach
    (E) fur : animal

12. GOBBLE : TURKEY : :
    (A) shed : cobra
    (B) chop : tree
    (C) graze : elephant
    (D) twitter : bird
    (E) sleep : lion

13. SELL : PURCHASE : :
    (A) pay : charge
    (B) offer : bid
    (C) buy : earn
    (D) donate : demand
    (E) give : receive

14. NOVEL : BOOK : :
    (A) act : play
    (B) article : magazine
    (C) mitten : hand
    (D) sock : foot
    (E) loafer : shoe

15. TEMERITY : CAUTION : :
    (A) trepidation : fear
    (B) effrontery : shame
    (C) cacophony : dissonance
    (D) capriciousness : whimsy
    (E) adulation : praise

Directions: Each passage below is followed by a set of questions. Read each passage; then answer the accompanying questions, basing your answers on what is stated or implied in the passage and in any introductory material provided. Mark the letter of your choice on your answer sheet.

Questions 16–22 are based on the following passage.

The principles of classical architecture have endured over time. Modern buildings built in the classical style still adhere to architectural principles established during the times of the ancient Romans. The following passage considers some of those principles.

Classical architecture, the origins of which can be traced to ancient Rome, was the type of architecture embraced by the very highest social levels of that ancient civilization. As such, classical architecture was
(5) characterized by a rigorous adherence to the principles of coherence, exactness, and detail.

The basis of the classical style was the manner in which a building's space was divided so as to create a coherent whole. An example of a plan for the division
(10) of a building's space was the *tripartite* plan, which would divide the space in a particular building into three equal parts. Such a plan would be followed no matter what the purpose of the building—churches, homes, or public government buildings could all be designed with
(15) such a plan. Even gardens, designed in the classical style, might have a three-part plan. It is interesting, too, that the classical *tripartite* plan spilled over from architecture to other arts—music, poetry, and dance—so that it is not uncommon to have a three-part hierarchy within
(20) those artistic areas as well.

Once the framework of a building designed in the classical style was established, architectural elements were added. Columns are fairly typical architectural elements, with the five most common column types
(25) being the *Doric, Ionic, Corinthian, Tuscan,* and *Composite*. Each column was distinctive and of a certain specified proportion, base to top. Just as the building itself might embody a tripartite plan, so did the columns themselves have a three-part organization. Above the
(30) column is a horizontal piece, called the *entablature*, then comes the column itself which is tall and cylindrical, and finally comes the three-step platform upon which the column rests, called the crepidoma. The top piece is further divided into three parts—the cornice, the frieze,
(35) and the architrave. The column breaks down into three parts—the capital, the shaft, and the base. The crepidoma maintains the three-part division with its three steps.

Symmetry was also an important element in classical architecture. The relationship between architectural el-
(40) ements and the whole edifice was conceived, studied, and implemented with a great deal of attention paid at each stage of the plan to assuring that balance was achieved. Proportion and parallelism were critical in the achievement of the plan's coherence as well.

(45) Classical architecture was filled with conventions, scrupulously adhered to, which although perhaps not obvious to the viewer become apparent upon closer analysis. For example, classical buildings must stand free; they cannot touch the sides of other buildings. This
(50) is so because in the view of the classicist, the building was a world within a world of its own. Thus, the building had to stand alone, an example of its singular world. Consequently, groups of classical buildings became problematic because of perceived violations of spatial
(55) conventions that troubled rule-based classical architects. The classical mode required an adherence to formal patterns and symmetry sometimes not possible to impose on groups of buildings.

Classical architects longed to bring order to the world
(60) through designs that struggled for consistency and completeness. The classical plan was a disciplined plan

GO ON TO THE NEXT PAGE

requiring the ability to divide, relate, and align elements. The resulting building was thus created in a way pleasing to the eye and appropriate to the time and place
(65) in which it was placed.

16. The origins of classical architecture date back to the time of ancient
    (A) Egypt
    (B) Greece
    (C) Sumeria
    (D) Rome
    (E) Mesopotamia

17. Classical architecture is characterized by all of the following EXCEPT
    (A) attention to detail
    (B) rigorous exactness
    (C) different spatial divisions for different types of buildings
    (D) attention to a coherent whole
    (E) use of a *tripartite* division of spaces

18. The word *tripartite* in line 10 most nearly means
    (A) geometric
    (B) three-part
    (C) political
    (D) spatial
    (E) mathematical

19. All of the following are column types EXCEPT
    (A) Egyptian
    (B) Doric
    (C) Ionic
    (D) Tuscan
    (E) Corinthian

20. Which of the following is one of the three parts of the column proper?
    (A) The cornice
    (B) The capital
    (C) The frieze
    (D) The architave
    (E) The detail

21. The word *symmetry* in line 38 most nearly means
    (A) absence of proportion
    (B) lack of parallelism
    (C) spatial qualities
    (D) architectural element
    (E) balance

22. The main idea of this passage is that
    (A) classical architecture is out of fashion
    (B) the classical approach to architecture allows for much freedom of expression
    (C) there is no place for architectural elements in the classical scheme
    (D) the Ionic column is the most perfect example of a classical element
    (E) the conventions of classical architecture are scrupulously followed

Questions 23–31 are based on the following passage.

Angel Decora was born Hinookmahiwi-kilinaka on the Winnebago Reservation in Nebraska in 1871. She worked as a book illustrator, particularly on books by and about Native Americans, and lectured and wrote about Indian art. The story from which this excerpt is taken, "The Sick Child," may be autobiographical.

It was about sunset when I, a little child, was sent with a handful of powdered tobacco leaves and red feathers to make an offering to the spirit who had caused the sickness of my little sister. It had been a long, hard
(5) winter, and the snow lay deep on the prairie as far as the eye could reach. The medicine-woman's directions had been that the offering must be laid upon the naked earth, and that to find it I must face toward the setting sun.

I was taught the prayer: "Spirit grandfather, I offer
(10) this to thee. I pray thee restore my little sister to health." Full of reverence and a strong faith that I could appease the anger of the spirit, I started out to plead for the life of our little one.

But now where was a spot of earth to be found in all
(15) that white monotony? They had talked of death at the house. I hoped that my little sister would live, but I was afraid of nature.

I reached a little spring. I looked down to its pebbly bottom, wondering whether I should leave my offering
(20) there, or keep on in search of a spot of earth. If I put my

offering in the water, would it reach the bottom and touch the earth, or would it float away, as it had always done when I made my offering to the water spirit?

(25) Once more I started on in my search of the bare ground.

The surface was crusted in some places, and walking was easy; in other places I would wade through a foot or more of snow. Often I paused, thinking to clear the snow away in some place and there lay my offering. But no, *(30)* my faith must be in nature, and I must trust to it to lay bare the earth. It was a hard struggle for so small a child.

I went on and on; the reeds were waving their tasselled ends in the wind. I stopped and looked at them. A reed, whirling in the wind, had formed a space round its *(35)* stem, making a loose socket. I stood looking into the opening. The reed must be rooted in the ground, and the hole must follow the stem to the earth. If I poured my offerings into the hole, surely they must reach the ground; so I said the prayer that I had been taught, and *(40)* dropped my tobacco and red feathers into the opening that nature itself had created.

No sooner was the sacrifice accomplished than a feeling of doubt and fear thrilled me. What if my offering should never reach the earth? Would my little *(45)* sister die?

Not till I turned homeward did I realize how cold I was. When at last I reached the house they took me in and warmed me, but did not question me, and I said nothing. Everyone was sad, for the little one had *(50)* grown worse.

The next day the medicine-woman said my little sister was beyond hope; she could not live. Then bitter remorse was mine, for I thought I had been unfaithful, and therefore my little sister was to be called to the spirit *(55)* land. I was a silent child, and did not utter my feelings; my remorse was intense. . . .

23. The word *offering* (line 3) means
    (A) proposal
    (B) bid
    (C) advance
    (D) tribute
    (E) suggestion

24. By "naked earth" (line 7), the medicine-woman meant
    (A) the bare ground
    (B) an eroded streambed
    (C) a treeless plain
    (D) the dirt floor of the house
    (E) a patch of snow

25. The narrator's journey could be called a
    (A) reverie
    (B) retreat
    (C) junket
    (D) quest
    (E) jaunt

26. "White monotony" (line 15) refers to the fact that
    (A) the family lives on a reservation
    (B) white people find Nebraska dull
    (C) snow covers the landscape
    (D) the narrator is blind
    (E) nothing happens in the story

27. Line 31 ("It was a hard struggle for so small a child") is
    (A) an aside by an omniscient narrator
    (B) the adult narrator's realization that saving her sick sister was too big a task for the child
    (C) an ironic statement by an outside observer
    (D) the adult narrator's excuse for placing the feathers and tobacco in a poor spot
    (E) the adult narrator's explanation for the young girl's silent remorse

28. The word *thrilled* (line 43) is used to mean
    (A) delighted
    (B) exhilarated
    (C) inflamed
    (D) enraptured
    (E) inspired

GO ON TO THE NEXT PAGE

29. The narrator's remorse is due to her
    (A) uncaring attitude toward her sister
    (B) mixed feelings toward her own religion
    (C) secret longing for attention
    (D) perceived failure at following instructions
    (E) mistrust of the medicine-woman

30. If her sister died, you would expect the narrator to feel
    (A) relieved
    (B) elated
    (C) surprised
    (D) confused
    (E) guilty

31. What feeling does the narrator have toward the child?
    (A) shame
    (B) bewilderment
    (C) forgiveness
    (D) irritation
    (E) anxiety

STOP

END OF SECTION 1. IF YOU HAVE ANY TIME LEFT, GO OVER YOUR WORK IN THIS SECTION ONLY. DO NOT WORK IN ANY OTHER SECTION OF THE TEST.

SECTION 2

25 Questions • Time—30 Minutes

Directions: Solve the following problems using any available space on the page for scratchwork. On your answer sheet fill in the choice which best corresponds to the correct answer.

Notes: The figures accompanying the problems are drawn as accurately as possible unless otherwise stated in specific problems. Again, unless otherwise stated, all figures lie in the same plane. All numbers used in these problems are real numbers. Calculators are permitted for this test.

Reference Information

Circle: $C = 2\pi r$, $A = \pi r^2$
Rectangle: $A = lw$
Rectangular Solid: $V = lwh$
Cylinder: $V = \pi r^2 h$
Triangle: $A = \frac{1}{2}bh$
$a^2 + b^2 = c^2$

45°-45°-90° triangle: sides x, x, $x\sqrt{2}$
30°-60°-90° triangle: sides x, $x\sqrt{3}$, $2x$

The number of degrees of arc in a circle is 360.
The measure in degrees of a straight angle is 180.
The sum of the measures in degrees of the angles of a triangle is 180.

---

1. Which of the following fractions is more than $\frac{3}{4}$?

    (A) $\frac{35}{71}$

    (B) $\frac{13}{20}$

    (C) $\frac{71}{101}$

    (D) $\frac{19}{24}$

    (E) $\frac{15}{20}$

2. If $820 + R + S - 610 = 342$, and if $R = 2S$, then $S =$

    (A) 44
    (B) 48
    (C) 132
    (D) 184
    (E) 192

3. What is the cost, in dollars, to carpet a room x yards long and y yards wide, if the carpet costs five dollars per square foot?

    (A) xy
    (B) $5xy$
    (C) $25xy$
    (D) $30xy$
    (E) $45xy$

4. If $7M = 3M - 20$, then $M + 7 =$

    (A) 0
    (B) 2
    (C) 5
    (D) 12
    (E) 17

GO ON TO THE NEXT PAGE

5. In circle O below, AB is the diameter, angle BOD contains 15°, and angle EOA contains 85°. Find the number of degrees in angle ECA.

   (A) 15
   (B) 35
   (C) 50
   (D) 70
   (E) 85

6. What is the smallest positive number, other than 2, which, when it is divided by 3, 4, or 5, will leave a remainder of 2?

   (A) 22
   (B) 42
   (C) 62
   (D) 122
   (E) 182

7. A taxi charges 75 cents for the first quarter of a mile and 15 cents for each additional quarter of a mile. The charge, in cents, for a trip of d miles is

   (A) $75 + 15d$
   (B) $75 + 15(4d - 1)$
   (C) $75 + 75d$
   (D) $75 + 4(d - 1)$
   (E) $75 + 75(d - 1)$

8. In a certain army post, 30% of the enlistees are from New York State, and 10% of these are from New York City. What percentage of the enlistees in the post are from New York City?

   (A) .03
   (B) .3
   (C) 3
   (D) 13
   (E) 20

9. The diagonal of a rectangle is 10. What is the area of the rectangle?

   (A) 24
   (B) 48
   (C) 50
   (D) 100
   (E) It cannot be determined from the information given.

10. In triangle PQR below, angle RPQ is greater than angle RQP, and the bisectors of angle P and angle Q meet in S. Therefore,

    Note: Figure not drawn to scale.

    (A) SQ > SP
    (B) SQ = SP
    (C) SQ < SP
    (D) SQ SP
    (E) No conclusion concerning the relative lengths of SQ and SP can be determined from the information given.

11. Which of the following is equal to 3.14×10^6?

    (A) 314
    (B) 3140
    (C) 31,400
    (D) 314,000
    (E) 3,140,000

12. $\dfrac{36}{29 - \frac{4}{0.2}}$

   (A) $\dfrac{3}{4}$

   (B) $\dfrac{4}{3}$

   (C) 2

   (D) 4

   (E) 18

13. In terms of the square units in the figure below, what is the area of the semicircle?

   (A) 32π
   (B) 16π
   (C) 8π
   (D) 4π
   (E) 2π

14. The sum of three consecutive odd numbers is always divisible by

   I. 2
   II. 3
   III. 5
   IV. 6

   (A) I only
   (B) II only
   (C) I and II only
   (D) I and III only
   (E) II and IV only

15. In the diagram, triangle ABC is inscribed in a circle and CD is tangent to the circle. If angle BCD is 40°, how many degrees are there in angle A?

   (A) 20
   (B) 30
   (C) 40
   (D) 50
   (E) 60

16. If a discount of 20% off the marked price of a jacket results in a savings of $15, what is the discounted price of the jacket?

   (A) $35
   (B) $60
   (C) $75
   (D) $150
   (E) $300

17. While researching a term paper, a student read pages 7 through 49 and pages 101 through 157 of a particular source book. Altogether, how many pages from this book did this student read?

   (A) 98
   (B) 99
   (C) 100
   (D) 101
   (E) 102

GO ON TO THE NEXT PAGE

18. If $\dfrac{P}{Q} = \dfrac{4}{5}$ what is the value of $2P + Q$?

   (A) 14
   (B) 13
   (C) 3
   (D) –1
   (E) It cannot be determined from the information given.

19. A 15-gallon mixture of 20% alcohol has 5 gallons of water added to it. The strength of the mixture, as a percent, is approximately

   (A) $12\dfrac{1}{2}$
   (B) $13\dfrac{1}{3}$
   (C) 15
   (D) $16\dfrac{2}{3}$
   (E) 20

20. In the figure below, QXRS is a parallelogram and P is any point on side QS. What is the ratio of the area of triangle PXR to the area of QXRS?

   (A) 1 : 4
   (B) 1 : 3
   (C) 1 : 2
   (D) 2 : 3
   (E) 3 : 4

21. If $x(p + 1) = M$, then $p =$

   (A) $M - 1$
   (B) M
   (C) $\dfrac{M-1}{x}$
   (D) $M - x - 1$
   (E) $\dfrac{M}{x} - 1$

22. If T tons of snow fall in 1 second, how many tons fall in M minutes?

   (A) $60MT$
   (B) $MT + 60$
   (C) MT
   (D) $\dfrac{60M}{T}$
   (E) $\dfrac{MT}{60}$

23. Which of the following is the graph of $x \geq -2$ and $x \leq 3$?

24. From 9 A.M. to 2 P.M., the temperature rose at a constant rate from −14°F to +36°F. What was the temperature at noon?

(A) −4°
(B) +6°
(C) +16°
(D) +26°
(E) +31°

25. What is the sum of ∠EBA + ∠DCF?

(A) 160°
(B) 180°
(C) 195°
(D) 200°
(E) It cannot be determined from the information given.

STOP

END OF SECTION 2. IF YOU HAVE ANY TIME LEFT, GO OVER YOUR WORK IN THIS SECTION ONLY. DO NOT WORK IN ANY OTHER SECTION OF THE TEST.

SECTION 3

35 Questions • Time—30 Minutes

Directions: Each of the following questions consists of an incomplete sentence followed by five words or pairs of words. Choose that word or pair of words which, when substituted for the blank space or spaces, *best* completes the meaning of the sentence and mark the letter of your choice on your answer sheet.

Example:

In view of the extenuating circumstances and the defendant's youth, the judge recommended ----.

(A) conviction
(B) a defense
(C) a mistrial
(D) leniency
(E) life imprisonment

Ⓐ Ⓑ Ⓒ ● Ⓔ

1. Human survival is a result of mutual assistance, since people are essentially ---- rather than ----.
   (A) superior..inferior
   (B) cooperative..competitive
   (C) individualistic..gregarious
   (D) physical..mental
   (E) dependent..insensate

2. For centuries, malnutrition has been ---- in the drought-stricken areas of Africa.
   (A) impalpable
   (B) evasive
   (C) endemic
   (D) divisive
   (E) redundant

3. Even as they ---- their pledges of support, they secretly planned a betrayal; their actions ---- their words.
   (A) demonstrated..echoed
   (B) confirmed..reinforced
   (C) compromised..precluded
   (D) reiterated..belied
   (E) submitted..emphasized

4. The day will come when our ---- will look back upon us and our time with a sense of superiority.
   (A) antecedents
   (B) descendants
   (C) predecessors
   (D) ancestors
   (E) contemporaries

5. Their ---- debate, billed as a(n) ---- of their opinions, was only needless repetition.
   (A) senseless..exoneration
   (B) national..travesty
   (C) incessant..distillation
   (D) primary..renunciation
   (E) final..clarification

6. With the ---- of winter storms, all drivers should take extra ---- while on the road.
   (A) demise..caution
   (B) approach..precautions
   (C) waning..care
   (D) proximity..leisure
   (E) duration..heed

7. Despite our ----, Eva ---- the stranger for directions.
   (A) compliance..harrassed
   (B) encouragement..questioned
   (C) entreaties..pinioned
   (D) intentions..assailed
   (E) warnings..approached

8. The young man was very unlikely to be hired; his appearance was disheveled, slovenly, and ----.
   (A) tousled
   (B) harried
   (C) beleaguered
   (D) mortified
   (E) despondent

9. The use of trained bears in circuses was once a ---- but has now almost ----.
   (A) menace..diminished
   (B) precedent..extinguished
   (C) sinecure..vanquished
   (D) commonplace..ceased
   (E) legacy..vanished

10. Although he has a reputation for aloofness, his manner on that occasion was so ---- that everyone felt perfectly at ease.
    (A) reluctant
    (B) gracious
    (C) malign
    (D) plausible
    (E) spurious

Directions: Each of the following questions consists of a capitalized pair of words followed by five pairs of words lettered A to E. The capitalized words bear some meaningful relationship to each other. Choose the lettered pair of words whose relationship is most similar to that expressed by the capitalized pair and mark its letter on your answer sheet.

Example:

DAY : SUN : :
(A) sunlight : daylight
(B) ray : sun
(C) night : moon
(D) heat : cold
(E) moon : star

Ⓐ Ⓑ ● Ⓓ Ⓔ

11. NEST : BIRD : :
    (A) lair : lion
    (B) kennel : dog
    (C) ring : elephant
    (D) corral : horse
    (E) coop : chicken

12. HAMMER : HIT : :
    (A) screw : replace
    (B) wrench : leak
    (C) glue : paste
    (D) saw : cut
    (E) heat : melt

13. ANGER : DISPLEASURE : :
    (A) ignorance : knowledge
    (B) hatred : understanding
    (C) ecstasy : happiness
    (D) patience : fury
    (E) indicate : triumph

14. TRICKLE : GUSH : :
    (A) flow : stream
    (B) listen : hear
    (C) soar : dive
    (D) touch : collide
    (E) drive : ride

GO ON TO THE NEXT PAGE

15. WINK : EYE : :
    (A) swallow : food
    (B) tap : toe
    (C) flirt : hand
    (D) hit : nail
    (E) smell : nose

16. BOWLING : PIN : :
    (A) basketball : center
    (B) tennis : racket
    (C) baseball : glove
    (D) archery : arrow
    (E) golf : hole

17. LAKE : WET : :
    (A) electricity : nuclear
    (B) ice : cold
    (C) fog : unavoidable
    (D) sand : dry
    (E) jewel : expensive

18. TOOTH : COMB : :
    (A) book : store
    (B) horse : race
    (C) cog : gear
    (D) hair : brush
    (E) dog : hound

19. MISER : STINGINESS : :
    (A) dilettante : skill
    (B) demagogue : passivity
    (C) tyrant : dignity
    (D) altruist : selflessness
    (E) miscreant : honesty

20. CHIVALROUS : GALLANT : :
    (A) sanguine : cheerful
    (B) doleful : happy
    (C) tardy : early
    (D) mercurial : slow
    (E) rich : degenerate

21. LAVA : VOLCANO : :
    (A) snow : mountain
    (B) water : spring
    (C) balloon : air
    (D) eyes : makeup
    (E) chimney : smoke

22. DIFFIDENT : CONFIDENCE : :
    (A) magnificent : beauty
    (B) voluminous : size
    (C) gloomy : cheer
    (D) meticulous : care
    (E) athletic : strength

23. CONDUCTOR : ORCHESTRA : :
    (A) violinist : bow
    (B) pianist : hands
    (C) author : books
    (D) president : country
    (E) school : principal

Questions 24–35 are based on the following passage.

Stephen Crane (1871–1900) wrote a number of novels, short stories, and poems in his short life, as well as working as a war correspondent overseas. "The Bride Comes to Yellow Sky" (1898) is the story of a small-town sheriff who brings home a bride, changing his frontier home forever. It opens with this scene.

The great Pullman was whirling onward with such dignity of motion that a glance from the window seemed simply to prove that the plains of Texas were pouring eastward. Vast flats of green grass, dull-hued
(5) spaces of mesquit and cactus, little groups of frame houses, woods of light and tender trees, all were sweeping into the east, sweeping over the horizon, a precipice.

A newly married pair had boarded this coach at San
(10) Antonio. The man's face was reddened from many days in the wind and sun, and a direct result of his new black clothes was that his brick-colored hands were constantly performing in a most conscious fashion. From time to time he looked down respectfully at his
(15) attire. He sat with a hand on each knee, like a man waiting in a barber's shop. The glances he devoted to other passengers were furtive and shy.

The bride was not pretty, nor was she very young. She wore a dress of blue cashmere, with small reser-
(20) vations of velvet here and there, and with steel buttons abounding. She continually twisted her head to regard her puff sleeves, very stiff, straight, and high. They embarrassed her. It was quite apparent that she had cooked, and that she expected to cook, dutifully. The
(25) blushes caused by the careless scrutiny of some passengers as she had entered the car were strange to see upon this plain, under-class countenance, which was drawn in placid, almost emotionless lines.

They were evidently very happy. "Ever been in a
(30) parlor-car before?" he asked, smiling with delight.

"No," she answered; "I never was. It's fine, ain't it?"

"Great! And then after a while we'll go forward to the diner, and get a big lay-out. Finest meal in the
(35) world. Charge a dollar."

"Oh, do they?" cried the bride. "Charge a dollar? Why, that's too much—for us—ain't it Jack?"

"Not this trip, anyhow," he answered bravely. "We're going to go the whole thing."

(40) Later he explained to her about the trains. "You see, it's a thousand miles from one end of Texas to the other; and this train runs right across it, and never stops but for four times." He had the pride of an owner. He pointed out to her the dazzling fittings of the coach;
(45) and in truth her eyes opened wider as she contemplated the sea-green figured velvet, the shining brass, silver, and glass, the wood that gleamed as darkly brilliant as the surface of a pool of oil. At one end a bronze figure sturdily held a support for a separated
(50) chamber, and at convenient places on the ceiling were frescoes in olive and silver.

To the minds of the pair, their surroundings reflected the glory of their marriage that morning in San Antonio; this was the environment of their new estate;
(55) and the man's face in particular beamed with an elation that made him appear ridiculous to the negro porter. This individual at times surveyed them from afar with an amused and superior grin. On other occasions he bullied them with skill in ways that did
(60) not make it exactly plain to them that they were being bullied. He subtly used all the manners of the most unconquerable kind of snobbery. He oppressed them; but of this oppression they had small knowledge, and they speedily forgot that infrequently a number of
(65) travelers covered them with stares of derisive enjoyment. Historically there was supposed to be something infinitely humorous in their situation.

24. Crane highlights the newlyweds'
    (A) tactlessness
    (B) unsophistication
    (C) wealth
    (D) merriment
    (E) fear

25. The bride's dress is clearly
    (A) beautiful
    (B) torn
    (C) red
    (D) comfortable
    (E) unfamiliar

26. The line "It was quite apparent that she had cooked, and that she expected to cook, dutifully" (lines 23–24) shows the bride's
    (A) natural talent
    (B) submissiveness
    (C) commonness
    (D) both A and B
    (E) both B and C

27. When the bridegroom answers his bride "bravely" (line 38), the implication is that
    (A) he has overcome his fear of her
    (B) his usual posture is weak and sniveling
    (C) gallantry is his natural mode
    (D) he will conquer his anxiety about money for her sake
    (E) it takes courage to speak forthrightly

28. The line "He had the pride of an owner" (line 43) is ironic because
    (A) the bride has no sense of style
    (B) the bridegroom could never own anything so fine
    (C) Crane prefers workers to owners
    (D) the owners of the train take no pride in it
    (E) the bridegroom is not proud of his own belongings

29. The word *estate* (line 54) is used to mean
    (A) property
    (B) inheritance
    (C) status
    (D) statement
    (E) manor

30. The figure of the porter is used to indicate
    (A) a parallel between slavery and marriage
    (B) where the line between worker and owner is drawn
    (C) the absurdity of young love
    (D) that the newlyweds are not alone in the world
    (E) just how unworldly and lower-class the newlyweds are

31. The last sentence of the passage refers to
    (A) the fact that newlyweds are figures of fun
    (B) Crane's amusement at the behavior of the travelers
    (C) people's delight at others' misfortunes
    (D) the joy of the newlyweds despite their surroundings
    (E) readers' sympathy with the characters

32. Crane uses the word *historically* (line 66) to mean
    (A) importantly
    (B) famously
    (C) customarily
    (D) prominently
    (E) ritually

33. Crane's feeling toward the newlyweds is one of
    (A) amused sympathy
    (B) disgusted revulsion
    (C) weary resignation
    (D) scornful derision
    (E) honest hatred

34. Crane probably does not name the newlyweds in this part of the story
    (A) because he does not know who they are
    (B) to make them seem ordinary and universal
    (C) because he wants to surprise the reader
    (D) to prove that they are worthless in his eyes
    (E) to focus attention on the peripheral characters

35. The main goal of this passage is to
    (A) introduce characters and setting
    (B) illustrate a conflict between two characters
    (C) resolve a crisis
    (D) express an opinion
    (E) instruct the reader

STOP

END OF SECTION 3. IF YOU HAVE ANY TIME LEFT, GO OVER YOUR WORK IN THIS SECTION ONLY. DO NOT WORK IN ANY OTHER SECTION OF THE TEST.

SECTION 4

25 Questions • Time—30 Minutes

Directions: Solve the following problems using any available space on the page for scratchwork. On your answer sheet fill in the choice which best corresponds to the correct answer.

Notes: The figures accompanying the problems are drawn as accurately as possible unless otherwise stated in specific problems. Again, unless otherwise stated, all figures lie in the same plane. All numbers used in these problems are real numbers. Calculators are permitted for this test.

Reference Information

Circle: $C = 2\pi r$, $A = \pi r^2$

Rectangle: $A = lw$

Rectangular Solid: $V = lwh$

Cylinder: $V = \pi r^2 h$

Triangle: $A = \frac{1}{2}bh$

Right triangle: $a^2 + b^2 = c^2$

45°-45°-90° triangle: legs x, x; hypotenuse $x\sqrt{2}$

30°-60°-90° triangle: sides x, $x\sqrt{3}$, $2x$

The number of degrees of arc in a circle is 360.
The measure in degrees of a straight angle is 180.
The sum of the measures in degrees of the angles of a triangle is 180.

Part 1: Quantitative Comparison Questions

Directions: Questions 1–15 each consist of two quantities—one in Column A, the other in Column B. Compare the two quantities and mark your answer sheet as follows:

(A) if the quantity in Column A is greater;
(B) if the quantity in Column B is greater;
(C) if the two quantities are equal;
(D) if the relationship cannot be determined from the information given.

Notes:

(1) Information concerning one or both of the compared quantities will be centered above the two columns for some items.
(2) Symbols that appear in both columns represent the same thing in Column A as in Column B.
(3) Letters such as x, n, and k are symbols for real numbers.

Examples

	Column A	Column B	Answers
	$a > 0$		
	$x > 0$		
E1.	$a - x$	$a + x$	Ⓐ ● Ⓒ Ⓓ
E2.	The average of 17, 19, 21, 23	The average of 6, 18, 20, 22	● Ⓑ Ⓒ Ⓓ

DO NOT MARK CHOICE (E) FOR THESE QUESTIONS. THERE ARE ONLY FOUR ANSWER CHOICES.

Diagnostic Examination

	Column A	Column B
1.	$2x - 1$	$2x + 1$

2. $x < -1$

Column A	Column B
$\dfrac{1}{x^2}$	x

3.

[Triangle with angles $a°$, $b°$ at top, and $c°$, $d°$ where $d°$ is exterior]

Column A	Column B
$a + b + c$	$c + d$

4.

Column A	Column B
$\tfrac{1}{4}(a+b)c$	$\dfrac{ac + bc}{4}$

5.

[Triangle ABC with angle $b°$ at B, $a°$ at A, $c°$ at C]

Note: Figure not drawn to scale.

Column A	Column B
AB	AC

6.

[Annulus with inner radius 3 and outer ring of width 2]

Column A	Column B
The area of the shaded region	The area of the small circle

The sum of all the rows and all the columns are equal.

w	4	y
7	x	4
v	7	z

7.

Column A	Column B
$v + z$	$y + w$

8.

Column A	Column B
$(n + 1)^3$	$n^3 + 1$

9.

[Two parallel lines $a \parallel b$ cut by transversals, with angles m and $75°$ marked]

Column A	Column B
$180 - m$	$180 - 75$

10.

Column A	Column B
$(26 \times 39) + (39 \times 13)$	$(39)^2$

GO ON TO THE NEXT PAGE

56   Master the SAT

	Column A	**Column B**
11.	$x = 1$, $1 > y > 0$ $\quad \dfrac{1}{y}$	x

Figure: two lines cut by a transversal, with angles $x°$ on line l, and $y°$, $z°$ on line w; $l \parallel w$.

	Column A	**Column B**
12.	$x + y$	$x + z$

	Column A	**Column B**
13.	$(m^2 - 1)(2m + 2)$	$(m + 1)^2(2m - 2)$
14.	0.7% of 62	70% of 6,200
15.	The area of a square with side s	The area of an equilateral triangle with side $2s$

Part 2: Student-Produced Response Questions

Directions: Solve each of these problems. Write the answer in the corresponding grid on the answer sheet and fill in the ovals beneath each answer you write. Here are some examples.

Answer: $\dfrac{3}{4}$ (= .75; show answer either way)   Answer: 325

Note: A mixed number such as $3\tfrac{1}{2}$ must be gridded as 7/2 or as 3.5. If gridded as "31/2," it will be read as "thirty-one halves."

Note: Either position is correct.

16. In the figure below, $l_1 \parallel l_2$. If the measure of $\angle x = 70°$ and the measure of $\angle y = 105°$, what is the measure of $\angle r$? (Disregard the degree symbol when you grid your answer.)

17. What is the value of $-x^2 - 2x^3$ when $x = -1$?

18. Jessica received marks of 87, 93, and 86 on three successive tests. What grade must she receive on a fourth test in order to have an average of 90?

19. In a circle with radius 6, what is the measure (in degrees) of an arc whose length is 2π? (Disregard the degree symbol when you grid your answer.)

20. If $\dfrac{2x}{3\sqrt{2}} = \dfrac{3\sqrt{2}}{x}$, what is the positive value of x?

21. Using the table below, what is the median of the following data?

Score	Frequency
20	4
30	4
50	7

22. If $A * B$ is defined as $\dfrac{AB - B}{-B}$, what is the value of $-2 * 2$?

23. A man travels 320 miles in 8 hours. If he continues at the same rate, how many miles will he travel in the next 2 hours?

24. A booklet contains 30 pages. If 9 pages in the booklet have drawings, what percent of the pages in the booklet have drawings? (Disregard the percent symbol when you grid your answer.)

25. If 3 copier machines can copy 300 sheets in 3 hours, assuming the same rate, how long (in hours) will it take 6 such copiers to copy 600 sheets?

STOP

END OF SECTION 4. IF YOU HAVE ANY TIME LEFT, GO OVER YOUR WORK IN THIS SECTION ONLY. DO NOT WORK IN ANY OTHER SECTION OF THE TEST.

SECTION 5

12 Questions • Time—15 Minutes

Directions: The two passages given below deal with a related topic. Following the passages are questions about the content of each passage or about the relationship between the two passages. Answer the questions based upon what is stated or implied in the passages and in any introductory material provided. Mark the letter of your choice on your answer sheet.

Questions 1–12 are based on the following passages.

Matthew Henson was born in 1866 of free black parents in Maryland. He met Commander Robert Peary in 1888 and became first his servant and then his assistant on Peary's major expeditions to the Arctic. In these two passages, Henson and Peary describe the same area in Greenland, a place known as Karnah.

Passage 1—from Henson's Account of the 1908 Expedition

We stopped at Kookan, the most prosperous of the Esquimo settlements, a village of five tupiks (skin tents), housing twenty-four people, and from there we sailed to the ideal community of Karnah.

(5) Karnah is the most delightful spot on the Greenland coast. Situated on a gently southward sloping knoll are the igloos and tupiks, where I have spent many pleasant days with my Esquimo friends and learned much of the folklore and history. Lofty mountains, sublime in their (10) grandeur, overtower and surround this place, and its only exposure is southward toward the sun. In winter its climate is not severe, as compared with other portions of this country, and in the perpetual daylight of summer, life here is ideal. Rivulets of clear, cold water, the beds (15) of which are grass- and flower-covered, run down the sides of the mountain and, but for the lack of trees, the landscape is as delightful as anywhere on earth.

Passage 2—from Peary's Account of the 1891 Expedition

From the eastern point of Academy Bay the main shore of the gulf extends, due east, to the face of the great (20) Heilprin Glacier, and then on beside the great ice-stream, until the crests of the cliffs disappear under the white shroud of the "Great Ice." From here on, the eastern and northern sides of the head of the gulf are an almost continuous glacier face, six great ice-streams, (25) separated by as many precipitous nunataks, flowing down from the interior ice-cap to discharge an enormous fleet of bergs. As a result of this free discharge, the great white viscosity of the interior has settled down into a huge, and in clear weather easily (30) discernible, semi-circular basin, similar to those of Tossukatek, Great Kariak, and Jacobshavn. In this head of the gulf, situated some in the face of the glaciers, and others a short distance beyond them, are seven or eight islands, most of which bear proof of former glaciation. (35) Along the north-western shore of the gulf, the vertical cliffs resume their sway, back of which rise the trio of striking peaks, Mounts Daly, Adams, and Putname. The cliffs continue westward for some little distance, then gradually merge into a gentle slope, which is in turn (40) succeeded by the face of the Hubbard Glacier. West of the glacier, cliffs of a different character (red and grey sandstone) occur, and extend to the grand and picturesque red-brown Castle Cliffs at the entrance to Bowdoin Bay. At these cliffs, the shore takes an abrupt turn to (45) the northward, into the now familiar but previously unknown Bowdoin Bay, in which was located the headquarters of my last Expedition.

This bay has an extreme length of eleven miles, and an average width of between three and four miles. What (50) with its southern exposure, the protection from the wind afforded by the cliffs and bluffs which enclose it, and the warmth of colouring of its shores, it presents one of the most desirable locations for a house. The scenery is also varied and attractive, offering to the eye greater (55) contrasts, with less change of position, than any other locality occurring to me. Around the circuit of the bay are seven glaciers with exposures to all points of the compass, and varying in size from a few hundred feet to over two miles in width.

(60) The ice-cap itself is also in evidence here, its vertical face in one place capping and forming a continuation of a vertical cliff which rises direct from the bay. From the western point of the bay, a line of grey sandstone

cliffs—the Sculptured Cliffs of Karnah—interrupted
(65) by a single glacier in a distance of eight miles, and
carved by the restless arctic elements into turrets, bastions, huge amphitheatres, and colossal statues of men
and animals, extends to Cape Ackland, the Karnah of
the natives. Here the cliffs end abruptly, and the shore
(70) trending north-westward to Cape Cleveland, eighteen
miles distant, consists of an almost continuous succession of fan-shaped, rocky deltas formed by glacier
streams. Back of the shoreline is a gradually sloping
foreshore, rising to the foot of an irregular series of hills,
(75) which rise more steeply to the ice-cap lying upon their
summits. In almost every depression between these
hills, the face of a glacier may be seen, and it is the
streams from these that have made the shore what it is,
and formed the wide shoals off it, on which every year
(80) a numerous fleet of icebergs becomes stranded.

1. Henson uses the word *exposure* (line 11) to mean
   (A) denunciation
   (B) unmasking
   (C) emptiness
   (D) danger
   (E) openness

2. Henson's main impression of Karnah is one of
   (A) apprehension
   (B) dismay
   (C) indifference
   (D) pleasure
   (E) tolerance

3. Henson might prefer that Karnah
   (A) were not so far north
   (B) were warmer
   (C) were uninhabited
   (D) lay further inland
   (E) had more trees

4. Peary admires Bowdoin Bay for its
   (A) diverse vistas
   (B) incredible length
   (C) calm waters
   (D) impressive tides
   (E) great ice-streams

5. Peary compares the arctic elements to
   (A) avenging Furies
   (B) athletic challenges
   (C) stonecarvers
   (D) wild horses
   (E) ice palaces

6. Future explorers might use Peary's description to
   (A) locate their ships in Karnah's harbor
   (B) find their way around Greenland's shoreline
   (C) decide the future of native settlements
   (D) identify trees and vegetation on the island
   (E) reenact Peary's discovery of the North Pole

7. In general, Peary's description is in
   (A) chronological order, according to his various trips
   (B) spatial order, proceeding along the coastline
   (C) chronological order, moving from past to present
   (D) spatial order, moving from west to east
   (E) spatial order, moving in a circle around the ship

8. The "lofty mountains" described by Henson (line 9) are probably Peary's
   (A) Sculptured Cliffs (line 64)
   (B) Cape Cleveland (line 70)
   (C) Heilprin Glacier (line 20)
   (D) Mount Daly (line 37)
   (E) Great Kariak (line 31)

GO ON TO THE NEXT PAGE

9. Unlike Henson, Peary seems intent on
    (A) snubbing the natives
    (B) discussing flora and fauna
    (C) focusing on geology
    (D) raising political issues
    (E) extolling the delights of Karnah

10. Peary and Henson seem to agree on
    (A) the severity of Greenland's weather
    (B) the area's attractiveness
    (C) the need for future exploration
    (D) both A and B
    (E) both B and C

11. Unlike Peary's account, Henson's tone is primarily
    (A) humorous
    (B) objective
    (C) scientific
    (D) appreciative
    (E) technical

12. Unlike Henson's account of his 1908 expedition, Peary pays considerable attention to
    (A) Esquimo settlements
    (B) Esquimo folklore
    (C) Esquimo dietary restrictions
    (D) glaciers and ice formations
    (E) Karnah's overall physical characteristics

STOP

END OF SECTION 5. IF YOU HAVE ANY TIME LEFT, GO OVER YOUR WORK IN THIS SECTION ONLY. DO NOT WORK IN ANY OTHER SECTION OF THE TEST.

SECTION 6

10 Questions • Time—15 Minutes

Directions: Solve the following problems using any available space on the page for scratchwork. On your answer sheet fill in the choice which best corresponds to the correct answer.

Notes: The figures accompanying the problems are drawn as accurately as possible unless otherwise stated in specific problems. Again, unless otherwise stated, all figures lie in the same plane. All numbers used in these problems are real numbers. Calculators are permitted for this test.

Reference Information

Circle: $C = 2\pi r$, $A = \pi r^2$
Rectangle: $A = lw$
Rectangular Solid: $V = lwh$
Cylinder: $V = \pi r^2 h$
Triangle: $A = \frac{1}{2}bh$
$a^2 + b^2 = c^2$

45°-45°-90° triangle: sides x, x, $x\sqrt{2}$
30°-60°-90° triangle: sides x, $x\sqrt{3}$, $2x$

The number of degrees of arc in a circle is 360.
The measure in degrees of a straight angle is 180.
The sum of the measures in degrees of the angles of a triangle is 180.

---

1. The coordinates of vertices X and Y of an equilateral triangle XYZ are $(-4,0)$ and $(4,0)$ respectively. The coordinates of Z may be

    (A) $(0, 2\sqrt{3})$
    (B) $(0, 4\sqrt{3})$
    (C) $(4, 4\sqrt{3})$
    (D) $(0, 4)$
    (E) $(4\sqrt{3}, 0)$

2. There are just two ways in which 5 may be expressed as the sum of two different positive (nonzero) integers, namely, $5 = 4 + 1 = 3 + 2$. In how many ways may 9 be expressed as the sum of two different positive (nonzero) integers?

    (A) 3
    (B) 4
    (C) 5
    (D) 6
    (E) 7

3. A board 7 feet 9 inches long is divided into three equal parts. What is the length of each part?

    (A) 2 ft. $6\frac{1}{3}$ in.
    (B) 2 ft. 7 in.
    (C) 2 ft. 8 in.
    (D) 2 ft. $8\frac{1}{3}$ in.
    (E) 2 ft. 9 in.

4. What is the smallest possible integer $K > 1$ such that $R^2 = S^3 = K$, for some integers R and S?

    (A) 4
    (B) 8
    (C) 27
    (D) 64
    (E) 81

GO ON TO THE NEXT PAGE

5. The number of square units in the area of triangle RST is
   (A) 10
   (B) 12.5
   (C) 15.5
   (D) 17.5
   (E) 20

6. Which of the following has the same value as $\frac{P}{Q}$?
   (A) $\frac{P-2}{Q-2}$
   (B) $\frac{1+P}{1+Q}$
   (C) $\frac{P^2}{Q^2}$
   (D) $\frac{3P}{3Q}$
   (E) $\frac{P+3}{Q+3}$

7. In the accompanying figure, ACB is a straight angle and DC is perpendicular to CE. If the number of degrees in angle ACD is represented by x, the number of degrees in angle BCE is represented by

   Note: Figure not drawn to scale.

   (A) $90 - x$
   (B) $x - 90$
   (C) $90 + x$
   (D) $180 - x$
   (E) $45 + x$

Questions 8 and 9 refer to the following drawing:

8. In parallelogram ABCD, what is the ratio of the shaded area to the unshaded area?
   (A) 1 : 2
   (B) 1 : 1
   (C) 4 : 3
   (D) 2 : 1
   (E) It cannot be determined from the information given.

9. If the ratio of AB to BC is 4 : 9, what is the area of parallelogram ABCD?
   (A) 36
   (B) 26
   (C) 18
   (D) 13
   (E) It cannot be determined from the information given.

10. A store owner buys eggs for M cents per dozen and sells them for $\frac{M}{6}$ cents apiece. At this rate, what is the profit on a dozen eggs?
    (A) $\frac{M}{12}$ cents
    (B) $\frac{M}{6}$ cents
    (C) $\frac{M}{2}$ cents
    (D) M cents
    (E) $2M$ cents

STOP

END OF SECTION 6. IF YOU HAVE ANY TIME LEFT, GO OVER YOUR WORK IN THIS SECTION ONLY. DO NOT WORK IN ANY OTHER SECTION OF THE TEST.

DIAGNOSTIC EXAMINATION
Answer Key

Section 1: Verbal

1. B
2. B
3. C
4. E
5. D
6. C
7. A
8. B
9. A
10. B
11. B
12. D
13. E
14. E
15. B
16. D
17. C
18. B
19. A
20. B
21. E
22. E
23. D
24. A
25. D
26. C
27. B
28. C
29. D
30. E
31. C

Section 2: Math (Code: A = Arithmetic; AL = Algebra; G = Geometry; O = Other)

1. D (A)
2. A (AL)
3. E (G)
4. B (AL)
5. B (G)
6. C (O)
7. B (AL)
8. C (A)
9. E (G)
10. A (G)
11. E (A)
12. D (A)
13. D (G)
14. B (O)
15. C (G)
16. B (A)
17. C (O)
18. E (A)
19. C (A)
20. C (G)
21. E (AL)
22. A (A)
23. E (O)
24. C (A)
25. A (G)

Section 3: Verbal

1. B
2. C
3. D
4. B
5. E
6. B
7. E
8. A
9. D
10. B
11. A
12. D
13. C
14. D
15. B
16. E
17. B
18. C
19. D
20. A
21. B
22. C
23. D
24. B
25. E
26. E
27. D
28. B
29. C
30. E
31. A
32. C
33. A
34. B
35. A

Section 4: Math

Part 1

1. B
2. A
3. C
4. C
5. B
6. A
7. B
8. D
9. B
10. C
11. A
12. C
13. C
14. B
15. B

Part 2

16. 35
17. 1
18. 94
19. 60
20. 3
21. 30
22. 3
23. 80
24. 30
25. 3

Section 5: Verbal
1. E
2. D
3. E
4. A
5. C
6. B
7. B
8. A
9. C
10. D
11. D
12. D

Section 6: Math (Code: A = Arithmetic; AL = Algebra; G = Geometry; O = Other)
1. B (G)
2. B (O)
3. B (G)
4. D (A)
5. D (G)
6. D (AL)
7. A (G)
8. B (G)
9. E (G)
10. D (AL)

DIAGNOSTIC EXAMINATION
Explanatory Answers

Note: A following a math answer explanation indicates that a calculator could be helpful in solving that particular problem.

Section 1

1. **(B)** A position that provides authority to award contracts is also likely to allow the holder to *incur* (take on) obligations to pay bills.
2. **(B)** A witness who reveals very little information, even when questioned by an experienced attorney, is *recalcitrant* (stubborn).
3. **(C)** The word *although* signifies a shift in meaning. Even though *substantial* (large) resources had been applied, the solution was still *elusive* (hard to determine).
4. **(E)** The only logical choice is the one in which both words have the same connotation; both must be either positive or negative. Only choice (E) satisfies this condition with two positive words.
5. **(D)** The word in the first blank must be a synonym for *kept*. *Retained* and *received* both might satisfy this condition, but only *insured* makes sense in the second blank.
6. **(C)** The first blank needs a positive word to describe the way the agent calmed the travelers; the second blank needs a negative word to describe the delayed travelers. Only choice (C) meets both conditions.
7. **(A)** The lover of democracy has an aversion or antipathy toward totalitarianism.
8. **(B)** This answer needs either two negative or two positive words. The other four choices have a combination of positive and negative words. Since choice (B) has two negative words describing the situation, it is the only correct response.
9. **(A)** The words need to be opposites. One word needs to be supportive of free individuals and the other needs to undermine it.
10. **(B)** Those who are *powerful* are also *mighty*. Those that are *mediocre* are also *ordinary*.
11. **(B)** A *horse* is a four-legged animal that is covered with an outer growth of *hair*. A *sheep* is a four-legged animal that is covered with an outer growth of *wool*.
12. **(D)** A gobble is a sound made by a particular kind of bird, a *turkey*. A *twitter* is a sound made by some *birds*.
13. **(E)** One *sells* something to someone, who thereby *purchases* it. One *gives* something to someone, who thereby *receives* it.
14. **(E)** A *novel* is a type of *book*, just as a *loafer* is a type of *shoe*.
15. **(B)** *Temerity* is a lack of *caution*; *effrontery* is a lack of *shame*.
16. **(D)** The roots of classical architecture date back to ancient Rome, when people of the highest social orders embraced its style.
17. **(C)** This answer is the exception because just the opposite is true—the same spatial divisions were applied no matter what the type of building.
18. **(B)** The context of the sentence indicates that *three-part* is the only possible answer.
19. **(A)** The passage mentions all of the columns by name with the exception of Egyptian. (See lines 25–26.)

20. **(B)** Capital is the answer. Lines 35–36 define the parts of the column as the capital, the shaft, and the base.
21. **(E)** The context of the sentence indicates that *balance* is the only possible answer.
22. **(E)** Throughout the passage the idea that classical architecture is filled with rules that must be followed is stressed.
23. **(D)** The word is used several times to refer to the feathers and leaves with which the narrator will appease the spirit. It is thus a *tribute* rather than any of the other synonyms.
24. **(A)** This interpretation question is quite literal. Go with your first answer on questions of this kind. The narrator's entire dilemma surrounds the difficulty of finding *bare ground* in a snowy landscape.
25. **(D)** It is a *quest*, because she is looking for a patch of bare ground where she can perform a religious rite.
26. **(C)** This is the essential problem of the story: How can bare ground be found in this snowy landscape?
27. **(B)** Looking back on the events, the adult narrator feels sorry for the small child she was. She now sees that the task was too great for someone so small—that a child could not hope or be expected to save her sister's life.
28. **(C)** Try the various synonyms in context, and you will see that only *inflamed* makes any sense.
29. **(D)** The child is afraid that the offering did not reach the ground, and therefore, her sister will not be saved. If it did not reach the ground, perhaps it is because she did not have faith in nature to show her a bare patch of ground and did not follow the medicine-woman's instructions.
30. **(E)** If you understand question 28, you probably answered this question correctly. The small child blames herself for her lack of faith, which she sees as causing her sister's turn for the worse.
31. **(C)** This evaluation question is a restatement of interpretation question 26. Throughout the passage, the reader is made aware of the child's struggle and her essential decency. The author wants us to like the child and forgive her as she herself has done.

Section 2

1. **(D)** $\frac{3}{4} = .75$

    $\frac{35}{71}$ is slightly less than $\frac{35}{70} = .5$

    $\frac{13}{20} = \frac{13 \times 5}{20 \times 5} = \frac{65}{100} = .65$

    $\frac{71}{101}$ is very close to $\frac{7}{10}$ or .7

    $\frac{15}{20} = \frac{15 \times 5}{20 \times 5} = \frac{75}{100} = .75$

    $\frac{19}{24} = 24 \overline{)19.00}$ which is more than $\frac{3}{4}$

    .79
    168
    220
    216

2. **(A)** $820 + R + S - 610 = 342$

    $R + S + 210 = 342$

    $R + S = 132$

    If $R = 2S$, then $2S + S = 132$

    $3S = 132$

    $S = 44$

3. **(E)**

```
          x yd.
      ┌─────────┐
y yd. │         │
      │         │
      └─────────┘
```

Area = xy sq. yd. = $9xy$ sq. ft.

$9xy \cdot 5 = 45xy$

4. **(B)** $7M = 3M - 20$

$\qquad 4M = -20$

$\qquad M = -5$

$M + 7 = -5 + 7 = 2$

5. **(B)** Arc $EA = 85°$ and arc $BD = 15°$. Since a central angle is measured by its arc, then

$$\begin{aligned} \text{angle } ECA &= \tfrac{1}{2}(AE - BD) \\ &= \tfrac{1}{2}(85 - 15) \\ &= \tfrac{1}{2} \cdot 70 \\ &= 35° \end{aligned}$$

6. **(C)** The smallest positive number divisible by 3, 4, or 5 is $3 \cdot 4 \cdot 5 = 60$. Hence, the desired number is $60 + 2 = 62$.

7. **(B)** Since there are $4d$ quarter miles in d miles the charge = $75 + 15(4d - 1)$.

8. **(C)** Assume that there are 100 enlistees on the post; then 30 are from New York State and $\tfrac{1}{10} \times 30$ are from New York City. $\tfrac{3}{100} = 3$

9. **(E)** If you know only the hypotenuse of a right triangle, you cannot determine its legs. Hence, the area of the rectangle cannot be determined from the data given.

10. **(A)** If angle RPQ > angle RQP, then $\tfrac{1}{2}$ angle P > $\tfrac{1}{2}$ angle Q; then angle SPQ > angle SQP. Since the larger side lies opposite the larger angle, it follows that $SQ > SP$.

11. **(E)** $3.14 \times 10^6 = 3.14 \times 1{,}000{,}000$

$\qquad\qquad = 3{,}140{,}000$

12. **(D)** $\dfrac{36}{29 - \tfrac{4}{0.2}} = \dfrac{36}{29 - 20} = \dfrac{36}{9} = 4$

13. **(D)** Diameter = $4\sqrt{2}$, since it is the hypotenuse of a right isosceles triangle of leg 4.

Then the radius = $2\sqrt{2}$

Area of semicircle = $\tfrac{1}{2} \times \pi \quad (2\sqrt{2})^2$

$\qquad\qquad\qquad = \tfrac{1}{2} \times \pi 8 = 4\pi$

14. **(B)** Consecutive odd numbers may be represented as

$\qquad 2n + 1$

$\qquad 2n + 3$

$\qquad \underline{2n + 5}$

Sum = $6n + 9$

Always divisible by 3. Thus, only II.

15. **(C)** Angle *BCD* is formed by tangent and chord and is equal to one-half of arc *BC*. Angle *A* is an inscribed angle and is also equal to one-half of arc *BC*. Hence, angle *A* = angle *BCD* = 40°.

16. **(B)** Let *x* = amount of marked price. Then

    $\frac{1}{5}x = 15$

    $x = 7$

    75 − 15 = $60

17. **(C)** This problem cannot be solved by simply doing subtraction. To give an example: if you read pages 1 and 2 of a book, how many pages have you read? The answer is obviously 2; we can conclude then that we do not obtain the answer by subtracting 1 from 2. Instead we subtract 1 from 2 and add 1.

    49 − 7 + 1 = 43
    157 − 101 + 1 = 57
    43 + 57 = 100

18. **(E)** If $\frac{P}{Q} = \frac{4}{5}$, then 5*P* = 4*Q*. However, there is no way of determining from this the value of 2*P* + *Q*.

19. **(C)** The new solution is $\frac{3}{20}$ pure alcohol or 15%.

    Starting Sol.   Resulting Sol.

20. **(C)** Area of *QXRS* = *XR* × altitude from *P* to *XR*. Area of △*PXR* = $\frac{1}{2}$ *XR* × altitude from *P* to *XR* Hence, ratio of area of △ to *QXRS* = 1 : 2.

21. **(E)** *x*(*p* + 1) = *M*

    Divide both sides by *x*.

    $p + 1 = \frac{M}{x}$ or $p = \frac{M}{x} - 1$

22. **(A)** $\frac{T}{1} = \frac{x}{60M}$

    x = 60*MT*

23. **(E)** It can be helpful to graph each of the inequalities and then put the two graphs together to find the overlapping area.

24. **(C)** Rise in temperature = 36 − (−14) = 36 + 14 = 50°. $\frac{50}{5}$ = 10° (hourly rise). Hence, at noon, temperature = −14 + 3(10) = −14 + 30 = +16°.

25. **(A)** When we are asked for the sum of two items, we often *cannot* state the values of the individual items. This is the case in this problem. We can say ∠BAD is 75° and ∠CDA is 85°. We also know that ABCD is a quadrilateral and must contain 360°. Therefore, ∠ABC + ∠BCD = 200°

$$\angle EBA + \angle ABC = 180°$$
$$\angle BCD + \angle DCF = 180°$$
$$\angle EBA + \angle ABC + \angle BCD + \angle DCFC = 360°$$
$$\angle EBA + 200° + \angle DCF = 360°$$
$$\angle EBA + \angle DCF = 160°$$

Section 3

1. **(B)** "Mutual assistance" implies that people are *cooperative*. Since "rather than" indicates a shift in meaning, the word in the second blank must have an opposing connotation; only *competitive* satisfies this condition.

2. **(C)** A condition that has existed for a long time in a particular place is said to be *endemic* to that location.

3. **(D)** The first blank could logically be filled by any of the choices. However, the secret betrayal implies that the actions *belied* (showed to be untrue) the words of the *reiterated* (repeated) pledges of support.

4. **(B)** Of the choices, the only one that could "look back upon us and our time" is our *descendants*.

5. **(E)** Choices (B), (D), and (E) are possibilities for the first blank. However, the second words in choices (B) and (D) make no logical sense. A *final* debate is likely to offer *clarification* of opinions.

6. **(B)** This is the only logical answer. "With the *duration*" is poor diction.

7. **(E)** The sentence establishes an opposition between "our" wishes and Eva's action. Only (E) satisfies this requirement.

8. **(A)** A key word in this sentence is *appearance*. The words following all tell how a person physically looks. Choices (B), (C), (D), and (E) describe feelings or behaviors. The only word describing physical appearance is *tousled* (A), which means "unkempt."

9. **(D)** The word *but* is your clue that the two words must have opposite connotations. The only choice that satisfies this condition is (D): the use of trained bears was once a *commonplace* (ordinary occurrence) but has now almost *ceased* (stopped).

10. **(B)** The word *although* signals that the second part of the sentence will describe the opposite of *aloofness* (coldness of manner). Therefore, the correct answer is *gracious* (courteous and kind).

11. **(A)** A *nest* is a structure built by a *bird* as a place to live and raise young. A *lair*, or *den*, is a place created by a *lion* for similar purpose. All the other choices include structures that are man-made.

12. **(D)** A *hammer* is used to *hit* an object. A *saw* is used to *cut* an object.

13. **(C)** The capitalized words are degrees of one another. And *ecstasy* is a stronger form of *happiness*.

14. **(D)** To *trickle* is to flow slowly; to *gush*, to flow profusely. Similarly, to *touch* is to come into gentle contact and to *collide* is to come into violent contact.

15. **(B)** We intentionally use the *eye* to *wink* and the *toe* to *tap* but we couldn't be said to intentionally use the *nose* to *smell*.

16. **(E)** In *bowling* you aim at the *pin* as in *golf* you aim at the *hole*.

17. **(B)** A *lake* will necessarily be experienced as *wet*, and *ice* necessarily as *cold*.

18. **(C)** A *tooth* is part of a *comb*; a *cog* is part of a *gear*.

19. **(D)** A *miser* is characterized by *stinginess*. An *altruist* (a person concerned with the welfare of others) is characterized by *selflessness*.

20. **(A)** One who is *chivalrous* is *gallant* and one who is *sanguine* is *cheerful*. Answers (B), (C), and (D) are antonyms.

21. **(B)** *Lava* flows out of a *volcano* and *water* flows out of a *spring*. Although answer choice (E) has some appeal, it reverses the order.

22. **(C)** To be *diffident* (timid) is to be lacking in *confidence*. Similarly, to be *gloomy* is to be lacking in *cheer*.

23. **(D)** A *conductor* leads an *orchestra* and a *president* leads a *country*.

24. **(B)** Their preoccupation with their stiff, new clothing, their awe at the train's typical conveniences, and their blushes at the glances of travelers—all of these combine to paint the picture of an innocent, unworldly pair.

25. **(E)** The bride constantly "twisted her head to regard her puff sleeves" (lines 20–21) and is embarrassed by them. Her dress is probably brand new, and she is certainly unused to such finery.

26. **(E)** With this single line, Crane paints a life of hard work and resignation.

27. **(D)** The bridegroom is putting on a brave face for the sake of his bride, who is even more unsophisticated than he.

28. **(B)** The bridegroom's pride is part of his delight in his "new estate" of marriage. He can show off for his bride, but there is no doubt that such elegance is rare for him.

29. **(C)** The charmingly decorated train is thought by the newlyweds to be indicative of their new status in life. Because they feel exalted by their new marriage, they imagine that they deserve such luxury.

30. **(E)** The porter is a lower-class working man, and is probably looked down upon by travelers, but he welcomes this opportunity to sneer at those lower on the ladder than himself.

31. **(A)** Travelers look at the newlyweds with "derisive enjoyment" (line 63). It is clear that they are just married, and there is something amusing about this.

32. **(C)** Customarily, people in the position of the newlyweds are amusing to others. None of the other synonyms makes sense in this context.

33. **(A)** Crane is not derisive (D); he leaves that to the other travelers and the porter. On the contrary, his attitude seems to be a slightly detached air of sympathy at the newlyweds' embarrassment and innocence.

34. **(B)** Their names are unimportant; what is vital is their provincialism and ordinariness. The reader can thus identify a type without feeling overly empathetic.

35. **(A)** This is, in fact, the beginning of the story, and, as with most short stories, its object is to introduce characters and setting. No opinion is expressed (D); the passage is simply descriptive.

Section 4

Part 1

1. **(B)** Since $2x$ is the same in both columns, adding 1 to $2x$ will surely be larger than subtracting 1 from it. The answer is (B).

2. **(A)** In Column A, x^2 will be a positive number, therefore $\frac{1}{x^2}$ will also be positive. In Column B, x will always be negative, so (A) is greater.

3. **(C)** $a + b + c$ is the sum of the angles of a triangle and therefore equals 180°. $c + d$ is the sum of supplementary angles and, therefore, also equals 180°.

4. **(C)** Using the distributive property in Column A, $(a + b)c = ac + bc$. Therefore $\frac{1}{4}(ac + bc) = \frac{ac+bc}{4}$. Column A and Column B are equal.

5. **(B)** Angle b is the largest in the triangle, so the side opposite b, side AC, is the largest side of the triangle. Therefore AC is larger than AB. Answer (B) is correct.

6. **(A)** The area of the small circle is $\pi(3)^2 = 9\pi$. The area of the shaded region is the area of the large circle minus that of the small circle. The area of the large circle is $\pi(5)^2 = 25\pi$. The area of the shaded region is $25\pi - 9\pi = 16\pi$. The area of the shaded region is larger than that of the smaller circle. Hence, answer (A) is correct.

7. **(B)** We are told that the sums of all the rows and columns are the same. We could set up an equation:

$$\frac{v + z + 7}{-4} = \frac{w + y + 4}{-4}$$

$$v + z + 3 \qquad w + y$$

Therefore, $w + y$ must be greater than $v + z$.

8. **(D)** It is impossible to determine which is larger. Taking two examples: $n = -\frac{1}{2}$; $(n + 1)^3 = (\frac{1}{2})^3 = \frac{1}{8}$ and $n^3 + 1 = (-\frac{1}{2})^3 + 1 = -\frac{1}{8} + 1 = \frac{7}{8}$. In this example, Column B is greater than Column A. However, $n = \frac{1}{2}$, $(n + 1)^3 = (1\frac{1}{2})^3 = 3\frac{3}{8}$ and $n^3 + 1 = (\frac{1}{2})^3 + 1 = 1\frac{1}{8}$. In this example, Column A is greater than Column B.

9. **(B)** m and n are alternate interior angles, so $m = n$. n and $75°$ are supplementary angles, so $n = 180° - 75° = 105° = m$ and $180° - m = 75°$. Therefore, $180° - 75° > 180° - m$, and (B) is the correct choice.

10. **(C)** Using the distributive property, $(26 \times 39) + (39 \times 13) = 39(26 + 13) = 39 \times 39 = (39)^2$. Therefore, Column A and Column B are equal.

11. **(A)** Since y is a positive fraction less than 1, $\frac{1}{y}$ is a positive fraction greater than 1. Therefore, $\frac{1}{y} > x$. Answer (A) is the correct choice.

12. **(C)** y and z are vertical angles and therefore equal angles. Thus, $x + y$ and $x + z$ are equal sums.

13. **(C)** Factoring Column A $(m^2 - 1)(2m + 2) = (m - 1)(m + 1) \cdot 2(m + 1)$. Rearrange the factor so that $(m + 1)^2 \cdot 2(m - 1) = (m + 1)^2(2m - 2)$, which is equal to Column B.

14. **(B)** In Column A, 0.7% of 62 is $(0.007) \times (62) = 0.434$. In Column B, 70% of 6200 is 4340. Column B is larger.

15. **(B)** The area of a square with side s is s^2. The height of the triangle, using the Pythagorean Theorem, is $\sqrt{(2s)^2 + s^2} = \sqrt{3s^2} = s\sqrt{3}$. The area of the triangle is $\frac{1}{2}(2s)(s\sqrt{3}) = s^2\sqrt{3}$. Thus, the area of the triangle (Column B) is larger.

Part 2

16. The measure of $\angle b = 70°$. It is an alternate interior angle with angle x.

    The measure of $\angle a = 75°$. It is the supplement of angle y.

    $\angle r + \angle a + \angle b = 180°$. They form a triangle.

    $\angle r + 75° + 70° = 180°$.

    $\angle r = 35°$

17. $-x^2 - 2x^3$

    Substitute the value -1 for x

    $-(-1)^2 - 2(-1)^3 =$

    $-(-1) - 2(-1) =$

    $-1 + 2 = 1$

18. Average = $\dfrac{\text{Sum of the test scores}}{\text{Quantity of tests}}$

    $90 = \dfrac{87 + 93 + 86 + x}{4}$

    By cross-multiplication:

    $4(90) = 87 + 93 + 86 + x$

    $360 = 266 + x$

    $x = 94$

19. Circumference $= 2\pi r = 2\pi(6) = 12\pi$. 2π is $\dfrac{2\pi}{12\pi} = \dfrac{1}{6}$ of the circumference. In turn, the central angle is $\dfrac{1}{6}(360°) = 60°$, or $\dfrac{\text{arc length}}{\text{circumference}} = \dfrac{x°}{360°}$.

    $\dfrac{2\pi}{12\pi} = \dfrac{x}{360}$

    $\dfrac{1}{6} = \dfrac{x}{360}$

    $6x = 360$

    $x = 60$

20. $\dfrac{2x}{3\sqrt{2}} = \dfrac{3\sqrt{2}}{x}$

   By cross-multiplication
   $2x(x) = (3\sqrt{2})(3\sqrt{2})$
   $2x^2 = 9(2) = 18$
   $x^2 = 9$
   $x = \pm 3$

   The positive value of x is 3.

21. The median is the "middle" data element when the data is arranged in numerical order.
   20, 20, 20, 20, 30, 30, 30, 30, 50, 50, 50, 50, 50, 50, 50
                          ↑

   The "middle" data element is 30.

22. $A * B = \dfrac{AB - B}{-B}$

   $-2 * 2 = \dfrac{(-2)(2) - 2}{-2} = \dfrac{-4 - 2}{-2} = \dfrac{-6}{-2} = 3$

23. distance = rate × time → rate = $\dfrac{\text{distance}}{\text{time}}$

   $\dfrac{320 \text{ miles}}{8 \text{ hrs}} = 40 \text{ mph}$

   40 mph × 2 hrs = 80 miles

24. $\dfrac{\text{part}}{\text{whole}} \times 100 = \dfrac{9}{30} \times 100 = 30\%$

25. The number of sheets is directly proportional to the number of machines and also directly proportional to the amount of time. Mathematically this can be expressed as:

   $\dfrac{\text{sheets}}{(\text{number of machines})(\text{time})} = \dfrac{\text{sheets}}{(\text{number of machines})(\text{time})}$

   $\dfrac{300}{3(3)} = \dfrac{600}{6(t)}$

   $\dfrac{300}{9} = \dfrac{600}{6t}$

   Reduce the fractions and then cross-multiply:

   $\dfrac{100}{3} = \dfrac{100}{t}$

   $100t = 300$

   $t = 3$

Section 5

1. **(E)** The town's only exposure is southward toward the sun; it is open only on the south side.
2. **(D)** Henson calls Karnah "pleasant," "delightful," even "ideal."
3. **(E)** The lack of trees (lines 16–17) is the only thing that keeps Karnah from having a landscape "as delightful as anywhere on earth."
4. **(A)** "The scenery is also varied and attractive, offering to the eye greater contrasts. . . ." (lines 53–55), writes Peary. This diversity is one of the attractions of the bay.
5. **(C)** Lines 66–67 describe the "restless arctic elements" carving the cliffs into "turrets, bastions, huge amphitheatres, and colossal statues. . . ."
6. **(B)** Peary does not talk about vegetation (D), nor is this passage about the North Pole (E). The passage follows the coast of Greenland with enough specific detail that a reader could use it as a map.
7. **(B)** The description of the geology and scenery of Greenland seems to be from the vantage point of a ship traveling along the coastline. Everything that is mentioned is along the shore.
8. **(A)** Henson's "lofty mountains" surround Karnah; the only mention of landmarks around Karnah in Peary's description is to the "Sculptured Cliffs of Karnah."
9. **(C)** Peary's descriptions are much more technical than Henson's; his purpose is not to write a simple travelogue, but to detail an expedition for future explorers.
10. **(D)** Both writers mention the severity of most of the arctic, Henson in comparing it to Karnah's more moderate climate (lines 11–13), and Peary in his description of the restless arctic elements. Both, too, remark on the unusual attractiveness of Karnah and the bay.
11. **(D)** As was previously mentioned, Peary's descriptions are more objective and technical than those of Henson. Henson's sound more like the appreciative words of a casual traveler.
12. **(D)** Although Henson's account discusses the "rivulets of clear, cold water," he does not focus on the impact of glacier and iceberg activity as does his counterpart.

Section 6

1. **(B)** Since Z is equidistant from X and Y, it must lie on the y-axis. Then $\triangle OZY$ is a 30°-60°-90° triangle with $YZ = 8$. Hence $OZ = \frac{8}{2}\sqrt{3} = 4\sqrt{3}$.

    Coordinates of Z are $(0, 4\sqrt{3})$.

2. **(B)** $9 = 8 + 1 = 7 + 2 = 6 + 3 = 5 + 4$.

    Thus, 4 ways.

3. **(B)** $\dfrac{7\text{ ft. }9\text{ in.}}{3} = \dfrac{6\text{ ft. }21\text{ in.}}{3} = 2$ ft. 7 in.

4. **(D)** Since K is an integer and R and S are integers, K must be a perfect square and perfect cube. The smallest such number listed is $64 = 8^2 = 4^3$.

5. **(D)** The $\triangle RST$ has a base of 7 and an altitude of 5. Hence the area = $\frac{1}{2} \cdot 7 \cdot 5 = 17\frac{1}{2}$

6. **(D)** $\dfrac{3P}{3Q}$ is obvious reducible to $\dfrac{P}{Q}$. The others cannot be reduced.

7. **(A)** Since ACB is a straight angle and angle DCE is a right angle, then angle ACD and angle BCE are complementary. Hence $BCE = 90 - x$.

8. **(B)** When a triangle is inscribed in a parallelogram or a rectangle, the area inside the inscribed triangle will always be the same as the area outside the inscribed triangle. All three triangles have the same altitude. Since AE plus ED equals BC, the two shaded triangles combined have the same base as the unshaded triangle. If the base and the altitude are the same, then the area is the same.

9. **(E)** The most important point here is that we do not know the altitude of the parallelogram; the area of a parallelogram is altitude times base. A secondary point would be that we do not know the lengths of AB and BC; we only know the ratio of the two sides. The actual lengths of the sides could be, for example, 8 and 18.

10. **(D)** If a dozen eggs cost M cents, then 1 egg costs $\frac{M}{12}$ cents (there are 12 items in a dozen). The profit per egg would be Selling Price – Cost or $\frac{M}{6} - \frac{M}{12}$. Using a common denominator of 12, the profit per egg would be $\frac{M}{12}$ cents. Then the profit on a dozen eggs would be $(\frac{M}{12}) \times 12$, which is M cents.

COMPUTING YOUR SCORES ON THE DIAGNOSTIC EXAM

To get a sense of where you are scoring, you need to compute individual verbal and mathematical raw scores. Once you have computed these, turn to the later section, "Conversion Scales for the Diagnostic Examination," to compute your SAT scaled scores (200–800). Keep in mind that these formulas have been simplified to give you a "quick and dirty" sense of where you are scoring, not a perfectly precise score.

To Compute Your Raw Scores:

1. Enter the number of correct answers for each verbal and mathematical reasoning section into the boxes marked "Number of Questions Correct."
2. Enter the number of incorrect answers (not blanks) for each verbal and mathematical reasoning section into the boxes marked "Number of Questions Incorrect."
3. Total the number correct and number incorrect.
4. Follow this formula: Take the total correct and minus one-quarter of the total incorrect. Round up in your favor to compute your Raw Score.

Verbal Section	Total Number of Questions	Number of Questions Correct	Number of Questions Incorrect
1	31		
3	35		
5	12		
Totals	78	Total Correct:	Total Incorrect:

Verbal Raw Score = Total Correct − ($\frac{1}{4}$ × Total Incorrect) = _____

Math Section	Total Number of Questions	Number of Questions Correct	Number of Questions Incorrect
2	25		
4	25		
6	10		
Totals	60	Total Correct:	Total Incorrect:

Math Raw Score = Total Correct − ($\frac{1}{4}$ × Total Incorrect) = _____

PINPOINTING RELATIVE STRENGTHS AND WEAKNESSES ON THE DIAGNOSTIC EXAM
VERBAL QUESTION TYPES
Sentence Completions

1. Count up the number of sentence completions you answered correctly (Section 1: 1–9 and Section 3: 1–10).
2. Write that number in the box marked "Number of Questions Correct."
3. Divide that number by "Total Number of Questions" and write down your percentage in the shaded box.

Analogies

1. Count up the number of analogies you answered correctly (Section 1: 10–15 and Section 3: 11–23).
2. Write that number in the box marked "Number of Questions Correct."
3. Divide that number by "Total Number of Questions" and write down your percentage in the shaded box.

Critical Reading

1. Count up the number of critical reading questions you answered correctly.
2. Write that number in the box marked "Number of Questions Correct."
3. Divide that number by "Total Number of Questions" and write down your percentage in the shaded box.

Type of Verbal Question	Number of Questions Correct	Total Number of Questions	Percent Correct (number correct/total)
Sentence Completions		19	
Analogies		19	
Critical Reading		40	

Compare these three percentages to assess your relative strengths and weaknesses. If any individual percentage was considerably lower than others, you should concentrate your further study of SAT Verbal topics in that area. You can do so by reading the appropriate strategy chapter in Part 3 and completing the exercises that accompany it.

If sentence completions and/or analogies gave you difficulty, you should work through Part 5 to bolster your vocabulary. Learning vocabulary words is a critical step to improving on these sections.

MATH QUESTION TYPES
Multiple-Choice Math

1. Count up the number of multiple-choice questions you answered correctly (Sections 2 and 6).
2. Write that number in the box marked "Number of Questions Correct."
3. Divide that number by the "Total Number of Questions" and write down your percentage in the shaded box.

Quantitative Comparisons

1. Count up the number of quantitative comparisons you answered correctly (Section 4: 1–15).
2. Write that number in the box marked "Number of Questions Correct."
3. Divide that number by the "Total Number of Questions" and write down your percentage in the shaded box.

Grid-Ins

1. Count up the number of grid-ins you answered correctly (Section 4: 16–25).
2. Write that number in the box marked "Number of Questions Correct."
3. Divide that number by the "Total Number of Questions" and write down your percentage in the shaded box.

Type of Math Question	Number of Questions Correct	Total Number of Questions	Percent Correct (number correct/total)
Multiple Choice		35	
Quantitative Comparison		15	
Grid-In		10	

Compare these three percentages to assess your relative strengths and weaknesses. If any individual section produced a percentage that was considerably lower than others, that's a weakness you can—and should—eliminate. To improve your skills in any area of SAT math, read the appropriate strategy chapter in Part 4 and do the exercises.

MATH SUBTOPICS

To get an even more in-depth look at your performance, look back at the answer key to the multiple-choice math questions (Sections 2 and 6). You'll notice that each question has been subdivided into one of four categories—arithmetic, algebra, geometry, and other.

Arithmetic

1. Count up the number of arithmetic multiple-choice questions you answered correctly.
2. Write that number in the box marked "Number of Questions Correct."
3. Divide that number by the "Total Number of Questions" and write down your percentage in the shaded box.

Algebra

1. Count up the number of algebra multiple-choice questions you answered correctly.
2. Write that number in the box marked "Number of Questions Correct."
3. Divide that number by the "Total Number of Questions" and write down your percentage in the shaded box.

Geometry

1. Count up the number of geometry multiple-choice questions you answered correctly.
2. Write that number in the box marked "Number of Questions Correct."
3. Divide that number by the "Total Number of Questions" and write down your percentage in the shaded box.

Type of Math Subtopic	Number of Questions Correct	Total Number of Questions	Percent Correct (number correct/total)
Arithmetic		10	
Algebra		6	
Geometry		14	

Compare these three percentages to assess your relative strengths and weaknesses by mathematical subcategory. If an individual percentage is considerably lower than others, you've found an area for further study. Read the appropriate math chapter in Part 6 and do the exercises.

MEASURING YOUR PROGRESS

As you visit chapters and do exercises, don't forget to compare your performance on those exercises with the verbal and mathematical percentages you calculated here. Down the road, you can also measure your progress very easily by comparing how you did on this test with how you do on other practice examinations.

Take note of whether you had difficulty finishing any particular part of the test. It might be that you are spending too long on certain questions and not allotting enough time for others. This should improve as you work through the strategy sections of this book and increase your familiarity with the test and question format. If you are worried about spending too long on particular question types, see Part 7 for a discussion of Timing Drills.

CONVERSION SCALES FOR DIAGNOSTIC EXAMINATION

VERBAL REASONING

Raw Score	Scaled Score	Raw Score	Scaled Score
75	800	40	540
70	740	35	510
65	690	30	480
60	650	25	450
55	620	20	410
50	600	15	380
45	570	10	340
		5	290
		0	230

MATHEMATICAL REASONING

Raw Score	Scaled Score	Raw Score	Scaled Score
60	800	25	470
55	730	20	440
50	670	15	400
45	620	10	360
40	580	5	310
35	550	0	240
30	510		

Although you now have some idea of what your scores would look like had they been scaled according to unofficial ETS standards, you will probably want to know how to interpret your Raw Scores in more familiar terms. If so, use the following Self-Evaluation Charts to see what your Raw Scores actually mean.

SELF-EVALUATION CHARTS

VERBAL REASONING: Raw Score

Excellent	60 – 75
Good	50 – 60
Average	30 – 50
Fair	20 – 30
Poor	0 – 20

MATHEMATICAL REASONING: Raw Score

Excellent	50 – 60
Good	40 – 50
Average	20 – 40
Fair	10 – 20
Poor	0 – 10

PART 3

SAT Verbal Strategies

CHAPTER 5

CHAPTER 6

CHAPTER 7

PREVIEW

SAT Analogies Strategies

SAT Sentence Completions Strategies

SAT Critical Reading Strategies

Chapter

SAT Analogies Strategies

Analogy questions test your vocabulary as well as your ability to form relationships. In this type of question, you are asked to form a relationship between two capitalized words and apply that relationship to the answer choices. In this chapter, you will develop the ability to form effective relationships. And you will also learn the most effective strategies for solving analogies, even when you don't know what the capitalized words mean!

A CLOSER LOOK AT ANALOGIES

Analogies test your ability recognize the relationships between pairs of words. You'll be given a pair of words in capital letters (the stem pair) that have a particular relationship to one another. You'll then be given five additional pairs of words, labeled (A), (B), (C), (D), and (E) (the answer choices). Your job is to select that answer choice with a pair of words whose relationship is similar to the relationship between the words in the stem pair.

SAT ANALOGY QUESTIONS

Your SAT examination will probably have a total of 19 analogy questions. In one verbal section, you can expect six analogies out of 30 total questions; in another verbal section, expect 13 analogies out of 35 total questions.

QUESTION FORMAT

A sample analogy question has been provided below to help you to familiarize yourself with the format.

> **Directions:** Each question below consists of a related pair of words or phrases, followed by five pairs of words or phrases labeled A through E. Select the pair that *best* expresses a relationship similar to that expressed in the original pair.

ROAD MAP

- *Take a closer look at analogies*
- *Learn to solve analogies*
- *Solve analogies even when you don't know the capitalized words!*
- *Review what you need to know about analogies*
- *Practice your skills on analogies exercises*

> **NOTE**
> Analogies are 19 out of 78 total verbal questions. They count as 24% of your overall verbal score.

Example:

> **Q** CRUMB : BREAD : :
>   (A) ounce : unit
>   (B) splinter : wood
>   (C) water : bucket
>   (D) twine : rope
>   (E) cream : butter
>
>   Ⓐ ● Ⓒ Ⓓ Ⓔ

The correct answer is (B).

SOLVING ANALOGIES: STRATEGIES THAT REALLY WORK
BUILD A BRIDGE

A bridge is a short sentence that contains both words in the stem pair and shows how they are related. Let's call the two words in the stem pair "X" and "Y." A typical bridge would define X in terms of Y. So, for the sample question from the directions above, the bridge might say, "A CRUMB is a very small piece that falls off or breaks off a piece of BREAD." Notice how this sentence explains the relationship between the two words. It also defines CRUMB (tells what a crumb is) in terms of BREAD. A lovely bridge! (No wonder: It's the test-makers' own example.)

> **NOTE**
> A strong bridge explicitly defines the relationship between the two words in the stem pair. By building a bridge, you force yourself to explain (to yourself) exactly how the two words logically fit together—the first step to solving any analogy question.

Here are a couple of other examples. Suppose the stem pair was "OPERA : MUSIC." (By the way, you would read this aloud, "opera is to music.") The bridge might say, "An OPERA is a long, elaborate, classical work of MUSIC." If the stem pair was "SURGEON : SCALPEL," the bridge might be, "A SURGEON is a professional who uses a SCALPEL." Get the idea?

PLUG IN THE ANSWER CHOICES

After you've created a bridge, turn to the answer choices. One by one, try to plug in the words from the answer choices into the same sentence. If your bridge is a strong one, only one pair of words will make sense.

Try this with the five answer choices for the sample question above. Only the words in choice (B) fit comfortably into the bridge: "A SPLINTER is a very small piece that falls off or breaks off of a piece of WOOD." Think about the others. Is an OUNCE a very small piece of a UNIT (choice A)? No; an ounce is a kind of unit—a unit of weight. Is WATER a very small piece of a BUCKET (choice C)? No; water might be carried in a bucket. The same with the other answers. So (B) is correct. (By the way, you would read the stem pair and the correct answer this way: "CRUMB is to BREAD as SPLINTER is to WOOD.")

What if our stem pair is OPERA : MUSIC?

> Which of these five answer choices fits the same bridge?
> (A) novel : artistry
> (B) painting : landscape
> (C) oboe : instrument
> (D) epic : poetry
> (E) microphone : recording

The correct answer is (D), because only that word pair fits into the same bridge: "An EPIC is a long, elaborate, classical work of POETRY."

GET NARROW AS NEEDED

Sometimes the differences among the answer choices will be subtle—so subtle that the first bridge you've built won't eliminate the wrong answers. When that's the case, two or more answer choices may fit the bridge. Here's an example:

> SURGEON : SCALPEL : :
> (A) judge : gavel
> (B) painter : canvas
> (C) executive : computer
> (D) farmer : fertilizer
> (E) carpenter : saw

If you built the bridge, "A SURGEON is a professional who uses a SCALPEL" and then tried plugging each of the answer pairs (A) through (E), you'd be dismayed to find that all five answer pairs could fit the bridge! A judge uses a gavel (it's the hammer a judge uses to pound on the bench); a painter (often) uses a canvas; an executive (often) uses a computer; a farmer uses fertilizer; and a carpenter uses a saw. Based on this bridge, all five answer choices could be considered correct! Now what?

Solution: narrow your bridge—that is, add details to the sentence to make it more specific. In this case, you might narrow the bridge in this way: "A SURGEON is a professional who uses a SCALPEL as a tool for cutting." Now plug in the answer choices. Only one fits the new, narrower bridge: choice (E). That's the correct answer.

Of course, picking the correct answer depends on your narrowing the bridge correctly. You could concoct a misleading bridge that included details that pointed to a different answer. For example, you could say, "A SURGEON is a professional who wears a protective smock while using a SCALPEL." With that bridge, answer (B) is arguably correct, since artists,

TIP
Think of analogies as resembling proportions in math. A proportion like $\frac{2}{3} = \frac{4}{6}$ also describes analogous logical relationships among things. Do you see the similarity?

> **TIP**
>
> If the correct answer for an analogy "jumps out at you" without the bridge-building step, great—go for it! But the more you practice bridge-building *before* the test, the faster your instincts will supply answers on SAT day.

like surgeons, do often wear protective smocks. (The robe a judge wears isn't "protective," so answer (A) doesn't work. And the people in the other choices don't wear smocks at all.) Does this mean that answer (B) is just as good as answer (E)?

No—in fact, if you think about it, you probably find answer (B), and the bridge we made up that points to it, a little silly. The smock that a surgeon (or an artist) wears isn't central to his or her work; and it certainly has little to do with the use of the scalpel. The first narrow bridge we created—the one that refers to the scalpel as a cutting tool—seems more sensible. It defines exactly what the scalpel does in the hands of the surgeon—which is similar to what the saw does in the hands of the carpenter.

The point is that it takes a bit of judgment to build the right bridge. You want to focus on the central, basic nature of the relationship between the two words—not on side issues that are irrelevant (like the surgeon's smock). It's a little subjective, yes. But nine times out of ten, devising the right bridge will strike you as a matter of "common sense."

In fact, in the example we've been looking at, you may have been able to "see" the similarity between SURGEON : SCALPEL and carpenter : saw even without consciously building the new, narrow bridge. That's fine. But as you prepare for the test, practice your bridge-building technique. It'll give you crucial help on the handful of really tough analogies your test will contain.

LOOK FOR THE TEST-MAKERS' FAVORITE RELATIONSHIPS

Pity the drudges at ETS. They write test questions by the hundred, week in and week out. Like anyone else, they eventually start to repeat themselves. (Ever notice how the third album by your favorite rock band sounds a lot like their first and second albums—only less interesting?) But this is a good thing for you, the test-taker. It means that analogies fall into repeated patterns that you can practice and learn. If you know and understand the test-makers' favorite analogy relationships, you'll quickly pounce on them if they pop up on your exam. And they will, they will!

Here are the top nine analogy relationships we've found on past and current SATs. (If any of the examples that follow contain words you're not sure about, you know what to do: Grab your dictionary!)

Part : Whole

In this kind of analogy, one word names something that is part of what's named by the other word—usually a specific kind of part. Here are a couple of examples:

> LID : POT : : roof : house
> MOVEMENT : SYMPHONY : : scene : play

Opposites

Here, the two words in the pair are opposite or opposed in meaning. Examples:

> NAIVE : SOPHISTICATED : : untutored : educated
> WATER : DROUGHT : : food : famine

Actor : Action

This kind of analogy links a person or thing with what they commonly do. Examples:

> COUNTERFEITER : FAKE : : blackmailer : extort
> DETERGENT : CLEAN : : bleach : whiten

Actor : Acted Upon

The word pair includes a person or thing and another person or thing that is commonly acted upon or affected by the first. Examples:

> TEACHER : CLASS : : orator : audience
> NET : FISH : : trap : game

Action : Acted Upon

Here, an action is paired with the person or thing that commonly receives or is affected by the action. Examples:

> ALPHABETIZE : FILES : : catalog : books
> RAZE : BUILDING : : fell : tree

Action : Emotion

One of the words describes an action, the other an emotion commonly associated with it. Examples:

> LOSS : MOURN : : triumph : celebrate
> TREMBLE : FEAR : : shiver : cold

Thing : Description

This kind of word-pair includes one word that names a person or thing, another that describes it. Examples:

> MISER : STINGY : : spendthrift : wasteful
> GLADE : SHADY : : clearing : open

Description : Quality

Here, an adjective that describes a particular quality is paired with a noun that names the quality. Examples:

> LIFELIKE : VIVIDNESS : : truthful : honesty
> ARROGANT : PRIDE : : modest : humility

Differing Connotations

In this kind of analogy, two words are linked that have similar meanings but different feelings, moods, or nuances—in other words, different connotations. Examples:

> CAR : JALOPY : : house : shanty
> HIGH : SHRILL : : bright : blinding

Not every analogy on your exam will fit into one of these nine categories, but three quarters of them will. Those that don't will embody "miscellaneous" relationships of their own, like these examples:

> MUSICIAN : CONCERT : : poet : reading

Here, a type of artist is paired with an event at which he or she might perform.

> BOTANY : PLANT : : astronomy : star

A field of science is paired with a typical object that is studied in that field.

> GAUNTLET : HAND : : helmet : head

A gauntlet is an armored glove worn, of course, on the hand; a helmet is an armored hat worn on the head.

SOLVING ANALOGIES: THE BEST TIPS
USE THE ANALOGY STRUCTURE TO GUESS WORDS YOU DON'T KNOW

On some analogies, you may encounter words whose meaning you aren't sure of. Don't worry. You can use the analogy structure to help you guess the meaning of the unknown words. First, realize that all the word pairs contain words that are the same parts of speech. For example, if the stem pair contains a noun and a verb, like this:

> TYRANT : OPPRESS

then each of the other word pairs will also contain a noun and a verb, in that order. So in any analogy with an unknown word, by looking at any of the other word pairs, you can tell whether the unknown word is a noun, verb, adjective, or any other part of speech—which in itself can be helpful in guessing its meaning.

Next, try using what you know about analogy relationships—and the words in the question that you *do* understand—to make a smart guess as to the meaning of the unknown word. Look at this example:

ETYMOLOGY : WORD : :
(A) etiology : disease
(B) history : event
(C) literature : author
(D) microscopy : microbe
(E) psychology : insanity

(We've deliberately included some difficult, specialized words in this analogy, to illustrate a point; actually, a word like *etiology* is unlikely to be used in an analogy on the real SAT.) You may or may not know what ETYMOLOGY means in the stem pair, but you can tell by glancing at the other word pairs that it must be a noun, since the first word in every pair is a noun. And you can probably guess, from the way the word looks, that it refers to a study or science of some kind. (Words that end in *-ology*, like *biology* and *anthropology*, usually do.)

Now, ETYMOLOGY is paired with WORD. From what you know of analogy relationships, you obviously know that ETYMOLOGY has something to do with a word or words. Given that fact, what's a possible meaning of ETYMOLOGY? Your first guess is likely to be that ETYMOLOGY is "the science or study of words." As it happens, that's not quite correct; but never mind. This guess is probably close enough to enable you to eliminate answers (B), (C), and (E) as clearly wrong. History can't be defined as "the science of events"; it's the study of the past, including events, people, forces, trends, and so on. Literature isn't "the science of authors"; it's the study of what authors produce, namely books and other writings. And psychology isn't "the science of insanity"; psychology studies the mind and human behavior, including both sane and insane subjects. So by sheer guesswork—and a modicum of word-sense—you can narrow your choices to two, giving you great odds for guessing, even if you have little or no idea what *etiology* and *microscopy* mean.

The correct answer, by the way, is (A). ETYMOLOGY is actually the study of word origins—where words come from. Similarly, *etiology* is the study of the origins of disease—where particular illnesses come from. So the analogy is close. (Microscopy has nothing to do with the origin of microbes, if you're wondering.)

Not every obscure word in an analogy may be positioned quite so well for guessing. But many will be. Don't let one or more unknown words in a question alarm you; work from what you do know to make reasonable guesses as to the meaning of the new words, and don't be afraid to base your answer choice on these guesses.

TIP
More students hurt themselves on the SAT by shunning the "obvious" than by taking it for granted. Don't be shy about guessing at word relationships! The test-makers are predictable, and the obvious connection is usually the right one.

TIP
On some analogies, you may find that your bridge enables you to eliminate two or three answer choices, leaving two or three possible answers. If that happens, try working backward from each of the live possibilities. Look at each word pair, build a bridge that defines their relationship, and then try to plug the stem pair into that bridge. It'll probably work with only one of the answer pairs—and that, of course, is the correct answer.

DON'T FEAR THE FLIP FLOP

The logical relationship in the stem pair will "run" a certain way; the relationships in the answer choices will run the same way. For example, suppose you face this stem pair:

> PROLIFIC : CREATOR

The relationship here is "Description : Thing," and it might be summarized by the bridge, "A PROLIFIC CREATOR is one that produces a lot (of offspring, ideas, artworks, or whatever)." Your job would be to find the answer choice with the same "Description : Thing" relationship, preferably using words that fit nicely into the same bridge. Choosing the right answer, as you've already seen, may at times be subtle, even tricky. But one kind of trick you *don't* have to worry about is the "flip-flop." The test-makers do *not* try to trick you by giving you a correct word pair in reverse order, like this:

> SOURCE : ABUNDANT

As we said before, on the SAT, you'll find that all the answer choices match the stem pair in their parts of speech. Similarly, you'll find that relationship reversals are not used to try to trick you. So don't worry about flip-flops—they don't turn up on the SAT.

WHEN ALL ELSE FAILS . . .

Sometimes, you won't be able to find the one best answer for an analogy question. Remember, the questions get harder as you move through a batch; so in a batch of 13 analogies, you're likely to find the last three or four to be quite hard. And you may encounter words whose meaning you don't know, and can't guess, even using the clues provided by the analogy structure. When this happens, work by elimination. Build the best bridge you can and plug in the answer choices. Eliminate any answer pairs that don't seem to fit, and guess from among the remaining answers.

Occasionally you may find that you've eliminated all the answers you understand, leaving only an answer that contains words you don't know. Don't be afraid—choose it!

SOLVING ANALOGIES: THE MOST IMPORTANT WARNINGS
IGNORE THE TOPICS OF THE WORD PAIRS

It's easy to go wrong by focusing on the surface meanings of the words in the word pairs rather than on their underlying relationship. Consider this example:

WING : FEATHER : :
(A) turtle : shell
(B) eagle : talon
(C) fish : fin
(D) roof : shingle
(E) bird : flight

The words in the stem pair refer to parts of a bird, of course. A hasty glance at the answer choices shows that four of them also refer to animals of one kind or another, and two (answers B and E) refer specifically to birds. So you might be tempted to pick one of these answers, misled by the surface similarity.

The correct answer, however, is choice (D). A well-thought-out bridge will tell you why. The relationship between the words in the stem pair might be described this way: "The WING of a bird is covered by many small, overlapping segments, each called a FEATHER." Only choice (D) fits the same bridge: "The ROOF of a house is [or may be] covered by many small, overlapping segments, each called a SHINGLE." Can you picture the similarity? No such similarity exists when you picture the turtle and its shell, the eagle and its talon (or claw), or any of the other items named in the answer choices.

BE PREPARED TO JUMP FROM THE CONCRETE TO THE ABSTRACT

The test-makers sometimes like to make you connect a pair of words that are concrete—related to the physical world—with a pair that are abstract—related to the world of ideas. Practice recognizing such analogies. Here are a couple of examples:

SPARK : FIRE : : inspiration : invention

SPARK and FIRE are concrete, physical things; a SPARK is a small thing that helps to create a larger, more powerful force, a FIRE. *Inspiration* and *invention* are abstract ideas that have much the same relationship.

RETRACE : PATH : : reiterate : argument

When you RETRACE a PATH, you are walking over the same steps you took before, in a physical sense. When you *reiterate* an *argument*, you are repeating the same ideas you stated before, in an abstract sense.

The following exercise gives you an opportunity to practice identifying answers that *could* be right. As you've just learned, this skill can help you solve SAT analogies—even when you don't know the meaning of the capitalized words.

TIP
Test-makers call wrong answers "distractors." You can see why. The wrong answers are deliberately designed to "distract" the unwary test-taker from the correct answer—which, on its surface, may appear far-fetched. Don't focus on the surface. Go deeper, focusing on the logical relationship between the words. That's what counts.

EXERCISE: IDENTIFYING POSSIBLE RIGHT ANSWERS

Directions: Of the 30 pairs of words below, only 10 are possible correct answers because they exhibit a clear-cut connection. The other pairs are NOT possible right answers. Place a checkmark by those that could be correct answers and an "X" by those that could not be correct.

1. DISTRACT : IGNORANCE
2. STOMACH : FLU
3. COURTESY : CHILD
4. PROSECUTION : DIRECTOR
5. SHOVEL : EXCAVATE
6. PENCIL : POCKET
7. SCALES : JUSTICE
8. CANDLE : POVERTY
9. SIMPLIFY : VALUABLE
10. NULLIFY : VALIDITY
11. SNIP : SCISSORS
12. PRECIOUS : WORRIED
13. TIME : CLOCK
14. ACCESSIBLE : VOYAGE
15. CONTRITE : FAVORITE
16. WHISPER : SHOUT
17. TOTAL : APPLICATION
18. AIR : SUFFOCATION
19. ROMANTIC : INTEREST
20. ILLUMINATE : PALE
21. SHREWD : RESENT
22. PARAGRAPH : ESSAY
23. QUIET : DESPERATION
24. UNIFORM : ERRONEOUS
25. ANTHOLOGY : DESCRIPTIVE
26. ILLNESS : VISION
27. DESTITUTE : MONEY
28. RANDOM : SINCERE
29. CREDULOUS : TRUST
30. PREPARE : DELIGHT

EXERCISE ANSWERS

The following list shows the "possible" right answers from the preceding exercise—and explains the relationship between the paired words.

5. A *shovel* is a tool used to *excavate*.
7. *Scales* are the symbols of *justice*.
10. To *nullify* something is to take away its *validity*.
11. *Scissors* are a tool used to *snip*.
13. A *clock* is a device used to measure *time*.
16. A *shout* is a louder form of communication than a *whisper*.
18. *Suffocation* occurs from lack of *air*.
22. A *paragraph* is a part of an *essay*.
27. To be *destitute* is to lack *money*.
29. To be *credulous* is more extreme than to be *trusting*.

Let's try one more SAT analogy to practice using the "clear-cut connection" test and to fine tune our guessing strategy:

ICONOCLAST: TRADITION : :
(A) science: fiction
(B) impostor: identity
(C) libertarian: tyranny
(D) stranger: domination
(E) soldier: satisfaction

Chances are good that you know the meaning of the word TRADITION. However, even if you have heard of the word ICONOCLAST (or icon), you probably cannot form a satisfactory sentence between the two words. Don't make up a random sentence because the wrong relationship will do you no good. Instead, work backwards by using the clear-cut connection test.

In this question, three choices drop out because they lack strong relationships. So you should be down to choices (B) and (C). You probably don't know exactly what a *libertarian* is, so you should probably focus your attention on choice (B). By definition, an impostor is someone who **fakes** his identity. If you think that an ICONOCLAST is someone who **fakes** his TRADITION, pick (B). That does not seem highly likely, though. How does a person fake his tradition, anyway? So if you doubt the likelihood of (B), you have to guess choice (C), even if it contains words whose meanings you don't know! As it turns out, choice (C) is correct. An ICONOCLAST is someone who strongly opposes TRADITION and a *libertarian* is someone who strongly opposes *tyranny*.

So what's our guessing strategy on difficult analogies? If you like the relationship between words you know, pick that choice. But if the relationship seems unlikely, you have to have the guts to choose the choice that contains the most difficult vocabulary. Statistically speaking, this will be to your benefit.

Summary: What You Need to Know About Analogies

- Analogies test your ability to find the relationship between paired words.
- The 19 analogy questions on the scored portion of the SAT count for about one-quarter of your verbal score.
- When you don't know the capitalized words, work backwards:
  1. Use the clear-cut connection test to rule out answer choices.
  2. Guess from the remaining choices. If easy words appear to work, select that choice. If easy words do not appear to fit exactly, guess the choice with the hardest words.

EXERCISES: ANALOGIES

Exercise 1

35 Questions • 25 Minutes

Directions: Each of the following questions consists of a capitalized pair of words followed by five pairs of words lettered A to E. The capitalized words bear some meaningful relationship to each other. Choose the lettered pair of words whose relationship is most similar to that expressed by the capitalized pair. Circle the letter that appears before your answer.

Example:

DAY : SUN : :
(A) sunlight : daylight
(B) ray : sun
(C) night : moon
(D) heat : cold
(E) moon : star

Ⓐ Ⓑ ● Ⓓ Ⓔ

1. HAIR : BALD : :
   (A) wig : curly
   (B) egg : cooked
   (C) rain : arid
   (D) skin : scarred
   (E) medicine : healthy

2. DINGHY : BOAT : :
   (A) novel : book
   (B) canoe : paddle
   (C) oar : water
   (D) deck : stern
   (E) land : sea

3. APPLE : TREE : :
   (A) silver : ore
   (B) bronze : copper
   (C) plank : wood
   (D) glass : sand
   (E) pearl : oyster

4. CARNIVORE : MEAT : :
   (A) carnivore : vegetables
   (B) herbivore : plants
   (C) vegetarian : vitamins
   (D) botanist : herbs
   (E) pollinator : plants

5. MAUVE : COLOR : :
   (A) basil : spice
   (B) salt : sugar
   (C) light : dark
   (D) tan : brown
   (E) blue : rainbow

6. MUFFLE : SILENCE : :
   (A) cover : report
   (B) sound : alarm
   (C) cry : hear
   (D) stymie : defeat
   (E) glimpse : look

7. DEARTH : PAUCITY : :
   (A) individual : person
   (B) scarcity : shortage
   (C) shortage : plethora
   (D) prairie : forest
   (E) commodity : expectation

8. WATERMARK : PAPER : :
   (A) landmark : monument
   (B) birthmark : person
   (C) tide : character
   (D) line : signal
   (E) signature : author

9. BRIGHT : BRILLIANT : :
   (A) orange : red
   (B) tall : high
   (C) warm : light
   (D) white : cold
   (E) happy : ecstatic

10. DISCIPLINE : ORDER : :
    (A) military : rank
    (B) authority : follower
    (C) parent : child
    (D) teacher : student
    (E) training : preparation

11. NEWS REPORT : DESCRIPTIVE : :
    (A) weather report : unpredictable
    (B) editorial : one-sided
    (C) feature story : newsworthy
    (D) commercial : prescriptive
    (E) joke : funny

12. AGREEMENT : CONSENSUS : :
    (A) discord : harmony
    (B) pleasure : hatred
    (C) tranquility : peace
    (D) argument : solution
    (E) action : conclusion

13. WATER : HYDRAULIC : :
    (A) energy : atomic
    (B) power : electric
    (C) gasoline : inflammable
    (D) pressure : compressible
    (E) air : pneumatic

14. STABLE : HORSE : :
    (A) pond : duck
    (B) sty : pig
    (C) fold : ram
    (D) coop : hen
    (E) zoo : lioness

15. ROLE : ACTOR : :
    (A) aria : soprano
    (B) private : soldier
    (C) melody : singer
    (D) position : ballplayer
    (E) character : part

16. PROW : SHIP : :
    (A) snout : hog
    (B) nose : airplane
    (C) bird : beak
    (D) wheel : car
    (E) point : shaft

17. MAXIMUM : MINIMUM : :
    (A) pessimistic : chauvinistic
    (B) minimum : optimum
    (C) best : good
    (D) most : least
    (E) waning : less

18. SENSATION : ANESTHETIC : :
    (A) breath : lung
    (B) drug : reaction
    (C) satisfaction : disappointment
    (D) poison : antidote
    (E) observation : sight

19. DISEMBARK : SHIP : :
    (A) board : train
    (B) dismount : horse
    (C) intern : jail
    (D) discharge : navy
    (E) dismantle : clock

20. PROTEIN : MEAT : :
    (A) calories : cream
    (B) energy : sugar
    (C) cyclamates : diet
    (D) starch : potatoes
    (E) fat : cholesterol

21. NECK : NAPE : :
    (A) foot : heel
    (B) head : forehead
    (C) arm : wrist
    (D) stomach : back
    (E) eye : lid

22. GRIPPING : PLIERS : :
    (A) appealing : picture
    (B) breaking : hammer
    (C) elevating : jack
    (D) killing : knife
    (E) fastening : screwdriver

23. RADIUS : CIRCLE : :
    (A) rubber : tire
    (B) bisector : angle
    (C) equator : earth
    (D) cord : circumference
    (E) spoke : wheel

24. MISDEMEANOR : FELONY : :
    (A) police : prison
    (B) thief : burglar
    (C) murder : manslaughter
    (D) mishap : catastrophe
    (E) crime : degree

25. HYGROMETER : HUMIDITY : :
    (A) clock : second
    (B) gauge : air
    (C) odometer : speed
    (D) barometer : weather
    (E) thermometer : temperature

26. ASTUTE : STUPID : :
    (A) pedantic : idiotic
    (B) agile : clumsy
    (C) lonely : wary
    (D) dull : ignorant
    (E) intelligent : smart

27. WHALE : FISH : :
    (A) collie : dog
    (B) fly : insect
    (C) bat : bird
    (D) alligator : crocodile
    (E) mako : shark

28. GOLD : PROSPECTOR : :
    (A) medicine : doctor
    (B) prayer : preacher
    (C) wood : carpenter
    (D) clue : detective
    (E) iron : machinist

29. COUPLET : POEM : :
    (A) letter : page
    (B) sentence : paragraph
    (C) address : house
    (D) epic : poetry
    (E) biography : novel

30. ENTREPRENEUR : PROFIT : :
    (A) interloper : trade
    (B) business : monopoly
    (C) miner : ore
    (D) nemesis : peace
    (E) captain : boat

31. RUDDER : SHIP : :
    (A) wheel : car
    (B) motor : truck
    (C) oar : boat
    (D) string : kite
    (E) wing : plane

32. STALLION : ROOSTER : :
    (A) buck : doe
    (B) filly : colt
    (C) horse : chicken
    (D) foal : calf
    (E) mare : hen

33. READ : BOOK : :
    (A) taste : salt
    (B) attend : movie
    (C) smell : odor
    (D) listen : record
    (E) touch : paper

34. PARROT : SPARROW : :
    (A) dog : poodle
    (B) elephant : ant
    (C) goldfish : guppy
    (D) lion : cat
    (E) eagle : butterfly

35. BONE : LIGAMENT : :
    (A) fracture : cast
    (B) muscle : tendon
    (C) fat : cell
    (D) knuckle : finger
    (E) knee : joint

Exercise 2

15 Questions • 10 Minutes

Directions: Each of the following questions consists of a capitalized pair of words followed by five pairs of words lettered A to E. The capitalized words bear some meaningful relationship to each other. Choose the lettered pair of words whose relationship is most similar to that expressed by the capitalized pair. Circle the letter that appears before your answer.

Example:

Q DAY : SUN : :
    (A) sunlight : daylight
    (B) ray : sun
    (C) night : moon
    (D) heat : cold
    (E) moon : star

    (A) (B) ● (D) (E)

1. SPICY : INSIPID : :
    (A) peppery : salty
    (B) hot : creamy
    (C) keen : dull
    (D) pickled : sweet
    (E) bland : chewy

2. SCYTHE : DEATH : :
    (A) fall : winter
    (B) knife : murder
    (C) sickle : grain
    (D) harvest : crops
    (E) arrow : love

3. YEAST : LEAVEN : :
    (A) soda : bubble
    (B) iodine : antiseptic
    (C) aspirin : medicine
    (D) flour : dough
    (E) penicillin : plant

4. POLYGLOT : LANGUAGE : :
    (A) teacher : students
    (B) tourist : countries
    (C) linguist : words
    (D) polygamist : children
    (E) factotum : trades

5. EXPURGATE : PASSAGES : :
    (A) defoliate : leaves
    (B) cancel : checks
    (C) incorporate : ideas
    (D) invade : privacy
    (E) till : fields

6. PHARMACIST : DRUGS : :
    (A) psychiatrist : ideas
    (B) mentor : drills
    (C) mechanic : troubles
    (D) chef : foods
    (E) nurse : diseases

7. CONQUER : SUBJUGATE : :
    (A) esteem : respect
    (B) slander : vilify
    (C) discern : observe
    (D) ponder : deliberate
    (E) free : enslave

8. ENGRAVING : CHISEL : :
    (A) printing : paper
    (B) photography : camera
    (C) lithography : stone
    (D) printing : ink
    (E) etching : acid

9. DECIBEL : SOUND : :
    (A) calorie : weight
    (B) volt : electricity
    (C) temperature : weather
    (D) color : light
    (E) area : distance

10. HOMONYM : SOUND : :
    (A) antonym : confusion
    (B) synonym : meaning
    (C) acronym : ideas
    (D) pseudonym : fake
    (E) synopsis : summary

11. WHET : KNIFE : :
    (A) file : spur
    (B) chop : ax
    (C) hone : razor
    (D) stab : sword
    (E) fence : rapier

12. VALUELESS : INVALUABLE : :
    (A) miserly : philanthropic
    (B) frugal : wealthy
    (C) thrifty : cheap
    (D) costly : cut-rate
    (E) incomprehensible : unreadable

13. TRIANGLE : PRISM : :
    (A) sphere : earth
    (B) square : rhomboid
    (C) rectangle : building
    (D) circle : cylinder
    (E) polygon : diamond

14. YOKE : OX : :
    (A) saddle : stallion
    (B) tether : cow
    (C) herd : sheep
    (D) brand : steer
    (E) harness : horse

15. SYMPHONY : CODA : :
    (A) drama : prologue
    (B) letter : introduction
    (C) music : note
    (D) opera : aria
    (E) novel : epilogue

ANSWER KEYS AND EXPLANATIONS

Exercise 1

1. C	8. B	15. D	22. C	29. B
2. A	9. E	16. B	23. E	30. C
3. E	10. E	17. D	24. D	31. A
4. B	11. D	18. D	25. E	32. E
5. A	12. C	19. B	26. B	33. D
6. D	13. E	20. D	27. C	34. C
7. B	14. B	21. A	28. D	35. B

1. **(C)** To be *bald* is to lack hair. To be *arid* is to lack *rain*.
2. **(A)** A *dinghy* is a type of *boat*, and a *novel* is a type of *book*.
3. **(E)** An *apple* is produced by a *tree*, and a *pearl* is produced by an *oyster*.
4. **(B)** A *carnivore* eats only *meat*, and an *herbivore* eats only *plants*.
5. **(A)** *Mauve* is a *color*, and *basil* is a *spice*.
6. **(D)** To *muffle* something is almost to *silence* it. To *stymie* something is almost to *defeat* it.
7. **(B)** *Paucity* is a synonym for *dearth*, as is *shortage* for *scarcity*.
8. **(B)** *Paper* is sometimes identified by a *watermark*, and a *person* by a *birthmark*.
9. **(E)** A person who is extremely *bright* is *brilliant*. A person who is extremely *happy* is *ecstatic*.
10. **(E)** *Discipline* brings about order rather than *disorder*. *Training* brings about *preparation* rather than lack of preparation.
11. **(D)** A *news report* is *descriptive* of an event, but a *commercial* is *prescriptive*, recommending rather than describing.
12. **(C)** In a case of *consensus* among individuals, there is necessarily an *agreement*. Where there is *tranquility* among individuals, there is also *peace*.
13. **(E)** *Hydraulic* describes something that is operated by means of *water*; *pneumatic* describes something that is operated by means of *air*.
14. **(B)** A *horse* is usually kept and fed in a *stable*; a *pig* is usually kept and fed in a *sty*.
15. **(D)** The *actor* plays a *role*, as a *ballplayer* plays a *position*.
16. **(B)** The *prow* is the forward part of the *ship*, as the *nose* is the forward part of the *airplane*.
17. **(D)** *Maximum* and *minimum* mark extremes in quantity, as do *most* and *least*.
18. **(D)** One can counteract a *sensation* with an *anesthetic* and a *poison* with an *antidote*.
19. **(B)** One leaves a *ship* by *disembarking* and a *horse* by *dismounting*.
20. **(D)** *Meat* is a food that supplies us with *protein*; *potatoes* are a food that supplies us with *starch*.
21. **(A)** The *nape* is the back of the *neck*, and the *heel* is the back of the *foot*.
22. **(C)** *Pliers* are designed for *gripping*, as is a *jack* for *elevating*.
23. **(E)** The *radius* is a line extending from the center of the *circle* to the edge, as the *spoke* is a bar extending from the center of the *wheel* to the edge.
24. **(D)** A *misdemeanor* is not as serious as a *felony*. A *mishap* is not as serious as a *catastrophe*.
25. **(E)** A *hygrometer* is used to measure *humidity*, as a *thermometer* measures *temperature*.

26. **(B)** As *astute* is in emphatic opposition to *stupid*, so is *agile* in opposition to *clumsy*. Both terms go beyond simple denials of the opposing terms.
27. **(C)** A *whale* is a mammal that is mistakenly thought to be a *fish*, and a *bat* is a mammal that is mistakenly thought to be a *bird*.
28. **(D)** A *prospector* seeks *gold*, and a *detective* seeks a *clue*.
29. **(B)** A *couplet* makes up part of a *poem*, and a *sentence* makes up part of a *paragraph*.
30. **(C)** The goal of an *entrepreneur* is to obtain *profit*, just as the goal of a *miner* is to obtain *ore*.
31. **(A)** A *rudder* is used in directing a *ship*. A *wheel* is used in directing a *car*.
32. **(E)** A *stallion* and a *rooster* are two different animals of the same sex, as are a *mare* and a *hen*.
33. **(D)** We assimilate a *book* through *reading*, and a *record* through *listening*.
34. **(C)** A *parrot* and a *sparrow* are two different sorts of birds. A *goldfish* and a *guppy* are two different sorts of fish.
35. **(B)** *Muscles* are connected to bones by *tendons*, just as *bones* are connected to bones by *ligaments*.

Exercise 2

1. C	6. D	11. C
2. E	7. B	12. A
3. B	8. E	13. D
4. E	9. B	14. E
5. A	10. B	15. E

1. **(C)** *Spicy* is the opposite of *insipid* as *keen* is the opposite of *dull*.
2. **(E)** A *scythe* is used as a symbol of *death*, and an *arrow* is used as a symbol of *love*.
3. **(B)** *Yeast* is used as a *leaven* and *iodine* as an *antiseptic*. These functions are more specific than aspirin's function as a medicine.
4. **(E)** A *polyglot* is adept at many *languages* as a *factotum* is adept at many skilled jobs, or *trades*.
5. **(A)** *Passages* can be eliminated by *expurgation* and *leaves* by *defoliation*.
6. **(D)** The basic materials of a *pharmacist* are *drugs*; the basic materials of a *chef* are *foods*.
7. **(B)** To *conquer* someone is to *subjugate* that person. To *slander* someone is to *vilify* him or her. In both cases, the subject is hostile toward the object.
8. **(E)** A *chisel* can be used to cut out an *engraving*. *Acid* can be used to cut through a surface to create an *etching*.
9. **(B)** *Sound* is measured in *decibels*, and *electricity* in *volts*.
10. **(B)** *Sound* determines whether two words are *homonyms*. *Meaning* determines whether two words are *synonyms*.
11. **(C)** One *whets* a *knife* to sharpen it. One *hones* a *razor* to sharpen it.
12. **(A)** At one extreme something can be *valueless*, and at another extreme something can be *invaluable*. At one extreme an individual can be *miserly*, and, at another extreme, *philanthropic*.
13. **(D)** A *triangle* has three sides, and a *prism* is a three-sided solid figure. A *circle* is circular, and a *cylinder* is a solid figure that is circular.
14. **(E)** An *ox* is controlled by means of a *yoke*. A *horse* is controlled by means of a *harness*.
15. **(E)** A *symphony* can end with a *coda*, as can a *novel* with an *epilogue*.

Chapter

SAT Sentence Completions Strategies

Sentence completion questions test your vocabulary as well as your ability to understand what you read. In this kind of question, you are given a sentence that has one or more blanks, and you're asked to choose the best word or pair of words to "fill-in" those blanks. In this chapter, you become familiar with the format of sentence completion questions, and you learn the most effective strategies for finding the right answers on this portion of the SAT.

A CLOSER LOOK AT SENTENCE COMPLETIONS

Are you drawing a blank? Get used to it, because you'll see a lot of them in the sentence completion questions on the SAT. In this kind of question, you are given a sentence that has one or more blanks. A number of words or pairs of words are suggested to fill in the blank spaces. It's up to you to select the word or pair of words that will best complete the meaning of the sentence. Sentence completion questions test your vocabulary as well as your ability to understand what you read. In a typical sentence completion question, several of the choices could be inserted into the blank spaces. However, only one answer will make sense and carry out the full meaning of the sentence.

SENTENCE COMPLETION QUESTIONS AND THEIR FORMAT

Your SAT will probably have a total of 19 sentence completions. In one verbal section, you can expect 9 sentence completions out of 30 total questions; in another verbal section, expect 10 sentence completions out of 35 total questions.

Every section of questions will be preceded by a set of directions and an example for your reference, like the example listed below:

ROAD MAP

- *Take a closer look at sentence completions*
- *Learn the basic steps for solving sentence completions*
- *Learn the best strategies for tackling difficult sentence completion questions*
- *Practice your skills in solving sentence completions*

NOTE

Don't forget that you're being tested on your ability to find the *best* answer. Though more than one answer may seem to work, only one is correct; be sure to make your choice very carefully.

Directions: Each of the sentences below contains one or two blanks. Each blank indicates that a word (or words) has been omitted. Following the sentence are five lettered words or phrases labeled A through E. Choose the word or phrase that *best* fits the meaning of the sentence as a whole.

Example:

Medieval kingdoms did not become constitutional republics overnight; on the contrary, the change was ——.

(A) unpopular
(B) unexpected
(C) advantageous
(D) sufficient
(E) gradual

Ⓐ Ⓑ Ⓒ Ⓓ ●

The correct answer is (E). The word "overnight" indicates that the blank should be filled by a word dealing with an period of time. As a result, "gradual" should have been your choice.

METHODS AND STRATEGIES FOR SOLVING SENTENCE COMPLETIONS

Are you ready to start filling in some of those blanks? The following steps will help you answer sentence completion questions:

1. Read the sentence carefully.
2. Think of a word or words that will fit the blank appropriately.
3. Look through the five answer choices for that word(s). If it's not there, move on to step 4.
4. Examine the sentence for clues to the missing word.
5. Eliminate any answer choices that are ruled out by the clues.
6. Try the ones that are left and pick whichever is best.

Now that you know how to approach these questions most effectively, try a few sample SAT sentence completion questions:

Those who feel that war is stupid and unnecessary think that to die on the battlefield is ——.

(A) courageous
(B) pretentious
(C) useless
(D) illegal
(E) heroic

Now, follow the steps to find the correct answer:

1. Read the sentence.
2. Think of your own word to fill in the blank. You're looking for a word that completes the logic of the sentence. You might come up with something like "stupid" or "dumb."
3. Look for *dumb* in the answer choices. It's not there, but *useless* is. That's pretty close, so mark it and go on.
4. If you couldn't guess the word, take your clue from the words *stupid* and *unnecessary* in the sentence. They definitely point toward some negative-sounding word.
5. The clues immediately eliminate (A) *courageous* and (E) *heroic*, which are both positive words.
6. Try the remaining choices in the sentence, and you'll see that *useless* fits best.

Here's another question:

> Unruly people may well become —— if they are treated with —— by those around them.
>
> (A) angry..kindness
> (B) calm..respect
> (C) peaceful..abuse
> (D) interested..medicine
> (E) dangerous..love

Now, here are your steps for finding the right answer:

1. Read the sentence. This time there are two blanks, and the missing words need to have some logical connection.
2. Think of your own words to fill in the blanks. You might guess that the unruly people will become "well-behaved" if they are treated with consideration.
3. Now look for your guesses in the answer choices. They're not there, but there are some possibilities.
4. Go back to the sentence and look for clues. *Become* signals that the unruly people will change their behavior. How that behavior changes will depend on how they are treated.
5. You can eliminate choices (A) and (E) because a negative behavior change (*angry* and *dangerous*) doesn't logically follow a positive treatment (*kindness* and *love*). Likewise, you can eliminate (C) because a *peaceful* behavior change is not likely to follow from *abuse*. Finally, you can eliminate (D) because *interested* and *medicine* have no logical connection.
6. The only remaining choice is (B), which fits the sentence and must be the correct answer.

CAUTION

Don't let sentence completions hold you up. In the 30-minute SAT verbal sections, sentence completion questions always come first. Try to spend no more than 45 to 50 seconds on any sentence completion, so you have time to get through the rest of the test.

THE BEST STRATEGIES FOR SENTENCE COMPLETION QUESTIONS

The six-step method for solving sentence completion questions is a tried-and-true approach to solving these questions on the SAT. But, because you want to move through these questions as quickly as you can (while choosing the right answers, of course), you also need to arm yourself with some basic strategies for tackling even the most difficult sentence completion questions. The following sections offer some very simple—and effective—strategies for quickly and accurately answering sentence completion questions.

Thinking up your own answer is the way to start

If you've thought up the best answer before you even look at the choices, you've started solving the problem in advance and have saved time. To test this theory, look at this typical SAT sentence completion question:

Robert was extremely —— when he received a B on the exam, for he was almost certain he had gotten an A.

(A) elated
(B) dissatisfied
(C) fulfilled
(D) harmful
(E) victorious

In this example, it is obvious that Robert would be "dissatisfied" with the grade he received. You may have come up with a different word, such as "discouraged" or "frustrated," but you can quickly deduce that (B) is the correct answer by the relationship of the answer choice to the word you guessed.

The words in the surrounding sentence offer clues to the missing word

When it comes to sentence completion questions, the word that does *not* appear is the key to the meaning of the sentence. But by thinking about the words that *do* appear, we can see the connection between the two parts of the sentence. Most sentences contain not only a collection of words but also a number of *ideas* that are connected to one another in various ways. When you understand how these ideas are connected, you can say that you really understand the sentence.

Some blanks go with the flow

The missing word may be one that supports another thought in the sentence, so you need to look for an answer that "goes with the flow."

TIP

Thinking up your own answer will help you kill two birds with one stone. You will save precious time because you will not need to read the sentence through five separate times to check five separate answer choices; you already will have formed an accurate expectation of what belongs in the blank. Thinking up your own answer will also help you avoid choices which merely "sound good," but have no logical or grammatical reason to be the right answer.

SAT Sentence Completions Strategies

The service at the restaurant was so slow that by the time the salad had arrived we were ———.

(A) ravenous
(B) excited
(C) incredible
(D) forlorn
(E) victorious

Where is this sentence going? The restaurant service is very slow. That means you have to wait a long time for your food, and the longer you wait, the hungrier you'll get. So the word in the blank should be something that completes this train of thought. Answer choice (A), "ravenous," which means very hungry, is the best answer. It works because it "goes with the flow."

Here's another example:

As a teenager, John was withdrawn, preferring the company of books to that of people; consequently, as a young adult John was socially ———.

(A) successful
(B) uninhibited
(C) intoxicating
(D) inept
(E) tranquil

The word "consequently" signals that the second idea is an outcome of the first, so again, you are looking for a word that completes the train of thought. What might happen if you spent too much time with your nose stuck in a book (except for this one, of course)? Most likely you would be more comfortable with books than with people. Choice (D), "inept," meaning awkward, is a good description of someone who lacks social graces, making this the right answer.

Here's yet another example:

A decision that is made before all of the relevant data are collected can only be called ———.

(A) calculated
(B) insincere
(C) laudable
(D) unbiased
(E) premature

The word "called" tells you that the blank is the word that the rest of the sentence describes. A decision that is made before all the facts are collected can only be described as premature, choice (E).

Some blanks shift gears

The missing word may be one that reverses a thought in the sentence, so you need to look for an answer that "shifts gears." Try this technique in the following question example:

> The advance of science has demonstrated that a fact that appears to contradict a certain theory may actually be ——— a more advanced formulation of that theory.
>
> (A) incompatible with
> (B) in opposition to
> (C) consistent with
> (D) eliminated by
> (E) foreclosed by

The correct answer is (C). Look at the logical structure of the sentence. The sentence has set up a contrast between what appears to be and what is actually true. This indicates that the correct answer will "shift gears" and be the opposite of "contradict." The choice "consistent with" provides this meaning. The other choices do not.

Here's another example:

> Although she knew that the artist's work was considered by some critics to be ———, the curator of the museum was anxious to acquire several of the artist's paintings for the museum's collection.
>
> (A) insignificant
> (B) important
> (C) desirable
> (D) successful
> (E) retroactive

The correct answer is (A). The very first word of the sentence, "although," signals that the sentence is setting up a contrast between the critics and the curator. The critics had one opinion, but the curator had a different one. Since the curator liked the artworks well enough to acquire them, you can anticipate that the critics disliked the artworks. So the blank requires a word with negative connotations, and choice (A), "insignificant," is the only one that works.

Here's another example of this type of contrast in a sentence completion question:

> After witnessing several violent interactions between the animals, the anthropologist was forced to revise her earlier opinion that the monkeys were ———.
>
> (A) peaceable
> (B) quarrelsome

(C) insensitive
(D) prosperous
(E) unfriendly

Where do you begin? The words "forced to revise" clearly signal a shift in the anthropologist's ideas. Her discovery that the monkeys were violent made her abandon an earlier contrasting opinion. Among the answer choices, the only contrast to "violent" is choice (A), "peaceable."

The right answer must be both logical and grammatically correct

When answering sentence completion questions, you can always simply toss out any answer choices that do not make sense in the sentence or that would not be grammatically correct. Try this technique in the following example:

> An advocate of consumer rights, Nader has spent much of his professional career attempting to —— the fraudulent claims of American business.
>
> (A) expose
> (B) immortalize
> (C) reprove
> (D) construe
> (E) import

What would you do with a fraudulent claim? Immortalize it? Import it? Not likely. These choices are not logical. The only logical answer is (A). You would *expose* a fraudulent claim.

Two-blank questions give you two ways to get it right

Most SAT sentence completions—about two-thirds—have two blanks rather than one. This provides another way of working by elimination. Sometimes you can guess the meaning of one blank, but not the other. Good! Scan the answer choices, looking only for the word you've guessed. Eliminate the answers that *don't* include it (or a near-synonym). Cross them out with your pencil if you like (this saves time if you look back at the question later. Then guess from what remains.

Difficult questions generally have difficult answers

As with analogy questions, easier sentence completions typically have easier answers and harder sentence completions typically have harder answers. This does not mean that you should always guess the hardest words on the hardest questions. However, if you have absolutely no idea which of 2, 3, or 4 remaining choices is correct, it is to your benefit to select the choice with the most difficult vocabulary.

NOTE
Why do difficult questions typically have difficult answers? Because the test-writers know what they're doing. They know that students prefer to pick answer choices that contain familiar vocabulary. After all, it's human nature to be afraid of words we don't know. So don't fall into their trap. Have the intestinal fortitude to guess the hardest words when all else fails!

Summary: What You Need to Know About Sentence Completions

- The scored portion of the SAT contains 19 sentence completion questions, arranged in order of easiest to most difficult.

- Sentence completion questions test your vocabulary and your reading comprehension skills by presenting sentences with one or two blanks and asking you to choose the best words to fill the blanks.

- In general, you follow these steps to answer sentence completion questions:

    1. Read the sentence carefully.
    2. Think of a word or words that will fit the blank appropriately.
    3. Look through the five answer choices for that word(s). If it's not there, move on to step 4.
    4. Examine the sentence for clues to the missing word.
    5. Eliminate any answer choices that are ruled out by the clues.
    6. Try the ones that are left and pick whichever is best.

- Eliminate choices that are illogical or grammatically incorrect, and use both words within a two-word choice to "test" for the best response.

- Try to spend no more than 45 to 50 seconds on any one sentence completion question.

EXERCISES: SENTENCE COMPLETIONS

Exercise 1

35 Questions • 25 Minutes

Directions: Each of the following questions consists of an incomplete sentence followed by five words or pairs of words. Choose that word or pair of words which, when substituted for the blank space or spaces, best completes the meaning of the sentence. Circle the letter that appears before your answer.

SAT Sentence Completions Strategies

Example:

> **Q** In view of the extenuating circumstances and the defendant's youth, the judge recommended ----.
> (A) conviction
> (B) a defense
> (C) a mistrial
> (D) leniency
> (E) life imprisonment
>
> (A) (B) (C) ● (E)

1. The ---- workroom had not been used in years.
   (A) derelict
   (B) bustling
   (C) bereft
   (D) bereaved
   (E) stricken

2. Tempers ran hot among the old-timers, who ---- the young mayor and his ---- city council.
   (A) despised..attractive
   (B) admired..elite
   (C) resented..reforming
   (D) forgave..activist
   (E) feared..apathetic

3. With the discovery of ---- alternative fuel source, oil prices dropped significantly.
   (A) a potential
   (B) a feasible
   (C) a possible
   (D) a variant
   (E) an inexpensive

4. The product of a ---- religious home, he often found ---- in prayer.
   (A) zealously..distraction
   (B) devoutly..solace
   (C) vigorously..comfort
   (D) fanatically..misgivings
   (E) pious..answers

5. Our ---- objections finally got us thrown out of the stadium.
   (A) hurled
   (B) modest
   (C) wary
   (D) vocal
   (E) pliant

6. We should have ---- trouble ahead when the road ---- into a gravel path.
   (A) interrogated..shrank
   (B) anticipated..dwindled
   (C) expected..grew
   (D) enjoyed..transformed
   (E) seen..collapsed

7. The ---- of the house, fresh lobster, was all gone, so we ---- ourselves with crab.
   (A) suggestion..resolved
   (B) embarrassment..consoled
   (C) recommendation..contented
   (D) specialty..pelted
   (E) regret..relieved

8. ---- mob began to form, full of angry men ---- incoherent threats.
   (A) An excited..whispering
   (B) A listless..shouting
   (C) An ugly..gesturing
   (D) A lynch..muttering
   (E) A huge..waving

9. In the ---- downpour, the women managed to ---- us and disappear.
   (A) ensuing..evade
   (B) incessant..pervade
   (C) uncouth..escape
   (D) torrential..provoke
   (E) insipid..avoid

10. As a staunch ---- of our right to leisure time, Ken had few ----.
    (A) proponent..friends
    (B) advocate..defenders
    (C) disciple..rivals
    (D) defender..equals
    (E) opponent..duties

11. A single wall still stood in mute ---- to Nature's force.
    (A) evidence
    (B) tribute
    (C) remainder
    (D) memory
    (E) testimony

12. With the current wave of crime, tourists are ---- to make sure their passports are secure.
    (A) required
    (B) invited
    (C) permitted
    (D) forbidden
    (E) urged

13. Over the ---- of the sirens, you could still hear the hoarse ---- of his voice.
    (A) babble..roar
    (B) drone..power
    (C) gibbering..cries
    (D) wail..sound
    (E) groaning..whisper

14. Working ---- under the pressure of time, Edmond didn't notice his ---- mistake.
    (A) leisurely..stupid
    (B) frantically..inevitable
    (C) rapidly..careless
    (D) sporadically..simple
    (E) continually..redundant

15. Held up only by a ---- steel cable, the chairlift was ---- to carry only two people.
    (A) slender..instructed
    (B) single..intended
    (C) sturdy..obliged
    (D) massive..designed
    (E) narrow..appointed

16. After completing her usual morning chores, Linda found herself ---- tired.
    (A) surprisingly
    (B) erratically
    (C) buoyantly
    (D) forcibly
    (E) unceasingly

17. With a ---- roar, the Concorde took off from New York on its ---- flight to Europe.
    (A) deafening..subterranean
    (B) thunderous..transoceanic
    (C) sickening..transcontinental
    (D) frightening..perennial
    (E) supersonic..eventual

18. The cheerful, lively sound of dance music ---- almost everyone.
    (A) accosted
    (B) drained
    (C) flaunted
    (D) revived
    (E) expired

19. With ---- grin, Mark quickly ---- his way through the crowd toward us.
    (A) an infectious..demolished
    (B) a sappy..devoured
    (C) an irrepressible..maneuvered
    (D) a surly..crawled
    (E) a hapless..lost

20. Though a ---- of four campaigns, he had never seen action on the front lines.
    (A) veteran
    (B) victim
    (C) volunteer
    (D) reveler
    (E) recruit

21. The ---- of the early morning light ---- the room, making it larger and cozier at once.
    (A) brilliance..shattered
    (B) softness..transformed
    (C) harshness..transfigured
    (D) warmth..disfigured
    (E) glare..annihilated

22. As ---- of the original team, Mickey had free ---- for all their games.
    (A) a survivor..advice
    (B) a scholar..passage
    (C) an institution..admission
    (D) an organizer..submission
    (E) a member..entrance

23. From his ---- manner, we could all tell that he was of ---- birth.
    (A) boorish..noble
    (B) aristocratic..humble
    (C) regal..royal
    (D) refined..common
    (E) courteous..illegitimate

24. The presence of armed guards ---- us from doing anything disruptive.
    (A) defeated
    (B) excited
    (C) irritated
    (D) prevented
    (E) encouraged

25. A careful ---- of the house revealed no clues.
    (A) dissemination
    (B) incineration
    (C) autopsy
    (D) dereliction
    (E) examination

26. For his diligent work in astronomy, Professor Wilson was ---- at the banquet as ---- of the Year.
    (A) taunted..Teacher
    (B) praised..Lobotomist
    (C) lauded..Scientist
    (D) honored..Astrologer
    (E) welcomed..Administrator

27. Because of his ---- sense of his own importance, Larry often tried to ---- our activities.
    (A) exaggerated..monopolize
    (B) inflated..autonomize
    (C) insecure..violate
    (D) modest..dominate
    (E) egotistic..diffuse

28. After such ---- meal, we were all quick to ---- Arlene for her delicious cooking.
    (A) a fearful..congratulate
    (B) an enormous..console
    (C) a delightful..avoid
    (D) a heavy..thank
    (E) a wonderful..applaud

29. If you hear the ---- of a gun, don't worry; it's only my car backfiring.
    (A) burst
    (B) report
    (C) retort
    (D) flash
    (E) volume

30. He demanded ---- obedience from us, and was always telling us we must be ---- subjects.
    (A) total..foolish
    (B) partial..cringing
    (C) formal..rigorous
    (D) complete..compliant
    (E) marginal..loyal

31. The ---- of the *Titanic* could have been avoided if more safety ---- had been taken.
    (A) tragedy..precautions
    (B) embargo..preservers
    (C) disaster..reservations
    (D) crew..measures
    (E) fiasco..inspectors

32. We are ---- going to have to face the reality that the resources of Earth are ----.
    (A) finally..worthless
    (B) gradually..limitless
    (C) eventually..finite
    (D) quickly..unavailable
    (E) seldom..vanished

33. A native wit, Angela never ---- for her words.
    (A) groaned
    (B) breathed
    (C) asked
    (D) groped
    (E) worried

34. With ---- a thought for his own safety, Gene ---- dashed back across the courtyard.
    (A) even..quickly
    (B) scarcely..nimbly
    (C) barely..cautiously
    (D) seldom..swiftly
    (E) hardly..randomly

35. As she ---- retirement, Laura became more thoughtful and withdrawn.
    (A) circled
    (B) sighted
    (C) withdrew
    (D) neared
    (E) derived

EXERCISE 2

15 Questions • 10 Minutes

Directions: Each of the following questions consists of an incomplete sentence followed by five words or pairs of words. Choose that word or pair of words which, when substituted for the blank space or spaces, best completes the meaning of the sentence. Circle the letter that appears before your answer.

Example:

Q In view of the extenuating circumstances and the defendant's youth, the judge recommended ----.
    (A) conviction
    (B) a defense
    (C) a mistrial
    (D) leniency
    (E) life imprisonment
    Ⓐ Ⓑ Ⓒ ● Ⓔ

1. Though many thought him a tedious old man, he had a ---- spirit that delighted his friends.
    (A) perverse
    (B) juvenile
    (C) meek
    (D) leaden
    (E) youthful

2. ----, the factories had not closed, and those who needed work most were given a chance to survive during the economic disaster.
    (A) Unintentionally
    (B) Mercifully
    (C) Blithely
    (D) Importunately
    (E) Tragically

3. There was a ---- all about the estate, and the ---- concerned the guards.
    (A) pall..shroud
    (B) focus..scrutiny
    (C) hush..quiet
    (D) coolness..temper
    (E) talent..genius

4. The stubborn families feuded for generations, and ---- feelings are still fixed in their ----.
   (A) begrudging..acceptance
   (B) bitter..generosity
   (C) inimical..antagonism
   (D) suspicious..relief
   (E) chary..helplessness

5. As the archaeologist expected, living conditions in the ancient culture were ---- worse than those of today.
   (A) awfully
   (B) surprisingly
   (C) significantly
   (D) begrudgingly
   (E) boldly

6. Our reunion was completely ----; who'd have guessed we would have booked the same flight?
   (A) illogical
   (B) fortuitous
   (C) expected
   (D) abandoned
   (E) usurped

7. There is one ---- thing about them: They have nothing in common and never will have.
   (A) immutable
   (B) atypical
   (C) indiscriminate
   (D) indigenous
   (E) alliterative

8. Always one for a long, pleasant talk, Nancy went on ---- for hours.
   (A) volubly
   (B) tiresomely
   (C) incessantly
   (D) relentlessly
   (E) articulately

9. He should be ---- to complain, since his salary is ---- with his productivity.
   (A) right..proportionate
   (B) brought..balanced
   (C) foolish..gratuitous
   (D) loath..commensurate
   (E) entitled..alleviated

10. Paul's ---- at work is a natural product of his ---- nature.
    (A) wastefulness..unpleasant
    (B) thoughtfulness..rarefied
    (C) diligence..sedulous
    (D) candor..familial
    (E) stubbornness..intrepid

11. Blustery winds knocked off hats and rattled windows, and the adventurous children were ----.
    (A) frightened
    (B) terrified
    (C) improved
    (D) anxious
    (E) delighted

12. The ---- youngster thought old people should be polite to him!
    (A) impertinent
    (B) classless
    (C) cultured
    (D) submissive
    (E) alternate

13. Wild beasts roamed the deserted country, which had not been ---- for hundreds of years.
    (A) temperate
    (B) active
    (C) winnowed
    (D) lived in
    (E) civilized

14. At night, the inn turned into a theater, not one of actors and actresses, but one of the ---- of real people.
    (A) sciences
    (B) psychologies
    (C) dramas
    (D) jokes
    (E) novels

15. "He who laughs last laughs ----."
    (A) least
    (B) fast
    (C) best
    (D) never
    (E) softest

ANSWER KEYS AND EXPLANATIONS

Exercise 1

1. A	8. D	15. B	22. E	29. B
2. C	9. A	16. A	23. C	30. D
3. E	10. D	17. B	24. D	31. A
4. B	11. E	18. D	25. E	32. C
5. D	12. E	19. C	26. C	33. D
6. B	13. D	20. A	27. A	34. B
7. C	14. C	21. B	28. E	35. D

1. **(A)** *Derelict* in this sense means "empty," or "abandoned." Only people are bereaved or bereft.

2. **(C)** This sentence implies discord between the old-timers and the young mayor. Old-timers are likely to resent those officials who are trying to change, or reform, things.

3. **(E)** There may be many possible alternative fuel sources, but unless they are inexpensive, they won't affect the price of oil.

4. **(B)** To say a pious religious home is redundant. Only (B) completes the thought and intent of the sentence.

5. **(D)** The objections mentioned must have been vocal to get them thrown out.

6. **(B)** Most people do not enjoy trouble, and you can't interrogate it, but you may logically conclude that they foresaw, or anticipated, trouble. A road doesn't grow into a path; nor does it collapse into one.

7. **(C)** No restaurant would advertise an embarrassment of the house, but you may logically conclude that lobster was their recommendation.

8. **(D)** In this item, the final two words are the key. It is impossible to gesture or wave incoherent threats. An excited mob wouldn't whisper and a listless mob wouldn't shout.

9. **(A)** In this question, only (A) logically completes the thought of the sentence.

10. **(D)** This sentence assumes that most people support having leisure time, ruling out (A) and (B). A *staunch disciple* is bad usage. That an opponent of leisure would have few duties is illogical.

11. **(E)** A single wall implies that, formerly, there were other walls. That only one wall still stood is testimony, not a tribute, to Nature's power. *Evidence to* is poor diction.

12. **(E)** Checking your passport can only be a suggestion, not an order. As losing your passport can pose serious problems to a tourist, *urged* is a better choice than *invited*.

13. **(D)** Sirens may drone or wail, but they don't babble, gibber, or groan. *Hoarse sound* is a better choice than *hoarse power*.

14. **(C)** The pressure of time indicates a need to work quickly. Assuming that mistakes are not inevitable or redundant, answer (C) is the only logical choice.

15. **(B)** This sentence is concerned with the design of the lift. As it says "held up only by," you may assume that the cable is not large, which eliminates (C) and (D). Of the three remaining options, only *intended* (B) completes the sentence logically.

16. **(A)** Assuming that routine activity is not exhausting, it would be surprising to find yourself exhausted by it one day.

17. **(B)** A transoceanic flight is one that goes over an ocean, in this case, the Atlantic.

18. **(D)** This sentence assumes that cheerful, lively music has a positive effect on people.

19. **(C)** As there is no such thing as a surly, or sullen, grin, choice (C) is the only answer that supplies the appropriate words for Mark's expression as well as for the manner in which he made his way through the crowd.

20. **(A)** One may be a veteran without ever having seen action, but a victim has to have seen it.

21. **(B)** For the light to make the room cozier, it must be soft, not harsh. This implies that the light enhanced the room, rather than disfigured it.

22. **(E)** A person may be an institution, but not an institution of a team. It is more likely that a member of the original team rather than a scholar would have a free pass.

23. **(C)** This is the only answer in which the first and second words are consistent.

24. **(D)** Armed guards are intended to prevent any kind of disruption. Answer (D) is the only logical and grammatical choice.

25. **(E)** The sentence implies that the house was being searched, and since you don't perform an autopsy on a house, (E) is the best choice.

26. **(C)** An astronomer would not be honored as an astrologer, much less as an administrator.

27. **(A)** Someone with a high opinion of his own importance tends to try to run others' activities. Choice (A) best reflects this attitude.

28. **(E)** One doesn't generally avoid or console someone for a tasty meal. Thus, (E) is the only logical answer.

29. **(B)** The sound of an explosion, whether from a gun or a car, is called a report.

30. **(D)** You may assume that no one demands partial or marginal obedience. *Compliant* is the best adjective for subjects.

31. **(A)** The loss of the *Titanic* is best described as a tragedy or a disaster. *Precautions*, not *reservations*, is the second word that is required, making (A) the correct response.

32. **(C)** As the Earth's resources are not limitless, worthless, or unavailable, only (C) logically completes this sentence.

33. **(D)** A person may grope for words; to say that he or she worries for them is bad usage.

34. **(B)** If Gene dashed across the courtyard, he must have run swiftly or nimbly. He couldn't have taken time to think of himself.

35. **(D)** Retirement has no physical presence, so it can't be either circled or sighted. One approaches, or nears, retirement.

Exercise 2

1. E	6. B	11. E
2. B	7. A	12. A
3. C	8. A	13. E
4. C	9. D	14. C
5. C	10. C	15. C

1. **(E)** A meek spirit may comfort or console people, but it won't delight them. A juvenile spirit is immature and thus is also inappropriate. A youthful spirit, however, may be mature as well as vigorous.

2. **(B)** According to the sense of this sentence, it was merciful, not unintentional, blithe, importunate, or tragic, that the factories remained open.

3. **(C)** It follows that a hush or a quiet about an estate would concern the guards, not a pall, focus, coolness, or talent.

4. **(C)** This sentence describes enmity and a persistence of ill will. Answer (C) best completes the thought of this sentence.

5. **(C)** The archaeologist would expect conditions to be significantly worse, not surprisingly, awfully, begrudgingly, or boldly worse.

6. **(B)** The sentence implies that the reunion occurred by chance, so it was fortuitous.

7. **(A)** *Immutable* means "unchanging." Since the second part of the sentence concerns finality and since the other choices are not appropriate, (A) is the answer.

8. **(A)** According to the sentence, Nancy is "one for a long, pleasant talk." *Voluble* means "garrulous," but does not necessarily imply unpleasantness, while *tiresome, incessant,* and *relentless* all imply offense. *Articulate* is simply speaking clearly.

9. **(D)** He should be loath (or reluctant) to complain if his salary is commensurate with (or equal to) his productivity.

10. **(C)** "Natural product" in this sentence means "logical extension or outgrowth of" and joins like characteristics. *Diligence* and *sedulousness* are synonyms.

11. **(E)** Adventurous children will be delighted by blustery winds and rattling windows.

12. **(A)** This sentence describes a rebellious attitude. *Impertinence* means "insolence."

13. **(E)** This sentence concerns a wilderness and an absence of people, or civilization. *Lived in* has a meaning similar to *civilized*, but it implies a home or a town and not a countryside.

14. **(C)** The concept of theater is satisfied by dramas, not sciences, psychologies, jokes, or novels.

15. **(C)** The last (i.e., "end-of-line") position in certain activities connotes a positive result or a favored position. Some examples are: having the last word; being assigned the last (closing) spot in a show; being up last in baseball; or having a last (final) rebuttal in a debate. Laughing last, then, could not imply laughing least, fast, never, or softest, because these are not positive terms. The person who laughs last laughs best, because being last by definition precludes any possibility of someone else laughing back.

Chapter

SAT Critical Reading Strategies

So now you're probably thinking, "Who are these people and why are they testing my reading? If I couldn't read, I couldn't take the test. Geez!" Well, they're not really testing your reading. They are testing how much you understand when you read, especially when you read something unfamiliar (and under incredible pressure, too). In this chapter, you get a chance to see—and work with—SAT critical reading questions. You learn about the format of the questions, the best strategies for answering these questions quickly and accurately, and you get a chance to practice what you've learned.

A CLOSER LOOK AT CRITICAL READING

The scored portion of the SAT contains five critical reading passages. Two of the passages appear in one verbal section, one passage appears in another, and the paired passages appear in a third section. Each passage or passage pair is followed by 5 to 13 questions, for a total of 40 scored critical reading questions. That means that critical reading accounts for more than half of your SAT verbal score.

The questions test your ability to quickly read the passage and understand its content. These questions *don't* test your ability to memorize details or become expert in the topics discussed in the passages. And, you don't have to be an expert in the areas of fiction, humanities, social studies, or science—the four subject areas from which the passages are drawn.

SAT READING PASSAGES

SAT reading passages can be anywhere from 400 to 850 words long, and they are taken from four topic areas: fiction, humanities, social studies, and science. Each one begins with a short introduction that gives you some idea of where the passage came from and often when it was written. Each passage contains all the information you need to answer the questions about it.

Once on every test you will see a pair of passages on subjects that relate to each other. These paired passages will be followed by a single set of questions that refer to each passage individually or to the two passages together.

ROAD MAP

- *Take a closer look at critical reading*
- *Learn how to answer critical reading questions*
- *Learn the most important critical reading strategies*
- *Learn specific strategies for specific question types*
- *Review what you need to know about critical reading*
- *Practice your skills with critical reading exercises*

118 Master the SAT

> **NOTE**
>
> Note that the critical reading questions are not arranged in order of difficulty. The questions for each passage are arranged in the order in which the information is presented in the passage. In other words, the first questions deal with the early parts of the passage, and later questions deal with the later parts of the passage.

QUESTION FORMAT

On the SAT, each critical reading passage and question set starts with directions that look like this:

> **Directions:** Each passage below is followed by a set of questions. Read each passage and then answer the accompanying questions, basing your answers on what is stated or implied in the passage and in any introductory material provided. Mark the letter of your choice on your answer sheet.

or

> **Directions:** The two passages given below deal with a related topic. Following the passages are questions about the content of each passage or about the relationship between the two passages. Answer the questions based upon what is stated or implied in the passages and in any introductory material provided. Mark the letter of your choice on your answer sheet.

The questions that follow each passage are in the standard multiple-choice format with five answer choices each. They are presented in the order in which information appears in the passage. Most often, these questions ask you to do one of the following:

- identify the main idea or the author's purpose
- define a word based on its meaning in the passage
- choose a phrase that best restates an idea in the passage
- draw inferences from ideas in the passage
- identify the author's tone or mood

BEST STRATEGIES FOR ANSWERING CRITICAL READING QUESTIONS

As you read these passages, notice special things about the words or the information. For instance, keep an eye out for an unfamiliar word that is defined right there in the sentence; you'll probably find a question about it. Also, be alert for similes and metaphors. Those often have questions about them, too. And, notice the line numbers along the left-hand side of the passage. Use them! They'll help you find answers more quickly.

To answer critical reading questions, follow these steps:

1. Read the introduction, if one is provided.
2. Read the passage.
3. Read the questions and their answer choices. Go back into the passage to find answers.

4. For any question you're not sure of, eliminate obviously wrong answers and take your best guess.

Let's look at this process in more detail.

1. You don't want to blow past the introductory paragraph because it can be very helpful to you. It might provide some important background information about the passage or it might "set the stage" so you know what you're reading about.
2. Now read the passage pretty quickly. Try to pick up main ideas, but don't get bogged down in the factual trivia. After all, you won't even be asked about most of the material in the passage!
3. Read the questions with their answer choices, and answer every question you can. Remember, all the answers are somewhere in the passage, so go back and reread any sections that will help you!
4. Here's the process of elimination again. If you're still not sure of an answer, toss the ones that are obviously wrong and take your best guess from the choices that are left.

Now that you're familiar with how to approach critical reasoning passages and questions, let's try a few.

SAMPLE CRITICAL READING PASSAGE

The following is an excerpt from a short story, "Miss Tempy's Watchers," by Sarah Orne Jewett, a novelist and short story writer who lived from 1849–1909. In the story, two women watch over their deceased friend on the evening before her funeral and share their memories of her.

The time of year was April; the place was a small farming town in New Hampshire, remote from any railroad. One by one the lights had been blown out in the scattered houses near Miss Tempy Dent's, but as her neighbors took a last look out of doors, their eyes turned with instinctive curiosity toward the old house where
(5) a lamp burned steadily. They gave a little sigh. "Poor Miss Tempy!" said more than one bereft acquaintance; for the good woman lay dead in her north chamber, and the lamp was a watcher's light. The funeral was set for the next day at one o'clock.

The watchers were two of her oldest friends. Mrs. Crowe and Sarah Ann Binson. They were sitting in the kitchen because it seemed less awesome than the unused
(10) best room, and they beguiled the long hours by steady conversation. One would think that neither topics nor opinions would hold out, at that rate, all through the long spring night, but there was a certain degree of excitement just then, and the two women had risen to an unusual level of expressiveness and confidence. Each had already told the other more than one fact that she had determined to keep secret; they
(15) were again and again tempted into statements that either would have found impossible by daylight. Mrs. Crowe was knitting a blue yarn stocking for her husband; the foot was already so long that it seemed as if she must have forgotten to narrow it at the proper time. Mrs. Crowe knew exactly what she was about, however; she was of a much cooler disposition than Sister Binson, who made futile
(20) attempts at some sewing, only to drop her work into her lap whenever the talk was most engaging.

NOTE

Just to give you an idea of the breadth of the subject areas covered within the critical reading portion of the SAT, here are some of the topics that have been the subject of reading passages on recent exams: Chinese-American women writers, the classificiation of species, pioneer life on the Great Plains, the relationship between plants and their environment, the meaning of *Robinson Crusoe*, and the philosophy of science.

> **TIP**
>
> Never skip the introduction. The introduction is likely to contain some important information about both the passage and the types of questions that accompany it. The introduction will identify the type of passage being presented, the source or author of the passage, the era in which the passage was written, or the event that the passage describes. All of this information will help you focus your reading and find the correct answers to the questions.

Their faces were interesting—of the dry, shrewd, quick-witted New England type, and thin hair twisted neatly back out of the way. Mrs. Crow could look vague and benignant, and Miss Binson was, to quote her neighbors, a little too sharp-set,
(25) but the world knew that she had need to be, with the load she must carry supporting an inefficient widowed sister and six unpromising and unwilling nieces and nephews. The eldest boy was at last placed with a good man to learn the mason's trade. Sarah Ann Binson, for all her sharp, anxious aspect never defended herself, when her sister whined and fretted. She was told every week of her life that the poor
(30) children would never have had to lift a finger if their father had lived, and yet she had kept her steadfast way with the little farm, and patiently taught the young people many useful things for which, as everybody said, they would live to thank her. However pleasureless her life appeared to outward view, it was brimful of pleasure to herself.

(35) Mrs. Crowe, on the contrary, was well-to-do, her husband being a rich farmer and an easy-going man. She was a stingy woman, but for all of that she looked kindly; and when she gave away anything, or lifted a finger to help anybody, it was thought a great piece of beneficence, and a compliment, indeed, which the recipient accepted with twice as much gratitude as double the gift that came from a poorer and more
(40) generous acquaintance. Everybody liked to be on good terms with Mrs. Crowe. Socially, she stood much higher than Sarah Ann Binson.

1. The word *bereft* (line 6) means
   (A) without hope
   (B) greedy
   (C) anxious
   (D) sad
   (E) lonesome

The introduction and the rest of the sentence talk about the death of a well-liked person. Sadness would probably be the first thing you'd feel after someone died, so the best answer is choice (D).

2. The author implies that the two women have divulged secrets to each other because
   (A) they are lonely
   (B) it is nighttime
   (C) it is a sad occasion
   (D) they trust each other
   (E) it is the only time they talk to each other

We already know that folks are sad, but the author doesn't say anything about the women being trusting or lonely, or only talking because of the situation. The author does makes a specific reference to the time of day. Reread that sentence and you'll see why the best answer is choice (B).

3. If Mrs. Crowe were confronted with an emergency, you would expect her to
   (A) remain calm
   (B) ask Miss Binson for help
   (C) become distracted
   (D) panic
   (E) run away

The passage has clues to Mrs. Crowe's character, talking about her knowing "exactly what she was about" (line 18) and her "cooler disposition" (line 19). Now you can see that choice (A) is clearly the best answer.

4. The phrase "a little too sharp-set" (line 24) means
   (A) thin
   (B) stern and anxious-looking
   (C) strong-featured
   (D) angular
   (E) well-defined

The description of Miss Binson's everyday life with her nieces and nephews illustrates that she runs a tight ship and keeps them all in line. So choice (B) is the best answer.

5. Sarah Ann Binson seems to be a woman who is
   (A) terribly unhappy
   (B) jealous of Mrs. Crowe
   (C) disloyal
   (D) quite wealthy
   (E) self-contented

To all outward appearances, Miss Binson seemed to have an especially hard life. However, the author ends that sentence saying that "it was brimful of pleasure to herself." Since Miss Binson was pretty happy with her life, choice (E) is the best answer.

SAMPLE PAIRED CRITICAL READING PASSAGES

Among the great loves in history are those of the composer Robert Schumann for his wife, Clara, and of Napoleon Bonaparte for his wife, Josephine. Their love is public knowledge due to the hundreds of love letters they left behind. The excerpts that follow are from letters. The first one is from Schumann to his then-fiancée and the second is from Napoleon on the battlefield to his wife at home.

Passage 1—Robert Schumann to Clara Wieck (1838)

I have a hundred things to write to you, great and small, if only I could do it neatly, but my writing grows more and more indistinct, a sign, I fear, of heart weakness. There are terrible hours when your image forsakes me, when I wonder anxiously

whether I have ordered my life as wisely as I might, whether I had any right to bind
(5) you to me, my angel, or can really make you as happy as I should wish. These doubts
all arise, I am include to think, from your father's attitude towards me. It is so easy
to accept other people's estimate of oneself. Your father's behaviour makes me ask
myself if I am really so bad—of such humble standing—as to invite such treatment
from anyone. Accustomed to easy victory over difficulties, to the smiles of fortune,
(10) and to affection, I have been spoiled by having things made too easy for me, and now
I have to face refusal, insult, and calumny. I have read of many such things in novels,
but I thought too highly of myself to imagine I could ever be the hero of a family
tragedy of the Kotzebue sort myself. If I had ever done your father an injury, he
might well hate me; but I cannot see why he should despise me and, as you say, hate
(15) me without any reason. But my turn will come, and I will then show him how I love
you and himself; for I will tell you, as a secret, that I really love and respect your
father for his many great and fine qualities, as no one but yourself can do. I have a
natural inborn devotion and reverence for him, as for all strong characters, and it
makes his antipathy for me doubly painful. Well, he may some time declare peace,
(20) and say to us, "Take each other, then."

You cannot think how your letter has raised and strengthened me . . . You are
splendid, and I have much more reason to be proud of you than of me. I have made
up my mind, though, to read all your wishes in your face. Then you will think, even
though you don't say it, that your Robert is a really good sort, that he is entirely
(25) yours, and loves you more than words can say. You shall indeed have cause to think
so in the happy future. I still see you as you looked in your little cap that last evening.
I still hear you call me *du*. Clara, I heard nothing of what you said but that *du*. Don't
you remember?

Passage 2—Napoleon Bonaparte to Josephine Bonaparte (1796)

I have not spent a day without loving you; I have not spent a night without
embracing you; I have not so much as drunk a single cup of tea without cursing the
pride and ambition which force me to remain separated from the moving spirit of
my life. In the midst of my duties, whether I am at the head of my army or inspecting
(5) the camps, my beloved Josephine stands alone in my heart, occupies my mind, fills
my thoughts. If I am moving away from you with the speed of the Rhône torrent,
it is only that I may see you again more quickly. If I rise to work in the middle of
the night, it is because this may hasten by a matter of days the arrival of my sweet
love. Yet in your letter of the 23rd and 26th Ventôse, you call me *vous*. *Vous*
(10) yourself! Ah! wretch, how could you have written this letter? How cold it is! And
then there are those four days between the 23rd and the 26th; what were you doing
that you failed to write to your husband?...Ah, my love, that *vous*, those four days
make me long for my former indifference. Woe to the person responsible! May he,
as punishment and penalty, experience what my convictions and the evidence
(15) (which is in your friend's favour) would make me experience! Hell has no torments
great enough! *Vous! Vous!* Ah! How will things stand in two weeks? . . . My spirit
is heavy; my heart is fettered and I am terrified by my fantasies. . . You love me less;
but you will get over the loss. One day you will love me no longer; at least tell me;
then I shall know how I have come to deserve this misfortune. . .

1. In Passage 1, the word *calumny* (line 11) means
   (A) remorse
   (B) chance
   (C) victory
   (D) kindness
   (E) slander

Here's a prime example of context to the rescue. Take a look at the sentence and then test each choice in place of *calumny*. Basically, Schumann is talking about the hard time he is having with Clara's father, so you would not choose a positive word; eliminate choices (C) and (D). Out goes choice (B) because it makes no sense in the sentence. Choice (A) technically makes sense, but it is not a roadblock to success like insults and refusals are. Therefore, the remaining answer is the best one—choice (E).

2. To what does Napoleon refer in Passage 2 when he writes of "the moving spirit of my life" (lines 3–4)?
   (A) France
   (B) ambition
   (C) the army
   (D) his wife
   (E) the Rhône River

Now you have to do some interpretation using the information in the passage. To do this you must know the author's intent. After you find the phrase, read the sentences around it. They all deal with Napoleon's love for Josephine. Since he curses his pride and ambition, choice (B) is out. He is with his army in France, so you can toss out choices (A) and (C). Choice (E) doesn't make sense, so the only choice is (D), his beloved wife.

3. How do the authors feel about being separated from their lovers?
   (A) Separation raises doubts and fears.
   (B) Separation is due to parental disapproval.
   (C) Separations never last long.
   (D) Separations improve a relationship.
   (E) Separations between lovers are inevitable.

This is where the comparison comes into play. The question asks about both authors, so you have to think about both passages and find the similarities. Let's start eliminating choices. The first to go are (D) and (E), since neither author mentions these at all. Choice (C) goes out because the authors don't tell us anything about the length of their separations. We know that while Robert Schumann has a big problem with Clara's dad, Napoleon doesn't seem to have a parental problem; choice (B) is gone. Why is choice (A) the best answer? Take a look back at both passages. Schumann mentions his doubts, and Napoleon tells Josephine that he is "terrified." Choice (A) is the only answer that fits both authors' thoughts.

4. Why do the writers refer to the words *du* and *vous*?

   (A) To remind their readers of their rank

   (B) To refer to their lovers' intimacy or form-ality

   (C) To ask their lovers to be faithful

   (D) To demonstrate their knowledge of languages

   (E) To address their unborn children

This is the kind of question that can send you into a panic. Calm down—you don't really have to know what the two words mean, you just have to figure out why the authors put them in. Reread the sentences in which the authors mention these special words. Are both authors happy about hearing the words? Are they both upset? Do they feel differently about hearing their sweethearts use these words? Aha! That's the key; Schumann is pleased that Clara used the word *du* (which is an informal word in German), but Napoleon is insulted and worried because Josephine used *vous* (a formal French word). Only choice (B) indicates that the authors might feel differently; the other choices aren't supported at all by a rereading of the information.

LEARN THE MOST IMPORTANT CRITICAL READING TIPS

Critical reading questions can eat up a lot of your time. But you can use some specific strategies and techniques to move through this portion of the SAT efficiently. Check out these tips for smarter solutions to solving critical reading questions quickly and accurately.

DO THE CRITICAL READING QUESTIONS LAST

In addition to the critical reading questions, the verbal section of the SAT also contains analogies and sentence completions. Because the critical reasoning questions require the most time to complete, you should save these questions for last. You've already learned time-saving tips for the analogies and sentence completions, so do those questions first. That way, you'll save extra time for critical reading.

ANSWER ALL OF THE QUESTIONS BEFORE YOU MOVE ON TO THE NEXT PASSAGE

There won't be time to go back to these passages at the end of this section, so you'll want to answer every question that you can about the passage before moving on. If you skip a question and try to come back to it later, you might have to reread the whole passage to find the answer—and you'll be out of time. Guess if you have to, but finish all the questions that you can before you move on to the next passage.

REMEMBER THAT THE QUESTIONS FOLLOW THE ORDER OF THE PASSAGE

The questions are like a map to the passage; in other words, the order of the questions follows the order of the information in the passage. The first questions refer to the early part of the passage, and later questions refer to later parts of the passage. If there are two passages, the first questions are for Passage 1, the next are for Passage 2, and the end questions refer to both. This helps you locate the information quickly.

DO DOUBLE PASSAGES ONE PASSAGE AT A TIME

Since the questions are arranged like a map, take advantage! Read Passage 1 then answer the questions that relate to Passage 1. Then read Passage 2 and answer the questions that relate to Passage 2. Finally, answer the comparative questions. In this way, you won't have to read too much at once and you won't confuse the message of Passage 1 with that of Passage 2.

DON'T PANIC WHEN YOU READ AN UNFAMILIAR PASSAGE

The passages are supposed to be unfamiliar. In their attempt to be fair, the SAT people purposely choose passages that are from the darkest recesses of the library. This helps make sure that no test-taker has ever seen them before. Remember, you're not being tested on your knowledge of the topic, but on how well you:

- figure out the meaning of an unfamiliar word from its context
- determine what an author means by noting certain words and phrases
- understand the author's assumptions, point of view, and main idea
- analyze the logical structure of a piece of writing

REMEMBER THAT EVERYTHING YOU NEED TO KNOW IS RIGHT THERE IN FRONT OF YOU

The introductory paragraph and the passage have all the information you'll need to answer the questions. Even if the passage is about the price of beans in Bulgaria or the genetic makeup of a wombat, don't worry. It's all right there on the page.

START WITH THE PASSAGES THAT INTEREST YOU

The passages that interest you are easier to work on. If there's a choice, it's best to start with the passage that's more interesting to you, whether it's fiction, a science article, or whatever. If the style appeals to you, you will probably go through the passage more quickly and find the questions easier to deal with.

CAUTION
Don't choose answers that only work for one of a pair of passages. When you're working with paired passages, some questions ask you to identify a common idea. When that happens, you can immediately reject any answer choice that only applies to one of the passages.

USE YOUR PENCIL TO HIGHLIGHT IMPORTANT INFORMATION AS YOU READ THE PASSAGE

It pays to be an active reader. When you read, use your pencil actively to highlight important names, dates, and facts. Though you aren't required to memorize specific details, the questions are likely to reference the more important information in the passage. If you've highlighted those pieces of information, you'll be able to find them easily when you need them to answer the questions.

DON'T GET BOGGED DOWN IN THE DETAILS

Remember, you don't have to understand every bit of information. You just have to find the information you need to answer the questions. Don't waste your time trying to analyze or memorize technical details or information that the questions don't ask for.

DON'T CONFUSE A "TRUE" ANSWER WITH A "CORRECT" ANSWER

The fact that an answer choice is true, doesn't mean it's right. What does that mean? It means that a certain answer choice may be perfectly true—in fact all of the answer choices may be true. But the *right* answer must be the correct answer to the question that's being asked. Only one of the answer choices will be correct and, therefore, the right choice. Read carefully—and don't be fooled!

STRATEGIES FOR ANSWERING SPECIFIC QUESTION TYPES

As you learned earlier in this chapter, critical reading questions ask you to do one of five things:

- identify the main idea or the author's purpose
- define a word based on its meaning in the passage
- choose a phrase that best restates an idea in the passage
- draw inferences from ideas in the passage
- identify the author's tone or mood

The next six tips present real strategies for dealing with the specific categories of critical reading questions. Before you move to the strategies, however, read the introductory paragraph and the passage below; the tips and questions that follow relate to this passage.

John Dewey, an American educator and philosopher of education, was a prolific writer on the subject. He was particularly interested in the place of education in a democratic republic.

The place of public education within a democratic society has been widely discussed and debated through the years. Perhaps no one has written more widely on the subject in the United States than John Dewey, sometimes called "the father of public education," whose theories of education have a large social component, (5) that is, an emphasis on education as a social act and the classroom or learning environment as a replica of society.

Dewey defined various aspects or characteristics of education. First, it was a necessity of life inasmuch as living beings needed to maintain themselves through a process of renewal. Therefore, just as humans needed sleep, food, water, and (10) shelter for physiological renewal, they also needed education to renew their minds, assuring that their socialization kept pace with physiological growth.

A second aspect of education was its social component, which was to be accomplished by providing the young with an environment that would provide a nurturing atmosphere to encourage the growth of their as yet undeveloped social (15) customs.

A third aspect of public education was the provision of direction to youngsters, who might otherwise be left in uncontrolled situations without the steadying and organizing influences of school. Direction was not to be of an overt nature, but rather indirect through the selection of the school situations in which the youngster (20) participated.

Finally, Dewey saw public education as a catalyst for growth. Since the young came to school capable of growth, it was the role of education to provide opportunities for that growth to occur. The successful school environment is one in which a desire for continued growth is created—a desire that extends throughout (25) one's life beyond the end of formal education. In Dewey's model, the role of education in a democratic society is not seen as a preparation for some later stage in life, such as adulthood. Rather, education is seen as a process of growth that never ends, with human beings continuously expanding their capacity for growth. Neither did Dewey's model see education as a means by which the past was recapitulated. (30) Instead education was a continuous reconstruction of experiences, grounded very much in the present environment.

Since Dewey's model places a heavy emphasis on the social component, the nature of the larger society that supports the educational system is of paramount importance. The ideal larger society, according to Dewey, is one in which the (35) interests of a group are all shared by all of its members and in which interactions with other groups are free and full. According to Dewey, education in such a society should provide members of the group a stake or interest in social relationships and the ability to negotiate change without compromising the order and stability of the society.

(40) Thus, Dewey's basic concept of education in a democratic society is based on the notion that education contains a large social component designed to provide direction and assure children's development through their participation in the group to which they belong.

REMEMBER THAT THE ANSWER TO A MAIN IDEA QUESTION IS NEITHER TOO GENERAL NOR TOO SPECIFIC

For a question about the main idea or the author's purpose, look for an answer choice that states it. Don't be too general or too specific.

1. The main idea of this passage can best be stated as:
    (A) The role of education is extremely complex.
    (B) Dewey's notion of education contains a significant social component.
    (C) Dewey's model of education is not relevant today.
    (D) Direction provided in education must not be overt.
    (E) Public education should be a catalyst for growth.

Choices (A) and (C) are very general; you'd be hard-pressed to find any supporting information in the passage for those main ideas. Choices (D) and (E) seem as if they were single sentences plucked right out of the passage; too specific! Choice (B)—the correct choice—gives an overall statement and you could find supporting details for it as a main idea.

CHECK THE INTRODUCTORY AND CONCLUSION PARAGRAPHS FOR THE MAIN IDEA OF THE PASSAGE

Look in the first or last (or both) paragraphs of the passage for answers to main idea/author's purpose questions. Choice (B) above is stated in the last sentence of the first paragraph and restated in the last paragraph. Remember to mark stuff like this as you read. Though the main idea may occur elsewhere in the passage, most often you'll find it in the first or last paragraph.

PLUG IN CHOICES TO SOLVE VOCABULARY-IN-CONTEXT QUESTIONS

For vocabulary-in-context questions, plug the choices into the original sentence and don't be fooled by the obvious synonym.

2. The word *nurturing* (line 14) means
    (A) nourishing
    (B) educational
    (C) critical
    (D) supportive
    (E) motivational

Take a look at the sentence in the passage—"... nurturing atmosphere to encourage the growth..."—and then try each of the answer choices. You might be tempted to just pick *nourishing*, but (D) is the choice that makes sense and supports the idea of the sentence.

FIND THE RIGHT RESTATEMENT BY FIRST RESTATING AN AUTHOR'S PHRASE IN YOUR OWN WORDS

3. The phrase "a continuous reconstruction of experiences" (line 30) used in reference to education means that education is
   (A) based in life experiences
   (B) a never-ending process
   (C) a meaning-based endeavor
   (D) an individual pursuit
   (E) something unattainable

Not to put words in your mouth, but if you had stated this phrase in your own words you might have used *ongoing* as a substitute for *continuous*. If you take it one more step, you come to (B), "a never-ending process."

READ BETWEEN THE LINES TO DRAW INFERENCES FROM THE PASSAGE

4. While not directly stated, the passage suggests that
   (A) true education fosters the desire for lifelong learning
   (B) a truly educated person has an understanding of physics
   (C) Dewey was a radical philosopher
   (D) education must cease at some point
   (E) Dewey's model has been embraced by all

When a critical reading question asks for something the author has suggested, implied, or not stated directly, you have to use the information in the passage and draw your own conclusions. Read between the lines to see if the author has given any hints that would lead you to the correct answer. In this question, the correct answer is (A) because the author's stated positions together logically lead to this statement. Choice (B) is a pretty far-fetched conclusion to make, and (C), (D), and (E) are not logical extensions of the information in the passage.

CAUTION
Don't expect the answer to a vocabulary-in-context question to rely upon the most common meaning of a word. More often, you can count on the question revolving around an unusual or uncommon usage of the word.

LOOK FOR DESCRIPTIVE WORDS TO CLUE YOU IN TO THE TONE OR MOOD OF THE PASSAGE

5. The tone of this passage can best be described as
   (A) humorous
   (B) serious
   (C) dramatic
   (D) informal
   (E) frivolous

This passage probably did not make you even chuckle, so (A) can be eliminated right off the bat. The topic is not frivolous, and the language was quite formal, so you can drop (E) and (D). There were no episodes or scenes that could be considered dramatic (C), so the best answer is, of course, (B). Take a minute to go back and scan the passage, look at the kind of language you find, and see how it sets the tone.

Summary: What You Need to Know About Critical Reading

- All of the information you need is right in the passage.
- Read the introduction, if one is provided.
- Read the passage without getting bogged down in details.
- Read the questions and their answer choices. Go back into the passage to find answers.
- Critical reading questions follow the order of information in the passage. Unlike other verbal questions, they are not arranged in order of difficulty.
- Answer every question for a passage before starting the next passage.
- For any question you're not sure of, eliminate obviously wrong answers and take your best guess.

EXERCISES: CRITICAL READING

Directions: The passage below is followed by questions based on its content. Answer the questions on the basis of what is *stated* or *implied* in the passage and in any introductory material that may be provided.

Exercise 1

30 Questions • 35 Minutes

In the eleventh century, the Muslim empire was taken over by Turks of the Seljuk tribes. The main Seljuk sultan had as his advisor a Persian called Nizam al-Mulk. Nizam al-Mulk took it upon himself to reform the government, writing many of his ideas in a treatise called The Book of Government. This passage is from a chapter entitled "Advice to Governors."

When ambassadors come from foreign countries, nobody is aware of their movements until they actually arrive at the city gates; nobody gives any information [that they are coming] and nobody makes any
(5) preparation for them; and they will surely attribute this to our negligence and indifference. So officers at the frontiers must be told that whenever anyone approaches their stations, they should at once dispatch a rider and find out who it is who is coming,
(10) how many men there are with him, mounted and unmounted, how much baggage and equipment he has, and what is his business. A trustworthy person must be appointed to accompany them and conduct them to the nearest big city; there he will hand them
(15) over to another agent who will likewise go with them to the next city (and district), and so on until they reach the court. Whenever they arrive at a place where there is cultivation, it must be a standing order that officers, tax-collectors and assignees should
(20) give them hospitality and entertain them well so that they depart satisfied. When they return, the same procedure is to be followed. Whatever treatment is given to an ambassador, whether good or bad, it is as if it were done to the very king who sent him; and
(25) kings have always shown the greatest respect to one another and treated envoys well, for by this their own dignity has been enhanced. And if at any time there has been disagreement or enmity between kings, and if ambassadors have still come and gone as occasion
(30) requires, and discharged their missions according to their instructions, never have they been molested or treated with less than usual courtesy. Such a thing would be disgraceful, as God (to Him be power and glory) says [in the Quran 24.53], "The messenger has
(35) only to convey the message plainly."

It should also be realized that when kings send ambassadors to one another their purpose is not merely the message or the letter which they communicate openly, but secretly they have a hundred other
(40) points and objects in view. In fact they want to know about the state of roads, mountain passes, rivers and grazing grounds, to see whether an army can pass or not; where fodder is available and where not; who are the officers in every place; what is the size of that
(45) king's army and how well it is armed and equipped; what is the standard of his table and company; what is the organization and etiquette of his court and audience hall; does he play polo and hunt; where are his qualities and manners, his designs and intentions,
(50) his appearance and bearing; is he cruel or just, old or young; is his country flourishing or decaying; are the peasants rich or poor; is he avaricious or generous; is he alert or negligent in affairs. . . .

1. What alarms the author about the way ambassadors are currently treated upon their arrival?
   (A) An ambassador might assume that the natives are discourteous and negligent in regard to foreigners.
   (B) Ambassadors may use the opportunity to spy on the natives.
   (C) Ambassadors are often molested at the border.
   (D) No one checks to see if ambassadors are smuggling arms.
   (E) Ambassadors can easily become lost because no one guides them.

2. The word *stations* (line 8) is used to mean
   (A) levels
   (B) ranks
   (C) depots
   (D) posts
   (E) postures

3. Why does Nizam al-Mulk want to hand ambassadors from one agent to the next?
   (A) To watch their every move
   (B) To make sure their needs are met
   (C) To remove them from the country quickly
   (D) To keep them from seeing the king
   (E) To stop their complaints

4. The word *envoys* (line 26) means
   (A) methods
   (B) heralds
   (C) substitutes
   (D) accounts
   (E) representatives

5. Which of these phrases best summarizes the main idea of paragraph 1?
   (A) Favor everyone with equal care.
   (B) Never molest an ambassador.
   (C) Kings must respect each other.
   (D) Politeness pays.
   (E) Be sure to treat envoys well.

6. Unlike paragraph 1, paragraph 2 deals with
   (A) ambassadors
   (B) kings
   (C) messages
   (D) intelligence
   (E) procedures

7. By "objects in view" (line 40) Nizam al-Mulk means
   (A) goals in mind
   (B) disagreements with opinions
   (C) commodities to investigate
   (D) complaints in mind
   (E) artwork to see

8. The word *fodder* (line 43) means
   (A) light
   (B) animal food
   (C) armaments
   (D) trees
   (E) tobacco

9. The phrase "standard of his table" (line 46) refers to the king's
   (A) flag
   (B) requirements
   (C) hospitality
   (D) performance
   (E) language

10. The word *avaricious* (line 52) means
    (A) savage
    (B) stingy
    (C) violent
    (D) fickle
    (E) charitable

"The Goodman Who Saved Another from Drowning" is a French tale from the Middle Ages. In today's litigious times, the lesson it teaches remains relevant.

It happened one day that a fisherman putting out to sea in a boat was just about to cast a net, when right in front of him he saw a man on the point of drowning. Being a stout-hearted and at the same time an
(5) agile man, he jumped up and, seizing a boathook, thrust it towards the man's face. It caught him right in the eye and pierced it. The fisherman hauled the man into the boat and made for the shore without casting any of his nets. He had the man carried to his
(10) house and given the best possible attention and treatment, until he had got over his ordeal.

For a long time, that man thought about the loss of his eye, considering it a great misfortune. "That wretched fellow put my eye out, but I didn't do him
(15) any harm. I'll go and lodge a complaint against him—why, I'll make things really hot for him!" Accordingly he went and complained to the magistrate, who fixed a day for the hearing. They both waited till the day came round, and then went to the
(20) court. The one who had lost an eye spoke first, as was appropriate. "Gentlemen," he said, "I'm bringing a complaint against this worthy, who, only the other day, savagely struck me with a boathook and knocked my eye out. Now I'm handicapped. Give me justice,
(25) that's all I ask. I've nothing more to say."

The other promptly spoke up and said, "Gentlemen, I cannot deny that I knocked his eye out, but if what I did was wrong, I'd like to explain how it all happened. This man was in mortal danger in the sea,
(30) in fact he was on the point of drowning. I went to his aid. I won't deny I struck him with my boathook, but I did it for his own good: I saved his life on that occasion. I don't know what more I can say. For God's sake, give me justice!"

(35) The court was quite at a loss when it came to deciding the rights of the case, but a fool who was present at the time said to them, "Why this hesitation? Let the first speaker be thrown back into the sea on the spot where the other man hit him in the face,
(40) and if he can get out again, the defendant shall compensate him for the loss of his eye. That I think, is a fair judgment." Then they all cried out as one man, "You're absolutely right! That's exactly what we'll do!" Judgment was then pronounced to that
(45) effect. When the man heard that he was to be thrown into the sea, just where he had endured all that cold water before, he wouldn't have gone back there for all the world. He released the goodman from any liability, and his earlier attitude came in for much
(50) criticism.

In the light of this incident, you can take it from me that it's a waste of time to help a scoundrel. Release a guilty thief from the gallows, and he will never like you for it. A wicked man will never be grateful to
(55) anyone who does him a good turn: he'll forget all about it; it will mean nothing to him. On the contrary, he would be only too glad to make trouble for his benefactor if he ever saw him at a disadvantage.

11. The word *cast* (line 2) is used to mean

    (A) tint
    (B) perform
    (C) hurl
    (D) mold
    (E) copy

12. Paragraph 1 makes it clear that the fisherman is

    (A) essentially well-meaning
    (B) clumsy and foolish
    (C) fat but nimble
    (D) hard-working and honest
    (E) basically unlucky

13. The word *fixed* (line 18) is used to mean

    (A) corrected
    (B) secured
    (C) set
    (D) mended
    (E) attached

14. The word *worthy* (line 22) is used to mean

    (A) caliber
    (B) significance
    (C) morality
    (D) gentleman
    (E) prize

15. Paragraph 3 concerns
    (A) the narrator's beliefs
    (B) the court's wishes
    (C) the one-eyed man's complaint
    (D) the fisherman's plea
    (E) the magistrate's judgment

16. The fool's suggested solution to the case was
    (A) pitiless and spiteful
    (B) absurd but lawful
    (C) harsh but fair
    (D) just and merciful
    (E) sensible but unjust

17. The phrase "as one man" (lines 42–43) means
    (A) manfully
    (B) as someone once said
    (C) one by one
    (D) together
    (E) as he believed

18. "In the light of this incident" (line 51) means
    (A) Thanks to that event
    (B) Because of this tale
    (C) Without further ado
    (D) As darkness falls
    (E) As you can see from this story

19. The narrator clearly believes that the one-eyed man
    (A) showed good sense
    (B) had bad luck
    (C) deserved better
    (D) was a scoundrel
    (E) did the right thing

20. The moral of this story might be
    (A) "Do unto others as you would have them do unto you."
    (B) "A wicked man is never satisfied."
    (C) "You can only be good so long."
    (D) "There is no such thing as justice."
    (E) "The one-eyed man is king."

Because of its enormous size, the United States is a country of contrasts. Nowhere are the differences between the eastern and western United States so profound as in terms of climate and availability of water.

The eastern and western United States differ in many ways, but perhaps the most significant difference between the two regions is climate. The East receives enough rainfall to sustain agriculture, while
(5) the West does not receive adequate rainfall to do so. Additionally, there are widely disparate climatic variations within smaller regions in the West than there are in the East. The mountains, the Sierra Nevadas and the Cascades, that impede the Pacific
(10) Ocean's ability to cool in the summer and warm in the winter, as well as the fronts that bring moisture in the form of rain and snow, have much to do with the extremes of climate found in the West. Elevations in the interior West also affect climate because even the
(15) mountainous flatlands have elevations higher than a mile.

Because of these extremes, particularly in the area of rainfall (there can be as much as 150 inches of precipitation annually on the western side of the
(20) Sierra-Cascade range as contrasted with as little as four inches annually on the eastern side), irrigation becomes critical if the area is to remain viable for human habitation. Actually, it is so hot in some portions of the western desert that even when rain
(25) clouds form, it does not rain because the earth's reflected heat dissipates the moisture before it can reach the ground. Any drops that actually reach the ground quickly evaporate. While the arid Central Plains of the United States can use water for irrigation
(30) from the Ogallala Aquifer, a closed-basin aquifer, discovered after World War I, the western regions are too far away to benefit from this trapped run-off from several Ice Ages that is confined in gravel beds, stretching from South Dakota to West Texas. No
(35) wonder then that water is so precious to the people and farmlands of this area and that the population of this area presses for national, state, and local funding for irrigation projects that will store and reroute water for them.

(40) The Colorado River, with its various tributaries, including, for example, the Gunnison, the Green, and the Gila, has long been the source of most irrigation projects in the desert areas of the West.

Much of the water from the Colorado River goes into
(45) the state of California to irrigate the Imperial and San Joaquin Valleys. On its route from high in the Rockies to the Gulf of California, the river is diverted in many areas to irrigate fields. Unfortunately, when it returns after having passed through deposits of mineral
(50) salts in the soil that was irrigated, the salinity content of the water has increased dramatically. The amount of salt in the water can then have a detrimental effect on the crops if proper drainage systems are not built. Not only is a proper drainage system exorbitantly
(55) expensive, but drainage systems also create a run-off, which must be handled in some efficient way. By the time the water is drained, this run-off would not only contain salt, but probably pesticides as well, and the question of what to do with the run-off becomes
(60) an issue.

Despite the years of better than average rainfall in the late 70s and early to mid-80s that even caused the Great Salt Lake in Utah to flood, the situation in the western desert areas, particularly California, remains
(65) critical. It is not uncommon for droughts in the state to last several years. Consequently, water, not only for crops, but for human consumption itself, is at stake. Thus, it becomes a serious mandate to solve the water problem in this area if the area is to survive.

21. The word *disparate* (line 6) means
    (A) distinct
    (B) different
    (C) unusual
    (D) analogous
    (E) similar

22. According to the passage, one of the mountain ranges that affects rainfall in the West is the
    (A) Rockies
    (B) Appalachian
    (C) Colorado
    (D) Blue Ridge
    (E) Sierra Nevadas

23. According to the passage, another factor influencing climate in the West is
    (A) desert plants
    (B) the Pacific Ocean
    (C) elevation
    (D) the Colorado River
    (E) plateaus

24. According to the passage, what has become critical on the eastern side of the Sierra-Cascade range?
    (A) crop rotation
    (B) truck farming
    (C) crop dusting
    (D) irrigation
    (E) drainage

25. In some areas of the arid western desert, the formation of rain clouds doesn't assure rain because
    (A) earth's reflected heat dissipates moisture
    (B) mountains are too high
    (C) desert winds blow clouds away
    (D) plateaus are too dry
    (E) riverbeds are too deep

26. The arid Central Plains are able to irrigate with water from
    (A) the Ogallala Aquifier
    (B) the Colorado River
    (C) the Rio Grande River
    (D) the Dakota River
    (E) the Green River

27. Which of the following is a tributary of the Colorado River?
    (A) San Joaquin River
    (B) Aspen River
    (C) Gila River
    (D) Cascade River
    (E) Dakota River

28. Most of the water from the Colorado River goes into the state of
    (A) Nevada
    (B) New Mexico
    (C) Arizona
    (D) California
    (E) Utah

29. The word *salinity* (line 50) means
    (A) mineral
    (B) pesticide
    (C) oxide
    (D) salt
    (E) vegetable

30. Which of the following statements expresses an opinion the author of this passage might have?
    (A) Irrigation projects are an unnecessary expense.
    (B) The situation in the desert of the West is hopeless.
    (C) If this area is to survive as a viable place of habitation, the water problem must be solved.
    (D) The water supply from the Colorado River is completely adequate to take care of the irrigation needs of the area.
    (E) Only the Imperial and San Joaquin Valleys should be irrigated.

Exercise 2

14 Questions • 18 Minutes

The Library of Congress in Washington, D.C., is noteworthy in many ways. In this passage, the history of the Library is traced, and the manner in which the Library evolved is considered.

The Library of Congress is the world's largest and most open library. With collections numbering more than 97 million items, it includes materials in 460 languages; the basic manuscript collections of 23
(5) Presidents of the United States, maps and atlases that have aided explorers and navigators in charting both the world and outer space; and the earliest motion pictures and examples of recorded sound, as well as the latest databases and software packages. The
(10) Library's services extend not only to members and committees of Congress, but to the executive and judicial branches of government, to libraries throughout the nation and the world, and to scholars, researchers, artists, and scientists who use its resources.

(15) This was not always the case. When President John Adams signed the bill that provided for the removal of the seat of government to the new capital city of Washington in 1800, he created a reference library for Congress only. The bill provided, among
(20) other items, $5,000 "for the purchase of such books as may be necessary for the use of Congress—and for putting up a suitable apartment for containing them therein...."

After this small congressional library was de-
(25) stroyed by fire along with the Capitol building in 1814, former President Thomas Jefferson offered as a replacement his personal library, accumulated over a span of 50 years. It was considered to be one of the finest in the United States. Congress accepted
(30) Jefferson's offer. Thus the foundation was laid for a great national library.

By the close of the Civil War, the collections of the Library of Congress had grown to 82,000 volumes and were still principally used by members of Con-
(35) gress and committees. In 1864 President Lincoln appointed as Librarian of Congress a man who was to transform the Library: Ainsworth Rand Spofford, who opened the Library to the public and greatly expanded its collections. Spofford successfully ad-
(40) vocated a change in the copyright law so that the Library would receive two free copies of every book, map, chart, dramatic or musical composition, engraving, cut, print, or photograph submitted for copyright. Predictably, Spofford soon filled all the
(45) Capitol's library rooms, attics, and hallways. In 1873, he then won another lobbying effort, for a new building to permanently house the nation's growing collection and reading rooms to serve scholars and the reading public. The result was the Thomas
(50) Jefferson Building, completed in 1897. Since then, two more buildings have been constructed to house the Library's ever-expanding collection.

The first Librarian in the new building was a newspaperman with no previous library experience,
(55) John Russell Young. He quickly realized that the Library had to get control of the collections that had been overflowing the rooms in the Capitol. Young

set up organizational units and devised programs that changed the Library from essentially an acqui-
(60) sitions operation into an efficient processing factory that organized the materials and made them useful.

Young was succeeded after only two years by Herbert Putnam, formerly head of the Boston Public Library, who served as Librarian of Congress for 40
(65) years. While Librarian Spofford had collected the materials, and Young had organized them, Putnam set out to insure that they would be used. He took the Library of Congress directly into the national library scene and made its holdings known and available to
(70) the smallest community library in the most distant part of the county.

About 1912 both Librarian Putnam and members of Congress became concerned about the distance that was widening between the Library and its em-
(75) ployer, the Congress. Various states had begun to set up "legislative reference bureaus," which brought together skilled teams of librarians, economists, and political scientists whose purpose was to respond quickly to questions that arose in the legislative
(80) process. Congress wanted the same kind of service for itself, so Putnam designed such a unit for the Library of Congress. Called the Legislative Reference Service, it went into operation in 1914 to prepare indexes, digests, and compilations of law
(85) that the Congress might need, but it quickly became a specialized reference unit for information transfer and research. This service was the forerunner of the Library's current Congressional Research Service.

1. By saying that the Library of Congress is "the world's most open library" (lines 1–2), the author means that

    (A) the Library has branches all over the world
    (B) anyone who wants to can use any of the resources of the Library
    (C) the Library maintains hours from very early in the morning to very late at night
    (D) the Library's services are available to a wide variety of institutions and individuals
    (E) the Thomas Jefferson Building contains several reading rooms for public use

2. Which of the following kinds of materials is NOT mentioned in the passage as being part of the collection of the Library of Congress?

    (A) computer software
    (B) every book published in English
    (C) musical recordings
    (D) Congressional research
    (E) every photograph copyrighted in the United States

3. Thomas Jefferson's donation of his personal library to Congress can be seen as

    (A) an attempt to outdo John Adams
    (B) an indication of Jefferson's disenchantment with the library
    (C) a well-meant but inadequate effort to replace what had been lost
    (D) the largest single contribution by an individual to the Library of Congress
    (E) the seed from which the present Library of Congress grew

4. Which of the following made the collections of the Library of Congress available to the public?

    (A) Thomas Jefferson
    (B) Ainsworth Rand Spofford
    (C) John Adams
    (D) Herbert Putnam
    (E) John Russell Young

5. Ainsworth Rand Spofford wanted to build a new building for the Library of Congress because

    (A) his efforts to expand the collection were so successful that there was no longer room for it in the Capitol
    (B) he wanted to leave a lasting legacy of his tenure as Librarian of Congress
    (C) housing the collection in the Capitol building made the library inaccessible to the public
    (D) there were no reading rooms in the Capitol
    (E) there was an overwhelming request from the populace for such a building

6. According to the passage, the Library of Congress now uses how many buildings?
   (A) three
   (B) two
   (C) one
   (D) five
   (E) four

7. A comparison between Ainsworth Rand Spofford and John Russell Young, as they are described in the passage, shows that
   (A) Young made a greater effort to expand the collection of the Library of Congress than Spofford did
   (B) Spofford had more library experience at the time of his appointment as Librarian of Congress than Young did
   (C) Spofford served as Librarian of Congress longer than Young did
   (D) Young was more concerned with housing the collection of the Library of Congress than Spofford was
   (E) Spofford was more interested in building a memorial to himself

8. Herbert Putnam's contributions to the Library of Congress included which of the following?
   I. Giving other libraries access to the Library of Congress's resources
   II. Creating distinct organizational units within the Library
   III. Instigating the Legislative Reference Service
   (A) II only
   (B) III only
   (C) I and II only
   (D) II and III only
   (E) I and III only

9. One difference between John Russell Young and Herbert Putnam is
   (A) their level of personal wealth
   (B) the extent to which they focused on expanding the Library's collection
   (C) their ability to lobby Congress on the Library's behalf
   (D) their interest in making the Library's resources available to the public
   (E) the kind of experience they brought to the post of Librarian of Congress

10. The purpose of the Legislative Reference Service was
    (A) to encourage members of Congress to use the Library's collection more fully
    (B) to replace the states' legislative reference bureaus
    (C) more broadly defined than that of any other unit of the Library
    (D) similar to the purpose for which the Library was originally established
    (E) to assist lawyers in preparing trial briefs

Directions: The two passages below deal with a related topic. Following the passages are questions about the content of each passage or about the relationship between the two passages. Answer the questions based upon what is stated or implied in the passages and in any introductory material provided.

Fanny Wright was a reformer, author, and orator, unusual occupations for a woman in the early nineteenth century. Young Robert Emmet was condemned to death for treason after organizing a rebellion against the English in Ireland. He, too, had achieved fame as an orator, with speeches decrying tyranny.

Passage 1—Fanny Wright to a Fourth-of-July Audience at New Harmony, Indiana (1828)

In continental Europe, of late years, the words patriotism and patriot have been used in a more enlarged sense than it is usual here to attribute to them, or than is attached to them in Great Britain. Since the political (5) struggles of France, Italy, Spain, and Greece, the word patriotism has been employed, throughout continental Europe, to express a love of the public good; a preference for the interests of the many to those of the few; a desire for the emancipation of the human race from the (10) thrall of despotism, religious and civil: in short, patriotism there is used rather to express the interest felt in the human race in general than that felt for any country, or inhabitants of a country, in particular. And patriot, in like manner, is employed to signify a lover of human (15) liberty and human improvement rather than a mere lover of the country in which he lives, or the tribe to which he belongs. Used in this sense, patriotism is a virtue, and a patriot is a virtuous man. With such an interpretation, a patriot is a useful member of society, (20) capable of enlarging all minds and bettering all hearts with which he comes in contact; a useful member of the human family, capable of establishing fundamental principles and of merging his own interests, those of his associates, and those of his nation in the interests of the (25) human race. Laurels and statues are vain things, and mischievous as they are childish; but could we imagine them of use, on such a patriot alone could they be with any reason bestowed. . . .

Passage 2—Robert Emmet to the Court That Condemned Him to Death (1803)

I am charged with being an emissary of France. An (30) emissary of France! and for what end? It is alleged that I wish to sell the independence of my country; and for what end? Was this the object of my ambition? . . . No; I am no emissary; and my ambition was to hold a place among the deliverers of my country, not in power nor in (35) profit, but in the glory of the achievement. Sell my country's independence to France! and for what? Was it a change of masters? No, but for ambition. Oh, my country! was it personal ambition that could influence me? Had it been the soul of my actions, could I not, by (40) my education and fortune, by the rank and consideration of my family, have placed myself amongst the proudest of your oppressors? My country was my idol! To it I sacrificed every selfish, every endearing sentiment; and for it I now offer up myself, O God! No, my lords; I acted (45) as an Irishman, determined on delivering my country from the yoke of a foreign and unrelenting tyranny, and the more galling yoke of a domestic faction, which is its joint partner and perpetrator in the patricide, from the ignominy existing with an exterior of splendor and a (50) conscious depravity. It was the wish of my heart to extricate my country from this double riveted despotism—I wished to place her independence beyond the reach of any power on earth. I wished to exalt her to that proud station in the world. Connection with France was, (55) indeed, intended, but only as far as mutual interest would sanction or require. Were the French to assume any authority inconsistent with the purest independence, it would be the signal for their destruction. . . .

Let no man dare, when I am dead, to charge me (60) with dishonor; let no man attaint my memory by believing that I could have engaged in any cause but that of my country's liberty and independence; or that I could have become the pliant minion of power in the oppression and misery of my country. The proclamation of the (65) provisional government speaks for our views; no inference can be tortured from it to countenance barbarity or debasement at home, or subjection, humiliation, or treachery from abroad. I would not have submitted to a foreign oppressor, for the same reason that I would (70) resist the foreign and domestic oppressor. In the dignity of freedom, I would have fought upon the threshold of my country, and its enemy should enter only by passing over my lifeless corpse. And am I, who lived but for my country, and who have subjected myself (75) to the dangers of the jealous and watchful oppressor, and the bondage of the grave, only to give my countrymen their rights, and my country its independence—am I to be loaded with calumny, and not suffered to resent it? No; God forbid!

11. In Passage 1, the word *thrall* (line 10) is used to mean
    (A) freedom
    (B) bondage
    (C) tremor
    (D) excitement
    (E) stimulation

12. How could you restate Wright's last sentence?
    (A) Laurels and statues are silly, but if they had any meaning at all, a patriot like the one I describe might deserve them.
    (B) Tributes make men vain, but such a man could wear them wisely.
    (C) We decorate men in vain, but a useful man could be called a patriot.
    (D) A patriot such as the one I have mentioned will have no need for statues and laurels.
    (E) In vain do we search for appropriate laurels and statues with which to reward such a patriot.

13. In what way does Emmet fail to fit Wright's definition of a patriot?
    (A) He prefers the despotism of France to that of England.
    (B) He wants to free his people.
    (C) He idolizes his own country over all.
    (D) He declares the court's sentence to be unjust.
    (E) He sees no dishonor in his actions.

14. Emmet's speech moves from
    (A) a plea for mercy to acceptance
    (B) interpretation to description
    (C) polite refusal to calm denial
    (D) impassioned denial to angry challenge
    (E) expressions of remorse to expressions of fear

ANSWER KEYS AND EXPLANATIONS

Exercise 1

1. A	7. A	13. C	19. D	25. A
2. D	8. B	14. D	20. B	26. A
3. B	9. C	15. D	21. B	27. C
4. E	10. B	16. C	22. E	28. D
5. E	11. C	17. D	23. C	29. D
6. D	12. A	18. E	24. D	30. C

1. **(A)** The answer to this is found in paragraph 1, lines 5–6. The author never mentions spying, molestation, or lost ambassadors; he is just worried that the messengers will think his countrymen negligent and indifferent.

2. **(D)** This multiple-meaning word has only one synonym given that fits the context of the sentence. If you plug the choices into the line cited, you will easily make the correct choice.

3. **(B)** The author's concerns have to do with behaving in a dignified and appropriate manner. He apparently wants to make sure the ambassadors are led to their destination courteously and swiftly.

4. **(E)** *Envoy* and *ambassador* are used interchangeably by the author to refer to representatives of foreign lands.

5. **(E)** This is an accurate summing up of paragraph 1. (A) is irrelevant, as is (C). (B) is not hinted at here, and (D) is never directly stated.

6. **(D)** In the connotation of information gleaned by visiting a foreign land, intelligence is precisely the subject of paragraph 2. Even if you do not know the word, you should be able to eliminate the other choices as irrelevant or incorrect.

7. **(A)** Plug the choices into the context of the sentence to determine the correct response. Only (A) makes sense.

8. **(B)** If this is a familiar word, you will have no problem. If not, substitute the choices into the sentence to find the one that makes the most sense.

9. **(C)** The phrase uses *standard* to mean "measure"; the ambassador is interested in gauging the measure of the king's table and company—the extent of his hospitality and the quality of his companions.

10. **(B)** The passage sets up a list of opposites. If you recognize this, it should be easy enough to find the word among the choices that is the opposite of *generous*; that is, *stingy*.

11. **(C)** It is used in relation to nets, so the only appropriate synonym for *cast* is *hurl* (C).

12. **(A)** The fisherman may be (D), but that is never made clear. He is certainly not (B), and he is stout-hearted, not stout (C). There is no support for (E). The only answer possible is (A), and, in fact, the narrator makes it clear that the fisherman has done everything possible to help the drowning man.

13. **(C)** *Fixed* has many meanings, and each choice is a possible synonym. However, in the context of "[fixing] a day for the hearing," only (C) makes sense.

14. **(D)** This archaic term means "man of worth," or gentleman. Testing the choices in context should lead you to this conclusion.

15. **(D)** All of paragraph 3 is given over to the fisherman's tale of what happened.

16. **(C)** The fool's suggestion to throw the one-eyed man back into the sea may have been harsh, but it offered a certain rough justice.

17. **(D)** Try the choices in context, and you will find that *together* is the only meaningful substitute.

18. **(E)** Choice (B) is incorrect—the narrator did not draw this conclusion because of the incident, but rather uses the incident to illustrate a moral.

19. **(D)** The scoundrel mentioned in line 52 is a reference to the man helped in the story—the one-eyed man.
20. **(B)** This is a reasonable paraphrase of the final paragraph. When you see the word *moral*, you know that you need to draw conclusions about the theme of what you have read. It may help to look back at the end of the story to see whether the author has done that for you, as in this case.
21. **(B)** The context of the sentence, particularly the use of the word *variations* supports the choice of (B).
22. **(E)** The two mountain ranges mentioned in the passage are Sierra Nevadas and the Cascades.
23. **(C)** While the Pacific Ocean (B) is mentioned as a potential source of moisture for the area, *elevation* is the critical factor influencing climate.
24. **(D)** Because of the virtual absence of rainfall on the eastern side, *irrigation* (D) is critical.
25. **(A)** The passage specifically states that moisture is dissipated by the earth's heat.
26. **(A)** The underground aquifier is the source of much of the water used for irrigation in the Central Plains.
27. **(C)** Only the *Gila* is a tributary of the Colorado River, according to the passage.
28. **(D)** The passage specifically states that most of the water for irrigation from the Colorado River is used by the state of *California*.
29. **(D)** The context of the sentence, which indicates that the water passes through deposits of mineral salts supports the choice of (D), *salt*.
30. **(C)** If you have understood the main idea of the passage, you will know that the author believes that the water problem in the area must be solved if the area is to survive.

Exercise 2

1. D	6. A	11. B
2. B	7. C	12. A
3. E	8. E	13. C
4. B	9. E	14. D
5. A	10. D	

1. **(D)** In the last sentence of the first paragraph, the author explains what is meant by an "open library" by describing who can use the Library of Congress's resources.
2. **(B)** Computer software is mentioned in line 9, musical recordings in line 8 combined with lines 41–42, Congressional research in line 86, and copyrighted photographs in lines 43–44. Every book *copyrighted in the United States* is put into the Library's collection, but many books published in English are not copyrighted in the United States.
3. **(E)** This answer uses a different metaphor to say what the author says in lines 30–31: "the foundation was laid for a great national library."
4. **(B)** See lines 36–37.
5. **(A)** This answer can be inferred from the previous sentences, particularly lines 37–39, which say that Spofford "greatly expanded [the Library's] collections," and lines 44–45, which say that all the Capitol's space had been filled.
6. **(A)** The three buildings are the Thomas Jefferson Building (lines 49–50) and "two more" constructed "since then" (lines 50–52).
7. **(C)** Young served as Librarian of Congress for two years (line 62). The length of Spofford's tenure is not mentioned, but he served at least from 1864 (line 35) to 1873 (line 46).
8. **(E)** Answer I is supported in lines 67–71 and answer III in the last paragraph. Creating distinct organizational units was the work of John Russell Young (lines 57–58).

9. **(E)** Young was a newspaperman (lines 53–54), and Putnam was a librarian (lines 63–64).

10. **(D)** According to the second paragraph, the Library's original purpose was to provide Congress with information necessary to its work. The purpose of the Legislative Reference Service, as described in lines 84–87, is also to provide Congress with reference information.

11. **(B)** This is a vocabulary-in-context question. Replace the word cited with the five choices and choose the word that best fits the context. In this case, only one of the words has the same meaning as the italicized word. At times, all five choices will be synonyms, but only one will fit the shade of meaning in the citation. Here, Wright speaks of emancipating the human race "from the thrall of despotism." If you know that emancipating means "freeing" and that despotism is "dictatorship," you will know to look for a word that implies the opposite of freeing—in this case, choice (B), *bondage*. Even if you do not recognize the words emancipating or despotism, reading the entire sentence will help you understand the meaning of the italicized word.

12. **(A)** This kind of interpretation question asks you to paraphrase a phrase or sentence. Often the language cited is archaic or difficult because of its use of figures of speech. If you merely read the choices above, (A), (B), (D), and (E) might make some kind of sense to you, in light of the passage you read. In order to choose correctly, you must return to the sentence in question and compare it piece by piece to the choices. Here, "Laurels and statues are vain things . . ." might be paraphrased "Laurels and statues are silly." "Could we imagine them of use" might be paraphrased "if they had any meaning at all," and so on. The choice that is closest to the original meaning is choice (A).

13. **(C)** This evaluation question requires you to use Passage 1 to evaluate Passage 2—in this case, to apply a definition from one passage to something in the other passage. In a science selection, you might be asked to apply one writer's hypothesis to another writer's results or to compare two theories. Here, first you must look at Wright's definition of a patriot. She believes that a patriot is a lover of human liberty in general rather than a lover of country in particular. Next, you must look at the choices in light of what you recall about Passage 2. Choice (A) has nothing to do with Wright's definition, and in terms of Emmet's speech, it is simply wrong. He does not prefer one type of tyranny; he hates all tyranny. Choice (B) is certainly true of Emmet, but it does not contradict Wright's definition, and you are looking for some aspect of Emmet's speech that does. The answer is choice (C)—Wright does not believe in blind chauvinism, but Emmet continually repeats the point that everything he has done, he has done for his country alone. In fact, Emmet supported the French Revolution and probably would have been admired by Fanny Wright, but you must base your answer solely on the material given in the passages. Neither (D) nor (E) discusses actions or attitudes that are part of Wright's definition of patriotism.

14. **(D)** This kind of synthesis/analysis question asks you to look at the flow of a passage and analyze the author's intent in light of the structure of the work. Skim the passage and look for a point where the tone or intent of the passage changes. Usually this will happen between paragraphs, so the paragraphing of the passage is a definite clue. Paragraph 1 of Passage 2 begins with a statement of the charge against Emmet and his denial of that charge. The tone is impassioned rather than polite (C). He never asks for mercy (A) or expresses remorse (E). Nor could this paragraph be termed "interpretation" (B). To test whether choice (D) is correct, go on to paragraph 2. Here, Emmet begins with the words "Let no man dare," angrily challenging those who might call him a dishonorable man. Choice (D) is the only possible answer.

PART 4

SAT Math Strategies

PREVIEW

CHAPTER 8 — *SAT Multiple-Choice Math Strategies*

CHAPTER 9 — *SAT Quantitative Comparisons Strategies*

CHAPTER 10 — *SAT Grid-In Strategies*

Chapter **8**

SAT Multiple-Choice Math Strategies

WHY MULTIPLE-CHOICE MATH IS EASIER

How can one kind of math possibly be easier than another? Well, SAT multiple-choice math is easier than the math tests you take in school. Why? First of all, SAT math focuses on basic arithmetic, elementary algebra, and basic geometry. You won't have to think about trigonometry, calculus, or any other advanced stuff. Also, because it's multiple-choice, the correct answer is always on the page in front of you. So even if you are estimating, you'll be able to narrow down the choices and improve your guessing odds.

SAT MULTIPLE-CHOICE MATH QUESTIONS

The scored portion of the SAT contains 35 standard multiple-choice questions, 25 in one section and 10 in another. Within each question set, the questions are arranged in order from easiest to most difficult. The questions don't stick to one content area. They jump around from arithmetic to algebra to geometry in no particular pattern.

ROAD MAP

- *Understand why multiple-choice math is easier*
- *Learn to solve multiple-choice math questions*
- *Know when to use your calculator*
- *Learn the most important multiple-choice tips*
- *Review what you need to know about multiple-choice math*
- *Practice your skills with multiple-choice math exercises*

QUESTION FORMAT

On the SAT, each set of multiple-choice math questions starts with directions and a reference section that look like this:

> **Directions:** Solve the following problems using any available space on the page for scratchwork. On your answer sheet fill in the choice which *best* corresponds to the correct answer.
>
> **Notes:** The figures accompanying the problems are drawn as accurately as possible unless otherwise stated in specific problems. Again, unless otherwise stated, all figures lie in the same plane. All numbers used in these problems are real numbers. Calculators are permitted for this test.

Reference Information

Circle: $C = 2\pi r$, $A = \pi r^2$

Rectangle: $A = lw$

Rectangular Solid: $V = lwh$

Cylinder: $V = \pi r^2 h$

Triangle: $A = \frac{1}{2}bh$

$a^2 + b^2 = c^2$

Special right triangles: 45°-45°-90° with sides x, x, $x\sqrt{2}$; 30°-60°-90° with sides x, $x\sqrt{3}$, $2x$.

The number of degrees of arc in a circle is 360.
The measure in degrees of a straight angle is 180.
The sum of the measures in degrees of the angles of a triangle is 180.

The information in the reference section should all be familiar to you from your schoolwork. Know that it's there in case you need it. But remember: The formulas themselves aren't the answers to any problems. You have to know when to use them and how to apply them.

Some multiple-choice questions are straight calculations, while others are presented in the form of word problems. Some include graphs, charts, or tables that you will be asked to interpret. All of the questions have five answer choices. These choices are arranged in order by size from smallest to largest or occasionally from largest to smallest.

SOLVING MULTIPLE-CHOICE MATH QUESTIONS

These five steps will help you solve multiple-choice math questions:

Multiple-Choice Math: Getting It Right

1. Read the question carefully and determine what's being asked.
2. Decide which math principles apply and use them to solve the problem.
3. Look for your answer among the choices. If it's there, mark it and go on.
4. If the answer you found is not there, recheck the question and your calculations.
5. If you still can't solve the problem, eliminate obviously wrong answers and take your best guess.

> **NOTE**
> **The answers line up by size.** The quantities in math multiple-choice answer choices either go from larger to smaller or the other way around. Remember that when you're trying to eliminate or test answers.

Now let's try out these steps on a couple of SAT-type multiple-choice math questions.

PQ = PS

In the figure above, $x =$

(A) 15
(B) 30
(C) 40
(D) 60
(E) 75

1. The problem asks you to find the measure of one angle of right triangle PQR.
2. Two math principles apply: (1) the sum of the measures in degrees of the angles of a triangle is 180, and (2) 45-45-90 right triangles have certain special properties. Since $PQ = PS$, PQS is a 45-45-90 right triangle. Therefore, angle $PQS = 45°$ and angle $PQR = 45 + 15 = 60°$. Therefore, angle $x = 180 - 90 - 60 = 30°$.
3. The correct answer, 30, is choice (B).

If x and y are negative numbers, which of the following is negative?

(A) xy

(B) $(xy)^2$

(C) $(x-y)^2$

(D) $x + y$

(E) $\dfrac{x}{y}$

1. The problem asks you to pick an answer choice that is a negative number.
2. The principles that apply are those governing operations with signed numbers. Since x and y are negative, both (A) and (E) must be positive. As for (B) and (C), so long as neither x nor y is zero, those expressions must be positive. (Any number other than zero squared gives a positive result.) (D), however, is negative since it represents the sum of two negative numbers.
3. By applying the rules governing signed numbers to each answer choice, you can determine that choices (A), (B), (C), and (E) can only be positive numbers.

TIP
Remember the Reference Information! The Reference Information at the start of the math section provides valuable information about special right triangles.

Therefore, the correct answer must be choice (D). If you have trouble working with letters, try substituting easy numbers for *x* and *y* in each choice.

KNOW WHEN TO USE YOUR CALCULATOR

Calculators are allowed on the SAT, but you won't *need* a calculator to solve any SAT math questions. Calculators can be helpful in doing basic arithmetic computations, square roots, and percentages and in comparing and converting fractions. But remember that your calculator is not some sort of magic brain. If you don't understand the questions in the first place, the calculator won't give you some magic solution.

Calculators don't have to be fancy. They just have to add, subtract, multiply, and divide. Actually, the simpler the better, because you're less likely to hit some wacky function key by mistake.

The most important thing to remember is to set up your work on paper first, then plug the info into the calculator. For example, if you have a question that deals with an equation, set up the equation on your scratch paper. Then make your number substitutions on the calculator. This way, you always have something to refer to without having to think, "Oh, nuts, how did I set that up?" Really, you don't want to be doing that as the seconds tick by.

When you use your calculator, check the display each time you enter numbers to make sure you entered them correctly. And make sure to hit the Clear key after each finished operation, otherwise it could get ugly.

> **CAUTION**
> Don't automatically reach for your calculator. If it can't help you solve the problem, you'll just waste time fiddling with it. Save the calculator for what it does best, especially arithmetic calculations, percentages, and square roots.

LEARN THE MOST IMPORTANT MULTIPLE-CHOICE MATH TIPS

Some of these you've heard before, some will be new to you. Whatever the case, read them, learn them, love them. They will help you.

THE QUESTION NUMBER TELLS YOU HOW HARD THE QUESTION IS

Just as in most of the other SAT sections, the questions go from easy to hard as you work toward the end. The first third of the questions are easy, the middle third are average but harder, and the final third get more and more difficult. Take a look at these three examples. Don't solve them yet (you'll be doing that in a couple of minutes), just get an idea of how the level of difficulty changes from Question 1 to Question 12 to Question 25.

1. If $x - 2 = 5$, then $x =$

    (A) -10

    (B) -3

    (C) $\dfrac{5}{2}$

    (D) 3

    (E) 7

12. For how many integers x is $-7 < 2x < -5$?

    (A) None
    (B) One
    (C) Two
    (D) Three
    (E) Indefinite number

25. In a set of five books, no two of which have the same number of pages, the longest book has 150 pages and the shortest book has 130 pages. If x pages is the average (arithmetic mean) of the number of pages in the five-book set, which of the following best indicates all possible values of x and only possible values of x?

    (A) $130 < x < 150$
    (B) $131 < x < 149$
    (C) $133 < x < 145$
    (D) $134 < x < 145$
    (E) $135 < x < 145$

Can you see the difference? You can probably do Question 1 with your eyes closed. For Question 12 you probably have to open your eyes and do some calculations on scratch paper. Question 25 may cause you to wince a little, and then get started on some heavy-duty thinking.

> **TIP**
> **Look for shortcuts.** SAT math problems test your math reasoning, not your ability to make endless calculations. If you find yourself calculating too much, you've probably missed a shortcut that would have made your work easier.

EASY QUESTIONS HAVE EASY ANSWERS— DIFFICULT QUESTIONS DON'T

Duh, but with an explanation. The easy questions are straightforward and don't have any hidden tricks. The obvious answer is almost always the correct answer. So for Question 1 the answer is indeed choice (E).

When you hit the difficult stuff, you have to think harder. The information is not straightforward and the answers aren't obvious. You can bet that your first-choice, easy answer will be wrong. If you don't believe it, let's take a look at the solution for difficult Question 25.

25. In a set of five books, no two of which have the same number of pages, the longest book has 150 pages and the shortest book has 130 pages. If x pages is the average (arithmetic mean) of the number of pages in the five-book set, which of the following best indicates all possible values of x and only possible values of x?

(A) $130 < x < 150$
(B) $131 < x < 149$
(C) $133 < x < 145$
(D) $134 < x < 145$
(E) $135 < x < 145$

CAUTION
Beware of the obvious. Don't be fooled by what look like obvious answers to difficult questions. The answers to difficult questions require some digging. They never jump out at you.

Yes, it's difficult mostly because the process you have to use to find the solution is difficult. Let's start by eliminating answer choices. Choice (A) is for suckers. You see the same info as you see in the word problem so you figure it's got to be right. Wrong. All it does is say that the shortest book is 130 pages, the longest book is 150 pages, and the average is between 130 and 150. Simple and wrong.

Choice (B) illustrates the reasoning that "no two books have the same number of pages, so the average must be one page more than the shortest book and one page less than the longest." Remember, it's a difficult question, it's just not that easy an answer.

OK then, let's skip to the correct answer, which is (E), and find out how we got there. First, you want to find the minimum value for x so you assume that the other three books contain 131, 132, and 133 pages. So the average would be

$$\frac{130 + 131 + 132 + 133 + 150}{5} = \frac{676}{5} = 135.2$$

So x must be more than 135. Now assume that the other three books contain 149, 148, and 147 pages. Then the average length of all five books would be

$$\frac{150 + 149 + 148 + 147 + 130}{5} = \frac{724}{5} = 144.8$$

Then x would be greater than 135 but less than 145.

WHEN GUESSING AT HARD QUESTIONS, YOU CAN TOSS OUT EASY ANSWERS

Now that you know the difficult questions won't have easy or obvious answers, use a guessing strategy. (Use all the help you can get!) When you have less than a clue about a difficult question, scan the answer choices and eliminate the ones that seem easy or obvious, such as any that just restate the information in the question. Ditch those and then take your best guess.

QUESTIONS OF AVERAGE DIFFICULTY WON'T HAVE TRICK ANSWERS

Let's look again at Question 12:

12. For how many integers x is $-7 < 2x < -5$?

    (A) None
    (B) One
    (C) Two
    (D) Three
    (E) Indefinite number

This is a bit more difficult than Question 1, but it's still pretty straightforward. There is only one integer between -7 and -5, and that's -6. There's also only one value for integer x so that $2x$ equals -6, and that is -3. Get it? $2(-3) = -6$. So, (B) is the correct answer. Trust your judgment and your reasoning; no tricks here.

IT'S SMART TO WORK BACKWARDS

Every standard mutiple-choice math problem includes five answer choices. One of them has to be correct; the other four are wrong. This means that it's always possible to solve a problem by testing each of the answer choices. Just plug each choice into the problem and sooner or later you'll find the one that works! Testing answer choices can often be a much easier and surer way of solving a problem than attempting a lengthy calculation.

WHEN WORKING BACKWARDS, ALWAYS START FROM THE MIDDLE

When working on multiple-choice math questions, remember that all of the answer choices are presented in order—either smallest to largest, or vice-versa. As a result, it's always best to begin with the middle option, or choice (C). This way, if you start with (C) and it's too large, you'll only have to concentrate on the smaller choices. There, you've just knocked off at least three choices in a heartbeat! Now let's give it a test-run!

If a rectangle has sides of $2x$ and $3x$ and an area of 24, what is the value of x?

(A) 2
(B) 3
(C) 4
(D) 5
(E) 6

You know that one of these is right. Get started by testing (C), and assume that $x = 4$. Then the sides would have lengths $2(4) = 8$ and $3(4) = 12$ and the rectangle would have an area of $8 \times 12 = 96$. Since 96 is larger than 24 (the area in the question), start working with the smaller answer choices. (Which means, of course, that you can immediately forget about (D) and (E). Great!)

When you plug 3 into the figuring, you get $2(3) = 6$ and $3(3) = 9$ and $6 \times 9 = 54$; still too large. The only choice left is (A), and it works.

Now try this testing business with a more difficult question:

A farmer raises chickens and cows. If his animals have a total of 120 heads and a total of 300 feet, how many chickens does the farmer have?

(A) 50
(B) 60
(C) 70
(D) 80
(E) 90

Here goes—starting with (C). If the farmer has 70 chickens, he has 50 cows. (You know the farmer has 120 animals, because they each have only one head, right?) So now you're talking about $70 \times 2 = 140$ chicken feet and $50 \times 4 = 200$ cow feet, for a grand total of 340 animal feet. Well, that's more than the 300 animal feet in the question. How will you lose some of those feet? First, assume that the farmer has more chickens and fewer cows (cows have more feet than chickens do). Give (D)—80—a try. Test $80 \times 2 = 160$ and $40 \times 4 = 160$; your total is 320 feet, which is closer but not quite right. The only answer left is (E), and that's the correct one. Check it out: $90 \times 2 = 180$ and $30 \times 4 = 120$ and the total is . . . 300!

IT'S EASIER TO WORK WITH NUMBERS THAN WITH LETTERS

Because numbers are more meaningful than letters, try plugging them into equations and formulas in place of variables. This technique can make problems much easier to solve. Here are some examples:

> If $x - 4$ is 2 greater than y, then $x + 5$ is how much greater than y?
>
> (A) 1
> (B) 3
> (C) 7
> (D) 9
> (E) 11

Choose any value for x. Let's say you decide to make $x = 4$. All right, $4 - 4 = 0$, and 0 is 2 greater than y. So $y = -2$. If $x = 4$, then $x + 5 = 4 + 5 = 9$, and so $x + 5$ is 11 more than y. Therefore, the correct answer is choice (E).

> The unit cost of pens is the same regardless of how many pens are purchased. If the cost of p pens is d dollars, what is the cost, in dollars, of x pens?
>
> (A) xd
>
> (B) xpd
>
> (C) $\dfrac{xd}{p}$
>
> (D) $\dfrac{xp}{d}$
>
> (E) $\dfrac{pd}{x}$

TIP

Leave a paper trail! If you need to set up an equation, jot it down in your test booklet. That way, if you come back to recheck your work, you'll know what you were originally thinking.

Time to plug in some real numbers, since you need real money to buy anything, including pens. Say that four pens (p) cost $2.00 ($d$), so each pen ($x$) would cost 50 cents. And say that you really only need one pen, so you're spending only $0.50. Then $p = 4$, $d = 2$, and $x = 1$, and the right answer would be 0.5. Now, start using these numbers with the answer choices:

(A) $xd = (1)(2) = 2$ (Nope.)

(B) $xpd = (1)(4)(2) = 8$ (Nope, again.)

(C) $\dfrac{xd}{p} = \dfrac{(1)(2)}{4} = 0.5$ (Yes, there it is.)

(D) $\dfrac{xp}{d} = \dfrac{(1)(4)}{2} = 2$ (Nope.)

(E) $\dfrac{pd}{x} = \dfrac{(4)(2)}{1} = 8$ (Nope.)

If a question asks for an odd integer or an even integer, go ahead and pick any odd or even integer you like.

IT'S OK TO WRITE IN YOUR TEST BOOKLET, SO USE IT FOR SCRATCH WORK

The test booklet is yours, so feel free to use it for your scratchwork. Also, go ahead and mark up any diagrams with length or angle information; it helps. But don't waste time trying to redraw diagrams; it's just not worth it.

QUESTIONS IN THE THREE-STATEMENT FORMAT CAN BE SOLVED BY THE PROCESS OF ELIMINATION

You may find a three-statement format in certain questions in the multiple-choice math section. The best way to answer this kind of question is to tackle one statement at a time, marking it as either true or false. Here is an example:

If $x - y$ is positive, which of the following statements is true?

I. $0 > x > y$

II. $x > 0 > y$

III. $y > x > 0$

(A) I only
(B) II only
(C) III only
(D) I and II only
(E) II and III only

CAUTION
Don't pick "cannot be determined" for a hard question. The hard questions are supposed to test how much you know about complex math operations, so the answer can be determined—even if you can't determine it.

The answer choices all refer to the three statements. Let's start by checking statement I. If x and y are negative numbers so that x is greater than y, then y has a greater absolute value than x. Since both are negative numbers, $x - y$ is positive. For example, $-3 > -4$ and $-3 - (-4) = -3 + 4 = 1$, and $1 > 0$. Therefore, statement I will appear in the correct answer choice. Now, since (B), (C), and (E) don't contain statement I, you can eliminate them.

Now let's check out statement II. If x is positive and y is negative, then $x - y$ would be subtracting a negative number from a positive number, which will give you a positive number. (Subtracting a negative number is really adding a positive number.) Because statement II must appear in the correct answer, you can now eliminate answer choice (A). So, by the process of elimination, you know that (D) is correct, and you don't even have to test statement III.

THE AREA OF AN UNUSUAL SHAPE IS REALLY THE DIFFERENCE BETWEEN THE AREAS OF TWO REGULAR FIGURES

Here's a visual example that might help:

In the figure below, what is the area of the shaded region?

(A) $2\frac{1}{2}$

(B) 4

(C) $3\frac{1}{2}$

(D) 6

(E) 8

Try to isolate the shaded portion of the figure. When you do, you'll see it's a trapezoid. Now, you could try to remember the formula for the area of a trapezoid, but look at the figure you have left after you pull out the trapezoid. It's another, smaller triangle. What you really need to do is figure out the areas of the original large triangle and the smaller triangle and find the difference.

You know that the larger triangle has a right angle and two equal sides, so it's an isosceles right triangle. The smaller triangle has a right angle and its side is parallel to the side of the larger triangle, so it too is an isosceles triangle. Now use the information in the figure to find the areas and then subtract.

Area of smaller triangle = $\frac{1}{2}(3)(3) = \frac{9}{2}$

Area of larger triangle = $\frac{1}{2}(4)(4) = 8$

$8 - \frac{9}{2} = 3\frac{1}{2}$

> **TIP**
> Draw a diagram if none is supplied. Drawing a diagram is a great way to organize information. Mark it up with the information you're given, and you'll have a better idea of what you're looking for.

USING THE MEASURE OF AN ANGLE OR A SIDE OF ANOTHER SHAPE CAN HELP YOU FIND A MEASURE YOU NEED

In the figure, what is the length of NP?

(A) 3
(B) 8
(C) 9
(D) 12
(E) 15

This figure is really two right triangles, NMO and NMP. Since NM is a side of both triangles, once you find the length of that, you can find the length of NP. The Pythagorean Theorem is what you need:

$NM^2 + MO^2 = NO^2$

$NM^2 + 16^2 = (20)^2$

Note that 16 and 20 are multiples of 4 and 5, respectively, so you now know that this is a 3-4-5 right triangle, which means that NM = 12.

Since you just found out that triangle NMP has sides of 9 and 12, it's also a 3-4-5 right triangle, so NP must be 15.

A REALITY CHECK CAN HELP YOU ELIMINATE ANSWERS THAT CAN'T POSSIBLY BE RIGHT

Knowing whether your calculations should produce a number that's larger or smaller than the quantity you started with can point you toward the right answer. It's also an effective way of eliminating wrong answers. Here's an example:

> **TIP**
> For multiple-choice math questions, circle what's being asked so that you don't pick a wrong answer by mistake. That way, for example, you won't pick an answer that gives a perimeter when the question asks for an area.

Using his bike, Daryl can complete a paper route in 20 minutes. Francisco, who walks the route, can complete it in 30 minutes. How long will it take the two boys to complete the route if they work together, one starting at each end of the route?

(A) 8 minutes
(B) 12 minutes
(C) 20 minutes
(D) 30 minutes
(E) 45 minutes

Immediately you can see that choices (C), (D), and (E) are impossible because the two boys working together will have to complete the job in less time than either one of them working alone. In fact, the correct answer is choice (B), 12 minutes.

	Daryl	Francisco
$\dfrac{\text{Time actually spent}}{\text{Time needed to do entire job alone}}$	$\dfrac{x}{20}$	$\dfrac{x}{30}$

$$\frac{x}{20} + \frac{x}{30} = 1$$

Multiply by 60 to clear fractions:

$$3x + 2x = 60$$
$$5x = 60$$
$$x = 12$$

YOUR EYE IS A GOOD ESTIMATOR

Figures in the standard multiple-choice math section are always drawn to scale unless you see the warning "Note: Figure not drawn to scale." That means you can sometimes solve a problem just by looking at the picture and estimating the answer. Here's how this works:

In the rectangle PQRS shown, TU and WV are parallel to SR. If PS = 6, UV = 1, and PR (not shown) = 10, what is the area of rectangle TUVW?

(A) 8
(B) 12
(C) 16
(D) 24
(E) 32

To solve the problem, you will need to find the length of TU. You can do this by using the Pythagorean Theorem. The triangle PSR has sides of 6 and 10, so SR = 8. Since TU = SR, TU = 8, so the area of the small rectangle is equal to $1 \times 8 = 8$.

As an alternative, you could simply estimate the length of TU. TU appears to be longer than PS (6), and TU must be shorter than PR (10). Therefore, TU appears to be approximately 8. And the area must be approximately $1 \times 8 = 8$. Is that sufficiently accurate to get the right answer? Look at the choices. (A) is 8, and it's the only choice that is even close to 8.

IF SOME QUESTIONS ALWAYS GIVE YOU TROUBLE, SAVE THEM FOR LAST

You know which little demons haunt your math skills. If you find questions that you know will give you nightmares, save them for last. They will take up a lot of your time, especially if you're panicking, and you can use that time to do more of the easier questions.

Summary: What You Need to Know About Multiple-Choice Math

- Follow the five-step plan for answering basic multiple-choice math questions:
    1. Read the question carefully and determine what's being asked.
    2. Decide which math principles apply and use them to solve the problem.
    3. Look for your answer among the choices. If it's there, mark it and go on.
    4. If the answer you found is not there, recheck the question and your calculations.
    5. If you still can't solve the problem, eliminate obviously wrong answers and take your best guess.
- Use a calculator where it can help the most: on basic arithmetic calculations, when calculating square roots and percentages, and in comparing and converting fractions.
- Always set up your work on paper, then enter the numbers in your calculator; that way, if your calculation becomes confused, you don't have to try to replicate your set-up from memory.
- The question number tells you how hard the question will be (on a 1 to 25 scale)
- Work backwards from the answer choices. When you do, start with choice (C).
- Try to work with numbers instead of letters. This will help you avoid unnecessary algebraic calculations.
- Figures in the math section are always drawn to scale unless you see a warning. So use your eye as an estimator if you need to.

EXERCISES: MULTIPLE-CHOICE MATH

Exercise 1

15 Questions • 18 Minutes

Directions: Solve the following problems using any available space on the page for scratchwork. Circle the letter that appears before your answer.

Notes: The figures accompanying the problems are drawn as accurately as possible unless otherwise stated in specific problems. Again, unless otherwise stated, all figures lie in the same plane. All numbers used in these problems are real numbers. Calculators are permitted for this test.

Reference Information

Circle: $C = 2\pi r$, $A = \pi r^2$
Rectangle: $A = lw$
Rectangular Solid: $V = lwh$
Cylinder: $V = \pi r^2 h$
Triangle: $A = \frac{1}{2}bh$
$a^2 + b^2 = c^2$

Special right triangles: 45°-45°-90° with sides x, x, $x\sqrt{2}$; 30°-60°-90° with sides x, $x\sqrt{3}$, $2x$.

The number of degrees of arc in a circle is 360.
The measure in degrees of a straight angle is 180.
The sum of the measures in degrees of the angles of a triangle is 180.

---

1. If $8 \times 8 = 4^x$, what is x?

   (A) 2
   (B) 3
   (C) 4
   (D) 5
   (E) 6

2. If $a > 2$, which of the following is the smallest?

   (A) $\dfrac{2}{a}$
   (B) $\dfrac{a}{2}$
   (C) $a + \dfrac{1}{2}$
   (D) $\dfrac{2}{a+1}$
   (E) $\dfrac{2}{a-1}$

3. Which of the following has the greatest value?

   (A) $\dfrac{1}{2}$
   (B) $\sqrt{.2}$
   (C) $.2$
   (D) $(.2)^2$
   (E) $(.02)^3$

4. If $\frac{a}{b} = \frac{3}{4}$, then $12a =$

   (A) b
   (B) $3b$
   (C) $9b$
   (D) $12b$
   (E) $16b$

5. If $a = b$ and $\frac{1}{c} = b$, then $c =$

   (A) a
   (B) $-a$
   (C) b
   (D) $\frac{1}{a}$
   (E) $-b$

6. If a building B feet high cast a shadow F feet long, then at the same time of day, a tree T feet high will cast a shadow how many feet long?

   (A) $\frac{FT}{B}$
   (B) $\frac{FB}{T}$
   (C) $\frac{B}{FT}$
   (D) $\frac{TB}{F}$
   (E) $\frac{T}{FB}$

7. The vertices of a triangle are (3, 1), (8, 1), and (8, 3). What is the area of this triangle?

   (A) 5
   (B) 10
   (C) 12
   (D) 14
   (E) 20

8. Of 60 employees at the Star Manufacturing Company, x employees are female. If $\frac{2}{3}$ of the remainder are married, how many unmarried men work for this company?

   (A) $40 - \frac{2}{3}x$
   (B) $40 - \frac{1}{3}x$
   (C) $40 + \frac{1}{3}x$
   (D) $20 - \frac{2}{3}x$
   (E) $20 - \frac{1}{3}x$

9. A circle whose center is at the origin passes through the point whose coordinates are (1, 1). What is the area of this circle?

   (A) π

   (B) 2π

   (C) $\sqrt{2\pi}$

   (D) $2\sqrt{2\pi}$

   (E) 4π

10. In triangle ABC, $AB = BC$ and AC is extended to D. If angle BCD contains 100°, find the number of degrees in angle B.

    (A) 20
    (B) 40
    (C) 50
    (D) 60
    (E) 80

11. $\dfrac{4\frac{1}{2}}{10\frac{1}{8}} =$

    (A) $\dfrac{2}{5}$

    (B) $\dfrac{4}{9}$

    (C) $\dfrac{4}{81}$

    (D) $\dfrac{3}{7}$

    (E) $\dfrac{15}{23}$

12. Which of the following is greater than $\dfrac{1}{3}$?

    (A) .33

    (B) $\left(\dfrac{1}{3}\right)^2$

    (C) $\dfrac{1}{4}$

    (D) $\dfrac{1}{.3}$

    (E) $\dfrac{.3}{2}$

13. What percent of a half dollar is a penny, a nickel, and a dime?

    (A) 8
    (B) 16
    (C) 20
    (D) 25
    (E) 32

14. If $\frac{1}{a} + \frac{1}{b} = \frac{1}{c}$, then $c =$

(A) $a + b$

(B) ab

(C) $\frac{a+b}{ab}$

(D) $\frac{ab}{a+b}$

(E) $\frac{1}{2}ab$

15. What percent of a is b?

(A) $\frac{100b}{a}$

(B) $\frac{a}{b}$

(C) $\frac{b}{100a}$

(D) $\frac{b}{a}$

(E) $\frac{100a}{b}$

Exercise 2

10 Questions • 12 Minutes

Directions: Solve the following problems using any available space on the page for scratchwork. Circle the letter that appears before your answer.

Notes: The figures accompanying the problems are drawn as accurately as possible unless otherwise stated in specific problems. Again, unless otherwise stated, all figures lie in the same plane. All numbers used in these problems are real numbers. Calculators are permitted for this test.

---

1. The average of two numbers is A. If one of the numbers is x, what is the other number?

    (A) $A - x$

    (B) $\dfrac{A}{2} - x$

    (C) $2A - x$

    (D) $\dfrac{A + x}{2}$

    (E) $x - A$

2. If $a = 5b$, then $\dfrac{3}{5}a =$

    (A) $\dfrac{5b}{3}$

    (B) $3b$

    (C) $\dfrac{3b}{5}$

    (D) $\dfrac{b}{3}$

    (E) $\dfrac{b}{5}$

3. A rectangular door measures 5 feet by 6 feet 8 inches. What is the distance from one corner of the door to the diagonally opposite corner?

    (A) 8'2"

    (B) 8'4"

    (C) 8'8"

    (D) 9'

    (E) 9'6"

4. Two ships leave from the same port at 11:30 A.M. If one sails due east at 20 miles per hour and the other due south at 15 miles per hour, how many miles apart are the ships at 2:30 P.M.?

    (A) 25
    (B) 50
    (C) 75
    (D) 80
    (E) 85

5. If m men can paint a house in d days, how many days will it take $m + 2$ men to paint the same house?

    (A) $d + 2$

    (B) $d - 2$

    (C) $\dfrac{m + 2}{md}$

    (D) $\dfrac{md}{m + 2}$

    (E) $\dfrac{md + 2d}{m}$

6. Ken received grades of 90, 88, and 75 on three tests. What grade must he receive on the next test so that his average for these four tests is 85?

    (A) 87
    (B) 89
    (C) 90
    (D) 92
    (E) 95

7. There is enough food at a picnic to feed 20 adults or 32 children. If there are 15 adults at the picnic, how many children can still be fed?

    (A) 6
    (B) 8
    (C) 12
    (D) 16
    (E) 18

8. In parallelogram $ABCD$, angle A contains 60°. What is the sum of angle B and angle D?

    (A) 60°
    (B) 180°
    (C) 240°
    (D) 280°
    (E) 300°

9. The area of circle O is 64π. What is the perimeter of square ABCD?

   (A) 32
   (B) 32π
   (C) 64
   (D) 16
   (E) 64π

10. If a train covers 14 miles in 10 minutes, what is the rate of the train in miles per hour?

    (A) 64
    (B) 76
    (C) 84
    (D) 90
    (E) 98

ANSWER KEYS AND EXPLANATIONS

Exercise 1

1. B
2. D
3. A
4. C
5. D
6. A
7. A
8. E
9. B
10. A
11. B
12. D
13. E
14. D
15. A

1. **(B)** $64 = 4^x$

   $x = 3 \quad (4 \times 4 \times 4 = 64)$

2. **(D)** Both (B) and (C) are greater than 1. (A), (D), and (E) all have the same numerator. In this case, the one with the largest denominator will be the smallest fraction.

3. **(A)** $\dfrac{1}{2} = .5$

   $\sqrt{.20} = .4^+$

   $(.2)^2 = .04$

   $(.02)^3 = .000008$

4. **(C)** Cross multiply.

   $4a = 3b$

   Multiply by 3.

   $12a = 9b$

5. **(D)** $a = b = \dfrac{1}{c}$

   $a = \dfrac{1}{c}$

   $ac = 1$

   $c = \dfrac{1}{a}$

6. **(A)** The ratio of height to shadow is constant.

   $\dfrac{B}{F} = \dfrac{T}{x}$

   $Bx = FT$

   $x = \dfrac{FT}{B}$

7. **(A)**

Right triangle area = $\frac{1}{2} \times 5 \times 2 = 5$

8. **(E)** $60 - x$ employees are male

$\frac{1}{3}$ of these are unmarried

$\frac{1}{3}(60 - x) = 20 - \frac{1}{3}x$

9. **(B)**

$1^2 + 1^2 = r^2$

$2 = r^2$

Area $= \pi r^2 = 2\pi$

10. **(A)** Angle BCA = Angle BAC = 80°

There are 20° left for angle B.

11. **(B)** $\frac{9}{2} \div \frac{81}{8} = \frac{9}{2} \times \frac{8}{81} = \frac{4}{9}$

12. **(D)** $\frac{1}{.3} = \frac{10}{3} = 3\frac{1}{3}$

13. **(E)** $\frac{16}{50} = \frac{32}{100} = 32\%$

14. **(D)** Multiply by abc.

$bc + ac = ab$

$c(b + a) = ab$

$c = \frac{ab}{b + a}$

15. **(A)** $\frac{b}{a} \times 100 = \frac{100b}{a}$

Exercise 2

1. C   5. D   9. C
2. B   6. A   10. C
3. B   7. B
4. C   8. C

1. **(C)** $\frac{x+y}{2} = A$

    $x + y = 2A$

    $y = 2A - x$

2. **(B)** $\frac{3}{\cancel{5}} \times \cancel{5}b = 3b$

3. **(B)** 5 feet = 60 inches

    6 feet 8 inches = 80 inches

    This is a 6-8-10 triangle, making the diagonal 100 inches, which is 8 feet 4 inches.

4. **(C)** In 3 hours, one ship went 60 miles, the other 45 miles. This is a 3-4-5 triangle as 45 = 3(15), 60 = 4(15). The hypotenuse will be 5(15), or 75.

5. **(D)** This is inverse variation.

    $m \times d = (m + 2) \times x$

    $\frac{md}{m+2} = x$

6. **(A)** He must score as many points above 85 as below. So far he has 8 above and 10 below. He needs another 2 above.

7. **(B)** If 15 adults are fed, $\frac{3}{4}$ of the food is gone. $\frac{1}{4}$ of the food will feed $\frac{1}{4} \times 32$, or 8 children.

8. **(C)** If angle $A = 60°$, then angle $B = 120°$.

    Angle B = Angle D. Their sum is 240°.

9. **(C)** Area of circle = $64\pi = \pi r^2$

    Radius of circle = 8

    Side of square = 16

    Perimeter of square = 64

10. **(C)** 10 minutes = $\frac{1}{6}$ hour

    In one hour, the train will cover 6(14), or 84 miles.

Chapter

9

SAT Quantitative Comparisons Strategies

GET TO KNOW THE QUANTITATIVE COMPARISON FORMAT

You picked up this book. You flipped through some pages. You got to this chapter and thought, "What the heck am I supposed to do with these weird questions? What do they want from me now?" Well, quantitative comparisons are not quite as wacky as they look. You can recognize quantitative comparison questions easily because they look very different from other math questions. Each one has two side-by-side boxes containing quantities that you must compare. Then you choose the correct answers from choices (A) through (D).

There are some good things to remember about these. First, the choices are always the same (check out the sample directions below). Second, you don't actually have to solve a problem. The questions are really testing knowledge of mathematical principles rather than your calculating skills. Third, sometimes the SAT folks give you a little help and provide a diagram or other information centered above the boxes with the information you are comparing. Oh, you can use a calculator, too, if you want.

ROAD MAP

- *Get to know the quantitative comparison format*
- *Learn to solve quantitative comparisons*
- *Learn the most important quantitative comparison tips*
- *Review what you need to know about quantitative comparisons*
- *Practice your skills with quantitative comparison exercises*

SAT QUANTITATIVE COMPARISON QUESTIONS

The scored portion of the SAT contains 15 quantitative comparisons, all grouped in a single section. Within each question set, the questions are arranged in order from easiest to most difficult. The questions cover the same mix of arithmetic, algebra, and geometry that appears in the multiple-choice math section.

QUESTION FORMAT

Each set of quantitative comparisons starts with directions that look like this:

> **Directions:** For each of the following questions, two quantities are given—one in Column A, the other in Column B. Compare the two quantities and mark your answer sheet as follows:
>
> (A) if the quantity in Column A is greater
>
> (B) if the quantity in Column B is greater
>
> (C) if the quantities are equal
>
> (D) if the relationship cannot be determined from the information given
>
> **Notes:**
>
> (1) Information concerning one or both of the compared quantities will be centered above the two columns for some items.
>
> (2) Symbols that appear in both columns represent the same thing in Column A as in Column B.
>
> (3) Letters such as x, n, and k are symbols for real numbers.

SOLVING QUANTITATIVE COMPARISONS

Your estimating and comparison skills, as well as the five steps shown below, will help you cope with these questions. Once you get used to the choices, things can move pretty quickly.

Quantitative Comparisons: Getting It Right

1. Try to remember all of the available answers.
2. For each question, compare the boxed quantities.
3. Consider all possibilities for any variables.
4. Decide which answer choice is best.
5. Carefully fill in the answer on the answer sheet.

TIP

Memorize the directions and the answer choices. Remember that the four answer choices for quantitative comparisons are always the same.

Now let's look at these steps in more detail.

1. Don't just learn the directions, try to memorize the answer choices. (Remember, they are always the same.) Then you can save time because you won't need to refer to them for every question.
2. Even though there are two quantities in each question, deal with one at a time. If there is extra information above the boxes, see how each quantity relates to it. Then do any figuring you need to do. (There won't be much.)
3. Consider all possibilities for any unknowns. Think what would happen if special numbers such as 0, negative numbers, or fractions were put into play.
4. Choose your answer. You shouldn't have to do involved calculations to get to the answer. If you're calculating endlessly, you've probably missed the mathematical principle the question is asking about.
5. Mark your answer sheet CAREFULLY! Did you notice that quantitative comparisons have only *four* answer choices? There is no choice (E), so don't mark (E) by mistake.

NOTE
Variables stay constant. A variable that appears in both columns means the same thing in each column.

Column A **Column B**

The price of a pound of cheese increased from $2.00 to $2.50.

| The percent increase in the price of cheese | 25% |

1. You already know the answer choices.
2. The centered information tells you that cheese increased in price from $2.00 to $2.50 per pound. Column A asks for the percent increase, which is $\frac{\$0.50}{\$2.00}$ = 25%. Column B requires no calculation, and it's equal to Column A.
3. There are no variables, so go on to Step 4.
4. Since the two columns are equal, the answer is choice (C).
5. Mark choice (C) on the answer sheet.

Column A **Column B**

| $x^2 + y^2$ | $(x + y)^2$ |

1. You already know the answer choices.
2. The expression in Column B is $(x + y)^2 = x^2 + 2xy + y^2$. This is the same as the expression in Column A with the addition of the middle term $2xy$.

CAUTION

Figures can be deceiving. If a figure carries a warning that it is not drawn to scale, don't depend on estimating or measuring to help you solve the question.

3. The terms x and y are variables that can be positive or negative or zero. For example, if x were 1 and y were 2, Column A would be $1^2 + 2^2 = 5$ and Column B would be $(1 + 2)^2 = 9$. The correct answer would then be choice (B). But if x were -1 and y were 2, Column A would be $-1^2 + 2^2 = 5$ and Column B would be $(-1 + 2)^2 = 1^2 = 1$. This time the correct answer would be choice (A).

4. Any time more than one answer can be true for a comparison—as is the case here—then the answer to that question must be choice (D), "the relationship cannot be determined from the information given."

5. Mark choice (D) on the answer sheet.

Remember that many quantitative comparisons can be solved without doing any calculating at all. In many cases, you should be able to arrive at the correct answer simply by applying your knowledge of basic math rules and principles. Look at these examples:

Column A   **Column B**

[triangle with vertices A, B, C; sides c (AB), a (BC), b (AC)]

$c > a$

	Column A	Column B
1.	$\angle A$	$\angle C$
2.	$\angle A$	$\angle B$
3.	$a + b$	c

1. If two sides of a triangle are unequal, the angles opposite them are unequal, and the larger angle is opposite the longer side. So, the answer for this question is (B).

2. Since we can't really tell whether a or b is greater, we can't tell which angle is greater, so (D) is the correct answer.

3. The sum of any two sides of a triangle must always be greater than the length of the third side. The only answer for this question is (A).

LEARN THE MOST IMPORTANT QUANTITATIVE COMPARISON TIPS

Quantitative comparisons may look complex, but if you come at them from the right angle (pardon the pun), you can streamline the answering process.

MAKE THE COLUMNS LOOK ALIKE

Start by doing whatever it takes to make the columns resemble one another. Only when the columns look alike—and therefore are comparable—can you easily tell which is greater. Here's a simple example:

Column A	Column B
a is 30% of b	
b is 40% of c	
Percent that a is of c	11

First, let's be clear what you're looking at. This question starts with two lines of information that is centered between Column A and Column B. This information isn't part of either column; instead, it is provided to help you interpret the values given in the columns. You're to assume that this information is true and that it applies to whatever quantities appear in the columns underneath.

Now look at the two quantities that you're supposed to compare. Column A *describes* a quantity: the "percent that a is of c." Column B, by contrast, *states* a quantity, in the simplest possible form: it's the integer 11. Can you tell, at a glance, which is greater? Probably not. The reason is that the two quantities are named in terms so different that they're not readily comparable.

To compare them, you need to make them look alike. Since Column B is already stated in the simplest possible form, your plan should be to make Column A look like Column B—that is, turn it into a simple number as well. To do that, you'll have to use your math skills. Since the shared information tells you that a is 30% of b and b is 40% of c, you can tell that a must be 30% of 40% of c. What is 30% of 40%? Multiply it out, using your calculator if you like:

$.30 \times .40 = .12$

So you can tell from the information given that a is 12% of c. Now we have a quantity for Column A—12—which can easily be compared with the quantity in Column B. Since 12 is greater than 11, Column A is greater, and (A) is the answer for this question.

> **TIP**
>
> When in doubt, try something! It may not be obvious what the test-makers want you to do with either quantity. If so, start messing around with the quantities, using whatever mathematical techniques strike you as natural or logical. Chances are good that some method you've used dozens of times in math class will yield the result the test-makers are looking for—even if you can't anticipate it when you start work.

Here's another example:

Column A	Column B
$(x+y)(x+y)$	$x^2 + y^2$

x and y are negative

In this question, neither column contains a quantity that's easy to measure—especially since we don't know the value of either unknown, x or y. But don't despair! It may still be possible to figure out how the two quantities compare, if we can make them appear similar and therefore comparable.

Which column can more easily be made to resemble the other? In this case, you can probably see how Column A can be made to look something like Column B. Two quantities contained in parentheses, like those in Column A, are practically crying out to be multiplied together. And you can probably tell that, when you multiply them out, you'll end up with a quantity that includes x^2 and y^2, not unlike Column B. Here's what happens to the comparison when the multiplication in Column A is carried out:

Column A	Column B
$x^2 + 2xy + y^2$	$x^2 + y^2$

We've used a basic algebra process here: when you multiply two binomials, like those in Column A, you end up with a trinomial like the one we've now created. See Chapter 14 if this procedure seems unfamiliar.

Now the two columns resemble one another, and we can compare them more easily. But, in this case, to determine which is greater, we need to use the second basic strategy for quantitative comparisons . . .

ELIMINATE WHATEVER THE COLUMNS SHARE

Remember, you're interested in figuring out the *difference* between the two quantities. That means that anything that the two quantities have in common—anything they share—is *irrelevant*.

Here's an analogy. Suppose you're trying to decide which of two used cars to buy. Also suppose that both cars are four-door models, about the same size, made in the same model year, with roughly the same amount of mileage on them. Since all of those factors are the *same*, they are all *irrelevant* to your choice—none of these will help you decide which car is better. Instead, you'll have to choose based on ways in which the two cars *differ*—price, for example, or appearance.

In the same way, when comparing two mathematical quantities on the SAT, you can eliminate as irrelevant anything both quantities share. Let's go back to the item we've been considering, with Column A transformed by having been multiplied out:

Column A	Column B
$x^2 + 2xy + y^2$	$x^2 + y^2$

At a glance, you can see that both columns now have two terms in common: x^2 and y^2. We don't know the numeric value of either of these terms, since we don't know the value of either x or y. Nonetheless, we can eliminate both x^2 and y^2 from the comparison, since they appear in both columns. The *difference* between the columns can't be contained in what they have in common!

Once we eliminate—remove—these two terms from both sides of the comparison, we can compare what remains:

Column A	Column B
$2xy$	0

Having eliminated x^2 and y^2 from Column A, all that's left there is $2xy$. And having made the same elimination from Column B, all that's left there is nothing—zero! So to answer the question, we simply have to decide whether $2xy$ is greater, less than, or equal to zero.

By using the information given above the two quantities, you can determine this. If both unknowns are negative, then when the two are multiplied together, the result is positive. (A negative times a negative is always a positive—a basic algebra principle you need to remember.) So xy is positive, and $2xy$, of course, will also be positive—which means it is greater than zero. So the answer to this question is A: Column A is greater than Column B. The quickest way to determine this is to eliminate what both columns have in common and then compare what's left—which is easy.

Here's another example of the principle of eliminating what the columns share:

Column A	Column B
$35 \times 112 \times 76$	$78 \times 56 \times 2 \times 35$

Whatever you do, *don't* start multiplying. It's time-consuming and may lead to a careless mistake—especially if you start rushing. Quantitative comparison items are generally written to minimize calculations, and this question is no exception; you can answer it with no figuring whatsoever. Here's how.

NOTE
Making the two columns resemble each other often requires you to *simplify* one or both quantities—for example, by reducing a fraction to lowest terms. It may also require you to *translate* one quantity so that both quantities are expressed in the same terms. For example, you might have to translate pounds into ounces, a fraction into a percentage, or minutes into hours.

> **CAUTION**
>
> In many Quantitative Comparison items, it's impossible to determine the precise value of one or both quantities. This may tempt you to opt for answer (D), "the relationship can not be determined." Not necessarily! Even imprecise or vague quantities can sometimes be compared. (You know the Sears Tower is taller than your local post office, even if you don't know the actual height of either building.)

First, notice that both "multiplication chains" have one factor in common—35. Eliminate it from both sides, either mentally or (better still) by physically crossing it out with your pencil. Now the comparison looks like this:

Column A	Column B
112×76	$78 \times 56 \times 2$

Now what? Do you have to start multiplying after all? Not if you're observant. The two columns now have something else in common. The term 112 in Column A is exactly the same in value as the two terms 56×2 in Column B! (You can probably "see" this even without calculating it.) So these values can be eliminated from the two columns as well. All that's left to compare now is:

Column A	Column B
76	78

Obviously, Column B is greater. Not a single multiplication is required.

One more example:

Column A	Column B
The number of prime numbers between 10 and 30	The number of prime numbers between 20 and 40

To answer this question, you need to figure out how many prime numbers there are between 10 and 30 and how many there are between 20 and 40—right? Not quite. Notice that there is an area of overlap between the range of numbers included in these two groups. Primes between 20 and 30 would fall into *both* categories. Therefore, they can be ignored! All you really need to consider are the primes between 10 and 20 (Column A) and the primes between 30 and 40 (Column B).

If you know the definition of a prime number—a number that can be evenly divided only by itself and 1—enumerating them isn't too difficult. The primes between 10 and 20 are 11, 13, 17, and 19. (Primes must be odd, of course, since all even numbers are divisible by two.) The primes between 30 and 40 are 31 and 37. There are more primes between 10 and 20, so the answer to this item is A. Notice the time we saved by, in effect, ignoring half of the question—the half that covered the overlap!

PLUG IN VALUES FOR X

Many quantitative comparisons include algebra-style unknowns: x, y, a, n, and so on. Often the quantitative comparison item itself will naturally suggest some algebraic operation; we saw an example in the second problem above, where it seemed natural to multiply out the binomials so as to produce a quantity that would be easier to compare with its counterpart.

Once you've taken all the obvious steps, however—multiplying to remove parentheses, reducing and simplifying fractions, consolidating like terms, and so on—you will usually still have the mysterious unknown quantity to reckon with. When this happens, take a few seconds to try plugging in a couple of possible values for the unknown and see what happens. Often the correct answer will jump out at you as a result.

Here's an example:

Column A	Column B
$3r - 4 > 11$	5

Of course, you need to understand the inequality sign here: it means, "is greater than," since it points toward the right side. If $3r - 4$ is greater than 11, what is a possible value of r? Could it be greater than the quantity you're supposed to compare it to, which is 5? Try plugging in an arbitrary value—6, for example—in place of r in the original inequality, and see whether it works:

$3(6) - 4 > 11$
$18 - 4 > 11$
$14 > 11$

Yes, that's correct—14 is greater than 11; so r could equal 6. But to make sure (B) is the right answer, also try plugging in a value of r that is less than 5:

$3(4) - 4 > 11$
$12 - 4 > 11$
$8 > 11$? NO WAY

Or try making r equal to 5 itself:

$3(5) - 4 > 11$
$15 - 4 > 11$
$11 > 11$? NO

> **NOTE**
> On the real exam, you *will* have time to plug in possible values on most quantitative comparison items. The math calculations are deliberately kept simple, because the testmakers are more concerned with whether you grasp the underlying arithmetic concepts rather than your ability to carry out the additions, subtractions, multiplications, and divisions. So unless you encounter an unusually complicated problem, don't hesitate to plug in numbers—on most quantitative comparison items you can do the figuring in your head within a few seconds.

The value eleven is not greater than *itself*, obviously. So by plugging in three possible values for the unknown—one greater, one less than, and one equal to the quantity given in the "opposite" column—you can determine that the answer to this question is (B).

Note: We've printed out the steps in our calculations here just for clarity's sake, to make it easy for you to follow. But notice how easy the calculations are. Most likely, you won't have to write anything on the test paper at all.

Here's one more example of plugging in numbers:

Column A	Column B
m^2	m^3

$0 < m < 1$

Again, we don't know the precise value of the unknown m. It doesn't matter. If you're not sure which of the two comparable quantities is greater, plug in a possible value and see what happens. In this case, we know that m is a positive fraction less than 1. Let's plug in the simplest possible value for m, $\frac{1}{2}$. (That will make the calculations a breeze.) If m is $\frac{1}{2}$, then $m^2 = (\frac{1}{2})(\frac{1}{2}) = \frac{1}{4}$, and $m^3 = (\frac{1}{2})(\frac{1}{2})(\frac{1}{2}) = \frac{1}{8}$. Since $\frac{1}{4}$ is greater than $\frac{1}{8}$, Column A is greater.

But before filling in the answer space, stop and ask: Will the answer be different if the value of m is different? In this case, no. If m is $\frac{1}{4}$, $\frac{3}{5}$, $\frac{11}{26}$, or any other positive fraction less than 1, the same relationship will exist—the value continues to go down as the fraction is multiplied repeatedly by itself. (That fact is what the question is designed to test.) But always ask that crucial question, "Will the answer be different if the value of the unknown is different?" when you plug in a number. That way, you won't be misled by an answer that just *happens* to be true with a particular value for x.

THE BEST TIPS
MEMORIZE THE ANSWER SYSTEM

You should practice quantitative comparisons enough before the day of the test so that the weird multiple-choice answer system begins to feel like second nature. You shouldn't have to read the directions or spend any time during the section thinking about what (A), (B), (C), and (D) stand for. And be sure never to absent-mindedly fill in answer (E) for any quantitative comparison item! That's an automatic wrong answer.

LOOK FOR MATH SHORTCUTS

We've already seen that most quantitative comparisons require few calculations and simple ones. This is deliberate: The test-makers are eager to measure your understanding of the underlying concepts rather than your ability to handle the calculations. (And keeping the math simple allows them to throw more questions at you in the same amount of time!) So avoid lengthy or complicated figuring; if a question seems to require it, you've probably overlooked a built-in shortcut.

Here's an example:

Column A	Column B
The average (arithmetic mean) of 5 integers m, n, o, p, and q is 19.	
The average (arithmetic mean) of m, n, o, p, q, and 17.5	19

On the principle of "When in doubt, try something," your first instinct may be to start working with the definition of "average." As you know, an average is calculated by taking the sum of a set of numbers and dividing it by the number of numbers in the set. In this case, if five integers have an average of 19, it would be possible to calculate the sum of those integers by multiplying the average by the number of numbers ($19 \times 5 = 95$). Then you could go ahead and calculate the sum of the set of six integers shown in Column A, with the sixth integer 17.5 thrown in, and finally divide that new sum by 6 to come up with the new average.

But stop! None of this is necessary. Look at the quantities being compared. All you need to figure out is whether the new average is more or less than 19—the old average. Now, what makes the new average different from the old average? It's simply the new member of the set, the sixth integer 17.5. And will that new member raise or lower the overall average? Since 17.5 is below the old average, it will drag the average down—it will lower it. Therefore, *with no calculations at all*, you can see that the answer will be (B): The old average, 19, is greater than the new average, *whatever it is*.

> **TIP**
> You need to work quantitative comparison items at the rate of one per minute. That's pretty fast, but it's possible, provided you don't get bogged down in lengthy calculations. If you find, after examining an item for fifteen seconds, that you can't see a way of tackling it, skip it for the moment—put an X next to the item in your question booklet and return to it at the end of the section.

THE MOST IMPORTANT WARNINGS
ASSUME NOTHING!

Quantitative comparisons are designed to test how quickly, creatively, and accurately you can think about a wide range of what might be called "math situations." As you've seen, these situations can be drawn from every area of math: arithmetic, algebra, geometry, word problems, etc., enabling the test-makers to test your knowledge of techniques in all of these areas. One key aspect of accuracy under these conditions is the ability to separate the *facts* you've been given from the *assumptions* you might make—which may or may not be correct.

> **NOTE**
> The real meaning of answer choice (D) is slightly hidden by its wording ("the relationship cannot be determined"). Don't think of it as meaning, "I don't know what the answer is." Instead, think of it as meaning, "More than one answer could be true." If any two answers—(A) and (B), (A) and (C), or (B) and (C)[md]are both possible, then the correct answer for the item is (D).

Let's consider a few examples.

Column A	Column B
In 1990, the price of a certain item was $50.00.	
The price of the same item in 1998	$50.00

It's tempting to answer this question based on what you know about the real world. Because of the economic phenomenon known as inflation, prices of most things tend to go up over time (though this is not true of everything: computers, for example, have consistently fallen in price during the 1980s and 1990s). Therefore, it's extremely likely that the "certain item" that cost $50.00 in 1990 cost more than that in 1998. The right answer, in that case, would be (A).

The logic is tempting—and wrong. You can't assume that inflation applies to this item *because you haven't been told to assume it.* We're not in the "real world" now but rather in SAT territory, where only the facts as stated in the question can be assumed to be true. The correct answer for this item is (D)—the relationship can't be determined.

Column A	Column B
Parking is legal on Pine Street only on even-numbered calendar days.	
Number of legal parking days in a calendar month	15

Obviously, the number of legal parking days in a calendar month will be somewhere around 15—since half the days are even-numbered days, and most months have around 30 days. But which month are we talking about? The question doesn't specify, so let's think it through. The month could be January or July, with 31 days, of which 15 are even-numbered (the 2nd, the 4th, the 6th,. . . the 30th); it could be June or September, with 30 days, of which the same 15 are even-numbered. The correct answer then would be (C): The number of legal parking days (Column A) would be equal to the number 15 (Column B). But the month could also be February, which has only 28 days (except in leap year), of which just 14 are even-numbered. In that case, the correct answer would be (B).

So there are two possible answers—(C) and (B)—and we don't know which is correct, because the question doesn't tell us. Sure, there are 11 chances out of 12 that the month is *not* February, but we can't make that assumption. Since answer (C) is correct under one possible assumption and answer (B) is correct under another, the correct answer is (D)—it cannot determined.

One more example of the danger of making assumptions:

Column A   **Column B**

On a certain day, 30 percent of the girls were absent and 50 percent of the boys were present in a history class.

| Number of girls present | Number of boys present |

From the information given, you can tell that the percentage of girls present was greater than the percentage of boys present (70 versus 50). But notice what you are being asked to compare not the percentage of girls and boys present, but the *number* present. We know nothing about this, because we don't know *how many* girls or boys were enrolled in the history class. You might, without much thought, assume that the number of girls and boys is approximately equal—but that's simply an assumption, with no special validity. The correct answer for this item is (D)—it can not be determined.

Strictly speaking, there *are* a few—a very few—facts you can safely assume on quantitative comparison items:

- Everyday facts like the number of inches in a foot and the number of days in a week are fair game.
- The basic formulas from geometry (for calculating the area of a circle or a triangle, for example) are not only assumed but provided as "Reference Information" at the start of each SAT math section. (You should know them by heart, however.)
- And you can assume, as the test-makers state, that all unknowns (like *x*) stand for "real numbers" (as opposed to "imaginary numbers," a special kind of number used only in certain quite specialized and advanced math operations).

Other than these facts, however, you should avoid assuming anything—as you've seen, it's dangerous.

WHEN THERE'S NO UNKNOWN, DON'T GUESS (D)

On quantitative comparison items, as on every other kind of question, there may be times when you have to guess. Perhaps you will find yourself running out of time but with several questions left to answer, or perhaps a couple of items will call for math skills you just can't recall. General guessing strategies for quantitative comparisons should be much the same as for other question types: follow a hunch, if you have one; when you can, eliminate answers and guess from what remains.

However, there's one special rule about guessing that applies only to quantitative comparisons. On about one third of quantitative comparison

CAUTION
Be careful about assumptions when plugging in numbers for an unknown quantity. We're so accustomed to the "counting numbers"—1, 2, 3, and so on—that we easily forget that *x* may equal zero, a negative number, or a fraction. Any of these possibilities may change the outcome of the comparison. So when plugging in possible values, be sure to include one of each of these number types, unless they have been specifically ruled out.

items, no unknown quantity is involved: there is no algebraic x or n, nor is there any geometric quantity (the degree measure of an angle or the length of a line segment, say) that is unknowable. Whenever this is true, the answer cannot be (D). Even if you, for whatever reason, can't figure out which quantity is greater, it is theoretically *possible* to figure it out—so (D) is an incorrect option.

Here's an example:

Column A	Column B
Price of a $320 stereo	$275 after a discount of 15%

If you've run out of time, or forgotten how to multiply by a percentage, you may not be able to answer this question. (Since $320 × 85% = $272, the answer is (B).) However, the question itself does not contain any unknown quantity. Therefore, if you have to guess on a question like this, don't guess (D). Since there is no unknown, only answers (A), (B), and (C) are possible.

Summary: What You Need to Know About Quantitative Comparisons

- Memorize the directions and the answer choices—they are identical for all quantitative comparison questions.

- For each question, compare the boxed quantities.

- Consider all possibilities for any variables.

- Remember that you don't need to do all of the calculations—for most of these questions, you can estimate or use your knowledge of basic mathematical principles.

- Remember that like the rest of the test, quantitative comparisons go from easy to hard.

EXERCISES: QUANTITATIVE COMPARISONS

Exercise 1

35 Questions • 35 Minutes

Directions: Compare the two quantities and write the correct answer next to the question number.

(A) if the quantity in Column A is greater;
(B) if the quantity in Column B is greater;
(C) if the two quantities are equal;
(D) if the relationship cannot be determined from the information given.

	Column A	Column B		Column A	Column B
1.	$\frac{2}{3} \times 2$	30%	6.	$(2+.2)(2-.2)\left(\frac{1}{5}\right)$	$(.2)(1.8)(2.2)$
2.	$\frac{4}{17}$	$\frac{2}{15}$	7.	$\sqrt{\frac{1}{4}+\frac{1}{9}}$	$\frac{1}{2}+\frac{1}{3}$
3.	$3\frac{1}{2}$ expressed as a percent	3.5%	8.	$m = 3, n = -2$ $(m+n)^2$	$(m-n)^2$
4.	$\sqrt{25.1}$	5.1		The distance from A to B is 3 miles. The distance from B to C is 4 miles.	
5.	Cost per egg if 2 dozen cost $1.90	9¢	9.	5 miles	The distance from A to C

	Column A	Column B		Column A	Column B
10.	x^5	x^2	18.	$a > b > 0$	
				$\dfrac{1}{a}$	$\dfrac{1}{b}$
11.	The area of a circle is 16π.		19.	$(2)(2)(a) = (3)(3)(3)$	
	Diameter of the circle	16		a	2
12.	The average of 5 numbers is 20.		20.	$-4 < x < -2$	
	The sum of the five numbers	110		$\dfrac{1}{x^4}$	$\dfrac{1}{x^5}$
13.	$\dfrac{1}{.5}$	$\dfrac{1}{.05}$	21.	$(16)(351)(10)$	$(15)(351)(11)$
14.	$.1\pi$	$\sqrt{.9}$	22.	$a^2 > 0$	
				a	0
15.	Area of a square having perimeter 32	Area of circle having radius 5	23.	A single discount of 10%	Two successive discounts of 5% and 5%
16.	$x = 8 = y^2 - 1$		24.	50%	$\dfrac{1}{.02}$
	x	y			
17.	$a^2 = 49$		25.	Time elapsed from 11:50 P.M. to 12:02 A.M.	$\dfrac{1}{3}$ hour
	a	7			

Column A	Column B

The diagram below applies to problems 26–29.

$AC \cong CD \cong AD \quad AC \perp CB$

26. | CD | DB |

27. | ∠A | ∠B |

28. | CD | CB |

29. | AD | DB |

Questions 30–31 refer to the figure below.

$AB \cong BC \qquad$ Angle B < Angle A

30. | ∠B | ∠C |

Column A	Column B

31. | AB | AC |

Questions 32–34 refer to the figure below.

$EC \perp AD$

32. | EC | ED |

33. | ∠EBA | ∠ECD |

34. | ∠A | ∠ECB |

$a > 0, b > 0, \dfrac{a}{b} < 1$

35. | a | b |

Exercise 2

15 Questions • 15 Minutes

Directions: Compare the two quantities in Column A and Column B and determine whether:

(A) the quantity is greater in Column A

(B) the quantity is greater in Column B

(C) both quantities are equal

(D) no comparison can be made with the information given

Write your answer next to the question number.

Notes:

(1) Information concerning one or both of the compared quantities will be centered between the two columns when given.

(2) Symbols that appear in both columns represent the same thing in Column A as in Column B.

(3) Letters such as x, n, and k are symbols for real numbers.

(4) Figures are not necessarily drawn to scale.

Column A	Column B

Questions 1–3 refer to the figure below.

ABCD is a parallelogram.

E is any point on AB.

1. Twice the area of triangle *DEC* | Area of parallelogram *ABCD*

2. ∠A | ∠B

3. AD | DC

Column A	Column B

Questions 4–6 apply to the figure below.

Radius of outer circle = 10

Radius of inner circle = 5

4. Twice area of inner circle | Area of shaded portion

5. Area of inner circle | 75

6. Circumference of inner circle | 50% of circumference of outer circle

SAT Quantitative Comparisons Strategies

	Column A	Column B
7.	105% of 200	50% of 400
8.	35%	$\dfrac{0.7}{2}$

$6x = 3y = 2z$

	Column A	Column B
9.	x	z

$a > b > c$

	Column A	Column B
10.	$2a$	$b + c$

$\dfrac{1}{x} > 1$

	Column A	Column B
11.	x	1

$\dfrac{1}{x} < 0$

	Column A	Column B
12.	x	0
13.	The percent of increase from $10 to $12	The percent of increase from $20 to $22

	Column A	Column B
14.	Sylvia's average rate if she drives 100 miles in 2 hours 30 minutes	Gloria's average rate if she drives 20 miles in 30 minutes

$m > 0, n > 0$

	Column A	Column B
15.	$(m+n)^2$	$m^2 + n^2$

ANSWER KEYS AND EXPLANATIONS

Exercise 1

1. A	8. B	15. B	22. D	29. C
2. A	9. D	16. A	23. A	30. B
3. A	10. D	17. D	24. B	31. A
4. B	11. B	18. B	25. B	32. B
5. B	12. B	19. A	26. C	33. A
6. C	13. B	20. A	27. A	34. B
7. B	14. B	21. B	28. B	35. B

1. **(A)** $\frac{2}{3} \div 2 = \frac{2}{3} \cdot \frac{1}{2} = \frac{1}{3} = 33\frac{1}{3}\%$

2. **(A)** To compare $\frac{a}{b}$ with $\frac{c}{d}$, compare ad with bc.

    If $ad < bc$, then the first fraction is smaller. If $ad = bc$, the fractions are equal. If $ad > bc$, then the first fraction is larger. 4 times 15 is greater than 17 times 2. Therefore, the first fraction is greater.

3. **(A)** $3\frac{1}{2} = 3.5 = 350\%$

4. **(B)** $(5.1)^2 = 26.01$
    $(\sqrt{25.1})^2 = 25.1$

5. **(B)** There are 24 eggs in 2 dozen.

    $$24 \overline{)1.90} \quad .079$$
    $$\underline{1\ 68}$$
    $$220$$

    Each egg costs almost 8 cents.

6. **(C)** $2 + .2 = 2.2$
    $2 - .2 = 1.8$
    $\frac{1}{5} = .2$

    Factors on both sides are the same.

7. **(B)** $\sqrt{\frac{1}{4} + \frac{1}{9}} = \sqrt{\frac{13}{36}} = \frac{\sqrt{13}}{6}$

    $\frac{1}{2} + \frac{1}{3} = \frac{5}{6}$

8. **(B)** $(m+n)^2 = (1)^2 = 1$
    $(m-n)^2 = (5)^2 = 25$

9. **(D)** There is no indication as to the direction from B to C.

10. **(D)** If $x > 1$, A is bigger. If $x = 1$, A and B are equal. If $x < 0$, B is bigger.

11. **(B)** Area of a circle $= \pi r^2$
    $16\pi = \pi r^2$
    $16 = r^2$
    $r = 4$
    diameter $= 8$

12. **(B)** If the average is 20, then the 5 numbers were added and the sum divided by 5 to give 20. The sum of these numbers must be 100.

13. **(B)** $\frac{1}{.5} = \frac{10}{5} = 2$
    $\frac{1}{.05} = \frac{100}{5} = 20$

14. **(B)** $.1(3.14) = .314$
    $.9$
    $\sqrt{.90}$

15. **(B)** Each side of the square is 8. Area of the square is 64. Area of the circle is 25π. $25(3.14)$ is greater than 64.

16. **(A)** $8 = y^2 - 1$
    $9 = y^2$
    $y = 3$ or -3

    Since $x = 8$, x is greater for either value of y.

17. **(D)** *a* may be either 7 or –7.

18. **(B)** When fractions have equal numerators, the fraction having the smaller denominator has the greater value.

19. **(A)** $4a = 27 \quad a = 6\frac{3}{4}$

20. **(A)** Since *x* is negative, any even power of *x* is positive, while any odd power of *x* is negative.

21. **(B)** (16)(10) is less than (15)(11).

22. **(D)** If a^2 is positive, *a* can be either negative or positive.

23. **(A)** Consider a marked price of $100. A single discount of 10% gives $10 off. An initial discount of 5% gives $5 off, making the new price $95. The second 5% discount is 5% of $95 or $4.75, making the total discount only $5 + $4.75 or $9.75.

24. **(B)** $50\% = \frac{1}{2}$

    $\frac{1}{.02} = \frac{100}{2} = 50$

25. **(B)** From 11:50 P.M. to 12:02 A.M. is 12 minutes. One third of an hour is 20 minutes.

26. **(C)**

    Triangle *ACD* is equilateral, making each angle 60°. Angle *DCB* is then 30°, and angle *CDB* is 120°, leaving 30° for angle *B*. Therefore, triangle *DCB* is isosceles.

27. **(A)** Angle *A* is 60° and angle *B* is 30°.

28. **(B)** In triangle *CDB*, *CD* is opposite a 30° angle, while *CB* is opposite 120°.

29. **(C)** Both of these segments are equal to *CD*.

30. **(B)** Since ∠*A* and ∠*C* must be equal, because the sides opposite are congruent, ∠*B* is also less than ∠*C*.

31. **(A)** Since ∠*B* is less than ∠*C*, *AC* will be less than *AB*.

32. **(B)** The shortest distance from a point to a line is the perpendicular.

33. **(A)** Angle *EBA* is an exterior angle of triangle *EBC* and is therefore greater than angle *ECB*. Since angle *ECD* is also a right angle, angle *EBA* will be greater than angle *ECD*.

34. **(B)** Triangle *ECA* has a right angle. Since there will be 90° left to divide between the two remaining angles, angle *A* must be less than 90°.

35. **(B)** If $\frac{a}{b}<1$, the denominator must be greater than the numerator.

Exercise 2

1. C	6. C	11. B
2. D	7. A	12. B
3. D	8. C	13. A
4. B	9. D	14. C
5. A	10. A	15. A

1. **(C)** The altitude of triangle EDC is equal to the altitude of the parallelogram. Both the triangle and the parallelogram have the same base. Since the area of a triangle is $\frac{1}{2}bh$ and the area of a parallelogram is bh, these quantities are equal.

2. **(D)** There is no way to tell which is greater.

3. **(D)** There is no way to tell which is greater.

4. **(B)** Area of outer circle = $\pi r^2 = 100\pi$
   Area of inner circle = 25π
   Shaded portion is outer circle minus inner circle, or 75π.

5. **(A)** Area of inner circle = $\pi r^2 = 25\pi$.
   $25(3.14)$ is more than 75.

6. **(C)** Circumference = πd
   Circumference of outer circle = $\pi(20)$
   Circumference of inner circle = $\pi(10)$
   $50\% = \frac{1}{2}$
   $\frac{1}{2}$ of outer circumference = 10π

7. **(A)** 105% of 200 is more than 200.
   50% or $\frac{1}{2}$ of 400 is 200.

8. **(C)** $35\% = .35$
   $\frac{0.7}{2} = .35$

9. **(D)** If $6x = 2z$, then $3x = z$, or $x = \frac{1}{3}z$. If either x or z is zero, both quantities are equal; if both are positive, z is larger. If both are negative, x is larger.

10. **(A)** $a > b$
    $a > c$
    $\overline{2a > b + c}$

11. **(B)** If $\frac{1}{x} > 1$, multiply each side by x to get $1 > x$. There should be no concern about reversing the inequality, as x must be positive if $\frac{1}{x} > 1$.

12. **(B)** If $\frac{1}{x}$ is to be negative, x must be negative, since a positive number divided by a negative number gives a negative quotient. 0 is larger than any negative number.

13. **(A)** Percent of increase = $\frac{\text{Amount of increase}}{\text{Original}} \cdot 100$
    The percent of increase in A is $\frac{2}{10} \cdot 100$. The percent of increase in B is $\frac{2}{20}$, or $\frac{1}{10} \cdot 100$.

14. **(C)** Average rate = $\frac{\text{Total distance}}{\text{Total time}}$
    Sylvia's average rate = $\frac{100}{2.5} = 40$
    Gloria's average rate = $\frac{20}{.5} = 40$

15. **(A)** $(m+n)^2 = m^2 + 2mn + n^2$. Since m and n are both positive, $2mn$ is positive.

Chapter

10

SAT Grid-In Strategies

WHY GRID-INS ARE EASIER THAN YOU THINK

You should be pretty good at filling in ovals by now, right? Here comes a new angle—grid-ins. These are officially named "student-produced responses," because you have to do the calculations and find the answer on your own; there are no multiple-choice answers to choose from. These special grids are the way to let the SAT people know which answer you came up with.

Many students get intimidated by grid-ins. Don't be! Grid-in questions test the exact same mathematical concepts as multiple-choice math. And there are only 10 of them to deal with, arranged in order from easy to hard. So you should only expect to have difficulty with a couple of questions.

SAT GRID-IN QUESTIONS

As we indicated, the scored portion of the SAT contains 10 grid-in questions. They are all grouped together in a single math section, where they are numbered from 16 through 25 (Questions 1 through 15 are quantitative comparisons).

Grid-ins test the same mix of arithmetic, algebra, and geometry concepts that are tested by multiple-choice math questions. The only difference is that there are no answer choices.

TAKE A LOOK AT A GRID

The special answer grid has some very different sections. There are blank boxes at the top so you can actually write in your answer. Below the boxes are some ovals that have fraction slashes and decimal points. You fill these in if your answer needs them. The largest section has ovals with numbers in them. You have to fill in the ovals to correspond to the answer you have written in the boxes. Yes, it's a lot to think about, but once you understand how to use them it's not a big deal. Here is a sample grid:

ROAD MAP

- *Understand why grid-ins are easier than you think*
- *Know how to record your answers*
- *Understand why guessing on grid-ins can't hurt you*
- *Review what you need to know about grid-ins*
- *Practice your skills with grid-in exercises*

NOTE

Grid-in no-nos. Remember that the student-produced responses will not be negative numbers and won't be greater than 9999.

HOW TO RECORD YOUR ANSWERS

On the SAT, each set of grid-in questions starts with directions that look approximately like this:

Directions: Solve each of these problems. Write the answer in the corresponding grid on the answer sheet and fill in the ovals beneath each answer you write. Here are some examples.

Answer: $\frac{3}{4}$ (= .75; show answer either way)   Answer: 325

Note: A mixed number such as $3\frac{1}{2}$ must be gridded as 7/2 or as 3.5. If gridded as "31/2," it will be read as "thirty-one halves."

Note: Either position is correct.

Once you get these rules down pat, you can concentrate just on solving the math problems in this section.

Gridding: Getting It Right

1. Write your answer in the boxes at the top of the grid.
2. Mark the corresponding bubbles, one per column.
3. Start in any column.
4. Work with decimals or fractions.
5. Express mixed numbers as decimals or improper fractions.
6. If more than one answer is possible, grid any one.

NOTE
Don't use a comma in a number larger than 999. Just fill in the four digits and the corresponding ovals. You only have ovals for numbers, decimal points, and fraction slashes; there aren't any for commas.

Now let's look at these rules in more detail:

1. **Write your answer in the boxes at the top of the grid.** Technically, this isn't required by the SAT. Realistically, it gives you something to follow as you fill in the ovals. Do it—it will help you.

2. **Make sure to mark the bubbles that correspond to the answer you entered in the boxes, one per column.** The machine that scores the test can only read the bubbles, so if you don't fill them in, you won't get credit. Just entering your answer in the boxes is not enough!

3. **You can start entering your answer in any column, if space permits.** Unused columns should be left blank; don't put in zeroes. Look at this example:

   Here are two ways to enter an answer of "150."

CAUTION
Take the time to write your answer in the spaces. It will lessen your chances of filling in an incorrect oval.

4. **You can write your answer as a decimal or as a fraction.** In other words, an answer can be expressed as $\frac{3}{4}$ or as .75. You don't have to put a zero in front of a decimal that is less than 1. Just remember that you have only four spaces to work with and that a decimal point or a fraction slash uses up one of the spaces.

For decimal answers, be as accurate as possible but keep it within four spaces. Say you get an answer of .1777; here are your options:

Answers .177 and .178 would both be marked as correct.

Answers .18 or .2 would be marked wrong because they could have been written more accurately in the space provided.

Fractions do not have to be reduced to lowest terms unless they don't fit in the answer grid. For example, you can grid $\frac{4}{10}$, but you can't grid $\frac{12}{16}$ because you'd need five spaces. So, you would reduce it and grid $\frac{3}{4}$.

5. A mixed number has to be expressed as a decimal or as an improper fraction. If you tried to grid $1\frac{3}{4}$, it would be scored as $\frac{13}{4}$, which would give you a wrong answer. Instead, you could grid the answer as 1.75 or as $\frac{7}{4}$.

These answers are acceptable.

This answer is unacceptable.

6. Sometimes the problems in this section will have more than one correct answer. Choose one and grid it.

    For example, if a question asks for a prime number between 5 and 13, the answer could be 7 or 11. Grid 7 or grid 11, but don't put in both answers.

    Either answer is acceptable, but not both.

TIP

Grid-in answers are either completely correct or completely wrong. But no points are deducted for wrong answers, so guessing is better than leaving a grid blank.

GUESSING ON GRID-INS CAN'T HURT YOU

Unfortunately, you cannot receive partial credit for grid-ins. Your answers are either completely correct or completely wrong. But no points are deducted for incorrect responses, so guessing is better than leaving a question blank.

Summary: What You Need to Know About Grid-Ins

- When you grid answers to student-produced response questions, follow these rules:
    1. Write your answer in the boxes at the top of the grid.
    2. Mark the corresponding bubbles, one per column.
    3. Start in any column.
    4. Work with decimals or fractions.
    5. Express mixed numbers as decimals or improper fractions.
    6. If more than one answer is possible, grid any one.
- Remember that grid-ins test the same concepts as multiple-choice math.
- Because there are only 10 grid-ins per test, you should be able to answer almost all of them correctly.
- The most important advice for grid-ins? Don't be intimidated.

EXERCISES: GRID-INS

Exercise 1

10 Questions • 15 Minutes

Directions: Solve each of these problems. Write the answer in the corresponding grid on the answer sheet and fill in the ovals beneath each answer you write. Here are some examples.

Answer: $\frac{3}{4}$ (= .75; show answer either way)

Answer: 325

Note: A mixed number such as $3\frac{1}{2}$ must be gridded as 7/2 or as 3.5. If gridded as "31/2," it will be read as "thirty-one halves."

Note: Either position is correct.

1. Reduced to lowest fractional terms, what part of a dime is a quarter?

2. Marion is paid $24 for 5 hours of work in the school office. Janet works 3 hours and makes $10.95. How much more per hour does Marion make than Janet? (Ignore the dollar sign in gridding your answer.)

3. If the outer diameter of a cylindrical oil tank is 54.28 inches and the inner diameter is 48.7 inches, what is the thickness of the wall of the tank, in inches?

4. What number added to 40% of itself is equal to 184?

5. If $r = 25 - s$, what is the value of $4r + s$?

6. A plane flies over Denver at 11:20 A.M. It passes over Coolidge, 120 miles from Denver, at 11:32 A.M. Find the rate of the plane in miles per hour.

7. 53% of the 1000 students at Jackson High are girls. How many boys are there in the school?

8. How many digits are there in the square root of a perfect square of 12 digits?

9. In May, Carter's Appliances sold 40 washing machines. In June, because of a special promotion, the store sold 80 washing machines. What is the percent of increase in the number of washing machines sold?

10. Find the value of $(3\sqrt{2})^2$.

Exercise 2

6 Questions • 8 Minutes

Directions: Solve each of these problems. Write the answer in the corresponding grid on the answer sheet and fill in the ovals beneath each answer you write. Here are some examples.

Answer: $\frac{3}{4}$ (= .75; show answer either way)

Answer: 325

Note: A mixed number such as $3\frac{1}{2}$ must be gridded as 7/2 or as 3.5. If gridded as "31/2," it will be read as "thirty-one halves."

Note: Either position is correct.

SAT Grid-In Strategies

1. If $\frac{8}{8}$ of $\frac{3}{8}$, what is the result?

2. If $2^{n-3} = 32$, what is the value of n?

3. In a group of 40 students, 25 applied to Columbia and 30 applied to neither Columbia nor Cornell. If 3 students applied to neither Columbia nor Cornell, how many students applied to both schools?

4. If $x^2 - y^2 = 100$ and $x - y = 20$, what is the value of $x + y$?

5. A gallon of water is added to 6 quarts of a solution that is 50% acid. What percent of the new solution is acid?

6. A gasoline tank is $\frac{1}{4}$ full. After adding 10 gallons of gasoline, the gauge indicates that the tank is $\frac{2}{3}$ full. Find the capacity of the tank in gallons.

ANSWER EXPLANATIONS

Exercise 1

1. $\frac{25}{10} = \frac{5}{2}$ **(answer)**

2. Marion's hourly wage is $\frac{\$24}{5}$ or $4.80.

   Janet's hourly wage is $\frac{\$10.95}{3}$ or $3.65.

   $4.80 − $3.65 = $1.15 **(answer)**

3. The difference of 5.58 must be divided between both ends. The thickness on each side is 2.79 **(answer)**.

4. $x + .40x = 84$

   $1.40x = 84$

   $14x = 840$

   $x = 60$ **(answer)**

5. $r + s = 25$

   $4(r + s) = 4(25) = 100$ **(answer)**

6. The plane covers 120 miles in 12 minutes or $\frac{1}{5}$ hour. In $\frac{5}{5}$ or 1 hour, it covers 5(120), or 600 miles. 600 **(answer)**

7. 47% of 1000 are boys.

   $(.47)(1000) = 470$ boys **(answer)**

8. For every pair of digits in a number, there will be one digit in the square root. 6 **(answer)**

9. Increase of 40

   Percent of Increase = [Amount of Increase/Original] × 100%

   $\frac{40}{40} \times 100\% = 100\%$ **(answer)**

10. $(3\sqrt{2})(3\sqrt{2}) = 9 \times 2 = 18$ **(answer)**

Exercise 2

1. $\frac{3}{8} + \frac{3}{8} = \frac{6}{8}$ or $\frac{3}{4}$ **(answers; both acceptable)**

2. $2^{n-3} = 2^5$

   $n - 3 = 5$

   $n = 8$ **(answer)**

3.

$$25 - x + x + 30 - x = 37$$
$$55 - x = 37$$
$$18 = x$$
18 **(answer)**

4. $x^2 - y^2 = (x-y)(x+y)$
$$100 = 20(x+y)$$
$$5 = (x+y)$$
5 **(answer)**

5.

	No. of quarts	% acid	= Amount of acid
Original	6	.50	3
Added	4	0	0
New	10		3

$\frac{3}{10} = 30\%$ **(answer)**

6. 10 gallons is $\frac{2}{3} - \frac{1}{4}$ of the tank.
$$\frac{2}{3} - \frac{1}{4} = \frac{8-3}{12} = \frac{5}{12}$$
$$\frac{5}{12}x = 10$$
$$5x = 120$$
$$x = 24 \text{ (answer)}$$

PART 5

SAT Vocabulary Prep Course

PREVIEW

CHAPTER 11 — *How Word Parts Work*

CHAPTER 12 — *The SAT "Top 500" Word List*

Chapter

11

How Word Parts Work

The SAT isn't a spelling test, and it isn't a "vocabulary bee." It is, however, a test of how much you *know* about vocabulary—how words are formed and the meanings of their parts. If you want to increase that knowledge (and, hello!, increase your score), you'll want to learn about the structure of words. This will help you figure out the meanings of unfamiliar words you come across in the verbal section of the SAT. In this chapter, you learn the basics of how words are built, what word parts mean and how they work together. You'll also get a crash-course list of common word parts that will help you understand the meanings of words you may encounter (maybe for the first time) on the SAT. The exercises at the end of this chapter help you practice your vocabulary skills, so you'll be ready to score high on the verbal sections of the SAT.

HOW WORDS ARE BUILT

Knowing what the parts of words mean is the key to deciphering words you've never seen before. Let's take a look at the word *biography* and its parts. You know that a biography is something written about a person's life. How do the word parts tell you this? Well, the second part of the word, *graphy*, comes from a Greek word that means "writing." The first part of the word, *bio*, is also from Greek and it means "life." Put them both together and you get . . . *biography,* the story of a person's life. If you add the Latin word for "self"—*auto*—you get . . . *autobiography,* a story you write about your own life. Think about some other words that use one or more of these parts, like *automobile, biochemistry,* and *autograph.* Can you see how the meaning fits the word parts?

ROAD MAP

- *Learn the vocabulary skills you need to succeed on the SAT*
- *Learn how words are built*
- *Learn how word parts work*
- *Learn common word parts to boost your SAT vocabulary*
- *Practice your skills with word parts exercises*

THE THREE BASIC WORD PARTS AND HOW THEY WORK

Different kinds of word parts work together to make a fully functioning word. Think about it: If your car is going to do more than just sit there, it needs a collection of parts put together in the right way. Two steering wheels won't do you any good if you don't have a gas tank.

Each kind of word part has a specific purpose. There are three basic types of word parts:

1. **Prefixes**—These parts attach to the beginning of a root word to alter its meaning or create a new word.
2. **Suffixes**—These parts attach to the end of a root word to change its meaning, help make it grammatically correct in context, or form a new word.
3. **Roots**—The basic element of a word that determines its meaning. Groups of words from the same root word are called word families.

A word can have a root, a prefix, and a suffix; it can have a root and two suffixes or a root and one prefix. The possibilities are endless (almost), but you must always have a root.

Use the word list that follows to expand your word horizons. Once you begin to learn the word parts on the list, you'll be able to take apart unfamiliar words like a master mechanic. As you make your way through the list, try to think of other words with the same parts. If you have time, check their meanings in a dictionary and take a look at the word origins in the entry.

> **TIP**
>
> When you know some common word parts and how they work, you have a formula for deciphering unfamiliar words. Just divide the word into its parts, then use the information you learn in this chapter to determine what the parts mean and how they work. Then, you're well on your way to recognizing the meaning of the word.

LIST OF COMMON WORD PARTS

PREFIXES

Prefix	Meaning	Example
a-	in, on, of, to	*abed*—in bed
a-, ab-, abs-	from, away	*abrade*—wear off
		absent—away, not present
a-, an-	lacking, not	*asymptomatic*—showing no symptoms
		anaerobic—able to live without air
ac-, ad-, af-, ag-, al-, an-, ap-, ar-, as-, at-	to, toward	*accost*—approach and speak to
		adjunct—something added to
		aggregate—bring together

Prefix	Meaning	Example
ambi-, amphi-	around, both	*ambidextrous*—using both hands equally *amphibious*—living both in water and on land
ana-	up, again, anew, throughout	*analyze*—loosen up, break up into parts *anagram*—word spelled by mixing up letters of another word
ante-	before	*antediluvian*—before the Flood
anti-	against	*antiwar*—against war
arch-	first, chief	*archetype*—first model
auto-	self	*automobile*—self-moving vehicle
bene-, ben-	good, well	*benefactor*—one who does good deeds
bi-	two	*bilateral*—two-sided
circum-	around	*circumnavigate*—sail around
com-, co-, col-, con-, cor-	with, together	*concentrate*—bring closer together *cooperate*—work with *collapse*—fall together
contra-, contro-, counter-	against	*contradict*—speak against *counterclockwise*—against the clock
de-	away from, down, opposite of	*detract*—draw away from
demi-	half	*demitasse*—half cup
di-	twice, double	*dichromatic*—having two colors
dia-	across, through	*diameter*—measurement across

Prefix	Meaning	Example
dis-, di-	not, away from	*dislike*—to not like *digress*—turn away from the subject
dys-	bad, poor	*dyslexia*—poor reading
equi-	equal	*equivalent*—of equal value
ex-, e-, ef-	from, out	*expatriate*—one who lives outside his or her native country *emit*—send out
extra-	outside, beyond	*extraterrestrial*—from beyond the earth
fore-	in front of, previous	*forecast*—tell ahead of time *foreleg*—front leg
geo-	earth	*geography*—science of the earth's surface
homo-	same, like	*homophonic*—sounding the same
hyper-	too much, over	*hyperactive*—overly active
hypo-	too little, under	*hypothermia*—state of having too little body heat
in-, il-, ig-, im-, ir-	not	*innocent*—not guilty *ignorant*—not knowing *illogical*—not logical *irresponsible*—not responsible
in-, il-, im-, ir-	on, into, in	*impose*—place on *invade*—go into
intra-, intro-	within, inside	*intrastate*—within a state
inter-	between, among	*interplanetary*—between planets
mal-, male-	bad, wrong, poor	*maladjust*—adjust poorly *malevolent*—ill-wishing

Prefix	Meaning	Example
mis-	badly, wrongly	*misunderstand*—understand wrongly
mis-, miso-	hatred	*misogyny*—hatred of women
mono-	single, one	*monorail*—train that runs on a single rail
neo-	new	*neolithic*—of the New Stone Age
non-	not	*nonentity*—a nobody
ob-	over, against, toward	*obstruct*—stand against
omni-	all	*omnipresent*—present in all places
pan-	all	*panorama*—a complete view
peri-	around, near	*periscope*—device for seeing all around
poly-	many	*polygonal*—many-sided
post-	after	*postmortem*—after death
pre-	before, earlier than	*prejudice*—judgment in advance
pro-	in favor of, forward, in front of	*proceed*—go forward *prowar*—in favor of war
re-	back, again	*rethink*—think again *reimburse*—pay back
retro-	backward	*retrospective*—looking backward
se-	apart, away	*seclude*—keep away
semi-	half	*semiconscious*—half conscious
sub-, suc-, suf-, sug-, sus-	under, beneath	*subscribe*—write underneath *suspend*—hang down *suffer*—undergo

Prefix	Meaning	Example
super-	above, greater	*superfluous*—overflowing, beyond what is needed
syn-, sym-, syl-, sys-	with, at the same time	*synthesis*—a putting together *sympathy*—a feeling with
tele-	far	*television*—machine for seeing far
trans-	across	*transport*—carry across a distance
un-	not	*uninformed*—not informed
vice-	acting for, next in rank to	*viceroy*—one acting for the king

SUFFIXES

Suffix	Meaning	Example
-able, -ble	able, capable	*acceptable*—able to be accepted
-acious, -cious	characterized by, having the quality of	*fallacious*—having the quality of a fallacy
-age	sum, total	*mileage*—total number of miles
-al	of, like, suitable for	*theatrical*—suitable for theater
-ance, -ancy	act or state of	*disturbance*—act of disturbing
-ant, -ent	one who	*defendant*—one who defends him- or herself
-ary, -ar	having the nature of, concerning	*military*—relating to soldiers *polar*—concerning the pole
-cy	act, state, or position of	*presidency*—position of president *ascendancy*—state of being raised up

Suffix	Meaning	Example
-dom	state, rank, that which belongs to	*wisdom*—state of being wise
-ence	act, state, or quality of	*dependence*—state of depending
-er, -or	one who, that which	*doer*—one who does *conductor*—that which conducts
-escent	becoming	*obsolescent*—becoming obsolete
-fy	to make	*pacify*—make peaceful
-hood	state, condition	*adulthood*—state of being adult
-ic, -ac	of, like	*demonic*—of or like a demon
-il, -ile	having to do with, like, suitable for	*civil*—having to do with citizens *tactile*—having to do with touch
-ion	act or condition of	*operation*—act of operating
-ious	having, characterized by	*anxious*—characterized by anxiety
-ish	like, somewhat	*foolish*—like a fool
-ism	belief or practice of	*racism*—belief in racial superiority
-ist	one who does, makes, or is concerned with	*scientist*—one concerned with science
-ity, -ty, -y	character or state of being	*amity*—friendship *jealousy*—state of being jealous
-ive	of, relating to, tending to	*destructive*—tending to destroy
-logue, -loquy	speech or writing	*monologue*—speech by one person *colloquy*—conversation

Suffix	Meaning	Example
-logy	speech, study of	*geology*—study of the earth
-ment	act or state of	*abandonment*—act of abandoning
-mony	a resulting thing, condition, or state	*patrimony*—property inherited from one's father
-ness	act or quality	*kindness*—quality of being kind
-ory	having the quality of; a place or thing for	*compensatory*—having the quality of a compensation *lavatory*—place for washing
-ous, -ose	full of, having	*glamorous*—full of glamour
-ship	skill, state of being	*horsemanship*—skill in riding *ownership*—state of being an owner
-some	full of, like	*frolicsome*—playful
-tude	state or quality of	*rectitude*—state of being morally upright
-ward	in the direction of	*homeward*—in the direction of home
-y	full of, like, somewhat	*wily*—full of wiles

ROOTS

Root	Meaning	Examples
acr	bitter	*acrid, acrimony*
act, ag	do, act, drive	*action, react, agitate*
acu	sharp, keen	*acute, acumen*
agog	leader	*pedagogue, demagogic*
agr	field	*agronomy, agriculture*
ali	other	*alias, alienate, inalienable*

Root	Meaning	Examples
alt	high	*altitude, contralto*
alter, altr	other, change	*alternative, altercation, altruism*
am, amic	love, friend	*amorous, amiable*
anim	mind, life, spirit	*animism, animate, animosity*
annu, enni	year	*annual, superannuated, biennial*
anthrop	man	*anthropoid, misanthropy*
apt, ept	fit	*apt, adapt, ineptitude*
aqu	water	*aquatic, aquamarine*
arbit	judge	*arbiter, arbitrary*
arch	chief	*anarchy, matriarch*
arm	arm, weapon	*army, armature, disarm*
art	skill, a fitting together	*artisan, artifact, articulate*
aster, astr	star	*asteroid, disaster, astral*
aud, audit, aur	hear	*auditorium, audition, auricle*
aur	gold	*aureate, aureomycin*
aut	self	*autism, autograph*
bell	war	*antebellum, belligerent*
ben, bene	well, good	*benevolent, benefit*
bibli	book	*bibliography, bibliophile*
bio	life	*biosphere, amphibious*
brev	short	*brevity, abbreviation*
cad, cas, cid	fall	*cadence, casualty, occasion, accident*
cand	white, shining	*candid, candle, incandescent*

Root	Meaning	Examples
cant, chant	sing, charm	*cantor, recant, enchant*
cap, capt, cept, cip	take, seize, hold	*capable, captive, accept, incipient*
capit	head	*capital, decapitate, recapitulate*
carn	flesh	*carnal, incarnate*
cede, ceed, cess	go, yield	*secede, exceed, process, intercession*
cent	hundred	*percentage, centimeter*
cern, cert	perceive, make certain, decide	*concern, certificate, certain*
chrom	color	*monochrome, chromatic*
chron	time	*chronometer, anachronism*
cide, cis	cut, kill	*genocide, incision*
cit	summon, impel	*cite, excite, incitement*
civ	citizen	*uncivil, civilization*
clam, claim	shout	*clamorous, proclaim, claimant*
clar	clear	*clarity, clarion, declare*
clin	slope, lean	*inclination, recline*
clud, clus, clos	close, shut	*seclude, recluse, closet*
cogn	know	*recognize, incognito*
col, cul	till	*colony, cultivate, agriculture*
corp	body	*incorporate, corpse*
cosm	order, world	*cosmetic, cosmos, cosmopolitan*
crac, crat	power, rule	*democrat, theocracy*
cre, cresc, cret	grow	*increase, crescent, accretion*

Root	Meaning	Examples
cred	trust, believe	*credit, incredible*
crux, cruc	cross	*crux, crucial, crucifix*
crypt	hidden	*cryptic, cryptography*
culp	blame	*culprit, culpability*
cur, curr, curs	run, course	*occur, current, incursion*
cura	care	*curator, accurate*
cycl	wheel, circle	*bicycle, cyclone*
dec	ten	*decade, decimal*
dem	people	*demographic, demagogue*
dent	tooth	*dental, indentation*
derm	skin	*dermatitis, pachyderm*
di, dia	day	*diary, quotidian*
dic, dict	say, speak	*indicative, edict, dictation*
dign	worthy	*dignified, dignitary*
doc, doct	teach, prove	*indoctrinate, docile, doctor*
domin	rule	*predominate, domineer, dominion*
dorm	sleep	*dormitory, dormant*
du	two	*duo, duplicity, dual*
duc, duct	lead	*educate, abduct, ductile*
dur	hard, lasting	*endure, obdurate, duration*
dyn	force, power	*dynamo, dynamite*
ego	I	*egomania, egotist*
equ	equal	*equation, equitable*
erg, urg	work, power	*energetic, metallurgy, demiurge*

Root	Meaning	Examples
err	wander	*error, aberrant*
ev	time, age	*coeval, longevity*
fac, fact, fect, fic	do, make	*facility, factual, perfect, artifice*
fer	bear, carry	*prefer, refer, conifer, fertility*
ferv	boil	*fervid, effervesce*
fid	belief, faith	*infidelity, confidant, perfidious*
fin	end, limit	*finite, confine*
firm	strong	*reaffirm, infirmity*
flect, flex	bend	*reflex, inflection*
flor	flower	*florescent, floral*
flu, fluct, flux	flow	*fluid, fluctuation, influx*
form	shape	*formative, reform, formation*
fort	strong	*effort, fortitude*
frag, fract	break	*fragility, infraction*
fug	flee	*refuge, fugitive*
fus	pour, join	*infuse, transfusion*
gam	marry	*exogamy, polygamous*
ge, geo	earth	*geology, geode, perigee*
gen	birth, kind, race	*engender, general, generation*
gest	carry, bear	*gestation, ingest, digest*
gon	angle	*hexagonal, trigonometry*
grad, gress	step, go	*regress, gradation*
gram	writing	*grammar, cryptogram*
graph	writing	*telegraph, graphics*

Root	Meaning	Examples
grat	pleasing, agreeable	*congratulate, gratuitous*
grav	weight, heavy	*gravamen, gravity*
greg	flock, crowd	*gregarious, segregate*
habit, hibit	have, hold	*habitation, inhibit, habitual*
heli	sun	*helium, heliocentric, aphelion*
hem	blood	*hemoglobin, hemorrhage*
her, hes	stick, cling	*adherent, cohesive*
hydr	water	*dehydration, hydrofoil*
iatr	heal, cure	*pediatrics, psychiatry*
iso	same, equal	*isotope, isometric*
it	journey, go	*itinerary, exit*
ject	throw	*reject, subjective, projection*
jud	judge	*judicial, adjudicate*
jug, junct	join	*conjugal, juncture, conjunction*
jur	swear	*perjure, jurisprudence*
labor	work	*laborious, belabor*
leg	law	*legal, illegitimate*
leg, lig, lect	choose, gather, read	*illegible, eligible, select, lecture*
lev	light, rise	*levity, alleviate*
liber	free	*liberal, libertine*
liter	letter	*literate, alliterative*
lith	rock, stone	*eolithic, lithograph*
loc	place	*locale, locus, allocate*
log	word, study	*logic, biology, dialogue*

Root	Meaning	Examples
loqu, locut	talk, speech	*colloquial, loquacious, interlocutor*
luc, lum	light	*translucent, pellucid, illumine, luminous*
lud, lus	play	*allusion, ludicrous, interlude*
magn	large, great	*magnificent, magnitude*
mal	bad, ill	*malodorous, malinger*
man, manu	hand	*manifest, manicure, manuscript*
mar	sea	*maritime, submarine*
mater, matr	mother	*matrilocal, maternal*
medi	middle	*intermediary, medieval*
mega	large, million	*megaphone, megacycle*
ment	mind	*demented, mental*
merg, mers	plunge, dip	*emerge, submersion*
meter, metr, mens	measure	*chronometer, metronome, geometry, commensurate*
micr	small	*microfilm, micron*
min	little	*minimum, minute*
mit, miss	send	*remit, admission, missive*
mon, monit	warn	*admonish, monument, monitor*
mor	custom	*mores, immoral*
mor, mort	death	*mortify, mortician*
morph	shape	*amorphous, anthropomorphic*
mov, mob, mot	move	*removal, automobile, motility*
multi	many	*multiply, multinational*
mut	change	*mutable, transmute*

Root	Meaning	Examples
nasc, nat	born	*native, natural, nascent, innate*
nav	ship, sail	*navy, navigable*
necr	dead, die	*necropolis, necrosis*
neg	deny	*renege, negative*
neo	new	*neologism, neoclassical*
nomen, nomin	name	*nomenclature, cognomen, nominate*
nomy	law, rule	*astronomy, antinomy*
nov	new	*novice, innovation*
ocul	eye	*binocular, oculist*
omni	all	*omniscient, omnibus*
onym	name	*pseudonym, eponymous*
oper	work	*operate, cooperation, inoperable*
ora	speak, pray	*oracle, oratory*
orn	decorate	*adorn, ornate*
orth	straight, correct	*orthodox, orthopedic*
pan	all	*panacea, pantheon*
pater, patr	father	*patriot, paternity*
path, pat, pass	feel, suffer	*telepathy, patient, compassion, passion*
ped	child	*pedagogue, pediatrics*
ped, pod	foot	*pedestrian, impede, tripod*
pel, puls	drive, push	*impel, propulsion*
pend, pens	hang	*pendulous, suspense*
pet, peat	seek	*petition, impetus, repeat*

Root	Meaning	Examples
phil	love	*philosopher, Anglophile*
phob	fear	*phobic, agoraphobia*
phon	sound	*phonograph, symphony*
phor	bearing	*semaphore, metaphor*
phot	light	*photograph, photoelectric*
pon, pos	place, put	*component, repose, postpone*
port	carry	*report, portable, deportation*
pot	power	*potency, potential*
press	press	*pressure, impression*
prim	first	*primal, primordial*
proto, prot	first	*proton, protagonist*
psych	mind	*psychic, metempsychosis*
pyr	fire	*pyrite, pyrophobia*
quer, quir, quis, ques	ask, seek	*query, inquiry, inquisitive, quest*
reg, rig, rect	straight, rule	*regulate, dirigible, corrective*
rid, ris	laugh	*deride, risible, ridiculous*
rog	ask	*rogation, interrogate*
rupt	break	*erupt, interruption, rupture*
sanct	holy	*sacrosanct, sanctify, sanction*
sci, scio	know	*nescient, conscious, omniscience*
scop	watch, view	*horoscope, telescopic*
scrib, script	write	*scribble, proscribe, description*
sed, sid, sess	sit, seat	*sedate, residence, session*
seg, sect	cut	*segment, section, intersect*

Root	Meaning	Examples
sent, sens	feel, think	*nonsense, sensitive, sentient, dissent*
sequ, secut	follow	*sequel, consequence, consecutive*
sign	sign, mark	*signature, designate, assign*
sol	alone	*solitary, solo, desolate*
solv, solu, solut	loosen	*dissolve, soluble, absolution*
somn	sleep	*insomnia, somnolent*
son	sound	*sonorous, unison*
soph	wise, wisdom	*philosophy, sophisticated*
spec, spic, spect	look	*specimen, conspicuous, spectacle*
spir	breathe	*spirit, conspire, respiration*
stab, stat	stand	*unstable, status, station, establish*
stead	place	*instead, steadfast*
string, strict	bind	*astringent, stricture, restrict*
stru, struct	build	*construe, structure, destructive*
sum, sumpt	take	*presume, consumer, assumption*
tang, ting, tact, tig	touch	*tangent, contingency, contact, tactile, contiguous*
tax, tac	arrange, arrangement	*taxonomy, tactic*
techn	skill, art	*technique, technician*
tele	far	*teletype, telekinesis*
tempor	time	*temporize, extemporaneous*
ten, tain, tent	hold	*tenant, tenacity, retention, contain*

Root	Meaning	Examples
tend, tens, tent	stretch	contend, extensive, intent
tenu	thin	tenuous, attenuate
term	end	terminal, terminate
terr, ter	land, earth	inter, terrain
test	witness	attest, testify
the	god	polytheism, theologist
therm	heat	thermos, isotherm
tom	cut	atomic, appendectomy
tort, tors	twist	tortuous, torsion, contort
tract	pull, draw	traction, attract, protract
trib	assign, pay	attribute, tribute, retribution
trud, trus	thrust	obtrude, intrusive
turb	agitate	perturb, turbulent, disturb
umbr	shade	umbrella, penumbra, umbrage
uni	one	unify, disunity, union
urb	city	urbane, suburb
vac	empty	vacuous, evacuation
vad, vas	go	invade, evasive
val, vail	strength, worth	valid, avail, prevalent
ven, vent	come	advent, convene, prevention
ver	true	aver, veracity, verity
verb	word	verbose, adverb, verbatim
vert, vers	turn	revert, perversion
vest	dress	vestment

Root	Meaning	Examples
vid, vis	see	*video, evidence, vision, revise*
vinc, vict	conquer	*evince, convict, victim*
viv, vit	life	*vivid, revive, vital*
voc, vok	call	*vociferous, provocative, revoke*
vol	wish	*involuntary, volition*
voly, volut	roll, turn	*involve, convoluted, revolution*
vulg	common	*divulge, vulgarity*
zo	animal	*zoologist, paleozoic*

Summary: What You Need to Know About Word Parts

- Words have three basic parts: *roots*, *suffixes*, and *prefixes*
- Each word part has a specific purpose.
- Word parts work together to form the meaning and function of the word in which they occur
- When you recognize common word parts, you can deconstruct any word to determine its meaning.

EXERCISES: WORD PARTS

Directions: In each of the following exercises, the words in the left-hand column are built on roots given in the word-part list. Match each word with its definition from the right-hand column. Refer to the list if necessary. Can you identify the roots of each word? If you can't figure out a word, look it up in a dictionary.

Exercise 1

1. mutable
2. culpable
3. interminable
4. amiable
5. vacuous
6. vital
7. primeval
8. tenacious
9. tangible
10. inoperable
11. risible
12. indissoluble

A. able to be touched
B. laughable
C. empty of meaning or interest
D. of the first age
E. holding firmly
F. necessary to life
G. unending
H. stable, not able to be loosened or broken up
I. changeable
J. friendly
K. blameworthy
L. not working, out of order

Exercise 2

1. infinity
2. duplicity
3. levity
4. brevity
5. ejection
6. edict
7. infraction
8. genocide
9. agenda
10. annuity
11. microcosm
12. doctrine

A. list of things to be done
B. sum paid yearly
C. a throwing out or from
D. shortness
E. endlessness
F. body of teachings
G. killing of a race
H. lightness of spirit
I. a breaking
J. double-dealing
K. official decree; literally, a speaking out
L. world in miniature

Exercise 3

1. recede
2. abdicate
3. homogenize
4. illuminate
5. supervise
6. verbalize
7. liberalize
8. legislate
9. intervene
10. inter
11. aver
12. protract

A. state as the truth
B. throw light on
C. forswear, give up a power
D. put into words
E. make freer
F. go away
G. bury
H. oversee
I. make laws
J. draw out
K. make the same throughout
L. come between

Exercise 4

1. abduction
2. fortitude
3. consequence
4. confluence
5. compression
6. locus
7. status
8. disunity
9. veracity
10. revival
11. advent
12. adjunct

A. arrival, a coming to
B. a pressing together
C. a flowing together
D. something added to
E. a coming back to life
F. place
G. truthfulness
H. that which follows as a result
I. strength
J. lack of oneness
K. a leading away, kidnapping
L. standing, position

Exercise 5

1. nascent
2. centennial
3. prospective
4. circumspect
5. multinational
6. clamorous
7. antebellum
8. contrary
9. impassioned
10. credulous
11. obdurate
12. nominal

A. being born
B. before the war
C. believing easily
D. going against
E. in name only
F. hard, unyielding
G. looking, forward
H. careful, looking in all directions
I. hundred year anniversary
J. have interests in many countries
K. full of strong feeling
L. shouting

ANSWER KEYS

Exercise 1
1. I
2. K
3. G
4. J
5. C
6. F
7. D
8. E
9. A
10. L
11. B
12. H

Exercise 2
1. E
2. J
3. H
4. D
5. C
6. K
7. I
8. G
9. A
10. B
11. L
12. F

Exercise 3
1. F
2. C
3. K
4. B
5. H
6. D
7. E
8. I
9. L
10. G
11. A
12. J

Exercise 4
1. K
2. I
3. H
4. C
5. B
6. F
7. L
8. J
9. G
10. E
11. A
12. D

Exercise 5
1. A
2. I
3. G
4. H
5. J
6. L
7. B
8. D
9. K
10. C
11. F
12. E

Chapter

12

The SAT "Top 500" Word List

As you learned in Chapter 11, a good vocabulary goes a long way in preparing you for success on the SAT. But that doesn't mean you have to memorize the dictionary before the test. This chapter lists and defines some of the words most commonly used on the SAT. It also shows you some of the best strategies for learning the words—and for choosing *which* words to learn. You also get an opportunity to practice your newly upgraded vocabulary skills in the exercises at the end of this chapter.

THE BEST WAYS TO LEARN NEW WORDS

Before you jump in headfirst, make sure you're taking a realistic approach to upgrading your vocabulary for the SAT. Let's face it—this chapter contains a lot of vocabulary words. You won't be able to learn all of these words, or all of the word parts, all at once. If you do want to try to learn the complete lists, give yourself plenty of time before the test date and break them down into manageable chunks. If you've decided to just concentrate on the words that seem most unfamiliar to you, it's still a good idea to work in smaller chunks to avoid information overload.

Here are a few techniques for designing a successful (and manageable) program for building your SAT vocabulary:

1. MAKE SOME PORTABLE LISTS

Take a look at the "SAT Word List" and choose 15 to 20 words that are new to you. Copy those words and their definitions on a separate sheet of paper. Now you've got a very portable list of words to learn. Once these words are comfortably lodged in your brain, make another list of new words.

ROAD MAP

- *Learn how the SAT tests your vocabulary*
- *Master the best ways to learn new words*
- *Hit list: Learn the top 500 SAT words*
- *Review a summary of everything you need to know about SAT words*
- *Practice your skills on SAT word exercises*

> **TIP**
>
> When you run into a word on the following SAT Word List that you can't define, think back to the information you learned in Chapter 11. Can you spot the word's root? Does it have a prefix or suffix that looks familiar to you? Apply the words skills you learned in Chapter 11. The word-part clues may help you define unfamiliar words.

2. MAKE FLASHCARDS

Gather up a batch of index cards and search the word list for words you don't know. Write one word on each index card. Then, write the definition on the back of the card. Study the words and their meanings—in small batches, of course—and then test yourself. Look at a word on one of your cards and write the definition on a separate sheet of paper. Then turn the card over and see if you're correct. If you have a study partner (or a friend who is also starting to sweat about the SAT), you can test one another.

THE TOP 500 SAT WORDS

There have to be a kazillion words in the English language, right? (And by the way, *kazillion* isn't one of them.) How could you ever figure out which words would be on the SAT? You can use the handy-dandy word list that follows. It doesn't contain every word you'll encounter on the exam, but it does represent the Top 500 SAT words from recent tests.

It's also not a bad idea to start reading some newspapers such as *The New York Times* or the *Washington Post*. They use the kind of vocabulary that you'll find on the SAT, and these newspapers are usually available in the library.

You might also do some random thesaurus searching. Think of a word and then find it in the thesaurus. See what some of the synonyms are and how their construction corresponds in word parts and meaning to the word you know.

THE SAT WORD LIST

-A-

aberration *(noun)* Deviation from what is correct or right.

abeyance *(noun)* Suspension of an activity; postponement.

abstemious *(adj)* Sparing in use of food or drink; moderate.

abstruse *(adj)* Concealed; difficult to comprehend; obscure.

accolade *(noun)* Embrace; award; commendation.

acerbic *(adj)* Bitter; harsh; caustic.

acrimonious *(adj)* Sarcastic; caustic; angry; mordant.

acuity *(noun)* Sharpness; acuteness; keenness.

acute *(adj)* 1. Perceptive. 2. Excruciating.
adept *(adj)* Proficient; masterful; expert.
adherent *(noun)* Believer; supporter; devotee.
adjunct *(noun)* 1. Attachment; appendage. 2. Subordinate or auxiliary capacity.
admonish *(verb)* Caution; reprove mildly; reprimand.
adroit *(adj)* Dexterous; proficient; skillful.
adulation *(noun)* Excessive flattery; adoration; idolization.
adulterate *(verb)* Make impure or inferior by adding improper ingredients; contaminate; pollute.
advocate *(verb)* 1. Argue for a cause; defend. 2. Support; uphold.
aesthete *(noun)* Person who cultivates beauty or art; connoisseur.
aggrandize *(verb)* Make more powerful; amplify; increase.
alacrity *(noun)* Eagerness; zeal; speed.
altruistic *(adj)* Concerned about the general welfare of others; charitable; generous.
ambivalence *(noun)* Uncertainty; doubt; indecisiveness.
ambulatory *(adj)* Able to walk; not stationary.
ameliorate *(verb)* Make better; improve.
amiable *(adj)* Cordial; of pleasant disposition; friendly.
amorphous *(adj)* Without structure; shapeless; nebulous.
animate *(verb)* Energize; enliven.
anomaly *(noun)* Abnormality; deviation from the general rule; irregularity.
antediluvian *(adj)* Ancient; antiquated; obsolete.
antipathy *(noun)* Feeling of opposition or repugnance; aversion; dislike.
apathy *(noun)* Lack of concern, emotion or interest; indifference.
aperture *(noun)* Gap; opening; orifice.
apocryphal *(adj)* False; unauthenticated; disputed.
apotheosis *(noun)* 1. Essence; epitome. 2. Canonization.
appease *(verb)* Satisfy; make peace; placate.
approbatory *(adj)* Expressing approval.
arable *(adj)* Suitable for cultivation or plowing.
arrogant *(adj)* Feeling superior to other people; egotistical.
ascetic *(adj)* Strict; austere.
assuage *(verb)* Ease; make less burdensome; mitigate.
atrophy *(verb)* Waste away from lack of use; degenerate.
audacity *(noun)* Boldness or adventurousness; gall.
authoritarian *(noun)* 1. Person who acts like a dictator; tyrant. 2. Disciplinarian.
avarice *(noun)* Extreme desire for wealth; greed; acquisitiveness.
aviary *(noun)* Large enclosure confining birds.
avouch *(verb)* Guarantee; take responsibility for; affirm.
avow *(verb)* Affirm; assert; declare; acknowledge.

-B-

baleful *(adj)* Sorrowful; sinister; evil.

balm *(noun)* Soothing ointment for pain or healing; salve.

banal *(adj)* Trite; insipid; ordinary.

bane *(noun)* Deadly affliction; curse; plague.

barbarity *(noun)* Cruel action; inhuman act; harsh conduct.

barren *(adj)* 1. Infertile; impotent. 2. Arid; unproductive.

befuddle *(verb)* Stupefy or confuse; misconstrue.

belated *(adj)* Tardy; overdue.

beleaguer *(verb)* Besiege; surround.

belittle *(verb)* Humiliate; tease; diminish in importance.

bemoan *(verb)* 1. Experience pain or distress. 2. Express pity for; mourn.

bemused *(adj)* Preoccupied by thought; bewildered; perplexed.

bilk *(verb)* Defraud; deceive; hoodwink.

blandishment *(noun)* Cajolery; enticement.

bliss *(noun)* Gaiety; happiness; enjoyment.

blithe *(adj)* Happy; pleased; delighted.

boisterous *(adj)* Noisy; loud; violent; rowdy.

boorish *(adj)* Ill-mannered; rude; gauche.

brevity *(noun)* Briefness; succinctness; terseness.

broach *(verb)* Introduce; bring up; mention.

browbeat *(verb)* Intimidate; harass; dominate.

bungle *(verb)* Botch; mismanage; spoil.

buttress *(noun)* Truss; foundation; support.

-C-

cacophonous *(adj)* Discordant; dissident; harsh.

callow *(adj)* Inexperienced; immature; naive.

candid *(adj)* Frank; blunt; open.

carouse *(verb)* Drink to excess; live it up.

cease *(verb)* Stop; end; halt.

celerity *(noun)* Swift motion; speed; alacrity.

censorious *(adj)* Critical; attacking; denouncing.

charlatan *(noun)* Fraud; person claiming knowledge he/she does not have; humbug; fake; hustler.

chary *(adj)* Careful; cautious.

chasten *(verb)* Castigate; punish; reprove.

cherubic *(adj)* Sweet; kind; innocent.

chimerical *(adj)* Fanciful; whimsical; playful.

chronic *(adj)* Compulsive; typical; habitual; inveterate.

churlish *(adj)* Selfish; rancorous; surly.

circuitous *(adj)* Indirect; roundabout; rambling.

clamor *(noun)* Loud noise or complaint; commotion; din.

clandestine *(adj)* Furtive; surreptitious; secret.

clemency *(noun)* Lenience; mercy; compassion.

cloister *(noun)* Convent; monastery; religious place.

coagulate *(verb)* Congeal; curdle; clot.

coalesce *(verb)* Combine; incorporate; merge.

coddle *(verb)* Pamper; overindulge; baby; spoil.

coercion *(noun)* Intimidation; duress; force; compulsion.

cognate *(adj)* Related by blood; having the same origin.

commensurate *(adj)* Equal in measure; of the same duration or size.

compile *(verb)* Collect data; accumulate; amass.

concomitant *(adj)* Concurrent; attendant; occurring with something else.

concordance *(noun)* Agreement; treaty; accord.

confluence *(noun)* Nexus; union; meeting; conflux.

confound *(verb)* Perplex; baffle; confuse.

conglomerate *(noun)* Corporation; partnership; firm.

conjugal *(adj)* Matrimonial; nuptial; marital.

constrict *(verb)* Squeeze; pinch; obstruct; block.

contentious *(adj)* Argumentative; pugnacious; quarrelsome.

contrite *(adj)* Penitent; apologetic; remorseful.

conundrum *(noun)* Mystery; puzzle.

convoke *(verb)* Convene; assemble.

copious *(adj)* Plentiful; ample; profuse.

corpulence *(noun)* Stoutness; obesity.

coterie *(noun)* Small group of people who share interests and meet frequently.

crass *(adj)* Vulgar, grossly ignorant; indelicate.

credulous *(adj)* Gullible; unsuspecting; naive.

cryptic *(adj)* Enigmatic; obscure; secret; puzzling.

ctenoid *(adj)* Comblike; having narrow segments.

cuboid *(adj)* Having the shape of a cube.

cucullate *(adj)* Hood-shaped.

curmudgeon *(noun)* Cantankerous person.

-D-

daub *(verb)* Blur; smear; spread.

dawdle *(verb)* Procrastinate; loiter; idle; dally.

dearth *(noun)* Paucity; shortage; deficiency.

debased *(adj)* Lowered in status or character; degenerate.

decipher *(verb)* Solve or figure out a puzzle; translate; untangle.

declivity *(noun)* Downward slope.

decorum *(noun)* Appropriate conduct; polite or proper behavior, protocol.

delectable *(adj)* Delicious; delightful; savory.

deleterious *(adj)* Destructive; poisonous; unhealthy.

delineate *(verb)* Describe; outline; depict.

delusion *(noun)* Untrue belief; hallucination; fallacy; misconception.

demagogue *(noun)* Incendiary; agitator; opportunist.

denounce *(verb)* Reprove; accuse; condemn.

depravity *(noun)* Perverted disposition; wickedness; vileness; corruption.

deprecatory *(adj)* Disapproving; belittling.

desecrate *(verb)* Contaminate; profane; defile.

desist *(verb)* Discontinue or stop; cease; renounce.

desolate *(adj)* Alone; without hope or comfort; forsaken.

despoil *(verb)* Ravage; rob; loot.

despot *(noun)* Dictator; tyrant; totalitarian.

diatribe *(noun)* Extreme, bitter, and abusive speech; vituperation; tirade.

didactic *(adj)* Pedantic; academic; for teaching.

diffidence *(noun)* Self-doubt; timidity; shyness.

dilatory *(adj)* Lackadaisical; lazy; remiss.

diligent *(adj)* Assiduous; studious; hard-working.

diminution *(noun)* Decrease; reduction.

disaffected *(adj)* Disillusioned; dissatisfied; discontented.

disapprobation *(noun)* Dislike; reservation; denunciation.

disband *(verb)* Disperse; dissipate; scatter; dispel.

discontent *(adj)* Unhappy; displeased; miserable.

discursive *(adj)* Circuitous; digressive; rambling.

dishearten *(verb)* Dismay; daunt; depress.

disinterment *(noun)* Exhumation; removal of a body from a grave.

disoblige *(verb)* Slight or offend.

disparage *(verb)* Deprecate; belittle or abuse.

dispassionate *(adj)* Imperturbable; unemotional; calm; composed.

disputatious *(adj)* Quarrelsome; contentious; argumentative.

dissemble *(verb)* Disguise; conceal; mask; camouflage.

dissension *(noun)* Conflict; disagreement; strife.

dissonant *(adj)* Cacophonous; inharmonious; discordant; strident.

dissuade *(verb)* Obstruct; hinder; deter.

distend *(verb)* Bloat, bulge; swell; stretch.

dither *(noun)* Commotion; turmoil.

divination *(noun)* Prediction; prophecy; forecast.
dolt *(noun)* Cretin; fool; dimwit; idiot.
dotard *(noun)* Senile person.
dubious *(adj)* Irresolute; uncertain; moot.
duplicity *(noun)* Cunning; fraud; trickery; deception.

-E-

edify *(verb)* Instruct; enlighten; educate.
efface *(verb)* Cancel; delete; obliterate.
effervescent *(adj)* Lively; volatile.
effigy *(noun)* Mannequin; likeness; image.
effrontery *(noun)* Impudence; nerve; gall.
egregious *(adj)* Flagrant; glaring; outrageous.
elegiac *(adj)* Mournful; sorrowful; sad.
elucidate *(verb)* Interpret; define; clarify; explain.
emanate *(verb)* Radiate; flow from; emit.
emasculate *(verb)* Deprive of strength.
embroil *(verb)* Implicate; enmesh; involve.
emcee *(noun)* Master of ceremonies.
empathize *(verb)* Identify with; understand.
emulate *(verb)* Model; pattern.
enervate *(verb)* Exhaust or weaken; debilitate.
engender *(verb)* Generate; produce; cause.
enigmatic *(adj)* Cryptic; baffling; mysterious.
enmesh *(verb)* Tangle or involve.
ennui *(noun)* Dullness; boredom; monotony.
enthrall *(verb)* Mesmerize; captivate; thrill.
entrench *(verb)* Fortify; reinforce; secure.
ephemeral *(adj)* Transitory; fleeting; passing; temporary.
epicure *(noun)* Person devoted to luxurious living; person with refined tastes.
epithet *(noun)* Word used to describe or characterize a person or thing.
equilibrium *(noun)* Balance; stability; poise.
equivocate *(verb)* Prevaricate; dodge; evade; hedge.
erudition *(noun)* Learning; knowledge; enlightenment.
escapade *(noun)* Adventurous conduct; unusual behavior.
esoteric *(adj)* Confidential; personal; private; privileged.
espouse *(verb)* Embrace; defend; support.
ethereal *(adj)* Incorporeal; intangible; airy.
eulogy *(noun)* Commendation; speech giving great tribute.

euphonic *(adj)* Agreeable to the ear.

evanescent *(adj)* Ephemeral; fading; brief.

exigent *(adj)* Pressing; insistent; urgent.

exonerate *(verb)* Acquit; vindicate; free from responsibility.

exorcise *(verb)* Cast out evil spirits; expel demons.

expatriate *(verb)* Send into exile; renounce one's own country.

expedite *(verb)* Speed up matters; accelerate; quicken.

expunge *(verb)* Obliterate; remove; erase; exterminate.

expurgate *(verb)* Remove erroneous or objectionable material; delete; edit.

extemporaneous *(adj)* Spontaneous; impromptu.

extol *(verb)* Praise; laud; hail; glorify.

extradite *(verb)* Transfer a person to another jurisdiction for possible prosecution for an alleged offense.

extricate *(verb)* Remove; loosen; untie.

-F-

fallible *(adj)* Faulty; imperfect.

fallow *(adj)* Idle; dormant.

fastidious *(adj)* Meticulous; exacting.

fathom *(verb)* Measure; discover; perceive.

fatuous *(adj)* Ludicrous; inane; idiotic; silly.

fecund *(adj)* Prolific; productive; fruitful.

felicity *(noun)* Great happiness; bliss.

fetid *(adj)* Possessing an offensive smell; malodorous; foul; gamey.

fetter *(verb)* Restrain; restrict; curb.

fickle *(adj)* Capricious; erratic; spasmodic.

fledgling *(noun)* Young or inexperienced person; young bird.

flippant *(adj)* Nonchalant; frivolous, superficial; light.

florid *(adj)* Ornate; flushed with rosy color; ruddy.

flout *(verb)* Ridicule; scoff; mock; scorn.

foible *(noun)* Frailty; imperfection; weakness.

forswear *(verb)* Repudiate; forsake; eschew.

fulsome *(adj)* Loathsome; excessive.

fume *(noun)* Gas; vapor; harmful or irritating smoke.

furtive *(adj)* Clandestine; secretive; surreptitious; covert.

-G-

gambol *(verb)* Play; frolic; romp.

garble *(verb)* Confuse; scramble; distort.

garish *(adj)* Gaudy; ostentatious; excessive.
garner *(verb)* Collect; receive; attain; acquire.
giddy *(adj)* Scatterbrained; silly; frivolous.
goad *(verb)* Incite; pressure; irk; arouse; awaken.
grandiloquence *(noun)* Pompous or bombastic speech; lofty, welling language.
grisly *(adj)* Frightening; ghastly; gory; hideous.
grovel *(verb)* Act in a servile way; cringe; kneel.
guile *(noun)* Wiliness; deceit; cunning.
guzzle *(verb)* Gulp; swill; consume to excess.

-H-

hackneyed *(adj)* Trite; common; overdone; banal.
haggle *(verb)* Dicker; barter; make a deal.
hallow *(verb)* Make holy; consecrate; sanctify.
hamper *(verb)* Hinder; frustrate; impede.
harbor *(verb)* Preserve; conceal; secure; shelter.
hardy *(adj)* Stalwart; robust; sturdy.
haughty *(adj)* Arrogant; disdainful; blatantly proud; contemptuous.
hearten *(verb)* Encourage; give strength.
hedge *(verb)* Enclose; surround; fence.
hedonism *(noun)* Intemperance; self-indulgence; excess.
herald *(verb)* Announce; broadcast; report.
heretic *(noun)* Nihilist; infidel; radical; dissenter.
hiatus *(noun)* Interruption; pause; gap.
hilarity *(noun)* Boisterous merriment; enjoyment.
histrionic *(adj)* Pertaining to actors; melodramatic.
hoary *(adj)* Frosted; grey; grizzled.
hyperbole *(noun)* Exaggeration; fanciful statement; enhancement.

-I-

iconoclasm *(noun)* Attack on religious values or symbols.
ignoramus *(noun)* Moron; fool; dimwit.
immutable *(adj)* Incorruptible; enduring; unchanging.
impecunious *(adj)* Poor; destitute; penniless.
imperturbable *(adj)* Even-tempered; level-headed; calm.
impervious *(adj)* Airtight; sealed; impenetrable.
impetuous *(adj)* Hasty; rash; impulsive.
impregnable *(adj)* Invincible; invulnerable; unable to be captured or entered.

impromptu *(adj)* Makeshift; spontaneous.
improvident *(adj)* Reckless; rash.
impugn *(verb)* Denounce; censor; attack.
inauspicious *(adj)* Unfavorable.
inaudible *(adj)* Faint; soft; hard to hear.
incipient *(adj)* Embryonic; developing; in the beginning stages.
incisive *(adj)* Perceptive; astute.
inclusive *(adj)* All-encompassing; broad in scope; comprehensive.
incoherent *(adj)* Illogical; inconsistent.
incongruous *(adj)* Inconsistent; unsuitable; contradictory.
incorrigible *(adj)* Unruly; delinquent; incapable of reform.
indecorous *(adj)* Inappropriate; indelicate; unseemly.
indefatigable *(adj)* Diligent; persistent; inexhaustible.
indenture *(noun)* Contract binding a person to work for another.
indolence *(noun)* Lethargy; idleness; sloth.
inebriation *(noun)* Drunkenness; intoxication.
ingenuous *(adj)* Genuine; open; candid; frank.
inimical *(adj)* Antagonistic; hurtful; harmful; adverse.
innocuous *(adj)* Dull; harmless; innocent.
inscrutable *(adj)* Mysterious; perplexing.
insipid *(adj)* Dull; banal; tasteless.
insolvent *(adj)* Bankrupt; unable to pay debts.
intercede *(verb)* Intervene; negotiate.
intonate *(verb)* Speak or utter with a particular tone.
intractable *(adj)* Unruly; disobedient.
intrinsic *(adj)* Inherent; natural; innate.
inveigh *(verb)* Abuse; criticize; rebuke.
inveterate *(adj)* Habitual; chronic.
irascible *(adj)* Testy; touchy; irritable.
issue *(verb)* Discharge; emerge; emanate.

-J-

jettison *(verb)* Eliminate; discharge.
jollity *(noun)* Gaiety; merriment.
judicious *(adj)* Logical; reasonable; clever.
juncture *(noun)* Joint; seam; intersection; joining.
juxtapose *(verb)* Place side by side.

-K-

kinetic *(adj)* Caused by motion; dynamic.
kitsch *(noun)* Art or writing of a pretentious but shallow nature.
kiosk *(noun)* A small structure used as a newsstand, bandstand, etc.
knave *(noun)* A dishonest, deceitful person; a rogue.
knotty *(adj)* Snarled; tangled.
knoll *(noun)* Hillock; mound.
kudos *(noun)* Credit or praise for an achievement; glory.

-L-

labyrinth *(noun)* Maze; network; puzzle.
lachrymose *(adj)* Weepy; tearful.
laconic *(adj)* Concise; terse; curt.
lamentation *(noun)* Complaint; moan.
lampoon *(verb)* Mock; ridicule.
languish *(verb)* Decline; diminish; weaken.
largess *(noun)* Charity; philanthropy; gift.
lassitude *(noun)* Fatigue; weariness; debility.
laudable *(adj)* Commendable; admirable; exemplary.
laxity *(noun)* Carelessness; indifference.
lethargy *(noun)* Idleness; listlessness; passivity.
levity *(noun)* Lightness; frivolity.
linger *(verb)* Loiter; remain; hesitate.
lithe *(adj)* Flexible; agile; mobile; bendable.
loutish *(adj)* Clumsy; idiotic; buffoonlike.
ludicrous *(adj)* Outlandish; silly; ridiculous.
lurid *(adj)* Shockingly vivid; horrifying; sensational.

-M-

maladroit *(adj)* Clumsy; unskilled.
malapropism *(noun)* Inappropriate or ludicrous use of a word.
malevolent *(adj)* Venomous; spiteful; malignant.
malinger *(verb)* Feign illness to escape work; shirk.
marred *(adj)* Having blemishes; damaged; defaced.
maudlin *(adj)* Overemotional; mushy.
meander *(verb)* Twist; bend; zigzag.
mendicant *(noun)* Almsman; beggar; leech; parasite.
meticulous *(adj)* Precise; scrupulous; particular.

mettle *(noun)* Stamina; bravery; courage.
mince *(verb)* Chop; mitigate.
mire *(noun)* Mud; slime; muck.
moribund *(adj)* Failing; waning; ailing.
motley *(adj)* Multicolored; spotted; mixed.
multifarious *(adj)* Diverse; many-sided; multiple.
mundane *(adj)* Boring; ordinary; typical; tedious.
munificent *(adj)* Generous; extravagant; philanthropic.

-N-

nadir *(noun)* Lowest point.
naive *(adj)* Foolishly simple; childlike.
nascent *(adj)* Beginning; embryonic; incipient.
nebulous *(adj)* Unclear; vague; indefinite.
needle *(verb)* Provoke.
nefarious *(adj)* Evil; vile; sinister; wicked.
nemesis *(noun)* Just punishment; retribution.
neologism *(noun)* Newly coined phrase or expression.
noisome *(adj)* Noxious to health.
noxious *(adj)* Harmful; malignant.

-O-

obdurate *(adj)* Stubborn; intractable.
obsequious *(adj)* Servile; groveling.
obviate *(verb)* Make unnecessary.
odious *(adj)* Detestable; loathsome; revolting; sickening.
officious *(adj)* Meddlesome.
opaque *(adj)* Impenetrable by light; dull; dark; obscure.
optimum *(noun)* Peak or prime; ideal.
opulent *(adj)* Affluent; well-to-do; plentiful.
ostentatious *(adj)* Conspicuous; showy.
ostracize *(verb)* Exclude; isolate; bar; shun.

-P-

palpable *(adj)* Noticeable; obvious; apparent.
paltry *(adj)* Minor; petty; insignificant.
panegyric *(noun)* Elaborate praise, public compliment.
paragon *(noun)* Model or standard of excellence.

pariah *(noun)* Outcast; misfit; refugee.
parochial *(adj)* Religious; restricted.
parsimony *(noun)* Miserliness; unusually excessive frugality.
partisan *(noun)* Fan or supporter; enthusiast supporting a particular cause or issue.
pastiche *(noun)* Hodgepodge; literary or musical piece imitating other works.
paucity *(noun)* Scarcity; shortage; dearth.
peccadillo *(noun)* Small sin or fault.
pedantic *(adj)* Stuffy or dogmatic; meticulous; academic.
peevish *(adj)* Irritable; grouchy; ill-tempered.
pejorative *(adj)* Degrading; derogatory; negative.
percipient *(adj)* Able to perceive or see things as they actually are.
perfidy *(noun)* Deliberate breach of faith or trust; treachery.
peripheral *(adj)* Marginal; outer; surrounding.
perspicacious *(adj)* Astute; keen; perceptive.
philistine *(noun)* Barbarian; person lacking artistic judgment.
pique *(verb)* Irritate; miff; offend.
pithy *(adj)* 1. Substantial; profound. 2. Brief; concise.
placid *(adj)* Sincere; tranquil; composed; sedate.
plaintive *(adj)* Sad; mournful; pathetic.
platitude *(noun)* 1. Triteness. 2. Cliché; trivial remark.
plaudit *(noun)* Enthusiastic expression.
pliable *(adj)* Limber; malleable; flexible.
poignant *(adj)* Intense; powerful; biting; piercing.
polemical *(adj)* Controversial; argumentative; debatable.
polyphony *(noun)* Music with two or more melodies blended together.
porous *(adj)* Permeable; absorbent; having holes.
posthumous *(adj)* Arising or continuing after someone's death.
potable *(adj)* Drinkable.
prattle *(verb)* Gab; babble.
precocious *(adj)* Showing premature development.
precursor *(noun)* Forerunner.
prescient *(adj)* Showing foresight; predicting events before they occur.
primeval *(adj)* Belonging to a primitive age.
primordial *(adj)* Belonging to a primitive age; first in time.
proclivity *(noun)* Tendency; inclination; propensity.
procrastinate *(verb)* Postpone; stall; defer.
prodigious *(adj)* Exceptional; impressive; of huge quantity; immense.
proficient *(adj)* Skillful; masterful; expert.
progeny *(noun)* Heir; descendant; offspring.

prolific *(adj)* Fruitful; abundant; fertile.
prosaic *(adj)* Common; routine; ordinary.
protean *(adj)* Taking many forms; changeable; variable.
protract *(verb)* Elongate; lengthen; prolong.
prudent *(adj)* Careful; cautious; judicious.
puerile *(adj)* Juvenile; immature; childish.
pugilism *(noun)* Boxing.
pugnacity *(noun)* Eagerness to fight; belligerence.
pulchritude *(noun)* Beauty; physical appeal.
pulverize *(verb)* Grind; crush; smash.

-Q-

quagmire *(noun)* Marsh; quicksand; swamp.
quandary *(noun)* Dilemma; mire; entanglement.
querulous *(adj)* Difficult; testy; disagreeable.
quibble *(verb)* Argue or bicker.
quixotic *(adj)* Romantic; whimsical; unrealistic.

-R-

rabid *(adj)* Berserk; diseased; sick.
ramble *(verb)* Meander; roam.
rancorous *(adj)* Antagonistic; hostile; spiteful.
rarefy *(verb)* Make thin; purify; make less dense.
raucous *(adj)* Harsh; annoying; piercing; shrill.
raze *(verb)* Demolish; level; topple.
reactionary *(adj)* Opposing progress; characterized by reaction.
recalcitrant *(adj)* Headstrong; disobedient; stubborn.
recant *(verb)* Rescind; retract; take back.
reconciliation *(noun)* Settlement or resolution.
redundant *(adj)* Excessive; repetitious; unnecessary.
refractory *(adj)* Unmanageable; obstinate; not responsive to treatment.
refurbish *(verb)* Overhaul; remodel.
regimen *(noun)* Administration; government; system.
remedial *(adj)* Restorative; corrective; healing.
remuneration *(noun)* Compensation; wages.
rend *(verb)* Rip; tear; splinter.
reprobate *(noun)* Degenerate; person without morals.
repudiate *(verb)* Recant; disclaim; reject; disavow.

rescind *(verb)* Cancel; repeal; veto.
resilient *(adj)* Elastic; stretchy; rebounding.
resonant *(adj)* Reverberant; ringing.
resplendent *(adj)* Dazzling; glorious; intense.
restive *(adj)* Nervous; restless; uneasy.
retrospection *(noun)* Contemplation of past things.
reverent *(adj)* Devout; solemn; worshipful.
ribald *(adj)* Lewd; obscene; irreverent.
rudiment *(noun)* Beginning; foundation or source.
ruffian *(noun)* Brutal person; cruel and sadistic person.
ruminate *(verb)* Contemplate; think about.

-S-

saccharine *(adj)* Sugary; syrupy.
savant *(noun)* Intellectual; scholar; philosopher.
scanty *(adj)* Meager; scarce.
scoff *(verb)* Mock; ridicule.
sequester *(verb)* Separate; isolate; segregate.
soporific *(adj)* Hypnotic; lethargic; causing sleep.
spurious *(adj)* Bogus; false.
spurn *(verb)* Defy; reject.
squalor *(noun)* 1. Severe poverty. 2. Filthiness.
stratagem *(noun)* Plot; tactic; deception.
strident *(adj)* Discordant; harsh; piercing.
strife *(noun)* Conflict; turmoil; struggle.
stultify *(verb)* Inhibit; make ineffective; cripple.
supercilious *(adj)* Egotistic; proud; arrogant.
surfeit *(noun)* Overabundance; excess; surplus.
surly *(adj)* Choleric; rude; sullen.
surreptitious *(adj)* Covert; furtive; acquired by stealthy means.
svelte *(adj)* Graceful; slim.
sybarite *(noun)* Someone devoted to luxury; pleasure-seeker.
sycophant *(noun)* Flatterer.

-T-

taciturn *(adj)* Reserved; shy; uncommunicative.
tantamount *(adj)* Indistinguishable; equivalent.
taper *(verb)* Diminish; thin; narrow.

tawdry *(adj)* Gaudy; showy; loud.
temerity *(noun)* Rashness; audacity; recklessness.
tensile *(adj)* Pertaining to tension; stretchable; ductile.
tenuous *(adj)* Attenuated; flimsy; thin.
tirade *(noun)* Diatribe; angry speech.
torpor *(noun)* Lethargy; apathy; dormancy.
trepidation *(noun)* Anxiety; alarm; apprehension.
truant *(adj)* Indolent; absent; idle.
turgid *(adj)* Swollen; bombastic; distended.
turpitude *(noun)* Depravity; baseness; shamefulness.

-U-

undulate *(verb)* Move in a wavy manner.
unfathomable *(adj)* Baffling; puzzling; incomprehensible.
unkempt *(adj)* Uncombed; messy; untidy.
unscathed *(adj)* Unhurt; uninjured.
unwieldy *(adj)* Clumsy; awkward; unmanageable.
upbraid *(verb)* Rebuke; scold; criticize.
upshot *(noun)* Final result; conclusion; end.

-V-

vacillate *(verb)* Hedge; waver; fluctuate.
variegated *(adj)* Multicolored; polychromatic; varied.
vehement *(adj)* Fierce; emphatic; intense.
venerate *(verb)* Admire; show respect.
veracity *(noun)* Truth; sincerity; honesty; candor.
verbose *(adj)* Wordy; talkative; profuse.
verdant *(adj)* Lush; thick with vegetation; leafy.
viable *(adj)* Living; alive; feasible.
vigilance *(noun)* Attentiveness; prudence; care.
vilify *(verb)* Defame; denigrate.
virulent *(adj)* Fatal; lethal; toxic.
vitriolic *(adj)* Scathing; caustic.
vociferous *(adj)* Clamorous; outspoken; noisy; vocal.
voluble *(adj)* Verbose; wordy; garrulous.
voluminous *(adj)* Huge; immense; bulky.
voracious *(adj)* 1. Enthusiastic; overly eager. 2. Starving.
vouchsafe *(verb)* Confer; grant; permit.

-W-

wan *(adj)* Anemic; colorless; pale.
waver *(verb)* Totter; fluctuate.
whet *(verb)* Stimulate; sharpen; intensify.
wistful *(adj)* Yearning; pensive; sad.
woe *(noun)* Anguish; grief; affliction.
writhe *(verb)* Squirm; twist.

-X-

xenophobe *(noun)* One who dislikes strangers or foreigners.

-Y-

yeoman *(noun)* Peasant; ordinary person.
yore *(noun)* Time long past.
yowl *(noun)* Long, mournful cry or howl.

-Z-

zealot *(noun)* Fanatic; radical; enthusiast.
zenith *(noun)* Apex; summit; peak.

Summary: What You Need to Know About SAT Words

- Whether you attempt to learn the entire SAT Word List or just parts of the list, break the words into manageable groups of 15 to 20 words, and study one group at a time.
- Portable lists and flashcards can help you study word groups—wherever you are.
- Use the word skills you learned in Chapter 11 to try to define unfamiliar words.
- Read good newspapers and other well-written books and periodicals to help broaden your vocabulary. Keep a dictionary or thesaurus nearby, so you can look up unfamiliar words.

EXERCISES: SAT WORDS

Exercise 1

35 Questions • 15 Minutes

Directions: For each of the following questions, select the one word that has most nearly the same meaning as the italicized word in the context of the sentence. Circle the letter that precedes your answer choice. Stop working at the end of the allotted time, then score your work. Afterward, return to the exercises and complete those questions you didn't finish.

1. The young girl listened to her grandfather's endless and repetitious stories with *laudable* patience.
   (A) exorbitant
   (B) meticulous
   (C) unwavering
   (D) exemplary
   (E) intractable

2. When the right job comes along, act with *celerity* to take advantage of the opportunity.
   (A) alacrity
   (B) resourcefulness
   (C) pragmatism
   (D) compunction
   (E) diligence

3. His *diffidence* caused him to miss many opportunities.
   (A) ignorance
   (B) timidity
   (C) indifference
   (D) indolence
   (E) arrogance

4. The business survived on a *tenuous* relationship with one customer.
   (A) tentative
   (B) insubstantial
   (C) lucrative
   (D) salient
   (E) amatory

5. He asked for compensation *commensurate* to his work.
   (A) approximate
   (B) previous
   (C) equal
   (D) appropriate
   (E) incongruous

6. Visitors to impoverished countries are often shocked at the number of *mendicants* in the streets.
   (A) beggars
   (B) criminals
   (C) vendors
   (D) drunkards
   (E) soldiers

7. It will take more than good intentions to *ameliorate* the conditions in the schools.
   (A) understand
   (B) counteract
   (C) eliminate
   (D) camouflage
   (E) improve

8. *Ephemeral* pleasures may leave long-lasting memories.
   (A) enervated
   (B) irresolute
   (C) frivolous
   (D) adventurous
   (E) transitory

9. The critic *belittled* her talent by suggesting that her beauty, rather than her acting ability, was responsible for her success.
   (A) illuminated
   (B) disparaged
   (C) declared
   (D) diminished
   (E) inveighed

10. The father *upbraided* his children for their extravagance.
    (A) scolded
    (B) scorned
    (C) advocated
    (D) bolstered
    (E) flouted

11. Imagination and curiosity are the antidotes for *ennui*.
    (A) inactivity
    (B) indolence
    (C) boredom
    (D) jollity
    (E) woe

12. His friends *dissuaded* him from that unwise course of action.
    (A) protected
    (B) ostracized
    (C) deterred
    (D) sequestered
    (E) enmeshed

13. They *rescinded* their offer of aid when they became disillusioned with the project.
    (A) renegotiated
    (B) withdrew
    (C) reinstated
    (D) rethought
    (E) validated

14. The novel told a *lurid* tale of murder and lust.
    (A) sensational
    (B) nonsensical
    (C) esoteric
    (D) unrealistic
    (E) dubious

15. She made many enemies because of her *acerbic* wit.
    (A) boorish
    (B) caustic
    (C) inane
    (D) ingratiating
    (E) magnanimous

16. The ancient town was a *labyrinth* of narrow, winding streets.
    (A) confusion
    (B) model
    (C) maze
    (D) collection
    (E) path

17. I will *ruminate* on your proposal and let you know my decision next week.
    (A) ameliorate
    (B) linger
    (C) report
    (D) procrastinate
    (E) contemplate

18. One *contentious* student can disrupt an entire class.
    (A) rambunctious
    (B) vociferous
    (C) quarrelsome
    (D) humorous
    (E) garrulous

19. The hot, humid weather can *enervate* even hearty souls.
    (A) intimidate
    (B) invigorate
    (C) weaken
    (D) incite
    (E) impugn

20. Insisting on a luxury car you cannot afford is *fatuous*.
    (A) inane
    (B) avarice
    (C) nefarious
    (D) impetuous
    (E) pretentious

21. They had to *jettison* the cargo to lighten the plane.
    (A) relocate
    (B) divide
    (C) eject
    (D) disregard
    (E) consume

22. His ideas were *quixotic* and thoroughly useless.
    (A) erroneous
    (B) dubious
    (C) incomprehensible
    (D) unrealistic
    (E) incoherent

23. He was *candid* about his financial difficulties.
    (A) incredulous
    (B) apprehensive
    (C) enigmatic
    (D) blunt
    (E) ambiguous

24. Because of the drug's *soporific* effect, you should not drive after taking it.
    (A) noxious
    (B) sedative
    (C) inimical
    (D) poignant
    (E) incongruous

25. He is always *chary* with a new acquaintance.
    (A) eager
    (B) amiable
    (C) impudent
    (D) baleful
    (E) cautious

26. An *intractable* person is slow to adapt to a new way of life.
    (A) timid
    (B) bemused
    (C) ascetic
    (D) stubborn
    (E) antediluvian

27. She responded with *alacrity* to every customer request.
    (A) indignation
    (B) aggression
    (C) laxity
    (D) diffidence
    (E) zeal

28. Knowing how sensitive she was about money, he did not *broach* the subject of who should pay for the ticket.
    (A) introduce
    (B) avoid
    (C) postpone
    (D) prolong
    (E) bemoan

29. United States law *emanates* from English common law.
    (A) fluctuates
    (B) merges
    (C) mitigates
    (D) originates
    (E) amasses

30. He was expelled from the club because of his *nefarious* activities.
    (A) unsolicited
    (B) questionable
    (C) sinister
    (D) unauthorized
    (E) pejorative

31. They met *surreptitiously* in the night to exchange information.
    (A) clandestinely
    (B) egregiously
    (C) punctiliously
    (D) exigently
    (E) indecorously

32. Only a personal apology will *appease* his rage at having been slighted.
    (A) control
    (B) entrench
    (C) placate
    (D) obviate
    (E) modify

33. Health benefits are part of the *remuneration* that goes with the position.
    (A) paucity
    (B) surfeit
    (C) pay
    (D) advantages
    (E) package

34. The band of terrorists threatened to *despoil* the town unless it surrendered.
    (A) infiltrate
    (B) ravage
    (C) scoff
    (D) browbeat
    (E) stultify

35. She was surprised to find that the *callow* youth had grown into a sophisticated man.
    (A) awkward
    (B) immature
    (C) banal
    (D) gauche
    (E) coddled

Exercise 2

15 Questions • 7 Minutes

Directions: For each of the following questions, select the one word that has most nearly the same meaning as the italicized word in the context of the sentence. Circle the letter that precedes your answer choice. Stop working at the end of the allotted time, then score your work. Afterward, return to the exercises and complete those questions you didn't finish.

1. *Impetuous* actions often lead to trouble.
   (A) contentious
   (B) malicious
   (C) irrational
   (D) dilatory
   (E) impulsive

2. A *recalcitrant* child is a difficult pupil.
   (A) indefatigable
   (B) churlish
   (C) unfocused
   (D) impudent
   (E) obdurate

3. *Brevity* is the essence of journalistic writing.
   (A) continuity
   (B) opacity
   (C) succinctness
   (D) incisiveness
   (E) hedonism

4. Supporting her *impecunious* aunt was a drain on her resources.
   (A) extravagant
   (B) thrifty
   (C) munificent
   (D) eccentric
   (E) destitute

5. The silly costumes and party hats epitomized the *levity* of the occasion.
   (A) inebriation
   (B) frivolity
   (C) emotion
   (D) banality
   (E) mettle

6. The jury's deliberation was *protracted* because of their confusion over a point of law.
   (A) lengthened
   (B) befuddled
   (C) decided
   (D) illuminated
   (E) distended

7. She had a *proclivity* for getting into trouble.
   (A) compulsion
   (B) propensity
   (C) guile
   (D) antipathy
   (E) vulnerability

8. Only a few scrubby trees clung to the rocky soil of that *barren* landscape.
   (A) verdant
   (B) undesirable
   (C) odious
   (D) arid
   (E) insolvent

9. The *dearth* of rain can create a desert in a few years.
   - (A) contamination
   - (B) deficiency
   - (C) hiatus
   - (D) equilibrium
   - (E) abundance

10. The rock sample was a *conglomerate* of quartz pebbles.
    - (A) mixture
    - (B) collusion
    - (C) emulation
    - (D) paragon
    - (E) apotheosis

11. Squeezing through the *aperture* between the rocks, she found herself in a cool, dark cave.
    - (A) chasm
    - (B) confluence
    - (C) path
    - (D) orifice
    - (E) anomaly

12. Sometimes a *circuitous* route is the best way to reach your destination.
    - (A) scenic
    - (B) alternative
    - (C) roundabout
    - (D) audacious
    - (E) desolate

13. To *expedite* delivery of the letter, he sent it by overnight mail.
    - (A) accelerate
    - (B) assure
    - (C) efface
    - (D) extradite
    - (E) secure

14. The *adroit* juggler held the attention of the crowd.
    - (A) inept
    - (B) stunning
    - (C) magnificent
    - (D) confident
    - (E) skillful

15. The confession of one prisoner *exonerated* the other suspects.
    - (A) infuriated
    - (B) acquitted
    - (C) condemned
    - (D) implicated
    - (E) denounced

ANSWER KEYS

Exercise 1

1.	D	8.	E	15.	B	22.	D	29.	D
2.	A	9.	B	16.	C	23.	D	30.	C
3.	B	10.	A	17.	E	24.	B	31.	A
4.	B	11.	C	18.	C	25.	E	32.	C
5.	C	12.	C	19.	C	26.	D	33.	C
6.	A	13.	B	20.	A	27.	E	34.	B
7.	E	14.	A	21.	C	28.	A	35.	B

Exercise 2

1.	E	4.	E	7.	B	10.	A	13.	A
2.	E	5.	B	8.	D	11.	D	14.	E
3.	C	6.	A	9.	B	12.	C	15.	B

PART 6

SAT Math Review

PREVIEW

CHAPTER 13 *SAT Arithmetic Review*

CHAPTER 14 *SAT Algebra Review*

CHAPTER 15 *SAT Geometry Review*

Chapter

SAT Arithmetic Review

1. OPERATIONS WITH INTEGERS AND DECIMALS

The four basic arithmetic operations are addition, subtraction, multiplication, and division. The results of these operations are called **sum, difference, product,** and **quotient,** respectively. Because these words are often used in problems, you should be thoroughly familiar with them.

ADDING. When adding integers and/or decimals, remember to keep your columns straight and to write all digits in their proper columns, according to place value.

Q Add 43.75, .631, and 5

```
  43.75
   .631
   5.
  ------
  49.381
```

A 49.381

SUBTRACTING. When subtracting integers and/or decimals, it is likewise important to put numbers in their proper columns. Be particularly careful in subtracting a longer decimal from a shorter one.

Q Subtract .2567 from 3.8

```
  3.8000
   .2567
  ------
  3.5433
```

A 3.5433

In order to perform this subtraction, zeros must be added to the top number to extend it to equal length with the bottom number. The zeros in this case are only place fillers and in no way change the value of the number.

MULTIPLYING. When multiplying integers, pay particular attention to zeros.

Q Find the product of 403 and 30.

```
    403
  × 30
  ------
  12,090
```

A 12,090

ROAD MAP

- *Operations with integers and decimals*
- *Operations with fractions*
- *Verbal problems involving fractions*
- *Variation*
- *Finding percents*
- *Verbal problems involving percent*
- *Averages*

When multiplying decimals, remember that the number of decimal places in the product must be equal to the sum of the number of decimal places in the numbers being mutiplied.

Q Find the product of 4.03 and .3

A
$$\begin{array}{r} 4.03 \\ \times\ .3 \\ \hline 1.209 \end{array}$$

DIVIDING. When dividing, it is also important to watch for zeros.

Q Divide 4935 by 7

A $7\overline{)4935}^{\ 705}$

Since 7 divides evenly into 49, there is no remainder to carry to the next digit. However, 7 will not divide into 3, so you must put a 0 into the quotient. Carrying the 3, you can then divide 7 into 35 evenly.

When dividing by a decimal, always change the decimal to an integer by moving the decimal point to the end of the divisor. To do this, multiply the divisor by a power of 10. (Multiplying by 10 moves a decimal point one place to the right. Multiplying by 100 moves it two places to the right, and so forth.) Then multiply the number in the division sign by the same power of 10. Since division can always be written as a fraction in which the divisor is the denominator and the number being divided is the numerator, when you remove a decimal point from the divisor, you are really multiplying both parts of the fraction by the same number, which changes its form, but not its value.

Q Divide 4.935 by .07

A $.07\overline{)4.935}$

(Multiply by 100 to move the decimal point two places to the right.)

$7\overline{)493.5}^{\ 70.5}$

> **TIP**
> To find out whether *A* is a divisor of *B*, simply divide *A* into *B* and see if there's any remainder. If the remainder is zero, then *B* is divisible by *A*.

EXERCISE: OPERATIONS WITH INTEGERS AND DECIMALS

Directions: Work out each problem on scratch paper.

Add:

1. 6 + 37 + 42,083 + 125
2. .007 + 32.4 + 1.234 + 7.3
3. .37 + .037 + .0037 + 37

Subtract:

4. 3701 − 371
5. 1000 − 112
6. 40.37 − 6.983

Multiply:

7. 3147 by 206
8. 2.137 by .11
9. .45 by .06

Divide:

10. 12,894 by 42
11. 34.68 by 3.4
12. .175 by 25

SOLUTIONS

1.
```
    6
   37
42083
+ 125
-----
42251
```

2.
```
  .007
 32.4
  1.234
+ 7.3
------
 40.941
```

3.
```
  .37
  .037
  .0037
+37.
-------
 37.4107
```

4.
```
 3701
− 371
-----
 3330
```

5.
```
 1000
− 112
-----
  888
```

6.
```
 40.370
− 6.983
-------
 33.387
```

7.
```
  3147
× 206
------
 18882
 62940
------
648282
```

8.
```
  2.137
×  .11
------
  2137
  2137
------
 .23507
```

9.
```
  .45
× .06
-----
.0270
```

10.
```
      307
   ┌──────
42 )12894
     126
     ---
      294
      294
```

11.
$$\begin{array}{r} 10.2 \\ 3.4 \overline{)34.68} \\ \underline{34} \\ 06 \\ \underline{0} \\ 68 \\ \underline{68} \end{array}$$

12.
$$\begin{array}{r} .007 \\ 25\overline{)175} \\ \underline{175} \end{array}$$

2. OPERATIONS WITH FRACTIONS

ADDING AND SUBTRACTING. In adding or subtracting fractions, you must remember that the numbers must have the same (common) denominator.

Q Add $\dfrac{1}{3} + \dfrac{2}{5} + \dfrac{3}{4}$

A The least number into which 3, 5, and 4 all divide evenly is 60. Therefore, use 60 as the common denominator. To add the fractions, divide each denominator into 60 and multiply the result by the given numerator.

$$\frac{20+24+45}{60} = \frac{89}{60}, \text{ or } 1\frac{29}{60}$$

$$\frac{a}{b} \times \frac{c}{d} = \frac{ad+bc}{bd}$$

A similar shortcut applies to subtraction.

$$\frac{a}{b} \times \frac{c}{d} = \frac{ad-bc}{bd}$$

$$\frac{3}{4} \times \frac{5}{7} = \frac{21-20}{28} = \frac{1}{28}$$

All fractions should be left in their lowest terms. That is, there should be no factor common to both numerator and denominator. Often in multiple-choice questions you may find that the answer you have correctly computed is not among the choices but an equivalent fraction is. Be careful!

In reducing fractions involving large numbers, it is helpful to be able to tell whether a factor is common to both numerator and denominator before a lengthy trial division. Certain tests for divisibility help with this.

> **TIP**
>
> To add or subtract two fractions quickly, remember that a sum can be found by adding the two cross-products and putting this answer over the denominator product.

Tests for Divisibility

To test if a number is divisible by:	Check to see:
2	if it is even
3	if the sum of the digits is divisible by 3
4	if the last two digits are divisible by 4
5	if it ends in 5 or 0
6	if it is even *and* the sum of the digits is divisible by 3
8	if the last three digits are divisible by 8
9	if the sum of the digits is divisible by 9
10	if it ends in 0

Q Reduce $\dfrac{3525}{4341}$

A This fraction is reducible by 3, since the sum of the digits of the numerator is 15 and those of the denominator add up to 12, both divisible by 3.

$$\frac{3525}{4341} = \frac{1175}{1447}$$

The resulting fraction meets no further divisibility tests and therefore has no common factor listed above. Larger divisors would be unlikely on an SAT test.

To add or subtract mixed numbers, it is again important to remember common denominators. In subtraction, you must borrow in terms of the common denominator.

Addition:
$$\begin{array}{r} 43\frac{2}{5} \\ +\ 8\frac{1}{3} \\ \hline \end{array} \qquad \begin{array}{r} 43\frac{6}{15} \\ +\ 8\frac{5}{15} \\ \hline 51\frac{11}{15} \end{array}$$

Subtraction:
$$\begin{array}{r} 43\frac{2}{5} \\ -\ 6\frac{2}{3} \\ \hline \end{array} \qquad \begin{array}{r} 43\frac{6}{15} \\ -\ 6\frac{10}{15} \\ \hline \end{array} \qquad \begin{array}{r} 42\frac{21}{15} \\ -\ 6\frac{10}{15} \\ \hline 36\frac{11}{15} \end{array}$$

MULTIPLYING: To multiply fractions, always try to cancel where possible before actually multiplying. In multiplying mixed numbers, always change them to improper fractions first.

Multiply: $\dfrac{2}{\cancel{5}} \cdot \dfrac{\cancel{10}^{2}}{\cancel{11}} \cdot \dfrac{\cancel{99}^{9}}{\cancel{110}_{55}} = \dfrac{18}{55}$

Multiply: $4\dfrac{1}{2} \cdot 1\dfrac{2}{3} \cdot 5\dfrac{1}{5}$

$\dfrac{\cancel{9}^{3}}{\cancel{2}} \cdot \dfrac{\cancel{5}}{\cancel{3}} \cdot \dfrac{\cancel{26}^{13}}{\cancel{5}} = 39$

DIVIDING: To divide fractions or mixed numbers, remember to invert the divisor (the number after the division sign) and multiply.

Divide: $4\dfrac{1}{2} \div \dfrac{3}{4} = \dfrac{\cancel{9}^{3}}{\cancel{2}} \cdot \dfrac{\cancel{4}^{2}}{\cancel{3}} = 6$

Divide: $62\dfrac{1}{2} \div 5 = \dfrac{\cancel{125}^{25}}{2} \cdot \dfrac{1}{\cancel{5}} = 12\dfrac{1}{2}$

To simplify complex fractions (fractions within fractions), multiply every term by the lowest number needed to clear all fractions in the given numerator and denominator.

Q $\dfrac{\dfrac{1}{2} + \dfrac{1}{3}}{\dfrac{1}{4} + \dfrac{1}{6}}$

A The lowest number which can be used to clear all fractions is 12. Multiplying each term by 12 yields:

$\dfrac{6+4}{3+2} = \dfrac{10}{5} = 2$

Q $\dfrac{\dfrac{3}{4} + \dfrac{2}{3}}{1 - \dfrac{1}{2}}$

A Again, multiply by 12.

$\dfrac{9+8}{12-6} = \dfrac{17}{6} = 2\dfrac{5}{6}$

EXERCISE: OPERATIONS WITH FRACTIONS

Directions: Work out each problem in the space provided.

Add:

1. $12\dfrac{5}{6} + 2\dfrac{3}{8} + 21\dfrac{1}{4}$

2. $\dfrac{1}{2} + \dfrac{1}{3} + \dfrac{1}{4} + \dfrac{1}{5} + \dfrac{1}{6}$

Subtract:

3. $5\dfrac{3}{4}$ from $10\dfrac{1}{2}$

4. $17\dfrac{2}{3}$ from 50

5. $25\dfrac{3}{5}$ from $30\dfrac{9}{10}$

Multiply:

6. $5\dfrac{1}{4} \cdot 1\dfrac{5}{7}$

7. $\dfrac{3}{4} \cdot \dfrac{3}{4} \cdot \dfrac{3}{4}$

8. $12\dfrac{1}{2} \cdot 16$

Divide:

9. $\dfrac{1}{5} \div 5$

10. $5 \div \dfrac{1}{5}$

11. $3\dfrac{2}{3} \div 1\dfrac{5}{6}$

Simplify:

12. $\dfrac{\dfrac{5}{6} - \dfrac{1}{3}}{2 + \dfrac{1}{5}}$

13. $\dfrac{3 + \dfrac{1}{4}}{5 - \dfrac{1}{2}}$

SOLUTIONS

1. $12\frac{5}{6} = \frac{20}{24}$
    $2\frac{3}{8} = \frac{9}{24}$
    $21\frac{1}{4} = \frac{6}{24}$
    $\overline{35 \quad \frac{35}{24}}$
    $36\frac{11}{24}$

2. $\frac{1}{2} = \frac{30}{60}$
    $\frac{1}{3} = \frac{20}{60}$
    $\frac{1}{4} = \frac{15}{60}$
    $\frac{1}{5} = \frac{12}{60}$
    $\frac{1}{6} = \frac{10}{60}$
    $\frac{87}{60} = 1\frac{27}{60} = 1\frac{9}{20}$

3. $10\frac{1}{2} = 9\frac{3}{2} = 9\frac{6}{4}$
    $\underline{-5\frac{3}{4}}$
    $4\frac{3}{4}$

4. $\overset{49}{5\cancel{0}}\frac{3}{3}$
    $17\frac{2}{3}$
    $\overline{32\frac{1}{3}}$

5. $\dfrac{30\frac{9}{10}}{25\frac{3}{5} = \frac{6}{10}}{5\frac{3}{10}}$

6. $\dfrac{\overset{3}{\cancel{21}}}{\cancel{4}} \cdot \dfrac{\overset{3}{\cancel{12}}}{\cancel{7}} = 9$

7. $\dfrac{3}{4} \cdot \dfrac{3}{4} \cdot \dfrac{3}{4} = \dfrac{27}{64}$

8. $\dfrac{25}{\cancel{2}} \cdot \overset{8}{\cancel{16}} = 200$

9. $\dfrac{1}{5} \cdot \dfrac{1}{5} = \dfrac{1}{25}$

10. $5 \cdot 5 = 25$

11. $\dfrac{\cancel{11}}{\cancel{3}} \cdot \dfrac{\overset{2}{\cancel{6}}}{\cancel{11}} = 2$

12. $\dfrac{25-10}{60+6} = \dfrac{15}{66} = \dfrac{5}{22}$
    Each term was multiplied by 30.

13. $\dfrac{12+1}{20-2} = \dfrac{13}{18}$
    Each term was multiplied by 4.

3. VERBAL PROBLEMS INVOLVING FRACTIONS

Fraction problems deal with parts of a whole.

Q If a class consists of 12 boys and 18 girls, what part of the class is boys?

A 12 out of 30 students, or $\frac{12}{30} = \frac{2}{5}$

Read all the questions carefully. Often a problem may require more than one calculation.

Q $\frac{1}{4}$ of this year's seniors have averages above 90. $\frac{1}{2}$ of the remainder have averages between 80 and 90. What part of the senior class have averages below 80?

A $\frac{1}{4}$ have averages above 90.

$\frac{1}{2}$ of $\frac{3}{4}$ or $\frac{3}{8}$ have averages between 80 and 90.

$\frac{1}{4} + \frac{3}{8} = \frac{2}{8} + \frac{3}{8} = \frac{5}{8}$ have averages above 80.

Therefore, $\frac{3}{8}$ of the class have averages below 80.

Q 14 is $\frac{2}{3}$ of what number?

A $14 = \frac{2}{3}x$

Multiply each side by $\frac{3}{2}$

$21 = x$

Q If John has p hours of homework and has worked for r hours, what part of his homework is yet to be done?

A If John had 5 hours of homework and had worked for 3 hours, you would first find he had 5 − 3 hours, or 2 hours, yet to do. This represents $\frac{2}{5}$ of his work. Using letters, his remaining work is represented by $\frac{p-r}{p}$.

TIP
If a problem is given with letters in place of numbers, the same reasoning must be used as if numbers were given. If you are not sure how to proceed, replace the letters with numbers to determine the steps that must be taken.

EXERCISE: VERBAL PROBLEMS INVOLVING FRACTIONS

Directions: Work out each problem. Circle the letter that appears before your answer.

1. A team played 30 games of which it won 24. What part of the games played did it lose?
   (A) $\frac{4}{5}$
   (B) $\frac{1}{4}$
   (C) $\frac{1}{5}$
   (D) $\frac{3}{4}$
   (E) $\frac{2}{3}$

2. If a man's weekly salary is $X and he saves $Y, what part of his weekly salary does he spend?
   (A) $\frac{X}{Y}$
   (B) $\frac{X-Y}{X}$
   (C) $\frac{X-Y}{Y}$
   (D) $\frac{Y-X}{X}$
   (E) $\frac{Y-X}{Y}$

3. What part of an hour elapses between 11:50 A.M. and 12:14 P.M.?
   (A) $\frac{2}{5}$
   (B) $\frac{7}{30}$
   (C) $\frac{17}{30}$
   (D) $\frac{1}{6}$
   (E) $\frac{1}{4}$

4. One-half of the employees of Acme Co. earn salaries above $18,000 annually. One-third of the remainder earn salaries between $15,000 and $18,000. What part of the staff earns below $15,000?
   (A) $\frac{1}{6}$
   (B) $\frac{2}{3}$
   (C) $\frac{1}{2}$
   (D) $\frac{1}{10}$
   (E) $\frac{1}{3}$

SAT Arithmetic Review

5. David received his allowance on Sunday. He spends $\frac{1}{4}$ of his allowance on Monday and $\frac{2}{3}$ of the remainder on Tuesday. What part of his allowance is left for the rest of the week?

    (A) $\frac{1}{3}$

    (B) $\frac{1}{12}$

    (C) $\frac{1}{4}$

    (D) $\frac{1}{2}$

    (E) $\frac{4}{7}$

6. 12 is $\frac{3}{4}$ of what number?

    (A) 16
    (B) 9
    (C) 36
    (D) 20
    (E) 15

7. A piece of fabric is cut into three sections so that the first is three times as long as the second and the second section is three times as long as the third. What part of the entire piece is the smallest section?

    (A) $\frac{1}{12}$

    (B) $\frac{1}{9}$

    (C) $\frac{1}{3}$

    (D) $\frac{1}{7}$

    (E) $\frac{1}{13}$

8. What part of a gallon is one quart?

    (A) $\frac{1}{2}$

    (B) $\frac{1}{4}$

    (C) $\frac{2}{3}$

    (D) $\frac{1}{3}$

    (E) $\frac{1}{5}$

9. A factory employs M men and W women. What part of its employees are women?

    (A) $\frac{W}{M}$

    (B) $\frac{M+W}{W}$

    (C) $\frac{W}{M-W}$

    (D) $\frac{W}{M+W}$

    (E) W

10. A motion was passed by a vote of 5 : 3. What part of the votes cast were in favor of the motion?

    (A) $\frac{5}{8}$

    (B) $\frac{5}{3}$

    (C) $\frac{3}{5}$

    (D) $\frac{2}{5}$

    (E) $\frac{3}{8}$

11. If the ratio of $x : y$ is 9 : 7, what is the value of $x + y$?

    (A) 2
    (B) 14
    (C) 16
    (D) 63
    (E) It cannot be determined from the information

12. In a certain class the ratio of men to women is 3 : 5. If the class has 24 people in it, how many are women?

    (A) 9
    (B) 12
    (C) 15
    (D) 18
    (E) 21

13. If the ratio of men to women in a class is 3 : 5 and the class contains 24 people, how many additional men would have to enroll to make the ratio of men to women 1 : 1?

    (A) 3
    (B) 6
    (C) 9
    (D) 12
    (E) 15

14. If x is $\frac{2}{3}$ of y and y is $\frac{3}{4}$ of z, what is the ratio of $z : x$?

    (A) 1 : 2
    (B) 1 : 1
    (C) 2 : 1
    (D) 3 : 2
    (E) 4 : 3

15. What fraction of 8 tons is 1,000 lbs?

    (A) $\frac{1}{32}$
    (B) $\frac{1}{16}$
    (C) $\frac{1}{8}$
    (D) $\frac{8}{1}$
    (E) $\frac{16}{1}$

SOLUTIONS

1. **(C)** The team lost 6 games out of 30. $\frac{6}{30} = \frac{1}{5}$

2. **(B)** The man spends $X - Y$ out of X. $\frac{X-Y}{X}$

3. **(A)** 10 minutes elapse by noon, and another 14 after noon, making a total of 24 minutes. There are 60 minutes in an hour. $\frac{24}{60} = \frac{2}{5}$

4. **(E)** One-half earn over $18,000. One-third of the other $\frac{1}{2}$, or $\frac{1}{6}$, earn between $15,000 and $18,000. This accounts for $\frac{1}{2} + \frac{1}{6}$, or $\frac{3}{6} + \frac{1}{6} = \frac{4}{6} = \frac{2}{3}$ of the staff, leaving $\frac{1}{3}$ to earn below $15,000.

5. **(C)** David spends $\frac{1}{4}$ on Monday and $\frac{2}{3}$ of the other $\frac{3}{4}$, or $\frac{1}{2}$, on Tuesday, leaving only $\frac{1}{4}$ for the rest of the week.

6. **(A)** $12 = \frac{3}{4} x$. Multiply each side by $\frac{4}{3}$.
    $16 = x$

7. **(E)** Let the third or shortest section = x. Then the second section = $3x$, and the first section = $9x$. The entire piece of fabric is then $13x$, and the shortest piece represents $\frac{x}{13x}$ or $\frac{1}{13}$ of the entire piece.

8. **(B)** There are four quarts in one gallon.

9. **(D)** The factory employs $M + W$ people, out of which W are women.

10. **(A)** For every 5 votes in favor, 3 were cast against. 5 out of every 8 votes cast were in favor of the motion.

11. **(E)** Remember, a ratio is a fraction. If x is 18 and y is 14, the ratio $x : y$ is 9 : 7, but $x + y$ is 32. The point of this problem is that x and y can take on *many* possible values, just as long as the ratio 9 : 7 is preserved. Given the multiplicity of possible values, it is not possible here to establish *one* definite value for the sum of x and y.

12. **(C)** The ratio of women to the total number of people is 5 : 8. We can set up a proportion. If $\frac{5}{8} = \frac{x}{24}$, then $x = 15$.

13. **(B)** From the previous problem we know that the class contains 15 women and 9 men. In order to have the same number of men and women, 6 additional men would have to enroll.

14. **(C)** There are several ways to attack this problem. If x is $\frac{2}{3}$ of y then y is $\frac{3}{2}$ of x. If y is $\frac{3}{4}$ of z then z is $\frac{4}{3}$ of y. Therefore, y is $\frac{3}{2}x$ and z is $2x$. The ratio of $z : x$ is 2 : 1. You could also plug in a real number and solve. If x is 2, figure out what y and z would be. y would be 3 and z would be 4, so the ratio of z to x is 2 : 1.

15. **(B)** A ton contains 2,000 pounds. So the fraction would be $\frac{1,000}{16,000}$, which is $\frac{1}{16}$.

4. VARIATION

DIRECT VARIATION. Two quantities are said to vary directly if they change in the same direction. As one increases, the other increases.

For example, the amount owed to the milkman varies directly with the number of quarts of milk purchased. The amount of sugar needed in a recipe varies directly with the amount of butter used. The number of inches between two cities on a map varies directly with the number of miles between the cities.

Q If a two-ounce package of peanuts costs 20¢, what is the cost of a pound of peanuts?

A Here you are comparing cents with ounces, so $\frac{20}{2} = \frac{x}{16}$

In solving a proportion, it is easiest to cross-multiply, remembering that the product of the means (the second and third terms of a proportion) is equal to the product of the extremes (the first and last terms of a proportion).

$2x = 320$

$x = 160$

Remember that the original units were cents, so the cost is $1.60.

When two fractions are equal, as in a proportion, it is sometimes easier to see what change has taken place in the given numerator or denominator and then to apply the same change to the missing term. In keeping fractions equal, the change will always involve multiplying or dividing by a constant. In the previous example, the denominator was changed from 2 to 16. This involved multiplication by 8; therefore, the numerator (20) must also be multiplied by 8, giving 160 as an answer without any written work necessary. Since time is a very important factor in this type of examination, shortcuts such as this could be critical.

Q If a truck can carry m pounds of coal, how many trucks are needed to carry p pounds of coal?

A You are comparing trucks with pounds. This again is a direct variation, because the number of trucks increases as the number of pounds increases.

$\frac{1}{m} = \frac{x}{p}$

$mx = p$

$x = \frac{p}{m}$

INVERSE VARIATION. Two quantities are said to vary inversely if they change in opposite directions. As one increases, the other decreases.

For example, the number of workers hired to paint a house varies inversely with the number of days the job will take. A doctor's stock of flu vaccine varies inversely with the number of patients injected. The number of days a given supply of cat food lasts varies inversely with the number of cats being fed.

> **TIP**
> Whenever two quantities vary directly, you can find a missing term by setting up a proportion. However, be very careful to compare the same units, in the same order, on each side of the equal sign.

> **TIP**
> Whenever two quantities vary inversely, you can find a missing term by using multiplication. Multiply the first quantity by the second and set the products equal.

Q If a case of cat food can feed 5 cats for 4 days, how long would it feed 8 cats?

A Since this is a case of inverse variation (the more cats, the fewer days), multiply the number of cats by the number of days in each instance and set them equal.

$5 \times 4 = 8 \times x$

$20 = 8x$

$2\frac{1}{2} = x$

EXERCISE: VARIATION

Directions: Work out each problem. Circle the letter that appears before your answer.

1. If 60 feet of uniform wire weighs 80 pounds, what is the weight of 2 yards of the same wire?

    (A) $2\frac{2}{3}$
    (B) 6
    (C) 2400
    (D) 120
    (E) 8

2. A gear 50 inches in diameter turns a smaller gear 30 inches in diameter. If the larger gear makes 15 revolutions, how many revolutions does the smaller gear make in that time?

    (A) 9
    (B) 12
    (C) 20
    (D) 25
    (E) 30

3. If x men can do a job in h days, how long would y men take to do the same job?

    (A) $\dfrac{x}{h}$
    (B) $\dfrac{xh}{y}$
    (C) $\dfrac{hy}{x}$
    (D) $\dfrac{xy}{h}$
    (E) $\dfrac{x}{y}$

4. If a furnace uses 40 gallons of oil in a week, how many gallons, to the nearest gallon, does it use in 10 days?

    (A) 57
    (B) 4
    (C) 28
    (D) 400
    (E) 58

5. A recipe requires 13 ounces of sugar and 18 ounces of flour. If only 10 ounces of sugar are used, how much flour, to the nearest ounce, should be used?

   (A) 13
   (B) 23
   (C) 24
   (D) 14
   (E) 15

6. If a car can drive 25 miles on two gallons of gasoline, how many gallons will be needed for a trip of 150 miles?

   (A) 12
   (B) 3
   (C) 6
   (D) 7
   (E) 10

7. A school has enough bread to feed 30 children for 4 days. If 10 more children are added, how many days will the bread last?

   (A) $5\frac{1}{3}$
   (B) $1\frac{1}{3}$
   (C) $2\frac{2}{3}$
   (D) 12
   (E) 3

8. At c cents per pound, what is the cost of a ounces of salami?

   (A) $\frac{c}{a}$
   (B) $\frac{a}{c}$
   (C) ac
   (D) $\frac{ac}{16}$
   (E) $\frac{16c}{a}$

9. If 3 miles are equivalent to 4.83 kilometers, then 11.27 kilometers are equivalent to how many miles?

   (A) $7\frac{1}{3}$
   (B) $2\frac{1}{3}$
   (C) 7
   (D) 5
   (E) $6\frac{1}{2}$

10. If p pencils cost d dollars, how many pencils can be bought for c cents?

    (A) $\frac{100pc}{d}$
    (B) $\frac{pc}{100d}$
    (C) $\frac{pd}{c}$
    (D) $\frac{pc}{d}$
    (E) $\frac{cd}{p}$

SOLUTIONS

1. **(E)** You are comparing *feet* with pounds. The more feet the more pounds. This is DIRECT. Remember to change yards to feet:
$$\frac{60}{80} = \frac{6}{x}$$
$$60x = 480$$
$$x = 8$$

2. **(D)** The larger a gear, the fewer times it revolves in a given period of time. This is INVERSE.
$$50 \cdot 15 = 30 \cdot x$$
$$750 = 30x$$
$$25 = x$$

3. **(B)** The more men, the fewer days. This is INVERSE.
$$x \cdot h = y \cdot ?$$
$$\frac{xh}{y} = ?$$

4. **(A)** The more days, the more oil. This is DIRECT. Remember to change the week to 7 days.
$$\frac{40}{7} = \frac{x}{10}$$
$$7x = 400$$
$$x = 57\frac{1}{7}$$

5. **(D)** The more sugar, the more flour. This is DIRECT.
$$\frac{13}{18} = \frac{10}{x}$$
$$13x = 180$$
$$x = 13\frac{11}{13}$$

6. **(A)** The more miles, the more gasoline. This is DIRECT.
$$\frac{25}{2} = \frac{150}{x}$$
$$25x = 300$$
$$x = 12$$

7. **(E)** The more children, the fewer days. This is INVERSE.
$$30 \cdot 4 = 40 \cdot x$$
$$120 = 40x$$
$$3 = x$$

8. **(D)** The more salami, the more it will cost. This is DIRECT. Remember to change the pound to 16 ounces.
$$\frac{c}{16} = \frac{x}{a}$$
$$x = \frac{ac}{16}$$

9. **(C)** The more miles, the more kilometers. This is DIRECT.
$$\frac{3}{4.83} = \frac{x}{11.27}$$
$$4.83x = 33.81$$
$$x = 7$$

10. **(B)** The more pencils, the more cost. This is DIRECT. Remember to change dollars to cents.
$$\frac{p}{100d} = \frac{x}{c}$$
$$x = \frac{pc}{100d}$$

5. FINDING PERCENTS

PERCENT EQUIVALENTS. "Percent" means "out of 100." If you understand this concept, it becomes very easy to change a percent to an equivalent decimal or fraction.

$$5\% = \frac{5}{100} = .05$$

$$2.6\% = \frac{2.6}{100} = .026$$

$$c\% = \frac{c}{100} = \frac{1}{100} \cdot c = .01c$$

$$\frac{1}{2}\% = \frac{\frac{1}{2}}{100} = \frac{1}{100} \cdot \frac{1}{2} = \frac{1}{100} \cdot .5 = .005$$

$$37\% = .37$$

$$.043 = 4.3\%$$

$$75\% = \frac{75}{100} = \frac{3}{4}$$

$$\frac{1}{8} = \frac{1}{8} \cdot 100\% = \frac{100}{8}\% = 12\frac{1}{2}\%$$

Certain fractional equivalents of common percents occur frequently enough that they should be memorized. Learning the values in the following table will make your work with percent problems much easier.

Percent–Fraction Equivalent Table

$$50\% = \frac{1}{2} \qquad 33\frac{1}{3}\% = \frac{1}{3} \qquad 12\frac{1}{2}\% = \frac{1}{8}$$

$$25\% = \frac{1}{4} \qquad 66\frac{2}{3}\% = \frac{2}{3} \qquad 37\frac{1}{2}\% = \frac{3}{8}$$

$$75\% = \frac{3}{4} \qquad 20\% = \frac{1}{5} \qquad 62\frac{1}{2}\% = \frac{5}{8}$$

$$10\% = \frac{1}{10} \qquad 40\% = \frac{2}{5} \qquad 87\frac{1}{2}\% = \frac{7}{8}$$

$$30\% = \frac{3}{10} \qquad 60\% = \frac{3}{5} \qquad 16\frac{2}{3}\% = \frac{1}{6}$$

$$70\% = \frac{7}{10} \qquad 80\% = \frac{4}{5} \qquad 83\frac{1}{3}\% = \frac{5}{6}$$

$$90\% = \frac{9}{10}$$

Most percentage problems can be solved by using the following proportion:

$$\frac{\%}{100} = \frac{\text{part}}{\text{whole}}$$

Although this method works, it often yields unnecessarily large numbers that are difficult to compute. Following are examples of the three basic types of percent problems and different methods for solving them.

TIP
To change a % to a decimal, remove the % sign and divide by 100. This has the effect of moving the decimal point two places to the LEFT.

TIP
To change a decimal to a %, add the % sign and multiply by 100. This has the effect of moving the decimal point two places to the RIGHT.

TIP
To change a % to a fraction, remove the % sign and divide by 100. This has the effect of putting the % over 100 and reducing the resulting fraction.

TIP
To change a fraction to a %, add the % sign and multiply by 100.

TO FIND A % OF A NUMBER

Q Find 27% of 92.

A

PROPORTION METHOD	SHORT METHOD
$\dfrac{27}{100} = \dfrac{x}{92}$ $100x = 2484$ $x = 24.84$	Change the % to its decimal or fraction equivalent and multiply. Use fractions only when they are among the familiar ones given in the previous chart. $\quad\quad 92$ $\quad\times .27$ $\overline{\quad 644}$ $\ 184\quad$ $\overline{24.84}$

Q Find $12\dfrac{1}{2}\%$ of 96.

A

PROPORTION METHOD	DECIMAL METHOD	FRACTION METHOD
$\dfrac{12\frac{1}{2}}{100} = \dfrac{x}{96}$ $100x = 1200$ $x = 12$	$\quad 96$ $\times .125$ $\overline{\ 480}$ $\ 192\ $ $\ 96\quad$ $\overline{12.000}$	$\dfrac{1}{8} \cdot 96 = 12$

Which method is easiest? It really pays to memorize those fractional equivalents.

TO FIND A NUMBER WHEN A % OF IT IS GIVEN

Q 7 is 5% of what number?

A

PROPORTION METHOD	SHORTER METHOD
$\dfrac{5}{100} = \dfrac{7}{x}$ $5x = 700$ $x = 140$	Translate the problem into an algebraic equation. In doing this, the % must be written as a fraction or decimal. $7 = .05x$ $700 = 5x$ $140 = x$

Q 20 is $33\frac{1}{3}$% of what number?

A PROPORTION METHOD　　　　　SHORT METHOD

$$\frac{33\frac{1}{3}}{100} = \frac{20}{x} \qquad\qquad 20 = \frac{1}{3}x$$

$$33\frac{1}{3}x = 2000 \qquad\qquad 60 = x$$

$$\frac{100}{3}x = 2000$$

$$100x = 6000$$

$$x = 60$$

Just think of the time you save and the number of extra problems you will get to solve if you know that $33\frac{1}{3}\% = \frac{1}{3}$.

TO FIND WHAT % ONE NUMBER IS OF ANOTHER

Q 90 is what % of 1500?

A PROPORTION METHOD　　　　　SHORT METHOD

$$\frac{x}{100} = \frac{90}{1500}$$

$$1500x = 9000$$

$$15x = 90$$

$$x = 6$$

Put the part over the whole. Reduce the fraction and multiply by 100.

$$\frac{90}{1500} = \frac{9}{150} = \frac{3}{50} \cdot 100 = 6$$

Q 7 is what % of 35?

A PROPORTION METHOD　　　　　SHORT METHOD

$$\frac{x}{100} = \frac{7}{35} \qquad\qquad \frac{7}{35} = \frac{1}{5} = 20\%$$

$$35x = 700$$

$$x = 20$$

Q 18 is what % of 108?

A

PROPORTION METHOD	SHORT METHOD
$\dfrac{x}{100} = \dfrac{18}{108}$	$\dfrac{18}{108} = \dfrac{9}{54} = \dfrac{1}{6} = 16\dfrac{2}{3}\%$
$108x = 1800$	
Time-consuming long division is necessary to get:	Once again, if you know the fraction equivalents of common percents, computation can be done in a few seconds.
$x = 16\dfrac{2}{3}$	

TO FIND A % OVER 100

Q Find 125% of 64.

A

PROPORTION METHOD	DECIMAL METHOD	FRACTION METHOD
$\dfrac{125}{100} = \dfrac{x}{64}$	$\begin{array}{r} 64 \\ \times 1.25 \\ \hline 320 \\ 128 \\ 64 \\ \hline 80.00 \end{array}$	$1\dfrac{1}{4} \cdot 64$
$100x = 8.000$		$\dfrac{5}{\cancel{4}} \cdot \cancel{64}^{16} = 80$
$x = 80$		

Q 36 is 150% of what number?

A

PROPORTION METHOD	DECIMAL METHOD	FRACTION METHOD
$\dfrac{150}{100} = \dfrac{36}{x}$	$36 = 1.50x$	$36 = 1\dfrac{1}{2}x$
$150x = 3600$	$360 = 15x$	$36 = \dfrac{3}{2}x$
$15x = 360$	$24 = x$	$72 = 3x$
$x = 24$		$24 = x$

Q 60 is what % of 50?

A

PROPORTION METHOD	FRACTION METHOD
$\dfrac{x}{100} = \dfrac{60}{50}$	$\dfrac{60}{50} = \dfrac{6}{5} = 1\dfrac{1}{5} = 120\%$
$50x = 6000$	
$5x = 600$	
$x = 120$	

EXERCISE: FINDING PERCENTS

Directions: Work out each problem. Circle the letter that appears before your answer.

1. Write .2% as a decimal.
   (A) .2
   (B) .02
   (C) .002
   (D) 2
   (E) 20

2. Write 3.4% as a fraction.
   (A) $\dfrac{34}{1000}$
   (B) $\dfrac{34}{10}$
   (C) $\dfrac{34}{100}$
   (D) $\dfrac{340}{100}$
   (E) $\dfrac{34}{10,000}$

3. Write $\tfrac{3}{4}$% as a decimal.
   (A) .75
   (B) .075
   (C) .0075
   (D) .00075
   (E) 7.5

4. Find 60% of 70.
   (A) 420
   (B) 4.2
   (C) $116\tfrac{2}{3}$
   (D) 4200
   (E) 42

5. What is 175% of 16?
   (A) $9\tfrac{1}{7}$
   (B) 28
   (C) 24
   (D) 12
   (E) 22

6. What percent of 40 is 16?
   (A) 20
   (B) $2\tfrac{1}{2}$
   (C) $33\tfrac{1}{3}$
   (D) 250
   (E) 40

7. What percent of 16 is 40?
   (A) 20
   (B) $2\tfrac{1}{2}$
   (C) 200
   (D) 250
   (E) 40

8. $4 is 20% of what?
   (A) $5
   (B) $20
   (C) $200
   (D) $5
   (E) $10

9. 12 is 150% of what number?

    (A) 18
    (B) 15
    (C) 6
    (D) 9
    (E) 8

10. How many sixteenths are there in $87\frac{1}{2}\%$?

    (A) 7
    (B) 14
    (C) 3.5
    (D) 13
    (E) 15

SOLUTIONS

1. **(C)** .2% = .002 The decimal point moves to the LEFT two places.

2. **(A)** $3.4\% = \frac{3.4}{100} = \frac{34}{1000}$

3. **(C)** $\frac{3}{4}\% = .75\% = .0075$

4. **(E)** $60\% = \frac{3}{5}$ $\frac{3}{5} \cdot 70 = 42$

5. **(B)** $175\% = 1\frac{3}{4}$ $\frac{7}{4} \cdot 16 = 28$

6. **(E)** $\frac{16}{40} = \frac{2}{5} = 40\%$

7. **(D)** $\frac{40}{16} = \frac{5}{2} = 2\frac{1}{2} = 250\%$

8. **(B)** $20\% = \frac{1}{5}$, so $4 = \frac{1}{5}x$ $20 = x$

9. **(E)** $150\% = 1\frac{1}{2}$ $\frac{3}{2}x = 12$ $3x = 24$ $x = 8$

10. **(B)** $87\frac{1}{2}\% = \frac{7}{8} = \frac{14}{16}$

6. VERBAL PROBLEMS INVOLVING PERCENT

Certain types of business situations are excellent applications of percent.

PERCENT OF INCREASE OR DECREASE

The **percent of increase or decrease** is found by putting the amount of increase or decrease over the original amount and changing this fraction to a percent, as explained in a previous section.

TIP
In word problems, *of* can usually be interpreted to mean *times* (in other words, *multiply*).

Q Over a five-year period, the enrollment at South High dropped from 1,000 students to 800. Find the percent of decrease.

A $\frac{200}{1000} = \frac{20}{100} = 20\%$

Q A company normally employs 100 people. During a slow spell, it fired 20% of its employees. By what percent must it now increase its staff to return to full capacity?

A $20\% = \frac{1}{5}$ $\frac{1}{5} \cdot 100 = 20$

The company now has 100 − 20 = 80 employees. If it then increases by 20, the percent of increase is $\frac{20}{80} = \frac{1}{4}$, or 25%.

DISCOUNT

A **discount** is usually expressed as a percent of the marked price that will be deducted from the marked price to determine the sale price.

Q Bill's Hardware offers a 20% discount on all appliances during a sale week. If they take advantage of the sale, how much must the Russells pay for a washing machine marked at $280?

A LONG METHOD

$$20\% = \frac{1}{5}$$

$$\frac{1}{5} \cdot 280 = \$56 \text{ discount}$$

$280 - \$56 = \$224$ sale price

The danger inherent in this method is that $56 is sure to be among the multiple-choice answers.

SHORTCUT METHOD

If there is a 20% discount, the Russells will pay 80% of the marked price.

$$80\% = \frac{4}{5}$$

$$\frac{4}{5} \cdot 280 = \$224 \text{ sale price}$$

Q A store offers a television set marked at $340 less discounts of 10% and 5%. Another store offers the same set with a single discount of 15%. How much does the buyer save by buying at the better price?

A In the first store, the initial discount means the buyer pays 90% or $\frac{9}{10}$ of 340, which is $306. The additional 5% discount means the buyer pays 95% of $306, or $290.70. Note that the second discount must be figured on the first sale price. Taking 5% off $306 is a smaller amount than taking the additional 5% off $340. The second store will therefore have a lower sale price. In the second store, the buyer will pay 85% of $340, or $289, making the price $1.70 less than in the first store.

COMMISSION

Many salespeople earn money on a commission basis. In order to encourage sales, they are paid a percentage of the value of goods sold. This amount is called a commission.

Q A salesperson at Brown's Department Store is paid $80 per week in salary plus a 4% commission on all her sales. How much will that salesperson earn in a week in which she sells $4,032 worth of merchandise?

A Find 4% of $4,032 and add this amount to $80.

  4032
  .04

$161.28 + \$80 = \$241.28$

CAUTION
Watch out! You should think of zero as an even number.

Q Bill Olson delivers newspapers for a dealer and keeps 8% of all money collected. One month he was able to keep $16. How much did he forward to the newspaper?

A First, determine how much he collected by finding the number that 16 is 8% of.
$$16 = .08x$$
$$1600 = 8x$$
$$200 = x$$
If Bill collected $200 and kept $16, he gave the dealer $200 − $16, or $184.

TAXES

Taxes are a percent of money spent or money earned.

Q Noname County collects a 7% sales tax on automobiles. If the price of a car is $8,532 before taxes, what will this car cost once sales tax is added in?

A Find 7% of $8,532 to determine tax and then add it to $8,532. This can be done in one step by finding 107% of $8,532.

```
    8532
    1.07
   59724
   85320
 $9129.24
```

Q If the tax rate in Anytown is $3.10 per $100, what is the annual real estate tax on a house assessed at $47,200?

A Annual tax = Tax rate × Assessed value
= ($3.10/$100)($47,200)
= (.031)   (47,200)
= $1463.20

EXERCISE: VERBAL PROBLEMS INVOLVING PERCENT

Directions: Work out each problem. Circle the letter that appears before your answer.

1. A suit marked at $80 is sold for $68. What is the rate of discount?

    (A) 15%

    (B) 12%

    (C) $17\frac{11}{17}\%$

    (D) 20%

    (E) 24%

2. What was the original price of a radio that sold for $70 during a 20%-off sale?

    (A) $84

    (B) $56

    (C) $87.50

    (D) $92

    (E) $90

3. How many dollars does a salesperson earn on a sale of s dollars at a commission of $r\%$?

    (A) rs

    (B) $\dfrac{r}{s}$

    (C) $100rs$

    (D) $\dfrac{r}{100s}$

    (E) $\dfrac{rs}{100}$

4. At a selling price of $273, a refrigerator yields a 30% profit on the cost. What selling price will yield a 10% profit on the cost?

    (A) $210

    (B) $231

    (C) $221

    (D) $235

    (E) $240

5. What single discount is equivalent to two successive discounts of 10% and 15%?

    (A) 25%

    (B) 24%

    (C) 24.5%

    (D) 23.5%

    (E) 22%

6. The net price of a certain article is $306 after successive discounts of 15% and 10% off the marked price. What is the marked price?

    (A) $234.09

    (B) $400

    (C) $382.50

    (D) $408

    (E) None of these

7. If a merchant makes a profit of 20% based on the selling price of an article, what percent does the merchant make on the cost?

    (A) 20

    (B) 40

    (C) 25

    (D) 80

    (E) None of these

8. A certain radio costs a merchant $72. At what price must the merchant sell this radio in order to make a profit of 20% of the selling price?
   (A) $86.40
   (B) $92
   (C) $90
   (D) $144
   (E) $148

9. A baseball team has won 40 games out of 60 played. It has 32 more games to play. How many of these must the team win to make its record 75% for the season?
   (A) 26
   (B) 29
   (C) 28
   (D) 30
   (E) 32

10. If prices are reduced 25% and sales increase 20%, what is the net effect on gross receipts?
    (A) They increase by 5%.
    (B) They decrease by 5%.
    (C) They remain the same.
    (D) They increase by 10%.
    (E) They decrease by 10%.

11. A salesperson earns 5% on all sales between $200 and $600, and 8% on all sales over $600. What is her commission in a week in which her sales total $800?
    (A) $20
    (B) $46
    (C) $88
    (D) $36
    (E) $78

12. If the enrollment at State U. was 3,000 in 1965 and 12,000 in 1990, what was the percent of increase in enrollment?
    (A) 125%
    (B) 25%
    (C) 300%
    (D) 400%
    (E) 3%

13. If 6 students, representing $16\frac{2}{3}\%$ of the class, failed algebra, how many students passed the course?
    (A) 48
    (B) 36
    (C) 42
    (D) 30
    (E) 32

14. If 95% of the residents of Coral Estates live in private homes and 40% of these live in air-conditioned homes, what percent of the residents of Coral Estates live in air-conditioned homes?
    (A) 3%
    (B) 30%
    (C) 3.8%
    (D) 40%
    (E) 38%

15. A salesperson receives a salary of $100 a week and a commission of 5% on all sales. What must be the amount of sales for a week in which the salesperson's total weekly income is $360?
    (A) $6,200
    (B) $5,200
    (C) $2,600
    (D) $720
    (E) $560

SOLUTIONS

1. **(A)** The amount of discount is $12. Rate of discount is figured on the original price.

   $$\frac{12}{80} = \frac{3}{20} \quad \frac{3}{20} \cdot 100 = 15\%$$

2. **(C)** $70 represents 80% of the original price.

   $$70 = .80x$$
   $$700 = 8x$$
   $$\$87.50 = x$$

3. **(E)** $r\% = \dfrac{r}{100}$

   The commission is $\dfrac{r}{100} \cdot s = \dfrac{rs}{100}$

4. **(B)** $273 represents 130% of the cost.

   $$1.30x = 273$$
   $$13x = 2730$$
   $$x = \$210 = \text{cost}$$

   The new price will add 10% of cost, or $21, for profit.

   New price = $231

5. **(D)** Work with a simple figure, such as 100.

   First sale price is 90% of $100, or $90.

   Final sale price is 85% of $90, or $76.50

   Total discount is $100 − $76.50 = $23.50

   % of discount = $\dfrac{23.50}{100}$ or 23.5%

6. **(B)** If marked price = m, first sale price = $.85m$ and net price = $.90(.85m) = .765m$

   $$.765m = 306$$
   $$m = 400$$

   In this case, it would be easy to work from the answer choices.

   15% of $400 is $60, making a first sale price of $340.

   10% of this price is $34, making the net price $306.

   Answers (A), (C), and (D) would not give a final answer in whole dollars.

7. **(C)** Use an easy amount of $100 for the selling price. If the profit is 20% of the selling price, or $20, the cost is $80. Profit based on cost is

   $$\frac{20}{80} = \frac{1}{4} = 25\%$$

8. **(C)** If the profit is to be 20% of the selling price, the cost must be 80% of the selling price.

   $$72 = .80x$$
   $$720 = 8x$$
   $$90 = x$$

9. **(B)** The team must win 75%, or $\frac{3}{4}$, of the games played during the entire season. With 60 games played and 32 more to play, the team must win $\frac{3}{4}$ of 92 games in all. $\frac{3}{4} \cdot 92 = 69$. Since 40 games have already been won, the team must win 29 additional games.

10. **(E)** Let original price = p, and original sales = s. Therefore, original gross receipts = ps. Let new price = $.75p$, and new sales = $1.20s$. Therefore, new gross receipts = $.90ps$. Gross receipts are only 90% of what they were.

11. **(D)** 5% of sales between $200 and $600 is .05(400) = $20. 8% of sales over $600 is .08(200) = $16. Total commission = $20 + $16 = $36.

12. **(C)** Increase is 9,000. Percent of increase is figured on original. $\frac{9000}{3000} = 3 = 300\%$

13. **(D)** $16\frac{2}{3}\% = \frac{1}{6}$

    $$6 = \frac{1}{6}x$$
    $$36 = x$$

    36 students in class. 6 failed. 30 passed.

14. **(E)** $40\% = \dfrac{2}{5}$

    $\dfrac{2}{5}$ of 95% = 38%

15. **(B)** Let s = sales

    $$\$100 + .05s = 360$$
    $$.05s = 260$$
    $$5s = 26{,}000$$
    $$s = \$5{,}200$$

7. AVERAGES

ADD, THEN DIVIDE. The concept of average is familiar to most students. To find the average of *n* numbers, simply add the numbers and divide by *n*.

Q Find the average of 32, 50, and 47.

A
```
  32          43
  50       3)129
  47
 ___
 129
```

A more frequently encountered type of average problem will give the average and ask you to find a missing term.

Q The average of three numbers is 43. If two of the numbers are 32 and 50, find the third number.

A Using the definition of average, write the equation

$$\frac{32 + 50 + x}{3} = 43$$
$$32 + 50 + x = 129$$
$$82 + x = 129$$
$$x = 47$$

WEIGHTED AVERAGE. Another concept to understand is the weighted average.

Q Andrea has four grades of 90 and two grades of 80 during the spring semester of calculus. What is her average in the course for this semester?

A
```
  90          or
  90
  90            90 • 4 = 360
  90            80 • 2 = 160
  80                   _____
  80                   6) 520
 ____                        2
 6) 520                    86 ―
       2                     3
    86 ―
       3
```

Be sure to understand that you cannot simply average 90 and 80, since there are more grades of 90 than 80.

AVERAGE RATE. The final concept of average that you should master is average rate. The average rate for a trip is the total distance covered, divided by the total time spent.

Q In driving from New York to Boston, Mr. Portney drove for 3 hours at 40 miles per hour and 1 hour at 48 miles per hour. What was his average rate for this portion of the trip?

A. Average rate = $\dfrac{\text{Total distance}}{\text{Total time}}$

Average rate = $\dfrac{3(40) + 1(48)}{3+1}$

Average rate = $\dfrac{168}{4}$ = 42 miles per hour

Since more of the trip was driven at 40 mph than at 48 mph, the average should be closer to 40 than to 48, which it is. This will help you to check your answer, or to pick out the correct choice in a multiple-choice question.

EXERCISE: AVERAGES

Directions: Work out each problem. Circle the letter that appears before your answer.

1. Dan had an average of 72 on his first four math tests. After taking the next test, his average dropped to 70. Which of the following is his most recent test grade?

    (A) 60
    (B) 62
    (C) 64
    (D) 66
    (E) 68

2. What is the average of $\sqrt{.64}$, .85, and $\frac{9}{10}$?

    (A) $\dfrac{21}{25}$
    (B) 3.25
    (C) 2.55
    (D) 85%
    (E) $\dfrac{4}{5}$

3. The average of two numbers is XY. If the first number is Y, what is the other number?

    (A) $2XY - Y$
    (B) $XY - 2Y$
    (C) $2XY - X$
    (D) X
    (E) $XY - Y$

4. 30 students had an average of X, while 20 students had an average of 80. What is the average for the entire group?

    (A) $\dfrac{X+80}{50}$
    (B) $\dfrac{X+80}{2}$
    (C) $\dfrac{50}{X+80}$
    (D) $\dfrac{3}{5}X + 32$
    (E) $\dfrac{30X + 80}{50}$

5. What is the average of the first 15 positive integers?
   (A) 7
   (B) 7.5
   (C) 8
   (D) 8.5
   (E) 9

6. A man travels a distance of 20 miles at 60 miles per hour and then returns over the same route at 40 miles per hour. What is his average rate for the round trip in miles per hour?
   (A) 50
   (B) 48
   (C) 47
   (D) 46
   (E) 45

7. A number p equals $\frac{3}{2}$ the average of 10, 12, and q. What is q in terms of p?
   (A) $\frac{2}{3}p - 22$
   (B) $\frac{4}{3}p - 22$
   (C) $2p - 22$
   (D) $\frac{1}{2}p + 11$
   (E) $\frac{9}{2}p - 22$

8. Susan has an average of 86 in three examinations. What grade must she receive on her next test to raise her average to 88?
   (A) 94
   (B) 90
   (C) 92
   (D) 100
   (E) 96

9. The heights of the five starters on Redwood High's basketball team are 5'11", 6'3", 6', 6'6", and 6'2". The average height of these players is
   (A) 6'1"
   (B) 6'2"
   (C) 6'3"
   (D) 6'4"
   (E) 6'5"

10. What is the average of all numbers from 1 to 100 that end in 2?
    (A) 46
    (B) 47
    (C) 48
    (D) 50
    (E) None of these

SOLUTIONS

1. **(B)** $\frac{4(72) + x}{5} = 70$

   $288 + x = 350$

   $x = 62$

2. **(D)** In order to average these three numbers, they should all be expressed as decimals.

   $\sqrt{.64} = .8$

   $.85 = .85$

   $\frac{9}{10} = .9$

   Average $= \frac{.8 + .85 + .9}{3} = \frac{2.55}{3} = .85$

   This is equal to 85%.

3. **(A)** $\frac{Y + x}{2} = XY$

   $Y + x = 2XY$

   $x = 2XY - Y$

4. **(D)** $\frac{30(X) + 20(80)}{50} = $ Average

   $\frac{30(X) + 1600}{50} = \frac{3X + 160}{5} = \frac{3}{5}X + 32$

5. **(C)** Positive integers begin with 1.

$$\frac{1+2+3+4+5+6+7+8+9+10+11+12+13+14+15}{15}$$

Since these numbers are evenly spaced, the average will be the middle number, 8.

6. **(B)** Average rate = $\frac{\text{Total distance}}{\text{Total time}}$

Total distance = 20 + 20 = 40

Since time = $\frac{\text{distance}}{\text{time}}$, time for first part of trip is $\frac{20}{60}$, or $\frac{1}{3}$ hour, while time for the second part of trip is $\frac{20}{40}$, or $\frac{1}{2}$ hour.

Total time = $\frac{1}{3} + \frac{1}{2}$, or $\frac{5}{6}$ hour.

Average rate $\frac{40}{\frac{5}{6}} = 40 \cdot \frac{6}{5} = 48$ mph

7. **(C)** $p = \frac{3}{2}\left(\frac{10+12+q}{3}\right)$

$p = \frac{10+12+q}{2}$

$2p = 22 + q$

$2p - 22 = q$

8. **(A)** $\frac{3(86)+x}{4} = 88$

$258 + x = 352$

$x = 94$

9. **(B)**
```
    5'11"
    6' 3"
    6'
    6' 6"
    6' 2"
29'22" = 5) 30' 10"
           6'2"
```

10. **(B)**

$$\frac{2+12+22+32+42+52+62+72+82+92}{10}$$

Since these numbers are equally spaced, the average is the middle number. However, since there is an even number of addends, the average will be halfway between the middle two. Halfway between 42 and 52 is 47.

Chapter 14

SAT Algebra Review

1. SIGNED NUMBERS

To solve algebra problems, you must be able to compute accurately with signed numbers.

Addition: To add signed numbers with the same sign, add the magnitudes of the numbers and keep the same sign. To add signed numbers with different signs, subtract the magnitudes of the numbers and use the sign of the number with the greater magnitude.

Subtraction: Change the sign of the number being subtracted and follow the rules for addition.

Multiplication: If there are an odd number of negative signs, the product is negative. An even number of negative signs gives a positive product.

Division: If the signs are the same, the quotient is positive. If the signs are different, the quotient is negative.

ROAD MAP

- *Signed numbers*
- *Linear equations*
- *Exponents*
- *Quadratic equations*
- *Literal expressions*
- *Roots and radicals*
- *Factoring and algebraic fractions*
- *Problem-solving in algebra*
- *Inequalities*
- *Defined operation problems*

EXERCISE: SIGNED NUMBERS

Directions: Work out each problem. Circle the letter that appears before your answer.

1. When +3 is added to –5, the sum is
   (A) –8
   (B) +8
   (C) –2
   (D) +2
   (E) –15

2. When –4 and –5 are added, the sum is
   (A) –9
   (B) +9
   (C) –1
   (D) +1
   (E) +20

3. Subtract + 3
              – 6
   (A) –3
   (B) +3
   (C) +18
   (D) –9
   (E) +9

4. When –5 is subtracted from +10 the result is
   (A) +5
   (B) +15
   (C) –5
   (D) –15
   (E) –50

5. (–6)(–3) equals
   (A) –18
   (B) +18
   (C) +2
   (D) –9
   (E) +9

6. The product of $(-6)(+\frac{1}{2})(-10)$ is
   (A) $-15\frac{1}{2}$
   (B) $+15\frac{1}{2}$
   (C) –30
   (D) +30
   (E) +120

7. When the product of (–4) and (+3) is divided by (–2), the quotient is
   (A) $\frac{1}{2}$
   (B) $3\frac{1}{2}$
   (C) 6
   (D) $-\frac{1}{2}$
   (E) – 6

SOLUTIONS

1. **(C)** In adding numbers with opposite signs, subtract their magnitudes (5 − 3 = 2) and use the sign of the number with the greater magnitude (negative).

2. **(A)** In adding numbers with the same sign, add their magnitudes (4 + 5 = 9) and keep the same sign.

3. **(E)** Change the sign of the bottom number and follow the rules for addition.

   $$+\quad 3$$
   $$+\ominus 6$$
   $$\overline{+\quad 9}$$

4. **(B)** Change the sign of the bottom number and follow the rules for addition.

   $$+\quad 10$$
   $$+\ominus 5$$
   $$\overline{+\quad 15}$$

5. **(B)** The product of two negative numbers is a positive number.

6. **(D)** The product of an even number of negative numbers is positive.

   $$(\cancel{6})\left(\frac{1}{\cancel{2}}\right)(10) = 30$$

7. **(C)** $(-4)(+3) = -12$

   Dividing a negative number by a negative number gives a positive quotient.

   $$\frac{-12}{-2} = +6$$

2. LINEAR EQUATIONS

The next step in solving algebra problems is mastering linear equations. Whether an equation involves numbers or only letters, the basic steps are the same.

Strategy

1. If there are fractions or decimals, remove them by multiplication.
2. Collect all terms containing the unknown for which you are solving on the same side of the equation. Remember that whenever a term crosses the equal sign from one side of the equation to the other, it must pay a toll. That is, it must change its sign.
3. Determine the coefficient of the unknown by combining similar terms or factoring when terms cannot be combined.
4. Divide both sides of the equation by this coefficient.

TIP
If you have a string of multiplications and divisions to do, if the number of negative factors is *even,* the result will be positive; if the number of negative factors is *odd*, the result will be negative.

Q Solve for x: $5x - 3 = 3x + 5$

A $2x = 8$
$x = 4$

Q Solve for x: $ax - b = cx + d$

A $ax - cx = b + d$
$x(a - c) = b + d$
$$x = \frac{b + d}{a - c}$$

Q Solve for x: $\frac{3}{4}x + 2 = \frac{2}{3}x + 3$

A Multiply by 12: $9x + 24 = 8x + 36$
$$x = 12$$

Q Solve for x: $.7x + .04 = 2.49$

A Multiply by 100: $70x + 4 = 249$
$$70x = 245$$
$$x = 3.5$$

SIMULTANEOUS EQUATIONS. In solving equations with two unknowns, you must work with two equations simultaneously. The object is to eliminate one of the two unknowns, and solve for the resulting single unknown.

Q Solve for x: $2x - 4y = 12$
$3x + 5y = 14$

A Multiply the first equation by 5:
$10x - 20y = 60$

Multiply the second equation by 4:
$12x + 20y = 56$

Since the y terms now have the same numerical coefficients, but with opposite signs, you can eliminate them by adding the two equations. If they had the same signs, you would eliminate them by subtracting the equations.

Add the equations:
$10x - 20y = 10$
$12x + 20y = 56$
$\overline{}$
$22x = 66$
$$x = 3$$

Since you were only asked to solve for x, stop here. If you were asked to solve for both x and y, you would now substitute 3 for x in either equation and solve the resulting equation for y.

$3(3) + 5y = 14$
$9 + 5y = 14$
$5y = 5$
$y = 1$

Q Solve for x:
$ax + by = c$
$dx + ey = f$

A Multiply the first equation by e:
$aex + bey = ce$

Multiply the second equation by b:

$bdx + bey = bf$

Since the y terms now have the same coefficient, with the same sign, eliminate these terms by subtracting the two equations.

$$\begin{aligned} aex + bey &= ce \\ -(bdx + bey &= bf) \\ \hline aex - bdx &= ce - bf \end{aligned}$$

Factor to determine the coefficient of x.

$x(ae - bd) = ce - bf$

Divide by the coefficient of x.

$$x = \frac{ce - bf}{ae - bd}$$

EXERCISE: LINEAR EQUATIONS

Directions: Work out each problem. Circle the letter that appears before your answer.

1. If $5x + 6 = 10$, then x equals

   (A) $\dfrac{16}{5}$

   (B) $\dfrac{5}{16}$

   (C) $-\dfrac{5}{4}$

   (D) $\dfrac{4}{5}$

   (E) $\dfrac{5}{4}$

2. Solve for x: $ax = bx + c, a \neq b$

   (A) $\dfrac{b+c}{a}$

   (B) $\dfrac{c}{a-b}$

   (C) $\dfrac{c}{b-a}$

   (D) $\dfrac{a-b}{c}$

   (E) $\dfrac{c}{a+b}$

3. Solve for k: $\dfrac{k}{3} + \dfrac{k}{4} = 1$

   (A) $\dfrac{11}{8}$

   (B) $\dfrac{8}{11}$

   (C) $\dfrac{7}{12}$

   (D) $\dfrac{12}{7}$

   (E) $\dfrac{1}{7}$

4. If $x + y = 8p$ and $x - y = 6q$, then x is

   (A) $7pq$

   (B) $4p + 3q$

   (C) pq

   (D) $4p - 3q$

   (E) $8p + 6q$

5. If $7x = 3x + 12$, then $2x + 5 =$
   (A) 10
   (B) 11
   (C) 12
   (D) 13
   (E) 14

6. In the equation $y = x^2 + rx - 3$, for what value of r will $y = 11$ when $x = 2$?
   (A) 6
   (B) 5
   (C) 4
   (D) $3\frac{1}{2}$
   (E) 0

7. If $1 + \frac{1}{t} = \frac{t+1}{t}$, what does t equal?
   (A) +1 only
   (B) +1 or −1 only
   (C) +1 or +2 only
   (D) No values
   (E) All values except 0

8. If $.23m = .069$, then $m =$
   (A) .003
   (B) .03
   (C) .3
   (D) 3
   (E) 30

9. If $35rt + 8 = 42rt$, then $rt =$
   (A) $\frac{8}{7}$
   (B) $\frac{8}{87}$
   (C) $\frac{7}{8}$
   (D) $\frac{87}{8}$
   (E) $-\frac{8}{7}$

10. For what values of n is $n + 5$ equal to $n - 5$?
    (A) No value
    (B) 0
    (C) All negative values
    (D) All positive values
    (E) All values

SOLUTIONS

1. **(D)** $5x = 4$ $x = \frac{4}{5}$

2. **(B)** $ax - bx = c$ $x(a-b) = c$ $x = \frac{c}{a-b}$

3. **(D)** Multiply by 12: $4k + 3k = 12$
   $7k = 12$
   $k = \frac{12}{7}$

4. **(B)** Add equations to eliminate y:
   $x + y = 8p$
   $\underline{x - y = 6q}$
   $2x = 8p + 6q$
   Divide by 2: $x = 4p + 3q$

5. **(B)** Solve for x:
   $4x = 12$
   $x = 3$
   $2x + 5 = 2(3) + 5 = 11$

6. **(B)** Substitute given values:
   $11 = 4 + 2r - 3$
   $10 = 2r$
   $r = 5$

7. **(E)** Multiply by t: $t + 1 = t + 1$
   This is an identity and is therefore true for all values. However, since t was a denominator in the given equation, t may not equal 0, because you can never divide by 0.

8. **(C)** Multiply by 100 to make coefficient an integer.
   $23x = 6.9$
   $x = .3$

9. **(A)** Even though this equation has two unknowns, you are asked to solve for *rt*, which may be treated as a single unknown.

$$8 = 7rt$$
$$\frac{8}{7} = rt$$

10. **(A)** There is no number such that when 5 is added, you get the same result as when 5 is subtracted. Do not confuse choices (A) and (B). Choice (B) would mean that the number 0 satisfies the equation, which it does not.

3. EXPONENTS

DEFINITIONS. An **exponent** is a mathematical notation indicating that a number, called the **base**, has been multiplied one or more times by itself. For example, in the term 2^3, the 2 is the base and the ^{3} is the exponent. This term means "2 times 2 times 2" and is read "two to the third power." The word **power** tells how many times the base number appears in the multiplication.

$x^3 = x$ times x times x
$x^2 = x$ times x
$x^1 = x$
$x^0 = 1$

The Rules of Exponents

1. To multiply powers of the same base, add the exponents.
   x^2 times $x^3 = x^{2+3} = x^5$
   x^5 times $x^4 = x^{5+4} = x^9$

2. To divide powers of the same base, subtract the exponent of the divisor from the exponent of the dividend.
   $$\frac{x^6}{x^2} = x^{6-2} = x^4$$
   $$\frac{x^{10}}{x^3} = x^{10-3} = x^7$$

3. To find the power of a power, multiply the exponents.
   $(x^2)^3 = x^{(2)(3)} = x^6$
   $(x^3 y^5)^2 = x^{(3)(2)} y^{(5)(2)} = x^6 y^{10}$

> **TIP**
> Commit to memory small powers of small numbers that come up in many questions. For example: The powers of 2: 2, 4, 8, 16, 32...; The powers of 3: 3, 9, 27, 81,... and so on.

A variable base with an even exponent has two values, one positive and one negative.

$x^2 = 25$ x could be positive 5 or negative 5.

A variable base can be zero (unless otherwise stated in the problem). In that case, no matter what the exponent, the value of the term is zero.

Is x^4 always greater than x^2? No; if x is zero, then x^4 and x^2 are equal.

When the base is a fraction between 0 and 1, the larger the exponent, the smaller the value of the term.

Which is greater, $(\frac{37}{73})$ or $(\frac{37}{73})^2$? The correct answer is $(\frac{37}{73})$. $(\frac{37}{73})$ is almost $\frac{1}{2}$, while $(\frac{37}{73})^2$ is about $\frac{1}{4}$.

EXERCISE: EXPONENTS

Directions: Work out the problem. Circle the letter that appears before your answer.

1. If x and y are not equal to 0, then $x^{12}y^6$ must be
   I. Positive
   II. Negative
   III. An integer
   IV. A mixed fraction
   (A) I only
   (B) II only
   (C) III only
   (D) IV only
   (E) I and III

2. $(x^2y^3)^4 =$
   (A) x^6y^7
   (B) x^8y^{12}
   (C) $x^{12}y^8$
   (D) x^2y
   (E) x^6y^9

3. $\frac{x^{16}y^6}{x^4y^2} =$
   (A) $x^{20}y^8$
   (B) x^4y^3
   (C) x^5y^6
   (D) $x^{12}y^3$
   (E) $x^{12}y^4$

4. If $x^4 = 16$ and $y^2 = 36$, then the *maximum* possible value for $x - y$ is
   (A) -20
   (B) 20
   (C) -4
   (D) 6
   (E) 8

5. $p^8 \times q^4 \times p^4 \times q^8 =$
   (A) $p^{12}q^{12}$
   (B) p^4q^4
   (C) $p^{32}q^{32}$
   (D) $p^{64}q^{64}$
   (E) $p^{16}q^{16}$

SOLUTIONS

1. **(A)** If x and y are not 0, then the even exponents would force x^{12} and y^6 to be positive.

2. **(B)** To raise a power to a power, multiply the exponents. $x^{(2)(4)}y^{(3)(4)} = x^8y^{12}$

3. **(E)** All fractions are implied division. When dividing terms with a common base and different exponents, subtract the exponents. $16 - 4 = 12$ and $6 - 2 = 4$.

4. **(E)** x could be positive 2 or negative 2. y could be positive 6 or negative 6. The four possible values for $x - y$ are as follows:

   $2 - 6 = -4$
   $2 - (-6) = 8$
   $-2 - 6 = -8$
   $-2 - (-6) = 4$
   The maximum value would be 8.

5. **(A)** The multiplication signs do not change the fact that this is the multiplication of terms with a common base and different exponents. Solve this kind of problem by adding the exponents.
   $p^{8+4} \times q^{4+8} = p^{12}q^{12}$

4. QUADRATIC EQUATIONS

ROOTS AND FACTORING. In solving quadratic equations, remember that there will always be two roots, even though these roots may be equal. A complete quadratic equation is of the form 0 and, in the SAT, can always be solved by factoring.

Q Factor: $x^2 + 7x + 12 = 0$

A $(x \quad)(x \quad) = 0$

The last term of the equation is positive; therefore, both factors must have the same sign, since the last two terms multiply to a positive product. The middle term is also positive; therefore, both factors must be positive, since they also add to a positive sum.
$(x + 4)(x + 3) = 0$
If the product of two factors is 0, each factor may be set equal to 0, yielding the values for x of -4 or -3

Q Factor: $x^2 + 7x - 18 = 0$

A $(x \quad)(x \quad) = 0$

Now you are looking for two numbers with a product of -18; therefore, they must have opposite signs. To yield +7 as a middle coefficient, the numbers must be +9 and −2.
$(x + 9)(x - 2) = 0$
This equation gives the roots −9 and +2.

Incomplete quadratic equations are those in which b or c is equal to 0.

Q Solve for x: $x^2 - 16 = 0$

A $x^2 = 16$
$x = \pm 4$ Remember, there must be 2 roots.

Q Solve for x: $4x^2 - 9 = 0$

A $4x^2 = 9$

$x^2 = \dfrac{9}{4}$

$x = \pm \dfrac{3}{2}$

Q Solve for x: $x^2 + 4x = 0$

A Never divide through an equation by the unknown, as this would yield an equation of lower degree having fewer roots than the original equation. Always factor this type of equation.
$x(x + 4) = 0$
The roots are 0 and −4.

Q Solve for x: $4x^2 - 9x = 0$

A $x(4x - 9) = 0$

The roots are 0 and $\dfrac{9}{4}$.

CAUTION

Don't forget: In working with any equation, if you move a term from one side of the equal sign to the other, you must change its sign.

RADICALS. In solving equations containing radicals, always get the radical alone on one side of the equation; then square both sides to remove the radical and solve. Remember that all solutions to radical equations must be checked, as squaring both sides may sometimes result in extraneous roots.

Q Solve for x: $\sqrt{x+5} = 7$
A $x + 5 = 49$
$x = 44$
Checking, we have $\sqrt{49} = 7$, which is true.

Q Solve for x: $\sqrt{x} = -6$
A $x = 36$
Checking, we have $\sqrt{36} = -6$, which is not true, as the radical sign means the positive, or principal, square root only. $\sqrt{36} = 6$, not -6, and therefore this equation has no solution.

Q Solve for x: $\sqrt{x^2+6} - 3 = x$
A $\sqrt{x^2+6} - 3 = x$

$$\sqrt{x^2+6} = x+3$$

$$x^2 + 6 = x^2 + 6x + 9$$

$$6 = 6x + 9$$

$$-3 = 6x$$

$$-\frac{1}{2} = x$$

Checking, we have $\sqrt{6\frac{1}{4}} - 3 = -\frac{1}{2}$

$$\sqrt{\frac{25}{4}} - 3 = -\frac{1}{2}$$

$$\frac{5}{2} - 3 = -\frac{1}{2}$$

$$2\frac{1}{2} - 3 = -\frac{1}{2}$$

$$-\frac{1}{2} = -\frac{1}{2}$$

This is a true statement. Therefore, $-\frac{1}{2}$ is a true root.

EXERCISE: QUADRATIC EQUATIONS

Directions: Work out each problem. Circle the letter that appears before your answer.

1. Solve for x: $x^2 - 2x - 15 = 0$
   (A) $+5$ or -3
   (B) -5 or $+3$
   (C) -5 or -3
   (D) $+5$ or $+3$
   (E) None of these

2. Solve for x: $x^2 + 12 = 8x$
   (A) $+6$ or -2
   (B) -6 or $+2$
   (C) -6 or -2
   (D) $+6$ or $+2$
   (E) None of these

3. Solve for x: $4x^2 = 12$
   (A) $\sqrt{3}$
   (B) 3 or -3
   (C) $\sqrt{3}$ or $-\sqrt{3}$
   (D) $\sqrt{3}$ or $\sqrt{-3}$
   (E) 9 or -9

4. Solve for x: $3x^2 = 4x$
   (A) $\dfrac{4}{3}$
   (B) $\dfrac{4}{3}$ or 0
   (C) $-\dfrac{4}{3}$ or 0
   (D) $\dfrac{4}{3}$ or $-\dfrac{4}{3}$
   (E) None of these

5. Solve for x: $\sqrt{x^2 + 7} - 2 = x - 1$
   (A) No values
   (B) $\dfrac{1}{3}$
   (C) $-\dfrac{1}{3}$
   (D) -3
   (E) 3

SOLUTIONS

1. **(A)** $(x - 5)(x + 3) = 0$
   $x = 5$ or -3

2. **(D)** $x^2 - 8x + 12 = 0$
   $(x - 6)(x - 2) = 0$
   $x = 6$ or 2

3. **(C)** $x^2 = 3$
   $x = \pm\sqrt{3}$

4. **(B)** $3x^2 - 4x = 0$
   $x(3x - 4) = 0$
   $x = 0$ or $\dfrac{4}{3}$

5. **(E)** $\sqrt{x^2 + 7} = x + 1$
   $x^2 + 7 = x^2 + 2x + 1$
   $6 = 2x$
   $x = 3$

   Checking: $\sqrt{16} - 2 = 3 - 1$
   $4 - 2 = 3 - 1$
   $2 = 2$

5. LITERAL EXPRESSIONS

If you can compute with numbers, working with letters should be easy. The computational processes are exactly the same. Just think of how you would do the problem with numbers and do exactly the same thing with letters.

Q Find the number of inches in 2 feet 5 inches.

A Since there are 12 inches in a foot, multiply 2 feet by 12 to change it to 24 inches and then add 5 more inches, giving an answer of 29 inches.

Q Find the number of inches in f feet and i inches.

A Doing exactly as you did above, multiply f by 12, giving $12f$ inches, and add i more inches, giving an answer of $12f + i$ inches.

Q A telephone call from New York to Chicago costs 85 cents for the first three-minutes and 21 cents for each additional minute. Find the cost of an eight-minute call at this rate.

A The first three minutes cost 85 cents. There are five additional minutes above the first three. These five are billed at 21 cents each, for a cost of $1.05. The total cost is $1.90.

Q A telephone call costs c cents for the first three minutes and d cents for each additional minute. Find the cost of a call which lasts m minutes if $m > 3$.

A The first three minutes cost c cents. The number of *additional* minutes is $(m - 3)$. These are billed at d cents each, for a cost of $d(m - 3)$ or $dm - 3d$. Thus the total cost is $c + dm - 3d$. Remember that the first three minutes have been paid for in the basic charge; therefore, you must subtract from the total number of minutes to find the *additional* minutes.

> **CAUTION**
> When people analyze statistics, they sometimes speak as if the mean, median, and mode are interchangeable—but they're not. Be careful to keep in mind the differences among these three terms.

EXERCISE: LITERAL EXPRESSIONS

Directions: Work out each problem. Circle the letter that appears before your answer.

1. David had d dollars. After a shopping trip, he returned with c cents. How many cents did he spend?

    (A) $d - c$
    (B) $c - d$
    (C) $100d - c$
    (D) $100c - d$
    (E) $d - 100c$

2. How many ounces are there in p pounds and q ounces?

    (A) $\dfrac{p}{16} + q$
    (B) pq
    (C) $p + 16q$
    (D) $p + q$
    (E) $16p + q$

3. How many passengers can be seated on a plane with r rows, if each row consists of d double seats and t triple seats?

   (A) rdt
   (B) $rd + rt$
   (C) $2dr + 3tr$
   (D) $3dr + 2tr$
   (E) $rd + t$

4. How many dimes are there in $4x - 1$ cents?

   (A) $40x - 10$
   (B) $\dfrac{2}{5}x - \dfrac{1}{10}$
   (C) $40x - 1$
   (D) $4x - 1$
   (E) $20x - 5$

5. If u represents the tens' digit of a certain number and t represents the units' digit, then the number with the digits reversed can be represented by

   (A) $10t + u$
   (B) $10u + t$
   (C) tu
   (D) ut
   (E) $t + u$

6. Joe spent k cents of his allowance and has r cents left. What was his allowance in dollars?

   (A) $k + r$
   (B) $k - r$
   (C) $100(k + r)$
   (D) $\dfrac{k + r}{100}$
   (E) $100kr$

7. If p pounds of potatoes cost $\$k$, find the cost (in cents) of one pound of potatoes.

   (A) $\dfrac{k}{p}$
   (B) $\dfrac{k}{100p}$
   (C) $\dfrac{p}{k}$
   (D) $\dfrac{100k}{p}$
   (E) $\dfrac{100p}{k}$

8. Mr. Rabner rents a car for d days. He pays m dollars per day for each of the first 7 days, and half that rate for each additional day. Find the total charge if $d > 7$.

   (A) $m + 2m(d - 7)$
   (B) $m + \dfrac{m}{2}(d - 7)$
   (C) $7m + \dfrac{m}{2}(d - 7)$
   (D) $7m + \dfrac{md}{2}$
   (E) $7m + 2md$

9. A salesperson earns 900 dollars per month plus a 10% commission on all sales over 1,000 dollars. One month she sells r dollars' worth of merchandise. How many dollars does she earn that month?

   (A) $800 + .1r$
   (B) $800 - .1r$
   (C) $900 + 1r$
   (D) $900 - .1r$
   (E) $810 + .1r$

10. Elliot's allowance was just raised to k dollars per week. He gets a raise of c dollars per week every 2 years. How much will his allowance be per week y years from now?

    (A) $k + cy$
    (B) $k + 2cy$
    (C) $k + \dfrac{1}{2}cy$
    (D) $k + 2c$
    (E) $ky + 2c$

SOLUTIONS

1. **(C)** Since the answer is to be in cents, change d dollars to cents by multiplying it by 100 and subtract from that the c cents he spent.

2. **(E)** There are 16 ounces in a pound. Therefore, you must multiply p pounds by 16 to change it to ounces and then add q more ounces.

3. **(C)** Each double seat holds 2 people, so d double seats hold $2d$ people. Each triple seat holds 3 people, so t triple seats hold $3t$ people. Therefore, each row holds $2d + 3t$ people. There are r rows, so multiply the number of people in each row by r.

4. **(B)** To change cents to dimes, divide by 10.
$$\frac{4x-1}{10} = \frac{4}{10}x - \frac{1}{10} = \frac{2}{5}x - \frac{1}{10}$$

5. **(A)** The original number would be $10u + t$. The number with the digits reversed would be $10t + u$.

6. **(D)** Joe's allowance was $k + r$ cents. To change this to dollars, divide by 100.

7. **(D)** This can be solved by using a proportion. Remember to change $\$k$ to $100k$ cents.
$$\frac{p}{100k} = \frac{1}{x}$$
$$px = 100k$$
$$x = \frac{100k}{p}$$

8. **(C)** He pays m dollars for each of 7 days, for a total of $7m$ dollars. Then he pays $\frac{1}{2}m$ dollars for $(d-7)$ days, for a cost of $\frac{m}{2}(d-7)$.
The total charge is $7m + \frac{m}{2}(d-7)$.

9. **(A)** She gets a commission of 10% of $(r-1000)$, or $.1(r-1000)$, which is $.1r - 100$. Adding this to 900 yields $800 + .1r$.

10. **(C)** Since he gets a raise only every 2 years, in y years, he will get $\frac{1}{2}y$ raises. Each raise is c dollars, so with $\frac{1}{2}y$ raises his present allowance will be increased by $c(\frac{1}{2}y)$.

6. ROOTS AND RADICALS

ADDING AND SUBTRACTING. Rules for adding and subtracting radicals are much the same as for adding and subtracting letters. Radicals must be exactly the same if they are to be added or subtracted, and they merely serve as a label that does not change.

$$4\sqrt{2} + 3\sqrt{2} = 7\sqrt{2}$$
$$\sqrt{2} + 2\sqrt{3} \text{ cannot be added.}$$
$$\sqrt{2} + \sqrt{3} \text{ cannot be added.}$$

Sometimes, when radicals are not the same, simplification of one or more radicals will make them the same. Remember that radicals are simplified by removing any perfect square factors.

$$\sqrt{27} + \sqrt{75}$$
$$\sqrt{9 \cdot 3} + \sqrt{25 \cdot 3}$$
$$3\sqrt{3} + 5\sqrt{3} = 8\sqrt{3}$$

MULTIPLYING AND DIVIDING. In multiplying and dividing, treat radicals in the same way as you treat letters. They are factors and must be handled as such.

$$\sqrt{2} \cdot \sqrt{3} = \sqrt{6}$$

$$2\sqrt{5} \cdot 3\sqrt{7} = 6\sqrt{35}$$

$$(2\sqrt{3})^2 = 2\sqrt{3} \cdot 2\sqrt{3} = 4 \cdot 3 = 12$$

$$\frac{\sqrt{75}}{\sqrt{3}} = \sqrt{25} = 5$$

$$\frac{10\sqrt{3}}{5\sqrt{3}} = 2$$

SIMPLIFYING. To simplify radicals that contain a sum or difference under the radical sign, add or subtract first, then take the square root.

$$\sqrt{\frac{x^2}{9} + \frac{x^2}{16}}$$

$$\sqrt{\frac{16x^2 + 9x^2}{144}} = \sqrt{\frac{25x^2}{144}} = \frac{5x}{12}$$

If you take the square root of each term before combining, you would have $\frac{x}{3} + \frac{x}{4}$, or $\frac{7x}{12}$, which is clearly not the same answer. Remember that $\sqrt{25}$ is 5. However, if you write that $\sqrt{25}$ as $\sqrt{16+9}$, you cannot say it is 4 + 3 or 7. *Always* combine the quantities within a radical sign into a single term before taking the square root.

FINDING SQUARE ROOTS. To find the number of digits in the square root of a number, remember that the first step in the procedure for finding a square root is to pair off the numbers in the radical sign on either side of the decimal point. Every pair of numbers under the radical gives one number in the answer.

$\sqrt{32\ 14\ 89}$ will have 3 digits.

Q The square root of 61504 is exactly

(A) 245
(B) 246
(C) 247
(D) 248
(E) 249

A The only answer among the choices which will end in 4 when squared is (D).

TIP

If you are given several choices for $\sqrt{321489}$, look first for a three-digit number. If there is only one among the answers, that is the one you should select. If there is more than one, you will have to reason further.

TIP

If a number ends in 9, such as in the example, its square root would have to end in a digit that would end in 9 when multiplied by itself. This might be either 3 or 7. Only one of these would probably be among the choices, as very few SAT problems call for much computation.

EXERCISE: ROOTS AND RADICALS

Directions: Work out each problem. Circle the letter that appears before your answer.

1. What is the sum of $\sqrt{12} + \sqrt{27}$?
   (A) $\sqrt{29}$
   (B) $3\sqrt{5}$
   (C) $13\sqrt{3}$
   (D) $5\sqrt{3}$
   (E) $7\sqrt{3}$

2. What is the difference between $\sqrt{150}$ and $\sqrt{54}$?
   (A) $2\sqrt{6}$
   (B) $16\sqrt{6}$
   (C) $\sqrt{96}$
   (D) $6\sqrt{2}$
   (E) $8\sqrt{6}$

3. What is the product of $\sqrt{18x}$ and $\sqrt{2x}$?
   (A) $6x^2$
   (B) $6x$
   (C) $36x$
   (D) $36x^2$
   (E) $6\sqrt{x}$

4. If $\frac{1}{x} = \sqrt{.25}$, what does x equal?
   (A) 2
   (B) .5
   (C) .2
   (D) 20
   (E) 5

5. If $n = 3.14$, find n^3 to the nearest hundredth.
   (A) 3.10
   (B) 30.96
   (C) 309.59
   (D) 3095.91
   (E) 30959.14

6. The square root of 24336 is exactly
   (A) 152
   (B) 153
   (C) 155
   (D) 156
   (E) 158

7. The square root of 306.25 is exactly
   (A) .175
   (B) 1.75
   (C) 17.5
   (D) 175
   (E) 1750

8. Divide $6\sqrt{45}$ by $3\sqrt{5}$.
   (A) 9
   (B) 4
   (C) 54
   (D) 15
   (E) 6

9. $\sqrt{\dfrac{y^2}{25} + \dfrac{y^2}{16}} =$

(A) $\dfrac{2y}{9}$

(B) $\dfrac{9y}{20}$

(C) $\dfrac{y}{9}$

(D) $\dfrac{y\sqrt{41}}{20}$

(E) $\dfrac{41y}{20}$

10. $\sqrt{a^2 + b^2}$ is equal to

(A) $a + b$
(B) $a - b$
(C) $(a + b)(a - b)$
(D) $\sqrt{a^2} + \sqrt{b^2}$
(E) None of these

SOLUTIONS

1. **(D)** $\sqrt{12} = \sqrt{4}\sqrt{3} = 2\sqrt{3}$
$\sqrt{27} = \sqrt{9}\sqrt{3} = 3\sqrt{3}$
$2\sqrt{3} + 3\sqrt{3} = 5\sqrt{3}$

2. **(A)** $\sqrt{150} = \sqrt{25}\sqrt{6} = 5\sqrt{6}$
$\sqrt{54} = \sqrt{9}\sqrt{6} = 3\sqrt{6}$
$5\sqrt{6} - 3\sqrt{6} = 2\sqrt{6}$

3. **(B)** $\sqrt{18x} \cdot \sqrt{2x} = \sqrt{36x^2} = 6x$

4. **(A)** $\sqrt{.25} = .5$
$\dfrac{1}{x} = .5$
$1 = .5x$
$10 = 5x$
$2 = x$

5. **(B)** $(3)^3$ would be 27, so the answer should be a little larger than 27.

6. **(D)** The only answer that will end in 6 when squared is (D).

7. **(C)** The square root of this number must have two digits before the decimal point.

8. **(E)** $\dfrac{6\sqrt{45}}{3\sqrt{5}} = 2\sqrt{9} = 2 \cdot 3 = 6$

9. **(D)** $\sqrt{\dfrac{y^2}{25} + \dfrac{y^2}{16}} = \sqrt{\dfrac{16y^2 + 25y^2}{400}}$
$= \sqrt{\dfrac{41y^2}{400}} = \dfrac{y\sqrt{41}}{20}$

10. **(E)** Never take the square root of a sum separately. There is no way to simplify $\sqrt{a^2 + b^2}$.

7. MONOMIALS AND POLYNOMIALS

When we add a collection of expressions together, each expression is called a *term*. *Monomial* means one term. For example, we might say that $2x + 3y^2 + 7$ is the sum of three terms or three monomials. When we talk about a monomial, we generally mean a term that is just the product of constants and variables, possibly raised to various powers. Examples might be $7, 2x, -3y^2$, and $4x^2z^5$. The constant factor is called the *coefficient* of the variable factor. Thus, in $-3y^2$, -3 is the coefficient of y^2.

If we restrict our attention to monomials of the form Axn, the sums of such terms are called *polynomials* (in one variable). Expressions like $3x + 5$, $2x^2 - 5x + 8$, and $x^4 - 7x^5 - 11$, are all examples of polynomials. The highest power of the variable that appears is called the *degree* of the polynomial. The three examples just given are of degree 1, 2, and 5 respectively.

In evaluating monomials and polynomials for negative values of the variable, the greatest pitfall is keeping track of the minus signs. Always remember that in an expression like $-x^2$, the power 2 is applied to the x, and the minus sign in front should be thought of as (-1) times the expression. If you want to have the power apply to $-x$, you must write $(-x)^2$.

Q Find the value of $3x - x^3 - x^2$, when $x = -2$.

A Substitute -2 every place you see an x, thus:

$$3(-2) - (-2)^3 - (-2)^2 = -6 - (-8) - (+4) = -6 + 8 - 4 = -2.$$

COMBINING MONOMIALS

Monomials with identical variable factors can be added together by adding their coefficients. So $3x^2 + 4x^2 = 7x^2$. of course, subtraction is handled the same way, thus:

$$3x^4 - 9x^4 = -6x^4$$

Monomials are multiplied by taking the product of their coefficients and taking the product of the variable part by adding exponents of factors with like bases. So $(3xy^2)(2xy^3) = 6x^2y^5$.

Monomial fractions can be reduced to lowest terms by dividing out common factors of the coefficients and then using the usual rules for subtraction of exponents in division. An example might be

$$\frac{6x^3y^5}{2x^4y^3} = \frac{3y^2}{x}$$

Q Combine into a single monomial $\frac{8x^3}{4x^2} - 6x$.

A The fraction reduces to $2x$, and $2x - 6x = -4x$.

COMBINING POLYNOMIALS AND MONOMIALS

Polynomials are added or subtracted by just combining like monomial terms in the appropriate manner. Thus,

$(3x^2 - 3x - 4) + (2x^2 + 5x - 11)$

is summed by removing the parentheses and combining like terms, to yield

$5x^2 + 2x - 15$

In subtraction, when you remove the parentheses with a minus sign in front, be careful to change the signs of *all* the terms within the parentheses. So:

$(3x^2 - 3x - 4) - (2x^2 + 5x - 11)$
$= 3x^2 - 3x - 4 - 2x^2 - 5x + 11$
$= x^2 - 8x + 7$

(Did you notice that $3x^2 - 2x^2 = 1x^2$ but the "1" is not shown?)

To multiply a polynomial by a monomial, use the distributive law to multiply each term in the polynomial by the monomial factor. For example, $2x(2x^2 + 5x - 11) = 4x^3 + 10x^2 - 22x$.

When multiplying a polynomial by a polynomial, you are actually repeatedly applying the distributive law to form all possible products of the terms in the first polynomial with the terms in the second polynomial. The most common use of this is in multiplying two *binomials* (polynomials with two terms), such as $(x + 3)(x - 5)$. In this case, there are four terms in the result, $x \times x = x^2$; $x(-5) = -5x$; $3 \times x = 3x$; and, $3 \times (-5) = -15$; but the two middle terms are added together to give $-2x$. Thus, the product is $x^2 - 2x - 15$.

This process is usually remembered as the FOIL method. That is, form the products of First, Outer, Inner, Last, as shown in the figure below.

$$(x + 3)(x - 5) = x^2 + (-5x + 3x) - 15$$

Q: If d is an integer, and $(x + 2)(x + d) = x^2 - kx - 10$, what is the value of $k + d$?

A: The product of the two last terms, $2d$, must be -10. Therefore, $d = -5$. If $d = -5$, then the sum of the outer and inner products becomes $-5x + 2x = -3x$, which equals $-kx$. Hence, $k = 3$, and $k + d = 3 + (-5) = -2$.

FACTORING MONOMIALS

Factoring a monomial simply involves reversing the distributive law. For example, if you are looking at $4x^2 + 12xy$, you should see that $4x$ is a factor of both terms. Hence, you could just as well write this as $4x(x + 3y)$. Multiplication using the distributive law will restore the original formulation.

Q If $3x - 4y = -2$, what is the value of $9x - 12y$?

A Although you seem to have one equation in two unknowns, you can still solve the problem, because you do not need to know the values of the individual variables. Just rewrite: $9x - 12y = 3(3x - 4y)$. Since $3x - 4y = -2$, $9x - 12y$ is 3 times -2, or -6.

EXERCISE: MONOMIALS AND POLYNOMIALS

Directions: Circle the letter that appears before your answer.

1. $6x^3(x^2)^3$
   - (A) $6x^7$
   - (B) $6x^8$
   - (C) $6x^9$
   - (D) $6x^{10}$
   - (E) $6x^{12}$

2. $(3w^2y^3)^4$
   - (A) $18w^8y^{12}$
   - (B) $18w^6y^7$
   - (C) $81w^6y^7$
   - (D) $81w^8y^{12}$
   - (E) $81w^8y^7$

3. $5x^3(-3x^8)$
   - (A) $15x^{11}$
   - (B) $-15x^{11}$
   - (C) $-15x^{24}$
   - (D) $15x^{24}$
   - (E) $15x^5$

4. $\dfrac{2}{3}^3$
   - (A) $\dfrac{8}{27}$
   - (B) $\dfrac{6}{9}$
   - (C) $\dfrac{4}{9}$
   - (D) $\dfrac{16}{27}$
   - (E) $\dfrac{16}{9}$

SOLUTIONS

1. **(C)** $6x^3(x^2)^3$
   $= 6 \times x^3 \times (x^2)^3$
   $= 6 \times x^3 \times x^{(2 \times 3)}$
   $= 6 \times x^3 \times x^6$
   $= 6 \times x^9$
   $= 6x^9$

2. **(D)** $(3w^2y^3)^4$
   $= (3)^4 \times w^{(2 \times 4)} \times y^{(3 \times 4)}$
   $= 81 \times w^8 \times y^{12}$
   $= 81w^8y^{12}$

3. **(B)** $5x^3(-3x^8)$
   $= 5 \times x^3 \times (-3) \times x^8$
   $= 5 \times (-3) \times x^3 \times x^8$
   $= -15 \times x^{3+8}$
   $= -15x^{11}$

4. **(A)** $\dfrac{2^3}{3}$
   $= \dfrac{2}{3} \times \dfrac{2}{3} \times \dfrac{2}{3}$
   $= 2 \times 2 \times \dfrac{2}{3} \times 3 \times 3$
   $= \dfrac{2^3}{3^3}$
   $= \dfrac{8}{27}$

8. PROBLEM-SOLVING IN ALGEBRA

When you are working with algebra word problems, remember that before you begin working you should be absolutely certain that you understand precisely what you are to answer. Once this is done, represent what you are looking for algebraically. Write an equation that translates the words of the problem to the symbols of mathematics. Then solve that equation by the techniques reviewed previously.

This section reviews the types of algebra problems most frequently encountered on the SAT. Thoroughly familiarizing yourself with the problems that follow will help you to translate and solve all kinds of verbal problems.

SOLVING TWO LINEAR EQUATIONS IN TWO UNKNOWNS

Many word problems lead to equations in two unknowns. Usually, one needs two equations to solve for both unknowns, although there are exceptions. There are two generally used methods to solve two equations in two unknowns. They are the method of *substitution* and the method of *elimination by addition and subtraction*.

We'll illustrate both methods via example. Here is one that uses the method of substitution.

Q Mr. Green took his four children to the local craft fair. The total cost of their admission tickets was $14. Mr. and Mrs. Molina and their six children had to pay $23. What was the cost of an adult ticket to the craft fair, and what was the cost of a child's ticket?

A Expressing all amounts in dollars, let x = cost of an adult ticket and let y = cost of a child's ticket.

For the Greens:

$x + 4y = 14$

For the Molinas:

$2x + 6y = 23$

The idea of the method of substitution is to solve one equation for one variable in terms of the other and then substitute that solution into the second equation. So we solve the first equation for x, because that is the simplest one to isolate:

$x = 14 - 4y$

and substitute into the second equation:

$2(14 - 4y) + 6y = 23$

This gives us one equation in one unknown that we can solve:

$28 - 8y + 6y = 23$
$-2y = -5; y = 2.5$

Now that we know $y = 2.5$, we substitute this into $x = 14 - 4y$ to get:

$x = 14 - 4(2.5) = 4$

Thus, the adult tickets were $4.00 each, and the children's tickets were $2.50 each.

Here is an example using the method of elimination.

Q Paul and Denise both have after-school jobs. Two weeks ago, Paul worked 6 hours, Denise worked 3 hours, and they earned a total of $39. Last week, Paul worked 12 hours, Denise worked 5 hours, and they earned a total of $75. What is each one's hourly wage?

A Again, let us express all amounts in dollars. Let x = Paul's hourly wage, and let y = Denise's hourly wage.

For the first week:

$6x + 3y = 39$

For the second week:

$12x + 5y = 75$

The idea of the method of elimination is that adding equal quantities to equal quantities gives a true result. So we want to add some multiple of one equation to the other one so that *if we add the two equations together,* one variable will be eliminated. In this case, it is not hard to see that if we multiply the first equation by –2, the coefficient of x will become –12. Now when we add the two equations, x will drop out.

–2 times the first equation is:

$$-12x - 6y = -78$$

the second equation is:

$$12x + 5y = 75$$

adding them:

$$-y = -3$$

Thus, $y = 3$. We now substitute this into either of the two equations. Let's use the first:

$6x + (3)(3) = 39; x = 5$

Thus, Denise makes only $3 per hour, while Paul gets $5.

WORD PROBLEMS IN ONE OR TWO UNKNOWNS

Word problems can be broken down into a number of categories. To do *consecutive integer* problems, you need to remember that consecutive integers differ by 1, so a string of such numbers can be represented as n, $n + 1, n + 2, \ldots$

Consecutive even integers differ by 2, so a string of such numbers can be represented as $n, n + 2, n + 4, \ldots$ Consecutive odd integers also differ by 2! So a string of such numbers can also be represented as $n, n + 2, n + 4, \ldots$

Rate-time-distance problems require you to know the formula $d = rt$. That is, distance equals rate times time.

Here are some examples of several types of word problems.

Q Sibyl is 5 years older than Moira. Three years ago, Sibyl was twice as old as Moira. How old is Sibyl?

A If you have trouble setting up the equations, try using numbers. Suppose that Moira is 11. If Sibyl is 5 years older than Moira, how old is Sibyl? She is 16. You got from 11 to 16 by *adding* 5. So, if S is Sibyl's age and M is Moira's age, $S = M + 5$. Three years ago, Sibyl was $S - 3$, and Moira was $M - 3$. So, from the second sentence, $S - 3 = 2(M - 3)$ or $S - 3 = 2M - 6$; or, adding 3 to both sides,

$S = 2M - 3$

Now, substituting $S = M + 5$,

$M + 5 = 2M - 3$

$M = 8$

Which means Sybil is 8 + 5 = 13.

Q Three consecutive integers are written in increasing order. If the sum of the first and second and twice the third is 93, what is the second number?

A Calling the smallest number x, the second is $x + 1$, and the third is $x + 2$. Therefore,

$$x + (x + 1) + 2(x + 2) = 93$$
$$x + x + 1 + 2x + 4 = 93$$
$$4x + 5 = 93$$
$$4x = 88; x = 22.$$

Hence the middle number is 22 + 1 = 23.

Q It took Andrew 15 minutes to drive downtown at 28 miles per hour to get a pizza. How fast did he have to drive back in order to be home in ten minutes?

A 15 minutes is $\frac{1}{4}$ of an hour. Hence, going 28 miles per hour, the distance to the Pizza Parlor can be computed using the formula $d = rt$; $d = (28)(\frac{1}{4}) = 7$ miles. Since ten minutes is $\frac{1}{6}$ of an hour, we have the equation $7 = r(\frac{1}{6})$ and multiplying by 6, $r = 42$ mph.

FRACTION PROBLEMS

A fraction is a ratio between two numbers. If the value of a fraction is $\frac{2}{3}$, it does not mean the numerator must be 2 and the denominator 3. The numerator and denominator could be 4 and 6, respectively, or 1 and 1.5, or 30 and 45, or any of infinitely many other combinations. All you know is that the ratio of numerator to denominator will be 2 : 3. Therefore, the numerator may be represented by $2x$, the denominator by $3x$, and the fraction by $\frac{2x}{3x}$.

Q The value of a fraction is $\frac{3}{4}$. If 3 is subtracted from the numerator and added to the denominator, the value of the fraction is $\frac{2}{5}$. Find the original fraction.

A Let the original fraction be represented by $\frac{3x}{4x}$. If 3 is subtracted from the numerator and added to the denominator, the new fraction becomes $\frac{3x-3}{4x+3}$. The value of the new fraction is $\frac{2}{5}$.

$$\frac{3x-3}{4x+3} = \frac{2}{5}$$

Cross multiply to eliminate fractions.
$$15x - 15 = 8x + 6$$
$$7x = 21$$
$$x = 3$$

Therefore, the original fraction is
$$\frac{3x}{4x} = \frac{9}{12}$$

EXERCISE: PROBLEM-SOLVING IN ALGEBRA

Directions: Circle the letter that appears before your answer.

1. A box contains five blocks numbered 1, 2, 3, 4, and 5. Johnnie picks a block and replaces it. Lisa then picks a block. What is the probability that the sum of the numbers they picked is even?

   (A) $\dfrac{9}{25}$ (C) $\dfrac{1}{2}$ (E) $\dfrac{3}{5}$

   (B) $\dfrac{2}{5}$ (D) $\dfrac{13}{25}$

2. If a fleet of m buses uses g gallons of gasoline every two days, how many gallons of gasoline will be used by 4 buses every 5 days?

   (A) $\dfrac{10g}{m}$ (C) $\dfrac{10m}{g}$ (E) $\dfrac{5g}{4m}$

   (B) $10gm$ (D) $\dfrac{20g}{m}$

3. A faucet is dripping at a constant rate. If, at noon on Sunday, 3 ounces of water have dripped from the faucet into a holding tank and, at 5 P.M. on Sunday, a total of 7 ounces have dripped into the tank, how many ounces will have dripped into the tank by 2:00 A.M. on Monday?

   (A) 10 (C) 12 (E) $\dfrac{81}{5}$

   (B) $\dfrac{51}{5}$ (D) $\dfrac{71}{5}$

4. If A and B are positive integers and $24AB$ is a perfect square, then which of the following CANNOT be possible?

   I. Both A and B are odd.
   II. AB is a perfect square
   III. Both A and B are divisible by 6

   (A) I only (C) III only (E) I, II, and III
   (B) II only (D) I and II only

SOLUTIONS

1. **(D)** Since each person had 5 choices, there are 25 possible pairs of numbers. The only way the sum could be odd is if one person picked an odd number and the other picked an even number. Suppose that Johnnie chose the odd number and Lisa the even one. Johnnie had 3 possible even numbers to select from, and for each of these, Lisa had 2 possible choices, for a total of $(3)(2) = 6$ possibilities. However, you could have had Johnnie pick an even number and Lisa pick an odd one, and there are also 6 ways to do that. Hence, out of 25 possibilities, 12 have an odd total, and 13 have an even total. The probability of an even total, then, is (D) $\dfrac{13}{25}$.

2. **(A)** Running m buses for 2 days is the same as running one bus for $2m$ days. If we use g gallons of gasoline, each bus uses $\dfrac{g}{2m}$ gallons each day. So if you multiply the number of gallons per day used by each bus by the number of buses and the number of days, you should get total gasoline usage. That is, $\dfrac{g}{2m} \times (4)(5) = \dfrac{10g}{m}$.

3. **(D)** In 5 hours, 4 ounces (7×3) have dripped. Therefore, the "drip rate" is $\dfrac{4}{5}$ of an ounce per hour. From 5:00 P.M. on Sunday until 2:00 A.M. on Monday is 9 hours, causing the total to be:

   $7 + \dfrac{4}{5} \times 9 = 7 + \dfrac{36}{5} = \dfrac{71}{5}$

4. **(D)** The prime factorization of 24 is $2^3 3$; hence, if $24AB$ is a perfect square, then AB must have a factor of 2 and a factor of 3. This means, first of all that both A and B cannot be odd. So I cannot be possible. II also cannot be possible, because if AB were a perfect square and $24AB$ were also a perfect square, then 24 would be a perfect square, which it is not. Of course, if, for example, A were 6 and B were 36, $24AB$ would be a perfect square with both A and B divisible by 6, so III is possible. Hence, the correct choice is (D).

9. INEQUALITIES

Algebraic inequality statements are solved just as equations are solved. However, you must remember that whenever you multiply or divide by a negative number, the order of the inequality, that is, the inequality symbol, must be reversed.

Q Solve for x: $3 - 5x > 18$

A Add -3 to both sides:
$-5x > 15$
Divide by -5, remembering to reverse the inequality:
$x < -3$

Q $5x - 4 > 6x - 6$

A Collect all x terms on the left and numerical terms on the right. As with equations, remember that if a term crosses the inequality symbol, the term changes sign.
$-x > -2$
Divide (or multiply) by -1:
$x < 2$

In working with geometric inequalities, certain postulates and theorems should be reviewed. The list follows:

POSTULATES AND THEOREMS

1. If unequal quantities are added to unequal quantities of the same order, the result is unequal quantities in the same order.
2. If equal quantities are added to, or subtracted from, unequal quantities, the results are unequal in the same order.
3. If unequal quantities are subtracted from equal quantities, the results are unequal in the opposite order.
4. Doubles, or halves, or unequals are unequal in the same order.
5. If the first of three quantities is greater than the second, and the second is greater than the third, then the first is greater than the third.
6. The sum of two sides of a triangle must be greater than the third side.
7. If two sides of a triangle are unequal, the angles opposite these sides are unequal, with the larger angle opposite the larger side.
8. If two angles of a triangle are unequal, the sides opposite these angles are unequal, with the larger side opposite the larger angle.
9. An exterior angle of a triangle is greater than either remote interior angle.

Q If *BCD* is a straight line and ∠*A* = 40°, then angle *ACD* contains
   (A) 40°
   (B) 140°
   (C) less than 40°
   (D) more than 40°
   (E) 100°

A The correct answer is (D), since an exterior angle of a triangle is always greater than either of the remote interior angles.

Q Which of the following statements is true regarding the triangle?
   (A) *AB* > *AC*
   (B) *AC* > *BC*
   (C) *AB* > *BC*
   (D) *AC* > *AB*
   (E) *BC* > *AB* + *AC*

A The correct answer is (D), since a comparison between two sides of a triangle depends upon the angles opposite these sides. The larger side is always opposite the larger angle. Since angle *A* contains 90°, the largest side of this triangle is *BC*, followed by *AC* and then *AB*.

EXERCISE: INEQUALITIES

Directions: Work out each problem. Circle the letter that appears before your answer.

1. If $x < y$, $2x = A$, and $2y = B$, then
   (A) $A = B$
   (B) $A < B$
   (C) $A > B$
   (D) $A < x$
   (E) $B < y$

2. If $a > b$ and $c > d$, then
   (A) $a = c$
   (B) $a < d$
   (C) $a + d = b + c$
   (D) $a + c < b + d$
   (E) $a + c > b + d$

3. If $ab > 0$ and $a < 0$, which of the following is negative?
   (A) b
   (B) $-b$
   (C) $-a$
   (D) $(a - b)$
   (E) $-(a + b)$

4. If $4 - x > 5$, then
   (A) $x > 1$
   (B) $x > -1$
   (C) $x < 1$
   (D) $x < -1$
   (E) $x = -1$

5. Point X is located on line segment AB and point Y is located on line segment CD. If AB = CD and AX > CY, then

   (A) XB > YD
   (B) XB < YD
   (C) AX > XB
   (D) AX < XB
   (E) AX > AB

6. If $w > x$, $y < z$, and $x > z$, which of the following must be true?

   (A) $w > x > y > z$
   (B) $w > x > z > y$
   (C) $x > z > y > w$
   (D) $z < y < x < w$
   (E) $z < x < y < w$

7. If x and y are positive integers such that $0 < (x + y) < 10$, which of the following must be true?

   (A) $x < 8$
   (B) $x > 3$
   (C) $x > y$
   (D) $x + y = 5$
   (E) $x - y < 7$

8. In the diagram below, which of the following is always true?

   I. $a > b$
   II. $c > a$
   III. $d > a$

   (A) I only
   (B) II and III only
   (C) I, II, and III
   (D) II only
   (E) None of these

9. If point X is on line segment AB, all of the following may be true except

   (A) $AX = XB$
   (B) $AX > XB$
   (C) $AX < XB$
   (D) $AB > XB$
   (E) $AX + XB < AB$

10. If $x > 0$, $y > 0$, and $x - y < 0$, then

    (A) $x > y$
    (B) $x < y$
    (C) $x + y < 0$
    (D) $y - x < 0$
    (E) $x = -y$

SOLUTIONS

1. **(B)** Doubles of unequals are unequal in the same order.

2. **(E)** If unequal quantities are added to unequal quantities of the same order, the results are unequal in the same order.

3. **(A)** If the product of two numbers is > 0 (positive), then either both numbers are positive or both are negative. Since $a < 0$ (negative), b must also be negative.

4. **(D)** $4 - x > 5$

   $-x > 1$. Divide by -1 and change the inequality sign.

   $x < -1$

5. **(B)**

   A ————————•———— B
              X

   C ————•———————— D
         Y

   If unequal quantities are subtracted from equal quantities, the results are unequal in the same order.

6. **(B)** The first and third statements prove:

   $w > x$ and $x > z$

   Therefore: $w > x > z$

   The second statement says that y is less than z.

   Therefore: $w > x > z > y$

7. **(E)** Perhaps using numbers is the easiest way to explain this item.

   (A) x could be 8 and y could be 1: $0 < (8+1) < 10$
   (B) x could be 3 and y could be 6: $0 < (3+6) < 10$
   (C) This is wrong as just shown above.
   (D) This too is wrong as shown above.
   (E) The largest possible value for x is 8, and the smallest possible value for y is 1. So the greatest possible value for $x - y$ is 7.

8. **(E)** An exterior angle of a triangle must be greater than either remote interior angle. There is no fixed relationship between an exterior angle and its adjacent interior angle.

9. **(E)** Point X could be so located to make each of the other choices true, but the whole segment AB will always be equal to the sum of its parts AX and XB.

10. **(B)** If x and y are both positive, but $x - y$ is negative, then y must be a larger number than x.

10. DEFINED OPERATION PROBLEMS

"Defined operation" is another name for "function." A function problem might look like this: The function of x is obtained by squaring x and then multiplying the result by 3. If you wanted to know $f(4)$, you would square 4 and multiply that product by 3; the answer would be 48. On the SAT the $f(x)$ symbol is not normally used. Instead the test-makers use arbitrary symbols and define what function they represent. You approach these symbols as you would a function: Ask yourself what the function does.

$!x = 2x + 4$

What does the "!" do in this problem? It takes x and doubles it and then adds four.

Q What is the value of $!6$?

A $!6 = 2(6) + 4 = 16$

EXERCISE: DEFINED OPERATION PROBLEMS

Directions: Work out each problem. Circle the letter that appears before your answer.

1. $\&x$ is such that $\&x = \frac{x^3}{2}$. What is the value of $\&4$?

   (A) 8
   (B) 16
   (C) 32
   (D) 40
   (E) 64

2. $\$x$ is such that $\$x$ is equal to the nearest low integer to x. What is the value of $\$6.99$ times $\$-2.01$?

   (A) 18
   (B) 12
   (C) −12
   (D) −18
   (E) −21

3. The operation # is defined in the following way for any two numbers:
   $p \# q = (p - q)$ times $(q - p)$.

   If $p \# q = -1$ then which of the following are true:

   I. p could equal 5 and q could equal 4
   II. p could equal 4 and q could equal 5
   III. p could equal 1 and q could equal -1
   IV. p could equal -1 and q could equal 1

   (A) I and II only
   (B) I and III only
   (C) II and IV only
   (D) III and IV only
   (E) I, II, III, IV

4. Every letter in the alphabet has a number value which is equal to its place in the alphabet; the letter A has a value of 1 and C a value of 3. The number value of a word is obtained by adding up the value of the letters in the word and then multiplying that sum by the length of the word. The word "DFGH" would have a number value of

   (A) 22
   (B) 44
   (C) 66
   (D) 100
   (E) 108

5. Let $\wedge x \wedge$ be defined such that $\wedge x \wedge = x + \frac{1}{x}$. The value of $\wedge 6 \wedge + \wedge 4 \wedge + \wedge 2 \wedge$ is

   (A) 12
   (B) $12\frac{7}{12}$
   (C) $12\frac{11}{12}$
   (D) $13\frac{1}{12}$
   (E) $13\frac{5}{12}$

SOLUTIONS

1. **(C)** $4^3 = 64$ and 64 divided by 2 is 32.

2. **(D)** The key phrase in the problem is "the nearest low integer." The nearest low integer to 6.99 is 6 (not 7, this problem does not say to round the numbers) and the nearest low integer to -2.01 is -3 (not -2 as -2 is higher than -2.01).

3. **(A)** The best way to solve this is to plug the values into the equation:
   $(5 - 4) \times (4 - 5) = -1$
   $(4 - 5) \times (5 - 4) = -1$
   $(1 - {}^-1) \times (-1 - 1) = -4$
   $(-1 - 1) \times (1 - {}^-1) = -4$
   Statements I and II give the stated value, -1.

4. **(D)** D = 4, F = 6, G = 7, and H = 8 so the sum of the letters would be 25. 25 multiplied by 4 (the length of the word) is 100.

5. **(C)** The work of this problem is adding up the reciprocals of the numbers.
   $6 + 4 + 2$ is clearly 12.
   $\frac{1}{6} + \frac{1}{4} + \frac{1}{2} = \frac{2}{12} + \frac{3}{12} + \frac{6}{12} = \frac{11}{12}$

Chapter

15

SAT Geometry Review

Here are some of the most important geometry formulas that you should know for the SAT.

1. AREAS

1. Rectangle = bh
   Area = $6 \cdot 3 = 18$

2. Parallelogram = bh
   Area = $8 \cdot 4 = 32$

3. Rhombus = $\frac{1}{2} d_1 d_2$

   If AC = 10 and BD = 8, then area is $\frac{1}{2}(10)(8) = 40$

4. Square = s^2 or $\frac{1}{2} d^2$
   Area = $6^2 = 36$

   Area = $\frac{1}{2}(10)(10) = 50$

ROAD MAP

- *Areas*
- *Perimeters*
- *Circles*
- *Volumes*
- *Triangles*
- *Right triangles*
- *Parallel lines*
- *Polygons*
- *Similar polygons*
- *Coordinate geometry*

CAUTION
Don't confuse the two formulas for calculating the circumference and area of circles. A good way to keep them straight is to remember the *square* in r². It should remind you that area must be in square units.

5. Triangle = $\frac{1}{2}bh$

   Area = $\frac{1}{2}(12)(4) = 24$

6. Equilateral triangle = $\frac{s^2}{4}\sqrt{3}$

   Area = $\frac{36}{4}\sqrt{3} = 9\sqrt{3}$

7. Trapezoid = $\frac{1}{2}h(b_1 + b_2)$

   Area = $\frac{1}{2}(5)(16) = 40$

8. Circle = πr^2

   Area = $\pi(6)^2 = 36\pi$

2. PERIMETERS

1. Any polygon = sum of all sides

   P = 5 + 8 + 11 = 24

2. Circle = πd
   (called circumference)

   Circle = $\pi(12) = 12$

3. The distance covered by a wheel in one revolution is equal to the circumference of the wheel.

In one revolution, this wheel covers $\pi \cdot \frac{14}{\pi}$, or 14 feet.

3. CIRCLES

1. A central angle is equal in degrees to its intercepted arc.

   If $\widehat{AB} = 80°$, then $\angle AOB = 80°$.

2. An inscribed angle is equal in degrees to one-half its intercepted arc.

   If $\widehat{AC} = 120°$, then $\angle ABC = 60°$.

3. An angle formed by two chords intersecting in a circle is equal in degrees to one-half the sum of its intercepted arcs.

   If $\widehat{AD} = 40°$ and $\widehat{CB} = 80°$, then $\angle CEB = 60°$.

4. An angle formed outside a circle by two secants, a secant and a tangent, or two tangents is equal in degrees to one-half the difference of its intercepted arcs.

If $\overset{\frown}{AD} = 120°$ and $\overset{\frown}{BD} = 70°$, then $\angle ACD = 25°$.

5. Two tangent segments drawn to a circle from the same external point are congruent.

If AC and CE are tangent to circle O at B and D, then $CB = CD$.

4. VOLUMES

1. The volume of a rectangular solid is equal to the product of its length, width, and height.

   $V = lwh$
   $V = (6)(2)(4) = 48$

2. The volume of a cube is equal to the cube of an edge.
   $V = e^3$
   $V = (5)^3 = 125$

3. The volume of a cylinder is equal to π times the square of the radius of the base times the height.

$V = \pi r^2 h$
$V = \pi (5)^2(3) = 75\pi$

5. TRIANGLES

1. If two sides of a triangle are congruent, the angles opposite these sides are congruent.

   If $AB \cong AC$, then
   $\angle B \cong \angle C$.

2. If two angles of a triangle are congruent, the sides opposite these angles are congruent.

   If $\angle B \cong \angle C$, then
   $AB \cong AC$

3. The sum of the measures of the angles of a triangle is 180°.

4. The measure of an exterior angle of a triangle is equal to the sum of the measures of the two remote interior angles.

   $\angle 1 = 130°$

5. If two angles of one triangle are congruent to two angles of a second triangle, the third angles are congruent.

   $\angle D \cong \angle A$

TIP
When an SAT problem asks you to find the area of a shaded region, you probably won't be able to calculate it directly. That's OK—instead, think of the shaded region as being whatever is left over when one region is subtracted or removed from a larger region. Use the formulas you know to find those two regions and perform the necessary subtraction.

6. RIGHT TRIANGLES

1. Pythagorean Theorem

$$(\text{leg})^2 + (\text{leg})^2 = (\text{hypotenuse})^2$$
$$4^2 + 5^2 = x^2$$
$$16 + 25 = x^2$$
$$41 = x^2$$
$$\sqrt{41} = x$$

2. Pythagorean triples: These are sets of numbers that satisfy the Pythagorean Theorem. When a given set of numbers such as 3, 4, 5 forms a Pythagorean triple ($3^2 + 4^2 = 5^2$), any multiples of this set such as 6, 8, 10 or 15, 20, 25 also form a Pythagorean triple. The most common Pythagorean triples, which should be memorized, are:

   3, 4, 5
   5, 12, 13
   8, 15, 17
   7, 24, 25

   Squaring these numbers in order to apply the Pythagorean Theorem would take too much time. Instead, recognize the hypotenuse as 3(13). Suspect a 5, 12, 13 triangle. Since the given leg is 3(5), the missing leg must be 3(12), or 36, with no computation and a great saving of time.

> **TIP**
> Remember the well-known *Pythagorean triples,* that is, sets of whole numbers such as 3-4-5 for which $a^2 + b^2 = c^2$. You'll encounter right triangles on the SAT with sides whose lengths correspond to these values. Other Pythagorean triples are: 5-12-13, 8-15-17, 17-24-25. Also watch for their multiples, such as 6-8-10 or 15-20-25.

3. The 30°-60°-90° triangle

   a) The leg opposite the 30° angle is $\frac{1}{2}$ hypotenuse.

   b) The leg opposite the 60° angle is $\frac{1}{2}$ hypotenuse • $\sqrt{3}$.

   c) An altitude in an equilateral triangle forms a 30°-60°-90° triangle and is therefore equal to $\frac{1}{2}$ hypotenuse • $\sqrt{3}$.

   $x = 4$ $y = 5\sqrt{3}$ $z = 12$ $x = 4\sqrt{3}$

4. The 45°-45°-90° triangle (isosceles right triangle)

   a) Each leg is $\frac{1}{2}$ hypotenuse • $\sqrt{2}$.

   b) Hypotenuse is leg • $\sqrt{2}$.

   c) The diagonal in a square forms a 45°-45°-90° triangle and is therefore equal to a side • $\sqrt{2}$.

   $w = 6$ $x = 8\sqrt{2}$ $y = 5\sqrt{2}$ $z = 6\sqrt{2}$

TIP
Remember that, in a right triangle, you can use the two *legs* (the two sides other than the hypotenuse) as base and altitude.

7. PARALLEL LINES

1. If two parallel lines are cut by a transversal, the alternate interior angles are congruent.

   If $AB \parallel CD$, then
   $\angle 1 \cong \angle 3$ and
   $\angle 2 \cong \angle 4$.

2. If two parallel lines are cut by a transversal, the corresponding angles are congruent.

   If $AB \parallel CD$, then
   $\angle 1 \cong \angle 5$,
   $\angle 2 \cong \angle 6$,
   $\angle 3 \cong \angle 7$, and
   $\angle 4 \cong \angle 8$.

3. If two parallel lines are cut by a transversal, interior angles on the same side of the transversal are supplementary.

   If $AB \parallel CD$, then
   $\angle 1$ is supplementary to $\angle 4$ and
   $\angle 2$ is supplementary to $\angle 3$.

8. POLYGONS

1. The sum of the measures of the angles of a polygon of n sides is $(n-2)180°$.

   Since ABCDE has 5 sides,

   $\angle A + \angle B + \angle C +$

   $\angle D + \angle E = (5-2)180 =$

   $3(180) = 540°$

2. In a parallelogram:
   a) Opposite sides are parallel.
   b) Opposite sides are congruent.
   c) Opposite angles are congruent.
   d) Consecutive angles are supplementary.
   e) Diagonals bisect each other.
   f) Each diagonal bisects the parallelogram into two congruent triangles.

3. In a rectangle, in addition to the properties listed in (2), above:
   a) All angles are right angles.
   b) Diagonals are congruent.

4. In a rhombus, in addition to the properties listed in (2), above:
   a) All sides are congruent.
   b) Diagonals are perpendicular.
   c) Diagonals bisect the angles.

5. A square has *all* of the properties listed in (2), (3), and (4), above.

6. The apothem of a regular polygon is perpendicular to a side, bisects that side, and also bisects a central angle.

   OX is an apothem.
   It bisects AB, is
   perpendicular to AB,
   and bisects $\angle AOB$.

7. The area of a regular polygon is equal to one-half the product of its apothem and perimeter.

$$A = \frac{1}{2}(3)(30) = 45$$

9. SIMILAR POLYGONS

1. Corresponding angles of similar polygons are congruent.
2. Corresponding sides of similar polygons are in proportion.

If triangle *ABC* is similar to triangle *DEF*, and the sides are given as marked, then *EF* must be equal to 6, as the ratio between corresponding sides is 4 : 8 or 1 : 2.

3. When figures are similar, all corresponding linear ratios are equal. The ratio of one side to its corresponding side is the same as perimeter to perimeter, apothem to apothem, altitude to altitude, etc.

4. When figures are similar, the ratio of their areas is equal to the square of the ratio between two corresponding linear quantities.

If triangle *ABC* is similar to triangle *DEF*, the area of triangle *ABC* will be 9 times as great as that of triangle *DEF*. The ratio of sides is 9 : 3, or 3 : 1. The ratio of areas will be the square of 3 : 1, or 9 : 1.

5. When figures are similar, the ratio of their volumes is equal to the cube of the ratio between two corresponding linear quantities.

The volume of the larger cube is 8 times as large as the volume of the smaller cube. If the ratio of sides is 3 : 6, or 1 : 2, the ratio of volumes is the cube of this, or 1 : 8.

10. COORDINATE GEOMETRY

1. Distance between two points

$$\sqrt{(x_2 - x_1)^2 + (y_2 - y_1)^2}$$

The distance from (–2, 3) to (4, –1) is

$$\sqrt{[4-(-2)]^2 + [-1-(3)]^2}$$

$$\sqrt{(6)^2 + (-4)^2} = \sqrt{36 + 16} = \sqrt{52}$$

2. The midpoint of a line segment

$$\left(\frac{x_1 + x_2}{2}, \frac{y_1 + y_2}{2} \right)$$

The midpoint of the segment joining (–2, 3) to (4, –1) is

$$\left(\frac{-2+4}{2}, \frac{3+(-1)}{2} \right) = \left(\frac{2}{2}, \frac{2}{2} \right) = 1, 1$$

EXERCISE: GEOMETRY

Directions: Work out each problem. Circle the letter that appears before your answer.

1. If the angles of a triangle are in the ratio 2 : 3 : 7, the triangle is

    (A) acute
    (B) isosceles
    (C) obtuse
    (D) right
    (E) equilateral

2. If the area of a square of side x is 5, what is the area of a square of side $3x$?

    (A) 15
    (B) 45
    (C) 95
    (D) 75
    (E) 225

3. If the radius of a circle is decreased by 10%, by what percent is its area decreased?

    (A) 10
    (B) 19
    (C) 21
    (D) 79
    (E) 81

4. A spotlight is 5 feet from one wall of a room and 10 feet from the wall at right angles to it. How many feet is it from the intersection of the two walls?

    (A) 15
    (B) $5\sqrt{2}$
    (C) $5\sqrt{5}$
    (D) $10\sqrt{2}$
    (E) $10\sqrt{5}$

5. A dam has the dimensions indicated in the figure. Find the area of this isosceles trapezoid.

    (A) 1300
    (B) 1560
    (C) 1400
    (D) 1440
    (E) It cannot be determined from the information given.

6. In parallelogram $PQRS$, angle P is four times angle Q. What is the measure in degrees of angle P?

    (A) 36
    (B) 72
    (C) 125
    (D) 144
    (E) 150

7. If $PQ \cong QS$, $QR \cong RS$ and angle $PRS = 100°$, what is the measure, in degrees, of angle QPS?

    (A) 10
    (B) 15
    (C) 20
    (D) 25
    (E) 30

8. A line segment is drawn from the point (3, 5) to the point (9, 13). What are the coordinates of the midpoint of this line segment?

   (A) (3, 4)
   (B) (12, 18)
   (C) (6, 8)
   (D) (9, 6)
   (E) (6, 9)

9. A rectangular box with a square base contains 6 cubic feet. If the height of the box is 18 inches, how many feet are there in each side of the base?

   (A) 1
   (B) 2
   (C) $\sqrt{3}$
   (D) $\frac{\sqrt{3}}{3}$
   (E) 4

10. The surface area of a cube is 150 square feet. How many cubic feet are there in the volume of the cube?

    (A) 30
    (B) 50
    (C) 100
    (D) 125
    (E) 150

11. Peter lives 12 miles west of school and Bill lives north of the school. Peter finds that the direct distance from his house to Bill's is 6 miles shorter than the distance by way of school. How many miles north of the school does Bill live?

    (A) 6
    (B) 9
    (C) 10
    (D) $6\sqrt{2}$
    (E) None of these

12. A square is inscribed in a circle of area 18. Find a side of the square.

    (A) 3
    (B) 6
    (C) $3\sqrt{2}$
    (D) $6\sqrt{2}$
    (E) It cannot be determined from the information given.

13. A carpet is y yards long and f feet wide. How many dollars will it cost if the carpet sells for x cents per square foot?

    (A) xyf
    (B) $3xyf$
    (C) $\frac{xyf}{3}$
    (D) $\frac{.03yf}{x}$
    (E) $.03xyf$

14. If a triangle of base 6 has the same area as a circle of radius 6, what is the altitude of the triangle?

    (A) 6
    (B) 8
    (C) 10
    (D) 12
    (E) 14

15. The vertex angle of an isosceles triangle is p degrees. How many degrees are there in one of the base angles?

    (A) $180 - p$
    (B) $90 - p$
    (C) $180 - 2p$
    (D) $180 - \frac{p}{2}$
    (E) $90 - \frac{p}{2}$

16. In a circle with center O, arc $RS = 132$ degrees. How many degrees are there in angle RSO?
    (A) 66
    (B) 20
    (C) 22
    (D) 24
    (E) 48

17. The ice compartment of a refrigerator is 8 inches long, 4 inches wide, and 5 inches high. How many ice cubes will it hold if each cube is 2 inches on an edge?
    (A) 8
    (B) 10
    (C) 12
    (D) 16
    (E) 20

18. In the figure, PSQ is a straight line and RS is perpendicular to ST. If angle $RSQ = 48°$, how many degrees are there in angle PST?
    (A) 48
    (B) 132
    (C) 90
    (D) 136
    (E) 138

19. A cylindrical pail has a radius of 7 inches and a height of 9 inches. If there are 231 cubic inches to a gallon, approximately how many gallons will this pail hold?
    (A) 6
    (B) $\frac{12}{7}$
    (C) 7.5
    (D) 8.2
    (E) 9

20. In triangle PQR, QS and SR are angle bisectors and angle $P = 80°$. How many degrees are there in angle QSR?
    (A) 115
    (B) 120
    (C) 125
    (D) 130
    (E) 135

SOLUTIONS

1. **(C)** Represent the angles as $2x$, $3x$, and $7x$.
   $$2x + 3x + 7x = 180$$
   $$12x = 180$$
   $$x = 15$$
   The angles are 30°, 45°, and 105°. Since one angle is between 90° and 180°, the triangle is called an obtuse triangle.

2. **(B)** If the sides have a ratio 1 : 3, the areas have a ratio 1 : 9. Therefore, the area of the large square is 9(5), or 45.

3. **(B)** If the radii of the two circles have a ratio of 10 : 9, the areas have a ratio of 100 : 81. Therefore, the decrease is 19 out of 100, or 19%.

4. **(C)** $5^2 + 10^2 = x^2$
   $$25 + 100 = x^2$$
   $$x^2 = 125$$
   $$x = \sqrt{125} = \sqrt{25}\sqrt{5} = 5\sqrt{5}$$

5. **(D)**

When altitudes are drawn from both ends of the upper base in an isosceles trapezoid, the figure is divided into a rectangle and two congruent right triangles. The center section of the lower base is equal to the upper base, and the remainder of the lower base is divided equally between both ends.

The altitude can then be found using the Pythagorean Theorem. In this case, we have a 5, 12, 13 triangle with all measures doubled, so the altitude is 24.

The area is $\frac{1}{2}(24)(120)$, or 1440.

6. **(D)** The consecutive angles of a parallelogram are supplementary, so
$$x + 4x = 180$$
$$5x = 180$$
$$x = 36$$
Angle P is 4(36), or 144°.

7. **(C)**

Since $QR \cong RS$, $\angle RQS \cong \angle RSQ$. There are 80° left in the triangle, so each of these angles is 40°. $\angle SQP$ is supplementary to $\angle SQR$, making it 140°. Since $QP \cong QS$, $\angle QPS \cong \angle QSP$. There are 40° left in the triangle, so each of these angles is 20°.

8. **(E)** Add the x values and divide by 2. Add the y values and divide by 2.

9. **(B)** Change 18 inches to 1.5 feet. Letting each side of the base be x, the volume is $1.5x^2$.
$$1.5x^2 = 6$$
$$15x^2 = 60$$
$$x^2 = 4$$
$$x = 2$$

10. **(D)** The surface area of a cube is made up of 6 equal squares. If each edge of the cube is x, then
$$6x^2 = 150$$
$$x^2 = 25$$
$$x = 5$$
Volume = (edge)^3 = 5^3 = 125

11. **(B)**

The direct distance from Peter's house to Bill's can be represented by means of the Pythagorean Theorem as $\sqrt{144 + x^2}$. Then
$$\sqrt{144 + x^2} = (12x + x) - 6$$
$$\sqrt{144 + x^2} = x + 6$$
Square both sides.
$$144 + x^2 = x^2 + 12x + 36$$
$$144 = 12x + 36$$
$$108 = 12x$$
$$9 = x$$

12. **(B)**

The diagonal of the square will be a diameter of the circle.
$$\pi r^2 = 18\pi$$
$$r^2 = 18$$
$$r = \sqrt{18} = \sqrt{9}\sqrt{2} = 3\sqrt{2}$$
The diameter is $6\sqrt{2}$ and, since the triangles are 45°-45°-90°, a side of the square is 6.

13. **(E)** To find the area in square feet, change y yards to $3y$ feet. The area is then $(3y)(f)$, or $3yf$ square feet. If each square foot costs x cents, change this to dollars by dividing x by 100. Thus, each square foot costs $\frac{x}{100}$ dollars.

The cost of $3yf$ square feet will be $(3yf)(\frac{x}{100})$, or $\frac{3xyf}{100}$.

Since $\frac{3}{100} = .03$, the correct answer is (E).

14. **(D)** The area of the circle is $(6)^2$, or 36.
In the triangle $\frac{1}{2}(6)(h) = 36$
$$3h = 36$$
$$h = 12$$

15. **(E)** There are $(180 - p)$ degrees left, which must be divided between 2 congruent angles. Each angle will contain $\frac{(180-p)}{2}$, or $90 - \frac{p}{2}$ degrees.

16. **(D)**

By extending *SO* until it hits the circle at *P*, arc *PRS* is a semicircle. Therefore, arc *PR* = 48°, and inscribed angle *RSO* = 24°.

17. **(D)**

The compartment will hold 2 layers, each of which contains 2 rows of 4 cubes each. This leaves a height of 1 inch on top empty. Therefore, the compartment can hold 16 cubes.

18. **(E)**

Since ∠*RST* is a right angle, 42° are left for ∠*QST*. Since *PSQ* is a straight angle of 180°, ∠*PST* contains 138°.

19. **(A)** The volume of the pail is found using the formula $V = \pi r^2 h$. Since the answers are not in terms of π, it is best to use $\frac{22}{7}$ as a value for π because the 7 will cancel with r^2: $V = \frac{22}{7} \cdot 49^7 \cdot 9$. Rather than multiply this out, which will take unnecessary time, divide by 231 and cancel wherever possible.

$$\frac{22^2 \cdot \cancel{7} \cdot 9^3}{\cancel{231} \atop \cancel{33} \atop \cancel{3}} = 6$$

20. **(D)** If ∠*P* = 80°, there are 100° left between ∠*PQR* and *PRQ*. If they are both bisected, there will be 50° between ∠*SQR* and *SRQ*, leaving 130° in triangle *SRQ* for ∠*QSR*.

PART 7

Practice Examinations

CHAPTER 16

CHAPTER 17

PREVIEW

How to Effectively Use the Practice Examinations

Seven Practice Examinations

Chapter 16

How to Effectively Use the Practice Examinations

The practice examinations in this book make up one of the most important parts of your SAT and PSAT preparation program. Use them as benchmarks as you work through the other chapters in this book. Each test gives you a great opportunity to gauge your progress and focus your ongoing study. Together, the tests map the growth of your skills and demonstrate your SAT "readiness." And, when you take the practice exams under simulated SAT test-taking conditions, they give you a wonderful opportunity to adjust to the test-taking environment. When you enter the SAT testing room, you'll know what to expect—and you'll be ready to score high on the exam.

HOW TO SIMULATE TEST-TAKING CONDITIONS

Above and beyond everything else, the seven practice exams in this part of the book help you prepare for the experience of taking a timed, standardized test. Taking these tests will improve your familiarity with the SAT, reduce your number of careless errors, and increase your overall level of confidence. To make sure that you get the most out of this practice, you should do everything in your power to simulate actual test-taking conditions. The following sections outline the best methods for simulating SAT testing conditions when you work through the practice exams.

FIND THREE QUIET HOURS

Because the SAT is administered in one long block of time, the best way to simulate test-taking conditions is to take an entire practice exam in one sitting. This means that you should set aside three consecutive hours to take a test. If you find it difficult to find three quiet hours at home, maybe take the test in the library or at a deserted location. If you decide to take a test at home, take precautions. Turn off the ringer on all nearby telephones, ask your parents to hold your calls, and convince siblings to stay out of your room. Easier said than done, right? Although infrequent interruptions won't completely invalidate your testing experience, you should try to avoid them.

ROAD MAP

- *Learn the best ways to use the practice exams*
- *Learn how to simulate test-taking conditions*
- *Learn how timing drills can help when you are short on time*
- *Review what you need to know to take practice tests and do timing drills*

WORK AT A DESK AND WEAR A WATCH

Don't take a practice examination while you are lounging on your bed. After all, the SAT people won't let you take the test lying down! Clear off sufficient space on a desk or table to work comfortably. Wear a watch to properly administer the sections under timed conditions. Remember that every section on the SAT takes 30 minutes with the exception of the two 15 minute "mini-sections." You are not allowed to explore other sections of the test while you are assigned to a particular section. So don't look back or press on. Take the full time to complete each individual section.

PRACTICE ON A WEEKEND MORNING

Since the SAT is typically administered at 8:30am on Saturday (or Sunday for religious observers), why not take the exam at the exact same time on a weekend morning? You should be most energetic in the morning anyway. If you are not a morning person, now is a good time to become one since that's when you'll have to take the actual SAT! When you take the practice exam, allow yourself two breaks. Give yourself a 5-minute break after Section 2 to run to the bathroom, scarf down a snack, and resharpen your pencils. After Section 4, give yourself a 1-minute stretch break. During this time on SAT day, you are not allowed to leave the room or speak with anyone. To simulate this, stand up after Section 4, take a minute to collect your thoughts, and then proceed to Section 5.

HOW TIMING DRILLS CAN HELP WHEN YOU ARE SHORT ON TIME

We know that it will be extremely difficult for you to find three consecutive hours during which to take full practice examinations. You have a life, after all—homework, social commitments, family responsibilities, etc. Maybe you'll only be able to take one or two complete examinations under simulated testing conditions. But you can do *timing drills* to get valuable practice in shorter periods of time. Timing drills are short groups of questions that allow you to work on your weaknesses under timed conditions.

MATH TIMING DRILLS

If you feel that you need work on a particular type of math question, the first thing you should do is revisit earlier portions of the book for review. For example, if multiple-choice math gives you difficulty, read Chapter 8 to review strategies and do exercises. The same can be said if you have difficulty with quantitative comparisons or grid-ins. Once you have done this, you can get extra valuable review by doing specific timing drills out of the seven practice exams.

TIP

If you are taking the practice exams at home, try to schedule them during your home's typical "quiet times." If your home doesn't have any "typical quiet times," maybe you can arrange some with your family. Be as resourceful as you can in finding a quiet space where you can spend three hours simulating a full-length SAT. It's one of the best ways you can prepare for the real exam.

TIP

If your watch has a beeper, it can help you keep track of the time during your practice exam. But remember, your watch can't beep during the real SAT or PSAT. You'll have to turn the beeper off, or wear a non-beeping watch, when you take the SAT.

If you want a good review of multiple-choice problems, find a 25-question section out of a practice test and give yourself a timing drill. Approach the section as you would approach the actual SAT. Allow exactly 30 minutes. Then check your answers, review your results, and look for patterns among your answers. (Try to determine whether you need to review your arithmetic, algebra, or geometry and revisit those chapters as necessary.) If you need to practice quantitative comparisons, find the section which contains the 15 quantitative comparisons and allow 15 minutes to do them. If grid-ins intimidate you, take 15 minutes to tackle the 10 of them.

VERBAL TIMING DRILLS

In verbal, you should also revisit earlier chapters to combat your weaknesses. Once you have, you can do the same kind of timing drills. If you feel that you need work on every type of verbal question and you don't have time to take an entire practice test, take a full 30-minute section. This will give you a chance to practice sentence completions, analogies, and critical reading questions in a timed format. If you find sentence completions particularly troubling, allow 7 minutes to answer a drill of 9 or 10 questions. If you want to review analogies, give yourself 9 minutes to do a group of 13 questions. And if critical reading is your stumbling block, allow 15 minutes to answer either a lengthy passage (10 or more questions) or a double passage.

Timing drills are an important way not only to address your weaknesses, but to work on them efficiently under testing conditions. We see timing drills sort of like exercise. You know how people say that if you exercise just 20 minutes per day, three times per week you can stay in shape? Well, if you do timing drills with regularity, it works the same way. In just 15 to 30 minutes per sitting, you can keep mentally fit for the SAT. Try 'em. They're relatively painless and extraordinarily effective.

A TABLE OF TIMING DRILLS

The following table puts all of the timing drill information in a "one-stop" format, so you can refer to it often when planning your SAT study time.

Type of Question	# of Questions	Time to Allot
Full Section Multiple-Choice Math	25	30 minutes
Quantitative Comparisons	15	15 minutes
Grid-Ins	10	15 minutes
Full Section Verbal	35 or 30	30 minutes
Sentence Completions	9 or 10	7 minutes
Analogies	13	9 minutes
Critical Reading	10 to 13	15 minutes

CAUTION

If you're worried that you won't be able to resist the temptation of checking the answer keys during the practice exams, rip the keys out and put them in a safe place. Don't allow yourself to become dependent upon a "sneak" look now and then. You won't have answer keys available on test day, and the main purpose of the practice exams is to prepare you for the real experience. If you know you can resist, leave the keys in the book. Otherwise...well, better safe than sorry.

NOTE

We know that doing all of this might appear to be excessive. But remember that your goal is to take these practice exams in as true an environment as possible so that you're prepared to take the real SAT. You will be accustomed to sitting for three hours and you will know when to take breaks. This knowledge will make you considerably less anxious on test day.

Summary: What You Need to Know to Take Practice Tests and Do Timing Drills

If you are going to take a full practice examination, try to simulate test-taking conditions by doing the following.

- To take a full-length practice exam, you'll need three quiet hours.
- Work at a desk and wear a watch when you take the practice exams.
- If temptation may lead you to "sneak a peak" at the answers during the exam, rip out the answer keys and put them in a safe place.
- Whenever possible, take the practice exams on weekend mornings.
- If you don't have the time to take a full test, or you need work on a specific type of question, take the appropriate timing drills.

PRACTICE EXAMINATION 1
Answer Sheet

If a section has fewer questions than answer ovals, leave the extra ovals blank.

Section 1

Section 2

Section 3
Answer spaces for Section 3 are on the back of this Answer Sheet.

Section 4

Section 5

Section 3

1. Ⓐ Ⓑ Ⓒ Ⓓ Ⓔ
2. Ⓐ Ⓑ Ⓒ Ⓓ Ⓔ
3. Ⓐ Ⓑ Ⓒ Ⓓ Ⓔ
4. Ⓐ Ⓑ Ⓒ Ⓓ Ⓔ
5. Ⓐ Ⓑ Ⓒ Ⓓ Ⓔ
6. Ⓐ Ⓑ Ⓒ Ⓓ Ⓔ
7. Ⓐ Ⓑ Ⓒ Ⓓ Ⓔ
8. Ⓐ Ⓑ Ⓒ Ⓓ Ⓔ
9. Ⓐ Ⓑ Ⓒ Ⓓ Ⓔ
10. Ⓐ Ⓑ Ⓒ Ⓓ Ⓔ
11. Ⓐ Ⓑ Ⓒ Ⓓ Ⓔ
12. Ⓐ Ⓑ Ⓒ Ⓓ Ⓔ
13. Ⓐ Ⓑ Ⓒ Ⓓ Ⓔ
14. Ⓐ Ⓑ Ⓒ Ⓓ Ⓔ
15. Ⓐ Ⓑ Ⓒ Ⓓ Ⓔ

Note: ONLY the answers entered on the grid are scored.

Handwritten answers at the top of the column are NOT scored.

16. [grid] 17. [grid] 18. [grid] 19. [grid] 20. [grid]

21. [grid] 22. [grid] 23. [grid] 24. [grid] 25. [grid]

Section 6

1. Ⓐ Ⓑ Ⓒ Ⓓ Ⓔ
2. Ⓐ Ⓑ Ⓒ Ⓓ Ⓔ
3. Ⓐ Ⓑ Ⓒ Ⓓ Ⓔ
4. Ⓐ Ⓑ Ⓒ Ⓓ Ⓔ
5. Ⓐ Ⓑ Ⓒ Ⓓ Ⓔ
6. Ⓐ Ⓑ Ⓒ Ⓓ Ⓔ
7. Ⓐ Ⓑ Ⓒ Ⓓ Ⓔ
8. Ⓐ Ⓑ Ⓒ Ⓓ Ⓔ
9. Ⓐ Ⓑ Ⓒ Ⓓ Ⓔ
10. Ⓐ Ⓑ Ⓒ Ⓓ Ⓔ
11. Ⓐ Ⓑ Ⓒ Ⓓ Ⓔ
12. Ⓐ Ⓑ Ⓒ Ⓓ Ⓔ
13. Ⓐ Ⓑ Ⓒ Ⓓ Ⓔ
14. Ⓐ Ⓑ Ⓒ Ⓓ Ⓔ
15. Ⓐ Ⓑ Ⓒ Ⓓ Ⓔ

Practice Examination 1

SECTION 1

25 Questions • Time—30 minutes

Directions: Solve the following problems using any available space on the page for scratchwork. On your answer sheet fill in the choice which best corresponds to the correct answer.

Notes: The figures accompanying the problems are drawn as accurately as possible unless otherwise stated in specific problems. Again, unless otherwise stated, all figures lie in the same plane. All numbers used in these problems are real numbers. Calculators are permitted for this test.

Reference Information

Circle: $C = 2\pi r$, $A = \pi r^2$
Rectangle: $A = lw$
Rectangular Solid: $V = lwh$
Cylinder: $V = \pi r^2 h$
Triangle: $A = \frac{1}{2}bh$
$a^2 + b^2 = c^2$
45°-45°-90° triangle: sides x, x, $x\sqrt{2}$
30°-60°-90° triangle: sides x, $x\sqrt{3}$, $2x$

The number of degrees of arc in a circle is 360.
The measure in degrees of a straight angle is 180.
The sum of the measures in degrees of the angles of a triangle is 180.

---

1. $0.2 \times 0.02 \times 0.002 =$

   (A) .08
   (B) .008
   (C) .0008
   (D) .00008
   (E) .000008

2. If it costs $1.30 a square foot to lay linoleum, what will be the cost of laying 20 square yards of linoleum? (3 ft. = 1 yd.)

   (A) $47.50
   (B) $49.80
   (C) $150.95
   (D) $249.00
   (E) $234.00

3. In a family of five, the heights of the members are 5 feet 1 inch, 5 feet 7 inches, 5 feet 2 inches, 5 feet, and 4 feet 7 inches. The average height is

   (A) 4 feet $4\frac{1}{5}$ inches
   (B) 5 feet
   (C) 5 feet 1 inch
   (D) 5 feet 2 inches
   (E) 5 feet 3 inches

4. Three times the first of three consecutive odd integers is 3 more than twice the third. Find the third integer.

   (A) 7
   (B) 9
   (C) 11
   (D) 13
   (E) 15

GO ON TO THE NEXT PAGE

5. In the figure below, the largest possible circle is cut out of a square piece of tin. The area, in square inches, of the remaining piece of tin is approximately

   (A) .14
   (B) .75
   (C) .86
   (D) 1.0
   (E) 3.14

6. The figure shows one square inside another and a rectangle of diagonal T. The best approximation to the value of T, in inches, is given by which of the following inequalities?

   (A) $8 < T < 9$
   (B) $9 < T < 10$
   (C) $10 < T < 11$
   (D) $11 < T < 12$
   (E) $12 < T < 13$

7. If nails are bought at 35 cents per dozen and sold at 3 for 10 cents, the total profits on $5\frac{1}{2}$ dozen is

   (A) 25 cents
   (B) $27\frac{1}{2}$ cents
   (C) $28\frac{1}{2}$ cents
   (D) $31\frac{1}{2}$ cents
   (E) 35 cents

8. The total number of eighths in $2\frac{3}{4}$ is

   (A) 11
   (B) 14
   (C) 19
   (D) 22
   (E) 24

9. What is the difference when $-x-y$ is subtracted from $-x^2 + 2y$?

   (A) $x^2 - x - 3y$
   (B) $-3x + y$
   (C) $x^2 + 3y$
   (D) $-x^2 + x - 3y$
   (E) $-x^2 + x + 3y$

10. If $2^m = 4x$ and $2^w = 8x$, what is m in terms of w?

    (A) $w - 1$
    (B) $w + 1$
    (C) $2w - 1$
    (D) $2w + 1$
    (E) w^2

11. $1\frac{1}{4}$ subtracted from its reciprocal is

    (A) $\frac{9}{20}$
    (B) $\frac{1}{5}$
    (C) $-\frac{1}{20}$
    (D) $-\frac{1}{5}$
    (E) $-\frac{9}{20}$

12. The total number of feet in x yards, y feet, and z inches is

    (A) $3x + y + \frac{z}{12}$
    (B) $12(x + y + z)$
    (C) $x + y + z$
    (D) $\frac{x}{36} + \frac{y}{12} + z$
    (E) $x + 3y + 36z$

13. If five triangles are constructed having sides of the lengths indicated below, the triangle that will NOT be a right triangle is:

    (A) 5, 12, 13
    (B) 3, 4, 5
    (C) 8, 15, 17
    (D) 9, 40, 41
    (E) 12, 15, 18

14. Of the following, the one that may be used correctly to compute $26 \times 3\frac{1}{2}$ is

    (A) $(26 \times 30) + (26 \times \frac{1}{2})$
    (B) $(20 \times 3) + (6 \times 3\frac{1}{2})$
    (C) $(20 \times 3\frac{1}{2}) + (6 \times 3)$
    (D) $(20 \times 3) + (26 \times \frac{1}{2}) + (6 \times 3\frac{1}{2})$
    (E) $(26 \times \frac{1}{2}) + (20 \times 3) + (6 \times 3)$

15. In the figure, ST is tangent to the circle at T. RT is a diameter. If $RS = 12$, and $ST = 8$, what is the area of the circle?

    (A) 5π
    (B) 8π
    (C) 9π
    (D) 20π
    (E) 40π

16. What would be the marked price of an article if the cost was $12.60 and the gain was 10% of the selling price?

    (A) $11.34
    (B) $12.48
    (C) $13.66
    (D) $13.86
    (E) $14.00

17. If the average weight of boys who are John's age and height is 105 lbs., and if John weighs 110% of the average, then how many pounds does John weigh?

    (A) 110
    (B) 110.5
    (C) 112
    (D) 114.5
    (E) 115.5

18. The radius of a circle that has a circumference equal to the perimeter of a hexagon whose sides are each 22 inches long is closest in length to which of the following?

    (A) 7
    (B) 14
    (C) 21
    (D) 24
    (E) 28

19. In the first year of the United States Stickball League, the Bayonne Bombers won 50% of their games. During the second season of the league the Bombers won 65% of their games. If there were twice as many games played in the second season as in the first, what percentage of the games did the Bombers win in the first two years of the league?

    (A) 115%
    (B) 60%
    (C) 57.5%
    (D) 55%
    (E) It cannot be determined from the information given.

20. If the total weight of an apple is $\frac{4}{5}$ of its weight plus $\frac{4}{5}$ of an ounce, what is its weight in ounces?

    (A) $1\frac{3}{5}$
    (B) $3\frac{1}{2}$
    (C) 4
    (D) $4\frac{4}{5}$
    (E) 5

GO ON TO THE NEXT PAGE

21. Nine playing cards from the same deck are placed as shown in the figure below to form a large rectangle of area 180 sq. in. How many inches are there in the perimeter of this large rectangle?

    (A) 29
    (B) 58
    (C) 64
    (D) 116
    (E) 210

22. If each of the dimensions of a rectangle is increased 100%, the area is increased

    (A) 100%
    (B) 200%
    (C) 300%
    (D) 400%
    (E) 500%

23. A recipe for a cake calls for $2\frac{1}{2}$ cups of milk and 3 cups of flour. With this recipe, a cake was baked using 14 cups of flour. How many cups of milk were required?

    (A) $10\frac{1}{3}$
    (B) $10\frac{3}{4}$
    (C) 11
    (D) $11\frac{3}{5}$
    (E) $11\frac{2}{3}$

24. In the figure below, M and N are midpoints of the sides PR and PQ, respectively, of $\triangle PQR$. What is the ratio of the area of $\triangle MNS$ to that of $\triangle PQR$?

    (A) 2 : 5
    (B) 2 : 9
    (C) 1 : 4
    (D) 1 : 8
    (E) 1 : 12

25. What is 10% of $\frac{1}{3}x$ if $\frac{2}{3}x$ is 10% of 60?

    (A) .1
    (B) .2
    (C) .3
    (D) .4
    (E) .5

STOP

END OF SECTION 1. IF YOU HAVE ANY TIME LEFT, GO OVER YOUR WORK IN THIS SECTION ONLY. DO NOT WORK IN ANY OTHER SECTION OF THE TEST.

SECTION 2

31 Questions • Time—30 Minutes

Directions: Each of the following questions consists of an incomplete sentence followed by five words or pairs of words. Choose that word or pair of words which, when substituted for the blank space or spaces, *best* completes the meaning of the sentence and mark the letter of your choice on your answer sheet.

Example:

In view of the extenuating circumstances and the defendant's youth, the judge recommended ----.

(A) conviction
(B) a defense
(C) a mistrial
(D) leniency
(E) life imprisonment

Ⓐ Ⓑ Ⓒ ● Ⓔ

1. Because the elder Johnson was regarded with much ---- by an appreciative public, the younger quite naturally received ----.

    (A) disdain..kudos
    (B) awe..respect
    (C) curiosity..familiarity
    (D) contemplation..abandonment
    (E) pleasantry..laughs

2. Her temperament was exceedingly ----, angry one minute but serene the next.

    (A) mercurial
    (B) steadfast
    (C) distraught
    (D) archetypal
    (E) circumspect

3. Traveling by automobile was ---- to him, but he thought nothing of bobsledding, which had been his ---- for many years.

    (A) tiresome..profession
    (B) tiring..outlet
    (C) harrowing..hobby
    (D) a threat..relief
    (E) exciting..fun

4. Perennial flowers such as irises remain ---- every winter, but they ---- in the spring.

    (A) fertile..wither
    (B) arable..congeal
    (C) dormant..burgeon
    (D) distended..contract
    (E) attenuated..rebound

5. The ---- customer was ---- by the manager's prompt action and apology.

    (A) pecuniary..appalled
    (B) weary..enervated
    (C) sedulous..consoled
    (D) intrepid..mortified
    (E) irate..mollified

6. His ---- manner served to hide the fact that he secretly indulged in the very vices he publicly ---- .

    (A) sedulous..dispelled
    (B) sanctimonious..condemned
    (C) dogmatic..espoused
    (D) stentorian..prescribed
    (E) candid..promulgated

7. Because of the ---- caused by the flood, living conditions in the area have ---- ; many people have lost all their belongings.

    (A) trepidation..augmented
    (B) morass..careened
    (C) censure..abated
    (D) devastation..deteriorated
    (E) vertigo..ameliorated

GO ON TO THE NEXT PAGE

8. Propaganda is a(n) ---- of truth, a mixture of half-truths and half-lies calculated to deceive.

   (A) revision
   (B) perversion
   (C) dissension
   (D) perception
   (E) invasion

9. Though brilliantly presented, the report was ---- since the information on which it was based was erroneous.

   (A) informative
   (B) erudite
   (C) laudable
   (D) worthless
   (E) verbose

Directions: Each of the following questions consists of a capitalized pair of words followed by five pairs of words lettered A to E. The capitalized words bear some meaningful relationship to each other. Choose the lettered pair of words whose relationship is most similar to that expressed by the capitalized pair and mark its letter on your answer sheet.

Example:

DAY : SUN : :

   (A) sunlight : daylight
   (B) ray : sun
   (C) night : moon
   (D) heat : cold
   (E) moon : star

   Ⓐ Ⓑ ● Ⓓ Ⓔ

10. NOSE : HEAD : :

    (A) hand : arm
    (B) foot : toe
    (C) eye : lid
    (D) wrist : finger
    (E) teeth : gums

11. WHEAT : GRAIN : :

    (A) cow : beef
    (B) orange : lime
    (C) carrot : vegetable
    (D) coconut : palm
    (E) hamburger : steak

12. COTTAGE : CASTLE : :

    (A) house : apartment
    (B) puppy : dog
    (C) dory : liner
    (D) man : family
    (E) poet : gentleman

13. OLD : ANTIQUE : :

    (A) new : modern
    (B) cheap : expensive
    (C) useless : useful
    (D) wanted : needed
    (E) rich : valuable

14. POSSIBLE : PROBABLE : :

    (A) likely : unlikely
    (B) best : better
    (C) willing : eager
    (D) quick : fast
    (E) frightened : worried

15. DIGRESS : RAMBLE : :

    (A) muffle : stifle
    (B) rust : weld
    (C) introduce : conclude
    (D) rest : stir
    (E) find : explain

Directions: Each passage below is followed by a set of questions. Read each passage, then answer the accompanying questions, basing your answers on what is stated or implied in the passage and in any introductory material provided. Mark the letter of your choice on your answer sheet.

Questions 16–22 are based on the following passage.

This passage is taken from the first book of short stories published by Willa Cather (1873–1947), better known for her novels of the western past such as O Pioneers! *For obvious reasons, "Paul's Case" is subtitled "A Study in Temperament."*

It was Paul's afternoon to appear before the faculty of the Pittsburgh High School to account for his various misdemeanors. He had been suspended a week ago, and his father had called at the Principal's (5) office and confessed his perplexity about his son. Paul entered the faculty room suave and smiling. His clothes were a trifle outgrown, and the tan velvet on the collar of his open overcoat was frayed and worn; but for all that there was something of the dandy in (10) him, and he wore an opal pin in his neatly knotted black four-in-hand, and a red carnation in his buttonhole. This latter adornment the faculty somehow felt was not properly significant of the contrite spirit befitting a boy under the ban of suspension.

(15) Paul was tall for his age and very thin, with high, cramped shoulders and a narrow chest. His eyes were remarkable for a certain hysterical brilliancy, and he continually used them in a conscious, theatrical sort of way, peculiarly offensive in a boy. (20) The pupils were abnormally large, as though he was addicted to belladonna, but there was a glassy glitter about them which that drug does not produce.

When questioned by the Principal as to why he was there Paul stated, politely enough, that he wanted (25) to come back to school. This was a lie, but Paul was quite accustomed to lying; found it, indeed, indispensable for overcoming friction. His teachers were asked to state their respective charges against him, which they did with such a rancor and aggrievedness (30) as evinced that this was not a usual case. Disorder and impertinence were among the offenses named, yet each of his instructors felt that it was scarcely possible to put into words the cause of the trouble, which lay in a sort of hysterically defiant manner of (35) the boy's; in the contempt which they all knew he felt for them, and which he seemingly made not the least effort to conceal. Once, when he had been making a synopsis of a paragraph at the blackboard, his English teacher had stepped to his side and attempted to guide (40) his hand. Paul had started back with a shudder and thrust his hands violently behind him. The astonished woman could scarcely have been more hurt and embarrassed had he struck at her. The insult was so involuntary and definitely personal as to be unforgettable. In one way (45) and another he had made all of his teachers, men and women alike, conscious of the same feeling of physical aversion. In one class he habitually sat with his hand shading his eyes; in another he always looked out the window during the recitation; in another he made a (50) running commentary on the lecture, with humorous intention.

His teachers felt this afternoon that his whole attitude was symbolized by his shrug and his flippantly red carnation flower, and they fell upon him without mercy, (55) his English teacher leading the pack. He stood through it smiling, his pale lips parted over his white teeth. (His lips were constantly twitching, and he had a habit of raising his eyebrows that was contemptuous and irritating to the last degree.) Older boys than Paul had broken (60) down and shed tears under that baptism of fire, but his set smile did not once desert him, and his only sign of discomfort was the nervous trembling of the fingers that toyed with the buttons of his overcoat, and an occasional jerking of the other hand that held his hat. (65) Paul was always smiling, always glancing about him, seeming to feel that people might be watching him and trying to detect something. This conscious expression, since it was as far as possible from boyish mirthfulness, was usually attributed to insolence or "smartness."

16. The subtitle "A Study in Temperament" suggests that Cather wants to examine

  (A) a certain type of character
  (B) reactions under pressure
  (C) how people change over time
  (D) people and their settings
  (E) inner rage

17. Cather makes it clear in the first paragraph that the faculty of the high school

    (A) are perplexed by Paul's actions
    (B) find Paul's demeanor inappropriate
    (C) cannot understand Paul's words
    (D) want only the best for Paul
    (E) are annoyed at Paul's disruption of their day

18. As it is used in lines 17 and 33–34, *hysterical* seems to imply

    (A) hilarious
    (B) raving
    (C) uncontrolled
    (D) frothing
    (E) delirious

19. To keep the reader from sympathizing with the faculty, Cather compares them metaphorically to

    (A) rabbits
    (B) wolves
    (C) dictators
    (D) comedians
    (E) warships

20. The word *smartness* (line 69) is used to mean

    (A) wit
    (B) intelligence
    (C) impudence
    (D) reasonableness
    (E) resoucefulness

21. Which adjective does *not* describe Paul as Cather presents him here?

    (A) paranoid
    (B) defiant
    (C) proud
    (D) flippant
    (E) candid

22. By the end of the selection, we find that the faculty

    (A) resent and loathe Paul
    (B) admire and trust Paul
    (C) struggle to understand Paul
    (D) are physically revolted by Paul
    (E) may learn to get along with Paul

Questions 23–31 are based on the following passage.

Thomas Jefferson wrote in 1787 to his nephew, Peter Carr, a student at the College of William and Mary. Here, Jefferson gives advice about Peter's proposed course of study.

Paris, August 10, 1787

Dear Peter, _____ I have received your two letters of Deccmb. 30. and April 18. and am very happy to find by them, as well as by letters from Mr. Wythe, that you have been so fortunate as to attract his notice and good
(5) will: I am sure you will find this to have been one of the more fortunate events of your life, as I have ever been sensible it was of mine. I inclose you a sketch of the sciences to which I would wish you to apply in such order as Mr. Wythe shall advise: I mention also the
(10) books in them worth your reading, which submit to his correction. Many of these are among your father's books, which you should have brought to you. As I do not recollect those of them not in his library, you must write to me for them, making out a catalogue of such
(15) as you think you shall have occasion for in 18 months from the date of your letter, and consulting Mr. Wythe on the subject. To this sketch I will add a few particular observations.

 1. *Italian.* I fear the learning of this language will
(20) confound your French and Spanish. Being all of them degenerated dialects of the Latin, they are apt to mix in conversation. I have never seen a person speaking the three languages who did not mix them. It is a delightful language, but late events having rendered the Spanish
(25) more useful, lay it aside to prosecute that.

 2. *Spanish.* Bestow great attention on this, and endeavor to acquire an accurate knowledge of it. Our future connections with Spain and Spanish America will render that language a valuable acquisition. The
(30) ancient history of a great part of America too is written in that language. I send you a dictionary.

 3. *Moral philosophy.* I think it lost time to attend lectures in this branch. He who made us would have been a pitiful bungler if he had made the rules of our
(35) moral conduct a matter of science. For one man of science, there are thousands who are not. What would have become of them? Man was destined for society. His morality therefore was to be formed to this object.

He was endowed with a sense of right and wrong
(40) merely relative to this. This sense is as much a part
of his nature as the sense of hearing, seeing, feeling;
it is the true foundation of morality. . . . The moral
sense, or conscience, is as much a part of man as his
leg or arm. It is given to all human beings in a
(45) stronger or weaker degree, as force of members is
given them in a greater or less degree. . . .State a
moral case to a ploughman and a professor. The
former will decide it as well, and often better than the
latter, because he has not been led astray by artificial
(50) rules. . . .

23. As he refers to Mr. Wythe, Jefferson seems to

   (A) affect an air of condescension
   (B) reject many of that man's opinions
   (C) warn his nephew not to repeat his mistakes
   (D) relive pleasant memories from his youth
   (E) dispute his nephew's preconceived notions

24. Jefferson uses the word *sciences* (line 8) to mean

   (A) Italian and Spanish only
   (B) moral philosophy and the physical sciences
   (C) school subjects in general
   (D) the subjects treated in his father's books
   (E) biology and chemistry

25. Jefferson's numbered points refer to

   (A) subjects in order of importance
   (B) academic courses
   (C) languages of the world
   (D) topics discussed in an earlier letter
   (E) items from a catalogue

26. Jefferson uses the word *confound* (line 20) to mean

   (A) fluster
   (B) misunderstand
   (C) curse
   (D) muddle
   (E) clarify

27. Jefferson encourages his nephew to study Spanish because

   (A) it is related to Latin
   (B) it will prove useful in international relations
   (C) there are many good dictionaries available
   (D) it will prove helpful in learning Italian
   (E) it is the language of history

28. By "lost time" (line 32), Jefferson means

   (A) wasted time
   (B) the past
   (C) missing time
   (D) youth
   (E) about time

29. Jefferson's main objection to attending lectures in moral philosophy is that

   (A) it could be taught as well by farmers
   (B) it is innate and cannot be taught
   (C) it is better practiced outside school
   (D) very few people understand what it means
   (E) parents, not professors, should be the instructors

30. The example of the ploughman and the professor is used to

   (A) illustrate the uselessness of education
   (B) demonstrate the path to true knowledge
   (C) explain the universality of morality
   (D) define the nature of conscience
   (E) disprove Mr. Wythe's theory of moral conduct

GO ON TO THE NEXT PAGE

31. Jefferson compares conscience to a physical limb of the body to show

   (A) that it is natural and present in all human beings
   (B) how easily we take it for granted
   (C) that without it, men are powerless
   (D) how mental and physical states are integrated
   (E) what is meant by "the arm of the law."

SECTION 3

25 Questions • Time—30 Minutes

Directions: Solve the following problems using any available space on the page for scratchwork. On your answer sheet fill in the choice which best corresponds to the correct answer.

Notes: The figures accompanying the problems are drawn as accurately as possible unless otherwise stated in specific problems. Again, unless otherwise stated, all figures lie in the same plane. All numbers used in these problems are real numbers. Calculators are permitted for this test.

Reference Information

Circle: $C = 2\pi r$, $A = \pi r^2$

Rectangle: $A = lw$

Rectangular Solid: $V = lwh$

Cylinder: $V = \pi r^2 h$

Triangle: $A = \frac{1}{2}bh$

$a^2 + b^2 = c^2$

45°-45°-90° triangle: sides x, x, $x\sqrt{2}$

30°-60°-90° triangle: sides x, $x\sqrt{3}$, $2x$

The number of degrees of arc in a circle is 360.
The measure in degrees of a straight angle is 180.
The sum of the measures in degrees of the angles of a triangle is 180.

Part 1: Quantitative Comparison Questions

Directions: For each of the following questions, two quantities are given—one in Column A, and the other in Column B. Compare the two quantities and mark your answer sheet as follows:

(A) if the quantity in Column A is greater
(B) if the quantity in Column B is greater
(C) if the two quantities are equal
(D) if the relationship cannot be determined from the information given.

Notes:

(1) Information concerning one or both of the compared quantities will be centered above the two columns for some items.
(2) Symbols that appear in both columns represent the same thing in Column A as in Column B.
(3) Letters such as x, n, and k are symbols for real numbers.

Examples

	Column A	Column B	Answers
	$a > 0$		
	$x > 0$		
E1.	$a - x$	$a + x$	(A) ● (C) (D)
E2.	The average of 17, 19, 21, 23	The average of 16, 18, 20, 22	● (B) (C) (D)

DO NOT MARK CHOICE (E) FOR THESE QUESTIONS. THERE ARE ONLY FOUR ANSWER CHOICES.

GO ON TO THE NEXT PAGE

352 Master the SAT

	Column A	Column B
1.	The number of sides in a polygon	The number of sides in a quadrilateral

Triangle with vertices A, B, C; AB = 4, BC = 6, AC = y

	Column A	Column B
2.	Length of side AC	10

$x(y + z) = 0$
$y = -z$

	Column A	Column B
3.	x	$y + z$

	Column A	Column B
4.	Area of a circle with a radius of $\frac{2r}{3}$	Area of a circle with a diameter of $\frac{4r}{3}$

$a \, \phi \, b = (a + b)(a - b)$

	Column A	Column B
5.	$2 \, \phi \, 2$	$-2 \, \phi \, -2$

p is an integer

	Column A	Column B
6.	The ratio of p to $(p + 1)$ if $5 < p < 10$	The ratio of p to $(p + 1)$ if $10 < p < 15$

Triangle A: right triangle with legs y and x
Triangle B: right triangle with legs $2y$ and $\frac{x}{2}$

	Column A	Column B
7.	Area of triangle A	Area of triangle B

Figure with angles a, b, c, d formed by intersecting lines

	Column A	Column B
8.	$\dfrac{a + b + c + d}{4}$	90

Questions 9 and 10 refer to the statement below.

In a sequence of N numbers the first is -1, the second is 1, the third is -2, the fourth is 2, and so on.

	Column A	Column B
9.	The ninth number times the eleventh number	The tenth number times the twelfth number
10.	The sum of the first through the fifth numbers	The sum of the sixth through the tenth numbers

$0 < k < 1$

	Column A	Column B
11.	$2k$	k^2

	Column A	Column B		Column A	Column B
	\multicolumn{2}{c	}{p is a positive integer}		\multicolumn{2}{c	}{$\dfrac{m^4}{3}=27$}
12.	The remainder when $3p + 5$ is divided by 3	The remainder when $7p + 8$ is divided by 7	14.	m	4
				\multicolumn{2}{c	}{$s > 1$}
13.	The number of prime numbers between 1 and 25	9	15.	The volume of a cube with a side of s	The volume of a rectangular solid with sides of s, $s + 1$, and $s - 1$

Part 2: Student-Produced Response Questions

Directions: Solve each of these problems. Write the answer in the corresponding grid on the answer sheet and fill in the ovals beneath each answer you write. Here are some examples.

Answer: $\dfrac{3}{4}$ (= .75; show answer either way)   Answer: 325

Note: A mixed number such as $3\frac{1}{2}$ must be gridded as 7/2 or as 3.5. If gridded as "3 1/2," it will be read as "thirty-one halves."

Note: Either position is correct.

GO ON TO THE NEXT PAGE

16. The average temperatures for five days were 82°, 86°, 91°, 79°, and 91°. What is the mode for these temperatures?

17. If $-2x + 5 = 2 - (5 - 2x)$, what is the value of x?

18. In the figure below, $BA \perp AD$ and $CD \perp AD$. Using the values indicated in the figure, what is the area of polygon $ABCD$?

19. In the figure below, $AC = BC$. If m $\angle B = 50°$, what is the measure of $\angle ECD$? (Do not grid the degree symbol.)

20. What is the value of $-m^2 n^3$, when m = -2 and n = -1?

21. Given a square, a rectangle, a trapezoid, and a circle, if one of these figures is selected at random, what is the probability that the figure has four right angles?

22. Given the concentric circles above, if radius JN is 3 times JU, then the ratio of the shaded area to the area of sector NJL is $1:b$. What is the value of b?

23. In a three-hour examination of 350 questions, there are 50 mathematical problems. If twice as much time should be allowed for each problem as for each of the other questions, how many minutes should be spent on the mathematical problems?

24. In a pantry there are 28 cans of vegetables. Eight of these have labels with white lettering, 18 have labels with green lettering, and 8 have labels with neither white nor green lettering. How many cans have both white and green lettering?

25. B, C and D divide AE into 4 equal parts. AB, BC, CD are divided into 4 equal parts as shown.

   DE is divided into 3 equal parts as shown.

   $$\frac{x+z}{y} =$$

STOP

END OF SECTION 3. IF YOU HAVE ANY TIME LEFT, GO OVER YOUR WORK IN THIS SECTION ONLY. DO NOT WORK IN ANY OTHER SECTION OF THE TEST.

SECTION 4

35 Questions • Time—30 Minutes

Directions: Each of the following questions consists of an incomplete sentence followed by five words or pairs of words. Choose that word or pair of words which, when substituted for the blank space or spaces, best completes the meaning of the sentence and mark the letter of your choice on your answer sheet.

Example:

In view of the extenuating circumstances and the defendant's youth, the judge recommended ----.

(A) conviction
(B) a defense
(C) a mistrial
(D) leniency
(E) life imprisonment

Ⓐ Ⓑ Ⓒ ● Ⓔ

1. He dashed into the house, ran for the phone, and answered ----, tripping over the cord.

   (A) hesitantly
   (B) nobly
   (C) soothingly
   (D) distantly
   (E) breathlessly

2. The criminal record of the witness caused the jury to ---- his testimony.

   (A) affirm
   (B) belie
   (C) retract
   (D) acquit
   (E) discredit

3. Although the storm left the family ----, it could not ---- their spirits.

   (A) discordant..raise
   (B) moribund..drench
   (C) destitute..dampen
   (D) sodden..excite
   (E) indolent..inhibit

4. By a stroke of luck the troops ----, avoiding a crushing ----.

   (A) converged..blow
   (B) prevailed..defeat
   (C) diverged..siege
   (D) retrenched..retreat
   (E) interceded..assault

5. You must act with ---- if you want to buy your airline ticket before tomorrow's price increase.

   (A) celerity
   (B) clemency
   (C) facility
   (D) lassitude
   (E) laxity

6. The ---- background music hinted of the dangers threatening the movie's heroine.

   (A) trenchant
   (B) ebullient
   (C) sardonic
   (D) portentous
   (E) precocious

7. Nineteenth-century advances in women's rights were gradual and ----; years might separate one advance from the next.

   (A) reticent
   (B) onerous
   (C) incumbent
   (D) docile
   (E) sporadic

8. Since several offices have been ---- across the street, the old directory is now ----.

   (A) refurbished..adequate
   (B) relocated..obsolete
   (C) deployed..reserved
   (D) transmuted..oblivious
   (E) removed..upgraded

9. The junta's promise of free elections was ----, a mere sop to world opinion.

   (A) spurious
   (B) contentious
   (C) unctuous
   (D) lucid
   (E) presumptuous

10. The woman acted in a ---- manner, pretending not to notice the nearby celebrities.

    (A) convivial
    (B) doleful
    (C) nonchalant
    (D) cogent
    (E) vicarious

Directions: Each of the following questions consists of a capitalized pair of words followed by five pairs of words lettered A to E. The capitalized words bear some meaningful relationship to each other. Choose the lettered pair of words whose relationship is most similar to that expressed by the capitalized pair and mark its letter on your answer sheet.

Example:

DAY : SUN ::

(A) sunlight : daylight
(B) ray : sun
(C) night : moon
(D) heat : cold
(E) moon : star

Ⓐ Ⓑ ● Ⓓ Ⓔ

11. LIBRARY : BOOKS : :

   (A) hotel : children
   (B) zoo : animals
   (C) office : sales
   (D) park : cars
   (E) school : buses

12. TINY : HUGE : :

   (A) small : little
   (B) great : grand
   (C) weak : strong
   (D) sad : gloomy
   (E) chaotic : confused

13. FRIGHTEN : SCARE : :

   (A) question : ask
   (B) look : see
   (C) terrorize : startle
   (D) brave : fear
   (E) upset : calm

14. SEARCH : FIND : :

   (A) fight : win
   (B) obey : believe
   (C) look : seek
   (D) write : read
   (E) listen : talk

15. DOOR : OPEN : :

   (A) cap : remove
   (B) knife : cut
   (C) blackboard : erase
   (D) gift : take
   (E) car : speed

16. DASTARD : COWARDICE : :

   (A) cipher : importance
   (B) scoundrel : immorality
   (C) native : intimacy
   (D) refugee : nationality
   (E) client : independence

17. TOE : FOOT : :

   (A) elbow : wrist
   (B) fist : hand
   (C) shoe : sock
   (D) pupil : eye
   (E) arm : leg

18. STRUM : GUITAR : :

   (A) tune : instrument
   (B) tighten : drum
   (C) polish : bugle
   (D) pedal : organ
   (E) hum : song

19. PUERILE : MATURITY : :

   (A) pungent : poignancy
   (B) poised : serenity
   (C) obscure : clarity
   (D) ostentatious : pretension
   (E) profuse : extravagance

20. HURTLE : TOSS : :

   (A) strike : tap
   (B) throw : bite
   (C) squelch : crush
   (D) quarrel : squabble
   (E) murmur : mumble

21. INFINITE : BOUNDS : :

   (A) intangible : property
   (B) kinetic : motion
   (C) nebulous : clarity
   (D) ponderous : bulk
   (E) propitious : favor

22. TIME : MINUTES : :
    (A) month : calendar
    (B) clock : faces
    (C) race : laps
    (D) yard : square
    (E) arms : legs

23. MOUNTAIN : TUNNEL : :
    (A) window : frame
    (B) river : bridge
    (C) door : handle
    (D) charcoal : fire
    (E) wall : window

GO ON TO THE NEXT PAGE

Questions 24–35 are based on the following passage.

A major step forward in the history of the novel, Don Quixote was penned by Miguel de Cervantes and first published in Spain in 1605. Driven mad by his constant perusal of tales of chivalry, Alonso Quijano changes his name to Don Quixote and rides off to seek adventure. This passage describes his First Expedition.

Once these preparations were completed, he was anxious to wait no longer before putting his ideas into effect, impelled to this by the thought of the loss the world suffered by his delay, seeing the grievances
(5) there were to redress, the wrongs to right, the injuries to amend, and the debts to discharge. So, telling nobody of his intentions, and quite unobserved, one morning before dawn—it was on one of those sweltering July days—he armed himself completely, mounted
(10) Rocinante, put on his badly-mended headpiece, slung on his shield, seized his lance and went out into the plain through the back gate of his yard, pleased and delighted to see with what ease he had started on his fair design. But scarcely was he in open country when
(15) he was assailed by a thought so terrible that it almost made him abandon the enterprise he had just begun. For he suddenly remembered that he had never received the honor of knighthood, and so, according to the laws of chivalry, he neither could nor should take
(20) arms against any knight, and even if he had been knighted he was bound, as a novice, to wear plain armour without a device on his shield until he should gain one by his prowess. These reflections made him waver in his resolve, but as his madness outweighed
(25) any other argument, he made up his mind to have himself knighted by the first man he met, in imitation of many who had done the same, as he had read in the books which had so influenced him. As to plain armor, he decided to clean his own, when he had time, till it
(30) was whiter than ermine. With this he quieted his mind and went on his way, taking whatever road his horse chose, in the belief that in this lay the essence of adventure.

As our brand-new adventurer journeyed along, he
(35) talked to himself, saying: "Who can doubt that in ages to come, when the authentic story of my famous deeds comes to light, the sage who writes of them will say, when he comes to tell of my first expedition so early in the morning: 'Scarce had the ruddy Apollo spread
(40) the golden threads of his lovely hair over the broad and spacious face of the earth, and scarcely had the forked tongues of the little painted birds greeted with mellifluous harmony the coming of the rosy Aurora who, leaving the soft bed of her jealous husband, showed
(45) herself at the doors and balconies of the Manchegan horizon, when the famous knight, Don Quixote de la Mancha, quitting the slothful down, mounted his famous steed Rocinante and began to journey across the ancient and celebrated plain of Montiel'?" That
(50) was, in fact, the road that our knight actually took, as he went on: "Fortunate the age and fortunate the times in which my famous deeds will come to light, deeds worthy to be engraved in bronze, carved in marble and painted on wood, as a memorial for posterity. And
(55) you, sage enchanter, whoever you may be, to whose lot it falls to be the chronicler of this strange history, I beg you not to forget my good Rocinante, my constant companion on all my rides and journeys!" And presently he cried again, as if he had really been
(60) in love: "O Princess Dulcinea, mistress of this captive heart! You did me great injury in dismissing me and inflicting on me the cruel rigour of your command not to appear in your beauteous presence. Deign, lady, to be mindful of your captive heart, which suffers such
(65) griefs for love of you."

He went on stringing other nonsense on to this, all after the fashion he had learnt in his reading, and imitating the language of his books as best he could. And all the while he rode so slowly and the sun's heat
(70) increased so fast that it would have been enough to turn his brain, if he had had any.

24. The word *redress* in line 5 most nearly means

  (A) to locate a residence
  (B) to put on clothes
  (C) to downplay
  (D) to correct
  (E) to confuse

25. As described in lines 19–24, Don Quixote was hesitant to fight because

    (A) he was afraid for his life
    (B) he didn't believe in violence
    (C) he would break the established code of chivalry
    (D) he would lose his wife if he fought for what he truly believed
    (E) he was indifferent to the cause

26. The word *device* in line 22 probably means

    (A) emblem
    (B) tool
    (C) gadget
    (D) trick
    (E) metal

27. The words that best describe the first speech Cervantes has Don Quixote make (lines 35–49) might be

    (A) informative and deliberate
    (B) profound and resolute
    (C) dull and ill-conceived
    (D) shocking and defamatory
    (E) flowery and overwrought

28. What does Don Quixote mean when he says "quitting the slothful down" (line 47)?

    (A) leaving the farm
    (B) climbing into the saddle
    (C) feeling happier and more energetic
    (D) recovering from illness
    (E) getting out of bed

29. The phrase "as if he had really been in love" (lines 59–60) is used to illuminate Don Quixote's

    (A) need for attention
    (B) starved spirit
    (C) dementia
    (D) unhappy childhood
    (E) inability to emote

30. Cervantes has his hero address his remarks to

    (A) God
    (B) the reader
    (C) his horse
    (D) a mythical historian and a princess
    (E) an unknown knight

31. The last line of the selection reminds us that

    (A) the story takes place in Spain
    (B) Don Quixote is mad
    (C) Rocinante has no destination in mind
    (D) other knights have taken this same route
    (E) the long day is about to end

32. We first suspect that Don Quixote is not quite the hero he seems when he recalls that

    (A) he left his armor at home
    (B) his horse is named Rocinante
    (C) he is not a real knight
    (D) Dulcinea holds him captive
    (E) he started his journey with ease

33. According to the author, Don Quixote's speech is affected by

    (A) romantic books he has read
    (B) the language of seventeenth-century Spain
    (C) letters received from Dulcinea
    (D) the speeches of Alfonso X
    (E) his night visions

34. Cervantes's opinion of the literature of his day seems to be that it is

    (A) written by madmen
    (B) argumentative and controversial
    (C) not up to the standards of the previous century
    (D) sentimental drivel
    (E) derivative

35. The best word to describe Cervantes's feeling toward his hero might be

    (A) disdainful
    (B) revolted
    (C) indifferent
    (D) mocking
    (E) appreciative

STOP

END OF SECTION 4. IF YOU HAVE ANY TIME LEFT, GO OVER YOUR WORK IN THIS SECTION ONLY. DO NOT WORK IN ANY OTHER SECTION OF THE TEST.

SECTION 5

10 Questions • Time—15 Minutes

Directions: Solve the following problems using any available space on the page for scratchwork. On your answer sheet fill in the choice which best corresponds to the correct answer.

Notes: The figures accompanying the problems are drawn as accurately as possible unless otherwise stated in specific problems. Again, unless otherwise stated, all figures lie in the same plane. All numbers used in these problems are real numbers. Calculators are permitted for this test.

Reference Information

Circle: $C = 2\pi r$, $A = \pi r^2$
Rectangle: $A = lw$
Rectangular Solid: $V = lwh$
Cylinder: $V = \pi r^2 h$
Triangle: $A = \frac{1}{2}bh$
$a^2 + b^2 = c^2$

Special right triangles: 45°-45°-90° with sides x, x, $x\sqrt{2}$; 30°-60°-90° with sides x, $x\sqrt{3}$, $2x$.

The number of degrees of arc in a circle is 360.
The measure in degrees of a straight angle is 180.
The sum of the measures in degrees of the angles of a triangle is 180.

---

1. The total savings in purchasing thirty 13-cent lollipops for a class party at a reduced rate of $1.38 per dozen is

    (A) $.35
    (B) $.38
    (C) $.40
    (D) $.45
    (E) $.50

2. A gallon of water is equal to 231 cubic inches. How many gallons of water are needed to fill a fish tank that measures 11" high, 14" long, and 9" wide?

    (A) 6
    (B) 8
    (C) 9
    (D) 14
    (E) 16

3. The area of a right triangle is 12 square inches. The ratio of its legs is 2:3. Find the number of inches in the hypotenuse of this triangle.

    (A) $\sqrt{13}$
    (B) $\sqrt{26}$
    (C) $3\sqrt{13}$
    (D) $\sqrt{52}$
    (E) $4\sqrt{13}$

4. A rectangular block of metal weighs 3 ounces. How many pounds will a similar block of the same metal weigh if the edges are twice as large?

    (A) $\frac{3}{8}$
    (B) $\frac{3}{4}$
    (C) $1\frac{1}{2}$
    (D) 3
    (E) 24

5. A college graduate goes to work for x dollars per week. After several months the company gives all the employees a 10% pay cut. A few months later the company gives all the employees a 10% raise. What is the college graduate's new salary?

   (A) $.90x$
   (B) $.99x$
   (C) x
   (D) $1.01x$
   (E) $1.11x$

6. What is the net amount of a bill of $428.00 after a discount of 6% has been allowed?

   (A) $432.62
   (B) $430.88
   (C) $414.85
   (D) $412.19
   (E) $402.32

7. A certain type of board is sold only in lengths of multiples of 2 feet, from 6 feet to 24 feet. A builder needs a larger quantity of this type of board in $5\frac{1}{2}$-foot lengths. For minimum waste, the lengths in feet to be ordered should be

   (A) 6
   (B) 12
   (C) 18
   (D) 22
   (E) 24

8. A cube has an edge which is four inches long. If the edge is increased by 25%, then the volume is increased by approximately

   (A) 25%
   (B) 48%
   (C) 73%
   (D) 95%
   (E) 122%

9. The ratio of $\frac{1}{4}$ to $\frac{3}{5}$ is

   (A) 1 to 3
   (B) 3 to 20
   (C) 5 to 12
   (D) 3 to 4
   (E) 5 to 4

10. Which of the following numbers is the smallest?

    (A) $\sqrt{3}$
    (B) $\dfrac{1}{\sqrt{3}}$
    (C) $\dfrac{\sqrt{3}}{3}$
    (D) $\dfrac{1}{3}$
    (E) $\dfrac{1}{3\sqrt{3}}$

STOP

END OF SECTION 5. IF YOU HAVE ANY TIME LEFT, GO OVER YOUR WORK IN THIS SECTION ONLY. DO NOT WORK IN ANY OTHER SECTION OF THE TEST.

SECTION 6

12 Questions • Time—15 Minutes

Directions: The two passages given below deal with a related topic. Following the passages are questions about the content of each passage or about the relationship between the two passages. Answer the questions based upon what is stated or implied in the passages and in any introductory material provided. Mark the letter of your choice on your answer sheet.

Questions 1–12 are based on the following passages:

The struggle of African Americans to make economic and political progress within the socio-economic structure of the United States has been long and filled with setbacks. These two passages document some of the events in that long struggle and seek to explain why the struggle was so difficult.

Passage 1—The Economic Scene

Because of slavery, which lasted until 1865, and undereducation, African Americans have been at a disadvantage in terms of socio-economic progress until well into the twentieth century. Segregated schools
(5) were often not on a par with the schools in which whites were educated; consequently, when African Americans competed for jobs with whites, they often found they could not.

Increased opportunities for African Americans fol-
(10) lowed in the wake of the civil rights movement, and as a result, African Americans were able to gain higher levels of education and achieve more managerial positions within the various professions. In the 1980s, African Americans moved into the upper middle class
(15) in large numbers.

Consistently in the last five decades, African Americans have moved into higher-status jobs, have opened their own businesses, and have increased their levels of education. Because of such progress, it is safe to
(20) assume that those African Americans who have become upwardly mobile would not be able to tolerate racial discrimination as it existed prior to the civil rights movement.

While progress has been made in some segments of
(25) the African-American population, less progress has occurred among low-income African Americans. Many low-income African Americans do not have a place in the class structure because of racial segregation and poverty, particularly in urban areas. When segrega-
(30) tion and poverty prevail, urban neighborhoods become places of high crime, poor schools, and poorly maintained homes.

Thus, what has emerged in the 1990s is a widening socio-economic gap between low-income African
(35) Americans and the African Americans who have been able to improve their socio-economic status.

Passage 2—The Political Scene

Only with the enforcement of the Reconstruction Act of 1867 and the ratification of the Fifteenth Amendment to the Constitution did African Ameri-
(40) cans first win seats in Congress. Hiram Revels of Mississippi became the first African American to serve in Congress when he took his seat in the Senate on February 25, 1870. Joseph Rainey of South Carolina became the first African American member of the
(45) House of Representatives later in 1870.

African Americans throughout the South became politically active soon after emancipation and the close of the Civil War. A generation of African American leaders emerged who nearly unanimously
(50) adhered to the Republican Party because it had championed the rights of African Americans. African Americans elected to Congress during Reconstruction found the national legislature an effective forum for the advocacy of political equality. Follow-
(55) ing the end of federal Reconstruction in 1877, African Americans continued to win election to Congress, and carried on the struggle for civil rights and economic opportunity.

During the 1890s and early 1900s, no African
(60) American won election to Congress, in part because of restrictive state election codes in some southern states.

During World War I and in the following decade, however, African American migration to northern cities established the foundations for political
(65) organization in urban centers. Over the next three decades African Americans won congressional seats in New York City, Detroit, and Philadelphia. In the wake of the civil rights movement and the enforcement of the Voting Rights Act of 1965, African
(70) Americans regained seats in the South. Since the 1930s, nearly all African American representatives have been Democrats.

Since the nineteenth century, African American members of Congress have served as advocates for
(75) all African Americans as well as representatives for their constituencies. During Reconstruction and the late nineteenth century, African American representatives called on their colleagues to protect the voting rights of African Americans. They also called for
(80) expanded educational opportunities and land grants for freed African Americans. In the mid-twentieth century, African American representatives turned to the needs of urban communities and urged federal programs for improved housing and job training.
(85) These representatives served as defenders of the civil rights movement and proponents of legislation to end segregation. The Congressional Black Caucus demonstrated a special concern for the protection of civil rights; the guarantee of equal opportunity in
(90) education, employment, and housing; and a broad array of foreign and domestic policy issues.

Since the victories of the civil rights movement in the 1960s, African American men and women have won election to Congress from increasingly diverse
(95) regions of the country. Whether from largely urban districts, suburban areas, or more recently from rural Mississippi, these members of Congress have maintained their common concern with economic issues that affect African Americans with the protection of
(100) civil rights.

The collected biographies of African Americans who served in the House and Senate provide an important perspective on the history of the Congress and the role of African Americans in American
(105) politics. Their stories offer eloquent testimony to the long struggle to extend the ideals of the founders to encompass all citizens of the United States.

1. The author's attitude in Passage 1 is primarily one of
   (A) complete detachment
   (B) unbridled outrage
   (C) indifference
   (D) disinterest
   (E) objectivity

2. Passage 1 indicates that socio-economic progress for African Americans has been slow because of
   (A) prejudice
   (B) insurmountable poverty
   (C) slavery and undereducation
   (D) generally slow economic progress in the United States
   (E) immigrants from Central America

3. The phrase "on a par" (line 5) means
   (A) in the same location
   (B) at odds with
   (C) in competition with
   (D) on the same level
   (E) on a different level

4. According to the passage, African Americans have done all of the following in the last five decades EXCEPT
   (A) move into higher-status jobs
   (B) open their own businesses
   (C) tolerate more racial discrimination
   (D) achieve more managerial positions
   (E) increase their level of education

5. While not directly stated, the passage implies that the civil rights movement
   (A) had no effect on African-American upward mobility
   (B) caused a setback for African-American socio-economic progress
   (C) was not supported by African Americans
   (D) had very little strong leadership
   (E) helped African Americans in their struggle to achieve economic goals

GO ON TO THE NEXT PAGE

6. The conclusion that the author ultimately reaches in Passage 1 is that
   (A) all African Americans have made socio-economic progress
   (B) upward mobility is no longer an issue with African Americans
   (C) the civil rights movement was not a success as far as most African Americans are concerned
   (D) poverty in the inner cities of the United States is insurmountable
   (E) the 1990s have seen a widening of the gap between low-income African Americans and those who have made economic progress

7. According to Passage 2, the first African American to serve in the House of Representatives was
   (A) a former slave
   (B) Hiram Revels
   (C) from Chicago
   (D) Joseph Rainey
   (E) Oscar DePriest

8. One difference between African American congressional representatives in the 19th century and those in the mid-20th century was
   (A) their commitment to education for African Americans
   (B) the political party to which they were likely to belong
   (C) the strength of their ties to the African American community as a whole
   (D) the extent to which they represented *all* African Americans
   (E) their ability to influence other congressional members

9. When the African American representatives "turned to" certain issues in the mid-twentieth century (line 79), they
   (A) became antagonistic toward those issues
   (B) reversed their positions on those issues
   (C) referred to those issues
   (D) devoted themselves to those issues
   (E) listened to criticisms of those issues

10. One reason cited in the passage for the election of African Americans to Congress from both southern states after Reconstruction and northern states after World War I is
    (A) strength of local African American political organizations
    (B) success of the civil rights movement
    (C) passage and enforcement of the Fifteenth Amendment
    (D) predominance of African Americans in certain districts
    (E) elimination of regional differences

11. The author expresses admiration for the African American congressional representatives discussed in the passage for their
    (A) political acumen
    (B) attempts to ensure the rights of all Americans
    (C) single-minded devotion to the struggle for civil rights
    (D) focus on providing economic opportunity for African Americans
    (E) ability to regularly secure re-election

12. The author of Passage 1 connects increased opportunity for African Americans with the civil rights movement of the 1960s while the author of Passage 2
    (A) believes that African American empowerment didn't occur until the 1980s
    (B) argues that since the American revolution blacks have had significant political opportunities
    (C) states that since the end of the Civil War, African Americans have enjoyed a steady rise in political power
    (D) points out that although political empowerment started in 1867, there have been bumps in the road to progress
    (E) claims that not until World War I did African Americans come to power

STOP

END OF SECTION 6. IF YOU HAVE ANY TIME LEFT, GO OVER YOUR WORK IN THIS SECTION ONLY. DO NOT WORK IN ANY OTHER SECTION OF THE TEST.

PRACTICE EXAMINATION 1

Answer Key

Section 1: Math
1. E	6. C	11. E	16. E	21. B
2. E	7. B	12. A	17. E	22. C
3. C	8. D	13. E	18. C	23. E
4. E	9. E	14. E	19. B	24. E
5. C	10. A	15. D	20. C	25. C

Section 2: Verbal
1. B	8. B	14. C	20. C	26. D
2. A	9. D	15. A	21. E	27. B
3. C	10. A	16. A	22. A	28. A
4. C	11. C	17. B	23. D	29. B
5. E	12. C	18. C	24. C	30. C
6. B	13. A	19. B	25. B	31. A
7. D				

Section 3: Math

Part 1
1. D	4. C	7. C	10. B	13. C
2. B	5. C	8. C	11. A	14. B
3. D	6. B	9. C	12. A	15. A

Part 2
16. 91	18. 30	20. 4	22. 9	24. 6
17. 2	19. 80	21. $\frac{1}{2}$ = .5	23. 45	25. 2

Section 4: Verbal
1. E	8. B	15. B	22. C	29. C
2. E	9. A	16. B	23. B	30. D
3. C	10. C	17. D	24. D	31. B
4. B	11. B	18. D	25. C	32. C
5. A	12. C	19. C	26. A	33. A
6. D	13. A	20. A	27. E	34. D
7. E	14. A	21. C	28. E	35. D

Section 5: Math

1. D	3. D	5. B	7. D	9. C
2. A	4. C	6. E	8. D	10. E

Section 6: Verbal

1. E	4. C	7. D	9. D	11. B
2. C	5. E	8. B	10. A	12. D
3. D	6. E			

PRACTICE EXAMINATION 1

Explanatory Answers

Note: A 🖩 following a math answer explanation indicates that a calculator could be helpful in solving that particular problem.

Section 1

1. **(E)** Count the number of decimal places in the terms to be multiplied; this adds up to 6. It should be clear that the last number must be 8. There must be six decimal places accounted for and thus there must be five zeros in front of the 8. 🖩

2. **(E)** 20 square yards = 180 square feet. At $1.30 per square foot, it will cost $234.00. 🖩

3. **(C)** 5 ft. 1 in.
    5 ft. 7 in.
    5 ft. 2 in.
    5 ft.
    4 ft. 7 in.
    24 ft. 17 in., or 25 ft. 5 in.

    Average = $\dfrac{25 \text{ ft. 5 in.}}{5}$ = 5 ft. 1 in. 🖩

4. **(E)** Let x = first integer
    $x + 2$ = second integer
    $x + 4$ = third integer
    $3(x) = 3 + 2(x + 4)$
    $3x = 3 + 2x + 8$
    $x = +11$

    The third integer is 15.

5. **(C)** Area of square = $2^2 = 4$
    Area of circle = $\pi \cdot 1^2 = \pi$
    Difference = $4 - \pi = 4 - 3.14 = .86$ 🖩

6. **(C)** The right triangle of which T is the hypotenuse has legs that are obviously 6 inches and 9 inches.
    Hence, $T^2 = 6^2 + 9^2$
    $T^2 = 36 + 81 = 117$
    $T = \sqrt{117}$
    or $10 < T < 11$ 🖩

7. **(B)** $5\frac{1}{2}$ dozen nails are bought for $5\frac{1}{2}$ dozen × 35 cents per dozen = 192.5 cents. There are 66 nails in $5\frac{1}{2}$ dozen and 66 ÷ 3 = 22 sets sold at 10 cents per set, so 22 sets × 10 cents per set = 220 cents. The profit is $220 - 192.5 = 27\frac{1}{2}$ cents. 🖩

8. **(D)** $2\dfrac{3}{4} \div \dfrac{1}{8} = \dfrac{11}{4} \div \dfrac{1}{8} = \dfrac{11}{4} \times 8 = 22.$ 🖩

9. **(E)** $-x^2 + 2y - (-x-y)$
    $= -x^2 + 2y + x + y$
    $= -x^2 + x + 3y$

10. **(A)** Multiply the equation $\quad 2^m = 4x$ by 2
    $2(2^m) = 2(4x)$
    $2^{m+1} = 8x = 2^w$
    $\therefore w = m + 1$ and $m = w - 1$

11. **(E)** The reciprocal of $1\frac{1}{4}$ is $\frac{4}{5}$. $\frac{4}{5} - \frac{5}{4} = \frac{16}{20} - \frac{25}{20} = -\frac{9}{20}$ 🖩

12. **(A)** x yards = $3x$ feet; y feet = y feet; z inches = $\frac{z}{12}$ feet. Therefore, x yards + y feet + z inches = $3x$ feet + y feet + $\frac{z}{12}$ feet, or $3x + y + \frac{z}{12}$ feet.

13. **(E)** If a triangle is a right triangle, then the squares of two sides will add up to the square of the hypotenuse. $12^2 = 144$. $15^2 = 225$. $18^2 = 324$. $144 + 225 \neq 324$. 🖩

14. **(E)** $26 \times 3\frac{1}{2} = (26 \times 3) + (26 \times \frac{1}{2})$ by the distributive law. $26 \times 3 = (20 \times 3) + (6 \times 3)$ by the distributive law. Therefore, $26 \times 3\frac{1}{2} = (26 \times \frac{1}{2}) + (20 \times 3) + (6 \times 3)$. 🖩

15. **(D)** Angle T is a right angle. By the Pythagorean Theorem, $RT^2 + ST^2 = RS^2$. Since $RS = 12$ and $ST = 8$, RT must equal $\sqrt{80}$ so, $OT = \frac{1}{2}\sqrt{80}$. By the formula for the area of a circle ($A = \pi r^2$),

area equals $(\pi) \left(\frac{1}{2}\right)^2 \left(\sqrt{80}\right)^2$, or $(\pi)\left(\frac{1}{4}\right)(80)$, which equals 20π.

16. **(E)** If the gain was 10% of the selling price, then $12.60 was 90%. Therefore, 100% was equal to $14.00.

17. **(E)** If John weighs 110% of the average, he weighs 10% more than the average weight of 105 lbs., or $.10 \times 105 = 10.5$ lbs. John weighs $105 + 10.5 = 115.5$ lbs.

18. **(C)** A hexagon with 22-inch sides has a perimeter of 6×22, or 132 inches.

$$C = 2\pi r$$
$$132 = 2\pi r$$
$$132 = 2(3.14)r$$
$$132 = 6.28r$$
$$21.02 = r$$

19. **(B)** We are not told how many games the Bombers played, but we know that the ratio of the number of games played in the 2nd year to that in the first is 2 : 1. Problems like this can be solved by plugging in real numbers. Let's say that there were 50 games in the first year, so they won 25. In the second year there were 100 games, so they won 65 games. Altogether they won 90 out of 150 games, and this fraction can be reduced to 3 out of 5, or 60%.

20. **(C)** Let x = weight in ounces of the apple.
Then $x = \frac{4}{5}x + \frac{4}{5}$
$$5x = 4x + 4$$
$$x = 4$$

21. **(B)** Let L = length of each card and W = width of each card. Then $5W$ = length of large rectangle and $L + W$ = width of large rectangle. Length of large rectangle = $4L$. Thus, $5W = 4L$.
$$5W(L + W) = 180, \text{ also}$$
$$9LW = 180 \text{ or } LW = 20$$
$$5LW + 5W^2 = 180$$
$$LW + W^2 = 36$$
$$20 + W^2 = 36$$
$$W^2 = 16$$
$$W = 4 \text{ and } L = 5$$
Thus, perimeter = $2[5W + (L + W)]$
$$= 2(20 + 9) = 58$$

22. **(C)** If each of the dimensions is doubled, the area of the new rectangle is four times the size of the original one. The increase is three times, or 300%.

23. **(E)** This is a proportion of $2\frac{1}{2} : 3 = x : 14$; $x = \frac{35}{3}$, or $11\frac{2}{3}$.

24. **(E)** $MN = \frac{1}{2}QR$ and MN is parallel to QR. Since $\triangle MNS \sim \triangle QSR$, it follows that the altitude from S to $NM = \frac{1}{2}$ the altitude from S to QR. Hence, the altitude from S to $NM = \frac{1}{3}$ of $\frac{1}{2}$ the altitude from P to QR, or $\frac{1}{6}$ of this altitude (h).

Thus $\triangle NMS = \frac{1}{2} \cdot MN \cdot$ alt. from S to MN
$= \frac{1}{2}(\frac{1}{2}QR)(\frac{1}{6}h)$
$= \frac{1}{2}(\frac{1}{12} QR \cdot h) = \frac{1}{12}(\frac{1}{2} \cdot QR \cdot h)$.
But $\frac{1}{2} \cdot QR \cdot h = \triangle PQR$
Hence, $\triangle NMS = \frac{1}{12} \cdot \triangle PQR$
Ratio is 1:12

25. **(C)** Given $\frac{2}{3}x = \frac{1}{10}(60) = 6$
$\therefore x = 9$

Find $\frac{1}{10}(\frac{1}{3}x) = \frac{1}{30}(9) = \frac{3}{10} = .3$

Section 2

1. **(B)** An "appreciative public" is likely to give the elder Johnson's son *respect*.

2. **(A)** A person who is angry one minute but serene the next is said to be *mercurial* (changeable).

3. **(C)** Irony or paradox is indicated by the phrase "but he thought nothing of." It is ironic that automobile travel should be *harrowing,* or frightening, to someone used to bobsledding, a dangerous sport.

4. **(C)** A perennial flower is one that blooms every year. In the winter it lies *dormant* (inactive), but the following spring it *burgeons* (sprouts) anew.

5. **(E)** A manager who apologizes must be dealing with an *irate* (angry) customer. As a result of the apology, the customer was *mollified* (soothed and pacified).

6. **(B)** Normally, vices are publicly condemned. Secret indulgence in them might, however, be hidden by a sanctimonious (excessively righteous) manner.

7. **(D)** A flood that destroys people's belongings causes devastation. Living conditions in the area can be said to have deteriorated (worsened).

8. **(B)** A perversion of the truth is a deviation from the truth, or the half-truths and half-lies mentioned in the second half of the sentence.

9. **(D)** As indicated by the word *though,* the sentence requires a contrast. Since the presentation was positive, the blank should be filled by a negative; worthless is the best choice to describe a report full of errors.

10. **(A)** The *nose* is part of the *head,* and the *hand* a part of the *arm.*

11. **(C)** *Wheat* is a type of *grain; carrot* is a type of *vegetable*. Both are foodstuffs.

12. **(C)** A *cottage* is a small house; a *castle* is a large and luxurious one. A *dory* is a modest rowboat; a *liner* is a large and luxurious passenger ship.

13. **(A)** Something *antique* is necessarily *old,* and something *modern* is necessarily *new.*

14. **(C)** Something that is *possible* might be, but is not necessarily, *probable*. Someone who is *willing* might be, but is not necessarily *eager.*

15. **(A)** To *digress* from a topic is to *ramble,* and to *muffle* a sound is to *stifle* it. The relationship is one of synonyms.

16. **(A)** Only the first choice explains the subtitle. The other choices may be included under the idea "A Study in Temperment," but they are not the main idea.

17. **(B)** The faculty may be perplexed (A), but the first paragraph focuses on their feeling that Paul's dress and behavior are not properly contrite.

18. **(C)** Paul seems to be unable to control his odd mannerisms, but he is not actually frenzied, as (B), (D), or (E) would suggest.

19. **(B)** The faculty "fell upon him without mercy, his English teacher leading the pack" (lines 54–55). The comparison is to a pack of wolves.

20. **(C)** All of these choices could mean "smartness," but only *impudence* makes sense in context.

21. **(E)** There is evidence for every other choice in the descriptions of Paul's actions. The point is made in lines 25–26 that Paul often lies; he cannot be called "candid."

22. **(A)** Paul is physically revolted by the faculty, not *vice versa* (D). The faculty's attack on Paul indicates their hatred for him.

23. **(D)** Jefferson is "ever sensible" that meeting and attracting the good will of Mr. Wythe was "one of the most fortunate events" of his life (lines 5–7).

24. **(C)** Jefferson uses the word *sciences* as a general term covering Italian, Spanish, and moral philosophy. Clearly, he is referring to school subjects in general.

25. **(B)** The numbered points are (1) Italian, (2) Spanish, and (3) Moral philosophy—courses that Peter proposes taking.

26. **(D)** This is part of Jefferson's argument that since Italian, French, and Spanish are related, people mix or muddle them in conversation.

27. **(B)** Jefferson says "Our future connections with Spain and Spanish America will render that language a valuable acquisition."

28. **(A)** Point 3 is all about the fact that no one needs to study moral philosophy. In other words, to study it is a waste of time.

29. **(B)** Lines 32–35 explain this reasoning.

30. **(C)** Jefferson's point is that either one is as likely to decide a moral argument fairly; morality is bred into everyone and does not require an advanced degree.

31. **(A)** Choices (B), (C), and (D) may be true, but Jefferson only covers the first point, that morality is as natural as an arm or leg, and is given to all "in a stronger or weaker degree" (lines 44–45).

Section 3

Part 1

1. **(D)** Since a polygon can have three or more sides, an answer is not possible.

2. **(B)** No one side of a triangle can be greater than or equal to the sum of the other two sides.

372 Master the SAT

3. **(D)** If y is the opposite of z, then we know that $y + z$ is equal to 0. We do not, however, know the value of x.

4. **(C)** The radius is equal to one-half the diameter. The circle in Column B has a diameter of $\frac{4r}{3}$, and $\frac{1}{2}$ of that is $\frac{2r}{3}$. Therefore, the columns are equal.

5. **(C)** Both columns are equal to 0.

6. **(B)** The largest fraction that Column A could be is $\frac{9}{10}$. The smallest fraction that Column B could be is $\frac{11}{12}$. Thus, Column B is always bigger.

7. **(C)** Triangle B has a height that is double that of Triangle A; it has a base that is half that of Triangle A. This will result in the two triangles having the same area.

8. **(C)** Since the opposite angles are equal, angles a and d can be moved inside the quadrilateral. All quadrilaterals contain 360 degrees. 360 divided by 4 is 90.

9. **(C)** In this problem it is easy to figure out that the ninth through twelfth numbers would be $-5, 5, -6$, and 6. $(-5) \times (-6) = 30$ and $5 \times 6 = 30$.

10. **(B)** Column A would equal -3. Column B would equal 3.

11. **(A)** If a fraction between 0 and 1 is squared, the result is always smaller than the original number.

12. **(A)** The question can be simplified. When you divide 5 by 3 the remainder is 2. When you divide 8 by 7, the remainder is 1.

13. **(C)** The prime numbers would be 2, 3, 5, 7, 11, 13, 17, 19, and 23.

14. **(B)** If you multiply both sides by 3, you find that $m^4 = 81$. Therefore, m can equal 3 or -3. In either case, m is less than 4.

15. **(A)** This is easily solved by substitution. Make s equal to 2. The volume of a cube with a side of 2 is 8. The volume of the rectangular block in Column B is $2 \times 1 \times 3 = 6$.

Part 2

16. The mode is the data element with the greatest frequency.
    mode = 91

17. $-2x + 5 = 2 - (5 - 2x)$
    $\qquad = 2 - 5 + 2x$
    $\qquad = -3 + 2x$
    $-2x + 5 = -3 + 2x$
    $\underline{+2x \quad\;\; = \quad +2x}$
    $5 = -3 + 4x$
    $\underline{+3 = +3}$
    $8 = 4x$
    $x = 2$

18.

    Area of rectangle $ABED$:
    $bh = 6(4) = 24$

    Area of $\triangle BEC$:
    $\frac{1}{2}bh = \frac{1}{2}(6)(2) = 6$

    Area of polygon = $24 + 6 = 30$

19.

    If $AC = BC$
    then m $\angle A$ = m $\angle B$ = 50º

    In $\triangle ABC$
    m $\angle ACB$ = 180º − (m $\angle A$ + m $\angle B$)
    m $\angle ACB$ = 80º

    m $\angle ACB$ = m $\angle ECD$ (vertical angles)
    m $\angle ECD$ = 80º

20. $-m^2 n^3 = -(-2)^2(-1)^3$
    $= -(4)(-1) = 4$

21.

    The square has four right angles.

    The rectangle has four right angles.

    The trapezoid does not have four right angles.

    The circle does not have four right angles.

    Probability of four right angles
    $= \dfrac{\text{number of successes}}{\text{number of possibilities}} = \dfrac{2}{4} = \dfrac{1}{2} = .5$

22.

    If $JU = x$, then $JN = 3x$ ∴ $NU = 2x$. The area of the smaller circle $= \pi(x)^2 = \pi x^2$. The area of the larger circle $= \pi(3x)^2 = 9x^2(\pi)$
    $= 9\pi x^2$.

    $\dfrac{\text{Area } JUS}{\text{Area } NJL} = \dfrac{\pi x^2}{9\pi x^2} = \dfrac{1}{9} = 1:9 = 1:b$

    ∴ $b = 9$

23. Letting m be the time per regular question, $2m$ is the time per math problem. $300m$ is the total time for all the regular questions and $50(2m)$ is the total time for all the math problems. Since the exam is 3 hours, or 180 minutes, $300m + 100m = 180$ minutes, $400m = 180$, and $m = \dfrac{180}{400} = \dfrac{9}{20}$. The time to do a math problem is $2\left(\dfrac{9}{20}\right) = \left(\dfrac{9}{10}\right)$. All 50 math problems can be done in $50\left(\dfrac{9}{10}\right) = 45$ minutes.

24.

    $a + b = 8$, $b + c = 18$, $d = 8$
    $\underbrace{\text{Total}}_{28} = \underbrace{a + b}_{8} + \underbrace{c + d}_{8}$
    $28 = 8 + c + 8$
    ∴ $c = 12$
    Since $b + c = 18$ and $c = 12$
    ∴ $b = 6$

25. $x = \dfrac{2}{4}, y = \dfrac{1}{4} + \dfrac{1}{3}, z = \dfrac{2}{3}$

    $\dfrac{x+z}{y} = \dfrac{\left(\frac{2}{4}\right) + \left(\frac{2}{3}\right)}{\frac{1}{4} + \frac{1}{3}} = \dfrac{2\left(\frac{1}{4} + \frac{1}{3}\right)}{\left(\frac{1}{4} + \frac{1}{3}\right)} = 2$

Section 4

1. **(E)** If he "dashed into the house," then he was in a hurry and probably out of breath.

2. **(E)** A criminal record may indeed cause a jury to *discredit* (disbelieve) a witness's testimony.

3. **(C)** A catastrophic storm might leave a family *destitute* (living in poverty). For the second blank, the word *although* indicates a shift in mood from negative to positive; poverty could not *dampen* (depress) the family's spirits.

4. **(B)** "By a stroke of luck" implies good fortune; the troops likely *prevailed* (were victorious), thereby avoiding a crushing *defeat*.

5. **(A)** If the price is going up tomorrow, you must do your buying with *celerity* (swiftness).

6. **(D)** If danger threatens, the music would likely be *portentous* (ominous).

7. **(E)** If years separated one advance from the next, progress in women's rights was *sporadic* (occasional or scattered over time).

8. **(B)** Offices that are now across the street have been *relocated* (moved). As a result, the directory is *obsolete* (out of date).

9. **(A)** Since the promise—a mere sop to world opinion—was unlikely to be kept, it was *spurious* (false).

10. **(C)** Pretending not to notice nearby celebrities is acting in a *nonchalant* (casually indifferent) manner.

11. **(B)** A *library* is a place for *books*, just as a *zoo* is a place for *animals*.

12. **(C)** Something *tiny* is much smaller in size than something *huge*. Something *weak* is much less in strength than something *strong*.

13. **(A)** To *frighten* someone is to *scare* that person; to *question* someone is to *ask* that person.

14. **(A)** *Finding* is a result of *searching*, and *winning* is a result of *fighting*.

15. **(B)** By means of a *door*, we can *open* something. By means of a *knife*, we can *cut* into something.

16. **(B)** A *dastard* is characterized by *cowardice*, just as a *scoundrel* is characterized by *immorality*.

17. **(D)** A *toe* is part of the *foot*, and the *pupil* is part of the eye.

18. **(D)** *Strumming* and *pedaling* are methods of playing an instrument. We strum the *guitar* and pedal the *organ*.

19. **(C)** *Puerile* means childish or lacking in *maturity*. *Obscure* means vague or lacking in *clarity*.

20. **(A)** To *hurtle* is to throw with force; to *toss* is to throw lightly. Similarly, to *strike* is to hit with force and to *tap* is to hit lightly.

21. **(C)** Something infinite (endless) lacks limits or bounds, just as something nebulous (vague) lacks clarity.

22. **(C)** *Time* is measured in *minutes* as a *race* is measured in *laps*.

23. **(B)** A *tunnel* is a roadway through a *mountain* and a *bridge* is a roadway over a *river*.

24. **(D)** In the text, the author discusses Quixote's desire to change wrongs to right and redress grievances. In this context, *redress* means to fix, change, or correct for the better.

25. **(C)** Because Don Quixote is not a knight, to take up arms against another knight would be a breach in the code of chivalry.

26. **(A)** Don Quixote is worried that he cannot wear armor with a *device* on his shield that denotes his knighthood. The only appropriate choice is (A).

27. **(E)** With such malapropisms as "forked tongues" of birds, Cervantes imbues his hero with language that mimics the flowery language of the romances he reads.

28. **(E)** In his florid, overblown language, Don Quixote tells of getting out of bed to ride off on his adventure. "The slothful down" seems to refer to the down mattress on which he sleeps.

29. **(C)** Don Quixote is talking to himself and calling on a woman who may or may not exist. His speech cries out for his love for Dulcinea, but Cervantes pulls the reader back with this line to show that Quixote is mad.

30. **(D)** Don Quixote speaks first to the "sage enchanter" who might chronicle his tale (lines 55–58) and then to Dulcinea, "mistress of this captive heart" (lines 60–65).

31. **(B)** The sun's heat "would have been enough to turn his brain, if he had had any." Cervantes is again reminding the reader that Don Quixote is out of his mind.

32. **(C)** The story up to this point might be the tale of any knight somewhat down on his luck, but in lines 17–18, Cervantes jolts the reader into realizing that Don Quixote is out of his mind—he is not even a real knight.

33. **(A)** Cervantes refers to the romantic books that fill Don Quixote's head in lines 27–28 and 67.

34. **(D)** Although he never comes right out and says so, Cervantes's mocking reproduction of the language

of romantic books makes it clear that he does not think much of the writing styles he imitates. The fact that the hero who speaks the way such writers write is completely mad is another ironic twist that reveals Cervantes's opinion.

35. **(D)** Throughout, Cervantes uses a gently mocking tone to show Don Quixote's ridiculousness. Examples such as lines 17–18, 25–26, and 66 show that Cervantes is amused by his hero but not contemptuous as (A) would suggest.

Section 5

1. **(D)** Buying the lollipops singly would cost: 30 pops × $.13 per pop = $3.90. The reduced rate is $1.38 per dozen. Thirty pops is $2\frac{1}{2}$ dozen, so the cost for 30 pops is $1.38 × 2.5 = $3.45. The savings with this reduced rate is $3.90 − $3.45 = $.45.

2. **(A)** The volume of the fish tank is 11" × 14" × 9" = 1,386 cu. in. The amount needed to fill the tank is 1,386 cu. in ÷ 231 cu. in./gal. = 6 gallons.

3. **(D)** Let legs be $2x$ and $3x$.
Then $(2x)^2 + (3x)^2 = $ (hypotenuse)^2 and
$$\frac{1}{2} \cdot 2x \cdot 3x = 12$$
$$3x^2 = 12$$
$$x^2 = 4$$
$$x = 2$$
Thus, $4^2 + 6^2 = $ (hypotenuse)^2
$$16 + 36 = 52$$
$$\text{hypotenuse} = \sqrt{52}$$

4. **(C)** The weights are proportional to the volumes, and the volumes vary as the cubes of their dimensions. If the edges are doubled, the volume becomes $2^3 = 8$ times as large. Hence, the weight $= 8 × 3 = 24$ ounces $= 1\frac{1}{2}$ lbs.

5. **(B)** The graduate starts at x dollars per week. After the pay cut the graduate receives 90% of the original salary. The 10% raise adds 9% to the salary (10% of 90%), so the new salary is $.99x$.

6. **(E)** $428.00 − (.06) $428.00 = $402.32

7. **(D)** There will be no waste if the lengths are multiples of $5\frac{1}{2}$ feet. This occurs between 6 and 24 feet only for 22 feet.

8. **(D)** A cube with an edge of 4 has a volume of 64 cubic inches. A cube with an edge of 5 has a volume of 125 cubic inches. The percentage increase is $\frac{61}{64}$, or approximately 95%.

9. **(C)** $\frac{1}{4} : \frac{3}{5} = \frac{1}{4} \div \frac{3}{5}$
$$= \frac{1}{4} \times \frac{5}{3}$$
$$= \frac{5}{12}$$
$$= 5 : 12$$

10. **(E)** $\sqrt{3} = 1.73$ (approx.)
$$\frac{1}{\sqrt{3}} = \frac{\sqrt{3}}{3} = \frac{1.73}{3} = .57$$
$$\frac{\sqrt{3}}{3} = \frac{1.73}{3} = .57$$
$$\frac{1}{3} = .3333.....$$
$$\frac{1}{3\sqrt{3}} = \frac{\sqrt{3}}{3 \times 3} = \frac{\sqrt{3}}{9} = \frac{1.73}{9} = .19$$
Thus, the smallest is $\frac{1}{3\sqrt{3}}$

Section 6

1. **(E)** Most of the choices are extremes, either extreme outrage or extreme lack of interest. The author takes more of an objective middle ground in outlining the history of African American economics.

2. **(C)** In the first sentence of the passage, the author indicates that slavery and undereducation hindered economic progress for African Americans until well into the twentieth century.

3. **(D)** The context of the sentence indicates that the best answer is "on the same level."

4. **(C)** On the contrary, in the last five decades African Americans have become much less tolerant of racial discrimination.

5. **(E)** The passage generally implies that the civil rights movement did help African Americans in their quest for economic and political equality.

6. **(E)** The passage acknowledges that progress has been made in some segments of the African American population but that the gap is widening between lower-income and higher-income African Americans.

7. **(D)** See lines 41–42. Hiram Revels was the first African American in Congress, but he was elected to the Senate. Answer (A) may be true, but it is not mentioned in the passage.

8. **(B)** Compare lines 47–50 and 68–69.

9. **(D)** The context makes it clear that "turned to" means "concentrated on" or "devoted themselves to."

10. **(A)** Political organizations in southern states in the nineteenth century are mentioned in lines 45–47; political organizations in northern states in the twentieth century are cited in lines 59–63.

11. **(B)** In this passage, the author expresses admiration only in the last paragraph, where the representatives' "long struggle to extend the ideals of the founders to encompass all citizens of the United States" is cited.

12. **(D)** Although the author of Passage 2 points out that political gain occurred immediately following the Civil War, he also indicates that African Americans suffered political powerlessness from 1890–1900. Therefore, there were bumps in the road.

COMPUTING YOUR SCORES ON PRACTICE EXAMINATION 1

To get a sense of your progress in preparing for the SAT, you need to compute individual verbal and mathematical raw scores for this first practice exam. Once you have computed these, use the conversion scales in the later section "Conversion Scales for Practice Examination 1," to compute your SAT scaled scores (200–800). Keep in mind that these formulas have been simplified to give you a "quick and dirty" sense of where you are scoring, not a perfectly precise score.

To Compute Your Raw Scores:

1. Enter the number of correct answers for each verbal and mathematical reasoning section into the boxes marked "Number of Questions Correct."
2. Enter the number of incorrect answers (not blanks) for each verbal and mathematical reasoning section into the boxes marked "Number of Questions Incorrect."
3. Total the number correct and number incorrect.
4. Follow this formula: Take the total correct and minus one-quarter of the total incorrect. Round up in your favor to compute your Raw Score.

Verbal Section	Total Number of Questions	Number of Questions Correct	Number of Questions Incorrect
2	31		
4	35		
6	12		
Totals	78	Total Correct:	Total Incorrect:

Verbal Raw Score = Total Correct − ($\frac{1}{4}$ × Total Incorrect) = _____

Math Section	Total Number of Questions	Number of Questions Correct	Number of Questions Incorrect
1	25		
3	25		
5	10		
Totals	60	Total Correct:	Total Incorrect:

Math Raw Score = Total Correct − ($\frac{1}{4}$ × Total Incorrect) = _____

CONVERSION SCALES FOR PRACTICE EXAMINATION 1

VERBAL REASONING

Raw Score	Scaled Score	Raw Score	Scaled Score
75	800	35	520
70	800	30	480
65	760	25	440
60	710	20	410
55	670	15	370
50	620	10	340
45	590	5	290
40	550	0	230

MATHEMATICAL REASONING

Raw Score	Scaled Score	Raw Score	Scaled Score
60	800	25	510
55	760	20	480
50	690	15	440
45	650	10	410
40	610	5	340
35	580	0	280
30	550		

Although you now have some idea of what your scores would like had they been scaled according to unofficial ETS standards, you will probably want to know how to interpret your Raw Scores in more familiar terms. If so, use the following Self-Evaluation Charts to see what your Raw Scores actually mean.

SELF-EVALUATION CHARTS

VERBAL REASONING: Raw Score

Excellent	60 – 75
Good	50 – 60
Average	30 – 50
Fair	20 – 30
Poor	0 – 20

MATHEMATICAL REASONING: Raw Score

Excellent	50 – 60
Good	40 – 50
Average	20 – 40
Fair	10 – 20
Poor	0 – 10

PRACTICE EXAMINATION 2

Answer Sheet

If a section has fewer questions than answer ovals, leave the extra ovals blank.

Section 1

Section 2

Section 3

Section 4

1. Ⓐ Ⓑ Ⓒ Ⓓ Ⓔ
2. Ⓐ Ⓑ Ⓒ Ⓓ Ⓔ
3. Ⓐ Ⓑ Ⓒ Ⓓ Ⓔ
4. Ⓐ Ⓑ Ⓒ Ⓓ Ⓔ
5. Ⓐ Ⓑ Ⓒ Ⓓ Ⓔ
6. Ⓐ Ⓑ Ⓒ Ⓓ Ⓔ
7. Ⓐ Ⓑ Ⓒ Ⓓ Ⓔ
8. Ⓐ Ⓑ Ⓒ Ⓓ Ⓔ
9. Ⓐ Ⓑ Ⓒ Ⓓ Ⓔ
10. Ⓐ Ⓑ Ⓒ Ⓓ Ⓔ
11. Ⓐ Ⓑ Ⓒ Ⓓ Ⓔ
12. Ⓐ Ⓑ Ⓒ Ⓓ Ⓔ
13. Ⓐ Ⓑ Ⓒ Ⓓ Ⓔ
14. Ⓐ Ⓑ Ⓒ Ⓓ Ⓔ
15. Ⓐ Ⓑ Ⓒ Ⓓ Ⓔ

Note: ONLY the answers entered on the grid are scored.

Handwritten answers at the top of the column are NOT scored.

16. [grid] 17. [grid] 18. [grid] 19. [grid] 20. [grid]

21. [grid] 22. [grid] 23. [grid] 24. [grid] 25. [grid]

Section 5

1. Ⓐ Ⓑ Ⓒ Ⓓ Ⓔ
2. Ⓐ Ⓑ Ⓒ Ⓓ Ⓔ
3. Ⓐ Ⓑ Ⓒ Ⓓ Ⓔ
4. Ⓐ Ⓑ Ⓒ Ⓓ Ⓔ
5. Ⓐ Ⓑ Ⓒ Ⓓ Ⓔ
6. Ⓐ Ⓑ Ⓒ Ⓓ Ⓔ
7. Ⓐ Ⓑ Ⓒ Ⓓ Ⓔ
8. Ⓐ Ⓑ Ⓒ Ⓓ Ⓔ
9. Ⓐ Ⓑ Ⓒ Ⓓ Ⓔ
10. Ⓐ Ⓑ Ⓒ Ⓓ Ⓔ
11. Ⓐ Ⓑ Ⓒ Ⓓ Ⓔ
12. Ⓐ Ⓑ Ⓒ Ⓓ Ⓔ
13. Ⓐ Ⓑ Ⓒ Ⓓ Ⓔ
14. Ⓐ Ⓑ Ⓒ Ⓓ Ⓔ
15. Ⓐ Ⓑ Ⓒ Ⓓ Ⓔ

Section 6

1. Ⓐ Ⓑ Ⓒ Ⓓ Ⓔ
2. Ⓐ Ⓑ Ⓒ Ⓓ Ⓔ
3. Ⓐ Ⓑ Ⓒ Ⓓ Ⓔ
4. Ⓐ Ⓑ Ⓒ Ⓓ Ⓔ
5. Ⓐ Ⓑ Ⓒ Ⓓ Ⓔ
6. Ⓐ Ⓑ Ⓒ Ⓓ Ⓔ
7. Ⓐ Ⓑ Ⓒ Ⓓ Ⓔ
8. Ⓐ Ⓑ Ⓒ Ⓓ Ⓔ
9. Ⓐ Ⓑ Ⓒ Ⓓ Ⓔ
10. Ⓐ Ⓑ Ⓒ Ⓓ Ⓔ
11. Ⓐ Ⓑ Ⓒ Ⓓ Ⓔ
12. Ⓐ Ⓑ Ⓒ Ⓓ Ⓔ
13. Ⓐ Ⓑ Ⓒ Ⓓ Ⓔ
14. Ⓐ Ⓑ Ⓒ Ⓓ Ⓔ
15. Ⓐ Ⓑ Ⓒ Ⓓ Ⓔ

Practice Examination 2

SECTION 1

31 Questions • Time—30 Minutes

Directions: Each of the following questions consists of an incomplete sentence followed by five words or pairs of words. Choose that word or pair or words which, when substituted for the blank space or spaces, *best* completes the meaning of the sentence and mark the letter of your choice on your answer sheet.

Example:

In view of the extenuating circumstances and the defendant's youth, the judge recommended ----.

(A) conviction
(B) a defense
(C) a mistrial
(D) leniency
(E) life imprisonment

Ⓐ Ⓑ Ⓒ ● Ⓔ

1. An audience that laughs in all the wrong places can ---- even the most experienced actor.

    (A) disparage
    (B) allay
    (C) disconcert
    (D) upbraid
    (E) satiate

2. Their assurances of good faith were hollow; they ---- on the agreement almost at once.

    (A) conferred
    (B) expiated
    (C) recapitulated
    (D) obtruded
    (E) reneged

3. If we ---- our different factions, then together we can gain the majority in their legislature.

    (A) amalgamate
    (B) manifest
    (C) preclude
    (D) alienate
    (E) deviate

4. The Eighteenth Amendment, often called the Prohibition Act, ---- the sale of alcoholic beverages.

    (A) prolonged
    (B) preempted
    (C) sanctioned
    (D) proscribed
    (E) encouraged

5. The police received a(n) ---- call giving them valuable information, but the caller would not give his name out of fear of ----.

    (A) private..impunity
    (B) anonymous..reprisals
    (C) professional..dissension
    (D) enigmatic..refusal
    (E) adamant..transgression

6. A person who is ---- is slow to adapt to a new way of life.

    (A) nonchalant
    (B) intractable
    (C) rabid
    (D) insolent
    (E) doughty

GO ON TO THE NEXT PAGE

7. Though they came from ---- social backgrounds, the newly married couple shared numerous interests and feelings.

   (A) desultory
   (B) obsolete
   (C) malleable
   (D) disparate
   (E) deleterious

8. The ---- was a ---- of gastronomic delights.

   (A) internist..progeny
   (B) gourmet..connoisseur
   (C) scientist..facilitator
   (D) xenophobe..promotor
   (E) tyro..master

9. Mrs. Jenkins, upon hearing that her arm was broken, looked ---- at the doctor.

   (A) jovially
   (B) plaintively
   (C) fortuitously
   (D) serendipitously
   (E) opportunely

Directions: Each of the following questions consists of a capitalized pair of words followed by five pairs of words lettered A to E. The capitalized words bear some meaningful relationship to each other. Choose the lettered pair of words whose relationship is most similar to that expressed by the capitalized pair and mark its letter on your answer sheet.

Example:

DAY : SUN : :

(A) sunlight : daylight   (B) ray : sun
(C) night : moon   (D) heat : cold
(E) moon : star   Ⓐ Ⓑ ● Ⓓ Ⓔ

10. THROAT : SWALLOW : :

    (A) teeth : chew
    (B) eyelid : wink
    (C) nose : point
    (D) ear : absorb
    (E) mouth : smile

11. GARNET : RED : :

    (A) pearl : round
    (B) diamond : solid
    (C) emerald : green
    (D) ivory : living
    (E) silver : shining

12. PATIENCE : VIRTUES : :

    (A) prudence : skills
    (B) sailing : crafts
    (C) grief : traits
    (D) temerity : vices
    (E) literature : arts

13. SOAR : ALIGHT : :

    (A) hop : stumble
    (B) crawl : run
    (C) lift : carry
    (D) walk : hike
    (E) sail : moor

14. OASIS : DESERT : :

    (A) canyon : gorge
    (B) savanna : steppe
    (C) island : ocean
    (D) tundra : icecap
    (E) channel : reef

15. COTTON : SOFT : :

    (A) wool : warm
    (B) iron : hard
    (C) nylon : strong
    (D) wood : polished
    (E) silk : expensive

Questions 16–23 are based on the following passage.

The Great Famine, which occurred in Ireland between 1845–1848, affected the country so profoundly that today, more than 100 years later, it is still discussed both in Irish-American communities in the United States and in Ireland. The passage presents a timeline of the famine and some of the events leading up to it.

During the mid-1840s, from 1845–1848, the potato crop in Ireland failed, creating a famine that ravaged the population. This event, the Great Famine, was one of the most significant events in the 8,000-year history
(5) of this island nation, and the effects of it continue to haunt the Irish, both those who still live in Ireland and those who live in the United States. The most immediate effect of the famine was the dramatic decline in the Irish population—either through death from star-
(10) vation and disease or through emigration to other countries.

In Ireland, the potato had historically been the mainstay of the diet of a large proportion of the rural population. Highly nutritional, the potato was easy to
(15) plant and easy to harvest. If a family of six had one acre of land, it could grow a potato crop that would feed them for almost a year. However, dependence on one crop had its downside as well. Potatoes could not be stored for long, and farmers who had grown so
(20) accustomed to dealing with this one crop neglected to plant other crops as a hedge against possible failures.

Rapid population increases in the years preceding the Great Famine had created a country whose expanding population was often poverty-stricken. Ex-
(25) panding population, coupled with landowners' lack of responsibility toward tenant-farmers, led to a system where tenant-farmers frequently subdivided their land so that they could gain a bit of rent themselves. Consequently, the rural areas were dotted with small
(30) plots of land, most of which were used for potato farming. Prior to the famine, urban areas in Ireland were also experiencing economic distress because of a decline in Irish industry that resulted in unemployment and poverty in cities such as Dublin.

(35) In 1845, the year the famine began, a good potato crop was expected, so it came as a great surprise when nearly half of the crop of the country failed because of a blight that had come from North America. This particular blight was unusual inasmuch as when the
(40) potato was dug from the ground, it appeared to be healthy; it was only after a day or two that the potato began to rot.

Despite the fact that only half the crop failed in 1845, starvation and disease plagued the entire coun-
(45) try because many starving people, some of whom were infected with contagious diseases, roamed the countryside looking for food and spreading disease. Then, in 1846, the crop failed completely. In 1847, there was another partial failure, but because people
(50) had eaten their seed potatoes in 1846, the crop was much smaller in 1847. Then again in 1848, the crop failed completely.

As if the crop failures were not enough, other factors affected the seriousness of the situation. Vari-
(55) ous contagious diseases such as typhus, dysentery, and several different types of fever spread rapidly. Landlords evicted tenant-farmers, and the government did very little to provide relief. Nor did it help that the winter of 1846–1847 was one of the coldest on
(60) record.

When the famine was over in 1849, a cholera epidemic struck Ireland, so that by 1850 the country found its population reduced from 8.5 million to 6.5 million. One million people had died from disease and
(65) starvation, and one million had left Ireland for Britain, Europe, or North America.

The results of the Great Famine were profound. Farming in Ireland changed from a one-crop economy to an agricultural economy that included livestock
(70) and other crops, such as grains. The seeds of animosity toward Great Britain, which had not helped the Irish in their time of need, were sown. And a pattern of emigration was established that lasts until today.

GO ON TO THE NEXT PAGE

16. The word *ravaged* (line 2) means

    (A) pillaged
    (B) devastated
    (C) wasted
    (D) sacked
    (E) assisted

17. According to the passage, the potato became a staple of the Irish diet for all of the following reasons EXCEPT

    (A) it was filled with nutrients
    (B) it was easy to plant
    (C) it was easy to harvest
    (D) the soil was good for potatoes
    (E) one acre could support a whole family

18. The passage implies that

    (A) dependence on one crop was sensible
    (B) the potato was not the only crop in Ireland
    (C) the dependence on one crop had no downside
    (D) the Irish were a happy people
    (E) dependence on one crop was dangerous

19. According to the passage, rural life in the years before the Great Famine can best be described as

    (A) prosperous
    (B) declining in population
    (C) harsh
    (D) decreasing in tenant-farmers
    (E) expanding in farm size

20. Irish farmers tended to subdivide their farms repeatedly because

    (A) the farms were getting too large
    (B) they had big families
    (C) it was easier to farm a smaller plot
    (D) they needed rent payments
    (E) they wanted to diversify their crops

21. The word *blight* (line 38) means

    (A) curse
    (B) disease
    (C) injury
    (D) omen
    (E) impairment

22. Disease plagued the Irish during the famine because

    (A) the potato was diseased
    (B) immigrants brought disease
    (C) starving Irish carried disease from place to place
    (D) living conditions were not sanitary
    (E) they were not prepared

23. All of the following were results of the famine EXCEPT

    (A) the Irish emigrated to new lands
    (B) the Irish began to raise livestock
    (C) the Irish were no longer dependent on one crop
    (D) the Irish became independent from Great Britain
    (E) the Irish became angered at the British

Questions 24–31 are based on the following passage.

Thomas Bulfinch (1796–1867) was a teacher and writer known for his popularization of myths and legends. In this excerpt from Bulfinch's Mythology, *he tells the story behind the Trojan War.*

Minerva was the goddess of wisdom, but on one occasion she did a very foolish thing; she entered into competition with Juno and Venus for the prize of beauty. It happened thus: At the nuptials of Peleus and
(5) Thetis all the gods were invited with the exception of Eris, or Discord. Enraged at her exclusion, the goddess threw a golden apple among the guests, with the inscription, "For the fairest." Thereupon Juno, Venus, and Minerva each claimed the apple. Jupiter, not
(10) willing to decide in so delicate a matter, sent the goddesses to Mount Ida, where the beautiful shepherd Paris was tending his flocks, and to him was committed the decision. The goddesses accordingly appeared before him. Juno promised him power and riches,
(15) Minerva glory and renown in war, and Venus the fairest of women for his wife, each attempting to bias his decision in her own favor. Paris decided in favour of Venus and gave her the golden apple, thus making the two other goddesses his enemies. Under the pro-
(20) tection of Venus, Paris sailed to Greece, and was hospitably received by Menelaus, king of Sparta. Now

Helen, the wife of Menelaus, was the very woman whom Venus had destined for Paris, the fairest of her sex. She had been sought as a bride by numerous (25) suitors, and before her decision was made known, they all, at the suggestion of Ulysses, one of their number, took an oath that they would defend her from all injury and avenge her cause if necessary. She chose Menelaus, and was living with him happily when Paris became (30) their guest. Paris, aided by Venus, persuaded her to elope with him, and carried her to Troy, whence arose the famous Trojan war, the theme of the greatest poems of antiquity, those of Homer and Virgil.

Menelaus called upon his brother chieftains of (35) Greece to fulfill their pledge, and join him in his efforts to recover his wife. They generally came forward, but Ulysses, who had married Penelope, and was very happy in his wife and child, had no disposition to embark in such a troublesome affair. He therefore (40) hung back and Palamedes was sent to urge him. When Palamedes arrived at Ithaca Ulysses pretended to be mad. He yoked an ass and an ox together to the plough and began to sow salt. Palamedes, to try him, placed the infant Telemachus before the plough, whereupon (45) the father turned the plough aside, showing plainly that he was no madman, and after that could no longer refuse to fulfill his promise. Being now himself gained for the undertaking, he lent his aid to bring in other reluctant chiefs, especially Achilles. This hero was the (50) son of that Thetis at whose marriage the apple of Discord had been thrown among the goddesses. Thetis was herself one of the immortals, a sea-nymph, and knowing that her son was fated to perish before Troy if he went on the expedition, she endeavoured to (55) prevent his going. She sent him away to the court of King Lycomedes, and induced him to conceal himself in the disguise of a maiden among the daughters of the king. Ulysses, hearing he was there, went disguised as a merchant to the palace and offered for sale female (60) ornaments, among which he had placed some arms. While the king's daughters were engrossed with the other contents of the merchant's pack, Achilles handled the weapons and thereby betrayed himself to the keen eye of Ulysses, who found no great difficulty in (65) persuading him to disregard his mother's prudent counsels and join his countrymen in the war.

24. Bulfinch describes Jupiter as unwilling to "decide in so delicate a matter" (lines 9–10), implying that

    (A) Jupiter is usually heavy-handed
    (B) any decision is bound to offend someone
    (C) Jupiter is overly sensitive
    (D) the problems are so obscure that no one can judge them
    (E) all three goddesses are fragile and dainty

25. The word *disposition* (line 38) is used to mean

    (A) inclination
    (B) nature
    (C) integrity
    (D) value
    (E) habit

26. The sowing of salt is used by Bulfinch to show

    (A) Ulysses's attempt to be found insane
    (B) the difficulty of cultivating in rocky soil
    (C) how the tears of the gods created the sea
    (D) the gods' punishment of those who disobey them
    (E) Ulysses's talent as a soldier rather than a farmer

27. When Palamedes "tries" Ulysses (line 43), he

    (A) finds him guilty
    (B) judges him
    (C) tests him
    (D) attempts to help him
    (E) taxes his patience

28. Bulfinch reveals that Thetis is a sea-nymph in order to explain

    (A) why she married Peleus
    (B) why she dislikes the idea of war
    (C) the effect of the apple of Discord
    (D) her love for Achilles
    (E) her ability to predict the future

29. Among the chieftains of Greece apparently are

    (A) Juno, Venus, and Minerva
    (B) Paris and Lycomedes
    (C) Ulysses, Achilles, and Menelaus
    (D) Eris and Thetis
    (E) Homer and Virgil

GO ON TO THE NEXT PAGE

30. Why does Ulysses display arms among the ornaments?

   (A) to test Achilles into revealing himself
   (B) as a declaration of war
   (C) to mislead the daughters of the king
   (D) to complete his disguise as a merchant
   (E) because he wants to start an altercation

31. A reasonable title for this narrative might be

   (A) "Disputes and Deceit"
   (B) "Achilles and Ulysses"
   (C) "Beauty and the Beast"
   (D) "The Pettiness of the Gods"
   (E) "The Apple of Discord Leads to War"

STOP

END OF SECTION 1. IF YOU HAVE ANY TIME LEFT, GO OVER YOUR WORK IN THIS SECTION ONLY. DO NOT WORK IN ANY OTHER SECTION OF THE TEST.

SECTION 2

25 Questions • Time—30 Minutes

Directions: Solve the following problems using any available space on the page for scratchwork. On your answer sheet fill in the choice which best corresponds to the correct answer.

Notes: The figures accompanying the problems are drawn as accurately as possible unless otherwise stated in specific problems. Again, unless otherwise stated, all figures lie in the same plane. All numbers used in these problems are real numbers. Calculators are permitted for this test.

Reference Information

Circle: $C = 2\pi r$, $A = \pi r^2$
Rectangle: $A = lw$
Rectangular Solid: $V = lwh$
Cylinder: $V = \pi r^2 h$
Triangle: $A = \frac{1}{2}bh$
$a^2 + b^2 = c^2$

Special right triangles: 45°-45°-90° with sides x, x, $x\sqrt{2}$; 30°-60°-90° with sides x, $x\sqrt{3}$, $2x$.

The number of degrees of arc in a circle is 360.
The measure in degrees of a straight angle is 180.
The sum of the measures in degrees of the angles of a triangle is 180.

---

1. One angle of a triangle is 82°. The other two angles are in the ratio 2 : 5. Find the number of degrees in the smallest angle of the triangle.

   (A) 14
   (B) 25
   (C) 28
   (D) 38
   (E) 82

2. Village A has a population of 6,800, which is decreasing at a rate of 120 per year. Village B has a population of 4,200, which is increasing at a rate of 80 per year. In how many years will the population of the two villages be equal?

   (A) 9
   (B) 11
   (C) 13
   (D) 14
   (E) 16

3. If *x is defined such that $*x = x^2 - 2x$, the value of $*2 - *1$ is

   (A) −1
   (B) 0
   (C) 1
   (D) 2
   (E) 4

4. In a right triangle, the ratio of the legs is 1 : 2. If the area of the triangle is 25 square units, what is the length of the hypotenuse?

   (A) $\sqrt{5}$
   (B) $5\sqrt{5}$
   (C) $5\sqrt{3}$
   (D) $10\sqrt{3}$
   (E) $25\sqrt{5}$

GO ON TO THE NEXT PAGE

5. In the graph below, the axes and the origin are not shown. If point P has coordinates (3,7), what are the coordinates of point Q, assuming each box is one unit?

   (A) (5, 6)
   (B) (1, 10)
   (C) (6, 9)
   (D) (6, 5)
   (E) (5, 10)

6. If $r = 5x$, how many tenths of r does $\frac{1}{2}$ of x equal?

   (A) 1
   (B) 2
   (C) 3
   (D) 4
   (E) 5

7. ABCD is a parallelogram, and DE = EC.

   What is the ratio of triangle ADE to the area of the parallelogram?

   (A) 2 : 5
   (B) 1 : 2
   (C) 1 : 3
   (D) 1 : 4
   (E) It cannot be determined from the information given.

8. In any square, the length of one side is

   (A) one-half the diagonal of the square
   (B) the square root of the perimeter of the square
   (C) about .7 the length of the diagonal of the square
   (D) the square root of the diagonal
   (E) one-fourth the area

9. A pulley having a 9-inch diameter is belted to a pulley having a 6-inch diameter, as shown in the figure. If the large pulley runs at 120 rpm, how fast does the small pulley run, in revolutions per minute?

   (A) 80
   (B) 100
   (C) 160
   (D) 180
   (E) 240

10. The number of degrees through which the hour hand of a clock moves in 2 hours and 12 minutes is

    (A) 66
    (B) 72
    (C) 126
    (D) 732
    (E) 792

11. The average of 8 numbers is 6; the average of 6 other numbers is 8. What is the average of all 14 numbers?

    (A) 6
    (B) $6\frac{6}{7}$
    (C) 7
    (D) $7\frac{2}{7}$
    (E) $8\frac{1}{7}$

12. If x is between 0 and 1, which of the following increases as x increases?

   I. $1 - x^2$
   II. $x - 1$
   III. $\dfrac{1}{x^2}$

   (A) I and II
   (B) II and III
   (C) I and III
   (D) II only
   (E) I only

13. In the series 3, 7, 12, 18, 25, ... the 9th term is

   (A) 50
   (B) 63
   (C) 75
   (D) 86
   (E) 88

14. Simplify $\dfrac{x^2 - y^2}{x - y}$

   (A) $\dfrac{xy}{x+y}$

   (B) $\dfrac{x+y}{xy}$

   (C) $x + y$

   (D) xy

   (E) $x^2 + y^2 - 1$

15. The front wheels of a wagon are 7 feet in circumference and the back wheels are 9 feet in circumference. When the front wheels have made 10 more revolutions than the back wheels, what distance, in feet, has the wagon gone?

   (A) 126
   (B) 180
   (C) 189
   (D) 315
   (E) 630

16. A rectangular flower bed, dimensions 16 yards by 12 yards, is surrounded by a walk 3 yards wide. The area of the walk in square yards is

   (A) 78
   (B) 93
   (C) 132
   (D) 204
   (E) 396

17. Doreen can wash her car in 15 minutes, while her younger brother Dave takes twice as long to do the same job. If they work together, how many minutes will the job take them?

   (A) 5
   (B) $7\dfrac{1}{2}$
   (C) 10
   (D) $22\dfrac{1}{2}$
   (E) 30

18. A circle is inscribed in a given square and another circle is circumscribed about the same square. What is the ratio of the area of the inscribed to the circumscribed circle?

   (A) 1 : 4
   (B) 4 : 9
   (C) 1 : 2
   (D) 2 : 3
   (E) 3 : 4

19. If $\dfrac{3}{7}$ of a bucket can be filled in 1 minute, how many minutes will it take to fill the rest of the bucket?

   (A) $\dfrac{7}{3}$
   (B) $\dfrac{4}{3}$
   (C) 1
   (D) $\dfrac{3}{4}$
   (E) $\dfrac{4}{7}$

GO ON TO THE NEXT PAGE

20. In the figure below, the side of the large square is 14. The four smaller squares are formed by joining the midpoints of opposite sides. Find the value of Y.

(A) 5

(B) 6

(C) $6\frac{5}{8}$

(D) $6\frac{2}{3}$

(E) 6.8

21. If the base of a rectangle is increased by 30% and the altitude is decreased by 20%, the area is increased by

(A) 4%
(B) 5%
(C) 10%
(D) 25%
(E) 104%

22. Using a 9 × 12-inch sheet of paper lengthwise, a typist leaves a 1-inch margin on each side and a $1\frac{1}{2}$-inch margin on top and bottom. What fractional part of the page is used for typing?

(A) $\frac{5}{12}$

(B) $\frac{7}{12}$

(C) $\frac{5}{9}$

(D) $\frac{3}{4}$

(E) $\frac{21}{22}$

23. In the figure, PQRS is a parallelogram, and ST = TV = VR. What is the ratio of the area of triangle SPT to the area of the parallelogram?

Note: Figure is not drawn to scale.

(A) $\frac{1}{6}$

(B) $\frac{1}{5}$

(C) $\frac{2}{7}$

(D) $\frac{1}{3}$

(E) It cannot be determined from the information given.

24. Given formula $A = P(1 + rt)$, then $t =$

    (A) $A - P - Pr$
    (B) $\dfrac{A + P}{Pr}$
    (C) $\dfrac{A}{P} - r$
    (D) $\dfrac{A - P}{Pr}$
    (E) $\dfrac{A - r}{Pr}$

25. If $p > q$ and $r < 0$, which of the following is (are) true?

    I. $pr < qr$
    II. $p + r > q + r$
    III. $p - r < q - r$

    (A) I only
    (B) II only
    (C) I and III only
    (D) I and II only
    (E) I, II, and III

STOP

END OF SECTION 2. IF YOU HAVE ANY TIME LEFT, GO OVER YOUR WORK IN THIS SECTION ONLY. DO NOT WORK IN ANY OTHER SECTION OF THE TEST.

Section 3

35 Questions • Time—30 Minutes

Directions: Each of the following questions consists of an incomplete sentence followed by five words or pairs of words. Choose that word or pair of words which, when substituted for the blank space or spaces, *best* completes the meaning of the sentence and mark the letter of your choice on your answer sheet.

Example:

In view of the extenuating circumstances and the defendant's youth, the judge recommended ----.

(A) conviction
(B) a defense
(C) a mistrial
(D) leniency
(E) life imprisonment   Ⓐ Ⓑ Ⓒ ● Ⓔ

1. The ---- was greatest when the pitcher paused before delivering the last strike.

   (A) game
   (B) crowd
   (C) cheering
   (D) sportsmanship
   (E) tension

2. Her ---- instincts led her to fund the construction of a hospital for the poor.

   (A) far-ranging
   (B) humanitarian
   (C) humble
   (D) popular
   (E) eclectic

3. After years of ---- war, the Great Wall was constructed to ---- the Chinese people.

   (A) internecine..instigate
   (B) destructive..resurrect
   (C) unceasing..protect
   (D) amicable..unite
   (E) pitiable..win

4. His remarks were so ---- that we could not decide which of the possible meanings was correct.

   (A) facetious
   (B) ambiguous
   (C) cogent
   (D) impalpable
   (E) congruent

5. In an attempt to ---- a strike, the two sides agreed to negotiate through the night.

   (A) arbitrate
   (B) herald
   (C) trigger
   (D) transmute
   (E) avert

6. Elder statesmen used to be ---- for their wisdom when respect for age was part of every person's upbringing.

   (A) deplored
   (B) exonerated
   (C) rebuked
   (D) venerated
   (E) exiled

7. Being less than perfectly prepared, she approached the exam with ----.

   (A) aplomb
   (B) trepidation
   (C) indifference
   (D) confidence
   (E) duplicity

8. As citizens, we would be ---- if we did not make these facts public.

   (A) derelict
   (B) pejorative
   (C) impersonal
   (D) private
   (E) derogatory

9. She was usually a model of ----, so her sudden burst of temper was atypical.

(A) veracity
(B) lucidity
(C) facility
(D) equanimity
(E) hostility

10. The ---- attitudes politicians have today cause them to ---- at the slightest hint of controversy.

(A) dauntless..recoil
(B) craven..cower
(C) pusillanimous..prevail
(D) undaunted..quail
(E) fractious..grovel

GO ON TO THE NEXT PAGE

Directions: Each of the following questions consists of a capitalized pair of words followed by five pairs of words lettered A to E. The capitalized words bear some meaningful relationship to each other. Choose the lettered pair of words whose relationship is most similar to that expressed by the capitalized pair and mark its letter on your answer sheet.

Example:

DAY : SUN : :

(A) sunlight : daylight
(B) ray : sun
(C) night : moon
(D) heat : cold
(E) moon : star

Ⓐ Ⓑ ● Ⓓ Ⓔ

11. FEEL : TOUCH : :

    (A) tickle : hurt
    (B) see : look
    (C) sprint : lift
    (D) giggle : laugh
    (E) shed : grow

12. CIRCLE : SQUARE : :

    (A) ball : bat
    (B) oval : rectangle
    (C) sphere : globe
    (D) angular : straight
    (E) volume : area

13. CHICKEN : ROOSTER : :

    (A) deer : doe
    (B) duck : drake
    (C) flock : hen
    (D) ewe : ram
    (E) pig : piglet

14. TRIGGER : PISTOL : :

    (A) bullet : gun
    (B) rifle : revolver
    (C) guard : police
    (D) switch : motor
    (E) fire : shoot

15. GOOD : ANGELIC : :

    (A) bad : poor
    (B) glad : joyous
    (C) mean : human
    (D) sweet : musty
    (E) correct : incorrect

16. CLARINET : WOODWIND : :

    (A) piano : key
    (B) symphony : composer
    (C) banjo : guitar
    (D) trumpet : brass
    (E) horn : tuba

17. GRIEF : DOLEFUL : :

    (A) melancholy : hopeful
    (B) greed : successful
    (C) anger : wrathful
    (D) fear : unintentional
    (E) reaction : involuntary

18. PAIL : WATER : :

    (A) milk : quart
    (B) eggs : dozen
    (C) gallon : container
    (D) river : ocean
    (E) shaker : salt

19. FISH : AQUARIUM : :

    (A) birds : aviary
    (B) car : garage
    (C) insects : ground
    (D) lightning : sky
    (E) dogs : pets

20. DISAGREEMENT : CONCORD : :

    (A) limitation : restriction
    (B) impartiality : bias
    (C) advantage : agreement
    (D) predicament : dilemma
    (E) predictability : routine

21. YEAR : CENTURY : :

    (A) inch : yard
    (B) mile : speed
    (C) week : month
    (D) cent : dollar
    (E) day : year

22. MULE : INTRACTABLE : :

   (A) horse : turbulent
   (B) fox : wily
   (C) dog : candid
   (D) wolf : fickle
   (E) tiger : inexorable

23. STUMBLE : WALK : :

   (A) creep : run
   (B) pain : hurt
   (C) stammer : speak
   (D) pitch : throw
   (E) smile : frown

Directions: The reading passage below is followed by a set of questions. Read the passage and answer the accompanying questions, basing your answers on what is stated or implied in the passage. Mark the letter of your choice on your answer sheet.

QUESTIONS 24–35 ARE BASED ON THE FOLLOWING PASSAGE.

Louisa May Alcott (1832–1888) was a beloved author of books for children, but she also wrote gothic tales and short stories for adults. This excerpt is from "Mrs. Gay's Prescription."

The poor little woman looked as if she needed rest but was not likely to get it; for the room was in a chaotic state, the breakfast table presented the appearance of having been devastated by a swarm of locusts,
(5) the baby began to fret, little Polly set up her usual whine of "I want sumpin to do," and a pile of work loomed in the corner waiting to be done.

"I don't see how I ever shall get through it all," sighed the despondent matron as she hastily drank a
(10) last cup of tea, while two great tears rolled down her cheeks, as she looked from one puny child to the other, and felt the weariness of her own tired soul and body more oppressive than ever.

"A good cry" was impending, when there came a
(15) brisk ring at the door, a step in the hall, and a large, rosy woman came bustling in, saying in a cheery voice as she set a flower-pot down upon the table, "Good morning! Nice day, isn't it? Came in early on business and brought you one of my Lady Washingtons, you are
(20) so fond of flowers."

"Oh, it's lovely! How kind you are. Do sit down if you can find a chair; we are all behind hand today, for I was up half the night with poor baby, and haven't energy enough to go to work yet," answered Mrs.
(25) Bennet, with a sudden smile that changed her whole face, while baby stopped fretting to stare at the rosy clusters, and Polly found employment in exploring the pocket of the new comer, as if she knew her way there.

"Let me put the pot on your stand first, girls are so
(30) careless, and I'm proud of this. It will be an ornament to your parlor for a week," and opening a door Mrs. Gay carried the plant to a sunny bay window where many others were blooming beautifully.

Mrs. Bennet and the children followed to talk and
(35) admire, while the servant leisurely cleared the table.

"Now give me that baby, put yourself in the easy chair, and tell me all about your worries," said Mrs. Gay, in the brisk, commanding way which few people could resist.

(40) "I'm sure I don't know where to begin," sighed Mrs. Bennet, dropping into the comfortable seat while baby changed bearers with great composure.

"I met your husband and he said the doctor had ordered you and these chicks off to Florida for the
(45) winter. John said he didn't know how he should manage it, but he meant to try."

"Isn't it dreadful? He can't leave his business to go with me, and we shall have to get Aunt Miranda to come and see to him and the boys while I'm gone, and
(50) the boys can't bear her strict, old-fashioned ways, and I've got to go that long journey all alone and stay among strangers, and these heaps of fall work to do first, and it will cost an immense sum to send us, and I don't know what is to become of me."

(55) Here Mrs. Bennet stopped for breath, and Mrs. Gay asked briskly, "What is the matter with you and the children?"

"Well, baby is having a hard time with his teeth and is croupy, Polly doesn't get over scarlet fever well, and
(60) I'm used up; no strength or appetite, pain in my side and low spirits. Entire change of scene, milder climate, and less work for me, is what we want, the doctor says. John is very anxious about us, and I feel regularly discouraged."

(65) "I'll spend the day and cheer you up a bit. You just rest and get ready for a new start tomorrow; it is a saving of time to stop short now and then and see where to begin next. Bring me the most pressing job of work. I can sew and see to this little rascal at the same
(70) time."

24. The "little woman" referred to in line 1 is

(A) Lady Washington
(B) Alcott's mother
(C) a servant
(D) Mrs. Bennet
(E) Mrs. Gay

25. When Alcott compares the breakfast table to something "devastated by a swarm of locusts" (line 4), she means

    (A) that it is a mess left by an uncaring mob
    (B) that children are no more meaningful than insects to Mrs. Bennet
    (C) to indicate Mrs. Bennet's flightiness
    (D) to illustrate the horror of Mrs. Bennet's life
    (E) that the Bennets are pests

26. All of the following contribute to the Bennet's "chaotic state" of affairs EXCEPT

    (A) the overall appearance of the breakfast table
    (B) the fretting of the baby
    (C) the contribution of Polly
    (D) the uncompleted pile of work
    (E) the optimism of Mrs. Gay

27. The word *despondent* in line 9 most nearly means

    (A) different
    (B) daring
    (C) excited
    (D) exasperated
    (E) dilapidated

28. Had Mrs. Gay not arrived when she did, Alcott leads us to suspect that

    (A) Mrs. Bennet would have gone back to bed
    (B) the children would have continued to cry
    (C) Mrs. Bennet would have accomplished little all day
    (D) sickness would have overtaken the entire family
    (E) the servant would have left the dishes untended

29. The "rosy clusters" in lines 26–27 are

    (A) Mrs. Gay's cheeks
    (B) Mrs. Bennet's cheeks
    (C) flowers
    (D) candies from Mrs. Gay's pockets
    (E) embroidered pockets

30. In lines 31–33 Alcott

    (A) reveals Mrs. Bennet's only talent
    (B) uses the sunny parlor as a symbol of hope
    (C) contrasts Mrs. Gay's sunniness with Mrs. Bennet's dullness
    (D) contrasts Mrs. Bennet's plants with her children
    (E) opens the door to Mrs. Bennet's despair

31. When Mrs. Bennet says that she's "used up" (line 60), she means that she

    (A) has no energy
    (B) is abused
    (C) is exploited
    (D) has spent all her money
    (E) has given up

32. The word *pressing* (line 68) means

    (A) heavy
    (B) ardent
    (C) forceful
    (D) important
    (E) concentrated

33. Mrs. Bennet's friend's disposition is indicated by

    (A) her name
    (B) her speech
    (C) her clothing
    (D) both A and B
    (E) both B and C

34. Alcott implies that Mrs. Bennet's real problem is

    (A) her inability to cope
    (B) a touch of fever
    (C) the cold winter weather
    (D) unsympathetic children
    (E) a lack of common sense

35. Mrs. Gay's primary quality seems to be her

    (A) lethargy
    (B) obliviousness
    (C) anxiety
    (D) dignity
    (E) practical nature

STOP

END OF SECTION 3. IF YOU HAVE ANY TIME LEFT, GO OVER YOUR WORK IN THIS SECTION ONLY. DO NOT WORK IN ANY OTHER SECTION OF THE TEST.

Section 4

25 QUESTIONS • TIME—30 MINUTES

Directions: Solve the following problems using any available space on the page for scratchwork. On your answer sheet fill in the choice which best corresponds to the correct answer.

Notes: The figures accompanying the problems are drawn as accurately as possible unless otherwise stated in specific problems. Again, unless otherwise stated, all figures lie in the same plane. All numbers used in these problems are real numbers. Calculators are permitted for this test.

Reference Information

Circle: $C = 2\pi r$, $A = \pi r^2$
Rectangle: $A = lw$
Rectangular Solid: $V = lwh$
Cylinder: $V = \pi r^2 h$
Triangle: $A = \frac{1}{2}bh$
$a^2 + b^2 = c^2$

45°-45°-90° triangle: sides x, x, $x\sqrt{2}$
30°-60°-90° triangle: sides x, $x\sqrt{3}$, $2x$

The number of degrees of arc in a circle is 360.
The measure in degrees of a straight angle is 180.
The sum of the measures in degrees of the angles of a triangle is 180.

Part 1: Quantitative Comparison Questions

Directions: For each of the following questions, two quantities are given—one in Column A, the other in Column B. Compare the two quantities and mark your answer sheet as follows:

(A) if the quantity in Column A is greater
(B) if the quantity in Column B is greater
(C) if the quantities are equal
(D) if the relationship cannot be determined from the information given

Notes:

(1) Information concerning one or both of the compared quantities will be centered above the two columns for some items.
(2) Symbols that appear in both columns represent the same thing in Column A as in Column B.
(3) Letters such as x, n, and k are symbols for real numbers.

Examples

	Column A	Column B	Answers
	$a > 0$		
	$x > 0$		
E1.	$a - x$	$a + x$	(A) ● (C) (D)
E2.	The average of 17, 19, 21, 23	The average of 16, 18, 20, 22	● (B) (C) (D)

DO NOT MARK CHOICE (E) FOR THESE QUESTIONS. THERE ARE ONLY FOUR ANSWER CHOICES.

their power to assure that the ecological balance is preserved in their areas. But in 1962, when Rachel
(65) Carson's *Silent Spring* was first published, this was not the case. Carson, a former marine biologist for the Fish and Game Service, disturbed many who had a vested interest in maintaining the status quo as far as the environment was concerned. Her credibility as a
(70) scientist and her deep and abiding personal courage enabled Carson to withstand the steady onslaught of criticism heaped on her during her lifetime. This criticism seemed to be directed at her on several levels—as a woman whose emotional response to the
(75) situation was getting in the way of scientific accuracy and as a scientist who believed that man should accommodate to nature rather than try to control it.

And what exactly was it that Rachel Carson did that was so disturbing? She pointed out the dangers of
(80) pesticides, DDT in particular, to the environment. Designed to contain insect pests in gardens and on farmland, the pesticides were permeating the soil, the rivers, and adhering to tree leaves and branches that were the home for various birds and unharmful in-
(85) sects.

Carson contended that the levels of chemical pesticides in major rivers, ground water, wildlife, soil, fish, earthworms, and humans, for example, were at levels that were alarming. The synthetic insecticides,
(90) according to Carson, were so potent that they were able to penetrate systems and remain there for years, perhaps leading to a breakdown in tissue and immune systems, and possibly causing malignancies.

Arsenic, the chief ingredient in insecticides and
(95) pesticides at the time of Carson's writing, is extremely toxic, causing reactions in livestock near areas dusted with arsenic sprays. Arsenic absorbed in the soil has even been found in plant tissues, thereby causing unsprayed plants to take up toxicity from the soil.
(100) As residue from the pesticides continues to build up in the soil over the years, more and more plant life is contaminated.

The furor caused by Carson's writing was mostly felt by the chemical companies that produced pesti-
(105) cides. Not willing to acknowledge the potential hazards of their products, they resisted by seeking to discredit Carson. And despite her credentials, Carson was discredited for a period of time. However, in 1970 with the establishment of the Environmental Protec-
(110) tion Agency, the nation became more concerned with issues that Carson had raised. Even though not as much progress has been made as Carson might have wished, DDT has been banned in the United States.

Rachel Carson, a scientist of vision and determina-
(115) tion, was able to change the course of history and bring environmental issues to the attention of the world.

1. According to Passage 1, the work of Mary Harris was particularly noteworthy because

    (A) she was an Irish immigrant
    (B) she fought for workers' rights
    (C) everyone was sure that she would fail
    (D) no one was supporting workers at that time
    (E) very few women worked in the public sector

2. The author implies that Mother Jones became a champion of workers' rights because

    (A) she experienced injustices in her native Ireland
    (B) no other work was open to her
    (C) the workers prevailed upon her to take up their cause
    (D) she knew how hard life in the textile mills was
    (E) workers were so mistreated in the mid-nineteenth century

3. Mother Jones' family responded to the oppression of the British by

    (A) joining the rebels
    (B) emigrating to Australia
    (C) becoming involved in local government
    (D) joining the Labor Party
    (E) establishing large land holdings

4. Mother Jones learned to become a radical union organizer through her association with

    (A) Irish rebels
    (B) the Knights of Labor
    (C) West Virginia coal miners
    (D) textile workers
    (E) County Cork Association

GO ON TO THE NEXT PAGE

5. When the passage refers to the *capriciousness of employers*, it means

   (A) employers were subject to no rules
   (B) employers were generous
   (C) employers were interested in profits
   (D) employers hired only nonunion workers
   (E) employers were not interested in workers' problems

6. According to Passage 1, Eugene V. Debs organized the

   (A) Knights of Labor
   (B) Textile Workers' Union
   (C) American Railway Union
   (D) Coal Miners' Union
   (E) Steel Workers' Union

7. In Passage 2, the word *constituencies* (line 62) means

   (A) an advisory committee
   (B) financial contributors
   (C) campaign workers
   (D) legislative body
   (E) a group of citizens

8. According to Passage 2, the reaction to Carson's findings and recommendations during her lifetime was

   (A) completely indifferent
   (B) highly supportive
   (C) somewhat critical
   (D) negative and hostile
   (E) positive and accepting

9. Rachel Carson pointed out the hazards to the environment associated with

   (A) pesticides
   (B) acid rain
   (C) smog
   (D) destruction of the rain forest
   (E) noise pollution

10. According to the passage, Carson maintained that the use of insecticides was responsible for all of the following EXCEPT

    (A) human tissue breakdown
    (B) breakdown of the immune system
    (C) breathing difficulties
    (D) malignancies
    (E) plant tissue contamination

11. One of the most toxic ingredients in insecticides, according to the passage, is

    (A) synthetic toxins
    (B) DDT
    (C) arsenic
    (D) Agent Orange
    (E) poisonous herbs

12. The authors of the two passages would agree that a quality shared by Mother Jones and Rachel Carson was

    (A) need for power
    (B) desire for the limelight
    (C) belief in a cause
    (D) understanding of the media
    (E) interest in monetary reward

STOP

END OF SECTION 5. IF YOU HAVE ANY TIME LEFT, GO OVER YOUR WORK IN THIS SECTION ONLY. DO NOT WORK IN ANY OTHER SECTION OF THE TEST.

SECTION 6

10 Questions • Time—15 Minutes

Directions: Solve the following problems using any available space on the page for scratchwork. On your answer sheet fill in the choice which best corresponds to the correct answer.

Notes: The figures accompanying the problems are drawn as accurately as possible unless otherwise stated in specific problems. Again, unless otherwise stated, all figures lie in the same plane. All numbers used in these problems are real numbers. Calculators are permitted for this test.

Reference Information

Circle: $C = 2\pi r$, $A = \pi r^2$
Rectangle: $A = lw$
Rectangular Solid: $V = lwh$
Cylinder: $V = \pi r^2 h$
Triangle: $A = \frac{1}{2}bh$
$a^2 + b^2 = c^2$

Special triangles: 45°-45°-90° with sides $x, x, x\sqrt{2}$; 30°-60°-90° with sides $x, x\sqrt{3}, 2x$.

The number of degrees of arc in a circle is 360.
The measure in degrees of a straight angle is 180.
The sum of the measures in degrees of the angles of a triangle is 180.

---

1. Which one of the following quantities has the lowest numerical value?

   (A) $\frac{4}{5}$
   (B) $\frac{7}{9}$
   (C) .76
   (D) $\frac{5}{7}$
   (E) $\frac{9}{11}$

2. A salesperson earns twice as much in December as in each of the other months of a year. What part of this salesperson's entire year's earnings are earned in December?

   (A) $\frac{1}{7}$
   (B) $\frac{2}{13}$
   (C) $\frac{1}{6}$
   (D) $\frac{2}{11}$
   (E) $\frac{3}{14}$

3. If $x = -1$, then $3x^3 + 2x^2 + x + 1 =$

   (A) −5
   (B) −1
   (C) 1
   (D) 2
   (E) 5

4. $.03\% \times .21 =$

   (A) .63
   (B) .063
   (C) .0063
   (D) .00063
   (E) .000063

GO ON TO THE NEXT PAGE

5. An equilateral triangle 3 inches on a side is cut up into smaller equilateral triangles one inch on a side. What is the greatest number of such triangles that can be formed?

   (A) 3
   (B) 6
   (C) 9
   (D) 12
   (E) 15

6. A square 5 units on a side has one vertex at the point (1,1). Which one of the following points *cannot* be diagonally opposite that vertex?

   (A) (6,6)
   (B) (−4,6)
   (C) (−4,−4)
   (D) (6,−4)
   (E) (4,−6)

7. Five equal squares are placed side by side to make a single rectangle whose perimeter is 372 inches. Find the number of square inches in the area of one of these squares.

   (A) 72
   (B) 324
   (C) 900
   (D) 961
   (E) 984

8. The water level of a swimming pool, 75 feet by 42 feet, is to be raised four inches. How many gallons of water must be added to accomplish this? (7.48 gal. = 1 cubic ft.)

   (A) 140
   (B) 7,854
   (C) 31,500
   (D) 94,500
   (E) 727,650

9. What part of the total quantity is represented by a 24-degree sector of a circle graph?

   (A) $6\frac{2}{3}\%$
   (B) 12%
   (C) $13\frac{1}{3}\%$
   (D) 15%
   (E) 24%

10. The square of a fraction between 0 and 1 is

    (A) less than the original fraction
    (B) greater than the original fraction
    (C) twice the original fraction
    (D) less than the cube of the fraction
    (E) not necessarily any of the preceding

STOP

END OF SECTION 6. IF YOU HAVE ANY TIME LEFT, GO OVER YOUR WORK IN THIS SECTION ONLY. DO NOT WORK IN ANY OTHER SECTION OF THE TEST.

PRACTICE EXAMINATION 2
Answer Key

Section 1: Verbal

1. C	8. B	14. C	20. D	26. A
2. E	9. B	15. B	21. B	27. C
3. A	10. A	16. B	22. C	28. E
4. D	11. C	17. D	23. D	29. C
5. B	12. E	18. E	24. B	30. A
6. B	13. E	19. C	25. A	31. E
7. D				

Section 2: Math

1. C	6. A	11. B	16. D	21. A
2. C	7. D	12. D	17. C	22. B
3. C	8. C	13. B	18. C	23. A
4. B	9. D	14. C	19. B	24. D
5. D	10. A	15. D	20. D	25. D

Section 3: Verbal

1. E	8. A	15. B	22. B	29. C
2. B	9. D	16. D	23. C	30. B
3. C	10. B	17. C	24. D	31. A
4. B	11. B	18. E	25. A	32. D
5. E	12. B	19. A	26. E	33. D
6. D	13. B	20. B	27. D	34. A
7. B	14. D	21. D	28. C	35. E

Section 4: Math

Part 1

1. C	4. B	7. C	10. A	13. B
2. A	5. A	8. A	11. B	14. D
3. D	6. C	9. B	12. D	15. D

Part 2

16. 2	18. 8.25	20. $\frac{31}{50} = .62$	22. 36	24. 11
17. 13	19. 70	21. 72	23. 7	25. $17.5 = \frac{35}{2}$

Section 5: Verbal

1. E
2. A
3. A
4. B
5. A
6. C
7. E
8. D
9. A
10. C
11. C
12. C

Section 6: Math

1. D
2. B
3. B
4. E
5. C
6. E
7. D
8. B
9. A
10. A

PRACTICE EXAMINATION 2
Explanatory Answers

Note: A 🖩 following a math answer explanation indicates that a calculator could be helpful in solving that particular problem.

Section 1

1. **(C)** Audience laughter at the wrong moment can easily disconcert (upset or confuse) an actor.

2. **(E)** Since the assurances of good faith were "hollow," it is not surprising that those who made them *reneged* on (went back on) their agreement.

3. **(A)** To win the majority, we must unite, or *amalgamate*, the different factions.

4. **(D)** A law known as the Prohibition Act would naturally be expected to *proscribe* (outlaw) something.

5. **(B)** A caller who will not give his name is by definition *anonymous*. Since he is giving information to the police, he may well fear *reprisals* (retaliation) by a criminal.

6. **(B)** An intractable, or stubborn, individual is likely to have trouble adapting to a new way of life. Choice (A), *nonchalant,* means *unconcerned.* Choice (C), *rabid,* means *furious.* Choice (D), *insolent,* means *rude.* And choice (E), *doughty,* means *valiant.*

7. **(D)** The key word *though* indicates that the word in the blank should be opposite in meaning from *shared.* The only choice that satisfies this condition is *disparate* (very different; having nothing in common).

8. **(B)** If you understand that *gastronomic* is an adjective having to do with eating, the only possible choice is (B). A *gourmet* (person who appreciates good food) is a *connoisseur,* or expert, in food.

9. **(B)** The phrase "her arm was broken" points to a negative word choice for this sentence. The only negative word is *plaintively,* which means *sadly.* All other choices are positive.

10. **(A)** A primary function of the *throat* is to *swallow,* and a primary function of the *teeth* is to *chew.*

11. **(C)** A *garnet* has the color *red,* and an *emerald* has the color *green.*

12. **(E)** *Patience* is considered one of the virtues, just as *literature* is considered one of the *arts.*

13. **(E)** An airplane that can *soar* will eventually *alight* on the ground. A boat that can *sail* will eventually *moor* at a dock.

14. **(C)** An *oasis* is a place of refuge in the middle of the *desert.* An *island* is a place of refuge in the middle of the *ocean.*

15. **(B)** *Cotton* is *soft* to the touch, as an *iron* is *hard* to the touch.

16. **(B)** While answers (A), (C), and (D) are all synonyms for *ravaged,* the context of the sentence supports the choice of *devastated.*

17. **(D)** Nowhere in the passage is the quality of the soil mentioned as a reason for the dependence on the potato as a staple.

18. **(E)** While not directly stated in the passage, the author certainly implies that the dependence on one crop was dangerous.

19. **(C)** The passage certainly describes Irish life as characterized by poverty and oppression from landlords, so *harsh* is the correct answer.

20. **(D)** The passage states that farmers were compelled to subdivide in order to make rent payments to their landlords.

21. **(B)** The best answer according the context of the sentence is *disease*, particularly since in the sentence the word applies to the crop.

22. **(C)** While some of the other responses may be true, they are not stated in the passage.

23. **(D)** The Irish did not gain their independence during this period; no reference to Irish independence is made in the passage.

24. **(B)** Jupiter is being asked to decide which of three goddesses is the fairest—it is a no-win decision, since it is bound to anger two of the three.

25. **(A)** Ulysses has no inclination to embark on the adventure, since he is happy at home with his family.

26. **(A)** "Ulysses pretended to be mad" (lines 41–42), and one of the methods he chose was to hitch up a mismatched team and sow something that could not grow.

27. **(C)** Palamedes doesn't buy Ulysses's mad act, and he thinks up a way to test him. Since Ulysses is unwilling to run over his own son, he is obviously not as mad as he pretends to be.

28. **(E)** Rather than say that Thetis, being a sea-nymph, can read the future, Bulfinch merely mentions her immortal status and expects the reader to understand that this means that she knows "her son was fated to perish."

29. **(C)** The names in (A) are those of goddesses. Paris is a "beautiful shepherd" (line 11). Eris is a goddess (line 6). Thetis is a sea-nymph (lines 51–52). Homer and Virgil are poets (lines 32–33). Only choice (C) names three chieftains of Greece.

30. **(A)** Again, Bulfinch expects his readers to understand Ulysses's clever ploy without its being spelled out. Achilles is disguised as a woman, but he is inappropriately interested in manly objects.

31. **(E)** This is an accurate summary of the main themes in the passage.

Section 2

1. **(C)** Let the other two angles be $2x$ and $5x$.

    Thus, $2x + 5x + 82 = 180$
    $$7x = 98$$
    $$x = 14$$
    $$2x = 28$$
    $$5x = 70$$
    Smallest angle $= 28°$

2. **(C)** Let $x =$ no. of years for 2 populations to be equal.

    Then $6800 - 120x = 4200 + 80x$
    $$2600 = 200x$$
    $$x = 13$$

3. **(C)** Simply plug the two values into the formula.

    $2^2 - 2(2) = 0$ and $1^2 - 2(1) = -1$
    $*2 - *1 = 0 - (-1) = 1$.

4. **(B)**

    $\frac{1}{2} \cdot x \cdot 2x = 25$

    $x^2 = 25$

    $x = 5$

    $2x = 10$

    $y^2 = 5^2 + 10^2$

    $y^2 = 25 + 100$

    $y^2 = 125$

    $y = \sqrt{125} = \sqrt{25 \times 5}$

    $y = 5\sqrt{5}$

5. **(D)** The abscissa of Q is 3 more than that of P. The ordinate of Q is 2 less than that of P. Hence, coordinates of Q are $(3+3, 7-2) = (6, 5)$

6. **(A)** $r = 5x$

    Divide both sides by 10

    $$\frac{r}{10} = \frac{5}{10}x$$

    or $\quad \frac{1}{10}r = \frac{1}{2}x$

    Hence, 1 is the answer.

7. **(D)** The area of triangle ADE equals the area of triangle AEC, since they have the same base and altitude. The area of triangle ABC equals that of triangle ADC, since the diagonal of a parallelogram divides it equally.

8. **(C)** If the side of a square is s, its diagonal is the hypotenuse of a right triangle with two sides as its legs. The length of the diagonal is $\sqrt{s^2 + s^2} = \sqrt{2}s$

    $0.7(\sqrt{2}s) \approx (0.7)(1.4)s \approx 1s = s$.

9. **(D)** This is an inverse proportion; that is:

    $$\frac{9}{6} = \frac{x}{120}$$

    $6x = 1080$

    $x = 180$

10. **(A)** Thinking of a clock in terms of degrees, there are 360 degrees from 12 noon to 12 midnight. In one hour there are 360 degrees ÷ 12 hours = 30 degrees per hour. In two hours the hour hand moves 2 hours × 30 degrees per hour = 60 degrees. Therefore, in 2 hours and 12 minutes the hour hand moves 66 degrees.

11. **(B)** $8 \times 6 = 48$

    $6 \times 8 = 48$

    $48 + 48 = 96$ (sum of all 14 numbers)

    Average $= \frac{96}{14} = 6\frac{6}{7}$

12. **(D)** I. As x increases, $(1 - x^2)$ decreases.

    II. As x increases, $(x - 1)$ increases

    III. As x increases, $\frac{1}{x^2}$ decreases.

    Hence, only II increases.

13. **(B)** 3, 7, 12, 18, 25,

    Differences are 4, 5, 6, 7, 8, . . . etc.

    Thus the series progresses as follows: 3, 7, 12, 18, 25, 33, 42, 52, 63

14. **(C)** The numerator is the difference between perfect squares. $x^2 - y^2$ is equal to the product of $(x + y)$ and $(x - y)$. Therefore,

    $$\frac{x^2 - y^2}{x - y} = \frac{(x+y)(x-y)}{x-y} = x + y$$

15. **(D)** The distance traveled is the circumference of the wheel times the number of revolutions. If r is the number of revolutions of the back wheel, $r + 10$ will be the number of revolutions of the front wheel. They will have traveled the same distance, so 7 ft. × $(r + 10)$ = 9 ft. × r, and $r = 35$. The wagon has gone 9 ft. × 35 revolutions = 315 ft.

16. **(D)** The dimensions of the flower bed including the walk are $(12 + 6)$ and $(16 + 6)$. Thus, the area is 18 yds. × 22 yds = 396 square yards. The area of the flower bed alone is $12 \times 16 = 192$ square yds. Therefore, the area of the walk is 396 square yds − 192 square yds. = 204 square yds.

17. **(C)** Dave takes 30 minutes to wash the car alone.

    $$\frac{x}{15} + \frac{x}{30} = 1$$

    $2x + x = 30$

    $3x = 30$

    $x = 10$

18. **(C)** Let r = radius of inscribed circle and s = radius of circumscribed circle. Then in right triangle OPQ, $PQ = OQ = r$ and $s = OP = r\sqrt{2}$.

Area of inscribed circle = πr^2

Area of circumscribed circle = $\pi s^2 = \pi(r\sqrt{2})^2 = 2\pi r^2$

Ratio = $\dfrac{\pi r^2}{2\pi r^2} = 1:2$

19. **(B)** Let x = no. of minutes to fill $\frac{4}{7}$ of bucket.

Then $\dfrac{\frac{3}{7}}{1} = \dfrac{\frac{4}{7}}{x}$, or $\dfrac{3}{1} = \dfrac{4}{x}$

$3x = 4 \qquad x = \dfrac{4}{3}$

20. **(D)** The similar triangles in the configuration produce the proportion

$\dfrac{3}{5} = \dfrac{4}{Y}$

$3Y = 20$

$Y = 6\dfrac{2}{3}$

21. **(A)** An increase of 30% in the base b means that the new base will be $b + .30b$. A 20% decrease in the new altitude a means that the new altitude will be $a - .20a$. The new area is $(b + .30b)(a - .20a) = 1.04ba$. The new area is 104% of the old, an increase of 104% − 100% = 4%.

22. **(B)** Typing space is 12 − 3 = 9 inches long and 9 − 2 = 7 inches wide. Part used =

$\dfrac{9 \times 7}{9 \times 12} = \dfrac{7}{12}$

23. **(A)** $\triangle SPT = \frac{1}{3} \triangle PSR$ since they have common altitude and the base $ST = \frac{1}{3}SR$.

But $\triangle PSR = \frac{1}{2} \square\, PQRS$

Hence $\triangle SPT = \frac{1}{3} \cdot \frac{1}{2}\square = \frac{1}{6}\square$

24. **(D)** $A = P(1 + rt)$

$A = P + Prt$

$A - P = Prt$

Divide both sides by Pr.

$t = \dfrac{A - P}{Pr}$

25. **(D)** I. If $p > q$ and $r < 0$, multiplying both sides by r reverses the inequality

$pr < qr$

II. Also $p + r > q + r$

III. However, subtracting r from both sides leaves inequality in same order.

Hence I and II only.

Section 3

1. **(E)** *Tension* is likely to mount before a pitcher delivers the last strike of a game—especially during a pause.

2. **(B)** Funding a hospital for the poor may properly be called a *humanitarian* act. It may or may not be popular.

3. **(C)** This is the only answer in which both words are correct in relation to each other as well as to the sense of the sentence.

4. **(B)** The word that means "having more than one meaning" is *ambiguous*.

5. **(E)** The two sides might negotiate, or bargain, through the night in an attempt to *avert*, or prevent, a strike.

6. **(D)** The missing word must mean the same as "respect for age." The correct choice is *venerated*.

7. **(B)** It is likely that someone who is unprepared would approach an exam with *trepidation*, or apprehension, not with *aplomb* (self-assurance), *indifference* (lack of concern), *confidence*, or *duplicity* (hypocrisy).

8. **(A)** The only word that makes sense in this context is *derelict*, meaning neglectful of duty, or remiss.

9. **(D)** If a show of temper is atypical or unusual, she must be something opposite in meaning. *Equanimity*, or calmness, is the correct choice.

10. **(B)** In this sentence, two negative words are needed, thus eliminating choices (A), (C) and (D), which have at least one positive response. Choice (E) makes no sense. The correct answer is (B), which includes two evidently negative responses. The *craven*, or cowardly, attitudes of politicians may cause them to *cower*, or shrink back, when there is controversy.

11. **(B)** When you *touch* something, you *feel* it. Similarly, when you *look* at something, you *see* it.

12. **(B)** The contrast in shape between a *circle* and a *square* is not unlike that between an *oval* and a *rectangle*.

13. **(B)** The male *chicken* is a *rooster*, and the male *duck* is a *drake*.

14. **(D)** A *trigger* activates a *pistol* and a *switch* a *motor*.

15. **(B)** *Angelic* is a greater degree of *good*, just as *joyous* is a greater degree of *glad*.

16. **(D)** The *clarinet* is a member of the *woodwind* family of instruments. The *trumpet* is a member of the *brass* family of instruments.

17. **(C)** To be *doleful* is to be full of *grief*, just as to be *wrathful* is to be full of *anger*. No other pair reflects a similar relationship.

18. **(E)** A *pail* holds *water* and water can be poured from a pail. A *shaker* holds *salt* and salt can be poured from a shaker.

19. **(A)** *Fish* kept in an artificial environment in captivity live in an *aquarium*. When *birds* are kept in captivity they live in an *aviary*. (B) is not a bad answer but it is not as good as (A) because a car is not alive.

20. **(B)** *Disagreement* is characterized by a lack of *concord* (harmony). Similarly, *impartiality* is characterized by a lack of *bias* (prejudice).

21. **(D)** A *year* is a hundredth of a *century*, and a *cent* is a hundredth of a *dollar*.

22. **(B)** A well-known characteristic of a *mule* is that it is *intractable* (stubborn). Likewise, the *fox* is known for being *wily* (sly and crafty).

23. **(C)** If we *stumble*, our *walking* is impeded, and if we *stammer*, our *speaking* is impeded.

24. **(D)** Introduced as the "little woman" and "despondent matron," Mrs. Bennet is named in paragraph 4. Alcott's epithets for Mrs. Bennet emphasize her weakness.

25. **(A)** Mrs. Bennet's family has left her this mess with as little concern as a swarm of insects might have. Locusts are not particularly horrible; had Alcott used a more potent simile, (D) might be correct.

26. **(E)** Mrs. Gay's presence has a beneficial effect on the chaotic Bennet. All of the other items either directly contribute to the chaos or are byproducts of it.

27. **(D)** In this context, *despondent* most nearly means sad, frustrated, or exasperated. This is explained in the context of lines 9–10 during which the reader learns that Mrs. Bennett is crying.

28. **(C)** Before Mrs. Gay's arrival, Mrs. Bennet was about to have "a good cry" (line 14). There is no indication that she would have been able to cope with her household duties.

29. **(C)** The flowers Mrs. Gay brings echo the rosiness of Mrs. Gay herself—she is earlier described as "a large rosy woman" (lines 15–16).

30. **(B)** In contrast to Mrs. Bennet's disorderly breakfast room, her front parlor is sunny and filled with blooming flowers, which contrast with her sickly children (D). (D) is not the correct response, however, because it only tells part of the story.

31. **(A)** Mrs. Bennet's lack of energy is her primary quality.

32. **(D)** Mrs. Gay, in her practical way, requests the job that is most vital, knowing that to get that job out of the way will improve Mrs. Bennet's spirits.

33. **(D)** Mrs. Gay has a name that suits her, and every speech she makes reveals her good humor and energy.

34. **(A)** Mrs. Bennet seems paralyzed by her situation. The "weariness of her own tired soul and body" oppresses her (line 12), and she surveys her household with despair.

35. **(E)** The last paragraph of the passage best expresses this quality. Mrs. Gay's get-things-done attitude is contrasted with Mrs. Bennet's ineffectiveness.

Section 4

Part 1

1. **(C)** Since dividing by 2 and multiplying by .5 have the same results, the quantities must be equal.

2. **(A)** Since the figure has 5 sides, it contains

    $180(5-2) = 540$ degrees
    $540 = x + 110 + 60 + 120 + 100$
    $540 = x + 390$
    $150 = x$

3. **(D)** The problem tells us only that the ratio of m to n is 7 to 10. It is possible, for example, that m is 700 and n is 1000.

4. **(B)** Simply plug the values into the formula.

    Column A $= \dfrac{(-3)(-2)}{-3-(-2)} = \dfrac{6}{-1} = -6$

    Column B $= \dfrac{(-2)(-3)}{-2-(-3)} = \dfrac{6}{1} = 6$

5. **(A)** Notice the right angle at $\angle BAC$. Side BC must be the longest side since it is opposite the largest angle. Since $\angle ADC$ is also a right angle, side AC must be longer than CD.

6. **(C)** Since there are three parallel lines, the corresponding angles are equal. If x, y and z are all the same, then $x + y$ must equal $y + z$.

7. **(C)** Since 3% = .03 and 4% = .04, then .03 × .04 = .0012.

8. **(A)** $7.88 divided by 2 equals $3.94. $11.79 divided by 3 equals $3.93.

9. **(B)** When an angle is inscribed in a circle, the arc is twice the angle. Arc AB equals 2 times 50, which is 100.

10. **(A)** $\sqrt{8}$ is almost 3. $\sqrt{24}$ is almost 5. Thus, Column A is close to 8. This is larger than $\sqrt{32}$ which is less than 6.

11. **(B)** Since there are more digits in Box B, it must contain more possibilities.

12. **(D)** There is no way to determine the relative values of a, b, and c.

13. **(B)** $p^2 - q^2 = (p+q)(p-q) = 4$. We can substitute -1 for $(p-q)$.
    $(p+q)(-1) = 4$
    $(p+q) = -4$

14. **(D)** The information tells us about percents only. We do not know how many boys or girls are in the class.

15. **(D)** While p, q, and r are positive, we do not know whether they are fractions. If the three variables were $\frac{1}{2}, \frac{1}{3}$ and $\frac{1}{4}$, the sum of the variables would be greater than the product.

Part 2

16. $(\sqrt{18} - \sqrt{8})^2$
$= (3\sqrt{2} - 2\sqrt{2})^2$
$= (\sqrt{2})^2 = 2$

17.

A radius drawn perpendicular to a chord bisects the chord. Construct the radius as shown above.

$5^2 + 12^2 = r^2$
$25 + 144 = r^2$
$r^2 = 169$
$r = 13$

18. $\dfrac{x}{11} = 15$
$x = 165$
$\dfrac{165}{20} = 8.25$

19.

An exterior angle of a triangle is equal to the sum of the two remote interior angles.

$8x + 40 = (9x - 40) + (4x + 30)$
$8x + 40 = 13x - 10$
$5x = 50$
$x = 10$
$m\angle J = (4x + 30)° = (40 + 30)° = 70°$

20. $\dfrac{2^2 + 3^2}{5^2} + \dfrac{1}{10} = \dfrac{4+9}{25} + \dfrac{1}{10}$
$= \dfrac{13}{25} + \dfrac{1}{10}$

The lowest common denominator is 50.

$= \dfrac{26}{50} + \dfrac{5}{50} = \dfrac{31}{50} = .62$

21. The shaded area is the area of the rectangle minus the area of the two circles.

Area of the rectangle $= 6(12) = 72$
Area of circle $= \pi r^2 = 9\pi$
Shaded area $= 72 - 2(9\pi)$
$= 72 - 18\pi$
$= a - b\pi$

$\therefore a = 72$ and $b = 18$

22.

Let $3x =$ the measure of one of the angles
$5x =$ the measure of the 2nd angle
$7x =$ the measure of the 3rd angle

$3x + 5x + 7x = 180$
$15x = 180$
$x = 12$

The smallest angle $= 3x = 36°$

23. $d = \sqrt{(x_2 - x_1)^2 + (y_2 - y_1)^2}$
$= \sqrt{(3-(-4))^2 + (-2-5)^2}$
$= \sqrt{7^2 + (-7)^2}$
$= \sqrt{49 + 49} = \sqrt{98} = \sqrt{49}\sqrt{2}$
$= 7\sqrt{2} = b\sqrt{2}$
$\therefore b = 7$

24. $\dfrac{9+9+10+x+y}{5} = 10$

$28 + x + y = 50$

$x + y = 22$

the average of x and y is

$\dfrac{x+y}{2} = \dfrac{22}{2} = 11$

25.

Area $\triangle NKL = \dfrac{1}{2}(b)(h)$

$= \dfrac{1}{2}(7)(5) = 17.5 = \dfrac{35}{2}$

Section 5

1. **(E)** The author makes the point that Mary's work was most unusual because women did not work in the public arena during the mid-nineteenth century.

2. **(A)** The passage, with its emphasis on Mary's history of standing up for human rights, certainly implies that previous injustices influenced her later work with workers.

3. **(A)** The passage clearly states that Mary's family joined the Irish rebels.

4. **(B)** When Mary found herself homeless (lines 25–26), she lived at the union hall and became involved with the Knights of Labor.

5. **(A)** The context of the sentence that mentions that employers could reduce wages whenever they wished, supports the choice of (A).

6. **(C)** The passage clearly states (lines 38–39) that Debs founded the American Railway Union.

7. **(E)** The context of the sentence indicates that "a group of citizens" is the best choice.

8. **(D)** During Carson's lifetime, the response to her work was negative and hostile; it was only later that her work was appreciated for its vision.

9. **(A)** Carson's work concerned the effect of pesticides on the environment (lines 79–80).

10. **(C)** Nowhere in the passage are breathing difficulties mentioned as a side effect of using insecticides.

11. **(C)** The passage mentions arsenic (lines 94–97) as the most toxic ingredient.

12. **(C)** The choice must be "belief in a cause," as the other choices are contrary to the picture painted of each of the women in the passages.

Section 6

1. **(D)** $\dfrac{4}{5} = .8$

$\dfrac{7}{9} = 9\overline{)7.00}\;\; .78$

$\dfrac{5}{7} = 7\overline{)5.00}\;\; .71$

$\dfrac{9}{11} = 11\overline{)9.00}\;\; .82$

Thus, $\dfrac{5}{7}$ is the smallest quantity.

2. **(B)** Let x = amount earned each month. $2x$ = amount earned in December.

Then $11x + 2x = 13x$ (entire earnings).

$\dfrac{2x}{13x} = \dfrac{2}{13}$

3. **(B)** $3x^3 + 2x^2 + x + 1$

$= 3(-1)^3 + 2(-1)^2 + (-1) + 1$

$= 3(-1) + 2(1) - 1 + 1$

$= -3 + 2 + 0$

$= -1$

4. **(E)** Convert the percent to decimal form before multiplying. $.03\% = .0003$

$.0003 \times .21 = .000063$

The number of decimal places in the product must be equal to the sum of the number of decimal places in the terms to be multiplied.

5. **(C)** Since the ratio of the sides is 3:1, the ratio of the areas is 9:1.

   The subdivision into 9△ is shown.

6. **(E)** The opposite vertices may be any of the number pairs $(1 \pm 5, 1 \pm 5)$, or $(6, 6), (-4, -4), (-4, 6),$ and $(6, -4)$.

   Thus, $(4, -6)$ is not possible.

7. **(D)**

   Perimeter of rectangle $= x + 5x + x + 5x$

   Thus, $12x = 372$

   $x = 31$

   Area of square $= 31^2 = 961$

8. **(B)** 4 inches is $\frac{1}{3}$ ft. The volume of the added level is $75 \times 42 \times \frac{1}{3} = 1050$ cubic ft. There are 7.48 gallons in 1 cubic ft., so 1050 cubic ft. $\times$ 7.48 gal./cubic ft. = 7,854 gallons.

9. **(A)** There are 360 degrees in a circle. A 24-degree sector is $\frac{24}{360} = .067$, or about $6\frac{2}{3}\%$ of a circle.

10. **(A)** In these fractions the numerator n is always less than the denominator d. After squaring the fraction $(\frac{n}{d})^2 = \frac{n^2}{d^2}$, the new fraction is less than the original since the denominator is getting larger faster than the numerator.

COMPUTING YOUR SCORES ON PRACTICE EXAMINATION 2

To check your progress in preparing for the SAT, you need to compute individual verbal and mathematical raw scores for this practice examination. Once you have computed these, use the conversion scales in the section that follows to compute your SAT scaled scores (200–800). Keep in mind that these formulas have been simplified to give you a "quick and dirty" sense of where you are scoring, not a perfectly precise score.

To Compute Your Raw Scores:

1. Enter the number of correct answers for each verbal and mathematical reasoning section into the boxes marked "Number of Questions Correct."
2. Enter the number of incorrect answers (not blanks) for each verbal and mathematical reasoning section into the boxes marked "Number of Questions Incorrect."
3. Total the number correct and number incorrect.
4. Follow this formula: Take the total correct and minus one-quarter of the total incorrect. Round up in your favor to compute your Raw Score.

Verbal Section	Total Number of Questions	Number of Questions Correct	Number of Questions Incorrect
1	31		
3	35		
5	12		
Totals	78	Total Correct:	Total Incorrect:

Verbal Raw Score = Total Correct − ($\frac{1}{4}$ × Total Incorrect) = _____

Math Section	Total Number of Questions	Number of Questions Correct	Number of Questions Incorrect
2	25		
4	25		
6	10		
Totals	60	Total Correct:	Total Incorrect:

Math Raw Score = Total Correct − ($\frac{1}{4}$ × Total Incorrect) = _____

CONVERSION SCALES FOR PRACTICE EXAMINATION 2

VERBAL REASONING

Raw Score	Scaled Score	Raw Score	Scaled Score
75	800	35	520
70	800	30	480
65	760	25	440
60	650	20	410
55	670	15	370
50	620	10	340
45	590	5	290
40	550	0	230

MATHEMATICAL REASONING

Raw Score	Scaled Score	Raw Score	Scaled Score
60	800	25	510
55	760	20	480
50	690	15	440
45	650	10	410
40	610	5	340
35	580	0	200
30	550		

Although you now have some idea of what your scores would look like had they been scaled according to unofficial ETS standards, you will probably want to know how to interpret your Raw Scores in more familiar terms. If so, use the following Self-Evaluation Charts to see what your Raw Scores actually mean.

SELF-EVALUATION CHARTS

VERBAL REASONING: Raw Score

Excellent	60 – 75
Good	50 – 60
Average	30 – 50
Fair	20 – 30
Poor	0 – 20

MATHEMATICAL REASONING: Raw Score

Excellent	50 – 60
Good	40 – 50
Average	20 – 40
Fair	10 – 20
Poor	0 – 10

PRACTICE EXAMINATION 3

Answer Sheet

If a section has fewer questions than answer ovals, leave the extra ovals blank.

Section 1

(Answer grid: questions 1–40, options A B C D E)

Section 2

(Answer grid: questions 1–40, options A B C D E)

Section 3

Answer spaces for Section 3 are on the back of this Answer Sheet.

Section 4

(Answer grid: questions 1–40, options A B C D E)

Section 5

(Answer grid: questions 1–15, options A B C D E)

Section 6

1. Ⓐ Ⓑ Ⓒ Ⓓ Ⓔ
2. Ⓐ Ⓑ Ⓒ Ⓓ Ⓔ
3. Ⓐ Ⓑ Ⓒ Ⓓ Ⓔ
4. Ⓐ Ⓑ Ⓒ Ⓓ Ⓔ
5. Ⓐ Ⓑ Ⓒ Ⓓ Ⓔ
6. Ⓐ Ⓑ Ⓒ Ⓓ Ⓔ
7. Ⓐ Ⓑ Ⓒ Ⓓ Ⓔ
8. Ⓐ Ⓑ Ⓒ Ⓓ Ⓔ
9. Ⓐ Ⓑ Ⓒ Ⓓ Ⓔ
10. Ⓐ Ⓑ Ⓒ Ⓓ Ⓔ
11. Ⓐ Ⓑ Ⓒ Ⓓ Ⓔ
12. Ⓐ Ⓑ Ⓒ Ⓓ Ⓔ
13. Ⓐ Ⓑ Ⓒ Ⓓ Ⓔ
14. Ⓐ Ⓑ Ⓒ Ⓓ Ⓔ
15. Ⓐ Ⓑ Ⓒ Ⓓ Ⓔ

Section 3

1. Ⓐ Ⓑ Ⓒ Ⓓ Ⓔ
2. Ⓐ Ⓑ Ⓒ Ⓓ Ⓔ
3. Ⓐ Ⓑ Ⓒ Ⓓ Ⓔ
4. Ⓐ Ⓑ Ⓒ Ⓓ Ⓔ
5. Ⓐ Ⓑ Ⓒ Ⓓ Ⓔ
6. Ⓐ Ⓑ Ⓒ Ⓓ Ⓔ
7. Ⓐ Ⓑ Ⓒ Ⓓ Ⓔ
8. Ⓐ Ⓑ Ⓒ Ⓓ Ⓔ
9. Ⓐ Ⓑ Ⓒ Ⓓ Ⓔ
10. Ⓐ Ⓑ Ⓒ Ⓓ Ⓔ
11. Ⓐ Ⓑ Ⓒ Ⓓ Ⓔ
12. Ⓐ Ⓑ Ⓒ Ⓓ Ⓔ
13. Ⓐ Ⓑ Ⓒ Ⓓ Ⓔ
14. Ⓐ Ⓑ Ⓒ Ⓓ Ⓔ
15. Ⓐ Ⓑ Ⓒ Ⓓ Ⓔ

Note: ONLY the answers entered on the grid are scored. Handwritten answers at the top of the column are NOT scored.

[Grid-in answer boxes for questions 16–25]

Practice Examination 3   423

...e space on the page for scratchwork. On your answer
... answer.

...accurately as possible unless otherwise stated in specific
...he same plane. All numbers used in these problems are

Triangle:

$A = \frac{1}{2}bh$ $a^2 + b^2 = c^2$

...180.

1. ...
   $18x + 5$?

   (A) 46
   (B) 41
   (C) 36
   (D) 32
   (E) It cannot be determined from the information given.

Note: Figure not drawn to scale.

2. In the figure above, $x =$

   (A) 35
   (B) 50
   (C) 70
   (D) 90
   (E) 110

GO ON TO THE NEXT PAGE

3. If $2y = \frac{1}{3}$, then $\frac{1}{4y} =$

   (A) $\frac{3}{2}$
   (B) $\frac{3}{4}$
   (C) $\frac{2}{5}$
   (D) $\frac{1}{5}$
   (E) $\frac{4}{3}$

4. Pieces of wire are soldered together so as to form the edges of a cube, whose volume is 64 cubic inches. The number of inches of wire used is

   (A) 24
   (B) 48
   (C) 64
   (D) 96
   (E) 120

5. If a box of note paper costs $4.20 after a 40% discount, what was its original price?

   (A) $2.52
   (B) $4.60
   (C) $5.33
   (D) $7.00
   (E) $10.50

6. A is 15 years old. B is one-third older. How many years ago was B twice as old as A?

   (A) 3
   (B) 5
   (C) 7.5
   (D) 8
   (E) 10

7. The distance, s, in feet that an object falls in t seconds when dropped from a height is obtained by use of the formula $s = 16t^2$. How many feet will an object fall in 8 seconds?

   (A) 256
   (B) 1,024
   (C) 2,048
   (D) 15,384
   (E) 16,000

8. Three circles are tangent externally to each other and have radii of 2 inches, 3 inches, and 4 inches, respectively. How many inches are in the perimeter of the triangle formed by joining the centers of the three circles?

   (A) 9
   (B) 12
   (C) 15
   (D) 18
   (E) 21

9. One-tenth is what part of three-fourths?

   (A) $\frac{3}{40}$
   (B) $\frac{1}{8}$
   (C) $\frac{2}{15}$
   (D) $\frac{15}{2}$
   (E) $\frac{40}{3}$

10. The area of square PQRS is 49. What are the coordinates of Q?

    (A) $(\frac{7}{2}\sqrt{2}, 0)$
    (B) $(0, \frac{7}{2}\sqrt{2})$
    (C) $(0, 7)$
    (D) $(7, 0)$
    (E) $(0, 7\sqrt{2})$

11. If one-half of the female students in a certain college eat in the cafeteria and one-third of the male students eat there, what fractional part of the student body eats in the cafeteria?

   (A) $\frac{5}{12}$
   (B) $\frac{2}{5}$
   (C) $\frac{3}{4}$
   (D) $\frac{5}{6}$
   (E) It cannot be determined from the information given.

12. A recent report states that if you were to eat each meal in a different restaurant in New York City, it would take you more than 19 years to cover all of New York City's eating places, assuming that you eat three meals a day. On the basis of this information, the number of restaurants in New York City

   (A) exceeds 20,500
   (B) is closer to 20,000 than 21,000
   (C) exceeds 21,000
   (D) exceeds 21,000 but does not exceed 21,500
   (E) is less than 20,500

13. In the figure below, $AB = BC$ and angle BEA is a right angle. If the length of DE is four times the length of BE, then what is the ratio of the area of $\triangle ACD$ to the area of $\triangle ABC$?

   (A) 1:4
   (B) 1:2
   (C) 2:1
   (D) 4:1
   (E) It cannot be determined from the information given.

14. A pound of water is evaporated from 6 pounds of sea water containing 4% salt. The percentage of salt in the remaining solution is

   (A) 3.6%
   (B) 4%
   (C) 4.8%
   (D) 5.2%
   (E) 6%

15. The product of 75^3 and 75^7 is

   (A) $(75)^5$
   (B) $(75)^{10}$
   (C) $(150)^{10}$
   (D) $(5625)^{10}$
   (E) $(75)^{21}$

16. The distance from City A to City B is 150 miles and the distance from City A to City C is 90 miles. Therefore, it is necessarily true that

   (A) the distance between B to C is 60 miles
   (B) six times the distance from A to B equals 10 times the distance from A to C.
   (C) the distance from B to C is 240 miles
   (D) the distance from A to B exceeds by 30 miles twice the distance from A to C
   (E) three times the distance from A to C exceeds by 30 miles twice the distance from A to B

GO ON TO THE NEXT PAGE

17. If $a+b=3$ and $ab=4$, then $\frac{1}{a}+\frac{1}{b}=$

(A) $\frac{3}{4}$

(B) $\frac{3}{7}$

(C) $\frac{4}{7}$

(D) $\frac{1}{7}$

(E) $\frac{1}{12}$

18. $(x)^6 + (2x^2)^3 + (3x^3)^2 =$

(A) $5x^5 + x^6$
(B) $17x^5 + x^6$
(C) $6x^6$
(D) $18x^6$
(E) $6x^{18}$

19. The scale of a map is $\frac{3}{4}$ inch = 10 miles. If the distance on the map between two towns is 6 inches, the actual distance in miles is

(A) 45
(B) 60
(C) 75
(D) 80
(E) 90

20. If $d = m - \frac{50}{m}$, and m is a positive number, then as m increases in value, d

(A) increases in value
(B) decreases in value
(C) remains unchanged
(D) increases, then decreases
(E) decreases, then increases

21. If a cubic inch of metal weighs 2 pounds, a cubic foot of the same metal weighs how many pounds?

(A) 8
(B) 24
(C) 96
(D) 288
(E) 3,456

22. If the number of square inches in the area of a circle is equal to the number of inches in its circumference, the diameter of the circle in inches is

(A) 4
(B) π
(C) 2
(D) $\frac{\pi}{2}$
(E) 1

23. John is now three time Pat's age. Four years from now John will be x years old. In terms of x, how old is Pat now?

(A) $\frac{x+4}{3}$
(B) $3x$
(C) $x+4$
(D) $x-4$
(E) $\frac{x-4}{3}$

24. When the fractions $\frac{2}{3}$, $\frac{5}{7}$, $\frac{8}{11}$, and $\frac{9}{13}$ are arranged in ascending order of size, the result is

(A) $\frac{8}{11}, \frac{5}{7}, \frac{9}{13}, \frac{2}{3}$

(B) $\frac{5}{7}, \frac{8}{11}, \frac{2}{3}, \frac{9}{13}$

(C) $\frac{2}{3}, \frac{8}{11}, \frac{5}{7}, \frac{9}{13}$

(D) $\frac{2}{3}, \frac{9}{13}, \frac{5}{7}, \frac{8}{11}$

(E) $\frac{9}{13}, \frac{2}{3}, \frac{8}{11}, \frac{5}{7}$

25. In a certain course a student takes eight tests, all of which count equally. When figuring out the final grade, the instructor drops the best and the worst grade and averages the other six. The student calculates that his average for all eight tests is 84%. After dropping the best and the worst grade the student averages 86%. What was the average of the best and the worst test?

(A) 68
(B) 72
(C) 78
(D) 88
(E) It cannot be determined from the information given.

STOP

END OF SECTION 1. IF YOU HAVE ANY TIME LEFT, GO OVER YOUR WORK IN THIS SECTION ONLY. DO NOT WORK IN ANY OTHER SECTION OF THE TEST.

SECTION 2

31 Questions • Time—30 minutes

Directions: Each of the following questions consists of an incomplete sentence followed by five words or pairs of words. Choose that word or pair of words which, when substituted for the blank space or spaces, *best* completes the meaning of the sentence and mark the letter of your choice on your answer sheet.

Example:

In view of the extenuating circumstances and the defendant's youth, the judge recommended ---- .

(A) conviction (B) a defense
(C) a mistrial (D) leniency
(E) life imprisonment   Ⓐ Ⓑ Ⓒ ● Ⓔ

1. Unsure of her skills in English, the young girl was ---- when called on to speak in class.

   (A) remunerative
   (B) transient
   (C) reticent
   (D) sartorial
   (E) resilient

2. Anyone familiar with the facts could ---- his arguments, which seemed logical but were actually ---- .

   (A) refute..specious
   (B) support..protracted
   (C) repeat..recumbent
   (D) review..cogent
   (E) elicit..prodigious

3. Each spring the ---- tree put out fewer and fewer leaves.

   (A) ambient
   (B) malignant
   (C) desultory
   (D) moribund
   (E) reclusive

4. The building had been ---- ; she could not even be sure exactly where it had stood.

   (A) jettisoned
   (B) debilitated
   (C) mitigated
   (D) berated
   (E) obliterated

5. The bully's menacing, ---- manner was actually just for show; in reality it was entirely ---- .

   (A) imperturbable..vapid
   (B) truculent..affected
   (C) stringent..credulous
   (D) supercilious..blatant
   (E) parsimonious..contentious

6. The municipality attracted the country's scientific elite and ---- them, insulating them entirely from the problems of ordinary civilian life.

   (A) cajoled
   (B) muted
   (C) mused
   (D) cosseted
   (E) impeded

7. Although the bank executive gave the appearance of a ---- businessman, he was really a ----.

   (A) dedicated..capitalist
   (B) respectable..reprobate
   (C) depraved..profligate
   (D) empathetic..philanthropist
   (E) churlish..miscreant

8. During a campaign, politicians often engage in ---- debate, attacking each other's proposals in a torrent of ---- words.

   (A) acerbic..amiable
   (B) acrimonious..angry
   (C) intensive..nebulous
   (D) garrulous..inarticulate
   (E) impassioned..vapid

9. He was uneven in his approach to the problem, at once ---- and ----.

   (A) surly..unwilling
   (B) sincere..well-meaning
   (C) harmonious..foolhardy
   (D) conscientious..frivolous
   (E) careless..insouciant

Directions: Each of the following questions consists of a capitalized pair of words followed by five pairs of words lettered A to E. The capitalized words bear some meaningful relationship to each other. Choose the lettered pair of words whose relationship is most similar to that expressed by the capitalized pair and mark its letter on your answer sheet.

Example:

DAY : SUN : :

(A) sunlight : daylight
(B) ray : sun
(C) night : moon
(D) heat : cold
(E) moon : star

Ⓐ Ⓑ ● Ⓓ Ⓔ

10. PEEL : APPLE : :

    (A) skin : knee
    (B) sail : boat
    (C) shell : lobster
    (D) pit : grape
    (E) coat : fur

11. FINGER : RING : :

    (A) neck : necklace
    (B) bandage : wound
    (C) bracelet : wrist
    (D) glove : hand
    (E) lip : tune

12. ADULT : CHILD : :

    (A) mother : baby
    (B) sheep : lamb
    (C) cow : calf
    (D) puppy : baby
    (E) buck : fawn

13. PEPPER : SEASON : :

    (A) cinnamon : prepare
    (B) sugar : sweeten
    (C) celery : plant
    (D) accent : cook
    (E) salt : taste

14. BEEF : JERKY : :

    (A) corn : flake
    (B) ham : pork
    (C) grape : raisin
    (D) meat : sausage
    (E) flesh : bone

15. SCHOOL : FISH : :

    (A) herd : cows
    (B) cars : traffic
    (C) dog : puppy
    (D) bird : wing
    (E) pig : barn

GO ON TO THE NEXT PAGE

Questions 16–23 are based on the following passage.

The following speech was delivered at the height of the 1960s civil rights movement by Dr. Martin Luther King, head of the Southern Christian Leadership Conference and the movement's most eloquent spokesperson.

We have come to this hallowed spot to remind America of the fierce urgency of now. This is no time to engage in the luxury of cooling off or to take the tranquilizing drug of gradualism. Now is the time to
(5) make real the promises of democracy. Now is the time to rise from the dark and desolate valley of segregation to the sunlit path of racial justice. Now is the time to lift our nation from the quicksand of racial injustice to the solid rock of brotherhood. Now is the time to make
(10) justice a reality for all of God's children.

It would be fatal for the nation to overlook the urgency of the moment. This sweltering summer of the Negro's legitimate discontent will not pass until there is an invigorating autumn of freedom and equal-
(15) ity. Those who hope that the Negro needed to blow off steam and will now be content will have a rude awakening if the nation returns to business as usual. There will be neither rest nor tranquility in America until the Negro is granted his citizenship rights. The
(20) whirlwinds of revolt will continue to shake the foundations of our nation until the bright day of justice emerges.

But that is something that I must say to my people who stand on the warm threshold which leads into the
(25) palace of justice. In the process of gaining our rightful place we must not be guilty of wrongful deeds. Let us not seek to satisfy our thirst for freedom by drinking from the cup of bitterness and hatred.

We must forever conduct our struggle on the high
(30) plane of dignity and discipline. We must not allow our creative protest to degenerate into physical violence. Again and again we must rise to the majestic heights of meeting physical force with soul force. The marvelous new militancy which has engulfed the Negro
(35) community must not lead us to a distrust of all white people, for many of our white brothers, as evidenced by their presence here today, have come to realize that their destiny is tied up with our destiny. And they have come to realize that their freedom is inextricably
(40) bound to our freedom. We cannot walk alone.

As we walk, we must make the pledge that we shall always march ahead. We cannot turn back. There are those who are asking the devotees of civil rights, "When will you be satisfied?" We can never be satis-
(45) fied as long as the Negro is the victim of the unspeakable horrors of police brutality. We can never be satisfied as long as the Negro's basic mobility is from a smaller ghetto to a larger one. We can never be satisfied as long as our children are stripped of their
(50) selfhood and robbed of their dignity by signs stating "For Whites Only." We cannot be satisfied as long as a Negro in Mississippi cannot vote and a Negro in New York believes he has nothing for which to vote. No, no, we are not satisfied, and we will not be satisfied until
(55) justice rolls down like waters and righteousness like a mighty stream.

I am not unmindful that some of you have come out of great trials and tribulations. Some of you have come fresh from narrow jail cells. Some of you have come
(60) from areas where your quest for freedom left you battered by the storms of persecution and staggered by the winds of police brutality. You have been the veterans of creative suffering. Continue to work with the faith that unearned suffering is redemptive.

(65) Go back to Mississippi, go back to Alabama, go back to South Carolina, go back to Louisiana, go back to the slums and ghettos of our Northern cities, knowing that somehow this situation can and will be changed. Let us not wallow in the valley of despair.

16. When King says in line 64 that "unearned suffering is redemptive," he means that it

    (A) provokes police brutality
    (B) confers sanctity, or holiness, upon the sufferer
    (C) is bound to continue forever
    (D) strips children of their dignity or self-worth
    (E) will never be repaid

17. In the passage, King's attitude is generally

    (A) prejudiced
    (B) cynical
    (C) fearful
    (D) optimistic
    (E) neutral

18. Which quotation best suggests the main idea of the speech?

    (A) ". . . we must not be guilty of wrongful deeds."
    (B) "We cannot walk alone."
    (C) "We can never be satisfied as long as the Negro's basic mobility is from a smaller ghetto to a larger one."
    (D) ". . . to remind America of the fierce urgency of now."
    (E) ". . . this situation can and will be changed."

19. The tone of this speech can best be described as

    (A) inspirational
    (B) boastful
    (C) defiant
    (D) sad
    (E) buoyant

20. King's attitude toward white Americans appears to be based on

    (A) noncommitment
    (B) contempt for authority
    (C) mutual distrust
    (D) mutual respect
    (E) negativism

21. King's remarks indicate that he considers the racial problem a national problem because

    (A) all white Americans are prejudiced
    (B) African-Americans are moving to the suburbs
    (C) all areas of American life are affected
    (D) the United States Constitution supports segregation
    (E) laws will be broken if the problem is left unattended

22. In the passage, King implies that the struggle for racial justice can be best won through

    (A) marching on Washington
    (B) civil disorder
    (C) creative protest
    (D) challenging unjust laws
    (E) doing nothing

23. In this speech, King specifically recommends

    (A) nonviolent resistance
    (B) faith in God
    (C) Communist ideas
    (D) social turmoil
    (E) turbulent revolt

Questions 24–31 are based on the following passage.

Agustín Yáñez was the author of many short stories, most of them based in or around Guadalajara, Mexico, his hometown. "Alda," from which this passage is excerpted, is from a collection entitled Archipiélago de mujeres.

I never met my first love. She must have been a sweet and sad child. Her photographs inspire my imagination to reconstruct the outlines of her soul, simple and austere as a primitive church, extensive as
(5) a castle, stately as a tower, deep as a well. Purity of brow, which, like the throat, the hands, the entire body, must have been carved in crystal or marble; the very soft lines of the face; the deep-set eyes with a look of surprise, sweet and sad, beneath the veil of the eye-
(10) lashes; a brief mouth with fine lips, immune to sensuality; docile hair, harmonious and still; simply dressed in harmony with the obvious distinction and nobility of her bearing; all of her, aglow with innocence and a certain gravity in which are mixed the delights of
(15) childhood and the reverie of first youth. Her photographs invite one to try to imagine the timbre and rhythm of her voice, the ring of her laughter, the depth of her silences, the cadence of her movements, the direction and intensity of her glances. Her arms must
(20) have moved like the wings of a musical and tranquil bird; her figure must have yielded with the gentleness of a lily in an April garden. How many times her translucent hands must have trimmed the lamps of the vigilant virgins who know not the day or the hour; in
(25) what moments of rapture did her mouth and eyes accentuate their sadness? When did they emphasize her sweet smile?

No, I never met her. And yet, even her pictures were with me for a long time after she died. Long before
(30) then, my life was filled with her presence, fashioned of unreal images, devoid of all sensation; perhaps more faithful, certainly more vivid, than these almost faded

GO ON TO THE NEXT PAGE

photographs. Hers was a presence without volume, line or color; an elusive phantom, which epitomized
(35) the beauty of all faces without limiting itself to any one, and embodied the delicacy of the best and loftiest spirits, indefinitely.

I now believe that an obscure feeling, a fear of reality, was the cause of my refusal to exchange the
(40) formless images for a direct knowledge of her who inspired them. How many times, just when the senses might have put a limit to fancy did I avoid meeting her; and how many others did Fate intervene! On one of the many occasions that I watched the house in which
(45) my phantom lived, I decided to knock; but the family was out.

24. What does Yáñez mean when he says "I never met my first love" (line 1)?

    (A) He loved unconditionally.
    (B) His first love died young.
    (C) He never fell in love.
    (D) He fell in love with someone he never really knew.
    (E) His first love was not a human being.

25. The description in paragraph 1 moves from

    (A) sound to sight
    (B) smell to sight to sound
    (C) sight to touch
    (D) sight to sound to movement
    (E) touch to sound to sight

26. The word *docile* (line 11) is used to imply

    (A) wildness
    (B) conformity
    (C) manageability
    (D) indifference
    (E) willingness

27. In paragraph 1, to what does Yáñez compare Alda's soul?

    (A) A series of buildings
    (B) Crystal and marble
    (C) The wings of a bird
    (D) A flower in a garden
    (E) A photograph

28. When Yáñez says he is "devoid of all sensation" (line 30), he means that he

    (A) has no sense of who Alda might be
    (B) does not see, hear, or touch Alda
    (C) cannot be sensible where Alda is concerned
    (D) has little judgment
    (E) feels nothing for Alda

29. The word *faithful* (line 32) is used to mean

    (A) loyal
    (B) constant
    (C) devoted
    (D) firm
    (E) reliable

30. Unlike the previous paragraphs, paragraph 3

    (A) suggests an explanation for the author's behavior
    (B) describes the author's photographs of Alda
    (C) mentions the elusive qualities of Alda
    (D) compares Alda to someone the author loved later
    (E) expresses regret for losing Alda's love

31. How might you reword the phrase "the senses might have put a limit to fancy" (lines 41–42)?

    (A) if I were sensible, I would not have fantasized
    (B) my good taste enabled me to dream without limits
    (C) good sense would have made things plainer
    (D) I could sense that she wanted to end my dreams
    (E) seeing her might have stopped my fantasies

STOP

END OF SECTION 2. IF YOU HAVE ANY TIME LEFT, GO OVER YOUR WORK IN THIS SECTION ONLY. DO NOT WORK IN ANY OTHER SECTION OF THE TEST.

SECTION 3

25 Questions • Time—30 Minutes

Directions: Solve the following problems using any available space on the page for scratchwork. On your answer sheet fill in the choice which best corresponds to the correct answer.

Notes: The figures accompanying the problems are drawn as accurately as possible unless otherwise stated in specific problems. Again, unless otherwise stated, all figures lie in the same plane. All numbers used in these problems are real numbers. Calculators are permitted for this test.

Reference Information

Circle: $C = 2\pi r$, $A = \pi r^2$

Rectangle: $A = lw$

Rectangular Solid: $V = lwh$

Cylinder: $V = \pi r^2 h$

Triangle: $A = \tfrac{1}{2}bh$

$a^2 + b^2 = c^2$

45°-45°-90°: sides x, x, $x\sqrt{2}$

30°-60°-90°: sides x, $x\sqrt{3}$, $2x$

The number of degrees of arc in a circle is 360.
The measure in degrees of a straight angle is 180.
The sum of the measures in degrees of the angles of a triangle is 180.

Part 1: Quantitative Comparison Questions

Directions: For each of the following questions, two quantities are given—one in Column A, the other in Column B. Compare the two quantities and mark your answer sheet as follows:

(A) if the quantity in Column A is greater
(B) if the quantity in Column B is greater
(C) if the quantities are equal
(D) if the relationship cannot be determined from the information given

Notes:

(1) Information concerning one or both of the compared quantities will be centered above the two columns for some items.
(2) Symbols that appear in both columns represent the same thing in Column A as in Column B.
(3) Letters such as x, n, and k are symbols for real numbers.

Examples

	Column A	Column B	Answers
	$a > 0$		
	$x > 0$		
E1.	$a - x$	$a + x$	(A) ● (C) (D)
E2.	The average of 17, 19, 21, 23	The average of 16, 18, 20, 22	● (B) (C) (D)

DO NOT MARK CHOICE (E) FOR THESE QUESTIONS. THERE ARE ONLY FOUR ANSWER CHOICES.

GO ON TO THE NEXT PAGE

Column A | **Column B** | | **Column A** | **Column B**

1. $a - y$ | x

(Triangle with angles $x°$, $y°$, and exterior angle $a°$)

Questions 2–3 refer to the following definition.

$\boxed{u} = u^2 - u$

2. $\boxed{3}$ | $\boxed{-3}$

3. $\boxed{u+1}$ | $\boxed{u-1}$

(Figure: lines l, m, n cut by transversals s, t with angles x and y)

$l \parallel m \parallel n$

$s \parallel t$

4. $\angle x$ | $\angle y$

5. Area of square with side 4 | Twice the area of a triangle with base 4 and height 4

(Triangle ABC with angle $A = 60°$, angle $C = 30°$, side $AB = 1$)

6. $\sqrt{3}$ | BC

$3x + 4 = y$

x is a positive integer less than or equal to 7

7. The number of values for y which are prime numbers | 2

r is the radius of a given circle.

8. r^2 | r^3

9. $9 + 3(-2)(4-5) + 1$ | $(3-6)[2 - 5(3-4)]$

10. The average of the degrees in all the angles in a quadrilateral | The average of the degrees in all the angles of *two* triangles

$s = 1$
$t = 4$
$r = -3$

11. $4s + 3t$ | $2t - 2r$

	Column A	Column B
12.	12% of 72,000	7% of 37,000
13.	The average of 17, 19, 21, 23, 25, 27	The average of 18, 20, 22, 24, 26

	Column A	Column B
14.	Area of circle A	12
15.	$\frac{1}{6}\left(\frac{3}{8} + \frac{9}{24}\right)$	$\left(\frac{1}{6}\right)\left(\frac{3}{8}\right) + \left(\frac{9}{24}\right)\left(\frac{1}{6}\right)$

(Circle A with radius 2)

Part 2: Student-Produced Response Questions

Directions: Solve each of these problems. Write the answer in the corresponding grid on the answer sheet and fill in the ovals beneath each answer you write. Here are some examples.

Answer: $\frac{3}{4}$ (= .75; show answer either way)

Answer: 325

Note: A mixed number such as $3\frac{1}{2}$ must be gridded as 7/2 or as 3.5. If gridded as "3 1/2," it will be read as "thirty-one halves."

Note: Either position is correct.

GO ON TO THE NEXT PAGE

16. Joshua bought two dozen apples for 3 dollars. At this rate, how much will 18 apples cost? (Do not grid the dollar sign.)

17. What is $\frac{1}{10}$% of $\frac{1}{10}$ of 10?

18. $\dfrac{\frac{-1}{3}}{3} - \dfrac{3}{-\frac{1}{3}} =$

19. Dawn's average for four math tests is 80. What score must she receive on her next exam to increase her average by three points?

20. In the figure below, square WXYZ is formed by connecting the midpoints of the sides of square ABCD. If the length of AB = 6, what is the area of the shaded region?

21. Thirty thousand two hundred and forty minutes is equivalent to how many weeks?

22. In the figure below, line l_1 is parallel to l_2. Transversals t_1 and t_2 are drawn. What is the value of $a + b + c + d$? (Do not grid the degree symbol.)

23. A car travels from town A to town B, a distance of 360 miles, in 9 hours. How many hours would the same trip have taken had the car travelled 5 mph faster?

24. In the figure below, KJ bisects ∠J. The measure of ∠K is 40° and the measure of ∠L is 20°. What is the measure of ∠N? (Do not grid the degree symbol.)

25. The area of a circle that is inscribed in a square with a diagonal of 8 is $a\pi$. What is the value of a?

STOP

END OF SECTION 3. IF YOU HAVE ANY TIME LEFT, GO OVER YOUR WORK IN THIS SECTION ONLY. DO NOT WORK IN ANY OTHER SECTION OF THE TEST.

SECTION 4

35 Questions • Time—30 minutes

Directions: Each of the following questions consists of an incomplete sentence followed by five words or pairs of words. Choose that word or pair of words which, when substituted for the blank space or spaces, *best* completes the meaning of the sentence and mark the letter of your choice on your answer sheet.

Example:

In view of the extenuating circumstances and the defendant's youth, the judge recommended ----.

(A) conviction
(B) a defense
(C) a mistrial
(D) leniency
(E) life imprisonment

Ⓐ Ⓑ Ⓒ ● Ⓔ

1. Her clear ---- of the situation kept the meeting from breaking up into ----.

   (A) grasp..chaos
   (B) vision..anarchy
   (C) knowledge..uproar
   (D) control..harmony
   (E) idea..laughter

2. The mayor remained ---- in her commitment to ---- the rise of unemployment among her constituents.

   (A) firm..uphold
   (B) wavering..identify
   (C) steadfast..stem
   (D) uncertain..staunch
   (E) alone..approach

3. A ---- old stone farmhouse, it had been a landmark since before the Civil War.

   (A) corrupt
   (B) sturdy
   (C) rickety
   (D) ramshackle
   (E) vital

4. Because she thought her hateful cousin's behavior was ----, it ---- her to hear the adults praise him.

   (A) intangible..thrilled
   (B) putative..baffled
   (C) laconic..encouraged
   (D) insipid..demeaned
   (E) obnoxious..galled

5. A public official must be ---- in all his or her actions to avoid even the appearance of impropriety.

   (A) redolent
   (B) unctuous
   (C) baleful
   (D) circumspect
   (E) propitious

6. So many people turned out for the meeting that there were not enough seats to ---- them all.

   (A) count
   (B) ascertain
   (C) accommodate
   (D) delineate
   (E) delegate

7. The editorial accused the mayor of ---- for making promises he knew he could not ----.

   (A) hypocrisy..fulfill
   (B) revulsion..condone
   (C) impunity..reprise
   (D) liability..improve
   (E) petulance..verify

8. She was ---- as a child, accepting without question everything she was told.

   (A) obstreperous
   (B) recalcitrant
   (C) credulous
   (D) truculent
   (E) tearful

9. Warned by an anonymous phone call that an explosion was ----, the police ---- the building immediately.

   (A) expected..filled
   (B) ubiquitous..purged
   (C) eminent..checked
   (D) imminent..evacuated
   (E) insidious..obviated

10. Route 71 has always been known to wind its ---- way through steep mountain passes and coarse terrain.

    (A) neat
    (B) indirect
    (C) evasive
    (D) tortuous
    (E) deceitful

Directions: Each of the following questions consists of a capitalized pair of words followed by five pairs of words lettered A to E. The capitalized words bear some meaningful relationship to each other. Choose the lettered pair of words whose relationship is most similar to that expressed by the capitalized pair and mark its letter on your answer sheet.

Example:

DAY : SUN : :
(A) sunlight : daylight (B) ray : sun
(C) night : moon (D) heat : cold
(E) moon : star
Ⓐ Ⓑ ● Ⓓ Ⓔ

11. CRACK : SMASH : :

    (A) merge : break
    (B) run : hover
    (C) whisper : scream
    (D) play : work
    (E) tattle : tell

12. SURGEON : DEXTEROUS : :

    (A) clown : fat
    (B) actress : beautiful
    (C) athlete : tall
    (D) acrobat : agile
    (E) man : strong

13. SPECTATOR : SPORT : :

    (A) jury : trial
    (B) witness : crime
    (C) soloist : music
    (D) player : team
    (E) fan : grandstand

14. WALK : AMBLE : :

    (A) work : tinker
    (B) play : rest
    (C) run : jump
    (D) jog : trot
    (E) go : come

15. HILT : BLADE : :

    (A) holster : gun
    (B) sheath : knife
    (C) leash : dog
    (D) stem : leaf
    (E) petal : branch

16. RULER : DISTANCE : :

    (A) king : country
    (B) yardstick : dimension
    (C) barometer : weather
    (D) microscope : size
    (E) thermometer : temperature

17. HAMMER : TOOL : :

    (A) tire : wheel
    (B) wagon : vehicle
    (C) nail : screw
    (D) stick : drum
    (E) saw : wood

18. FLIPPERS : DIVER : :

    (A) baton : runner
    (B) cap : ballplayer
    (C) gloves : skater
    (D) tights : dancer
    (E) spikes : golfer

19. BRAGGART : DIFFIDENCE : :

    (A) benefactor : generosity
    (B) pariah : esteem
    (C) partisan : partiality
    (D) savant : wisdom
    (E) sycophant : flattery

20. DIATRIBE : BITTERNESS : :

    (A) dictum : injury
    (B) critique : even-handedness
    (C) polemic : consonance
    (D) encomium : praise
    (E) concordance : disagreement

21. TRAVESTY : RIDICULE : :

    (A) reproduction : provoke
    (B) forgery : deceive
    (C) imitation : feign
    (D) treachery : reprieve
    (E) poetry : comprehend

22. AUTHOR: NOVEL : :

(A) composer: piano
(B) artist: easel
(C) sculptor: statue
(D) painter: color
(E) mechanic: oil

23. MAGNANIMOUS: PETTY : :

(A) arrogant: insolent
(B) valiant: belligerent
(C) passionate: blase
(D) munificent: generous
(E) circumspect: prudent

GO ON TO THE NEXT PAGE

Questions 24–35 are based on the following passage.

Alexander Wilson was a poet and a naturalist. Born in Scotland in 1766, he emigrated to Pennsylvania in 1794 and soon became a full-time naturalist. This excerpt on hummingbird nests is from a nine-volume work titled American Ornithology, *published in 1808–1814.*

About the twenty-fifth of April the Hummingbird usually arrives in Pennsylvania; and about the tenth of May begins to build its nest. This is generally fixed on the upper side of a horizontal branch, not among the
(5) twigs, but on the body of the branch itself. Yet I have known instances where it was attached by the side to an old moss-grown trunk; and others where it was fastened on a strong rank stalk, or weed, in the garden; but these cases are rare. In the woods it very often
(10) chooses a white oak sapling to build on; and in the orchard, or garden, selects a pear tree for that purpose. The branch is seldom more than ten feet from the ground. The nest is about an inch in diameter, and as much in depth. A very complete one is now lying
(15) before me, and the materials of which it is composed are as follows: —The outward coat is formed of small pieces of bluish grey lichen that vegetates on old trees and fences, thickly glued on with the saliva of the bird, giving firmness and consistency to the whole, as well
(20) as keeping out moisture. Within this are thick matted layers of the fine wings of certain flying seeds, closely laid together; and lastly, the downy substance from the great mullein, and from the stalks of the common fern, lines the whole. The base of the nest is continued round
(25) the stem of the branch, to which it closely adheres; and, when viewed from below, appears a mere mossy knot or accidental protuberance. The eggs are two, pure white, and of equal thickness at both ends. . . . On a person's approaching their nest, the little proprietors
(30) dart around with a humming sound, passing frequently within a few inches of one's head; and should the young be newly hatched, the female will resume her place on the nest even while you stand within a yard or two of the spot. The precise period of incubation I am
(35) unable to give; but the young are in the habit, a short time before they leave the nest, of thrusting their bills into the mouths of their parents, and sucking what they have brought them. I never could perceive that they carried them any animal food; tho, from circum-
(40) stances that will presently be mentioned, I think it highly probable they do. As I have found their nest with eggs so late as the twelfth of July, I do not doubt but that they frequently, and perhaps usually, raise two broods in the same season.

24. In line 3, the word "fixed" most nearly means

   (A) changed
   (B) improved
   (C) found
   (D) understood
   (E) undermined

25. According to the author, all of the following are places where one could find a hummingbird EXCEPT

   (A) on the upper side of a branch
   (B) on a moss grown trunk
   (C) on a white oak sapling
   (D) on a pear tree
   (E) in the meadow

26. Why does Wilson mention the "old moss-grown trunk" and "strong rank stalk" (lines 7–8)?

   (A) To compare relative sizes of birds
   (B) To establish the birds' eating patterns
   (C) To illustrate nontypical nesting behaviors
   (D) To delineate plant life in Pennsylvania
   (E) To complete a list of related flora

27. When Wilson remarks that the birds' nests resemble an "accidental protuberance" (line 27), he implies that

   (A) the nests are messily constructed
   (B) nests may be destroyed accidently
   (C) the nests are usually invisible
   (D) the nests are designed to blend into their surroundings
   (E) most nests resemble the beak of the bird itself

28. The phrase "little proprietors" (line 29) refers to

    (A) children in the orchard
    (B) eggs
    (C) naturalists
    (D) shopowners
    (E) nesting pairs of hummingbirds

29. When Wilson remarks that he "never could perceive" hummingbirds feeding their nestlings animal food (lines 38–39), he is suggesting

    (A) that his eyesight is failing
    (B) his limitations as an observer
    (C) that animal food may, in fact, be eaten
    (D) that no animal food is eaten
    (E) that hummingbirds eat only at night

30. The fact that Wilson has found nests with eggs "so late as the twelfth of July" indicates that

    (A) birds do not lay eggs before June
    (B) most eggs are found earlier than July 12
    (C) the eggs are not likely to hatch
    (D) the birds began nesting late in the season
    (E) some birds abandon their nests

31. The hummingbirds' nest is composed of all of the following EXCEPT

    (A) moss
    (B) lichen
    (C) the wings of flying seeds
    (D) a downy substance from fern stalks
    (E) hummingbird saliva

32. How does Wilson reconstruct the makeup of the nest?

    (A) By taking apart a nest that hangs in the orchard
    (B) By watching a hummingbird build a nest in the stable
    (C) By reading a report by John Audubon
    (D) By inspecting a nest that lies on his desk
    (E) By making a copy of a nest he has observed

33. Which of the following can be inferred about the hummingbirds' habits?

    (A) They flourish only in Pennsylvania.
    (B) Their broods each consist of a single egg.
    (C) They migrate in the spring.
    (D) They always raise two broods in a season.
    (E) They spend the winter in Pennsylvania.

34. The main purpose of this passage is to describe

    (A) the nesting behavior of the hummingbird
    (B) the mating behavior of the hummingbird
    (C) the relative size of the hummingbird
    (D) hummingbirds in Pennsylvania
    (E) young hummingbird fledglings

35. If Wilson were to study crows, he would be likely to

    (A) stuff and mount them
    (B) observe them in the wild
    (C) read all about them
    (D) mate them in a laboratory
    (E) dissect them

STOP

END OF SECTION 4. IF YOU HAVE ANY TIME LEFT, GO OVER YOUR WORK IN THIS SECTION ONLY. DO NOT WORK IN ANY OTHER SECTION OF THE TEST.

SECTION 5

10 Questions • Time—15 Minutes

Directions: Solve the following problems using any available space on the page for scratchwork. On your answer sheet fill in the choice which best corresponds to the correct answer.

Notes: The figures accompanying the problems are drawn as accurately as possible unless otherwise stated in specific problems. Again, unless otherwise stated, all figures lie in the same plane. All numbers used in these problems are real numbers. Calculators are permitted for this test.

Reference Information

Circle: $C = 2\pi r$, $A = \pi r^2$
Rectangle: $A = lw$
Rectangular Solid: $V = lwh$
Cylinder: $V = \pi r^2 h$
Triangle: $A = \frac{1}{2}bh$
$a^2 + b^2 = c^2$

Special right triangles: 45°-45°-90° (x, x, $x\sqrt{2}$); 30°-60°-90° (x, $x\sqrt{3}$, $2x$)

The number of degrees of arc in a circle is 360.
The measure in degrees of a straight angle is 180.
The sum of the measures in degrees of the angles of a triangle is 180.

---

1. In the figure, what percent of the area of rectangle *PQRS* is shaded?

    (A) 20
    (B) 25
    (C) 30
    (D) $33\frac{1}{3}$
    (E) 35

2. One wheel has a diameter of 30 inches and a second wheel has a diameter of 20 inches. The first wheel traveled a certain distance in 240 revolutions. In how many revolutions did the second wheel travel the same distance?

    (A) 120
    (B) 160
    (C) 360
    (D) 420
    (E) 480

3. The one of the following to which 1.86×10^5 is equivalent is

    (A) 18,600
    (B) 186,000
    (C) 18,600,000
    (D) $186 \times 500,000$
    (E) 1,860,000

4. How many of the numbers between 100 and 300 begin or end with 2?

    (A) 20
    (B) 40
    (C) 100
    (D) 110
    (E) 180

5. The area of a square is $49x^2$. What is the length of a diagonal of the square?

   (A) $7x$
   (B) $7x\sqrt{2}$
   (C) $14x$
   (D) $7x^2$
   (E) $\dfrac{7x}{\sqrt{2}}$

6. If shipping charges to a certain point are 62 cents for the first five ounces and 8 cents for each additional ounce, the weight of a package, in pounds, for which the charges are $1.66 is

   (A) $\dfrac{7}{8}$
   (B) 1
   (C) $1\dfrac{1}{8}$
   (D) $1\dfrac{1}{4}$
   (E) $1\dfrac{1}{2}$

7. If 15 cans of food are needed for seven adults for two days, the number of cans needed to feed four adults for seven days is

   (A) 15
   (B) 20
   (C) 25
   (D) 30
   (E) 35

8. A rectangular sign is cut down by 10% of its height and 30% of its width. What percent of the original area remains?

   (A) 30
   (B) 37
   (C) 57
   (D) 63
   (E) 70

9. If the average (arithmetic mean) of a series of numbers is 20 and their sum is 160, how many numbers are in the series?

   (A) 8
   (B) 16
   (C) 32
   (D) 48
   (E) 80

10. If the result of squaring a number is less than the number, the number is

    (A) negative and greater than -1
    (B) negative and less than -1
    (C) a positive fraction greater than 1
    (D) positive and less than 1
    (E) 1 and only 1

STOP

END OF SECTION 5. IF YOU HAVE ANY TIME LEFT, GO OVER YOUR WORK IN THIS SECTION ONLY. DO NOT WORK IN ANY OTHER SECTION OF THE TEST.

SECTION 6

12 Questions • Time—15 minutes

Directions: The two passages below deal with a related topic. Following the passages are questions about the content of each passage or about the relationship between the two passages. Answer the questions based upon what is stated or implied in the passages and in any introductory material provided. Mark the letter of your choice on your answer sheet.

Questions 1–12 are based on the following passages.

Achilles, the Greek hero, and Cuchulain, the Champion of Ireland, achieved mythical status because of their acts of courage. The following passages compare the two heroes and their heroic feats.

Passage 1—Achilles, Defender of Honor

... When Achilles heard that his friend Patroclus had been killed in battle, he became so despondent that his friends feared he might end his own life. When word of his complete and agonizing distress reached
(5) his mother, Thetis, in the depths of the ocean where she resided, she raced to his side. She found him in a highly distraught state, feeling guilty that he, in some way, might have been responsible for his friend's demise. His only consolation were thoughts of re-
(10) venge for which he needed the help of Hector. However, his mother reminded him that he was without armor, having lost his recently in battle. His mother, however, promised him that she would procure for him a suit of armor from Vulcan far superior to the one
(15) he had lost. Achilles agreed and Thetis immediately repaired to Vulcan's palace. Thetis found Vulcan busy at his forge making magical tripods that moved forward when they were wanted, and retreated when dismissed. Vulcan immediately honored Thetis's re-
(20) quest for a set of armor for her son, and ceasing his own work, hastened to meet her de-mands. Vulcan created a magnificent suit of armor for Achilles. The shield was adorned with elaborate ornaments. The helmet had a gold crest, and the body of the armor was
(25) perfectly suited to his body and of the very finest workmanship. The armor was completed in one night. When Thetis received it, she descended to earth, and laid it down at Achilles' feet at the first dawn of day.
    Seeing the armor brought the first signs of life to
(30) Achilles that he had felt since the death of his friend Patroclus. The armor was so splendid that Achilles was stunned at the sight of it. Achilles went into battle with his new armor, consumed with rage and thirst for vengeance that made him an unbeatable foe. The
(35) bravest warriors fled from him or were killed by his lance.

Passage 2—Cuchulain, Champion of Ireland

In days of yore, the men of Ulster sought to choose a champion. They enlisted the help of Curoi of Kerry, a wise man, to help them reach their decision. Three
(40) brave men, Laegire, Connall Cearnach, and Cuchulain indicated that they wished to be considered. Each was told that he would have to meet the challenge of a terrible stranger. When the stranger arrived, all were in awe of him. "Behold my axe," the stranger said. "My
(45) challenge is this. Whoever will take the axe today may cut my head off with it, provided that I may, in like manner, cut off his head tomorrow. If you have no champions who dare face me, I will say that the men of Ulster have lost their courage and should be
(50) ashamed."
    Laegire was the first to accept the challenge. The giant laid his head on a block. With one blow the hero severed it from the body. Thereupon the giant arose, took the head and the axe, and headless, walked slowly
(55) from the hall. The following night the giant returned, sound as ever, to claim the fulfillment of Laegires' promise. However, Laegire did not come forward. The stranger scoffed at the men of Ulster because their great champion showed no courage. He could not face
(60) the blow he should receive in return for the one he gave.

The men from Ulster were sorely ashamed, but Conall Cearnach, the second aspiring champion, made another pact with the stranger. He, too, gave a blow (65) which beheaded the giant. But again, when the giant returned whole and sound on the following evening, the champion was not there.

Now it was the turn of Cuchulain, who as the others had done, cut off the giant's head at one stroke. The (70) next day everyone watched Cuchulain to see what he would do. They would not have been surprised if he had not appeared. This champion, however, was there. He was not going to disgrace Ulster. Instead, he sat with great sadness in his place. "Do not leave this place (75) till all is over," he said to his king. "Death is coming to me soon, but I must honor my promise, for I would rather die than break my word."

At the end of the day the giant appeared.

"Where is Cuchulain?' he cried.

(80) "Here I am," answered Cuchulain.

"Cuchulain, your speech is morose, and the fear of death is obviously foremost in your thoughts, but at least you have honored your promise."

Cuchulain went towards the giant, as he stood with (85) his great axe ready, and knelt to receive the blow.

The would-be champion of Ulster laid his head on the block.

When the giant did not immediately use his axe, Cuchulain said, "Slay me now with haste, for I did not (90) keep you waiting last night."

The stranger raised his axe so high that it crashed upwards through the rafters of the hall, like the crash of trees falling in a storm. When the axe came down with a sound that shook the room, all men looked (95) fearfully at Cuchulain. But to the surprise of all, the descending axe had not even touched him; it had come down with the blunt side on the ground, and Cuchulain knelt there unharmed. Smiling at him and leaning on his axe, stood no terrible and hideous stranger, but (100) Curoi of Kerry, who had taken on the form of the giant to test the champions. He was now there to give his decision.

"Rise up, Cuchulain," said Curoi. "There is none among all the heroes of Ulster to equal you in courage (105) and loyalty and truth. The Championship is yours."

Thereupon Curoi vanished. The assembled warriors gathered around Cuchulain, and all with one voice acclaimed him the champion.

1. The word *despondent* in Passage 1 (line 2) means

   (A) very depressed
   (B) in need of food
   (C) angry
   (D) embarrassed
   (E) belligerent

2. Achilles' feelings of guilt were related to

   (A) the loss of his armor
   (B) the loss of his last battle
   (C) his estrangement from his mother
   (D) the death of his friend
   (E) his relationship with Vulcan

3. In line 16, the word "repaired" means

   (A) glazed
   (B) retired
   (C) replenished
   (D) returned
   (E) untouched

4. Although not stated directly in the passage, it is obvious that Vulcan

   (A) blames Achilles for his friend's death
   (B) is a lower-level god
   (C) is extremely powerful
   (D) loves Thetis
   (E) does not wish to help Achilles

5. Achilles' feeling as he went into battle can best be described as

   (A) guilty
   (B) nervous
   (C) confident
   (D) depressed
   (E) arrogant

6. According to Passage 2, when the men of Ulster wished to select a champion they enlisted the help of

   (A) Curoi
   (B) the king
   (C) Laegire
   (D) Connall
   (E) Cearnach

7. The challenge that the would-be champion had to meet involved

   (A) fighting a giant with an axe
   (B) beheading a giant
   (C) competing against other men of Ulster
   (D) winning a match with the king
   (E) fighting Curoi of Kerry

8. According to the passage, the giant was unusual because

   (A) he was so tall
   (B) he was so huge
   (C) he defeated all his opponents
   (D) he remained alive while headless
   (E) he had three eyes

9. The word *sorely* (line 62) means

   (A) feverishly
   (B) utterly
   (C) angrily
   (D) bitterly
   (E) pitifully

10. Cuchulain appeared as promised to meet the giant because

    (A) he was afraid
    (B) he knew the giant would not kill him
    (C) he knew the giant was Curoi
    (D) he did not wish to fail his king
    (E) he gave his word

11. In line 81, the word "morose" most nearly means

    (A) serious and somber
    (B) riotous and humorous
    (C) indifferent and detached
    (D) informed and knowledgeable
    (E) satisfied

12. Cuchulain is sometimes called the "Irish Achilles," probably because of his

    (A) honesty
    (B) bravery
    (C) strength
    (D) wisdom
    (E) intelligence

STOP

END OF SECTION 6. IF YOU HAVE ANY TIME LEFT, GO OVER YOUR WORK IN THIS SECTION ONLY. DO NOT WORK IN ANY OTHER SECTION OF THE TEST.

PRACTICE EXAMINATION 3

Answer Key

Section 1: Math

1. B	6. E	11. E	16. B	21. E
2. B	7. B	12. A	17. A	22. A
3. A	8. D	13. D	18. D	23. E
4. B	9. C	14. C	19. D	24. D
5. D	10. B	15. B	20. A	25. C

Section 2: Verbal

1. C	8. B	15. A	22. C	29. E
2. A	9. D	16. B	23. A	30. A
3. D	10. C	17. D	24. D	31. E
4. E	11. A	18. E	25. D	
5. B	12. B	19. A	26. C	
6. D	13. B	20. D	27. A	
7. B	14. C	21. C	28. B	

Section 3: Math

Part 1

1. C	4. C	7. A	10. A	13. C
2. B	5. C	8. D	11. A	14. A
3. D	6. C	9. A	12. A	15. C

Part 2

16. $2.25 = \frac{9}{4}$	18. $\frac{80}{9} = 8.89$	20. 18	22. 360	24. 60
17. .001	19. 95	21. 3	23. 8	25. 8

Section 4: Verbal

1. A	8. C	15. D	22. C	29. C
2. C	9. D	16. E	23. C	30. B
3. B	10. D	17. B	24. C	31. A
4. E	11. C	18. E	25. E	32. D
5. D	12. D	19. B	26. C	33. C
6. C	13. B	20. D	27. D	34. A
7. A	14. A	21. B	28. E	35. B

Section 5: Math

| 1. B | 3. B | 5. B | 7. D | 9. A |
| 2. C | 4. D | 6. C | 8. D | 10. D |

Section 6: Verbal

1. A	4. C	7. B	9. B	11. A
2. D	5. C	8. D	10. E	12. B
3. D	6. A			

PRACTICE EXAMINATION 3

Explanatory Answers

Note: A 🖩 following a math answer explanation indicates that a calculator could be helpful in solving that particular problem.

Section 1

1. **(B)** If $9x + 5 = 23$, $9x = 18$, or $x = 2$. Thus, $18x + 5 = 36 + 5 = 41$. 🖩

2. **(B)**

   $120 = 70 + x$
   $x = 50$

3. **(A)** $2y = \dfrac{1}{3}$

   $6y = 1$

   $y = \dfrac{1}{6}$

   $\dfrac{1}{4y} = \dfrac{1}{4\left(\dfrac{1}{6}\right)} = \dfrac{1}{\dfrac{2}{3}} = \dfrac{3}{2}$ 🖩

4. **(B)** The volume of a cube is $V = s^3$. The side s of this cube is $\sqrt[3]{64} = 4$ in. Since there are 12 edges to a cube, the amount of wire needed is 12×4 in., or 48 inches.

5. **(D)** Let x = original price.
   Then $.60x = \$4.20$
   or $6x = \$42.00$
   $x = \$7.00$

6. **(E)** $A = 15$

   $B = 15 + \dfrac{1}{3}(15) = 20$

   $15 - n$ is A's age n years ago
   $20 - n$ is B's age n years ago
   $(20 - n) = 2(15 - n)$
   $20 - n = 30 - 2n$
   $n = 10$

7. **(B)** By simple substitutions,
   $s = 16 \times 8 \times 8$, or 1,024. 🖩

8. **(D)** The line of center of two tangent circles passes through the point of tangency. Hence, perimeter of $\triangle = (2 + 3) + (3 + 4) + (4 + 2) = 5 + 7 + 6 = 18$. 🖩

9. **(C)** $\dfrac{1}{10} = x \cdot \dfrac{3}{4} = \dfrac{3x}{4}$

   $30x = 4$

   $x = \dfrac{2}{15}$ 🖩

10. **(B)** Since $QR = 7$, and QOR is a right isosceles triangle, $OQ = \dfrac{7}{\sqrt{2}} = \dfrac{7\sqrt{2}}{2}$.
    Hence, coordinates of Q are $(0, \tfrac{7}{2}\sqrt{2})$.

11. **(E)** There is no indication as to the exact percentage of students who eat in the cafeteria, since we do not know how many boys or girls there are.

12. **(A)** Three meals a day times 365 days per year means there are $3 \times 365 = 1,095$ meals in one year. Over 19 years there are $1,095 \times 19 = 20,805$ meals. Therefore, the number of restaurants in New York City exceeds 20,500.

13. **(D)** Both of the triangles share a common base, line segment AC. The difference in their area is accounted for by the difference in their altitudes. Since we are given a right angle we know that DE is the altitude of the larger triangle and BE is the altitude of the smaller triangle. Since the ratio of those two segments is 4:1, then the areas must be in the ratio of 4:1.

14. **(C)** The original 6 pounds contained .24 pounds of salt. Now, the same .24 pounds are in 5 pounds of solution, so the percentage is $\frac{.24}{5}(100) = 4.8\%$.

15. **(B)** By the Law of Exponents,
$(75)^3 \times (75)^7 = (75)^{3+7} = (75)^{10}$.

16. **(B)** Cities A, B, and C need not be on a straight line; therefore, one cannot add or subtract miles. Six times the distance between A and B is $150 \times 6 = 900$, which is 10 times the distance between A and C, or $10 \times 90 = 900$.

17. **(A)** $\frac{1}{a} + \frac{1}{b} = \frac{b+a}{ab} = \frac{3}{4}$

18. **(D)**
$x^6 + (2x^2)^3 + (3x^3)^2 = x^6 + 8x^6 + 9x^6 = 18x^6$

19. **(D)** Set up a proportion and solve for x:
$$\frac{\frac{3}{4} \text{ in.}}{6 \text{ in.}} = \frac{10 \text{ mi.}}{x \text{ mi.}}$$
$$\frac{3}{4}x = 60$$
$$x = 80$$

20. **(A)** If h is any positive quantity, then letting $d' = (m+h) - \frac{50}{m+h}$, we can see that d' is greater than d, since h is greater than zero, and $\frac{50}{m}$ is greater than $\frac{50}{m+h}$. Therefore, d increases as m does.

21. **(E)** One cubic foot equals 12^3 cubic inches, or 1,728. Thus, one cubic foot of the metal would weigh 3,456 pounds.

22. **(A)** The area of the circle is πr^2 and the circumference is $2\pi r$. If the area equals the circumference, solve the equation $\pi r^2 = 2\pi r$, or $r = 2$. The diameter is $2r$, or 4 inches.

23. **(E)** Let's substitute J for John and P for Pat.
(J is 3 times P) $J = 3P$
(J in four years) $x = J + 4$
(substitute $3P$ for J) $x = 3P + 4$
$$x - 4 = 3P$$
$$\frac{x-4}{3} = P$$

You can also reason this way: If John will be x years old in 4 years, then he is $x-4$ years old now. Since Pat's age is now one-third of John's, Pat is now $\frac{x-4}{3}$ years old.

24. **(D)** Converting to decimals, $\frac{2}{3} = .666\ldots$, $\frac{5}{7} = .7142\ldots$, $\frac{8}{11} = .7272\ldots$, $\frac{9}{13} = .6923\ldots$, so the order is $\frac{2}{3}, \frac{9}{13}, \frac{5}{7}, \frac{8}{11}$.

25. **(C)** If the average for the eight tests is 84%, then the sum of the eight tests must be 8 times 84, or 672. For the six tests the sum must be 6 times 86, or 516. The two dropped tests must have accounted for 156 points. 156 divided by 2 is 78.

Section 2

1. **(C)** If the young girl was unsure of her English skills, she was likely to be *reticent* (shy and restrained) when asked to speak.

2. **(A)** Arguments that only seemed logical were likely to be *specious* (false), and anyone familiar with the facts could *refute* (disprove) them.

3. **(D)** A tree that puts out fewer and fewer leaves is probably *moribund* (dying).

4. **(E)** If no trace of the building remained, it had been *obliterated* (destroyed completely).

5. **(B)** A manner that is menacing or threatening is said to be *truculent*. If, however, it is put on only for show, it is merely *affected*.

6. **(D)** Those who are protected from the harsh world around them are pampered, or cosseted. The other choices make no sense.

7. **(B)** The transitional word *although* sets up a contrast suggesting that one choice will be positive and one choice will be negative. The only possible choice is (B). Someone only appearing to be a respectable businessman may in reality be a reprobate, or a scoundrel.

8. **(B)** The word *attacking* indicates the need for two strong negative words. Only choice (B) satisfies this requirement with *acrimonious*, meaning harsh or bitter, and *angry*.

9. **(D)** *Conscientious* (extremely careful) and *frivolous* (silly) are opposing characteristics.

10. **(C)** The *peel* is the outer layer of an *apple*, just as the *shell* is the outer covering of a *lobster*.

11. **(A)** A *ring* is worn around the *finger* and a *necklace* is worn around the *neck*.

12. **(B)** A *child*, on becoming a fully mature person, is an *adult*. A *lamb* becomes a *sheep* on reaching full maturity. (*Cow* and *buck*, other mature animals, are specifically female and male, respectively.)

13. **(B)** *Pepper* is added to food to *season* it, and *sugar* to *sweeten* it.

14. **(C)** *Beef* can be dried to make *jerky*, and *grapes* can be dried to make *raisins*.

15. **(A)** A group of *fish* is called a *school* and a group of *cows* is called a *herd*.

16. **(B)** King urges his listeners to "continue to work with the faith that unearned suffering is redemptive." Even if you did not know the meaning of *redemptive*, you could infer that it promised something positive. Of the choices only (B) satisfies this condition.

17. **(D)** The last paragraph gives King's belief that "... this situation can and will be changed."

18. **(E)** This is stated in the last paragraph and sums up the point of the entire speech.

19. **(A)** King is attempting to inspire his listeners.

20. **(D)** Lines 35–38 state that this new attitude "...must not lead us to a distrust of all white people, for many of our white brothers ... have come to realize that their destiny is tied up with our destiny."

21. **(C)** King states in lines 18–19: "There will be neither rest nor tranquility in America until the Negro is granted his citizenship rights."

22. **(C)** Paragraph 4 specifically mentions creative protest.

23. **(A)** The second paragraph discusses "the whirlwinds of revolt" that will continue until justice prevails; the third paragraph urges listeners to obey the law, as "... we must not be guilty of wrongful deeds." Thus nonviolent resistance is the best response.

24. **(D)** This is a completely literal statement. As the rest of the passage makes clear, the narrator never really knew Alda.

25. **(D)** To answer this synthesis/analysis question will require looking back at the paragraph and tracing its structure. The narrator describes what Alda looked like, speculates on what she sounded like, and guesses what she moved like, in that order.

26. **(C)** *Docile* has several connotations, but a look back at the citation in question will tell you that only two of the choices could easily be applied to hair, and (A) is exactly opposite to the meaning the narrator intends.

27. **(A)** He compares her brow to (B) and he speaks of a flower (D) and a photograph (E). However, he compares her soul to a church, castle, and tower as well as to a well (see lines 4–5).

28. **(B)** Reread the surrounding text to remind yourself of the author's main point. Her presence has no sensation for him, because he has not really met her.

29. **(E)** Each choice is a possible synonym, but only choice (E) suits the idea of memory being more faithful than faded photographs.

30. **(A)** In the first sentence of paragraph 3, the author suggests that his fear of reality was the reason he failed to meet Alda. This is the first time he has made such a suggestion. Paragraph 3 might also be said to support (C), but so do paragraphs 1 and 2. Choices (D) and (E) are not supported anywhere in the passages.

31. **(E)** Here is an example of an oddly worded phrase that cannot be easily deciphered. By testing the choices in place of the phrase in context, however, the reasonable translation is clear.

Section 3

Part 1

1. **(C)** The exterior angle of a triangle is equal to the sum of the two interior nonadjacent angles. Thus, $x + y = a$ and $\therefore x = a - y$. Therefore, Column A and Column B are equal.

2. **(B)** $3^2 - 3 = 6$. $(-3)^2 - (-3) = 12$.

3. **(D)** This type of problem is most easily solved by plugging in small values.
   If $u = 0$ then $1^2 - 1 = 0$, while $(-1)^2 - (-1) = 2$.
   If $u = 1$ then $2^2 - 2 = 2$ while $(0)^2 - 0 = 0$. Since Column B is larger than Column A when $u = 0$, but smaller when $u = 1$, the answer must be (D).

4. **(C)** An alternate exterior angle of $\angle x$ is a vertical angle to an alternate exterior angle of $\angle y$. Since alternate exterior angles of two parallel lines cut by a transversal are equal, and vertical angles are always equal, $\angle x = \angle y$. Thus, the two columns are equal.

5. **(C)** The area of a square with side 4 is $4^2 = 16$. The area of the triangle in Column B is $(\frac{1}{2})(4)(4) = 8$. Twice this area is 16. Thus, the two areas are equal.

6. **(C)** Since two of the angles of this triangle total 90°, and there are 180° in a triangle, angle B must equal 90°, and this is a right triangle. In a right triangle in which the angles are 90°, 60°, and 30°, the length of the side opposite the 30° angle is one-half the length of the hypotenuse, and the length of the side opposite the 60° angle is one-half the length of the hypotenuse times $\sqrt{3}$. Side AB is opposite the 30° angle, and so must be one-half the hypotenuse. AB is 1; therefore, AC must be 2. BC, then, will be one-half the length of the hypotenuse times $\sqrt{3}$. So BC will be $\sqrt{3}$. Thus, the two columns are equal.

7. **(A)** x can range in value from 1 to 7. Plugging in each of those values, y can be 7, 10, 13, 16, 19, 22, and 25. Of these, 7, 13, and 19 are prime numbers.

8. **(D)** Since r is the radius of a circle, r cannot be negative. Thus $r^3 > r^2$. But, if $0 < r < 1$, $r^2 > r^3$. Hence, it cannot be determined which is larger.

9. **(A)** The values of Column A and Column B are 16 and -9, respectively. Therefore, Column A is greater than Column B.

10. **(A)** There are 360 degrees and 4 angles in all quadrilaterals and 360 divided by 4 is 90. A triangle contains 180 degrees and 3 angles. For two triangles the average would be 360 divided by 6, or 60.

11. **(A)** Substituting for s and t in Column A, $4(1) + 3(4) = 16$. Substituting t and r in Column B, $2(4) - 2(-3) = 14$. Therefore, Column A is larger than Column B.

12. **(A)** In Column A, 12% of 72,000 is $(.12)(72,000) = 8,640$. In Column B, 7% of 37,000 is $(.07)(37,000) = 2,590$. Therefore, Column A is greater than Column B.

13. **(C)** The average can be found by totaling the numbers in each column and dividing that sum by the number of terms.

    Column A $\dfrac{132}{6} = 22$.

    Column B $\dfrac{110}{5} = 22$.

Practice Examination 3

14. **(A)** The area of circle A with radius 2 is $\pi r^2 = 4\pi$. 4π is approximately 12.56, so Column A is bigger.

15. **(C)** The values of Column A and Column B are both $\frac{1}{8}$.

Part 2

16. Use a ratio of apples to dollars.

$$\frac{\text{apples}}{\text{dollars}} \rightarrow \frac{24}{3} = \frac{18}{x}$$

$$8 = \frac{18}{x}$$

$$8x = 18$$

$$x = 2.25 = \frac{9}{4}$$

17. $\frac{1}{10}\% = \frac{1}{1000}$

$$\frac{1}{1000} \cdot \frac{1}{10} \cdot \frac{10}{1} = \frac{1}{1000} = .001$$

18. $\dfrac{-\dfrac{1}{3}}{\dfrac{3}{3}} - \dfrac{\dfrac{3}{1}}{-\dfrac{1}{3}} = \dfrac{-\dfrac{1}{3}}{\dfrac{3}{3}} - \dfrac{\dfrac{3}{1}}{-\dfrac{1}{3}}$

$$= -\frac{1}{3}\left(\frac{1}{3}\right) - \frac{3}{1}\left(-\frac{3}{1}\right)$$

$$= -\frac{1}{9} + 9$$

$$= 8\frac{8}{9} = \frac{80}{9} = 8.89$$

19. The sum of Dawn's scores for the first four tests is $80(4) = 320$.

$$\frac{320 + x}{5} = 83$$

$$320 + x = 415$$

$$x = 95$$

20.

the area of a square $= (\text{side})^2$

or

$= \dfrac{(\text{diagonal})^2}{2}$

Area of $\square\ ABCD = (\text{side})^2 = 6^2 = 36$

Area of $\square\ WXYZ = \dfrac{(\text{diagonal})^2}{2} = \dfrac{6^2}{2} = 18$

Shaded area $= 36 - 18 = 18$

21. 1 week $=$ 7 days

1 day $=$ 24 hours

1 hour $=$ 60 minutes

$$\frac{30,240}{7(24)(60)} = 3$$

22. The sum of the interior angles of a quadrilateral is $360°$.

$\therefore a + b + c + d = 360$

23. Distance $=$ rate $\times$ time

$360 = r(9)$

$40 = r$

If r were $40 + 5 = 45$

$d = rt$

$360 = 45t$

$t = 8$

24.

$40 + 90 + a = 180$

$a = 50$

$m\angle J = 2(50) = 100°$

$m\angle N + m\angle J + m\angle L = 180°$

$m\angle N + 100° + 20° = 180°$

$m\angle N = 60°$

25.

$x^2 + x^2 = 8^2$

$2x^2 = 64$

$x = 4\sqrt{2}$

The side of the square $= 4\sqrt{2}$.

The radius of the circle $= \dfrac{1}{2}(4\sqrt{2}) = 2\sqrt{2}$.

$A = \pi r^2$

$= \pi(2\sqrt{2})^2 = 8\pi = a\pi \therefore a = 8$

Section 4

1. **(A)** Keeping a meeting from breaking up requires more than a clear *idea* or *vision*; it requires control, or a *grasp* of the situation.

2. **(C)** The word *commitment* signals the appropriate actions of the mayor; to be *steadfast* in her commitment, she must *stem*, or check, the increase of economic problems for the people who voted her into office.

3. **(B)** For the farmhouse to have been a landmark since before the Civil War, it must have been well built, or *sturdy*.

4. **(E)** If she thought her cousin was hateful, it is most likely that she found his behavior *obnoxious* (offensive) and that she was *galled*, or irritated, to hear him praised.

5. **(D)** *Circumspect*, meaning "watchful or wary," is the only choice that makes sense.

6. **(C)** *Accomodate*, meaning "to provide space for," is the only answer that makes sense.

7. **(A)** To make promises you know you cannot *fulfill* is *hypocrisy*. No other choice correctly fills both blanks.

8. **(C)** One who accepts without question is *credulous* (tending to believe readily).

9. **(D)** If the police know an explosion is *imminent* (about to happen), they are likely to *evacuate* (empty) the building quickly.

10. **(D)** The key word is *wind*. A road that winds is *tortuous* (D). (C) and (E) are wrong because they refer to other meanings of *tortuous*. Choices (A) and (B) make no sense.

11. **(C)** To *smash* something is to do much greater damage than merely *crack* it. To *scream* is to make a much greater noise than to *whisper*.

12. **(D)** A *surgeon* is necessarily *dexterous* (skillful in using the hands), and an *acrobat* is necessarily *agile*.

13. **(B)** A *sport* is viewed by a *spectator*, and a *crime* is viewed by a *witness*.

14. **(A)** To *amble* is to *walk* unhurriedly without a predetermined destination. To *tinker* is to *work* aimlessly without a predetermined direction.

15. **(D)** A *hilt* (handle) is the part of a sword to which the *blade* is attached. Similarly, the *stem* is part of a plant to which a *leaf* is attached.

16. **(E)** A *ruler* is used to measure *distance*, and a *thermometer* is used to measure *temperature*.

17. **(B)** A *hammer* is a *tool*, and a *wagon* is a *vehicle*.

18. **(E)** *Flippers* and *spikes* are each footgear for a sport: *flippers* for the *diver* and *spikes* for the *golfer*.

19. **(B)** A *braggart* (offensively boastful person) lacks *diffidence* (modesty), just as a *pariah* (outcast) lacks *esteem* (regard).

20. **(D)** A *diatribe* is a speech full of *bitterness*. An *encomium* is speech full of *praise*.

21. **(B)** A *travesty* is an imitation intended to *ridicule*. A *forgery* is an imitation intended to *deceive*.

22. **(C)** An *author* produces a *novel* while a *sculptor* makes a *statue*.

23. **(C)** One who is *magnanimous* (generous) is not *petty* (mean-spirited), just as one who is *passionate* (ardent) is not *blasé* (bored).

24. **(C)** In this context, the word *fixed* means situated or found, not its more common meaning—changed or altered.

25. **(E)** All of the other choices are explicitly mentioned by the author as the resting places of the hummingbird.

26. **(C)** Wilson states that nests are sometimes attached to such objects, but "these cases are rare" (lines 8–9).

27. **(D)** The nest is not easily seen, but it is not invisible, as (C) suggests. Wilson describes seeing it from below (lines 26–27).

28. **(E)** Wilson refers to the proprietors darting around to protect the nest (lines 29–31).

29. **(C)** Wilson believes that hummingbirds *do* feed their young such food, saying, "I think it highly probable they do" (lines 40–41). However, he has not seen it.

30. **(B)** Since Wilson takes this to mean that hummingbirds may raise two broods (lines 43–44), the only possible answer here is (B).

31. **(A)** According to the passage (lines 15–23), the nest is composed of bluish-grey lichen glued on with hummingbird saliva, the wings of flying seeds, and downy substances from fern stalks and from the great mullein (another kind of plant).

32. **(D)** Lines 14–15 show that Wilson is looking at something that "is now lying before me."

33. **(C)** It can inferred from the sentence that the hummingbirds migrate into Pennsylvania (presumably from the south) "about the twenty-fifth of April." None of the other choices is supported by the passage.

34. **(A)** Although other details about the hummingbird are included, the passage focuses on hummingbirds' nesting.

35. **(B)** Most of Wilson's observations in this piece happen in the wild; it is safe to assume that he would study crows the same way.

Section 5

1. **(B)**

Area of ΔI = Area of ΔII

Area of ΔI + ΔIII = Area of ΔIII + ΔII

PR and *SQ* are diagonals of rectangle *PQRS*. The diagonals of a rectangle divide the rectangle into four triangles of equal area.
∴ ΔIII + ΔII = 25% of rectangle *PQRS*.

2. **(C)** The number of revolutions is inversely proportional to size of wheel.

   Thus, $\dfrac{30}{20} = \dfrac{n}{240}$

   Where n = no. of revolutions for second wheel,

   $$20n = 7200$$

   $$n = 360$$

3. **(B)** $1.86 \times 10^5 = 1.86 \times 100,000 = 186,000$

4. **(D)** All the numbers from 200 to 299 begin with 2. There are 100 of these. Then all numbers like $102, 112, \ldots, 192$ end with 2. There are 10 of these.

   Hence, there are 110 such numbers.

5. **(B)** If the area is $49x^2$, the side of the square is $7x$. Therefore, the diagonal of the square must be the hypotenuse of a right isosceles triangle of leg $7x$.

   Hence, diagonal $= 7x\sqrt{2}$

6. **(C)** The amount paid for weight over 5 ounces is $1.66 - \$.62 = \$1.04$. At $.08$ for each additional ounce, $\dfrac{\$1.04}{\$.08} = 13$ ounces of additional weight. The total weight is 13 ounces + 5 ounces = 18 ounces × $(\dfrac{1 \text{ lb.}}{16 \text{ oz.}}) = 1\dfrac{1}{8}$ lbs.

7. **(D)** Each adult needs 15 cans/7 adults = $\dfrac{15}{7}$ cans in two days, or $(\dfrac{1}{2})(\dfrac{15}{7}) = \dfrac{15}{14}$ cans per adult per day. Multiply this by the number of adults and by the number of days.

   $(\dfrac{15}{14})(4 \text{ adults})(7 \text{ days}) = 30$ cans of food.

8. **(D)** Let the original sign be 10 by 10.

   [Diagram: Square 10×10, Area = 100; Square 9×7, Area = 63]

   Then the new sign is 9 by 7.

   $\dfrac{63}{100} = 63\%$

9. **(A)** The average is found by taking the sum of a list of numbers and dividing the sum by the number in the list. If n is the number of numbers in the series, $160 \div n = 20$, so $n = 8$ numbers.

10. **(D)** Squaring a negative number will make it positive, so choices (A) and (B) are not true. $1^2 = 1$, so choice (E) is not true. Squaring any number greater than 1 will always be larger than the number itself, but squaring a fraction less than 1, where the denominator is larger than the numerator, will make the denominator much larger than the numerator, thus making the whole fraction smaller.

Section 6

1. **(A)** The context of the sentence, with its reference to taking his own life, supports this choice.

2. **(D)** Sentence 3 specifically cites the cause of Achilles' feelings of guilt.

3. **(D)** In this context, Thetis is traveling or returning to Vulcan.

4. **(C)** The passage refers to Vulcan's palace and his ability to create magical tripods, indicating that he is quite powerful.

5. **(C)** With his new armor and his feelings of righteousness, Achilles is confident as he goes into battle.

6. **(A)** Sentence 2 in passage 2 states that they enlisted the help of Curoi of Kerry.

7. **(B)** The champion did not have to fight the giant; the champion had to behead the giant.

8. **(D)** Although choices (A) and (B) might be appealing, the fact that giant remained alive while headless was what made him so unusual.

9. **(B)** The context of the sentence supports definition (B), as the men of Ulster were completely or utterly ashamed.

10. **(E)** Cuchulain is a man to whom his word is his bond; he had to meet the giant because he gave his word.

11. **(A)** His speech is serious and sad because he is afraid of imminent death.

12. **(B)** The quality that Achilles and Cuchulain share is courage.

COMPUTING YOUR SCORES ON PRACTICE EXAMINATION 3

To check your SAT preparation progress at the end of this third practice examination, you need to compute individual verbal and mathematical raw scores. Once you have computed these, use the conversion scales in the section that follows to compute your SAT scaled scores (200–800). Keep in mind that these formulas have been simplified to give you a "quick and dirty" sense of where you are scoring, not a perfectly precise score.

To Compute Your Raw Scores:

1. Enter the number of correct answers for each verbal and mathematical reasoning section into the boxes marked "Number of Questions Correct."
2. Enter the number of incorrect answers (not blanks) for each verbal and mathematical reasoning section into the boxes marked "Number of Questions Incorrect."
3. Total the number correct and number incorrect.
4. Follow this formula: Take the total correct and minus one-quarter of the total incorrect. Round up in your favor to compute your Raw Score.

Verbal Section	Total Number of Questions	Number of Questions Correct	Number of Questions Incorrect
1	31		
3	35		
5	12		
Totals	78	Total Correct:	Total Incorrect:

Verbal Raw Score = Total Correct − ($\frac{1}{4}$ × Total Incorrect) = _____

Math Section	Total Number of Questions	Number of Questions Correct	Number of Questions Incorrect
2	25		
4	25		
6	10		
Totals	60	Total Correct:	Total Incorrect:

Math Raw Score = Total Correct − ($\frac{1}{4}$ × Total Incorrect) = _____

CONVERSION SCALES FOR PRACTICE EXAMINATION 3

VERBAL REASONING

Raw Score	Scaled Score	Raw Score	Scaled Score
75	800	35	520
70	800	30	480
65	760	25	440
60	710	20	410
55	670	15	370
50	620	10	340
45	590	5	290
40	550	0	230

MATHEMATICAL REASONING

Raw Score	Scaled Score	Raw Score	Scaled Score
60	800	25	510
55	760	20	480
50	690	15	440
45	650	10	410
40	610	5	340
35	580	0	200
30	550		

Although you now have some idea of what your scores would like had they been scaled according to unofficial ETS standards, you will probably want to know how to interpret your Raw Scores in more familiar terms. If so, use the following Self-Evaluation Charts to see what your Raw Scores actually mean.

SELF-EVALUATION CHARTS

VERBAL REASONING: Raw Score

Excellent	60 – 75
Good	50 – 60
Average	30 – 50
Fair	20 – 30
Poor	0 – 20

MATHEMATICAL REASONING: Raw Score

Excellent	50 – 60
Good	40 – 50
Average	20 – 40
Fair	10 – 20
Poor	0 – 10

PRACTICE EXAMINATION 4

Answer Sheet

If a section has fewer questions than answer ovals, leave the extra ovals blank.

Section 1

Section 2

Section 3

Section 4

Note: ONLY the answers entered on the grid are scored.
Handwritten answers at the top of the column are NOT scored.

Section 5

1. Ⓐ Ⓑ Ⓒ Ⓓ Ⓔ   6. Ⓐ Ⓑ Ⓒ Ⓓ Ⓔ   11. Ⓐ Ⓑ Ⓒ Ⓓ Ⓔ
2. Ⓐ Ⓑ Ⓒ Ⓓ Ⓔ   7. Ⓐ Ⓑ Ⓒ Ⓓ Ⓔ   12. Ⓐ Ⓑ Ⓒ Ⓓ Ⓔ
3. Ⓐ Ⓑ Ⓒ Ⓓ Ⓔ   8. Ⓐ Ⓑ Ⓒ Ⓓ Ⓔ   13. Ⓐ Ⓑ Ⓒ Ⓓ Ⓔ
4. Ⓐ Ⓑ Ⓒ Ⓓ Ⓔ   9. Ⓐ Ⓑ Ⓒ Ⓓ Ⓔ   14. Ⓐ Ⓑ Ⓒ Ⓓ Ⓔ
5. Ⓐ Ⓑ Ⓒ Ⓓ Ⓔ   10. Ⓐ Ⓑ Ⓒ Ⓓ Ⓔ   15. Ⓐ Ⓑ Ⓒ Ⓓ Ⓔ

Section 6

1. Ⓐ Ⓑ Ⓒ Ⓓ Ⓔ   6. Ⓐ Ⓑ Ⓒ Ⓓ Ⓔ   11. Ⓐ Ⓑ Ⓒ Ⓓ Ⓔ
2. Ⓐ Ⓑ Ⓒ Ⓓ Ⓔ   7. Ⓐ Ⓑ Ⓒ Ⓓ Ⓔ   12. Ⓐ Ⓑ Ⓒ Ⓓ Ⓔ
3. Ⓐ Ⓑ Ⓒ Ⓓ Ⓔ   8. Ⓐ Ⓑ Ⓒ Ⓓ Ⓔ   13. Ⓐ Ⓑ Ⓒ Ⓓ Ⓔ
4. Ⓐ Ⓑ Ⓒ Ⓓ Ⓔ   9. Ⓐ Ⓑ Ⓒ Ⓓ Ⓔ   14. Ⓐ Ⓑ Ⓒ Ⓓ Ⓔ
5. Ⓐ Ⓑ Ⓒ Ⓓ Ⓔ   10. Ⓐ Ⓑ Ⓒ Ⓓ Ⓔ   15. Ⓐ Ⓑ Ⓒ Ⓓ Ⓔ

Practice Examination 4

SECTION 1

35 Questions • Time—30 Minutes

Directions: Each of the following questions consists of an incomplete sentence followed by five words or pairs of words. Choose that word or pair of words which, when substituted for the blank space or spaces, best completes the meaning of the sentence and mark the letter of your choice on your answer sheet.

Example:

In view of the extenuating circumstances and the defendant's youth, the judge recommended ----.

(A) conviction (B) a defense
(C) a mistrial (D) leniency
(E) life imprisonment   Ⓐ Ⓑ Ⓒ ● Ⓔ

1. ---- by her family, the woman finally agreed to sell the farm.

    (A) Decimated
    (B) Importuned
    (C) Encumbered
    (D) Interpolated
    (E) Designated

2. The ghost of his royal father ---- the young Hamlet to avenge his murder.

    (A) enervates
    (B) parlays
    (C) marauds
    (D) exhorts
    (E) inculcates

3. Concerned for his children's safey, the father tried to ---- in them a ---- attitude toward strangers.

    (A) obviate..hospitable
    (B) ingratiate..assiduous
    (C) insinuate..salubrious
    (D) assimilate..benevolent
    (E) inculcate..wary

4. A life of hardship and poverty has ---- them to petty physical discomforts.

    (A) ascribed
    (B) inured
    (C) remonstrated
    (D) deferred
    (E) impugned

5. Displeased with the ---- of his novel, the author withdrew from the television project.

    (A) adaptation
    (B) compilation
    (C) transliteration
    (D) transfusion
    (E) resurgence

6. Because he changed his mind nearly every day, the governor had a reputation for ----.

    (A) impudence
    (B) impartiality
    (C) perspicuity
    (D) prevarication
    (E) vacillation

GO ON TO THE NEXT PAGE

7. Her ---- smile ---- all those who saw it.

   (A) devastating..replenished
   (B) penultimate..inured
   (C) radiant..obliged
   (D) sunny..tanned
   (E) bright..dazzled

8. Although he was known as a ---- old miser, his anonymous gifts to charity were always ----.

   (A) grasping..tasteless
   (B) spendthrift..gracious
   (C) gregarious..selfish
   (D) penurious..generous
   (E) stingy..mangy

9. With one ---- motion, Brian disarmed his assailant and gained his freedom.

   (A) maladroit
   (B) deft
   (C) ponderous
   (D) superfluous
   (E) brusque

10. The platypus is a biological ----; although it's classed as a mammal, it has a duck-like bill and lays eggs.

    (A) euphemism
    (B) exemplar
    (C) antidote
    (D) periphery
    (E) anomaly

Directions: Each of the following questions consists of a capitalized pair of words followed by five pairs of words lettered A to E. The capitalized words bear some meaningful relationship to each other. Choose the lettered pair of words whose relationship is most similiar to that expressed by the capitalized pair and mark its letter on your answer sheet.

Example:

DAY : SUN : :

(A) sunlight : daylight
(B) ray : sun
(C) night : moon
(D) heat : cold
(E) moon : star

Ⓐ Ⓑ ● Ⓓ Ⓔ

11. TEACHER : INSTRUCTION : :

   (A) lawyer : crime
   (B) army : regiment
   (C) doctor : disease
   (D) guard : protection
   (E) student : learning

12. USHER : THEATER : :

   (A) conductor : train
   (B) program : movie
   (C) aisle : row
   (D) friend : actor
   (E) pilot : airplane

13. SKATE : RINK : :

   (A) build : arena
   (B) sleep : lecture
   (C) repose : bed
   (D) park : stadium
   (E) draw : circle

14. SAPLING : TREE : :

   (A) weed : plant
   (B) grass : wheat
   (C) puppy : dog
   (D) seed : vegetable
   (E) acorn : oak

15. FRET : RELAX : :

   (A) worry : avoid
   (B) sob : cry
   (C) fight : submit
   (D) sing : laugh
   (E) frolic : play

16. STUTTER : TALK : :

   (A) worry : analyze
   (B) stumble : walk
   (C) walk : run
   (D) hear : understand
   (E) trip : fall

17. DAMAGE : DEMOLISH : :

   (A) whimper : wail
   (B) break : mar
   (C) loosen : cinch
   (D) punish : accept
   (E) plan : act

18. HOSE : WATER : :

   (A) lawn : grass
   (B) speaker : sound
   (C) window : air
   (D) vent : flap
   (E) chimney : smoke

19. EXERCISE : STRENGTH : :

   (A) concern : resource
   (B) practice : skill
   (C) success : loss
   (D) sport : contest
   (E) gym : weight

20. SERGEANT : SOLDIERS : :

   (A) captain : sports
   (B) colonel : tanks
   (C) coach : players
   (D) director : scripts
   (E) teacher : books

GO ON TO THE NEXT PAGE

21. VOLATILE : STABILITY : :

    (A) spontaneous : enthusiasm
    (B) voluble : glibness
    (C) wanton : restraint
    (D) reverent : respect
    (E) servile : humility

22. SCIENTIST : LABORATORY : :

    (A) chemist : test tube
    (B) lawyer : client
    (C) dentist : drill
    (D) teacher : classroom
    (E) actor : playwright

23. JOCULAR : SOLEMNITY : :

    (A) latent : visibility
    (B) pompous : spectacle
    (C) ruined : demolition
    (D) vindictive : enmity
    (E) lonely : insularity

Questions 24–35 are based on the following passage.

The history of a place is preserved in various ways, including through its landmarks, historic buildings, and public areas. The following passage discusses Los Angeles, and what is being done there to preserve its history of place.

An outsider approaches the subject gingerly, lest civic feelings be bruised. Los Angeles gives the impression of having erased much of its history by allowing the city's development to run unchecked. Insiders like
(5) Dolores Hayden ... pull no punches: "It is ... common," she wrote, "for fond residents to quote Gertrude Stein's sentence about Oakland when summing up urban design in Los Angeles: 'There's no there, there.'" Hayden has also acknowledged that Los Angeles is generally
(10) "the first (American city) singled out as having a problem about sense of place." Both statements come from a handsome brochure-*cum*-itinerary, drawn up by Hayden, Gail Dubrow, and Carolyn Flynn to introduce The Power of Place, a local nonprofit group with a
(15) mission to retrieve some of the city's misplaced "there."

Founded by Hayden in 1982, The Power of Place lays special emphasis on redressing an imbalance in memory—and memorials. As Hayden has pointed out, in 1987 less than half the population of Los Angeles was
(20) Anglo-American; yet almost 98 percent of the city's cultural historic landmarks were devoted to the history and accomplishments of Anglo-Americans. Even these personages come from a narrow spectrum of achievers—in Hayden's phrase, "a small minority of
(25) landholders, bankers, business leaders, and their architects"—almost all of whom were male . . . .

The likeliest explanation for this under-representation may be an urban variation on the great-man theory of history: History is what public figures do, and by their
(30) civic monuments shall ye know them—especially the structures they designed or built. In Hayden's view, however, "The task of choosing a past for Los Angeles is a political as well as an historic and cultural one," and the unexamined preference for architecture as the focus
(35) of historic preservation efforts can slight less conscious but perhaps equally powerful human forces. Hayden's goal has been to supplement the city's ample supply of monocultural landmarks and memorials with others representing its ethnic and gender-based diversity. Ac-
(40) cordingly, some sites need new status as official landmarks, others need reinterpretation. Other sites no longer contain structures emblematic of their histories or are located in blighted neighborhoods; these do not readily lend themselves to resuscitation through renovation
(45) and commercial development, as preservationists have managed elsewhere.

The Power of Place has identified nine places on which to concentrate in the first phase of its work: development of a walking tour of little-known Los
(50) Angeles sites, for which The Power of Place brochure serves as a guide.

The most ethnically evocative of these sites is probably Vignes Vineyard/Wolfskill Grove, neighboring plots that once supported a share of the vineyards and
(55) citrus groves abounding in early 19th-century Los Angeles. The first cultivators of the wine grapes and citrus were Franciscan missionaries and their Native American converts. The padres gave way to white entrepreneurs; the Native Americans to various waves
(60) of immigrants, including Chinese, then Japanese, and finally, Mexicans . . .

The Power of Place brochure concludes its summary of what is known about each stop on the walking tour with a postscript called Placemaking, which describes
(65) the site's current status and suggests ways to make it more redolent of its past. For the vineyard/grove complex, the current situation is not atypical: "Present uses...are commercial and industrial." Then comes word of what seems to be a minor miracle: "One tall slender
(70) grapefruit tree . . . has been preserved and relocated in the courtyard of the Japanese American Cultural and Community Center . . . ." Suggestions for recapturing more of the past proposed by The Power of Place include returning orange trees to the Wolfskill site and
(75) installing historical markers on the Vignes site.

24. Which of the following most accurately summarizes the main idea of the passage?

    (A) Multicultural landmarks are better than monocultural ones.
    (B) The Power of Place is attempting to correct an imbalance in Los Angeles historical landmarks.
    (C) Los Angeles has a limited sense of place because it has not adequately preserved its history.
    (D) Dolores Hayden has an iconoclastic viewpoint on the state of historical preservation in Los Angeles.
    (E) Los Angelenos do not care about their surroundings.

25. The author uses the phrase "civic feelings" (line 2) to mean the

    (A) allegiance of a city's residents to their city
    (B) emotions that breed courtesy and good behavior
    (C) respect for each other shown by people who think of themselves as civilized
    (D) defensiveness that city residents sometimes show toward outsiders
    (E) regularity with which citizens vote

26. What is the danger of allowing the development of Los Angeles to "run unchecked"? (line 4)

    (A) The roadways will become overrun with traffic.
    (B) Developers will use up all arable land.
    (C) Smog will become an even bigger environmental concern.
    (D) Much of the city's cultural history will be lost to modernization.
    (E) People will emigrate from Los Angeles in search of more suitable living conditions.

27. In quoting Gertrude Stein's saying, "There's no there, there" (line 8), Dolores Hayden most likely means to say that

    (A) the same lack of urban design that characterizes Oakland is also typical of Los Angeles
    (B) a sprawling city like Los Angeles often has no particular center where residents congregate

    (C) Los Angeles's historic monuments focus too exclusively on a particular segment of the population
    (D) Los Angeles is not an old city historically
    (E) Los Angeles seems to have no outstanding characteristics that define it as a place

28. According to Dolores Hayden, most of the historical landmarks of Los Angeles

    (A) do not enhance a sense of place among the people of Los Angeles
    (B) have been chosen according to political rather than aesthetic criteria
    (C) are not representative of the history of all of the people of Los Angeles
    (D) should be replaced by landmarks that celebrate the accomplishments of minorities and women
    (E) are not on a par with historical landmarks elsewhere

29. With which of the following statements about the people memorialized by most existing Los Angeles monuments would Dolores Hayden be most likely to agree?

    I. They were usually of a higher social class than were the people highlighted by The Power of Place.
    II. Their accomplishments are more conspicuous than are those of the people highlighted by The Power of Place.
    III. They made greater contributions to the economic development of Los Angeles than did the people highlighted by The Power of Place.

    (A) I only
    (B) I, II, and III
    (C) I and III
    (D) I and II
    (E) II only

30. Which of the following statements most accurately characterizes Hayden's view on historic preservation, as those views are described in the passage?

    (A) Political and economic considerations should have no place in the designation of cultural and historic landmarks.
    (B) Plants and other natural phenomena make better historic landmarks than do buildings and other human artifacts.
    (C) Some parts of history cannot be memorialized in surviving buildings and landmarks, so new ways must be found to more fully recapture the past.
    (D) The homes and workplaces of working people should be preserved whenever possible because the history of working people is more important than that of so-called "great men."
    (E) The past cannot be memorialized in anything but buildings and landmarks so that every care must be taken to preserve them.

31. Which one of the following is cited in the passage as a difficulty The Power of Place faces in preserving the history of women and minorities?

    (A) Most citizens of Los Angeles are uninterested in the preservation effort.
    (B) Few written records of the history of women and minorities have been preserved.
    (C) Women and minorities are not in support of the efforts on their behalf.
    (D) Many of the historical sites have completely changed in the intervening years.
    (E) Funding for historical preservation tends to go to groups that memorialize famous public figures.

32. The author of the passage seems to value the Vignes/Wolfskill site most for

    (A) its well-preserved state
    (B) the main uses the site has served over the years
    (C) its evocation of one of the most important industries in 19th-century Los Angeles
    (D) the variety of cultural groups whose history is represented there
    (E) its connection to the early founders of Los Angeles

33. For Hayden, "Placemaking" (line 64) most nearly means

    (A) finding ways to overcome urban blight
    (B) capturing the character of the city by evoking the past of all its people
    (C) restoring an historic site to its previous condition
    (D) showing the city's residents how particular sites have been used in the past
    (E) creating new landmarks

34. The author most likely refers to the existence of a grapefruit tree at the Vignes/Wolfskill site as "a minor miracle" (line 69) because

    (A) the tree's slenderness indicates that it has survived so far only because of exceptionally good care
    (B) grapefruit trees grow best in groves rather than singly
    (C) citrus trees, once common at the site, have been replaced by businesses and factories
    (D) grapefruit trees are not native to the area and often do not grow well there
    (E) the area has been so heavily vandalized

35. In the author's view, all of the following would most likely be *undervalued* cultural landmarks EXCEPT:

    (A) indigenous trees
    (B) endangered species of animal and plant life
    (C) historic buildings in dilapidated areas
    (D) city hall
    (E) china town

STOP

END OF SECTION 1. IF YOU HAVE ANY TIME LEFT, GO OVER YOUR WORK IN THIS SECTION ONLY. DO NOT WORK IN ANY OTHER SECTION OF THE TEST.

SECTION 2

25 Questions • Time—30 Minutes

Directions: Solve the following problems using any available space on the page for scratchwork. On your answer sheet fill in the choice which best corresponds to the correct answer.

Notes: The figures accompanying the problems are drawn as accurately as possible unless otherwise stated in specific problems. Again, unless otherwise stated, all figures lie in the same plane. All numbers used in these problems are real numbers. Calculators are permitted for this test.

Reference Information

Circle: $C = 2\pi r$, $A = \pi r^2$
Rectangle: $A = lw$
Rectangular Solid: $V = lwh$
Cylinder: $V = \pi r^2 h$
Triangle: $A = \frac{1}{2}bh$
$a^2 + b^2 = c^2$

Special right triangles: 45°-45°-90° with sides x, x, $x\sqrt{2}$; 30°-60°-90° with sides x, $x\sqrt{3}$, $2x$.

The number of degrees of arc in a circle is 360.
The measure in degrees of a straight angle is 180.
The sum of the measures in degrees of the angles of a triangle is 180.

---

1. If for all real numbers (a.b.c. − d.e.f.) = (a − d) × (b − e) × (c − f), then (4.5.6. − 1.2.3.) =

    (A) −27
    (B) 0
    (C) 27
    (D) 54
    (E) 108

2. The sum of an odd number and an even number is

    (A) sometimes an even number
    (B) always divisible by 3 or 5 or 7
    (C) always an odd number
    (D) always a prime number (not divisible)
    (E) always divisible by 2

3. If $6x + 12 = 9$, $x^2 =$

    (A) $\dfrac{21}{6}$
    (B) $-\dfrac{1}{2}$
    (C) $\dfrac{9}{12}$
    (D) $\dfrac{1}{4}$
    (E) $\dfrac{9}{6}$

4. Under certain conditions, sound travels at about 1,100 ft. per second. If 88 ft. per second is approximately equivalent to 60 miles per hour, the speed of sound in miles per hour under the above conditions is closest to

    (A) 730
    (B) 740
    (C) 750
    (D) 760
    (E) 780

5. If on a blueprint $\frac{1}{4}$ inch equals 12 inches, what is the actual length in feet of a steel bar that is represented on the blueprint by a line $3\frac{3}{8}$ inches long?

   (A) $2\frac{1}{2}$
   (B) $3\frac{3}{8}$
   (C) $6\frac{3}{4}$
   (D) 9
   (E) $13\frac{1}{2}$

6. If one angle of a triangle is three times a second angle and the third angle is 20 degrees more than the second angle, the second angle, in degrees, is

   (A) 64
   (B) 50
   (C) 40
   (D) 34
   (E) 32

7. If $x = \frac{3}{2}$ and $y = 2$, then $x + y^2 - \frac{1}{2} =$

   (A) 5
   (B) 10
   (C) $11\frac{1}{2}$
   (D) $9\frac{1}{2}$
   (E) $\frac{6}{2}$

8. A math class has 27 students in it. Of those students, 14 are also enrolled in history and 17 are enrolled in English. What is the minimum percentage of the students in the math class who are also enrolled in history *and* English?

   (A) 15%
   (B) 22%
   (C) 49%
   (D) 63%
   (E) 91%

9. A cylindrical container has a diameter of 14 inches and a height of 6 inches. Since one gallon equals 231 cubic inches, the capacity of the tank in gallons is approximately

   (A) $\frac{2}{3}$
   (B) $1\frac{1}{7}$
   (C) $2\frac{2}{7}$
   (D) $2\frac{2}{3}$
   (E) 4

10. If $\dfrac{1}{x+y} = 6$ and $x = 2$, then $y =$

    (A) $-\dfrac{11}{6}$
    (B) $-\dfrac{9}{4}$
    (C) -2
    (D) -1
    (E) 4

11. The number of grams in one ounce is 28.35. The number of grams in a kilogram is 1,000. Therefore the number of kilograms in one pound is approximately

    (A) 0.045
    (B) 0.45
    (C) 1.0
    (D) 2.2
    (E) 4.5

12. Which one of the following numbers is not the square of a rational number?

    (A) .0016
    (B) .16
    (C) 1.6
    (D) 16
    (E) 1,600

GO ON TO THE NEXT PAGE

13. In the figure above, lines l and m are parallel. Which of the following must be equal to 180 degrees?

   I. 1 plus 3
   II. 2 plus 4
   III. 5 plus 6
   IV. 7 plus 8
   V. 8 plus 6

   (A) I and II only
   (B) III and IV only
   (C) V only
   (D) I, II, III, IV only
   (E) I, II, III, IV, V

14. If x is a fraction which ranges from $\frac{1}{4}$ to $\frac{1}{2}$ and y is a fraction which ranges from $\frac{3}{4}$ to $\frac{11}{12}$, what is the maximum value for $\frac{x}{y}$?

   (A) $\frac{3}{16}$
   (B) $\frac{11}{48}$
   (C) $\frac{3}{8}$
   (D) $\frac{11}{24}$
   (E) $\frac{2}{3}$

15. These circles share a common center, point 0. The smallest circle has a radius of 2, the next circle a radius of 5, and the largest circle a radius of 9. What fraction of the area of the largest circle is the area of the shaded region?

   (A) $\frac{7}{27}$
   (B) $\frac{25}{81}$
   (C) $\frac{1}{3}$
   (D) $\frac{7}{11}$
   (E) $\frac{12}{17}$

16. If n and d represent positive whole numbers $(n > d > 1)$, the fractions

   I. $\frac{d}{n}$
   II. $\frac{d+1}{n+1}$
   III. $\frac{d-1}{n-1}$
   IV. $\frac{n}{d}$
   V. $\frac{n-1}{d-1}$

   arranged in ascending order of magnitude are represented correctly by

   (A) III, II, I, V, IV
   (B) IV, V, III, I, II
   (C) II, I, IV, III, V
   (D) III, V, IV, I, II
   (E) III, I, II, IV, V

17. A train running between two towns arrives at its destination 10 minutes late when it goes 40 miles per hour and 16 minutes late when it goes 30 miles per hour. The distance in miles between the towns is

   (A) $8\frac{6}{7}$
   (B) 12
   (C) 192
   (D) 560
   (E) 720

18. A square has a diagonal of x units. If the diagonal is increased by 2 units, what is the length of the side of the new square?

   (A) $x+2$
   (B) $(x+2)\sqrt{2}$
   (C) $\frac{(x+2)\sqrt{2}}{2}$
   (D) $(x+2)2$
   (E) $\frac{(x+2)\sqrt{2}}{4}$

19. PQRS is a square and PTS is an equilateral triangle. How many degrees are there in angle TRS?

   (A) 60
   (B) 75
   (C) 80
   (D) 90
   (E) It cannot be determined from the information given.

20. In the figure, line PQ is parallel to line RS, angle $y = 60°$, and angle $z = 130°$. How many degrees are there in angle x?

   (A) 90°
   (B) 100°
   (C) 110°
   (D) 120°
   (E) 130°

21. In the figure below, QOR is a quadrant of a circle. $PS = 6$ and $PT = 8$. What is the length of arc QR?

   (A) 5π
   (B) 10π
   (C) 20π
   (D) 24
   (E) It cannot be determined from the information given.

22. The ice compartment in a refrigerator is 8 inches deep, 5 inches high, and 4 inches wide. How many ice cubes will it hold if each cube is 2 inches on each edge?

   (A) 16
   (B) 20
   (C) 24
   (D) 80
   (E) 160

23. If Paul can paint a fence in 2 hours and Fred can paint the same fence in 3 hours, Paul and Fred working together can paint the fence in how many hours?

   (A) 2.5
   (B) $\frac{5}{6}$
   (C) 5
   (D) 1
   (E) 1.2

24. If one-third of the liquid contents of a can evaporates on the first day and three-fourths of the remainder evaporates on the second day, the fractional part of the original contents remaining at the close of the second day is

   (A) $\frac{1}{6}$
   (B) $\frac{1}{4}$
   (C) $\frac{5}{12}$
   (D) $\frac{1}{2}$
   (E) $\frac{7}{12}$

GO ON TO THE NEXT PAGE

25. A motorist drives 60 miles to her destination at an average speed of 40 miles per hour and makes the return trip at an average rate of 30 miles per hour. Her average speed in miles per hour for the entire trip is

(A) 17

(B) $34\frac{2}{7}$

(C) 35

(D) $43\frac{1}{3}$

(E) 70

STOP

END OF SECTION 2. IF YOU HAVE ANY TIME LEFT, GO OVER YOUR WORK IN THIS SECTION ONLY. DO NOT WORK IN ANY OTHER SECTION OF THE TEST.

SECTION 3

31 Questions • Time—30 Minutes

Directions: Each of the following questions consists of an incomplete sentence followed by five words or pairs of words. Choose that word or pair of words which, when substituted for the blank space or spaces, best completes the meaning of the sentence and mark the letter of your choice on the answer sheet.

Example:

In view of the extenuating circumstances and the defendant's youth, the judge recommended ----.

(A) conviction   (B) a defense
(C) a mistrial   (D) leniency
(E) life imprisonment

1. They acted in concert, each ---- for a(n) ---- of the plot.

    (A) reliable..source
    (B) responsible..element
    (C) unavailable..section
    (D) appointed..article
    (E) agreeable..felony

2. They were unwisely ---- during their education, and ---- was the result.

    (A) neglected..ignorance
    (B) interrupted..consistency
    (C) befriended..alienation
    (D) instructed..genius
    (E) taught..attendance

3. Most young children are highly conformist and will ---- a classmate whose appearance or manners are ----.

    (A) welcome..bizarre
    (B) shun..conventional
    (C) emulate..unusual
    (D) ostracize..different
    (E) deride..ordinary

4. The royal astrologers were commanded to determine the most ---- date for the king's coronation.

    (A) propitious
    (B) ostensible
    (C) aberrant
    (D) resplendent
    (E) obsequious

5. The poem by the great satirist was dripping with venom and was ---- with scorn.

    (A) contentious
    (B) discordant
    (C) redolent
    (D) sardonic
    (E) vicarious

6. The ---- rites of the fraternity were kept secret by the members and were never ---- to outsiders.

    (A) eclectic...delegated
    (B) esoteric..divulged
    (C) dubious..maligned
    (D) inscrutable..traduced
    (E) elusive..proscribed

7. The composer was ---- enough to praise the work of a musician he detested.

    (A) magnanimous
    (B) loquacious
    (C) munificient
    (D) parsimonious
    (E) surreptitious

GO ON TO THE NEXT PAGE

8. The goodwill of its customers is a genuine but ---- asset for a company.

(A) insensate
(B) redolent
(C) dismissive
(D) intangible
(E) vigilant

9. Though the law's ---- purpose was to curtail false advertising its actual result was to ---- free speech.

(A) potential..preclude
(B) mendacious..eschew
(C) ostensible..circumscribe
(D) illicit..reconcile
(E) recalcitrant..repress

Practice Examination 4

Directions: Each of the following questions consists of a capitalized pair of words followed by five pairs of words lettered A to E. The capitalized words bear some meaningful relationship to each other. Choose the lettered pair of words whose relationship is most similar to that expressed by the capitalized pair and mark its letter on your answer sheet.

Example:

DAY : SUN : :
(A) sunlight : daylight (B) ray : sun
(C) night : moon (D) heat : cold
(E) moon : star
Ⓐ Ⓑ ● Ⓓ Ⓔ

10. AWL : PUNCTURE : :

    (A) tire : ride
    (B) cleaver : cut
    (C) plane : soar
    (D) throttle : start
    (E) axle : steer

11. LUSH : JUNGLE : :

    (A) delicious : fruit
    (B) diligent : worker
    (C) barren : desert
    (D) hot : weather
    (E) obvious : wealth

12. HAND : GNARLED : :

    (A) tree : tall
    (B) foot : sore
    (C) flower : crushed
    (D) brow : creased
    (E) tire : round

13. PLANET : ROTATES : :

    (A) top : spins
    (B) star : shines
    (C) moon : glows
    (D) toy : plays
    (E) rocket : fires

14. MILK : SPOIL : :

    (A) metal : bend
    (B) water : filter
    (C) wood : rot
    (D) fish : swim
    (E) animal : rest

15. MUNIFICENT : GENEROSITY : :

    (A) dolorous : sorrow
    (B) domineering : timidity
    (C) indisputable : doubt
    (D) fortunate : haplessness
    (E) beguiled : judiciousness

GO ON TO THE NEXT PAGE

Questions 16–23 are based on the following passage.

John Adams Audubon (1785–1851) is known primarily for his bird studies, but as this passage from Ornithological Biography *shows, he was fascinated by the behavior of other animals as well.*

The Black Bear (*Ursus americanus*), however clumsy in appearance, is active, vigilant, and persevering; possesses great strength, courage, and address; and undergoes with little injury the greatest fatigues and
(5) hardships in avoiding the pursuit of the hunter. Like the Deer, it changes its haunts with the seasons, and for the same reason, namely, the desire of obtaining suitable food, or of retiring to the more inaccessible parts, where it can pass the time in security, unobserved by man, the
(10) most dangerous of its enemies. During the spring months, it searches for food in the low rich alluvial lands that border the rivers, or by the margins of such inland lakes as, on account of their small size, are called by us ponds. There it procures abundance of succulent roots, and of
(15) the tender juicy stems of plants, on which it chiefly feeds at that season. During the summer heat, it enters the gloomy swamps, passes much of its time in wallowing in the mud, like a hog, and contents itself with crayfish, roots, and nettles, now and then, when
(20) hard pressed by hunger, seizing on a young pig, or perhaps a sow, or even a calf. As soon as the different kinds of berries which grow on the mountain begin to ripen, the Bears betake themselves to the high grounds, followed by their cubs. In such retired parts of the
(25) country where there are no hilly grounds, it pays visits to the maize fields, which it ravages for a while. After this, the various species of nuts, acorns, grapes, and other forest fruits, that form what in the western country is called *mast*, attract its attention. The Bear is then seen
(30) rambling singly through the woods to gather this harvest, not forgetting to rob every Bee tree it meets with, Bears being, as you well know, expert at this operation. You also know that they are good climbers, and may have been told, or at least may now be told, that the
(35) Black Bear now and then houses itself in the hollow trunks of the larger trees for weeks together, when it is said to suck its paws. You are probably not aware of a habit in which it indulges, and which, being curious, must be interesting to you.

(40) At one season, the Black Bear may be seen examining the lower part of the trunk of a tree for several minutes with much attention, at the same time looking around, and snuffing the air, to assure itself that no enemy is near. It then raises itself on its hind legs,
(45) approaches the trunk, embraces it with its forelegs, and scratches the bark with its teeth and claws for several minutes in continuance. Its jaws clash against each other, until a mass of foam runs down both sides of the mouth. After this it continues its rambles.

(50) In various portions of our country, many of our woodsmen and hunters who have seen the Bear performing the singular operation just described, imagine that it does so for the purpose of leaving behind an indication of its size and power. They measure the
(55) height at which the scratches are made, and in this manner, can, in fact, form an estimate of the magnitude of the individual. My own opinion, however, is different. It seems to me that the Bear scratches on the trees, not for the purpose of showing its size or its
(60) strength, but merely for that of sharpening its teeth and claws, to enable it better to encounter a rival of its own species during the amatory season. The Wild Boar of Europe clashes its tusks and scrapes the earth with its feet, and the Deer rubs its antlers against the lower part
(65) of the stems of young trees or bushes, for the same purpose.

16. The bear migrates from one habitat to another in order to

    (A) teach its cubs to climb
    (B) locate a hollow tree
    (C) visit every bee tree
    (D) escape from the wild boar
    (E) find food and security

17. The fact that Audubon calls man the bear's "most dangerous" enemy (line 10) indicates that he

    (A) is himself a hunter
    (B) has some sympathy for hunted bears
    (C) is an animal rights activist
    (D) does not believe that bears are dangerous
    (E) thinks bears are more dangerous than people

18. The word *alluvial* (line 11) refers to

    (A) high grounds
    (B) rocky shorelines
    (C) river-deposited sediment
    (D) thick underbrush
    (E) maize fields

19. According to the passage, black bears eat all of the following *except*

    (A) bark
    (B) maize
    (C) mast
    (D) honey
    (E) crayfish

20. Audubon believes that bears scratch trees to

    (A) show their power
    (B) leave a mark
    (C) sharpen their claws
    (D) navigate
    (E) indicate their size

21. Audubon assumes that his reader knows about bears'

    (A) scratching behavior and threatening manner
    (B) eating of roots and berries
    (C) size and coloring
    (D) fear of man
    (E) climbing expertise and love of honey

22. Audubon compares the bear with deer twice,

    (A) once in relation to its migratory habits, and once in comparing its rubbing behavior
    (B) once in relation to its eating habits, and once in comparing its combative behavior
    (C) both times having to do with its habitat
    (D) both times having to do with hibernation
    (E) both times having to do with size and weight

23. From his description, it seems that Audubon's attitude toward black bears is one of

    (A) fear
    (B) respect
    (C) amusement
    (D) alarm
    (E) bewilderment

Questions 24–31 are based on the following passage.

The study of plant life is very different from the study of animal life because of unique plant characteristics. The following passage provides an overview of those characteristics along with some plant classifications that are of interest to scientists.

Compared to animals, plants present unique problems in demographic studies. The idea of counting living individuals becomes difficult given perennials that reproduce vegetatively by sending out runners or
(5) rhizomes, by splitting at the stem base, or by producing arching canes that take root where they touch the ground. In these ways some individuals, given sufficient time, can extend out over a vast area.

There are five typical plant life spans, and each has
(10) a basic associated life form. *Annual plants* live for 1 year or less. Their average life span is 1-8 months, depending on the species and on the environment where they are located (the same desert plant may complete its life cycle in 8 months one year, and in 1 month the next,
(15) depending on the amount of rain it receives). Annuals with extremely short life cycles are classified as *ephemeral* plants. An example of an ephemeral is *Boerrhavia repens* of the Sahara Desert, which can go from seed to seed in just 10 days. Annuals are herbaceous, which
(20) means that they lack a secondary meristem that produces lateral, woody tissue. They complete their life cycle after seed production for several reasons: nutrient depletion, hormone changes, or inability of nonwoody tissue to withstand unfavorable environmental condi-
(25) tions following the growing season. A few species can persist for more than a year in uncommonly favorable conditions.

Biennial plants are also herbaceous, but usually live for 2 years. Their first year is spent in vegetative growth,
(30) which generally takes place more below ground than above. Reproduction occurs in the second year, and this is followed by the completion of the life cycle. Under poor growing conditions, or by experimental

manipulation, the vegetative stage can be drawn out for more than 1 year.

Herbaceous perennials typically live for 20-30 years, although some species have been known to live for 400-800 years. These plants die back to the root system and root crown at the end of each growing season. The root system becomes woody, but the above-ground system is herbaceous. They have a juvenile, vegetative stage for the first 2-8 years, then bloom and reproduce yearly. Sometimes they bloom only once at the conclusion of their life cycle. Because herbaceous perennials have no growth rings, it is difficult to age them. Methods that have been used to age them include counting leaf scars or estimating the rate of spread in *tussock* (clumped) forms.

Suffrutescent shrubs (hemixyles) fall somewhere between herbaceous perennials and true shrubs. They develop perennial, woody tissue only near the base of their stems; the rest of the shoot system is herbaceous and dies back each year. They are small, and are short-lived compared to true shrubs.

Woody perennials (trees and shrubs) have the longest life spans. Shrubs live on the average 30-50 years. Broadleaf trees (angiosperm) average 200-300 years, and conifer (needles) trees average 500-1000 years. Woody perennials spend approximately the first 10% of their life span in a juvenile, totally vegetative state before they enter a combined reproductive and vegetative state, achieving a peak of reproduction several years before the conclusion of their life cycle.

Regardless of the life span, annual or perennial, one can identify about eight important age states in an individual plant or population. They are: (1) viable seed, (2) seedling, (3) juvenile, (4) immature, (5) mature, (6) initial reproductive, (7) maximum vigor (reproductive and vegetative), and (8) senescent. If a population shows all eight states, it is stable and is most likely a part of a *climax* community. If it shows only the last four states, it may not maintain itself and may be part of a *seral* community.

24. The author believes that plants present "unique problems in demographic studies" (lines 1–2) because

(A) they cannot be aged accurately
(B) it is difficult to define and identify an individual
(C) many have very short lifespans
(D) there has been little interest in such studies
(E) the scientific community is not capable of conducting them

25. The best definition of *ephemeral* (lines 16–17) might be

(A) resilient
(B) short-lived
(C) awkward
(D) uncomplicated
(E) shrub-like

26. Which of these statements is (are) true, according to paragraph 2 (lines 9–27)?

I. All herbaceous plants are annuals.
II. All annuals are herbaceous plants.
III. All annuals are ephemeral.

(A) I only
(B) III only
(C) II only
(D) I and III only
(E) I and II only

27. A plant that spends a year growing below ground and a year growing above ground before dying would be called

(A) an angiosperm
(B) a true shrub
(C) a meristem
(D) ephemeral
(E) a biennial

28. *Annual* and *perennial* are names of

    (A) plant life spans
    (B) plant species
    (C) woody plants
    (D) plant age states
    (E) plant life forms

29. Paragraph 5 deals mainly with

    (A) suffrutescent shrubs
    (B) a form of tree shrub
    (C) a form of herbaceous perennial
    (D) a woody biennial
    (E) none of the above

30. Which of the following is a woody perennial?

    (A) a tulip
    (B) a fern
    (C) a strawberry
    (D) an oak
    (E) an angiosperm

31. The best definition of *senescent* (line 69) might be

    (A) doddering
    (B) receptive
    (C) solitary
    (D) complicated
    (E) aged

STOP

END OF SECTION 3. IF YOU HAVE ANY TIME LEFT, GO OVER YOUR WORK IN THIS SECTION ONLY. DO NOT WORK IN ANY OTHER SECTION OF THE TEST.

SECTION 4

25 Questions • Time—30 Minutes

Directions: Solve the following problems using any available space on the page for scratchwork. On your answer sheet, fill in the choice which best corresponds to the correct answer.

Notes: The figures accompanying the problems are drawn as accurately as possible unless otherwise stated in specific problems. Again, unless otherwise stated, all figures lie in the same plane. All numbers used in these problems are real numbers. Calculators are permitted for this test.

Reference Information

Circle: $C = 2\pi r$, $A = \pi r^2$

Rectangle: $A = lw$

Rectangular Solid: $V = lwh$

Cylinder: $V = \pi r^2 h$

Triangle: $A = \frac{1}{2}bh$

$a^2 + b^2 = c^2$

45°-45°-90° triangle: sides x, x, $x\sqrt{2}$

30°-60°-90° triangle: sides x, $x\sqrt{3}$, $2x$

The number of degrees of arc in a circle is 360.
The measure in degrees of a straight angle is 180.
The sum of the measures in degrees of the angles of a triangle is 180.

Part 1: Quantitative Comparison Questions

Directions: For each of the following questions, two quantities are given—one in Column A, the other in Column B. Compare the two quantities and mark your answer sheet as follows:

(A) if the quantity in Column A is greater
(B) if the quantity in Column B is greater
(C) if the quantities are equal
(D) if the relationship cannot be determined from the information given

Notes:

(1) Information concerning one or both of the compared quantities will be centered above the two columns for some items.
(2) Symbols that appear in both columns represent the same thing in Column A as in Column B.
(3) Letters such as x, n, and k are symbols for real numbers.

Examples

	Column A	Column B	Answers
	$a > 0$		
	$x > 0$		
E1.	$a - x$	$a + x$	(A) ● (C) (D)
E2.	The average of 17, 19, 21, 23	The average of 16, 18, 20, 22	● (B) (C) (D)

DO NOT MARK CHOICE (E) FOR THESE QUESTIONS. THERE ARE ONLY FOUR ANSWER CHOICES.

Practice Examination 4   485

	Column A	Column B
	$r = -3$	
1.	$r^3 + 5r^2 - 6r + 4$	$3r^2 - 7r - 8$

	Column A	Column B
	$x \neq 0$	
2.	x	$\dfrac{1}{x}$

| 3. | The average of a, b, and c | b |

Triangle with vertex C at top, right angle at A (labeled $3m°$), angle at C labeled $2m°$, vertex B at right.

Note: Figure not drawn to scale.

| 4. | $\angle ABC$ | $\angle ACB$ |

Three parallel lines a, b, c with a transversal creating angles s, t, u, v.

$a \parallel b \parallel c$

$\angle u > \angle v$

| 5. | s | t |

	Column A	Column B
	$R > r$	
6.	Circumference of circle with radius r	Area of circle with radius R

| | $s > t$ | |
| 7. | s^2 | t^2 |

Questions 8–10 refer to the figure below.

Figure with lines C and D crossing lines A and B; angles labeled a, b at upper intersection and e, c, d at lower intersections.

$C \parallel D$

$A \parallel B$

$a = 100°$

| 8. | $a + b$ | $b + d$ |

| 9. | 180 | $b + c$ |

| 10. | d | $180 - a$ |

$$\left(\dfrac{1}{2}\right)x - \left(\dfrac{1}{2}\right)a = 4$$

| 11. | x | a |

GO ON TO THE NEXT PAGE

	Column A	Column B
12.	6% of 200	7% of 300

Side AB = Side AC

	Column A	Column B
13.	∠A	∠B

Points: C(-2,3), D(3,4), A(-2,-1), B(4,-1)

	Column A	Column B
14.	AB	CD

$$A * B = \frac{A}{4} + 2B$$

	Column A	Column B
15.	$\left(\frac{1}{4}\right) * 2$	$5 * \left(\frac{1}{2}\right)$

Part 2: Student-Produced Response Questions

Directions: Solve each of these problems. Write the answer in the corresponding grid on the answer sheet and fill in the ovals beneath each answer you write. Here are some examples.

Answer: $\frac{3}{4}$ (= .75; show answer either way)

Answer: 325

Note: A mixed number such as $3\frac{1}{2}$ must be gridded as 7/2 or as 3.5. If gridded as "3 1/2," it will be read as "thirty-one halves."

Note: Either position is correct.

16. What is the ratio of 6 minutes to 6 hours?

17. At Ungerville High School, the ratio of girls to boys is 2:1. If $\frac{3}{5}$ of the boys are on a team and the remaining 40 boys are not, how many girls are in the school?

18. Jerry grew 5 inches in 1993, and 2 inches more in 1994 before reaching his final height of 5 feet 10 inches. What percentage of his final height did his 1993–1994 growth represent?

19. Seth bought $4\frac{5}{6}$ pounds of peanuts. He gave $\frac{1}{4}$ of his purchase to his sister. How many pounds of peanuts did Seth keep for himself?

20. If $p = 2r = 3s = 4t$, then $\frac{pr}{st} =$

21. $\sqrt{7+9+7+9+7+9+7+9} =$

DA and *EA* trisect angle *A*.

22. If $\angle DMC = 80°$ and $\angle ENC = 60°$, then angle A =
(Do not grid the degree symbol.)

23. $\dfrac{\frac{7}{8} + \frac{7}{8} + \frac{7}{8}}{\frac{8}{7} + \frac{8}{7} + \frac{8}{7}} =$

24. The average of 8 numbers is 6; the average of 6 other numbers is 8. What is the average of all 14 numbers?

25. If the ratio of $4a$ to $3b$ is 8 to 9, what is the ratio of $3a$ to $4b$?

STOP

END OF SECTION 4. IF YOU HAVE ANY TIME LEFT, GO OVER YOUR WORK IN THIS SECTION ONLY. DO NOT WORK IN ANY OTHER SECTION OF THE TEST.

SECTION 5

12 Questions • Time—15 Minutes

Directions: The two passages given below deal with a related topic. Following the passages are questions about the content of each passage or about the relationship between the two passages. Answer the questions based upon what is stated or implied in the passages and in any introductory material provided. Mark the letter of your choice on your answer sheet.

Questions 1–12 are based on the following passages.

In 1848, a Woman's Rights Convention was held at Seneca Falls, New York. Sponsored by Lucretia Mott, Martha Wright, Elizabeth Cady Stanton, and Mary Ann McClintock, the convention featured the creation of a "Declaration of Sentiments," a document based on American's Declaration of Independence, in which men's unfair dominion over women was described. Crusader for the rights of African-Americans and women, Sojourner Truth was born a slave on a Dutch estate around 1797 and named Isabella. The first edition of her biography was written by Olive Gilbert, a white friend of hers, and published in 1850.

Passage 1—Declaration of Sentiments

The history of mankind is a history of repeated injuries and usurpations on the part of man toward woman, having in direct object the establishment of an absolute tyranny over her. To prove this, let facts be (5) submitted to a candid world.

He has never permitted her to exercise her inalienable right to the elective franchise.

He has compelled her to submit to laws, in the formation of which she had no voice. He has withheld (10) from her rights which are given to the most ignorant and degraded men—both natives and foreigners.

Having deprived her of this first right of a citizen, the elective franchise, thereby leaving her without representation in the halls of legislation, he has oppressed her (15) on all sides.

He has made her, if married, in the eye of the law, civilly dead.

He has taken from her all right in property, even to the wages she earns.

(20) He has made her, morally, an irresponsible being, as she can commit many crimes with impunity, provided they be done in the presence of her husband. In the covenant of marriage, she is compelled to promise obedience to her husband, he becoming, to all (25) intents and purposes, her master—the law giving him power to deprive her of her liberty, and to administer chastisement.

He has so framed the laws of divorce, as to what shall be the proper causes, and in the case of separation, to (30) whom the guardianship of the children shall be given, as to be wholly regardless of the happiness of women—the law, in all cases, going upon a false supposition of the supremacy of man, and giving all power into his hands.

(35) After depriving her of all rights as a married woman, if single, and the owner of property, he has taxed her to support a government which recognizes her only when her property can be made profitable to it.

He has endeavored, in every way that he could, to (40) destroy her confidence in her own powers, to lessen her self-respect, and to make her willing to lead a dependent and abject life.

Passage 2—Sojourner Truth

After emancipation had been decreed by the State, some years before the time fixed for its consummation, (45) Isabella's master told her if she would do well, and be faithful, he would give her "free papers," one year before she was legally free by statute. In the year 1826, she had a badly diseased hand, which greatly diminished her usefulness; but on the arrival of July 4, 1827, (50) the time specified for her receiving her "free papers," she claimed the fulfillment of her master's promise; but he refused granting it, on account (as he alleged) of the loss he had sustained by her hand. She plead that she had worked all the time, and done many things she was not

(55) wholly able to do, although she knew she had been less useful than formerly; but her master remained inflexible. Her very faithfulness probably operated against her now, and he found it less easy than he thought to give up the profits of his faithful Bell, who had so long done
(60) him efficient service.

But Isabella inwardly determined that she would remain quietly with him only until she had spun his wool—about one hundred pounds—and then she would leave him, taking the rest of the time to herself. "Ah!"
(65) she says, with emphasis that cannot be written, "the slaveholders are TERRIBLE for promising to give you this or that, or such and such a privilege, if you will do thus and so; and when the time of fulfillment comes, and one claims the promise, they, forsooth, recollect noth-
(70) ing of the kind; and you are, like as not, taunted with being a LIAR; or, at best, the slave is accused of not having performed *his* part or condition of the contract." "Oh!" said she, "I have felt as if I could not live through the *operation* sometimes. Just think of us! *so* eager for
(75) our pleasures, and just foolish enough to keep feeding and feeding ourselves up with the idea that we should get what had been thus fairly promised; and when we think it is almost in our hands, find ourselves flatly denied! Just think! how *could* we bear it?"

1. Both passages concern themselves with a kind of
   (A) tyranny
   (B) liberation
   (C) government
   (D) security
   (E) autonomy

2. The word *injuries* in line 2 of the Declaration of Sentiments might be replaced with the word
   (A) bruises
   (B) prejudice
   (C) mistreatment
   (D) wounds
   (E) shocks

3. The Declaration of Sentiments compares the status of women with those of "ignorant and degraded men" (lines 10–11) in order to
   (A) condemn people with weak bodies
   (B) poke fun at a segment of the population
   (C) argue that even undereducated men deserve a chance to express their opinions
   (D) state that they are equals
   (E) highlight the ludicrousness of women's position in society

4. When the Declaration of Sentiments states in line 17 that a married woman is "civilly dead," this probably means that
   (A) the law ignores married women
   (B) married women must treat their husbands courteously
   (C) women must give up their lives to their husbands
   (D) a man may kill his wife with impunity
   (E) married women must not show undue emotion

5. The word *her* as used throughout the Declaration of Sentiments refers to
   (A) an emancipated woman
   (B) a married woman
   (C) any woman
   (D) the author of the Declaration
   (E) a woman who is old enough to vote

6. According to the Declaration of Sentiments, women are only seen as useful to the government when they
   (A) promote discord
   (B) can provide it with profit
   (C) vote
   (D) marry
   (E) earn wages

7. In line 53, the word "sustained" most nearly means
   (A) experienced
   (B) maintained
   (C) improved
   (D) nourished
   (E) made plentiful

8. The narrative of Sojourner Truth implies that slaveholders' cruelty is based on
    (A) twisted emotions
    (B) desire for profit
    (C) fear of confrontation
    (D) racism
    (E) misunderstanding

9. Truth's main objection to her slaveholder is to his
    (A) harassment
    (B) brutality
    (C) unfairness
    (D) bigotry
    (E) rudeness

10. When Truth refers to "us" in line 74, she means
    (A) African-Americans
    (B) slaveholders
    (C) women
    (D) writers
    (E) slaves

11. The tone of both passages might be described as
    (A) resigned
    (B) calculating
    (C) fierce
    (D) embittered
    (E) hopeful

12. Would you expect Sojourner Truth to approve of the Declaration of Sentiments?
    (A) No, because the Declaration clearly represents only white women.
    (B) No, because slavery and sexual oppression have little in common.
    (C) Yes, because she, too, is taxed to support a government that does not represent her.
    (D) Yes, because she, too, is willing to be dependent.
    (E) Yes, because she understands as well as anyone what it means to have no rights.

STOP

END OF SECTION 5. IF YOU HAVE ANY TIME LEFT, GO OVER YOUR WORK IN THIS SECTION ONLY. DO NOT WORK IN ANY OTHER SECTION OF THE TEST.

SECTION 6

10 Questions • Time—15 Minutes

Directions: Solve the following problems using any available space on the page for scratchwork. On your answer sheet fill in the choice which best corresponds to the correct answer.

Notes: The figures accompanying the problems are drawn as accurately as possible unless otherwise stated in specific problems. Again, unless otherwise stated, all figures lie in the same plane. All numbers used in these problems are real numbers. Calculators are permitted for this test.

---

1. In the figure above, BW is one-third the length of AB. What is the area of triangle ACW?

    (A) 4
    (B) 5
    (C) 6
    (D) 8
    (E) 9

2. Of the following, the one that is *not* equivalent to 376 is

    (A) $(3 \times 100) + (6 \times 10) + 16$
    (B) $(2 \times 100) + (17 \times 10) + 6$
    (C) $(3 \times 100) + (7 \times 10) + 6$
    (D) $(2 \times 100) + (16 \times 10) + 6$
    (E) $(2 \times 100) + (7 \times 10) + 106$

3. Emily can pack 6 cartons in h days. At this rate she can pack $3h$ cartons in how many days?

    (A) 18
    (B) $2h$
    (C) h^2
    (D) $\dfrac{h^2}{2}$
    (E) $2h^2$

4. What is the total length of fencing needed to enclose a rectangular area 46 feet by 34 feet (3 ft. = 1 yd.)?

    (A) 26 yards 1 foot
    (B) $26\dfrac{2}{3}$ yards
    (C) 52 yards 2 feet
    (D) $53\dfrac{1}{3}$ yards
    (E) $37\dfrac{2}{3}$ yards

5. On an income of $15,000 a year, a clerk pays 15% in federal taxes and 10% of the remainder in state taxes. How much is left?

   (A) $9,750
   (B) $11,475
   (C) $12,750
   (D) $13,500
   (E) $14,125

6. $(x^a)^b =$

   (A) $x \cdot a \cdot b$
   (B) x^{a+b}
   (C) x^{ab}
   (D) $(ax)^b$
   (E) b^{xa}

7. A is 300 miles from B. The path of all points equidistant from A and B can best be described as

   (A) a line ∥ to AB and 150 miles north of AB
   (B) a transverse segment cutting through AB at a 45° angle
   (C) a circle with AB as its diameter
   (D) the perpendicular bisector of AB
   (E) the line AB

8. If $y = x^2$, $z = x^3$, and $w = xy$ then $y^2 + z^2 + w^2 =$

   (A) $x^4 + x^6 + x^{10}$
   (B) $x^4 + 2x^5$
   (C) $x^4 + 2x^6$
   (D) $2x^9$
   (E) $2x^{10}$

9. The number missing in the series 2, 6, 12, 20, ?, 42, 56, 72 is

   (A) 24
   (B) 30
   (C) 36
   (D) 38
   (E) 40

10. The square and the equilateral triangle in the above drawing both have a side of 6. If the triangle is placed inside the square with one side of the triangle directly on one side of the square, what is the area of the shaded region?

    (A) $36 - 18\sqrt{3}$
    (B) $36 - 9\sqrt{3}$
    (C) $36 - 6\sqrt{3}$
    (D) $36 + 6\sqrt{3}$
    (E) $36 + 9\sqrt{3}$

STOP

END OF SECTION 6. IF YOU HAVE ANY TIME LEFT, GO OVER YOUR WORK IN THIS SECTION ONLY. DO NOT WORK IN ANY OTHER SECTION OF THE TEST.

PRACTICE EXAMINATION 4
Answer Key

Section 1: Verbal

1. B	8. D	15. C	22. D	29. D
2. D	9. B	16. B	23. A	30. C
3. E	10. E	17. A	24. B	31. D
4. B	11. D	18. E	25. A	32. D
5. A	12. A	19. B	26. D	33. B
6. E	13. C	20. C	27. E	34. C
7. E	14. C	21. C	28. C	35. D

Section 2: Math

1. C	6. E	11. B	16. E	21. A
2. C	7. A	12. C	17. B	22. A
3. D	8. A	13. B	18. C	23. E
4. C	9. E	14. E	19. B	24. A
5. E	10. A	15. A	20. C	25. B

Section 3: Verbal

1. B	8. D	15. A	22. A	29. A
2. A	9. C	16. E	23. B	30. D
3. D	10. B	17. B	24. B	31. E
4. A	11. C	18. C	25. B	
5. C	12. D	19. A	26. C	
6. B	13. A	20. C	27. E	
7. A	14. C	21. E	28. A	

Section 4: Math

Part 1

1. C	4. A	7. D	10. C	13. D
2. D	5. A	8. A	11. A	14. A
3. D	6. D	9. B	12. B	15. A

Part 2

16. $\frac{1}{60}$
17. 200
18. 10
19. $\frac{29}{8} = 3.63$
20. 6
21. 8
22. 60
23. .766
24. $\frac{48}{7} = 6.86$
25. $\frac{1}{2}$

Section 5: Verbal
1. A
2. C
3. E
4. A
5. C
6. B
7. A
8. B
9. C
10. E
11. D
12. E

Section 6: Math
1. C
2. D
3. D
4. D
5. B
6. C
7. D
8. C
9. B
10. B

PRACTICE EXAMINATION 4
Explanatory Answers

Note: A 🖩 following a math answer explanation indicates that a calculator could be helpful in solving that particular problem.

Section 1

1. **(B)** The word *finally* suggests that the woman agreed to see the farm only after being *importuned*, or repeatedly urged, to do so by her family.

2. **(D)** The ghost urges, or *exhorts*, Hamlet to take revenge.

3. **(E)** Concern for the children's safety would logically lead a father to *inculcate* (teach by constant repetition) in them a *wary* attitude toward strangers.

4. **(B)** With a life full of hardship and poverty, they are surely *inured* (accustomed) to discomfort.

5. **(A)** The author probably withdrew from the project because he was displeased with the novel's *adaptation*, or change required to turn the novel into a television program.

6. **(E)** *Vacillation* means fluctuation of mind or changing from one purpose to another.

7. **(E)** A smile could be *devastating* or *bright*, but it could logically only *dazzle* all those who saw it.

8. **(D)** The word *although* indicates that the blanks will be filled by opposites as in choice (D): *penurious* (stingy) and *generous*.

9. **(B)** To disarm someone in a single motion requires sure and swift, or *deft*, action.

10. **(E)** The platypus, with its curious duckbill and habit of laying eggs, is a biological *anomaly* (abnormality).

11. **(D)** A *teacher* gives *instruction*, and a *guard* gives *protection*.

12. **(A)** An *usher* shows people to their seats in a *theater*, just as a *conductor* shows people to their seats on the *train*.

13. **(C)** A *rink* is a place to *skate*; a *bed* is a place to *repose*.

14. **(C)** A *sapling* is a young *tree*, and a *puppy* is a young *dog*.

15. **(C)** To *fret* is by definition not to *relax*, and to *fight* is necessarily not to *submit*.

16. **(B)** To *stutter* impedes *talking*; to *stumble* impedes *walking*.

17. **(A)** *Damage* is a much less intense degree of destruction than *demolish*. Similarly, *whimper* is much less intense than *wail*.

18. **(E)** A *hose* is used to conduct *water*, just as a *chimney* is used to conduct *smoke*.

19. **(B)** *Exercise* is a way to build *strength*. *Practice* is a way to build *skill*.

20. **(C)** A *sergeant* trains *soldiers* just as a *coach* trains *players*.

21. **(C)** *Volatile* means lacking in *stability* just as *wanton* means lacking in *restraint*.

22. **(D)** A *scientist* works in a *laboratory* and a *teacher* works in a *classroom*.

23. **(A)** To be *jocular* is to lack *solemnity*. To be *latent* is to lack *visibility*.

24. **(B)** The Power of Place is the main subject of the passage. Dolores Hayden (D) is important only because she is thdWñounder and spokesperson of this organization; while she would probably agree with answers (A) and (C), those answers are too broad.

25. **(A)** The juxtaposition in lines 1 and 2 of "outsider" and "Los Angeles" indicates that "civic" should be taken in its original sense of "having to do with the city." That the city's feelings might be "bruised" by a criticism suggests that these feelings consist of a loyalty to allegiance to one's home city.

26. **(D)** According to the author, the modernization of Los Angeles threatens to rob the city of its naturally diverse cultural history.

27. **(E)** See lines 2–4 and 9–10. Answers (A) and (B), while they may reflect Hayden's opinions, are not what she means while quoting Stein's statement.

28. **(C)** This answer summarizes Hayden's point in saying that 98 percent of landmarks memorialize Anglo-Americans while less than half the population of Los Angeles is Anglo-American (lines 18–22).

29. **(D)** Answer I is supported by the contrast between the "landholders, bankers, business leaders" of line 24 and the workers described in the fifth paragraph. Answer II is supported in lines 28–30. Answer III is not supported in the passage; in fact, Hayden's respect for the economic contributions of working people is mentioned in lines 31–35.

30. **(C)** This is the point of the third paragraph, especially lines 34–36.

31. **(D)** See lines 41–43.

32. **(D)** The author describes the site as "ethnically evocative" (line 52) and identifies several different ethnic groups that worked there.

33. **(B)** This answer summarizes Hayden's views as they are expressed not only in lines 31–38 but throughout the passage. "Placemaking" is intended to make the site "more redolent of its past" (line 66), and the point of this redolence, as described by the first three paragraphs, is to give Los Angeles a better sense of place.

34. **(C)** The tree is a miracle only in contrast to its surroundings as described in lines 69–72.

35. **(D)** Chances are that a monument such as city hall garners significant attention from the mainstream community. After all, it is an official government landmark. The other listed attributes are more likely to get lost in the shuffle.

Section 2

1. **(C)** This is easily solved by plugging in the numbers:
$$(4-1) \times (5-2) \times (6-3) = 3 \times 3 \times 3 = 27$$

2. **(C)** If $2n$ is an even number, $2n+1$ is odd.

3. **(D)** Solving the equation for x gives x a value of $-\frac{1}{2}$, and $x^2 = \left(-\frac{1}{2}\right)^2 = \frac{1}{4}$.

4. **(C)** Setting up a ratio,
$$\frac{88 \text{ ft./sec.}}{60 \text{ mi./hr.}} = \frac{1100 \text{ ft./sec.}}{x \text{ mi./hr.}}$$
$$88x = (1100)(60)$$
$$x = 750 \text{ mi./hr.}$$

5. **(E)** Setting up a ratio,
$$\frac{\frac{1}{4} \text{ in.}}{12 \text{ in.}} = \frac{3\frac{3}{8} \text{ in.}}{x \text{ in.}}$$
$$\left(\frac{1}{4}\right)x = (12)\left(3\frac{3}{8}\right)$$
$$x = 162 \text{ in.} = 13\frac{1}{2} \text{ ft.}$$

6. **(E)** Let x be the second angle. The first angle is $3x$, and the third angle is $x+20$. The angles of a triangle must equal 180°, so $3x + x + (x+20) = 180$, $5x = 160$, and $x = 32$.

7. **(A)** By substitution, $x + y^2 - \frac{1}{2}$ becomes
$$\frac{3}{2} + (2)^2 - \frac{1}{2} = \frac{3}{2} + 4 - \frac{1}{2} =$$
$$\frac{3}{2} + \frac{8}{2} - \frac{1}{2} = \frac{10}{2} = 5.$$

8. **(A)** $14 + 17 = 31$ Therefore, there are 4 students who must be enrolled in all three courses. $\frac{4}{27}$ is slightly larger than $\frac{4}{28}$. The answer must be slightly larger than $\frac{1}{7}$, which is $14\frac{2}{7}\%$.

Practice Examination 4   497

9. **(E)** The volume of the container is the area of the circle at one end times the height. The area of the circle is $A = \pi 7^2 \approx 154$ sq. in. The volume is $154 \times 6 = 924$ cu. in. The capacity of the tank is 924 cu. in. ÷ 231 cu. in./gal. = 4 gallons.

10. **(A)**
$$\frac{1}{x+y} = 6$$
$$\frac{1}{2+y} = 6$$
$$6(2+y) = 1$$
$$12 + 6y = 1$$
$$6y = -11$$
$$y = -\frac{11}{6}$$

11. **(B)** If there are 28.35 grams per ounce, then 28.35 grams per ounce ÷ 1,000 grams per kilogram = .02835 kilograms per ounce. Since there are 16 ounces to the pound, .02835 kilograms per ounce times 16 ounces per pound = 0.45 kilograms per pound.

12. **(C)** The square root of .16 is .4, so .16 is a perfect square. The square root of 16 is 4, so 16 is a perfect square. The square root of 1,600 is 40, so 1,600 is a perfect square. The square root of .0016 is .04, so .0016 is a perfect square. Only 1.6 is not a perfect square.

13. **(B)** Let's start by pointing out that we do not know the size of angles 1, 2, 3, or 4. We do know that the two lines are parallel and therefore 8 and 6 can be moved to their corresponding locations on the top line. Since all straight lines have 180 degrees, III and IV each equal 180 degrees.

14. **(E)** The maximum value is obtained by making x as large as possible and y as small as possible. Thus, we set up a fraction $\frac{\frac{1}{2}}{\frac{2}{3}} = \frac{1}{2} \times \frac{4}{3} = \frac{4}{6} = \frac{2}{3}$.

15. **(A)** Start by finding the area of the largest circle. The radius of the largest circle is 9, so the area is 81π. The middle circle has a radius of 5, so the area is 25π. The smallest circle has a radius of 2, so the area is 4π. To find the shaded region, subtract the smaller circle from the middle and get 21π. The fraction is thus $\frac{21\pi}{81\pi}$, which can be reduced to $\frac{7}{27}$.

16. **(E)** The answer can quickly be obtained by using a numerical example. Let $n = 5$ and $d = 2$.

   I. $\frac{2}{5}$
   II. $\frac{3}{6}$
   III. $\frac{1}{4}$
   IV. $\frac{5}{2}$
   V. $\frac{4}{1}$

   $\frac{1}{4} < \frac{2}{5} < \frac{3}{6} < \frac{5}{2} < 4$

17. **(B)** Let the time the train is scheduled to arrive be t. At 40 mph the train arrives in $t + \frac{10}{60} = t + \frac{1}{6}$ hours. At 30 mph the train takes $t + \frac{16}{60} = t + \frac{4}{15}$ hours. The distance is the speed times the time.

$$40\left(t + \frac{1}{6}\right) = 30\left(t + \frac{4}{15}\right)$$
$$40t + \frac{40}{6} = 30t + 8$$
$$10t = 8 - \frac{40}{6}$$
$$10t = 1\frac{1}{3} \text{ hr} = 80 \text{ min.}$$
$$t = 8 \text{ min.}$$

The distance between towns is:
$$d = (40 \text{ mph})\left(\frac{8}{60} + \frac{10}{60}\right) \text{ hr.}$$
$$= 40 \times \frac{18}{60}$$
$$= 12 \text{ miles}$$

18. **(C)** When you are given the diagonal of a square, you can find the length of the side by dividing the diagonal by 2 and multiplying by $\sqrt{2}$.

19. **(B)** $\angle TSP = 60°$
Since $PSR = 90°$, $\angle TSR = 90 - 60 = 30°$
Since $TS = PS = SR$, $\angle RTS = \angle TRS$. Thus,
$$\angle TRS = \frac{1}{2}(180° - 30°) = \frac{1}{2}(150°) = 75°.$$

20. **(C)**

Through point K, draw KM parallel to PQ and RS. Then

$\angle x = \angle MKV + \angle MKT$

$\angle MKV = \angle KVS = 180 - 130 = 50°$

$\angle MKT = \angle QTK = 60°$

$\angle x = 60° + 50° = 110°$

21. **(A)** Draw OP. Then in right triangle OPS,

$OP^2 = PS^2 + OS^2 = 6^2 + 8^2 = 10^2$.
$OP = 10$.

Then $\widehat{QR} = \frac{1}{4} \cdot 2\pi r = \frac{1}{4} \cdot 2\pi \cdot 10 = 5\pi$.

22. **(A)**

The 2-inch ice cube will fit only in the 8-inch by 4-inch by 4-inch part of the compartment. The upper inch cannot be used.

Hence, $\frac{8 \times 4 \times 4}{2 \times 2 \times 2} = 16$ cubes.

23. **(E)** Since it takes Paul 2 hours to paint 1 fence, he paints $\frac{1}{2}$ of the fence in one hour. Fred paints $\frac{1}{3}$ of the fence per hour. Together their speed is $\frac{1}{2} + \frac{1}{3} = \frac{5}{6}$ fence/hr. The time to paint this fence working together is 1 fence ÷ $\frac{5}{6}$ fence/hr. = 1.2 hours.

24. **(A)** $\frac{3}{4}$ evaporates the second day, therefore, there is $\frac{1}{4}$ of the $\frac{2}{3}$ of liquid left after evaporation the first day. $\frac{1}{4}$ of $\frac{2}{3} = \frac{1}{6}$, so $\frac{1}{6}$ of the original contents remains after two days.

25. **(B)** The time it takes the driver to arrive at her destination is 60 miles ÷ 40 miles per hour = $1\frac{1}{2}$ hours. The time it takes to return is 60 miles ÷ 30 miles per hour = 2 hours, making the total time for this 120-mile trip $1\frac{1}{2} + 2 = 3\frac{1}{2}$ hours. The average speed for the entire trip is 120 miles ÷ $3\frac{1}{2}$ hours = $34\frac{2}{7}$ miles per hour.

Section 3

1. **(B)** Acting together, those involved would each be *responsible* for an *element*.

2. **(A)** Unwise *neglect* during someone's education could result in *ignorance*.

3. **(D)** A conformist is conventional, acting in accordance with the prevailing customs. Children who are conventional are likely to *ostracize* (exclude) classmates who are *different* in behavior or dress.

4. **(A)** The date chosen for a king's coronation would most likely be *propitious* (lucky).

5. **(C)** A poem dripping with venom is apt to be *redolent* with (suggestive of) scorn.

6. **(B)** If the rites were kept secret, the members never *divulged* (revealed) them. Furthermore, fraternity rites are very likely to be *esoteric* (known to only a select few).

7. **(A)** A composer who praised the work of a musician he detested would be considered *magnanimous* (extremely generous).

8. **(D)** *Goodwill* is a genuine asset, but it is necessarily *intangible* (incapable of being touched in the physical sense).

9. **(C)** Clearly, the law's actual result was different from its *ostensible* (apparent) purpose. By curtailing false advertising, it also tended to *circumscribe* (limit) free speech.

10. **(B)** An *awl* is used to *puncture*, and a *cleaver* is used to *cut*.

11. **(C)** A *jungle* is characteristically *lush*; a *desert* is characteristically *barren*.

12. **(D)** *Hands* may become *gnarled* (knotted and twisted) with age, just as *brows* may become *creased* (wrinkled or ridged) with age.

13. **(A)** A *planet rotates* on its axis just as a *top spins*.

14. **(C)** *Milk* that *spoils* loses its original freshness. *Wood* that *rots* deteriorates from its original condition.

15. **(A)** Something *munificent* is characterized by great *generosity*. Something *dolorous* is characterized by great *sorrow*.

16. **(E)** According to the first paragraph, the bear "changes its haunts with the seasons" in order to obtain "suitable food" and security.

17. **(B)** This is the only possible conclusion one can reach among those listed. Nothing indicates that Audubon hunts (A), and he never denies that bears are dangerous (D).

18. **(C)** Low, rich lands bordering a river are likely to be composed largely of river-deposited sediments.

19. **(A)** The bears scratch bark with their teeth and claws, but they do not eat it. Each of the other choices is specifically mentioned.

20. **(C)** Lines 60–61 puts forth Audubon's theory. Others, he says, believe in theories (A), (B), and (E).

21. **(E)** Audubon draws back and addresses the reader directly in lines 32–33, remarking that "you well know" and "you also know" about bears' honey eating and ability to climb.

22. **(A)** The first comparison comes in lines 6–10 and the second comes at the end of the passage, in lines 58–65.

23. **(B)** Audubon makes much of the positive traits of the bear, focusing on its strength and pragmatism. He brushes over any indications that bears are fearsome (A) or alarming (D).

24. **(B)** A careful reading of paragraph 1 will tell you this. Although (B) and (C) are true in some cases, they have nothing to do with the opinion of the author.

25. **(B)** Whether or not you know this word in another context, you should be able to comprehend its meaning by reading the surrounding passage. The word is used to describe a plant with an extremely short life cycle.

26. **(C)** Not all herbaceous plants are annuals; line 28 refers to biennial herbaceous plants, and lines 36–48 cover herbaceous perennials. Thus statement 1 is false. Only very short-lived annuals are called *ephemeral*. Thus, statement III is false. Since only II is correct, the answer is (C).

27. **(E)** The definition of *biennial* appears in paragraph 3.

28. **(A)** This is a key idea in the passage, most of which deals with the five characteristic life spans of plants and their respective differences and similarities.

29. **(A)** The paragraph deals mainly with suffrutescent shrubs, which fall somewhere between herbaceous perennials and true shrubs.

30. **(D)** According to line 55, a woody perennial is a tree or shrub. Of the four choices given, only an oak fits this definition.

31. **(E)** Since it is the end of the eight-state life cycle, it should be easy to determine the meaning of *senescent*.

Section 4
Part 1

1. **(C)** Substituting $r = -3$ into Column A, $(-3)^3 + 5(-3)^2 - 6(-3) + 4 = -27 + 45 + 18 + 4 = 40$ Doing the same for Column B, $3(-3)^2 - 7(-3) - 8 = 27 + 21 - 8 = 40$. Therefore, Columns A and B are equal.

2. **(D)** If $x > 1$ or $-1 < x < 0$, then any number $x > \frac{1}{x}$. But if $x < -1$ or $0 < x < 1$ then any number $x < \frac{1}{x}$. Therefore, it is not possible to tell which column is larger.

3. **(D)** Without knowing the value of any of the variables, it is impossible to make a determination.

4. **(A)** The angles of triangle *ABC* are $2m + 3m + 90° = 180°$. $5m = 90°$ and $m = 18°$. Angle *ACB* is $2m = 2 \times 18 = 36°$. Angle *ABC* is $3m = 3 \times 18 = 54°$. Thus, angle *ABC* is the larger angle.

5. **(A)** Since $a \parallel b \parallel c$ angle t = angle v, being opposite exterior angles. Therefore, since angle u > angle v, angle u > angle t. Also angle s = angle u, since they are opposite exterior angles. Therefore, $u = s > t$. Column A is the larger.

6. **(D)** The circumference of a circle with radius r is $2\pi r$. The area of a circle with radius R is πR^2. If $R > r > \sqrt{2}$, then $\pi R^2 > 2\pi r$. But if $0 < r < R < \sqrt{2}$, then $2\pi r > \pi R^2$. Therefore, it is not possible to tell which column is larger.

7. **(D)** If $s > t > 0$, then $s^2 > t^2$. But if $0 > s > t$, then $s^2 < t^2$. It is not possible to tell which column is the larger.

8. **(A)** a and b are equal, so $a + b = 2a = 2(100°) = 200°$. b and d are supplementary angles, so $b + d = 180°$. Column A is larger than Column B.

9. **(B)** In Column B, $a = b = c$, so $b + c = 100° + 100° = 200°$, which is more than Column A's value of $180°$.

10. **(C)** Since a and d are supplementary angles, $d = 180° - a$.

11. **(A)** $\left(\frac{1}{2}\right)x - \left(\frac{1}{2}\right)a = 4$. Multiplying both sides of the equation by 2, $x - a = 8$, and $x = 8 + a$. Adding 8 to any real number will make it larger; therefore, x is the larger number.

12. **(B)** The values of Column A and Column B are 12 and 21 respectively. Therefore, Column B is the larger.

13. **(D)** Since side AB = side Ac, $\triangle ABC$ is isosceles, and it can be assumed that $\angle B$ and $\angle C$ are equal. This information, though, does not provide any clues as to which is bigger, $\angle A$ or $\angle B$.

14. **(A)** It is obvious that the length of AB is 6. The length of CD is $\sqrt{[3-(-2)]^2 + (4-3)^2} = \sqrt{26}$, or approximately 5.10. Therefore, AB is longer.

15. **(A)** The value of Columns A and B are $4\frac{1}{16}$ and $2\frac{1}{4}$ respectively. Therefore, Column A is larger than Column B.

Part 2

16. $\dfrac{6 \text{ minutes}}{6 \text{ hours}} = \dfrac{6 \text{ minutes}}{6(60) \text{ minutes}} = \dfrac{1}{60}$

17. $\frac{2}{5}$(Boys) = 40

    $\therefore$ Boys = 100.

    There are twice as many girls as boys.

    $\therefore$ girls = 200.

18. First convert Jerry's final height to inches:
    $5 \times 12 = 60 \quad 60 + 10 = 70$
    Jerry's 7-inch growth is 10% of 70 inches.

19. He kept $\frac{3}{4}$ of his peanuts. $\frac{3}{4}(4\frac{5}{6}) = \frac{3}{4}(\frac{29}{6}) = \frac{29}{8} = 3\frac{5}{8} = 3.625$.

    Use 3.63.

20. $\dfrac{pr}{st} = \dfrac{p\left(\frac{p}{2}\right)}{\left(\frac{p}{3}\right)\left(\frac{p}{4}\right)} = \dfrac{\frac{p^2}{2}}{\frac{p^2}{12}} = \dfrac{p^2}{2} \cdot \dfrac{12}{p^2} = 6$

21. $\sqrt{7+9+7+9+7+9+7+9} = \sqrt{4(7+9)} = \sqrt{4(16)} = \sqrt{64} = 8$

22.

$x + y = 60$ (Exterior angle = sum of the 2 remote interior angles.)

$2x + y = 80$ (Exterior angle = sum of the 2 remote interior angles.)

$$2x + y = 80$$
$$-(x + y = 60)$$
$$x = 20$$

$\therefore \angle A = 3x = 60$

23. $\dfrac{\frac{7}{8}+\frac{7}{8}+\frac{7}{8}}{\frac{8}{7}+\frac{8}{7}+\frac{8}{7}} = \dfrac{3\left(\frac{7}{8}\right)}{3\left(\frac{8}{7}\right)} = \dfrac{\frac{7}{8}}{\frac{8}{7}}$

$= \frac{7}{8} \cdot \frac{7}{8} = \frac{49}{64} = .766$

24. Average = $\dfrac{\text{Sum}}{\text{Number of items}}$

$\therefore$ Sum = (Avg.)(No. of items)

$48 = (8)(6)$
$+\ 48 = (6)(8)$
$\ \ 96$

Average = $\frac{96}{14} = 6\frac{6}{7} = \frac{48}{7} = 6.86$

25. $\dfrac{4a}{3b} = \dfrac{8}{9}$

Multiply each side of the equation by $\frac{9}{16}$.

$\dfrac{\cancel{4}a}{\cancel{3}b} \cdot \dfrac{\cancel{9}}{\cancel{16}} = \dfrac{\cancel{8}}{\cancel{9}} \cdot \dfrac{\cancel{9}}{\cancel{16}}$

(1, 3, 1, 1 / 1, 4, 1, 2)

$\dfrac{3a}{4b} = \dfrac{1}{2}$

Section 5

1. **(A)** The Declaration speaks of the tyranny of men over women; Truth speaks of the tyranny of the slaveholder over his slaves.

2. **(C)** The word *injuries* signifies general mistreatment of women by men. The forms of mistreatment that are listed are primarily legal and social; "bruises," "prejudice," "wounds," and "shocks" are never mentioned.

3. **(E)** The Declaration does not equate the two, as is argued in choice (D). The comparison is made to argue that if undereducated foreigners have basic rights, so too should the average American woman.

4. **(A)** "In the eye of the law" is the clue here; a woman who marries is dead in the law's eyes, or ignored by the law.

5. **(C)** Look back at the first paragraph and you will see that the authors of the Declaration are referring to the tyranny of man over woman throughout history. *He* is all men; *her* refers to all women.

6. **(B)** The proof of this is in lines 35-38, wherein the woman is taxed to "support a government which recognizes her only when her property can be made profitable to it."

7. **(A)** In this context, *sustained* means *experienced*. The master experienced a loss in productivity because of the slave's diseased hand.

8. **(B)** This opinion is implied in lines 52–53 ("the loss he had sustained by her hand"); and 58–59 ("to give up the profits of his faithful Bell . . . ").

9. **(C)** We see no signs of brutality (D), but Truth's owner is clearly pictured as unfair. He breaks his promises despite Isabella's faithfulness.

10. **(E)** Truth is referring to those who are eager for freedom but foolish enough to believe that they will get it—slaves, in other words.

11. **(D)** The passages as cited cannot be considered *resigned* (A) or *hopeful* (E). Each is essentially a catalog of sins by an aggrieved victim.

12. **(E)** In fact, Sojourner Truth went on to work hard for the rights of women. Even if you did not know that, however, you could predict her approval based on the fact that her description of slavery parallels so thoroughly the Declaration's description of sexual oppression.

Section 6

1. **(C)** Area = $\frac{1}{2}bh$. The base is AW, which is $\frac{2}{3}$ of AB, or $\frac{2}{3}(9) = 6$. The height is 2.

$a = \frac{1}{2}(6)(2) = 6$.

2. **(D)** $(2 \times 100) + (16 \times 10) + 6 = 200 + 160 + 6 = 366$.

3. **(D)** This is a direct proportion $\frac{\text{cartons}}{\text{days}} \Rightarrow \frac{6}{h} = \frac{3h}{x}$

$$6x = 3h^2$$

$$x = \frac{h^2}{2}$$

4. **(D)** The perimeter of a 46' × 34' rectangle is 160 feet, which equals $53\frac{1}{3}$ yards.

5. **(B)** After the 15% deduction, $12,750 is left. After the 10% is deducted from $12,750, $11,475 is left. Note that you cannot simply deduct 25% from the $15,000.

6. **(C)** By definition, $\left(x^a\right)^b$ is the same as $x^{a \bullet b}$.

7. **(D)** The path of all points equidistant from two points is the perpendicular bisector of the segment which connects the two points. Therefore, the line that is perpendicular to AB and intersects it at 150 miles from A is the perpendicular bisector of AB (Remember, A and B are 300 miles apart.)

8. **(C)** $w = xy = x(x^2) = x^3$

$y^2 + z^2 + w^2 = (x^2)^2 + (x^3)^2 + (x^3)^2$

$= x^4 + x^6 + x^6 = x^4 + 2x^6$

9. **(B)** The difference between the numbers increases by 2; therefore, ? − 20 = 10, so ? = 30.

10. **(B)** The area of the square is 36. Since the triangle is equilateral, we can use the 30 - 60 - 90 rule to solve. By dropping a perpendicular we find the altitude to be $3\sqrt{3}$. Then the area of the triangle is $9\sqrt{3}$. Thus the shaded area is $36 - 9\sqrt{3}$.

COMPUTING YOUR SCORES ON PRACTICE EXAMINATION 4

Now that you've completed the fourth practice examination, it's time to check your progress. To get a sense of your scores on this exam, you need to compute individual verbal and mathematical raw scores. Once you have computed these, use the conversion scales in the section that follows to compute your SAT scaled scores (200–800). Keep in mind that these formulas have been simplified to give you a "quick and dirty" sense of where you are scoring, not a perfectly precise score.

To Compute Your Raw Scores:

1. Enter the number of correct answers for each verbal and mathematical reasoning section into the boxes marked "Number of Questions Correct."
2. Enter the number of incorrect answers (not blanks) for each verbal and mathematical reasoning section into the boxes marked "Number of Questions Incorrect."
3. Total the number correct and number incorrect.
4. Follow this formula: Take the total correct and minus one-quarter of the total incorrect. Round up in your favor to compute your Raw Score.

Verbal Section	Total Number of Questions	Number of Questions Correct	Number of Questions Incorrect
1	35		
3	31		
5	12		
Totals	78	Total Correct:	Total Incorrect:

Verbal Raw Score = Total Correct − ($\frac{1}{4}$ × Total Incorrect) = _____

Math Section	Total Number of Questions	Number of Questions Correct	Number of Questions Incorrect
2	25		
4	25		
6	10		
Totals	60	Total Correct:	Total Incorrect:

Math Raw Score = Total Correct − ($\frac{1}{4}$ × Total Incorrect) = _____

CONVERSION SCALES FOR PRACTICE EXAMINATION 4

VERBAL REASONING

Raw Score	Scaled Score	Raw Score	Scaled Score
75	800	35	520
70	800	30	480
65	760	25	440
60	710	20	410
55	670	15	370
50	620	10	340
45	590	5	290
40	550	0	230

MATHEMATICAL REASONING

Raw Score	Scaled Score	Raw Score	Scaled Score
60	800	25	510
55	760	20	480
50	690	15	440
45	650	10	410
40	610	5	340
35	580	0	200
30	550		

Although you now have some idea of what your scores would look like had they been scaled according to unofficial ETS standards, you will probably want to know how to interpret your Raw Scores in more familiar terms. If so, use the following Self-Evaluation Charts to see what your Raw Scores actually mean.

SELF-EVALUATION CHARTS

VERBAL REASONING: Raw Score

Excellent	60 – 75
Good	50 – 60
Average	30 – 50
Fair	20 – 30
Poor	0 – 20

MATHEMATICAL REASONING: Raw Score

Excellent	50 – 60
Good	40 – 50
Average	20 – 40
Fair	10 – 20
Poor	0 – 10

Practice Examination 5

Answer Sheet

If a section has fewer questions than answer ovals, leave the extra ovals blank.

Section 1

(Answer bubbles 1–40, options A B C D E)

Section 2

(Answer bubbles 1–40, options A B C D E)

Section 3

Answer spaces for Section 3 are on the back of this Answer Sheet.

Section 4

(Answer bubbles 1–40, options A B C D E)

Section 5

(Answer bubbles 1–15, options A B C D E)

Section 6

1. Ⓐ Ⓑ Ⓒ Ⓓ Ⓔ
2. Ⓐ Ⓑ Ⓒ Ⓓ Ⓔ
3. Ⓐ Ⓑ Ⓒ Ⓓ Ⓔ
4. Ⓐ Ⓑ Ⓒ Ⓓ Ⓔ
5. Ⓐ Ⓑ Ⓒ Ⓓ Ⓔ
6. Ⓐ Ⓑ Ⓒ Ⓓ Ⓔ
7. Ⓐ Ⓑ Ⓒ Ⓓ Ⓔ
8. Ⓐ Ⓑ Ⓒ Ⓓ Ⓔ
9. Ⓐ Ⓑ Ⓒ Ⓓ Ⓔ
10. Ⓐ Ⓑ Ⓒ Ⓓ Ⓔ
11. Ⓐ Ⓑ Ⓒ Ⓓ Ⓔ
12. Ⓐ Ⓑ Ⓒ Ⓓ Ⓔ
13. Ⓐ Ⓑ Ⓒ Ⓓ Ⓔ
14. Ⓐ Ⓑ Ⓒ Ⓓ Ⓔ
15. Ⓐ Ⓑ Ⓒ Ⓓ Ⓔ

Section 3

1. Ⓐ Ⓑ Ⓒ Ⓓ Ⓔ
2. Ⓐ Ⓑ Ⓒ Ⓓ Ⓔ
3. Ⓐ Ⓑ Ⓒ Ⓓ Ⓔ
4. Ⓐ Ⓑ Ⓒ Ⓓ Ⓔ
5. Ⓐ Ⓑ Ⓒ Ⓓ Ⓔ
6. Ⓐ Ⓑ Ⓒ Ⓓ Ⓔ
7. Ⓐ Ⓑ Ⓒ Ⓓ Ⓔ
8. Ⓐ Ⓑ Ⓒ Ⓓ Ⓔ
9. Ⓐ Ⓑ Ⓒ Ⓓ Ⓔ
10. Ⓐ Ⓑ Ⓒ Ⓓ Ⓔ
11. Ⓐ Ⓑ Ⓒ Ⓓ Ⓔ
12. Ⓐ Ⓑ Ⓒ Ⓓ Ⓔ
13. Ⓐ Ⓑ Ⓒ Ⓓ Ⓔ
14. Ⓐ Ⓑ Ⓒ Ⓓ Ⓔ
15. Ⓐ Ⓑ Ⓒ Ⓓ Ⓔ

Note: ONLY the answers entered on the grid are scored. Handwritten answers at the top of the column are NOT scored.

16. [grid-in]
17. [grid-in]
18. [grid-in]
19. [grid-in]
20. [grid-in]
21. [grid-in]
22. [grid-in]
23. [grid-in]
24. [grid-in]
25. [grid-in]

Practice Examination 5

SECTION 1

31 Questions • Time—30 Minutes

Directions: Each of the following questions consists of an incomplete sentence followed by five words or pairs of words. Choose that word or pair of words which, when substituted for the blank space or spaces, best completes the meaning of the sentence and mark the letter of your choice on your answer sheet.

Example:

In view of the extenuating circumstances and the defendant's youth, the judge recommended ---- .

(A) conviction
(B) a defense
(C) a mistrial
(D) leniency
(E) life imprisonment

Ⓐ Ⓑ Ⓒ ● Ⓔ

1. ---- the activities of her employees, the director refused to ---- their methods.

    (A) Disarming..condone
    (B) Applauding..question
    (C) Repudiating..reward
    (D) Handling..oversee
    (E) Approving..arrogate

2. The ---- soldier ---- at the idea that he was to go to battle.

    (A) luckless..rejoiced
    (B) youthful..retired
    (C) unwilling..recoiled
    (D) frail..relapsed
    (E) vigorous..repined

3. The ---- treatment of the zoo animals resulted in community-wide ---- .

    (A) curious..apathy
    (B) popular..neglect
    (C) critical..distention
    (D) adequate..revulsion
    (E) inhumane..criticism

4. Unlike gold, paper money has no ---- value; it is merely a representation of wealth.

    (A) financial
    (B) inveterate
    (C) economic
    (D) intrinsic
    (E) fiscal

5. His untimely death, at first thought to be due to a ---- fever, was later ---- to poison.

    (A) degenerative..relegated
    (B) debilitating..ascribed
    (C) raging..reduced
    (D) sanguine..abdicated
    (E) pernicious..prescribed

GO ON TO THE NEXT PAGE

6. To strengthen her client's case, the lawyer sought to put the ---- of the witness in doubt.
    (A) laxity
    (B) posterity
    (C) probity
    (D) onus
    (E) sensitivity

7. During the campaign, the politicians engaged in ---- debate, accusing each other of gross misdeeds.
    (A) capricious
    (B) acrimonious
    (C) altruistic
    (D) facetious
    (E) chimerical

8. His carelessness produced a(n) ---- report which left everyone ----.
    (A) intelligent..inept
    (B) ambiguous..confused
    (C) complete..mollified
    (D) acceptable..angry
    (E) insipid..inspired

9. Only a ---- person could be ---- to the suffering of the starving child.
    (A) churlish..receptive
    (B) dour..disposed
    (C) placid..detrimental
    (D) pious..uncivil
    (E) callous..oblivious

Directions: Each of the following questions consists of a capitalized pair of words followed by five pairs of words lettered A to E. The capitalized words bear some meaningful relationship to each other. Choose the lettered pair of words whose relationship is most similar to that expressed by the capitalized pair and mark its letter on your answer sheet.

Example:

DAY : SUN : :

(A) sunlight : daylight
(B) ray : sun
(C) night : moon
(D) heat : cold
(E) moon : star

Ⓐ Ⓑ ● Ⓓ Ⓔ

10. MICROSCOPE : INSTRUMENT : :

    (A) autobiography : novel
    (B) hammer : metal
    (C) necktie : accessory
    (D) oar : boat
    (E) telescope : stars

11. SKETCH : PAINTING : :

    (A) original : replica
    (B) camera : photo
    (C) scene : play
    (D) draft : thesis
    (E) illustration : cartoon

12. GATE : PLANE : :

    (A) latch : door
    (B) fence : yard
    (C) track : train
    (D) highway : car
    (E) driver : bus

13. SWEAR : OATH : :

    (A) laugh : smile
    (B) grab : boulder
    (C) sign : contract
    (D) neglect : demand
    (E) disregard : notice

14. SPELUNKER : CAVE : :

    (A) astronaut : space
    (B) teacher : student
    (C) miner : ore
    (D) pilot : airplane
    (E) bear : den

15. LAUGHTER : AMUSEMENT : :

    (A) vigor : optimism
    (B) squalor : filth
    (C) stealth : openness
    (D) pride : humility
    (E) pallor : illness

GO ON TO THE NEXT PAGE ➤

Questions 16–23 are based on the following passage.

The following speech has been adapted from A Citizen is Entitled to Vote *by Susan B. Anthony, a nineteenth-century campaigner for women's rights. At the time of the speech, women were not guaranteed the right to vote.*

Friends and fellow citizens:—I stand before you tonight under indictment for the alleged crime of having voted at the last presidential election, without having a lawful right to vote.

(5) It shall be my work this evening to prove to you that in thus voting, I not only committed no crime, but instead, simply exercised my *citizen's rights,* guaranteed to me and all United States citizens by the National Constitution, beyond the power of any State to (10) deny.

The preamble of the Federal Constitution says: "We, the people of the United States, in order to form a more perfect union, establish justice, insure *domestic tranquility,* provide for the common defense, promote (15) the general welfare, and secure the blessings of liberty to ourselves and our posterity, do ordain and establish this Constitution for the United States of America."

It was we, the people, not we, the white male citizens; but we, the whole people, who formed the (20) Union. And we formed it, not to give the blessings of liberty, but to secure them; not to the half of ourselves and the half of our posterity but to the whole people—women as well as men. And it is a down-right mockery to talk to women of their enjoyment of the blessings of (25) liberty while they are denied the use of the only means of securing them provided by this democratic-republican government—the ballot.

For any State to make sex a qualification that must ever result in the disfranchisement of one entire half of (30) the people is a violation of the supreme law of the land. By it the blessings of liberty are forever withheld from women and their female posterity. To them this government has no just powers derived from the consent of the governed. To them this government is not a (35) democracy. It is not a republic. It is a hateful oligarchy of sex. An oligarchy of learning, where the educated govern the ignorant, might be endured; but this oligarchy of sex, which makes father, brothers, husband, sons, the oligarchs or rulers over the mother and (40) sisters, the wife and daughters of every household—which ordains all men sovereigns, all women subjects, carries dissension, discord and rebellion into every home of the nation.

Webster's Dictionary defines a citizen as a person (45) in the United States, entitled to vote and hold office.

The only question left to be settled now is, Are women persons? And I hardly believe any of our opponents will have the hardihood to say they are not. Being persons, then, women are citizens; and no State (50) has a right to make any law, or to enforce any old law, that shall abridge their privileges or immunities. Hence, every discrimination against women in the constitutions and laws of the several States is today null and void.

16. Anthony talks as if she were a

    (A) defendant on trial
    (B) chairperson of a committee
    (C) legislator arguing for a new law
    (D) judge ruling at a trial
    (E) lawyer in court

17. Anthony broadens her appeal to her audience by showing how her case could affect all

    (A) existing laws
    (B) United States citizens
    (C) women
    (D) uneducated persons
    (E) children

18. Anthony quotes the preamble to the Constitution in order to

    (A) impress the audience with her intelligence
    (B) share common knowledge with her audience
    (C) point out which part of the preamble needs to be changed
    (D) add force to her argument
    (E) utilize a common legalistic trick

19. According to this speech, one reason for forming the Union was to

    (A) establish an aristocracy
    (B) limit the powers of the states
    (C) insure domestic harmony
    (D) draw up a Constitution
    (E) provide an international power

20. Anthony argues that a government that denies women the right to vote is not a democracy because its powers do not come from

    (A) the Constitution of the United States
    (B) the rights of the states
    (C) the consent of the governed
    (D) the vote of the majority
    (E) both houses of Congress

21. According to this speech, an oligarchy of sex would cause

    (A) women to rebel against the government
    (B) men to desert their families
    (C) poor women to lose hope
    (D) problems to develop in every home
    (E) the educated to rule the ignorant

22. In this speech, a citizen is *defined* as a person who has the right to vote and also the right to

    (A) change laws
    (B) acquire wealth
    (C) speak publicly
    (D) hold office
    (E) pay taxes

23. Anthony argues that state laws which discriminate against women are

    (A) being changed
    (B) null and void
    (C) helpful to the rich
    (D) supported only by men
    (E) supported by the Constitution

Questions 24–31 are based on the following passage.

The Indianists were musicians who borrowed freely from Native American motifs, rhythms, and musical structures to create a style of music that was unique. The passage outlines a history of this movement.

In the late nineteenth and early twentieth centuries, Euro-American composers known as the "Indianist" school chose and adapted elements of Indian song for their own work. Certain elements of Indian song styles
(5) could easily be used by these American-born but typically European-trained composers; other elements were not assimilated so easily into musical structures built on harmony and into a musical aesthetic that preferred an open-throated singing style. For example,
(10) a choral setting of the "Navajo War Dance," composed by Arthur Farwell (1872–1952), does not give the illusion of being an actual Navajo song. But the elements of Navajo style that caught Farwell's attention are clear: the sparse sound (few harmonies), the
(15) typical Navajo melodic skips, the pulsing beat.

Farwell got his ideas about Indian music from visits to southwestern reservations and from studying transcriptions of melodies collected by Alice Fletcher, a noted scholar of Omaha ceremonial traditions. Other
(20) composers also borrowed material from Fletcher's collections. The opening motif and basic melodic outline for perhaps the most famous Indianist composition, Charles Wakefield Cadman's "From the Land of the Sky Blue Waters" (published in 1901), are fairly
(25) literal reproductions of an Omaha flute call and love song in Fletcher's collection. But, unlike Farwell, Cadman did not try to replicate Indian sounds. He embedded the tune in pure Euro-American harmonic structures and rhythms. What seems more "Indian" is
(30) the song's narrative, describing a fearless captive maid courted by a flute player.

It is the text that marks many Indianist compositions, but the words do not usually reflect direct tribal experience. The Indianists were Romantics who seized
(35) on universal themes of love, war, and death cloaked in American Indian dress. One could not know from these compositions that native peoples had an everyday world of work, education, childbearing, and food preparation. The images selected for Indianist compo-
(40) sitions are just that: selections from a much broader array of experiences.

GO ON TO THE NEXT PAGE

As the Indianist composers selected sounds from or notions about Native American music for their purposes, native groups chose and adapted items from
(45) Euro-American musical practice. For example, while many drum groups use a wooden drum covered with rawhide, others choose a Western-style bass drum turned on its side; in its decoration and use, it becomes a Native American instrument. Similarly, many Cana-
(50) dian and Alaskan indigenous people have adopted the fiddle as a means of cultural self-expression. This adaptation reflects Euro-American influence, but native traditions are also represented, for example, in the way songs are introduced, typically identifying the
(55) occasion for the song's composition, and in accompanying activities, such as community feasts.

Perhaps the most far-reaching result of European contact is the development of a pantribal style. The very concept of "American Indian" is probably a
(60) product of contact. Though there were tribal confederacies prior to contact with Europeans, there was no need for an identity that spanned a continent to include tribal neighbors, rivals, and strangers—and no outside view to lump together people as diverse as the Kwakiutl,
(65) the Hopi, the Cuna, the Pawnee, and the Natchez. However, "American Indian" and "Native American" are now recognized concepts both inside and outside the societies so identified. Though tribal affiliation is a primary source of identification for most individu-
(70) als, sometimes the category "American Indian" takes precedence.

One drum group that includes Arizona Pima and Kansas Potawatomi singers, for example, performs songs representative of the Northern Plains rather than
(75) of the Southwest or Central Plains. Indeed, the wide-range Northern Plains–style song has come to represent "American Indian" music. Its characteristic forms, sung with tense throat and pulsating voice, make it most different from Euro-American singing, and the
(80) most difficult aural pattern for a non-Indian to assimilate, let alone replicate. By differentiating as much as possible from the dominant culture, by staking out that which is most markedly unique and displaying it to the outside world, native musical groups that perform in
(85) the Northern Plains style confirm their cultural identity.

24. In using and adapting Native American music, the Indianist composers attempted to

(A) reflect the gamut of Native American experiences
(B) popularize Native American music among Euro-Americans
(C) reproduce faithfully the style and content of the music they were copying
(D) address universal concerns using Native American motifs
(E) indicate their appreciation of the musical form

25. According to the passage, both Arthur Farwell and Charles Wakefield Cadman

(A) studied with Native American musicians
(B) attempted to reproduce Native American harmonies and rhythms
(C) used material from Alice Fletcher's collections
(D) studied musical composition in Europe
(E) adapted Native American melodies to European harmonies

26. The word *marks* in line 32 most nearly means

(A) grades
(B) distinguishes
(C) notices
(D) imprints
(E) symbolizes

27. The use of a Western-style drum by some Native American drum groups is an example of how some Native Americans have

(A) put aside their own traditions in favor of Euro-American forms of cultural expression
(B) adopted some Euro-American material goods, but not other aspects of Euro-American culture
(C) borrowed aspects of European culture and adapted these aspects to their own use
(D) adapted to the scarcity of traditional instruments by using instruments that are more readily available
(E) indicated an inclination to embrace more and more Western forms

28. The "development of a pantribal style" of music (line 58) is an example of the way in which

    (A) cultural groups select and adapt aspects of each other's culture when two groups meet
    (B) Native American groups formed tribal confederacies to resist the advance of the Europeans
    (C) tribal identification transcends musical style
    (D) members of the Pima and Potawatomi peoples have learned to work together
    (E) a group's culture can be modified when the group meets another cultural group

29. In saying that the "very concept of 'American Indian' is probably a product of contact" (lines 59–60), the author means that

    (A) Native Americans could begin to think of themselves as "American Indians" only after they learned to speak English
    (B) across-cultural identity became necessary as Native American groups came into contact with each other
    (C) Europeans were the first to see the various Native American peoples as one group
    (D) Native Americans identify with their tribe and do not accept the Euro-American designation of "American Indian"
    (E) the American Indian did not exist prior to contact with Europeans

30. The passage suggests that the Indianist composers would have had the most difficulty in using and adapting which of the following aspects of Native American music?

    (A) melodic lines
    (B) harmonic styles
    (C) vocal techniques
    (D) rhythmical patterns
    (E) all of the above

31. According to the passage, the Northern Plains-style music has come to stand for Native American music in general because

    (A) the Northern Plains-style is so different from Euro-American musical styles that it sets the singers clearly apart as Native Americans
    (B) Europeans, when they first heard Northern Plains-style music, wrongly assumed that it was representative of all Native American music
    (C) Northern Plains–style music is more easily comprehended and enjoyed by Euro-Americans than most other styles of Native American music
    (D) Northern Plains tribes are predominant among Native American tribes today
    (E) Northern Plains music has been the most widely distributed music

STOP

END OF SECTION 1. IF YOU HAVE ANY TIME LEFT, GO OVER YOUR WORK IN THIS SECTION ONLY. DO NOT WORK IN ANY OTHER SECTION OF THE TEST.

SECTION 2

25 Questions • Time—30 Minutes

Directions: Solve the following problems using any available space on the page for scratchwork. On your answer sheet fill in the choice which best corresponds to the correct answer.

Notes: The figures accompanying the problems are drawn as accurately as possible unless otherwise stated in specific problems. Again, unless otherwise stated, all figures lie in the same plane. All numbers used in these problems are real numbers. Calculators are permitted for this test.

Reference Information

Circle: $C = 2\pi r$, $A = \pi r^2$
Rectangle: $A = lw$
Rectangular Solid: $V = lwh$
Cylinder: $V = \pi r^2 h$
Triangle: $A = \frac{1}{2}bh$
$a^2 + b^2 = c^2$

Special right triangles: 45°-45°-90° (x, x, $x\sqrt{2}$); 30°-60°-90° (x, $x\sqrt{3}$, $2x$)

The number of degrees of arc in a circle is 360.
The measure in degrees of a straight angle is 180.
The sum of the measures in degrees of the angles of a triangle is 180.

---

1. If $3x + 2 > 2x + 7$, then x is

   (A) 5
   (B) < 5
   (C) > 5
   (D) < 1
   (E) < −1

2. If $x \neq \frac{2}{3}$, then $\dfrac{6x^2 - 13x + 6}{3x - 2} =$

   (A) $3x - 2$
   (B) $3x - 3$
   (C) $2x - 6$
   (D) $2x - 3$
   (E) $2x^2 + 3x - 3$

3. [Graph showing points B(1,4), C(5,4), A(1,1)]

   What is the length of side AC?

   (A) $2\frac{1}{2}$
   (B) 5
   (C) 7
   (D) 11
   (E) 25

4. If 3! means 3•2•1 and 4! means 4•3•2•1, then what does $\frac{8!}{9!}$ equal?

   (A) 9
   (B) $\frac{8}{9}$%
   (C) $\frac{1}{9}$%
   (D) $\frac{1}{89}$
   (E) 0

5. If a distance estimated at 150 feet is really 140 feet, the percent of error in this estimate is

   (A) 10%
   (B) $7\frac{1}{7}$%
   (C) $6\frac{2}{3}$%
   (D) 1%
   (E) 0.71%

6. There are x cookies in a cookie jar. One child eats $\frac{1}{4}$ of all the cookies. A second child eats $\frac{1}{3}$ of the remaining cookies. If the remaining cookies are distributed among four other children, what fraction of the original number of cookies did each of the four children receive?

   (A) $\frac{7}{12}$
   (B) $\frac{1}{2}$
   (C) $\frac{5}{12}$
   (D) $\frac{1}{6}$
   (E) $\frac{1}{8}$

7. $|2y - 4| = 6$, $y =$

   (A) −5, 1
   (B) −8
   (C) −4, 3
   (D) 5, −1
   (E) 0

8. Given the system of equations $3x + 2y = 4$ and $6x - 3y = 6$, what does y equal?

   (A) 14
   (B) $\frac{14}{6}$
   (C) 2
   (D) $\frac{11}{7}$
   (E) $\frac{2}{7}$

9. If the radius of a circle is diminished by 20%, the area is diminished by

   (A) 20%
   (B) 36%
   (C) 40%
   (D) 64%
   (E) 400%

10. If $x - y = 10$ and $x + y = 20$ then what is the value of $x^2 - y^2$?

    (A) 400
    (B) 200
    (C) 100
    (D) 30
    (E) It cannot be determined from the information given.

GO ON TO THE NEXT PAGE

11. A semicircle surmounts a rectangle whose length a $2a$ and whose width is a, as shown in the diagram. A formula for finding the area of the whole figure is

(A) $2a^2 + \dfrac{\pi a^2}{2}$
(B) $2\pi a^2$
(C) $3\pi a^2$
(D) $2a^2 + \pi a^2$
(E) $2a^2 + 2\pi a^2$

12. An airplane flies 550 yards in 3 seconds. What is the speed of the airplane, expressed in miles per hour? (5,280 ft. = 1 mi.)

(A) 1,125
(B) 375
(C) 300
(D) 125
(E) 90

13. Given that 1 meter = 3.28 ft., the distance run in a 100-meter race approximates most closely

(A) 100 yards
(B) 90 yards
(C) 105 yards
(D) 110 yards
(E) 103 yards

14. Of the following sets of fractions, the set that is arranged in increasing order is

(A) $\dfrac{7}{12}, \dfrac{6}{11}, \dfrac{3}{5}, \dfrac{5}{8}$
(B) $\dfrac{6}{11}, \dfrac{7}{12}, \dfrac{5}{8}, \dfrac{3}{5}$
(C) $\dfrac{6}{11}, \dfrac{7}{12}, \dfrac{3}{5}, \dfrac{5}{8}$
(D) $\dfrac{3}{5}, \dfrac{5}{8}, \dfrac{6}{11}, \dfrac{7}{12}$
(E) $\dfrac{7}{12}, \dfrac{6}{11}, \dfrac{5}{8}, \dfrac{3}{5}$

15. If one pipe can fill a tank in $1\tfrac{1}{2}$ hours and another can fill the same tank in 45 minutes, then how many hours will it take the two pipes to fill the tank if they are working together?

(A) $\dfrac{1}{3}$
(B) $\dfrac{1}{2}$
(C) $\dfrac{5}{6}$
(D) 1
(E) $1\tfrac{1}{2}$

16. If the sum of the edges of a cube is 48 inches, the volume of the cube in cubic inches is

(A) 64
(B) 96
(C) 149
(D) 512
(E) 1,728

17. If the length of each side of a square is $\frac{2x}{3}+1$, the perimeter of the square is

   (A) $\frac{8x+4}{3}$
   (B) $\frac{8x+12}{3}$
   (C) $\frac{2x}{3}+4$
   (D) $\frac{2x}{3}+16$
   (E) $\frac{4x}{3}+2$

18. Equilateral triangle ABC has a perpendicular line drawn from A to point D. If the triangle is "folded over" on the perpendicular line so that points B and C meet, the perimeter of the new triangle is approximately what percent of the perimeter of the triangle before the fold?

   (A) 100%
   (B) 78%
   (C) 50%
   (D) 32%
   (E) It cannot be determined from the information given.

19. To find the radius of a circle whose circumference is 60 inches

   (A) multiply 60 by π
   (B) divide 60 by 2π
   (C) divide 30 by 2π
   (D) divide 60 by π and extract the square root of the result
   (E) multiply 60 by $\frac{\pi}{2}$

20. If the outer diameter of a metal pipe is 2.84 inches and the inner diameter is 1.94 inches, the thickness of the metal in inches is

   (A) .45
   (B) .90
   (C) 1.42
   (D) 1.94
   (E) 2.39

21. Line $a \| b$, while d is the distance between a and b at points C and D.

   The length of segment d

   (A) steadily increases as it is moved along lines a and b to the right
   (B) steadily decreases as it is moved toward the left
   (C) fluctuates in both directions
   (D) remains constant
   (E) none of the above

22. $(x+9)(x+2) =$

   (A) $x^2 + 18$
   (B) $11x$
   (C) $x^2 + 11$
   (D) $x^2 + 11x + 18$
   (E) $9(x+2) + 2(x+9)$

23. The points $(3,1)$ and $(5,y)$ are $\sqrt{13}$ units apart. What does y equal?

   (A) -3
   (B) 4
   (C) $\sqrt{17}$
   (D) 10
   (E) 17

GO ON TO THE NEXT PAGE

24. In a baseball game, a pitcher needs to throw nine strikes to complete an inning. If a pitcher is able to throw strikes on 85% of his pitches, how many pitches to the nearest whole number would it take for him to throw the necessary number of strikes for a nine-inning game?

   (A) 95
   (B) 97
   (C) 103
   (D) 105
   (E) 111

25. Corner *AFE* is cut from the rectangle as shown in the figure below. The area of the remaining polygon *ABCDE* in square inches is

   Note: Figure not drawn to scale.

   (A) 29
   (B) 68
   (C) 78
   (D) 88
   (E) 98

STOP

END OF SECTION 2. IF YOU HAVE ANY TIME LEFT, GO OVER YOUR WORK IN THIS SECTION ONLY. DO NOT WORK IN ANY OTHER SECTION OF THE TEST.

Practice Examination 5 519

SECTION 3

25 Questions • Time—30 Minutes

Directions: Solve the following problems using any available space on the page for scratchwork. On your answer sheet fill in the choice which best corresponds to the correct answer.

Notes: The figures accompanying the problems are drawn as accurately as possible unless otherwise stated in specific problems. Again, unless otherwise stated, all figures lie in the same plane. All numbers used in these problems are real numbers. Calculators are permitted for this test.

Reference Information

Circle:
$C = 2\pi r$
$A = \pi r^2$

Rectangle:
$A = lw$

Rectangular Solid:
$V = lwh$

Cylinder:
$V = \pi r^2 h$

Triangle:
$A = \frac{1}{2}bh$

$a^2 + b^2 = c^2$

45°-45°-90° triangle: sides x, x, $x\sqrt{2}$
30°-60°-90° triangle: sides x, $x\sqrt{3}$, $2x$

The number of degrees of arc in a circle is 360.
The measure in degrees of a straight angle is 180.
The sum of the measures in degrees of the angles of a triangle is 180.

Part 1: Quantitative Comparison Questions

Directions: For each of the following questions, two quantities are given—one in Column A, and the other in Column B. Compare the two quantities and mark your answer sheet as follows:

(A) if the quantity in Column A is greater
(B) if the quantity in Column B is greater
(C) if the two quantities are equal
(D) if the relationship cannot be determined from the information given.

Notes:

(1) Information concerning one or both of the compared quantities will be centered above the two columns for some items.
(2) Symbols that appear in both columns represent the same thing in Column A as in Column B.
(3) Letters such as x, n, and k are symbols for real numbers.

Examples

	Column A	Column B	Answers
	$a > 0$		
	$x > 0$		
E1.	$a - x$	$a + x$	(A) ● (C) (D)
E2.	The average of 17, 19, 21, 23	The average of 16, 18, 20, 22	● (B) (C) (D)

DO NOT MARK CHOICE (E) FOR THESE QUESTIONS. THERE ARE ONLY FOUR ANSWER CHOICES.

	Column A	Column B
	$s > t$	
1.	$s - t$	$t - s$
2.	The cost of a complete stereo system that is discounted 30%	The cost of a pair of speakers that is discounted 30%
	$p > 0$	
	$q < 0$	
3.	$p + q$	$p - q$
	Distance from A to B is 12 miles	
	Distance from A to C is 10 miles	
4.	Distance from A to B	Distance from B to C
5.	The number that 63 is 7% of	7% of 63
	$r = \dfrac{1}{2}$	
6.	$2r^3 - 12r + 7$	$r^2 + 1$
	$x \; 0$	
7.	$\dfrac{1}{x^2}$	x^2
	$m^3 = 64$	
	$\sqrt{n} = 16$	
8.	m	n

	Column A	Column B
9.	Note: Figure not drawn to scale. $x = y = z$ side s	side t
10.	Area of a rectangle with a length of 4 and a width of π	Area of a circle with radius 4
11.	Surface area of the cube (side 3)	Cutting the cube in half to form 2 smaller boxes: the sum of the surface area of both the boxes
	$r < 0 < s$	
12.	r^5	s^4
	$x^2 = 25$	
	$2y + 3 = 27$	
13.	x	y

Column A	Column B

Side AB = Side AC

14. | x | y |

Column A	Column B

$\angle MNQ$ is a right angle

15. | $\angle M + \angle Q$ | $45°$ |

Part 2: Student-Produced Response Questions

Directions: Solve each of these problems. Write the answer in the corresponding grid on the answer sheet and fill in the ovals beneath each answer you write. Here are some examples.

Answer: $\frac{3}{4}$ (= .75; show answer either way)

Answer: 325

Note: A mixed number such as $3\frac{1}{2}$ must be gridded as 7/2 or as 3.5. If gridded as "3 1/2," it will be read as "thirty-one halves."

Note: Either position is correct.

16. In the pentagon shown, what is the maximum number of different diagonals that can be drawn?

17. If $4x = 2(2 + x)$ and $6y = 3(2 + y)$, then $2x + 3y =$

GO ON TO THE NEXT PAGE

18. Let the "JOSH" of a number be defined as three less than three times the number. What number is equal to its "JOSH"?

19. Machine A produces flue covers at a uniform rate of 2,000 per hour. Machine B produces flue covers at a uniform rate of 5,000 in $2\frac{1}{2}$ hours. After $7\frac{1}{4}$ hours, Machine A has produced how many more flue covers than Machine B?

20. .01 is the ratio of .1 to what number?

21. In the figure above, AB is parallel to ED and $AC = BC$. If angle E is 50°, then $x =$

22. At NJL High School, $\frac{1}{4}$ of the school's population are seniors, $\frac{1}{5}$ are juniors and $\frac{1}{3}$ are sophomores. If there are 390 freshmen, what is the total school population?

23. From the town of Williston Park to Albertson there are 3 different roads. From the town of Albertson to Mineola there are 5 routes. How many different paths are there to go from Williston Park to Mineola through Albertson?

24. If 12 candies cost $1.70, how many of these candies can be bought for $10.20?

25. Two roads intersect at right angles. A pole is 30 meters from one road and 40 meters from the other road. How far (in meters) is the pole from the point where the roads intersect?

STOP

END OF SECTION 3. IF YOU HAVE ANY TIME LEFT, GO OVER YOUR WORK IN THIS SECTION ONLY. DO NOT WORK IN ANY OTHER SECTION OF THE TEST.

SECTION 4

35 Questions • Time—30 Minutes

Directions: Each of the following questions consists of an incomplete sentence followed by five words or pairs of words. Choose that word or pair of words which, when substituted for the blank space or spaces, best completes the meaning of the sentence and mark the letter of your choice on your answer sheet.

Example:

In view of the extenuating circumstances and the defendant's youth, the judge recommended ----.

(A) conviction (B) a defense
(C) a mistrial (D) leniency
(E) life imprisonment   Ⓐ Ⓑ Ⓒ ● Ⓔ

1. The society was not ---- and required much outside aid.

    (A) destitute
    (B) self-sufficient
    (C) democratic
    (D) impoverished
    (E) benevolent

2. The new regime immediately ---- laws implementing the promised reforms.

    (A) vouchsafed
    (B) ensconced
    (C) augmented
    (D) promulgated
    (E) parlayed

3. The machines were ----, and because of the below-zero temperature, it was feared they would ----.

    (A) frozen..dehydrate
    (B) brittle..shatter
    (C) frosty..slide
    (D) icy..capsize
    (E) shiny..expand

4. A long illness can ---- even the strongest constitution.

    (A) obviate
    (B) inculcate
    (C) bolster
    (D) enervate
    (E) disparage

5. With ---- attention to detail, the careful researcher churned out his reports.

    (A) prosaic
    (B) painless
    (C) meticulous
    (D) appealing
    (E) atypical

6. A shy look from the beautiful Laura ---- him, and soon they were married.

    (A) released
    (B) controlled
    (C) enchanted
    (D) ensconced
    (E) jilted

7. The city ---- to the advancing invaders without firing a single shot.

    (A) extolled
    (B) regressed
    (C) equivocated
    (D) dissembled
    (E) capitulated

GO ON TO THE NEXT PAGE

8. When the two opposing sides failed to reach a ----, the long-anticipated strike became ----.

   (A) consensus..impossible
   (B) transition..general
   (C) compromise..inevitable
   (D) rationale..culpable
   (E) precedent..potential

9. Her new neighbor was ---- and charming, the ---- of the bumbling yokel she had expected.

   (A) urbane..antithesis
   (B) callow..exemplar
   (C) provincial..precursor
   (D) obtuse..tableau
   (E) petulant..delegate

10. If you find peeling potatoes to be ----, perhaps you'd prefer to scrub the floors?

    (A) felicitous
    (B) remunerative
    (C) onerous
    (D) vilifying
    (E) redundant

Directions: Each of the following questions consists of a capitalized pair of words followed by five pairs of words lettered A to E. The capitalized words bear some meaningful relationship to each other. Choose the lettered pair of words whose relationship is most similiar to that expressed by the capitalized pair and mark its letter on your answer sheet.

Example:

DAY : SUN : :
- (A) sunlight : daylight
- (B) ray : sun
- (C) night : moon
- (D) heat : cold
- (E) moon : star

Ⓐ Ⓑ ● Ⓓ Ⓔ

11. OSCILLATE : PENDULUM : :
    - (A) obligate : promise
    - (B) float : fish
    - (C) turn : car
    - (D) spin : gyroscope
    - (E) learn : student

12. PREMIERE : MOVIE : :
    - (A) unveiling : statue
    - (B) rookie : football
    - (C) debutante : teenager
    - (D) ruler : subject
    - (E) celluloid : film

13. CARPENTER : AWL : :
    - (A) artist : canvas
    - (B) computer : disc
    - (C) film : camera
    - (D) gardener : hose
    - (E) miner : pick

14. ROOF : PITCH : :
    - (A) triangle : side
    - (B) basement : cement
    - (C) mountain : grade
    - (D) tree : sap
    - (E) ceiling : rafter

15. COG : WATCH : :
    - (A) plant : biome
    - (B) piston : engine
    - (C) scale : fish
    - (D) handle : pot
    - (E) leash : dog

16. EQUESTRIAN : HORSE : :
    - (A) veterinarian : hospital
    - (B) taxi : cab
    - (C) cyclist : bicycle
    - (D) cow : farmer
    - (E) camel : desert

17. RECLUSE : SOLITARY : :
    - (A) socialite : gregarious
    - (B) hermit : old
    - (C) monk : lowly
    - (D) soldier : political
    - (E) hut : squalid

18. DIFFUSE : CONCENTRATION : :
    - (A) spread : expansion
    - (B) diffident : shyness
    - (C) indelicate : coarseness
    - (D) incongruous : harmony
    - (E) anger : resentment

19. APPLE : FRUIT : :
    - (A) dog : bone
    - (B) tree : bush
    - (C) sparrow : bird
    - (D) robin : owl
    - (E) elm : birch

GO ON TO THE NEXT PAGE

20. TEN : DECADE : :

    (A) score : century
    (B) discount : percent
    (C) miles : odometer
    (D) era : eon
    (E) thousand : millennium

21. ZEALOT : FERVOR : :

    (A) charlatan : honesty
    (B) rogue : sobriety
    (C) fledgling : experience
    (D) dotard : youth
    (E) sage : wisdom

22. CURE : PHYSICIAN : :

    (A) prescribe : pharmacist
    (B) discuss : writer
    (C) entertain : comedian
    (D) train : athlete
    (E) trust : policeman

23. SYMPHONY : MOVEMENT : :

    (A) dollar : cent
    (B) strings : section
    (C) chorus : soloist
    (D) play : act
    (E) action : reason

Directions: The reading passage below is followed by a set of questions. Read the passage and answer the accompanying questions, basing your answers on what is stated or implied in the passage. Mark the letter of your choice on your answer sheet.

Questions 24–35 are based on the following passage.

Anton Chekhov is the Russian playwright responsible for some of our most enduring dramas—The Sea Gull, The Cherry Orchard, Uncle Vanya, and others. In this letter he writes to another important playwright, Maxim Gorky, about Gorky's latest work.

Moscow. Oct. 22, 1901

Five days have passed since I read your play (*The Petty Bourgeois*). I have not written to you till now because I could not get hold of the fourth act; I have kept waiting for it, and—I have still not got it. And so
(5) I have read only three acts, but that I think is enough to judge of the play. It is, as I expected, very good, written à la Gorky, original, very interesting; and, to begin by talking of the defects, I have noticed only one, a defect incorrigible as red hair in a red-haired
(10) man—the conservatism of the form. You make new and original people sing new songs to an accompaniment that looks second-hand; you have four acts, the characters deliver edifying discourses, there is a feeling of alarm before long speeches, and so on, and so
(15) on. But all that is not important, and it is all, so to speak, drowned in the good points of the play. Perchikhin—how living! His daughter is enchanting, Tatyana and Piotr also, and their mother is a splendid old woman. The central figure of the play, Nil, is
(20) vigorously drawn and extremely interesting! In fact, the play takes hold of one from the first act. Only, God preserve you from letting anyone act Perchikhin except Artyom, while Alekseyev-Stanislavsky must certainly play Nil. Those two figures will do just what's
(25) needed; Piotr—Meierkhold. Only, Nil's part, a wonderful part, must be made two or three times as long. You ought to end the play with it, to make it the leading part. Only, do not contrast him with Piotr and Tatyana, let him be by himself and them by themselves, all
(30) wonderful, splendid people independent of one another. When Nil tries to seem superior to Piotr and Tatyana, and says of himself that he is a fine fellow—the element so characteristic of our decent working man, the element of modesty, is lost. He boasts, he
(35) argues, but you know one can see what kind of man he is without that. Let him be merry, let him play pranks through the whole four acts, let him eat a great deal after his work—and that will be enough for him to conquer the audience with. Piotr, I repeat, is good.
(40) Most likely you don't even suspect how good he is. Tatyana, too, is a finished figure, only,—(a) she ought really to be a schoolmistress, ought to be teaching children, ought to come home from school, ought to be taken up with her pupils and exercise-books, and—(b)
(45) it ought to be mentioned in the first or second act that she has attempted to poison herself; then, after that hint, the poisoning in the third act will not seem so startling and will be more in place. Teterev talks too much: such characters ought to be shown bit by bit
(50) among others, for in any case such people are everywhere merely incidental—both in life and on the stage. Make Elena dine with all the rest in the first act, let her sit and make jokes, or else there is very little of her, and she is not clear. . . .

24. By "à la Gorky" (line 7) Chekhov seems to mean

(A) plagiarized from another playwright
(B) in the manner of Maxim's father
(C) quirky
(D) fascinating and creative
(E) full of defects

25. The word *incorrigible* (line 9) means

(A) offensive
(B) irreparable
(C) pessimistic
(D) alarming
(E) impossible

26. When Chekhov compares the book to the red-haired man in lines 8–10, his comments are

(A) inflammatory
(B) pessimistic
(C) harsh
(D) supportive
(E) condescending

GO ON TO THE NEXT PAGE

27. When Chekhov states that the "accompaniment looks second-hand" (lines 11–12), he means that

 (A) the music should be rewritten
 (B) the minor characters are stereotypes
 (C) the form of the play is old-fashioned
 (D) very few new characters are introduced
 (E) the set is shabby

28. By "all that" in line 15, Chekhov is referring to

 (A) the dramatic highlights of the play
 (B) the superior development of the play's characters
 (C) the work's traditional trappings
 (D) the poor acting
 (E) the bizarre elements of "The Petty Bourgeois"

29. When Chekhov refers to Perchikhin as "living" (line 16), he means that the character

 (A) dies later in the act
 (B) seems authentic
 (C) is incredibly active
 (D) lives well
 (E) seethes with rage

30. From the passage you can infer that Nil is most likely a(n)

 (A) intellectual
 (B) ordinary working man
 (C) aristocrat
 (D) murderer
 (E) revolutionary

31. Chekhov objects to Nil's lack of

 (A) willpower
 (B) contrast
 (C) superiority
 (D) modesty
 (E) energy

32. Chekhov's advice about Elena (lines 52–54) is meant to

 (A) elucidate her character
 (B) startle Gorky
 (C) remove her from the first act
 (D) contrast her behavior with that of Nil
 (E) lengthen the play

33. In line 51, the word *incidental* means

 (A) insignificant
 (B) accidental
 (C) coincidental
 (D) essential
 (E) characteristic

34. Chekhov expresses definite opinions on each of these points EXCEPT

 (A) who should play the part of Nil
 (B) whose part should be extended
 (C) what Tatyana should do for a living
 (D) how Teterev's part should be cut
 (E) how the third act should end

35. Chekhov suggests change in all of the following characters EXCEPT

 (A) Tatyana
 (B) Elena
 (C) Nil
 (D) Teterev
 (E) Piotr

STOP

END OF SECTION 4. IF YOU HAVE ANY TIME LEFT, GO OVER YOUR WORK IN THIS SECTION ONLY. DO NOT WORK IN ANY OTHER SECTION OF THE TEST.

SECTION 5

12 Questions • Time—15 Minutes

Directions: The two passages given below deal with related topics. Following the passages are questions about the content of each passage or about the relationship between the two passages. Answer the questions based upon what is stated or implied in the passages and in any introductory material provided. Mark the letter of your choice on your answer sheet.

Questions 1–12 are based on the following passages.

President Lincoln referred to Harriet Beecher Stowe as "the little woman who made the great war," largely because of the furor caused by the publication of her anti-slavery novel Uncle Tom's Cabin. *In Passage 1 Stowe reflects on the writing of that novel. In Passage 2, Frederick Douglass, a slave who fled to freedom, speaks of his fear on the eve of his second—and successful—attempt to escape to the North from slavery.*

Passage 1—Harriet Beecher Stowe, from a letter to Mrs. Follen (1853)

I had two little curly-headed twin daughters to begin with, and my stock in this line was gradually increased, till I have been the mother of seven children, the most beautiful and the most loved of whom (5) lies buried near my Cincinnati residence. It was at his dying bed and at his grave that I learned what a poor slave mother may feel when her child is torn away from her. In those depths of sorrow which seemed to me immeasurable, it was my only prayer to God that (10) such anguish might not be suffered in vain. There were circumstances about his death of such peculiar bitterness, of what seemed almost cruel suffering, that I felt that I could never be consoled for it unless this crushing of my own heart might enable me to work out some (15) great good to others. . . .

I allude to this here because I have often felt that much that is in that book ("Uncle Tom") had its root in the awful scenes and bitter sorrows of that summer. It has left now, I trust, no trace on my mind except a deep (20) compassion for the sorrowful, especially for mothers who are separated from their children. . .

I am now writing a work which will contain, perhaps, an equal amount of matter with "Uncle Tom's Cabin." It will contain all the facts and documents (25) upon which that story was founded, and an immense body of facts, reports of trial, legal documents, and testimony of people now living South, which will more than confirm every statement in "Uncle Tom's Cabin."

(30) I must confess that till I began the examination of facts in order to write this book, much as I thought I knew before, I had not begun to measure the depth of the abyss. The law records of courts and judicial proceedings are so incredible as to fill me with amaze- (35) ment whenever I think of them. It seems to me that the book cannot but be felt, and, coming upon the sensibility awaked by the other, do something.

I suffer exquisitely in writing these things. It may be truly said that I suffer with my heart's blood. Many (40) times in writing "Uncle Tom's Cabin" I thought my heart would fail utterly, but I prayed earnestly that God would help me till I got through, and still I am pressed beyond measure and above strength. . . .

Passage 2—Recollection of Frederick Douglass

. . . It is impossible for me to describe my feelings (45) as the time of my contemplated start grew near. I had a number of warm-hearted friends in Baltimore,— friends that I loved almost as I did my life,—and the thought of being separated from them forever was painful beyond expression. It is my opinion that thou- (50) sands would escape from slavery, who now remain, but for the strong cords of affection that bind them to their friends. The thought of leaving my friends was decidedly the most painful thought with which I had to contend. The love of them was my tender point, and (55) shook my decision more than all things else. Besides the pain of separation, the dread and apprehension of a failure exceeded what I had experienced at my first

GO ON TO THE NEXT PAGE

attempt. The appalling defeat I then sustained returned to torment me. I felt assured that, if I failed in this
(60) attempt, my case would be a hopeless one—it would seal my fate as a slave forever. I could not hope to get off with anything less than the severest punishment, and being placed beyond the means of escape. It required no very vivid imagination to depict the most
(65) frightful scenes through which I would have to pass, in case I failed. The wretchedness of slavery, and the blessedness of freedom, were perpetually before me. It was life and death with me. But I remained firm and according to my resolution, on the third day of Sep-
(70) tember, 1838, I left my chains, and succeeded in reaching New York without the slightest interruption of any kind.

1. Harriet Beecher Stowe traces her compassion for slave mothers to her

   (A) writing of *Uncle Tom's Cabin*
   (B) hatred of injustice
   (C) meeting a young woman in Cincinnati
   (D) reading of legal documents and testimony
   (E) loss of her own son

2. Stowe is writing a new book that will be

   (A) as long as *Uncle Tom's Cabin*
   (B) fictional, like *Uncle Tom's Cabin*
   (C) more successful than *Uncle Tom's Cabin*
   (D) both A and B
   (E) both B and C

3. By "the depth of the abyss" (lines 32–33), Stowe refers to

   (A) the endless array of documentation
   (B) the cruelty of the judicial process
   (C) the suffering of young mothers
   (D) the horrors of slavery
   (E) the immeasurable intensity of grief

4. In line 38, the word "exquisitely" most nearly means

   (A) lavishly
   (B) expensively
   (C) enormously
   (D) indefinitely
   (E) superficially

5. Stowe believes that her new book will

   (A) prompt readers to read her last book
   (B) arouse empathy in readers
   (C) cause readers intense suffering
   (D) console readers of *Uncle Tom's Cabin*
   (E) infuriate readers of *Uncle Tom's Cabin*

6. Why does Stowe want to write a follow-up to Uncle Tom's Cabin?

   I. She believes that the book needs a sequel to complete the story.
   II. She feels the need to substantiate claims that she made in the original novel.
   III. She feels that a presentation of more facts will deepen the reader's understanding of the first book.

   (A) I only
   (B) II only
   (C) I and II only
   (D) III only
   (E) II and III only

7. Stowe is obviously a writer who

   (A) wrote with little effort
   (B) conducted little research for her writing
   (C) was deeply and emotionally involved in her work
   (D) did not understand the demands of writing
   (E) was not an enduring literary force

8. The main idea of Passage 1 is that

   (A) Stowe was in the right place at the right time
   (B) a successful writer is born not made
   (C) Stowe was successful because she lived at a time when significant events were occurring in our nation
   (D) without Lincoln, Stowe would not have succeeded
   (E) a writer's life is a deeply felt one

9. In Passage 2, Douglass acknowledges which of the following as a reason for many slaves not attempting to escape?

   (A) fear
   (B) ties to their friends
   (C) lack of education
   (D) lack of courage
   (E) inability to make contact with people in the North

10. According to the passage, what, in particular, tormented Douglass as he waited to make his second attempt at escape?

    (A) fear of reprisals
    (B) memories of his failed first attempt to escape
    (C) the wretchedness of slavery
    (D) the blessedness of freedom
    (E) pain of separation

11. Douglass was especially frightened at this attempt to escape because

    (A) it was not as well planned as his first attempt
    (B) his northern contact had not been established
    (C) he was going alone
    (D) failure would result in the severest punishment
    (E) he was leaving his friends

12. From the picture of Douglass portrayed in Passage 2, which phrase below best describes him?

    (A) fearful and indecisive
    (B) bitter and angry
    (C) friendless and alone
    (D) confused and troubled
    (E) brave and persistent

STOP

END OF SECTION 5. IF YOU HAVE ANY TIME LEFT, GO OVER YOUR WORK IN THIS SECTION ONLY. DO NOT WORK IN ANY OTHER SECTION OF THE TEST.

SECTION 6

10 Questions • Time—15 Minutes

Directions: Solve the following problems using any available space on the page for scratchwork. On your answer sheet fill in the choice which best corresponds to the correct answer.

Notes: The figures accompanying the problems are drawn as accurately as possible unless otherwise stated in specific problems. Again, unless otherwise stated, all figures lie in the same plane. All numbers used in these problems are real numbers. Calculators are permitted for this test.

Reference Information

Circle: $C = 2\pi r$, $A = \pi r^2$
Rectangle: $A = lw$
Rectangular Solid: $V = lwh$
Cylinder: $V = \pi r^2 h$
Triangle: $A = \frac{1}{2}bh$
$a^2 + b^2 = c^2$

Special right triangles: 45°-45°-90° with sides x, x, $x\sqrt{2}$; 30°-60°-90° with sides x, $x\sqrt{3}$, $2x$.

The number of degrees of arc in a circle is 360.
The measure in degrees of a straight angle is 180.
The sum of the measures in degrees of the angles of a triangle is 180.

---

1. If a triangle of base 7 is equal in area to a circle of radius 7, what is the altitude of the triangle?

    (A) 8π
    (B) 10π
    (C) 12π
    (D) 14π
    (E) It cannot be determined from the information given.

2. If the following numbers are arranged in order from the smallest to the largest, what will be their correct order?

    I. $\frac{9}{13}$
    II. $\frac{13}{9}$
    III. 70%
    IV. $\frac{1}{.70}$

    (A) II, I, III, IV
    (B) III, II, I, IV
    (C) III, IV, I, II
    (D) II, IV, III, I
    (E) I, III, IV, II

3. The coordinates of the vertices of quadrilateral PQRS are P(0,0), Q(9,0), R(10,3), and S(1,3), respectively. What is the area of PQRS?

    (A) $9\sqrt{10}$
    (B) $\frac{9}{2}\sqrt{10}$
    (C) $\frac{27}{2}$
    (D) 27
    (E) It cannot be determined from the information given.

4. If $8x + 4 = 64$, then $2x + 1 =$

    (A) 12
    (B) 13
    (C) 16
    (D) 24
    (E) 60

5. A circle whose radius is 7 has its center at the origin. Which of the following points are outside the circle?

   I. (4,4)
   II. (5,5)
   III. (4,5)
   IV. (4,6)

   (A) I and II only
   (B) II and III only
   (C) II, III, and IV only
   (D) II and IV only
   (E) III and IV only

6. What is the difference in surface area between a square with side = 9 and a cube with edge = 3?

   (A) 516
   (B) 432
   (C) 72
   (D) 27
   (E) 18

7. A set of numbers is "quarked" if the sum of all the numbers in the set is evenly divisible by each of the numbers in the set. Which of the following sets is "quarked"?

   (A) (1, 3, 5, 7)
   (B) (4, 6, 8)
   (C) (6, 7, 8, 9)
   (D) (2, 4, 6)
   (E) (5, 10, 15, 20)

8. If $x \ne -2$, $\dfrac{3(x^2 - 4)}{x + 2} =$

   (A) $3x^2 + 4$
   (B) $3x - 2$
   (C) $x - 2$
   (D) $3x - 6$
   (E) $3x + 6$

9. An ice-cream truck runs down a certain street 4 times a week. This truck carries 5 different flavors of ice-cream bars, each of which comes in 2 different designs. Considering that the truck runs Monday through Thursday, and Monday was the first day of the month, by what day of the month could a person, buying one ice-cream bar each truck run, purchase all the different varieties of ice-cream bars?

   (A) 11th
   (B) 16th
   (C) 21st
   (D) 24th
   (E) 30th

10. If $N! = N(N-1)(N-2)\ldots[N-(N-1)]$, what does $\dfrac{N!}{(N-2)!}$ equal?

    (A) $N^2 - N$
    (B) $N^5 + N^3 - N^2 + \dfrac{N}{N^2}$
    (C) $N + 1$
    (D) 1
    (E) 6

STOP

END OF SECTION 6. IF YOU HAVE ANY TIME LEFT, GO OVER YOUR WORK IN THIS SECTION ONLY. DO NOT WORK IN ANY OTHER SECTION OF THE TEST.

PRACTICE EXAMINATION 5
Answer Key

Section 1: Verbal

1. B	8. B	14. A	20. C	26. B
2. C	9. E	15. E	21. D	27. C
3. E	10. C	16. A	22. D	28. E
4. D	11. D	17. B	23. B	29. C
5. B	12. C	18. D	24. D	30. C
6. C	13. C	19. C	25. C	31. A
7. B				

Section 2: Math

1. C	6. E	11. A	16. A	21. D
2. D	7. D	12. B	17. B	22. D
3. B	8. E	13. D	18. B	23. B
4. C	9. B	14. C	19. B	24. A
5. B	10. B	15. B	20. A	25. C

Section 3: Math

Part 1

1. A	4. D	7. D	10. B	13. B
2. D	5. A	8. B	11. B	14. C
3. B	6. C	9. C	12. B	15. A

Part 2

16. 5	18. $1.5 = \frac{3}{2}$	20. 10	22. 1800	24. 72
17. 10	19. 0	21. 80	23. 15	25. 50

Section 4: Verbal

1. B	8. C	15. B	22. C	29. B
2. D	9. A	16. C	23. D	30. B
3. B	10. C	17. A	24. D	31. D
4. D	11. D	18. D	25. B	32. A
5. C	12. A	19. C	26. D	33. A
6. C	13. E	20. E	27. C	34. E
7. E	14. C	21. E	28. C	35. E

Section 5: Verbal

1. E	4. C	7. C	9. B	11. D
2. A	5. B	8. E	10. B	12. E
3. D	6. E			

Section 6: Math

1. D	3. D	5. D	7. D	9. B
2. E	4. C	6. D	8. D	10. A

PRACTICE EXAMINATION 5
Explanatory Answers

Note: A 🖩 following a math answer explanation indicates that a calculator could be helpful in solving that particular problem.

Section 1

1. **(B)** If the director *applauds* her employees' activities, she is not likely to *question* their methods.

2. **(C)** An *unwilling* soldier would *recoil* at the idea of going to battle.

3. **(E)** The *inhumane* treatment of the zoo animals would result in *criticism*.

4. **(D)** Paper money is merely a representation of wealth; therefore, unlike gold, it has no *intrinsic* (inherent) value.

5. **(B)** The fever could be *degenerative*, *debilitating*, *raging*, or *pernicious*. However, only *ascribed* (attributed) makes sense in the second blank.

6. **(C)** If the lawyer can cast doubt on the *probity* (honesty or integrity) of the witness, she can probably strengthen her client's case.

7. **(B)** A debate in which candidates fling accusations at each other is likely to be *acrimonious* (harsh or bitter).

8. **(B)** Because they result from carelessness, both blanks should be filled by negative words. Carelessness is likely to produce an *ambiguous* (vague or unclear) report, which may leave everyone *confused*.

9. **(E)** Only a *callous* or insensitive person could be *oblivious* to, or unmindful of, the suffering of a starving child.

10. **(C)** A *microscope* is an *instrument*, and a *necktie* is an *accessory*.

11. **(D)** A *sketch* precedes a finished *painting* as a *draft* precedes a finished *thesis*.

12. **(C)** A *plane* arrives at and departs from an assigned *gate*, just as a *train* arrives at and departs from an assigned *track*.

13. **(C)** One *swears* an *oath* and *signs* a *contract*. Both actions show commitment.

14. **(A)** A *spelunker* is a person who explores a *cave*. An *astronaut* is one who explores *space*.

15. **(E)** *Laughter* is a sign of *amusement; pallor* is a sign of *illness*.

16. **(A)** The second sentence of the passage states: "I stand before you tonight under indictment for the alleged crime . . ." A defendant on trial would be under indictment for a supposed crime.

17. **(B)** The fourth paragraph discusses how ". . . not we, the white male citizens; but we, the whole people . . . formed the Union" to secure the blessings of liberty ". . . to the whole people—women as well as men."

18. **(D)** Quoting the preamble of the Constitution adds weight to her argument that all citizens, not merely white, male citizens, should have the right to vote.

19. **(C)** Lines 19–22 state: ". . . we, the whole people, who formed the Union . . . not to give the blessings of liberty, but to secure them . . . to the whole people. . . ."

20. **(C)** Lines 32–36 state: "To them this government has no just powers derived from the consent of the governed. . . . It is a hateful oligarchy of sex."

21. **(D)** Lines 41–43 describe an oligarchy of sex as a government where "all men [are] sovereigns [and] all women subjects, [inciting] dissension, discord and rebellion [in] every home."

22. **(D)** Lines 44–45 present the definition of a citizen "... as a person in the United States, entitled to vote and hold office."

23. **(B)** The last sentence of the passage states that "... every discrimination against women in the constitutions and laws of the several States is today null and void."

24. **(D)** As stated in lines 34–36, "The Indianists ... seized on universal themes ... cloaked in American Indian dress."

25. **(C)** Lines 16–18 say that Farwell used Fletcher's collections; lines 21–26 show that Cadman used melodies from the same collection.

26. **(B)** Substitution of each choice for the word *marks* in context shows that "It is the text that *distinguishes* many Indianist compositions."

27. **(C)** Lines 43–46 state the point of the examples in the fifth paragraph.

28. **(E)** The final paragraph contains the best explanation for this thesis. Answer (A), while it expresses the main idea of the passage as a whole, does not apply to the development of a pantribal style of music because in this case the Native Americans are not adapting a European cultural expression.

29. **(C)** Lines 61–66, directly following the quoted sentence, explain the author's meaning.

30. **(C)** Lines 6–9 say that "certain elements of Indian song styles" could not be easily assimilated into European "musical structures built on harmony and ... a musical aesthetic that preferred an open-throated singing style." The fact that Farwell used a Navaho harmonic style in "Navajo War Dance" (line 10) eliminates (B) as the best choice, while the discussion of Europeans' difficulty with Northern Plains-style singing "with tense throat and pulsating voice" in the final paragraph confirms that vocal techniques are the most difficult aspect of Native American music for Euro-American composers to assimilate.

31. **(A)** See lines 78–82.

Section 2

1. **(C)**
$$3x + 2 > 2x + 7$$
$$x + 2 > 7$$
$$x > 5$$

2. **(D)** By long division:

$$\begin{array}{r} 2x - 3 \\ 3x-2\overline{)6x^2 - 13x + 6} \\ \underline{6x^2 - 4x} \\ -9x + 6 \\ \underline{-9x + 6} \\ 0 \end{array}$$

3. **(B)** It can easily be seen that $AB = 3$ and $BC = 4$. By the Pythagorean theorem, $(3)^2 + (4)^2 = (AC)^2$ and $AC = 5$. Also, the distance formula can be used.

$$d = \sqrt{(x - x_1)^2 + (y - y_1)^2}$$
$$= \sqrt{(5-1)^2 + (4-1)^2}$$
$$= \sqrt{(4)^2 + (3)^2} = \sqrt{25} = 5.$$

4. **(C)** $\dfrac{8!}{9!} = \dfrac{8 \times 7 \times 6 \times 5 \times 4 \times 3 \times 2 \times 1}{9 \times 8 \times 7 \times 6 \times 5 \times 4 \times 3 \times 2 \times 1}$

Cancelling like terms in the numerator and denominator leaves $\frac{1}{9}$.

5. **(B)** There was an error of 150 ft. – 140 ft. = 10 ft. The percent of error is the error divided by the actual distance, 10 ft. ÷ 140 ft. = .0714 × 100% or about $7\frac{1}{7}\%$.

6. **(E)** The first child leaves $\frac{3}{4}$ of the cookies. The second child eats $\frac{1}{3}$ of $\frac{3}{4}$ and that leaves $\frac{1}{2}$. If the $\frac{1}{2}$ is divided among four children, then $\frac{1}{2}$ divided by 4 is $\frac{1}{8}$.

7. **(D)** $|2y - 4| = 6$ means that $2y - 4 = 6$ or $2y - 4 = -6$. Solving the first equation, $y = \frac{10}{2} = 5$, and solving the second equation gives y a value of -1. Therefore, $y =$ both 5 and/or -1.

8. **(E)** To solve this system of equations for y, the top equation must be multiplied by 2.

$$3x + 2y = 4 \rightarrow 6x + 4y = 8$$
$$6x - 3y = 6 \rightarrow 6x - 3y = 6$$

Subtracting the two equations on the right gives $7y = 2$. Therefore, $y = \frac{2}{7}$.

9. **(B)** If the radius r of a circle is diminished by 20%, the new radius is $r - .20r$. The new area is $\pi(r-.20r)^2 = \pi(.64r^2)$. The new area is 64% of the old area. Thus, the area was diminished by 100% − 64% = 36%.

10. **(B)** $x^2 - y^2 = (x+y)(x-y) = 10 \times 20 = 200$.

11. **(A)** The area of the rectangle is $(2a) \times a = 2a^2$. The area of a semicircle is $\frac{1}{2}$ the area of a circle. The radius of the semicircle is $\frac{1}{2}(2a) = a$; therefore, the area is $\frac{\pi a^2}{2}$. Add the areas of the rectangle and semicircle to get the total area, $2a^2 + \frac{\pi a^2}{2}$.

12. **(B)** In one second the plane flies about 550 yds. ÷ 3 sec. = 183 yd./sec. There are 3,600 seconds in one hour, so the plane flies 183 yd./sec. × 3,600 sec./hr. = 658,800 yd./hr. There are 1,760 yards in one mile, so the plane flies 658,800 yd./hr. ÷ 1,760 yd./mi. ≈ 375 mi./hr.

13. **(D)** One meter equals approximately 1.10 yards. 100 meters is 100 m. × 1.10 yds. per m. = 110 yards.

14. **(C)** The least common denominator of all the fractions is 1,320. Changing each fraction to have 1,320 as the denominator, we have
$\frac{6}{11} = \frac{720}{1320}, \frac{7}{12} = \frac{770}{1320}, \frac{3}{5} = \frac{792}{1320}$, and $\frac{5}{8} = \frac{825}{1320}$.

15. **(B)** The first pipe can fill the tank in $1\frac{1}{2}$ or $\frac{3}{2}$ hours, or it can do $\frac{2}{3}$ the work in 1 hour. The second pipe can fill the tank in 45 minutes or $\frac{3}{4}$ hour, doing $\frac{4}{3}$ of the job in 1 hour. Thus, together the two pipes can do $\frac{4}{3} + \frac{2}{3} = \frac{6}{3}$ of the job in 1 hour. Therefore, the pipes working together could fill the entire tank in $\frac{1}{2}$ hour.

16. **(A)** There are 12 edges on a cube, so each edge is 48 in. ÷ 12 = 4 inches. The volume of the cube is $(s)^3 = (4 \text{ in.})^3 = 64$ cu. in.

17. **(B)** Since the perimeter of a square is four times the length of a side, it is
$$4\left(\frac{2x}{3} + 1\right), \text{ or } \frac{8x+12}{3}$$

18. **(B)** This is more easily solved by using real numbers. If we assign a value of 6 to AB, then we can figure out that the perpendicular AD is $3\sqrt{3}$. The old perimeter was 18 and the new perimeter is $6 + 3 + 3\sqrt{3}$, or about 14.1. The fraction $\frac{14}{18}$ can be reduced to $\frac{7}{9}$, which is about 78%.

19. **(B)** If the circumference is 60 inches, since $C = 2\pi r$, substitute $C = 60$; therefore, $r = \frac{60}{2\pi}$.

20. **(A)** The radii of the pipe are 1.42 in. and 0.97 in. The thickness is their difference, or .45 in.

21. **(D)** By definition, parallel lines are everywhere equidistant. Therefore, the length of segment d remains constant.

22. **(D)** By using the foil method, $(x+9)(x+2)$
$= x^2 + 9x + 2x + 18$

By combining like terms, this is shortened to:
$x^2 + 11x + 18$.

23. **(B)** If the points (3,1) and (5,y) are $\sqrt{13}$ units apart, then by the distance formula, $\sqrt{13} = \sqrt{(5-3)^2 + (y-1)^2}$.

Solving for y: $13 = (2)^2 + (y-1)^2$
$9 = (y-1)^2$
$y = 4$

24. **(A)** The total number of strikes that a pitcher must throw in a game is 9×9, or 81. Since only 85% of his pitches are strikes, he must throw 81/.85, or 95, pitches a game.

25. **(C)** The area of the rectangle is length × width = 11" × 8" = 88 sq. in. The area of the triangle is $\frac{1}{2}$ (base) × (height). Its base is 8" − 3" = 5"; its height is 11" − 7" = 4". The area of the triangle is $\frac{1}{2} \times 5" \times 4" = 10$ sq. in. The area of the polygon is 88 − 10 = 78 sq. in.

Section 3

Part 1

1. **(A)** For any real numbers s and t, as long as $s > t$, the difference of the smaller from the larger, $s - t$, will always be greater than the larger from the smaller, $t - s$.

2. **(D)** There is no way to determine the cost of the total system or the speakers; therefore, there is no way to determine the discounted price.

3. **(B)** If $p > 0$ and $q < 0$, then $p - q$ is equivalent to $p + |q|$ and $p + q$ is equivalent to $p - |q|$. Since Column B is adding rather than subtracting, Column B is larger.

4. **(D)** Since we know nothing about the placement of A, B, and C, we cannot determine anything about their distances.

5. **(A)** The value of Column A is found by computing $\frac{63}{.07}$, which equals 900. The value of Column B is $(.07)(63) = 4.41$. Hence, Column A is larger.

6. **(C)** Substituting $\frac{1}{2}$ for r in Column A, $2r^3 - 12r + 7 = 2\left(\frac{1}{2}\right)^3 - 12\left(\frac{1}{2}\right) + 7 = 1\frac{1}{4}$. Doing the same in Column B, $r^2 + 1 = \left(\frac{1}{2}\right)^2 + 1 = 1\frac{1}{4}$. The columns are equal.

7. **(D)** We cannot judge which is the larger since if $-1 < x < 1$, $\frac{1}{x^2} > x^2$, but if $x > 1$ or $x < -1$, $x^2 > \frac{1}{x^2}$.

8. **(B)** Solving the two equations: first, $m^3 = 64$, $m = \sqrt[3]{64} = 4$, and second, $\sqrt{n} = 16$, $n = (16)^2 = 256$. Therefore, $n > m$, making Column B greater than Column A.

9. **(C)** Since the measures of angles x, y, and z are equivalent, the triangle is an equilateral triangle with all sides equal. Therefore, $s = t$.

10. **(B)** In Column A, the area of the rectangle is $4 \times \pi = 4\pi$. In Column B, the area of the circle is $\pi(4)^2 = 16\pi$. Therefore, the area of the circle is larger, and Column B is the correct choice.

11. **(B)** The surface area of the whole cube is $6(3)^2 = 54$. The new boxes formed by cutting the cube in half have the same surface area as the cube as a whole, but have added surface area on each cube where the cut was made. This is an addition of $3^2 = 9$ for each cube, making the total surface area $54 + 9 + 9 = 72$. Column B is the larger.

12. **(B)** Since r is a negative number, r^5 will also be a negative number. s^4 is always positive and, consequently, larger than r^5.

13. **(B)** If $x^2 = 25$, $x = \pm 5$. If $2y + 3 = 27$, $2y = 24$, so $y = 12$. y is larger whether x is $+5$ or -5.

14. **(C)** Triangle ABC is isosceles with sides AB and AC equal; therefore, angles ABC and ACB are equal. Angles x and y are supplementary angles of angles ABC and ACB, respectively, and thus must be equal to each other.

15. **(A)** The angles of all triangles add up to $180°$. Angle $MNO = 90°$; therefore, the sum of angles M and Q must also equal $90°$. Column A is larger than Column B.

Part 2

16. 5

17. $4x = 2(2 + x) \quad 6y = 3(2 + y)$
    $4x = 4 + 2x \qquad 6y = 6 + 3y$
    $2x = 4 \qquad\qquad 3y = 6$
    $2x + 3y = 4 + 6 = 10$

18. "JOSH" $= 3n - 3$
    $n = 3n - 3$
    $-2n = -3$
    $n = \frac{3}{2} = 1.5$

19. Machine A produces:

    2,000 flue covers/hour

    Machine B produces:

    $5{,}000 / \frac{5}{2}$ hr. $= 5{,}000 \left(\frac{2}{5}\right) = 2{,}000$ / hr.

Since the rates are the same, they produce the same amount of flue covers during any period of time.

20. $.01 = \dfrac{.1}{x}$

$\dfrac{1}{100} = \dfrac{\frac{1}{10}}{x} = \dfrac{1}{10} \cdot \dfrac{1}{x} = \dfrac{1}{10x}$

$\dfrac{1}{100} = \dfrac{1}{10x}$

$10x = 100$

$x = 10$

21.

Since $ED \parallel AB$
angle E = angle B = 50°
(alternate interior angles)
Since $AC = BC$, angle A = angle B = 50°.
(In a triangle opposite equal sides are equal angles.)

In $\triangle ABC$

$50 + 50 + x = 180$
$x = 80$

22. Let p = the school's population

$\dfrac{1}{4}p + \dfrac{1}{5}p + \dfrac{1}{3}p + 390 = p$

$\dfrac{15p + 12p + 20p}{60} + 390 = p$

$60\left(\dfrac{47p}{60} + 390\right) = p$

$47p + 390(60) = 60p$

$13p = 390(60)$

$p = \dfrac{\overset{30}{\cancel{390}}(60)}{\cancel{13}} = 30(60) = 1800$

23.

3 roads   5 roads

There are $3 \times 5 = 15$ different paths from Williston Park to Mineola through Albertson.

24. Establish a ratio of candies to cents.
Note: $1.70 = 170 cents and $10.20 = 1020 cents.

$\dfrac{\text{candies}}{\text{cents}} : \dfrac{12}{170} = \dfrac{x}{1020}$

$170x = 12(1020)$

$x = 72$

25.

Using the Pythagorean Theorem:

$(30)^2 + (40)^2 = x^2$

$900 + 1,600 = x^2$

$2,500 = x^2$

$x = 50$

Section 4

1. **(B)** The fact that the society required outside aid indicates that it could not totally support itself. In other words, it was not *self-sufficient*.

2. **(D)** Since the regime is new, the laws must be newly announced and put into effect, or *promulgated*.

3. **(B)** *Brittle* machines might *shatter*.

4. **(D)** When illness strikes, even a person with a strong constitution can be *enervated* (weakened and drained of energy).

5. **(C)** A careful researcher would be *meticulous*.

6. **(C)** A shy look might *enchant* someone into matrimony, but it would not *release*, *control*, *ensconce*, or *jilt* someone to that end.

7. **(E)** A city that has failed to fire a single shot against an invading army has clearly *capitulated* (surrendered).

8. **(C)** A *compromise* (agreement) between two opposing sides might avert a strike, but without one the strike becomes *inevitable* (unavoidable).

9. **(A)** A neighbor who is charming is also likely to be *urbane* (suave and sophisticated). Such a person would be the opposite, or *antithesis*, of a bumbling yokel.

10. **(C)** Peeling potatoes and scrubbing floors are both tasks that are *onerous* (burdensome and unpleasant).

11. **(D)** A *pendulum* is designed to *oscillate* and a *gyroscope* to *spin*.

12. **(A)** The first showing of a *movie* is its *premiere* and the first showing of a *statue* is its *unveiling*.

13. **(E)** An *awl* is a pointed tool used by a *carpenter* to make holes in wood. A *pick* is a pointed tool used by a *miner* to break up soil or rock.

14. **(C)** The degree of incline of a *roof* is its *pitch*. The degree of incline of a *mountain* is its *grade*.

15. **(B)** A *cog* is a moving part of a *watch* as a *piston* is a moving part of an *engine*.

16. **(C)** An *equestrian* rides a *horse*; a *cyclist* rides a *bicycle*.

17. **(A)** A *recluse* is *solitary*, preferring to be without company. A *socialite* is *gregarious*, or fond of company.

18. **(D)** *Diffuse* means lacking *concentration*. Similarly, *incongruous* means lacking *harmony*.

19. **(C)** An *apple* is a kind of *fruit* and a *sparrow* is a kind of *bird*.

20. **(E)** A *decade* is *ten* years just as a *millennium* is a *thousand* years.

21. **(E)** A *zealot* (ardent supporter of a cause) is characterized by *fervor* (passion) as a *sage* (wise man) is characterized by *wisdom*.

22. **(C)** A *physician cures* and a *comedian entertains*.

23. **(D)** Plays and symphonies are performed. A *movement* is a part of a *symphony*, and an *act* is part of a *play*.

24. **(D)** Chekhov is praising the play. He is presumably familiar with Gorky's style, and thus compares this play to previous plays with this compliment.

25. **(B)** Red hair on a red-haired man cannot be corrected; it is a natural "flaw." Chekhov means that the "defect" in the play is natural and cannot be repaired.

26. **(D)** Even though Chekhov is being critical in lines 9–11, he makes the point that the play's problems are unavoidable. As a result, his criticism is more supportive than it is negative.

27. **(C)** The play's only defect, according to Chekhov, is "the conservatism of the form" (line 10), which undermines Gorky's new and original characters.

28. **(C)** Chekhov explains that "all that"—the play's unavoidable flaws—stem from the work's conservative structure, i.e. its traditional trappings.

29. **(B)** Chekhov seems concerned throughout with realism. This answer is the only one that makes sense in context.

30. **(B)** As stated in lines 33–34, Nil's modesty is "the element so characteristic of our decent working man."

31. **(D)** Lines 33–34 reveal Chekhov's concern.

32. **(A)** Chekhov is concerned that Elena "is not clear" (lines 52–54); his suggestions attempt to correct that.

33. **(A)** "Both on life and on the stage," Chekhov considers characters such as Teterev unimportant. For this reason, he suggests that Teterev talk less.

34. **(E)** (A) is covered in lines 23–24, (B) in lines 25–26, (C) in lines 40–42, and (D) in lines 47–50. Chekhov has ideas about the ending of the play, which has four acts, but never discusses the ending of the third act.

35. **(E)** Chekhov comments that Piotr "is good. Most likely you don't even suspect how good he is." His only suggestion is that Piotr should be portrayed by the actor Meierkhold.

Section 5

1. **(E)** Stowe says as much in lines 5–7 and in paragraph 2.

2. **(A)** The book will "contain facts and documents" (line 24), so it will not be fictional (B). It will "contain, perhaps, an equal amount of matter" as the previous book (lines 22–23); in other words, it may be as long.

3. **(D)** Rereading this paragraph and the one before proves that Stowe is referring to the horrors of slavery, which she thought she knew, but now finds she "had not begun to measure."

4. **(C)** In this context, the word *exquisitely* means enormously, not its more conventional definitions—expensively, lavishly, or ostentatiously.

5. **(B)** "It seems to me that the book cannot but be felt. . . ." (lines 35–36). Stowe thinks that her readers will feel the pain she documents.

6. **(E)** Nowhere in the passage is it stated that Stowe feels that *Uncle Tom's Cabin* needs a sequel. But she does imply that a second book would support her original work (statement II) and that a presentation of more factual information will strengthen the reader's understanding.

7. **(C)** The passage vividly conveys the emotionalism with which Stowe approaches her writing.

8. **(E)** While there is some truth to (C), it is not implied in the passage. The entire passage concerns Stowe's deeply felt emotions concerning the evils of slavery.

9. **(B)** While all of the answers may have had something to do with slaves not escaping, only (B) is cited in the passage.

10. **(B)** The passage specifically states (lines 55–59) that Douglass's failed first attempt haunted him.

11. **(D)** Since this was his second attempt at escape, Douglass knew that he would be severely punished if he did not succeed.

12. **(E)** Although (D) has some appeal, it is obvious from the last sentence that "brave and persistent" is the best choice.

Section 6

1. **(D)** Since both areas are equal, $\frac{1}{2}bh = \pi r^2$. Thus, knowing the base of the triangle and radius of the circle, $\frac{1}{2}(7)h = \pi(7)^2$, so $h = 14\pi$.

2. **(E)** $70\% = \frac{70}{100} = \frac{7}{10} \cdot \frac{1}{.70} = \frac{100}{70} = \frac{10}{7} \cdot \frac{13}{9}$ and $\frac{1}{.70}$ are the only fractions larger than 1. Comparing them by finding a common denominator of 63, $\frac{10}{7} = \frac{90}{63}, \frac{13}{9} = \frac{91}{63}$, we find $\frac{10}{7} < \frac{13}{9}$. Comparing $\frac{9}{13}$ and $\frac{7}{10}$, which are both less than 1, we find $\frac{9}{13} = \frac{90}{130}, \frac{7}{10} = \frac{91}{130}$, so $\frac{9}{13} < \frac{7}{10}$. Therefore, $\frac{9}{13} < 70\% < \frac{1}{.70} < \frac{13}{9}$.

3. **(D)** The quadrilateral *PQRS* is a parallelogram as shown:

```
         (1,3)                        (10,3)
         ┌─────────────────────────────┐
         │3
       (0,0)                          (9,0)
```

It has a height of 3 and a base of 9. The area is, like that of a rectangle, *bh*, or 27.

Practice Examination 5   543

4. **(C)** One simple way to solve this problem is to divide each side of the given equation by 4.
$$\frac{8x+4}{4} = \frac{64}{4}$$
$$2x+1 = 16$$

5. **(D)** Since the center is at the origin, each coordinate point is the length of a leg of a triangle. The hypotenuse of each triangle is the radius of a new circle with its center at the origin. If the hypotenuse of the triangle is greater than 7, the points are outside the circle. (4,4):

$h = \sqrt{4^2 + 4^2} = 5.7$, so (4,4) is inside the circle. (5,5): $h = \sqrt{5^2 + 5^2} = 7.07$, so (5,5) is outside the circle. (4,5): $h = \sqrt{4^2 + 5^2} = 6.4$, so (4,5) is inside the circle. (4,6): $h = \sqrt{4^2 + 6^2} = 7.2$, so (4,6) is outside the circle.

6. **(D)** The surface area of a square with side = 9 is $9 \cdot 9 = 81$. The surface area of a cube with edge = 3 is $3 \cdot 3 \cdot 6 = 9 \cdot 6 = 54$. The difference, therefore, is $81 - 54 = 27$.

7. **(D)** $2+4+6 = 12$ and 12 is evenly divisible by all three.

8. **(D)**
$$\frac{3(x^2-4)}{(x+2)} = \frac{3(x+2)(x-2)}{(x+2)}$$
$$= 3(x-2)$$
$$= 3x-6$$

9. **(B)** There are $5 \times 2 = 10$ different varieties of ice cream bars on the truck. Since the truck only runs four times a week, it would take a person 2 weeks + 2 days to purchase all the different varieties of ice cream bars. Therefore, the day would be the 16th of the month.

10. **(A)**

$$\frac{N!}{(N-2)} =$$
$$\frac{N(N-1)(N-2)(N-3)(N-4)\ldots[N-(N-1)]}{(N-2)(N-3)(N-4)\ldots[N-(N-1)]}$$

Cancelling like factors in the numerator and the denominator leaves only

$$\frac{N(N-1)}{1} = N(N-1) = N^2 - N$$

COMPUTING YOUR SCORES ON PRACTICE EXAMINATION 5

You are now ready to check your progress by calculating your scores for the fifth practice examination. To begin, you need to compute individual verbal and mathematical raw scores. Once you have computed these, use the conversion scales in the section that follows to compute your SAT scaled scores (200–800). Keep in mind that these formulas have been simplified to give you a "quick and dirty" sense of where you are scoring, not a perfectly precise score.

To Compute Your Raw Scores:

1. Enter the number of correct answers for each verbal and mathematical reasoning section into the boxes marked "Number of Questions Correct."
2. Enter the number of incorrect answers (not blanks) for each verbal and mathematical reasoning section into the boxes marked "Number of Questions Incorrect."
3. Total the number correct and number incorrect.
4. Follow this formula: Take the total correct and minus one-quarter of the total incorrect. Round up in your favor to compute your Raw Score.

Verbal Section	Total Number of Questions	Number of Questions Correct	Number of Questions Incorrect
1	31		
4	35		
5	12		
Totals	78	Total Correct:	Total Incorrect:

Verbal Raw Score = Total Correct – ($\frac{1}{4}$ × Total Incorrect) = _____

Math Section	Total Number of Questions	Number of Questions Correct	Number of Questions Incorrect
2	25		
3	25		
6	10		
Totals	60	Total Correct:	Total Incorrect:

Math Raw Score = Total Correct – ($\frac{1}{4}$ × Total Incorrect) = _____

CONVERSION SCALES FOR PRACTICE EXAMINATION 5

VERBAL REASONING

Raw Score	Scaled Score	Raw Score	Scaled Score
75	800	35	520
70	800	30	480
65	760	25	440
60	710	20	410
55	670	15	370
50	620	10	340
45	590	5	290
40	550	0	230

MATHEMATICAL REASONING

Raw Score	Scaled Score	Raw Score	Scaled Score
60	800	25	510
55	760	20	480
50	690	15	440
45	650	10	410
40	610	5	340
35	580	0	200
30	550		

Although you now have some idea of what your scores would look like had they been scaled according to unofficial ETS standards, you will probably want to know how to interpret your Raw Scores in more familiar terms. If so, use the following Self-Evaluation Charts to see what your Raw Scores actually mean.

SELF-EVALUATION CHARTS

VERBAL REASONING: Raw Score

Excellent	60 – 75
Good	50 – 60
Average	30 – 50
Fair	20 – 30
Poor	0 – 20

MATHEMATICAL REASONING: Raw Score

Excellent	50 – 60
Good	40 – 50
Average	20 – 40
Fair	10 – 20
Poor	0 – 10

PRACTICE EXAMINATION 6

Answer Sheet

If a section has fewer questions than answer ovals, leave the extra ovals blank.

Section 1

(Answer grid: questions 1–40, options A B C D E)

Section 2

(Answer grid: questions 1–40, options A B C D E)

Section 3

Answer spaces for Section 3 are on the back of this answer sheet.

Section 4

(Answer grid: questions 1–40, options A B C D E)

Section 3

1. Ⓐ Ⓑ Ⓒ Ⓓ Ⓔ
2. Ⓐ Ⓑ Ⓒ Ⓓ Ⓔ
3. Ⓐ Ⓑ Ⓒ Ⓓ Ⓔ
4. Ⓐ Ⓑ Ⓒ Ⓓ Ⓔ
5. Ⓐ Ⓑ Ⓒ Ⓓ Ⓔ
6. Ⓐ Ⓑ Ⓒ Ⓓ Ⓔ
7. Ⓐ Ⓑ Ⓒ Ⓓ Ⓔ
8. Ⓐ Ⓑ Ⓒ Ⓓ Ⓔ
9. Ⓐ Ⓑ Ⓒ Ⓓ Ⓔ
10. Ⓐ Ⓑ Ⓒ Ⓓ Ⓔ
11. Ⓐ Ⓑ Ⓒ Ⓓ Ⓔ
12. Ⓐ Ⓑ Ⓒ Ⓓ Ⓔ
13. Ⓐ Ⓑ Ⓒ Ⓓ Ⓔ
14. Ⓐ Ⓑ Ⓒ Ⓓ Ⓔ
15. Ⓐ Ⓑ Ⓒ Ⓓ Ⓔ

Note: ONLY the answers entered on the grid are scored. Handwritten answers at the top of the column are NOT scored.

[Grid-in answer boxes for questions 16–25]

Section 5

1. Ⓐ Ⓑ Ⓒ Ⓓ Ⓔ
2. Ⓐ Ⓑ Ⓒ Ⓓ Ⓔ
3. Ⓐ Ⓑ Ⓒ Ⓓ Ⓔ
4. Ⓐ Ⓑ Ⓒ Ⓓ Ⓔ
5. Ⓐ Ⓑ Ⓒ Ⓓ Ⓔ
6. Ⓐ Ⓑ Ⓒ Ⓓ Ⓔ
7. Ⓐ Ⓑ Ⓒ Ⓓ Ⓔ
8. Ⓐ Ⓑ Ⓒ Ⓓ Ⓔ
9. Ⓐ Ⓑ Ⓒ Ⓓ Ⓔ
10. Ⓐ Ⓑ Ⓒ Ⓓ Ⓔ
11. Ⓐ Ⓑ Ⓒ Ⓓ Ⓔ
12. Ⓐ Ⓑ Ⓒ Ⓓ Ⓔ
13. Ⓐ Ⓑ Ⓒ Ⓓ Ⓔ
14. Ⓐ Ⓑ Ⓒ Ⓓ Ⓔ
15. Ⓐ Ⓑ Ⓒ Ⓓ Ⓔ

Section 6

1. Ⓐ Ⓑ Ⓒ Ⓓ Ⓔ
2. Ⓐ Ⓑ Ⓒ Ⓓ Ⓔ
3. Ⓐ Ⓑ Ⓒ Ⓓ Ⓔ
4. Ⓐ Ⓑ Ⓒ Ⓓ Ⓔ
5. Ⓐ Ⓑ Ⓒ Ⓓ Ⓔ
6. Ⓐ Ⓑ Ⓒ Ⓓ Ⓔ
7. Ⓐ Ⓑ Ⓒ Ⓓ Ⓔ
8. Ⓐ Ⓑ Ⓒ Ⓓ Ⓔ
9. Ⓐ Ⓑ Ⓒ Ⓓ Ⓔ
10. Ⓐ Ⓑ Ⓒ Ⓓ Ⓔ
11. Ⓐ Ⓑ Ⓒ Ⓓ Ⓔ
12. Ⓐ Ⓑ Ⓒ Ⓓ Ⓔ
13. Ⓐ Ⓑ Ⓒ Ⓓ Ⓔ
14. Ⓐ Ⓑ Ⓒ Ⓓ Ⓔ
15. Ⓐ Ⓑ Ⓒ Ⓓ Ⓔ

Practice Examination 6

SECTION 1

35 Questions • Time—30 Minutes

Directions: Each of the following questions consists of an incomplete sentence followed by five words or pairs of words. Choose that word or pair of words which, when substituted for the blank space or spaces, best completes the meaning of the sentence and mark the letter of your choice on your answer sheet.

Example:

In view of the extenuating circumstances and the defendant's youth, the judge recommended ----.

(A) conviction (B) a defense
(C) a mistrial (D) leniency
(E) life imprisonment   Ⓐ Ⓑ Ⓒ ● Ⓔ

1. His ---- record collection included everything from Bach to rock.

    (A) divisive
    (B) effusive
    (C) eclectic
    (D) intrinsic
    (E) laconic

2. The objective may be ----, but the plan presented for achieving it is far from practicable.

    (A) compensatory
    (B) laudable
    (C) insignificant
    (D) precarious
    (E) subversive

3. Her statements were so ---- that we were left in doubt as to her real intentions.

    (A) equitable
    (B) equivocal
    (C) innocuous
    (D) dogmatic
    (E) incisive

4. The Senator was under investigation because of accusations that he had filed ---- financial disclosure forms.

    (A) veritable
    (B) replicated
    (C) extraneous
    (D) duplicitous
    (E) muddled

5. The retiring teacher was ---- for his tireless efforts on behalf of his students.

    (A) paraphrased
    (B) involved
    (C) appointed
    (D) commended
    (E) directed

6. That particular economist ---- that government regulation ---- leads to higher prices.

    (A) teaches..unavailably
    (B) knows..insistently
    (C) feels..dubiously
    (D) sees..blindly
    (E) believes..inevitably

7. The teenagers were such ---- followers of the daytime soap opera that they taped every episode.

    (A) dexterous
    (B) flagrant
    (C) assiduous
    (D) retentive
    (E) adroit

GO ON TO THE NEXT PAGE

8. Scheherazade ---- by spinning tales for the Sultan, thus postponing her execution for a thousand and one nights.

   (A) eradicated
   (B) temporized
   (C) truncated
   (D) acclimated
   (E) transgressed

9. The supervisor prided herself on her ----, convinced that it was more important to be fair than to be liked by everyone.

   (A) cheerfulness
   (B) reticence
   (C) objectivity
   (D) superiority
   (E) congeniality

10. That field has become so ---- that researchers on different aspects of the same problem may be ---- each other's work.

    (A) secure..bombarded with
    (B) partial..surprised at
    (C) departmental..inimical to
    (D) specialized..unfamiliar with
    (E) secretive..knowledgeable of

Directions: Each of the following questions consists of a capitalized pair of words followed by five pairs of words lettered A to E. The capitalized words bear some meaningful relationship to each other. Choose the lettered pair of words whose relation-ship is most similar to that expressed by the capitalized pair and mark its letter on your answer sheet.

Example:

DAY : SUN : :
(A) sunlight : daylight (B) ray : sun
(C) night : moon   (D) heat : cold
(E) moon : star

Ⓐ Ⓑ ● Ⓓ Ⓔ

11. TRUMPET : TUBA : :

 (A) piano : keys
 (B) violin : bow
 (C) drum : cymbal
 (D) piccolo : bassoon
 (E) music : notes

12. DINGHY : WATER : :

 (A) barge : dock
 (B) oar : wing
 (C) river : boat
 (D) glider : air
 (E) parachute : plane

13. NAIL : PUNCTURE : :

 (A) scalpel : incision
 (B) drill : window
 (C) saw : tree
 (D) cleft : ax
 (E) wheel : axle

14. STAR : GALAXY : :

 (A) sun : moon
 (B) light : dawn
 (C) bird : flock
 (D) caravan : desert
 (E) plane : jet

15. SILVER : METAL : :

 (A) gold : alloy
 (B) plastic : container
 (C) helium : gas
 (D) sand : glass
 (E) sediment : rock

16. SPRINTER : SPEED : :

 (A) athlete : practice
 (B) ball : game
 (C) soccer : head
 (D) weight lifter : strength
 (E) gymnast : bars

17. INTERLOPER : MEDDLE : :

 (A) stranger : alienate
 (B) rogue : repent
 (C) avenger : punish
 (D) patron : teach
 (E) consumer : create

18. METEOROLOGY : WEATHER : :

 (A) ornithology : birds
 (B) chemistry : test tube
 (C) physics : calculus
 (D) meteors : earth
 (E) clouds : moisture

19. INNOVATION : PRECEDENT : :

 (A) inception : reality
 (B) illusion : veracity
 (C) conservation : simplicity
 (D) renovation : antiquity
 (E) invention : production

20. ANARCHIST : LAWLESS : :

 (A) policeman : cautious
 (B) lawyer : ominous
 (C) philosopher : escapist
 (D) animal : beauty
 (E) philistine : uncultured

21. DETRIMENTAL : PERNICIOUS : :

 (A) delightful : delicious
 (B) cheerful : exuberant
 (C) painful : sore
 (D) helpful : useful
 (E) fearful : timid

GO ON TO THE NEXT PAGE

22. ROBUST : VIGOR : :
    (A) massive : strength
    (B) sick : illness
    (C) farsighted : glasses
    (D) full : appetite
    (E) sanguine : hope

23. TRAITOROUS : PERFIDY : :
    (A) despicable : country
    (B) envious : green
    (C) devious : dourness
    (D) loyal : steadfastness
    (E) smart : average

Questions 24–35 are based on the following passage.

On July 4, 1852, former slave Frederick Douglass was asked to speak during a commemoration of the Declaration of Independence in Rochester, New York. His speech shocked many listeners and introduced one of the greatest orators of the Civil War era.

What, am I to argue that it is wrong to make men brutes, to rob them of their liberty, to work them without wages, to keep them ignorant of their relations to their fellow men, to beat them with sticks, to flay their flesh
(5) with the lash, to load their limbs with irons, to hunt them with dogs, to sell them at auction, to sunder their families, to knock out their teeth, to burn their flesh, to starve them into obedience and submission to their masters? Must I argue that a system thus marked with
(10) blood, and stained with pollution, is wrong? No! I will not. I have better employment for my time and strength than such arguments would imply.

What, then, remains to be argued? Is it that slavery is not divine; that God did not establish it; that our
(15) doctors of divinity are mistaken? There is blasphemy in the thought. That which is inhuman cannot be divine! Who can reason on such a proposition? They that can, may; I cannot. The time for such argument is past.

At a time like this, scorching iron, not convincing
(20) argument, is needed. O! had I the ability, and could I reach the nation's ear, I would today pour out a fiery stream of biting ridicule, blasting reproach, withering sarcasm, and stern rebuke. For it is not light that is needed, but fire; it is not the gentle shower, but
(25) thunder. We need the storm, the whirlwind, and the earthquake. The feeling of the nation must be quickened; the conscience of the nation must be roused; the propriety of the nation must be startled; the hypocrisy of the nation must be exposed; and its crimes against
(30) God and man must be proclaimed and denounced.

What, to the American slave, is your Fourth of July? I answer: a day that reveals to him, more than all other days in the year, the gross injustice and cruelty to which he is the constant victim. To him, your celebration is a
(35) sham; your boasted liberty, an unholy license; your national greatness, swelling vanity; your sounds of rejoicing are empty and heartless; your denunciation of tyrants, brass-fronted impudence; your shouts of liberty and equality, hollow mockery; your prayers and hymns,
(40) your sermons and thanksgiving, with all your religious parade and solemnity, are to him, mere bombast, fraud, deception, impiety, and hypocrisy—a thin veil to cover up crimes which would disgrace a nation of savages. There is not a nation on earth guilty of practices more
(45) shocking and bloody than are the people of the United States at this very hour.

Go where you may, search where you will, roam through all the monarchies and despotisms of the Old World, travel through South America, search out every
(50) abuse, and when you have found the last, lay your facts by the side of the everyday practices of this nation, and you will say with me that, for revolting barbarity and shameless hypocrisy, America reigns without a rival.

24. Douglass opens this section of his speech with a(n)

    (A) metaphor
    (B) rhetorical question
    (C) appeal to the gods
    (D) digression
    (E) apology

25. The word *lash* (line 5) is used to mean

    (A) whip
    (B) tie
    (C) tether
    (D) eyebrow
    (E) band

26. In line 6, what is the best definition of *sunder*?

    (A) surrender
    (B) supply
    (C) divide
    (D) affix
    (E) harbor

27. Which of the following best states Douglass's opinion of the theory that slavery is divinely ordained?

 (A) It may or may not be true.
 (B) It is blasphemous.
 (C) It is a question for the clergy to decide.
 (D) It has been proven by doctors of divinity.
 (E) The time has come to debate the theory.

28. Why does Frederick Douglass state that he has "better employment" (line 11) for his time than to make certain arguments against slavery?

 (A) Because the issue of slavery has already been neatly resolved.
 (B) Because these arguments will not have a significant impact.
 (C) Because he is now a freed man, he no longer cares about slavery.
 (D) Because the issues are too complex.
 (E) Because he is too tired to undertake the challenge.

29. Why does Douglass list violent natural phenomena in paragraph 3?

 (A) To appeal to Heaven for release
 (B) To expose the cruelty of man
 (C) To show that slavery is unnatural
 (D) To stress the need for drastic action
 (E) To compare natural and man-made disasters

30. How might you reword the phrase "the feeling of the nation must be quickened" (line 26)?

 (A) The opinion of the nation must be expedited.
 (B) The nation's approach must be impulsive.
 (C) The foreboding in the nation is accelerating.
 (D) The nation's beliefs must be perceptive.
 (E) The nation's passions must be aroused.

31. How does Douglass feel about the Fourth of July?

 (A) It is a fraud.
 (B) It is exciting.
 (C) It is a time for pride in the nation's heritage.
 (D) It is the best day to abolish slavery.
 (E) It is the ideal moment for a debate on slavery.

32. With the phrase "a nation of savages" (line 43), Douglass means to compare Americans who condone slavery to

 (A) slaves
 (B) citizens
 (C) barbarians
 (D) countrymen
 (E) foreigners

33. Why does Douglass mention South America (line 49)?

 (A) To contrast slavery in two locales
 (B) As an example of a place he considers more barbaric than the United States
 (C) To compare two forms of government
 (D) As an example of an innocent land
 (E) As an example of a place he considers less barbaric than the United States

34. Listeners probably found this speech shocking because of the speaker's

 (A) furious denunciation of the celebration
 (B) anger at elected officials
 (C) profane language and swearing
 (D) call for revolt against the government
 (E) appeal to rebels to lay down their arms

35. Frederick Douglass' overall attitude toward the United States is

 (A) resigned
 (B) scorching
 (C) indifferent
 (D) somewhat supportive
 (E) resoundingly patriotic

STOP

END OF SECTION 1. IF YOU HAVE ANY TIME LEFT, GO OVER YOUR WORK IN THIS SECTION ONLY. DO NOT WORK IN ANY OTHER SECTION OF THE TEST.

SECTION 2

25 Questions • Time—30 Minutes

Directions: Solve the following problems using any available space on the page for scratchwork. On your answer sheet fill in the choice which best corresponds to the correct answer.

Notes: The figures accompanying the problems are drawn as accurately as possible unless otherwise stated in specific problems. Again, unless otherwise stated, all figures lie in the same plane. All numbers used in these problems are real numbers. Calculators are permitted for this test.

1. If $\frac{2}{3} + \frac{3}{4} + \frac{5}{6} + p = 3$, then $p =$

   (A) $\frac{4}{3}$
   (B) $\frac{3}{4}$
   (C) $\frac{2}{3}$
   (D) $\frac{1}{2}$
   (E) $\frac{1}{3}$

2. In the figure below, $x + y =$

   (A) 360
   (B) 180
   (C) 130
   (D) 50
   (E) It cannot be determined from the information given.

3. If $P = QR$ and $Q = S + 2$, then which of the following is equal to $\frac{P}{R}$?

   (A) $S + 2$
   (B) S
   (C) $S - 2$
   (D) $Q(S + 2)$
   (E) SQ

4. If $x = -\frac{1}{2}$, then which of the following is the greatest?

   (A) x^5
   (B) x^4
   (C) x^3
   (D) x^2
   (E) x

GO ON TO THE NEXT PAGE

5. A man runs 5 miles per hour for one and one-half hours. If a woman runs the same distance in one hour, what is the woman's average speed in miles per hour?

   (A) 10
   (B) $9\frac{1}{2}$
   (C) $7\frac{1}{2}$
   (D) 5
   (E) $4\frac{1}{2}$

6. What is the sum of four integers whose average is 11?

   (A) 36
   (B) 38
   (C) 40
   (D) 42
   (E) 44

7. In a basket containing 180 pears, 9 are spoiled. What percent of the pears in the basket are not spoiled?

   (A) 95%
   (B) 90%
   (C) 50%
   (D) 25%
   (E) 20%

8. A number r is tripled, the new number is decreased by three, and that number is then divided by three. Which of the following reflects the above statements?

   (A) $3(r-3)$
   (B) $9r$
   (C) $r-3$
   (D) r
   (E) $r-1$

9. If $ABCD$ is a square with a side of 4, then what is the sum of the perimeter of $\triangle ABE$ and $\triangle DCF$?

   Note: Figure not drawn to scale.

   (A) 48
   (B) 36
   (C) 24
   (D) 12
   (E) 6

10. $\sqrt{\dfrac{3}{4} - \dfrac{3}{16}} =$

    (A) $\dfrac{4}{3}$
    (B) $\dfrac{3}{4}$
    (C) $\dfrac{9}{16}$
    (D) $\dfrac{1}{3}$
    (E) $\dfrac{1}{4}$

11. If $\{w, x, y, z\} = z(w + x + y)$, so that $\{1, 2, 3, 4\} = 4(1 + 2 + 3) = 24$, then all of the following are equal *except*

    (A) $\{2, 3, 4, 6\}$
    (B) $\{4, 3, 2, 6\}$
    (C) $\{3, 5, 1, 6\}$
    (D) $\{4, 1, 5, 6\}$
    (E) $\{1, 5, 3, 6\}$

12. If a pound contains 16 ounces, 16.4 ounces would be how many pounds?

    (A) 1.75
    (B) 1.5
    (C) 1.25
    (D) 1.025
    (E) 1.0025

13. If a certain circle has a circumference of x, then which of the following is the radius of the circle?

    (A) $\dfrac{x}{2\pi}$

    (B) $\dfrac{x}{\pi}$

    (C) $\dfrac{2x}{\pi}$

    (D) $2 \times \pi$

    (E) $4 \times \pi$

14. If $(x+1)(x-2)$ is positive, then

    (A) $x < -1$ or $x > 2$
    (B) $x > -1$ or $x < 2$
    (C) $-1 < x < 2$
    (D) $-2 < x < 1$
    (E) $x = -1$ or $x = 2$

15. If rectangle $ABCD$ has a length of 12 and a width of 8, what is the ratio of the area of $\triangle AED$ to the area of $ABCD$?

    (A) 1 : 6
    (B) 1 : 4
    (C) 2 : 5
    (D) 3 : 7
    (E) 1 : 2

16. A "full" number is one that is the sum of all the other numbers besides itself by which it can be divided without leaving a remainder. Which of the following is a "full" number?

    I. 6
    II. 12
    III. 28
    IV. 32

    (A) I only
    (B) I and II only
    (C) I and III only
    (D) III and IV only
    (E) I, III, and IV only

17. ANNUAL SALE OF CASSETTES
    ABC SOUND STORES

Year	Number Sold
1985	7,000
1986	9,000
1987	12,000
1988	16,000
1989	20,000
1990	24,000

    In the above table, which yearly period had the smallest percent increase in sales?

    (A) 1985–86
    (B) 1986–87
    (C) 1987–88
    (D) 1988–89
    (E) 1989–90

18. A student scored 70, 75, and 80 on three tests. If the student scored y on the fourth test, what is the average (arithmetic mean) of the four tests?

    (A) $\dfrac{225+y}{4}$

    (B) $\dfrac{225+y}{3}$

    (C) $\dfrac{75+y}{4}$

    (D) $\dfrac{75+y}{2}$

    (E) y

19. Two snails are three feet apart and directly facing each other. If one snail moves forward continuously at .04 inches per second and the other moves forward continuously at .05 inches per second, how many minutes will it take for the snails to touch?

   (A) $3\frac{1}{3}$ minutes

   (B) $6\frac{2}{3}$ minutes

   (C) 9 minutes

   (D) $12\frac{1}{2}$ minutes

   (E) 18 minutes

20. A person is hired for a job that pays $500 per month and receives a 10% raise in each following month. In the fourth month, how much will that person earn?

   (A) $550
   (B) $600.50
   (C) $650.50
   (D) $665.50
   (E) $700

21. John is now four times as old as Anne was six years ago. How old is Anne today if John is 20 years old?

   (A) 8
   (B) 11
   (C) 12
   (D) 14
   (E) 15

22. If $a^2 - 2ab + b^2 = 36$ and $a^2 - 3ab + b^2 = 22$, what is the value of ab?

   (A) 6
   (B) 8
   (C) 12
   (D) 14
   (E) It cannot be determined from the information given.

23. In the figure below, four semicircles are drawn on the four sides of a rectangle. What is the total area of the shaded portion?

   (A) 5π

   (B) $\dfrac{5\pi}{2}$

   (C) $\dfrac{5\pi}{4}$

   (D) $\dfrac{5\pi}{8}$

   (E) $\dfrac{5\pi}{16}$

24. $P = \frac{1}{2} + \frac{1}{3}$ and $Q = P^2$, what is $Q - P$?

(A) 1

(B) $\frac{5}{36}$

(C) 0

(D) $-\frac{5}{36}$

(E) $-\frac{25}{36}$

25. In the figure, the enclosed square has an area of

(A) 9
(B) 18
(C) 24
(D) 27
(E) 36

Note: Figure not drawn to scale.

STOP

END OF SECTION 2. IF YOU HAVE ANY TIME LEFT, GO OVER YOUR WORK IN THIS SECTION ONLY. DO NOT WORK IN ANY OTHER SECTION OF THE TEST.

SECTION 3

25 Questions • Time—30 Minutes

Directions: Solve the following problems using any available space on the page for scratchwork. On your answer sheet fill in the choice which best corresponds to the correct answer.

Notes: The figures accompanying the problems are drawn as accurately as possible unless otherwise stated in specific problems. Again, unless otherwise stated, all figures lie in the same plane. All numbers used in these problems are real numbers. Calculators are permitted for this test.

Reference Information

Circle: $C = 2\pi r$, $A = \pi r^2$
Rectangle: $A = lw$
Rectangular Solid: $V = lwh$
Cylinder: $V = \pi r^2 h$
Triangle: $A = \frac{1}{2}bh$
$a^2 + b^2 = c^2$

Special right triangles: 45°-45°-90° with sides x, x, $x\sqrt{2}$; 30°-60°-90° with sides x, $x\sqrt{3}$, $2x$.

The number of degrees of arc in a circle is 360.
The measure in degrees of a straight angle is 180.
The sum of the measures in degrees of the angles of a triangle is 180.

Part 1: Quantitative Comparison Questions

Directions: For each of the following questions, two quantities are given—one in Column A, and the other in Column B. Compare the two quantities and mark your answer sheet as follows:

(A) if the quantity in Column A is greater
(B) if the quantity in Column B is greater
(C) if the two quantities are equal
(D) if the relationship cannot be determined from the information given.

Notes:

(1) Information concerning one or both of the compared quantities will be centered above the two columns for some items.
(2) Symbols that appear in both columns represent the same thing in Column A as in Column B.
(3) Letters such as x, n, and k are symbols for real numbers.

Examples

	Column A	Column B	Answers
	$a > 0$		
	$x > 0$		
E1.	$a - x$	$a + x$	(A) ● (C) (D)
E2.	The average of 17, 19, 21, 23	The average of 16, 18, 20, 22	● (B) (C) (D)

DO NOT MARK CHOICE (E) FOR THESE QUESTIONS. THERE ARE ONLY FOUR ANSWER CHOICES.

8. It takes great ---- to leave a country and ---- a new life in a foreign land.

   (A) demands..forget
   (B) mandates..regret
   (C) courage..establish
   (D) conviction..designate
   (E) ability..relish

9. The military censors ---- any passages in the letters that they thought might ---- security.

   (A) obtruded..malign
   (B) impugned..nullify
   (C) rebutted..decimate
   (D) expunged..jeopardize
   (E) divulged..enjoin

Directions: Each of the following questions consists of a capitalized pair of words followed by five pairs of words lettered A to E. The capitalized words bear some meaningful relationship to each other. Choose the lettered pair of words whose relationship is most similar to that expressed by the capitalized pair and mark its letter on your answer sheet.

Example:

DAY : SUN : :

(A) sunlight : daylight (B) ray : sun
(C) night : moon (D) heat : cold
(E) moon : star

Ⓐ Ⓑ ● Ⓓ Ⓔ

10. HOUR : TIME : :

   (A) hand : clock
   (B) digit : electricity
   (C) gram : weight
   (D) speedometer : car
   (E) scale : diet

11. GEM : SETTING : :

   (A) diamond : gold
   (B) photo : camera
   (C) ring : necklace
   (D) picture : frame
   (E) painting : subject

12. SHIP : ARMADA : :

   (A) sail : wind
   (B) gun : sword
   (C) atom : molecule
   (D) chemical : reaction
   (E) violin : flute

13. CATERPILLAR : BUTTERFLY : :

   (A) tadpole : frog
   (B) bird : nest
   (C) egg : yolk
   (D) puppy : kitten
   (E) horse : zebra

14. TREMBLE : FEAR : :

   (A) scream : envy
   (B) smile : rage
   (C) demand : anger
   (D) follow : love
   (E) weep : grief

15. SPARK : CONFLAGRATION : :

   (A) match : light
   (B) oxygen : combustion
   (C) drizzle : downpour
   (D) sugar : sweetness
   (E) mountain : hill

Directions: Each passage below is followed by a set of questions. Read each passage, then answer the accompanying questions, basing your answers on what is stated or implied in the passage and in any introductory material provided. Mark the letter of your choice on your answer sheet.

Questions 16–24 are based on the following passage.

This passage presents an overview of the various types of interactions that certain types of organisms have with their environment.

The study of the interactions between organisms and their environment and the effects that these interactions have is called *ecology*. The different kinds of organisms living and interacting together in an area are called a
(5) *community*. An example of a community might be a pond where you might find fish, turtles, ducks, and algae all living together. The fish use the pond as a home. Turtles use the pond for a source of food, as do the ducks. The algae thrive in the wet environment.
(10) Obtaining food is one of the more obvious interactions between organisms in a community.

There are many kinds of communities. A tree is a community that may contain insects, woodpeckers, squirrels, and moss. We as humans are also part of a
(15) community. Dogs, cats, trees, birds, and insects are some of the organisms that exist in our community.

A *food chain* is a sequence of organisms in a community in which each member of the chain feeds on the member below it. Organisms feed upon other organisms
(20) and are then fed upon themselves. For example, insects may feed upon leaves and grass. Mice may in turn feed on the insects and then be fed upon by snakes, which may be eaten by hawks. This is just one example of a food chain. A community can have several food chains, and
(25) those food chains can be intertwined. This type of interaction of many food chains is called a *food web*.

Every member of a community plays a certain role in the food chain. The food chain is based on the lowest members, which are known as *producers*. Producers
(30) make their own food. Plants such as oak trees, algae, and grass are producers. They make their food from air, water, and light by photosynthesis. All members of a community depend either directly or indirectly on the producers.

(35) Consumers are organisms that do not make their own food. Some consumers eat producers; some consumers, like owls, snakes, and bobcats, eat other live consumers. And some consumers, such as vultures and some insects, eat dead consumers. Several consumers in a
(40) food web are the *decomposers*. Decomposers, which include bacteria, mushrooms, and molds, play an important role in the community by breaking down the bodies of dead organisms and the waste products of live organisms into simple chemical substances.

(45) *Symbiosis* is the relationship between two different organisms that interact closely. In some symbiotic relationships, both organisms benefit from the interaction. In other symbiotic relationships, only one of the organisms benefits from the interaction; such relation-
(50) ships are thought of as *parasitic* relationships. Parasites obtain food directly from the live organism (host) in or on which they live, harming the host by this interaction. *Competition* is another type of symbiotic relationship. Competition occurs when some necessity, such as food
(55) or shelter, is in short supply. Competing organisms may actually fight for a resource.

A much larger interacting system than the community is the ecosystem. An ecosystem contains all of the living and non-living things in an area. The non-living
(60) aspects of an ecosystem include the air, water, light, temperature, space, soil, rocks, and minerals. There is an interaction between the living and the non-living in an ecosystem. Voles burrow into the ground. Larger animals may live in caves. Living organisms also obtain
(65) chemical substances from the non-living environment. For example, producers make food and obtain water from the soil and the air. They also obtain nitrogen and phosphorus from the environment. These chemicals are imperative for growth, and are passed on to the consum-
(70) ers through the food chain.

Living organisms all have certain characteristics that help them survive in the environment. These characteristics are called *adaptations*. An adaptation may affect the way in which an organism blends into its
(75) surroundings or the ways in which that particular organism behaves under certain conditions.

GO ON TO THE NEXT PAGE

16. Which of the following might be considered an example of a community?

    (A) animals and plants in a meadow
    (B) a family of bobcats
    (C) rocks and cliffs on a mountainside
    (D) grass and rocks
    (E) a field of flowers

17. Which of the following shows a food chain from producer to decomposer?

    (A) grass—antelope—lion
    (B) lion—hyena—hunter
    (C) mouse—hawk—vulture—mold
    (D) oak tree—acorn—sapling—forester
    (E) clover—rabbit—fox—microbe

18. Which of the following conclusions is (are) suggested by paragraphs 4 and 5 (lines 27–37)?

    I. Consumers depend upon producers.
    II. Only producers make their own food.
    III. All consumers are animals.

    (A) I only
    (B) II only
    (C) I and II only
    (D) III only
    (E) II and III only

19. If you saw a crow feeding on a dead rabbit, you might conclude that

    (A) the crow was lower on the food chain
    (B) the animals had a competitive relationship
    (C) the animals had a symbiotic relationship
    (D) the crow was higher on the food chain
    (E) the rabbit had been unable to adapt

20. A parasitic relationship is

    (A) a relationship between equal organisms
    (B) a relationship of mutual benefit
    (C) a form of adaptation
    (D) a form of variation
    (E) a form of symbiosis

21. An example of competition might be

    (A) robins feeding worms to their nestlings
    (B) pine needles exuding a chemical that keeps other plants from growing nearby
    (C) woodpeckers pecking holes in trees in order to obtain insects
    (D) bats and bears sharing a single cave
    (E) a family of bobcats seeking food

22. Unlike a community, an ecosystem

    (A) includes both producers and consumers
    (B) includes inanimate objects
    (C) involves interactions among organisms
    (D) involves intertwined food webs
    (E) includes competitive relationships

23. All of the following might be considered adaptations EXCEPT

    (A) a butterfly whose pattern resembles an owl's face
    (B) a turkey's mating call
    (C) a human's hair color
    (D) a snowshoe hare's white winter coat
    (E) a chameleon's coloring

24. A good title for this article might be

    (A) "Symbiosis"
    (B) "All About Ecology"
    (C) "Examples of Interactions"
    (D) "Food Chains in our Ecosystem"
    (E) "Adapt or Perish"

Questions 25–31 are based on the following passage.

Stephen Crane (1871–1900) was an American fiction writer who specialized in realistic description. In the following story, originally printed in Harper's Magazine *in 1899, he recounts a harrowing tale of events in a schoolyard.*

"Oh! Oh! Oh! Jimmie Trescott's writing to his girl! Oh! Oh!"... She managed soon to shy through the door and out upon the playground, yelling, "Oh, Jimmie Trescott's been writing to his girl!"

(5) The unhappy Jimmie was following as closely as he was allowed by his knowledge of the decencies to be preserved under the eye of the teacher.

Jimmie himself was mainly responsible for the scene which ensued on the playground. It is possible that the (10) little girl might have run, shrieking his infamy, without exciting more than a general but unmilitant interest. These barbarians were excited only by the actual appearance of human woe; in that event they cheered and danced. Jimmie made the strategic mistake of pursuing (15) little Rose, and thus exposed his thin skin to the whole school. He had in his cowering mind a vision of a hundred children turning from their play under the maple trees and speeding toward him over the gravel with sudden wild taunts. Upon him drove a yelping (20) demonic mob, to which his words were futile. He saw in this mob boys that he dimly knew, and his deadly enemies, and his retainers, and his most intimate friends. The virulence of his deadly enemy was no greater than the virulence of his intimate friend. From the outskirts (25) the little informer could be heard still screaming the news, like a toy parrot with clock-work inside it. It broke up all sorts of games, not so much because of the mere fact of the letter-writing as because the children knew that some sufferer was at the last point, and like little (30) blood-fanged wolves, they thronged to the scene of his destruction. They galloped about him shrilly chanting insults. He turned from one to another, only to meet with howls. He was baited.

Then, in one instant, he changed all this with a blow. (35) Bang! The most pitiless of the boys near him received a punch, fairly and skillfully, which made him bellow out like a walrus, and then Jimmie laid desperately into the whole world, striking out frenziedly in all directions. Boys who could handily whip him, and knew it, (40) backed away from this onslaught. Here was intention—serious intention. They themselves were not in frenzy and their cooler judgment respected Jimmie's efforts when he ran amuck. They saw that it really was none of their affair. In the meantime the wretched little girl who (45) had caused the bloody riot was away by the fence, weeping because boys were fighting. . . .

Then upon the situation there pealed a brazen bell. It was a bell that these children obeyed, even as nations obey the formal law which is printed in calfskin. It (50) smote them into some sort of inaction; even Jimmie was influenced by its potency, although, as a finale, he kicked out lustily into the legs of an intimate friend who had been one of the foremost in the torture. . . .

The teacher looked carefully down at him. "Come up (55) to the desk. . . ."

He rose amid the awe of the entire schoolroom.

"Who have you been fighting?" she asked.

"I dunno, 'm."

Whereupon the empress blazed out in wrath. "You (60) don't know who you've been fighting?". . . She seemed about to disintegrate to mere flaming fagots of anger. "You don't know who you've been fighting?" she demanded, blazing. "Well, you stay in after school until you find out."

(65) As he returned to his place all the children knew by his vanquished air that sorrow had fallen upon the house of Trescott. When he took his seat he saw gloating upon him the satanic black eyes of the little Goldege girl.

25. Which of the following describes what really happened on the playground?

   (A) The little girl started the fight.
   (B) The boys who ran over were responsible for the fight.
   (C) Jimmie imagined the fight.
   (D) The teacher stopped the fight.
   (E) Jimmie's reactions started the fight.

26. "The virulence of his deadly enemy was no greater than the virulence of his intimate friend" (lines 23–24) means that

   (A) his friends taunted him just as fiercely as his enemies
   (B) the little girl became his deadly enemy
   (C) the whole school was to blame
   (D) the boys didn't like Jimmie
   (E) his best friend fought on his side

27. The sentence "He was baited" (line 33) means

   (A) he was hooked on a tree
   (B) he was goaded into fighting back
   (C) he made up his mind
   (D) he was ready to run
   (E) he held his breath

GO ON TO THE NEXT PAGE

28. Which of the following is an example of irony?

    (A) The little girl keeps yelling.
    (B) Decencies are preserved under the eye of the teacher.
    (C) Jimmie pursues little Rose.
    (D) The little girl weeps when the boys start fighting.
    (E) The teacher demands to know who took part in the fight.

29. All of the following participate in the action of the story EXCEPT

    (A) Jimmie's girlfriend
    (B) Jimmie's intimate friends
    (C) Rose
    (D) the teacher
    (E) Jimmie's deadly enemies

30. The "empress" (line 59) is

    (A) Rose
    (B) Jimmie's girlfriend
    (C) the teacher
    (D) the little Goldege girl
    (E) Jimmie's mother

31. The word *vanquished* (line 66) most nearly means

    (A) envious
    (B) defeated
    (C) repentant
    (D) combative
    (E) awesome

STOP

END OF SECTION 4. IF YOU HAVE ANY TIME LEFT, GO OVER YOUR WORK IN THIS SECTION ONLY. DO NOT WORK IN ANY OTHER SECTION OF THE TEST.

SECTION 5

10 Questions • Time—15 Minutes

Directions: Solve the following problems using any available space on the page for scratchwork. On your answer sheet fill in the choice which best corresponds to the correct answer.

Notes: The figures accompanying the problems are drawn as accurately as possible unless otherwise stated in specific problems. Again, unless otherwise stated, all figures lie in the same plane. All numbers used in these problems are real numbers. Calculators are permitted for this test.

Reference Information:

Circle: $C = 2\pi r$, $A = \pi r^2$
Rectangle: $A = lw$
Rectangular Solid: $V = lwh$
Cylinder: $V = \pi r^2 h$
Triangle: $A = \frac{1}{2}bh$
$a^2 + b^2 = c^2$
45°–45°–90°: sides x, x, $x\sqrt{2}$
30°–60°–90°: sides x, $x\sqrt{3}$, $2x$

The number of degrees of arc in a circle is 360.
The measure in degrees of a straight angle is 180.
The sum of the measures in degrees of the angles of a triangle is 180.

---

1. Which of the following is smaller than $-\frac{1}{2}$?

    (A) $-\frac{3}{5}$
    (B) $-\frac{3}{7}$
    (C) $-\frac{2}{5}$
    (D) $-\frac{1}{3}$
    (E) $-\frac{1}{4}$

2. $\frac{2}{3}$ of a certain number is 6 more than $\frac{1}{2}$ of the same number. What is the number?

    (A) 48
    (B) 36
    (C) 30
    (D) 24
    (E) 12

3. What percent is 10 of 2?

    (A) 20%
    (B) 50%
    (C) 200%
    (D) 400%
    (E) 500%

4. A quart of oil usually sells for $1.39. During a sale, the price is reduced to 59 cents. If a customer buys six quarts at the sale price, how much is she saving off the regular price?

    (A) $8.34
    (B) $6.40
    (C) $4.80
    (D) $3.54
    (E) $2.88

GO ON TO THE NEXT PAGE

5. If square *ABCD* has a side of *m*, then which of the following represents the shaded area?

(A) $m^2 - \dfrac{mn}{2}$

(B) $m^2 + \dfrac{mn}{2}$

(C) $mn + m^2$

(D) $m^2 - mn$

(E) $m^2 - 2n$

6. John is 6 inches taller than Henry, who is $\frac{3}{4}$ as tall as Mark. Which of the following could be the heights of the three boys?

   I. Mark = 4'   John = $3\frac{1}{2}$'   Henry = 3'
   II. Mark = 6'   John = $5\frac{1}{2}$'   Henry = $4\frac{1}{2}$'
   III. Mark = $5\frac{1}{2}$'   John = $4\frac{1}{2}$'   Henry = 4'

(A) I only
(B) I and II only
(C) II and III only
(D) I and III only
(E) None of the above

7. What is the average of $\frac{2}{3}$, $\frac{3}{4}$, and $\frac{5}{6}$?

(A) $\dfrac{7}{9}$

(B) $\dfrac{3}{4}$

(C) $\dfrac{2}{3}$

(D) $\dfrac{5}{12}$

(E) $\dfrac{5}{24}$

8. If $k = \frac{3}{4}j$ and both *j* and *k* are positive integers, *k* could be any of the following except

(A) 9
(B) 12
(C) 15
(D) 18
(E) 20

9. If *r* is an even integer greater than 2, then which of the following must also be even?

(A) $(r-1)^2$

(B) $(r+1)^2$

(C) $\dfrac{r}{2}+1$

(D) $2r + 1$

(E) $r^2 + r$

10. Segment *AB* is three times longer than segment *BC*, which is two times as long as segment *CD*. If segment *BC* is removed from the line and the other two segments are joined to form one line, then what is the ratio of the original line *AD* to the new line *AD*?

Note: Figure not drawn to scale.

(A) 3 : 2
(B) 9 : 7
(C) 5 : 4
(D) 7 : 6
(E) 11 : 10

STOP

END OF SECTION 5. IF YOU HAVE ANY TIME LEFT, GO OVER YOUR WORK IN THIS SECTION ONLY. DO NOT WORK IN ANY OTHER SECTION OF THE TEST.

SECTION 6

12 Questions • Time—15 Minutes

Directions: The two passages given below deal with a related topic. Following the passages are questions about the content of each passage or about the relationship between the two passages. Answer the questions based upon what is stated or implied in the passages and in any introductory material provided. Mark the letter of your choice on your answer sheet.

Questions 1–12 are based on the two passages that follow.

Passage 1 presents an overview of the philosophy underlying the formation of the Indian tribal council and its com-mitment to preserving the religious ceremonies of the tribes.

Passage 2 recounts part of the story of Black Elk, a holy man of the Ogalala Sioux. Black Elk was born in 1863 and lived through the upheavals in the Sioux Nation that culminated in the massacre at Wounded Knee in 1890. In the passage, Black Elk recounts the beginning of the end, a time when the whites (Wasichu) would not even allow the Indians to practice their religion.

Passage 1—The Creation of the Tribal Council

The tribal council government system of Native American cultures, with its dependence on custom and precedent, was incomprehensible to the Europeans who were seeking to govern the Indians in the West because
(5) their own system, with hierarchical levels of leadership, was so different from the Native American system. Because native tribes were somewhat homogeneous in terms of religion, economics, politics, and their belief that all aspects of life were interwoven, the most impor-
(10) tant tenet of governance was that decisions involving the people be consonant with tradition. The councils saw to it that this occurred. Europeans were also disturbed by the fact that most tribes did not write down their organizing social, political, and religious prin-
(15) ciples. Despite the fact that the Iroquois had a written constitution, which mentioned such things as referendums and equal suffrage, most tribes did not record their laws and beliefs. Instead, they depended on stories and anecdotes to assure proper tribal behavior. And the
(20) tribal council was the group that served to interpret these stories and anecdotes. Among the tribes, Ogalala Sioux, Navajo, Apache, one of the primary responsibilities of the chief and the tribal council was to see that religious ceremonies occurred regularly.

(25) With the western tribes, the conflict between the whites and the Indians over how the two systems of government might work was led by the Indian agent, who often sought to establish an informal council that would assist the federal government in achieving its
(30) goals—the chief of which was the assimilation of the tribes into the federal system. Agents often chose members of these councils from Indians who were more open to new ways rather than from Indians who were more traditional. Only the strength of a particular chief,
(35) such as Red Cloud at Pine Ridge, assured that the council would persist in its more traditional ways. Indeed, traditional ways of governing remained strong until the powerful chief's passing.

Passage 2—from Black Elk Speaks*

When Good Thunder and Kicking Bear came back
(40) in the spring from seeing the Wanekia, the Wasichus at Pine Ridge put them in prison awhile, and then let them go. This showed the Wasichus were afraid of something. In the Moon of Black Cherries (August) many people were dancing at No Water's Camp on Clay
(45) Creek, and the agent came and told them to stop dancing. They would not stop, and they said they would fight for their religion if they had to do it. The agent went away, and they kept on dancing. They called him Young-Man-Afraid-of-Lakotas.

(50) Later, I heard that the Brules were dancing over east of us; and then I heard that Big Foot's people were dancing on the Good River reservation; also that Kicking Bear had gone to Sitting Bull's camp on Grand River, and that people were dancing there too. Word
(55) came to us that the Indians were beginning to dance everywhere.

The people were hungry and in despair, and many believed in the good new world that was coming. The Wasichus gave us less than half the beef cattle they (60) promised us in the treaty, and these cattle were very poor. For a while our people would not take the cattle, because there were so few of them and they were so poor. But after a while they had to take them or starve to death. So we got more lies than cattle, and we could (65) not eat lies. When the agent told the people to quit dancing, their hearts were bad. . . .

When I came back from the Brules, the weather was getting cold. Many of the Brules came along when I came back, and joined the Ogalalas in the dancing on (70) Wounded Knee. We heard that there were soldiers at Pine Ridge and that others were coming all the time. Then one morning we heard that the soldiers were marching toward us, so we broke camp and moved west to Grass Creek. From there we went to White Clay and (75) camped awhile and danced.

There came to us Fire Thunder, Red Wound and Young American Horse with a message from the soldiers that this matter of the ghost dance must be looked into, and that there should be rulings over it; and that (80) they did not mean to take the dance away from us. But could we believe anything the Wasichus ever said to us? They spoke with forked tongues.

We moved in closer to Pine Ridge and camped. Many soldiers were there now, and what were they there (85) for?

There was a big meeting with the agent, but I did not go to hear. He made a ruling that we could dance three days every moon, and the rest of the time we should go and make a living for ourselves somehow. He did not (90) say how we could do that. But the people agreed to this.

The next day, while I was sitting in a teepee with Good Thunder, a policeman came to us and said: "I was not sent here, but I came for your good to tell you what I have heard—that they are going to arrest you two."

*Reprinted from *Black Elk Speaks*, by John G. Neihardt, by permission of the University of Nebraska Press. Copyright 1932, 1959, 1972, by John G. Neihardt. Copyright © 1961 by the John G. Neihardt Trust.

1. In line 11, the word *consonant* most nearly means

    (A) traditional
    (B) irrefutable
    (C) without vowels
    (D) controversial
    (E) consistent

2. According to Passage 1, Indian tribal government was not understandable to Europeans because

    (A) laws and principles were recorded
    (B) its decisions were based on custom and precedent
    (C) its procedures were barbaric
    (D) European government was centralized
    (E) it was hierarchical

3. According to the passage, the only tribe to have a written constitution were the

    (A) Iroquois
    (B) Ogalala Sioux
    (C) Navajo
    (D) Cherokee
    (E) Cree

4. One of the main responsibilities of the chief and tribal council was to see that

    (A) religious ceremonies occurred regularly
    (B) laws were followed
    (C) justice was dispensed
    (D) proper behavior was enforced
    (E) traditions were maintained

5. According to the passage, the councils that were successful in maintaining their traditional ways were

    (A) the councils of the Apaches
    (B) the ones with the strongest chiefs
    (C) the ones with written bylaws
    (D) councils with broad memberships
    (E) the ones led by seven members

6. The leader of the conflict with the tribal councils was

    (A) Red Cloud
    (B) Bad Wound
    (C) the U.S. government
    (D) the Iroquois
    (E) the Indian agent

7. According to Passage 2, dancing was occurring everywhere EXCEPT

    (A) No Water's Camp
    (B) among the Brules
    (C) Good River reservation
    (D) Grand River Camp
    (E) Pueblo Camp

8. When Black Elk says that the Indians' "hearts were bad" (line 66), he means that they were

    (A) ill and malnourished
    (B) afraid
    (C) sick at heart
    (D) about to die
    (E) rotten to the core

9. The Indians' refusal to stop dancing is apparently seen by the Wasichus as a form of

    (A) insurrection
    (B) brutality
    (C) intolerance
    (D) courage
    (E) rudeness

10. When Black Elk says that the Wasichus speak with "forked tongues" (line 82), he is referring to their tendency toward

    (A) chivalry
    (B) gloom
    (C) misrepresentation
    (D) accuracy
    (E) bluntness

11. The tone of Black Elk's narrative might be described as

    (A) amused
    (B) ominous
    (C) soothing
    (D) sullen
    (E) reassuring

12. Both passages clearly underscore

    I. The white man's lack of understanding of Native American tradition.
    II. The white man's oppression of the Native American.
    III. The importance of religion and dance to Native American culture.

    (A) I only
    (B) I and II only
    (C) II and III only
    (D) III only
    (E) I and III only

STOP

END OF SECTION 6. IF YOU HAVE ANY TIME LEFT, GO OVER YOUR WORK IN THIS SECTION ONLY. DO NOT WORK IN ANY OTHER SECTION OF THE TEST.

PRACTICE EXAMINATION 6

Answer Key

Section 1: Verbal

1. C	8. B	15. C	22. E	29. D
2. B	9. C	16. D	23. D	30. E
3. B	10. D	17. C	24. B	31. A
4. D	11. D	18. A	25. A	32. C
5. D	12. D	19. B	26. C	33. E
6. E	13. A	20. E	27. B	34. A
7. C	14. C	21. B	28. B	35. B

Section 2: Math

1. B	6. E	11. D	16. C	21. B
2. C	7. A	12. D	17. E	22. D
3. A	8. E	13. A	18. A	23. C
4. D	9. C	14. A	19. B	24. D
5. C	10. B	15. E	20. D	25. B

Section 3: Math

Part 1

1. D	4. D	7. B	10. C	13. B
2. C	5. D	8. A	11. B	14. A
3. B	6. C	9. C	12. A	15. A

Part 2

16. 22	18. 0	20. $\frac{36}{5}=7.2$	22. 30	24. 28
17. 85	19. 1	21. 35	23. 90	25. 5

Section 4: Verbal

1. D	8. C	14. E	20. E	26. A
2. E	9. D	15. C	21. B	27. B
3. C	10. C	16. A	22. B	28. D
4. A	11. D	17. E	23. C	29. A
5. C	12. C	18. C	24. C	30. C
6. A	13. A	19. D	25. E	31. B
7. C				

Section 5: Math

1. A	3. E	5. A	7. B	9. E
2. B	4. C	6. A	8. E	10. B

Section 6: Verbal

1. E	4. A	7. E	9. A	11. B
2. B	5. B	8. C	10. C	12. E
3. A	6. E			

PRACTICE EXAMINATION 6
Explanatory Answers

Note: A 🖩 following a math answer explanation indicates that a calculator could be helpful in solving that particular problem.

Section 1

1. **(C)** A record collection that includes all kinds of music can be described as *eclectic* (composed of materials from a variety of sources).

2. **(B)** The implication is that the objective is a good one although the plan for achieving it is not. Choice (B), *laudable* (or praiseworthy), is the correct completion of this sentence.

3. **(B)** A statement that is *equivocal* can have more than one interpretation and thus leave doubt about the speaker's intentions.

4. **(D)** One is investigated only if misconduct is suspected. Filing *duplicitous* or deceitful forms would be cause for investigation. It is not likely that one would be investigated for filing true (A), duplicate (B), unnecessary (C), or messy (E) forms.

5. **(D)** The sentence implies that the teacher is being praised. *Commend* is a synonym for praise.

6. **(E)** The first word in each choice is acceptable. Quickly plugging in the choices eliminates the wrong answers.

7. **(C)** Taping every episode implies that the teenagers were *assiduous* (extremely attentive) followers of the soap opera.

8. **(B)** The key word in the sentence is *postponing*. By spinning tales, Scheherazade *temporized* (delayed in order to gain time), thus stalling her planned execution.

9. **(C)** The key word is *fair*. The supervisor could be proud of any of the choices, but the only one that means "fairness" is *objectivity*.

10. **(D)** The only choice that makes sense is (D). When research becomes highly *specialized*, people working on different aspects of the same problem may be unaware of or *unfamiliar with* each other's work.

11. **(D)** A *trumpet* is a small brass instrument, while a *tuba* is a large brass instrument. A *piccolo* is a small wind instrument, while a *bassoon* is a large one.

12. **(D)** A *dinghy* is a small boat that operates in the water, and a *glider* is a small flying craft that operates in the *air*.

13. **(A)** A *nail* makes a *puncture*, and a *scalpel* makes an *incision*.

14. **(C)** A *galaxy* is made up of many *stars*, and a *flock* is made up of many *birds*.

15. **(C)** *Silver* is a *metal* and *helium* is a *gas*.

16. **(D)** A *sprinter* has great *speed*, and a *weightlifter* has great *strength*.

17. **(C)** An *interloper* seeks to *meddle* in the affairs of another. An *avenger* seeks to *punish* another.

18. **(A)** *Meteorology* is the study of *weather*, and *ornithology* is the study of *birds*.

19. **(B)** An *innovation* is the brand-new idea that lacks *precedent* (an earlier instance or example). Similarly, an *illusion* by definition lacks *veracity* (truthfulness).

20. **(E)** An *anarchist* is a *lawless* person; a *philistine* is an *uncultured* person.

21. **(B)** *Detrimental* means *harmful*. *Pernicious* means fatal, a greater degree of harm. *Cheerful* means happy. *Exuberant* means uninhibited or high-spirited, denoting a higher degree of joy.

22. **(E)** *Robust* means full of *vigor*, just as *sanguine* means full of *hope*.

23. **(D)** *Perfidy*, or betrayal of trust, is a characteristic of a *traitorous* person. *Steadfastness*, or constancy, is a characteristic of a *loyal* person.

24. **(B)** Each of the choices is a kind of rhetorical element, a form used in speech-making. In this case, the speaker asks what is called a rhetorical question, which is one that doesn't need an answer and is asked only for effect or emphasis. Even if you do not know this term, process of elimination and the fact that the first sentences of the passage are questions should make the answer evident.

25. **(A)** Substituting the choices in place of the italicized word will make your choice clear.

26. **(C)** If you know the word, only one choice is synonymous. If you do not know it, test the choices in context.

27. **(B)** Douglass states (B) in lines 15–16: "There is blasphemy in the thought." He also clearly believes that there is no further point in debating the issue and that arguments over whether or not God ordained slavery are futile.

28. **(B)** Douglass believes that to articulate the arguments in paragraph one is a complete waste of time because these words are not strong enough to fight slavery.

29. **(D)** Douglass refers to fire, thunder, storm, whirlwind, and earthquake to emphasize the need for drastic—and if necessary, violent—action.

30. **(E)** This kind of interpretation question may be easier to answer if you try restating the phrase in your own words and comparing them to the choices. Here, choices (A), (B), and (D) are relatively meaningless. Choice (C) may be true, but it is not a restatement of the phrase.

31. **(A)** Douglass says that to the American slave, the Fourth of July is a "sham," a "mockery," a "fraud," and a "deception." Nothing in the passage supports choices (B), (C), or (D), and as for (E), Douglass has said that the time for debate is passed.

32. **(C)** The crimes covered up by this thin veil are the crimes of a group worse than savages. Only choice (C) has this connotation.

33. **(E)** A careful reading of the text surrounding this citation shows that in Douglass's view, America compares unfavorably with every other nation, including South America.

34. **(A)** Paragraph 4 contains a furious denunciation of the Fourth of July as hypocritical at a time when some Americans are being held as slaves. Douglass's words most likely shocked and frightened his mostly white Rochester audience.

35. **(B)** Frederick Douglass criticizes the United States so strongly that "scorching" best describes the extent of his anger toward America.

Section 2

1. **(B)** First you must find a common denominator for 3, 4, and 6. The lowest common denominator would be 12.

$$\frac{8}{12} + \frac{9}{12} + \frac{10}{12} + p = 3$$

$$\frac{27}{12} + p = 3$$

$$p = \frac{36}{12} - \frac{27}{12}$$

$$p = \frac{9}{12}$$

$$p = \frac{3}{4}$$

2. **(C)** The 130-degree angle and the angle next to it must add up to 180 degrees, as they form a straight line. All triangles contain 180 degrees, so

$$180 = 50 + x + y$$
$$130 = x + y$$

Note that we can tell the value of $x + y$, but we cannot tell the value of x or y alone.

3. **(A)** Since $Q = S + 2$, we can substitute $S + 2$ in place of Q in the first equation.

Step 1: $P = QR$ is the same as $P = (S + 2)R$

Step 2: Divide both sides by R:

$$\frac{P}{R} = S + 2$$

4. **(D)** Answer choices (A), (C), and (E) must be negative, while (B) and (D) are positive. (B) is $\frac{1}{16}$, while (D) is $\frac{1}{4}$.

5. **(C)** $5 \times 1\frac{1}{2} = 7\frac{1}{2}$

    If the woman runs $7\frac{1}{2}$ miles in an hour, then that is her average miles per hour.

6. **(E)** If the average of the four numbers is 11, then the sum must be 4×11.

7. **(A)** If 9 pears spoiled, then 171 did not.

    $\frac{171}{180} = \frac{19}{20} = 95\%$

8. **(E)** Follow the instructions one step at a time.

    Step 1: $3r$

    Step 2: $3r - 3$

    Step 3: $\frac{3r-3}{3}$

    Step 4: The 3's divide out and leave $r - 1$.

9. **(C)** Since ABCD is a square, all of the sides must be 4. We know that the triangles are both right triangles since they are adjacent to the square. Therefore, they are both 3, 4, 5 triangles. $2(3 + 4 + 5) = 24$

10. **(B)** $\sqrt{\frac{3}{4} - \frac{3}{16}} = \sqrt{\frac{12}{16} - \frac{3}{16}} = \sqrt{\frac{9}{16}} = \frac{3}{4}$

11. **(D)** The easiest way to solve this is to substitute into the formula.

    Answer A = $6(2 + 3 + 4) = 54$
    Answer B = $6(4 + 3 + 2) = 54$
    Answer C = $6(3 + 5 + 1) = 54$
    Answer D = $6(4 + 1 + 5) = 60$
    Answer E = $6(1 + 5 + 3) = 54$

12. **(D)** This is solved by dividing 16.4 by 16.

    $$\begin{array}{r} 1.025 \\ 16\overline{)16.400} \\ \underline{16} \\ 40 \\ \underline{32} \\ 80 \\ \underline{80} \end{array}$$

13. **(A)** Circumference $= 2\pi r$

    $x = 2\pi r$ (substitute x)

    $\frac{x}{2\pi} = r$ (divide by 2π)

14. **(A)** The product of the terms can be positive if they are both negative or both positive. This chart shows the combinations.

	$x < -1$	$-1 < x < 2$	$x > 2$
$x + 1$	−	+	+
$x - 2$	−	−	+
$(x+1)(x-2)$	+	−	+

15. **(E)** Segment AD is the base of the triangle and the length of the rectangle. Segment CD is the height of the triangle and the width of the rectangle. Let's use l and w to represent length and width.

    Area $ABCD = l \times w$

    Area $\triangle AED = \frac{l \times w}{2}$

    Since the rectangle is twice as big as the triangle, the ratio is 1 : 2.

16. **(C)** Each of the choices will have to be considered.

    I. 6 can be divided by 1, 2, and 3.
       $1 + 2 + 3 = 6$
    II. 12 can be divided by 1, 2, 3, 4, and 6.
       $1 + 2 + 3 + 4 + 6 = 16$
    III. 28 can be divided by 1, 2, 4, 7, and 14.
       $1 + 2 + 4 + 7 + 14 = 28$
    IV. 32 can be divided by 1, 2, 4, 8, and 16.
       $1 + 2 + 4 + 8 + 16 = 31$

    Only I and III are full numbers.

17. **(E)** The formula for finding percent change is Difference divided by the Original Amount.

   (A) $\dfrac{2000}{7000} \cong 28\%$

   (B) $\dfrac{3000}{9000} = 33\dfrac{1}{3}\%$

   (C) $\dfrac{4000}{12000} = 33\dfrac{1}{3}\%$

   (D) $\dfrac{4000}{16000} = 25\%$

   (E) $\dfrac{4000}{20000} = 20\%$

18. **(A)** To compute an average, add the items to be averaged and then divide that sum by the number of items.

   $\dfrac{70 + 75 + 80 + y}{4} = \dfrac{225 + y}{4}$

19. **(B)** In order to use one measurement, convert 3 feet into 36 inches. Therefore, the two snails have to move a total of 36 inches.

   $.04d + .05d = 36$
   $.09d = 36$
   $d = 400$

   It will take 400 seconds, which is equal to $6\dfrac{2}{3}$ minutes.

20. **(D)** 1st month $= 500$
   2nd month $= 500 + .10(500) = 550$
   3rd month $= 550 + .10(550) = 605$
   4th month $= 605 + .10(605) = 665.50$

21. **(B)** The question translated into algebra would read $J = 4(A - 6)$.

   $20 = 4A - 24$
   $44 = 4A$
   $11 = A$

22. **(D)** Set these up as simultaneous equations and solve.

   $a^2 - 2ab + b^2 = 36$
   $\dfrac{-(a^2 - 3ab + b^2 = 22)}{ab \qquad = 14}$

23. **(C)** It makes the problem easier if you realize that the facing semicircles form two whole circles.

   The smaller circle has a diameter of 1 and, therefore, a radius of $\frac{1}{2}$.
   Area $= \pi(\frac{1}{2})^2 = \frac{\pi}{4}$
   The larger circle has a diameter of 2 and, therefore, a radius of 1. Area $= \pi(1)^2 = \pi$

   $\dfrac{4\pi}{4} + \dfrac{\pi}{4} = \dfrac{5\pi}{4}$

24. **(D)** $P = \dfrac{1}{2} + \dfrac{1}{3} = \dfrac{3}{6} + \dfrac{2}{6} = \dfrac{5}{6}$

   $Q = P^2 = \left(\dfrac{5}{6}\right)^2 = \dfrac{25}{36}$

   $Q - P = \dfrac{25}{36} - \dfrac{5}{6} = \dfrac{25}{36} - \dfrac{30}{36} = -\dfrac{5}{36}$

25. **(B)** There are several ways to solve this problem. One way would be to divide the square into four triangles each of which would be a 45°–45°–90° triangle.

   The ratio of the sides of a 45° : 45° : 90° is 1 : 1 : $\sqrt{2}$, giving sides of 3 : 3 : $3\sqrt{2}$ and an area of $3\sqrt{2} \times 3\sqrt{2} = 18$.

   OR diagonal $= 6$

   Area $= \dfrac{d^2}{2} = \dfrac{6^2}{2} = 18$.

Section 3

Part 1

1. **(D)** Each angle of a square is 90°; therefore, the sum of all angles is 360°. A polygon may have any number of sides, and angles, so the sum of all the angles cannot be determined.

2. **(C)** The missing angle measure is 180° – 70° – 55° = 55°. Therefore, the triangle is isosceles, with two equal angles of 55°. In an isosceles triangle, the sides opposite the equal angles are equal. Thus $x = y$.

3. **(B)** The area of the larger triangle is $\frac{1}{2}(9)(7) = 31\frac{1}{2}$. The area of the smaller triangle is $\frac{1}{2}(5)(3) = 7\frac{1}{2}$. The area of the shaded area is the area of the larger triangle minus that of the smaller, $31\frac{1}{2} - 7\frac{1}{2} = 24$. The shaded area has the larger area.

4. **(D)** If $x > 1$, then $\frac{1}{x} < x$. But if $0 < x < 1$, then $\frac{1}{x} > x$. Since the denominator in $\frac{1}{x}$ will be a fraction, it will be 1 times the reciprocal of x. This will be larger than x itself. We cannot tell which is the larger.

5. **(D)** Factoring the equation in Column B, we find $a^2 - 7a + 12 = (a-4)(a-3)$. If $a > 4$, Column A is larger. But if $a \leq 4$, Column B is larger. Therefore, we cannot determine which column is larger.

6. **(C)** The circumference of a circle with radius $2r$ is $2\pi(2r) = 4\pi r$. The perimeter of a square with side πr is $4\pi r$, so Column A and Column B are equal.

7. **(B)** In Column A,

$$\sqrt{\frac{1}{3} \times \frac{1}{6}} = \sqrt{\frac{1}{3} \times \frac{1}{3} \times \frac{1}{2}} = \frac{1}{3}\sqrt{\frac{1}{2}}.$$

In Column B,

$$\sqrt{\frac{1}{3} + \frac{1}{6}} = \sqrt{\frac{6}{18} + \frac{3}{18}} = \sqrt{\frac{9}{18}} = \sqrt{\frac{1}{2}}.$$

Column A is $\frac{1}{3}$ the value of Column B.

8. **(A)** Plugging in -2 we get $(-2-1)^2 + (-2) = 9 - 2 = 7$.

Plugging in 2 we get $(2-1)^2 + 2 = 1 + 2 = 3$

9. **(C)** $(0-1)^2 + 0 = 1$
$(1-1)^2 + 1 = 1$

10. **(C)** The easiest way to solve this is to realize that $(a+b) = (b+a)$ and $(c+d) = (d+c)$. You can also use the foil method to multiply out both sides.

11. **(B)** 42% of 165 is $165 \times 0.42 = 69.3$. The number which 80 is 20% of is $N \times 0.20 = 80$, or $N = \frac{80}{0.20} = 400$. Thus, Column B is larger than Column A.

12. **(A)** Each face of the small cube has an area of 1; each small cube thus has a surface area of 6. Each face of the large cube has an area of 4; the large cube thus has a surface area of 24. $\frac{24}{8} = 3$.

13. **(B)** In Column A, a positive number is multiplied by a negative number. In Column B, the negative of M is taken and divided by N, a negative number, thus resulting in a positive number. A positive number is always greater than a negative number.

14. **(A)** $p = \sqrt{8^2 - 4^2}$; hence, $p = \sqrt{48}$. Meanwhile, q is the hypotenuse of a right triangle, so $q = \sqrt{4^2 + 5^2}$. Hence $q = \sqrt{41}$. Therefore, p is larger.

15. **(A)** The value of Column A is -44. The value of Column B is -168. Therefore, Column A is larger.

Part 2

16.

```
        7
   ┌─────────┐
 4 │         │ 4
   └─────────┘
        7
```

Perimeter $= 4 + 7 + 4 + 7 = 22$

17. The median is the middle score when the data is arrayed in increasing order.

70, 70, 70, 70, 85, 85, 85, 90, 90, 95

85 is the median.

18. $\text{(-1)} = -1 - 1 = -2$, and $\boxed{1} = 2(1) = 2$

$\text{(-1)} + \boxed{1} = -2 + 2 = 0$

19. $x + y^2 - z = (-1) + (-1)^2 - (-1)$
$= (-1) + (1) - (-1)$
$= -1 + 1 + 1$
$= 1$

20. $\dfrac{\frac{1}{2} + \frac{1}{3}}{\frac{1}{2} + \frac{1}{3}} = \dfrac{\frac{1}{2} \cdot \frac{3}{3} + \frac{1}{3} \cdot \frac{2}{2}}{}$

$= \dfrac{\frac{3}{6} + \frac{2}{6}}{} = \dfrac{5}{6}$

$\dfrac{6}{\frac{1}{2} + \frac{1}{3}} = \dfrac{6}{\frac{5}{6}} = \dfrac{6}{1} \cdot \dfrac{6}{5} = \dfrac{36}{5}$

21. Angle *AOC* is a central angle. Arc *AC* = 70° as a central angle is equal to its intercepted arc.

An inscribed angle is equal to $\frac{1}{2}$ the measure of its intercepted arc.

$m\angle ABC = \frac{1}{2} mAC = \frac{1}{2}(70°) = 35°$

22. Dawnville H.S.

$x + y = 44$
$y + z = 46$
$x + y + z + \text{neither} = 70,$
$x + y + z + 10 = 70$
$x + y + z = 60$
but $x + y = 44 \therefore z = 16$
but $y + z = 46 \therefore x = 14$
$\therefore 14 + y + 16 = 60$
$y + 30 = 60$
$y = 30$

23. $\frac{\text{Sum of test scores}}{\text{Number of tests}} = \text{Average}$

$\frac{\text{Sum}}{5} = 70 \therefore \text{Sum} = 350$

If two tests are disregarded
the new sum = $350 - 50 - 30 = 270$
the new number of tests = $5 - 2 = 3$

The new average

$= \frac{\text{Sum}}{\text{Number of tests}} = \frac{270}{3} = 90$

24. $3a + 5b = 10$
$\underline{a - b = 6}$ (adding the equations)
$4a + 4b = 16$

$\frac{7}{4}(4a + 4b = 16)$ (multiply by $\frac{7}{4}$)

$7a + 7b = 28$

25. $a - b = b - c = c - a$
$a - b = b - c \rightarrow 2b = a + c$
$a - b = c - a \rightarrow 2a = c + b$
$2b = a + c$
$\therefore 4b = 2a + 2c$, but $2a = c + b$
$4b = (c + b) + 2c$ (substitute $(c + b)$ for $2a$)
$4b = 3c + b$
$3b = 3c$
$b = c$
$2b = a + c$ (substitute c for b)
$2c = a + c$
$c = a$
$\therefore a = b = c$
$\therefore \frac{2a + 3b}{c} = \frac{2a + 3a}{a} = \frac{5a}{a} = 5$

Section 4

1. **(D)** A person who leads a *secluded* life has no contact with the outside world and therefore would have to use *imagination* to explore it. None of the other choices makes sense.

2. **(E)** Spending all one's money will *preclude* (make impossible) a trip to the movies.

3. **(C)** One is unlikely to gain admission to a top college with an academic record that is *mediocre* (merely ordinary).

4. **(A)** The blue whale typically grows to *prodigious* (huge) size and must eat tons of plankton to *satiate* (satisfy) its huge appetite.

5. **(C)** A recklessly bold attempt is by definition characterized by *audacity* and was successful because the enemy failed to *anticipate* it.

6. **(A)** The pair of words must be contrasting due to the word *but*. Living in isolation is the opposite of living in a community.

7. **(C)** One's view is influenced by one's beliefs, or *philosophy*.

8. **(C)** This is the only pair that makes sense.

9. **(D)** The military censors are concerned about maintaining security. If they find passages in a letter that *jeopardize* (endanger) it, they would *expunge* (erase) those passages.

10. **(C)** An *hour* is a measure of *time*, while a *gram* is a measure of *weight*.

11. **(D)** A *gem* is placed within a *setting* in jewelry, just as a *picture* is placed within a *frame*.

12. **(C)** A *ship* is part of an *armada*, and an *atom* is part of a *molecule*.

13. **(A)** A *caterpillar* changes into a *butterfly*, and a *tadpole* turns into a *frog*.

14. **(E)** To *tremble* is a sign of *fear*, just as to *weep* is a sign of *grief*.

15. **(C)** A *conflagration* is a huge fire, while a *spark* is a very small fire. A *drizzle* is a very light rain, while a *downpour* is very heavy rain.

16. **(A)** A community is defined as "the different kinds of organisms living and interacting together in an area" (lines 3–4). The only answer that fits this definition is (A).

17. **(E)** A producer makes its own food. Grass (A) is one, an oak tree (D) is another, and clover (E) is a third. However, only (E) takes the chain all the way to a decomposer, as the rabbit eats the clover, the fox eats the rabbit, and the microbe eats the fox.

18. **(C)** "All members of a community depend...on the producers" (lines 32–34), so I is true. Consumers do not produce food, but producers do, so II is true. Some consumers mentioned include mushrooms and molds, which are not animals, so III is not true. Since I and II are true, the answer is (C).

19. **(D)** If you understand the definitions of terms in the passage, this is the only conclusion you might draw.

20. **(E)** Parasitism is defined as being a form of symbiosis wherein one organism benefits and the other is harmed.

21. **(B)** In competition, organisms fight over a resource. Only (B) hints at this kind of relationship.

22. **(B)** A community contains organisms, but an ecosystem contains "living and non-living things" (line 59).

23. **(C)** An adaptation is defined as a characteristic that helps the organism survive in the environment. All of the examples except (C) might be considered adaptations that improve chances of survival.

24. **(C)** Choices (A) and (B) are too broad, while choices (D) and (E) are too narrow; the title that best conveys the main idea of the passage is (C).

25. **(E)** In paragraph 3, it is clearly developed that Jimmie is the reason for the fight. The taunts of his schoolmates put him on the defensive and lead up to the point in paragraph 4 where he takes matters into his own hands "with a blow." He strikes out at friends and enemies alike.

26. **(A)** *Virulence* means "bitter hostility," and as the playground events developed, Jimmie's friends proved every bit as hostile to him as his enemies—or so it appeared to him.

27. **(B)** In the story, Jimmie is teased mercilessly by the other children until finally their taunts goad him into striking back. They *bait*, or *provoke*, him into starting the fight.

28. **(D)** Irony, in which the result is the opposite of what might be expected, is found in the behavior of the little girl. At the beginning of the passage she is gleefully taunting Jimmie, but once the fight starts, she begins weeping.

29. **(A)** In the opening paragraph, little Rose claims to have seen Jimmie writing to his girlfriend. However, the girlfriend never actually appears in the story.

30. **(C)** The "empress" who demands to know who took part in the fight is clearly the teacher.

31. **(B)** Since "sorrow had fallen upon the house of Trescott" when the teacher reprimanded Jimmie, the boy was clearly defeated.

Section 5

1. **(A)** The number line below shows the approximate location of the five fractions.

2. **(B)** Be careful in converting the words into an equation.
$$\frac{2}{3}x = 6 + \frac{1}{2}x$$
Subtract $\frac{1}{2}x$ from both sides:
$$\frac{1}{6}x = 6$$
$$x = 36$$

3. **(E)** 10 divided by 2 is equal to 5, which in percent form is 500%.

4. **(C)** The savings on one quart is $1.39 - $.59 = .80. The savings on six quarts is 6 × .80 = $4.80.

5. **(A)** Since the square has a side of m, its area is m^2. The unshaded triangle has an area of $\frac{mn}{2}$. The shaded area is equal to the whole square minus the unshaded portion.

6. **(A)** Proposition II is eliminated because it has John 12 inches taller than Henry. Proposition III is eliminated because it does not have Henry at $\frac{3}{4}$ of Mark's height.

7. **(B)** $\dfrac{\frac{2}{3} + \frac{3}{4} + \frac{5}{6}}{3} =$

$$\dfrac{\frac{8}{12} + \frac{9}{12} + \frac{10}{12}}{3} = \dfrac{\frac{27}{12}}{3} = \frac{27}{12} \cdot \frac{1}{3} = \frac{27}{36} = \frac{3}{4}$$

8. **(E)** Plug the answer choices into the equation until you find the one that does not allow j to be an integer.

Example: (A) $\frac{3}{4}j = 9$
$$j = 9\left(\frac{4}{3}\right)$$
$$j = 12$$

(E) $\frac{3}{4}j = 20$
$$j = 20\left(\frac{4}{3}\right)$$
$$j = \frac{80}{3} = 26\frac{2}{3}$$

9. **(E)** Plug the number 4 into the answer choices. (A) is 9, (B) is 25, (C) is 3, (D) is 9, and (E) is 12.

10. **(B)** Since a ratio is used, we are free to plug in any numbers that we wish so long as they fit the ratio. Since segment CD is the smallest, let's assign a value of 1 to that length. Segment BC is twice as long, so it will be 2. Segment AB is three times as long as segment BC, so it is 6. Segment AD has a total length of 9. If we subtract segment BC, it has a length of 7.

Section 6

1. **(E)** In context, the word *consonant* means consistent. So the decisions involved had to be consistent with tradition.

2. **(B)** Europeans, with their history, both in Europe and in the United States, of written law, found it very hard to understand a system of government based on custom and precedent that was largely transmitted through stories.

3. **(A)** See paragraph 1 (lines 15–17) for reference to the written constitution of the Iroquois.

4. **(A)** The tribal council was primarily a judicial council dedicated to seeing that proper behavior was assured; its primary function was to see that religious ceremonies occurred.

5. **(B)** The chief was the single element that determined whether traditional ways would be followed.

6. **(E)** The passage specifically cites the Indian agent as the leader of the conflict with the tribal councils.

7. **(E)** Nowhere in the passage are the Pueblo mentioned.

8. **(C)** This line refers to the people's despair rather than to their hunger or illness. Black Elk is saying that to give up their dance would be the last straw.

9. **(A)** The Wasichus would not throw people in jail and mass soldiers near the ridge if they saw the refusal simply as rudeness (E). They are afraid that one refusal will lead to others, and that insurrection is possible.

10. **(C)** The Wasichus have made and broken promises before (lines 58–61), and now Black Elk does not trust them.

11. **(B)** The scenes of wild dancing contrasted with the scenes of soldiers on the move lead to a feeling of tension. Clearly something bad is going to happen.

12. **(E)** It is tempting to believe that all three statements are true. But you have to base your answers on the passages, not your beliefs. Nowhere in the passages is the oppression of the Native American emphasized. Only I and III are supported by the passages.

COMPUTING YOUR SCORES ON PRACTICE EXAMINATION 6

To get a sense of your SAT preparation progress, you need to compute individual verbal and mathematical raw scores for the sixth practice examination. Once you have computed these, use the conversion scales in the section that follows to compute your SAT scaled scores (200–800). Keep in mind that these formulas have been simplified to give you a "quick and dirty" sense of where you are scoring, not a perfectly precise score.

To Compute Your Raw Scores:

1. Enter the number of correct answers for each verbal and mathematical reasoning section into the boxes marked "Number of Questions Correct."
2. Enter the number of incorrect answers (not blanks) for each verbal and mathematical reasoning section into the boxes marked "Number of Questions Incorrect."
3. Total the number correct and number incorrect.
4. Follow this formula: Take the total correct and minus one-quarter of the total incorrect. Round up in your favor to compute your Raw Score.

Verbal Section	Total Number of Questions	Number of Questions Correct	Number of Questions Incorrect
2	31		
4	35		
6	12		
Totals	78	Total Correct:	Total Incorrect:

Verbal Raw Score = Total Correct − ($\frac{1}{4}$ × Total Incorrect) = _____

Math Section	Total Number of Questions	Number of Questions Correct	Number of Questions Incorrect
1	25		
3	25		
5	10		
Totals	60	Total Correct:	Total Incorrect:

Math Raw Score = Total Correct − ($\frac{1}{4}$ × Total Incorrect) = _____

CONVERSION SCALES FOR PRACTICE EXAMINATION 6

VERBAL REASONING

Raw Score	Scaled Score	Raw Score	Scaled Score
75	800	35	520
70	800	30	480
65	760	25	440
60	710	20	410
55	670	15	370
50	620	10	340
45	590	5	290
40	550	0	230

MATHEMATICAL REASONING

Raw Score	Scaled Score	Raw Score	Scaled Score
60	800	25	510
55	760	20	480
50	690	15	440
45	650	10	410
40	610	5	340
35	580	0	280
30	550		

Although you now have some idea of what your scores would like had they been scaled according to unofficial ETS standards, you will probably want to know how to interpret your Raw Scores in more familiar terms. If so, use the following Self-Evaluation Charts to see what your Raw Scores actually mean.

SELF-EVALUATION CHARTS

VERBAL REASONING: Raw Score

Excellent	60 – 75
Good	50 – 60
Average	30 – 50
Fair	20 – 30
Poor	0 – 20

MATHEMATICAL REASONING: Raw Score

Excellent	50 – 60
Good	40 – 50
Average	20 – 40
Fair	10 – 20
Poor	0 – 10

FINAL PRACTICE EXAMINATION
Answer Sheet

If a section has fewer questions than answer ovals, leave the extra ovals blank.

Section 1

Section 2

Section 3
Answer spaces for Section 3 are on the back of this answer sheet.

Section 4

Section 3

1. Ⓐ Ⓑ Ⓒ Ⓓ Ⓔ
2. Ⓐ Ⓑ Ⓒ Ⓓ Ⓔ
3. Ⓐ Ⓑ Ⓒ Ⓓ Ⓔ
4. Ⓐ Ⓑ Ⓒ Ⓓ Ⓔ
5. Ⓐ Ⓑ Ⓒ Ⓓ Ⓔ
6. Ⓐ Ⓑ Ⓒ Ⓓ Ⓔ
7. Ⓐ Ⓑ Ⓒ Ⓓ Ⓔ
8. Ⓐ Ⓑ Ⓒ Ⓓ Ⓔ
9. Ⓐ Ⓑ Ⓒ Ⓓ Ⓔ
10. Ⓐ Ⓑ Ⓒ Ⓓ Ⓔ
11. Ⓐ Ⓑ Ⓒ Ⓓ Ⓔ
12. Ⓐ Ⓑ Ⓒ Ⓓ Ⓔ
13. Ⓐ Ⓑ Ⓒ Ⓓ Ⓔ
14. Ⓐ Ⓑ Ⓒ Ⓓ Ⓔ
15. Ⓐ Ⓑ Ⓒ Ⓓ Ⓔ

Note: ONLY the answers entered on the grid are scored.

Handwritten answers at the top of the column are NOT scored.

16. [grid-in]
17. [grid-in]
18. [grid-in]
19. [grid-in]
20. [grid-in]
21. [grid-in]
22. [grid-in]
23. [grid-in]
24. [grid-in]
25. [grid-in]

Section 5

1. Ⓐ Ⓑ Ⓒ Ⓓ Ⓔ
2. Ⓐ Ⓑ Ⓒ Ⓓ Ⓔ
3. Ⓐ Ⓑ Ⓒ Ⓓ Ⓔ
4. Ⓐ Ⓑ Ⓒ Ⓓ Ⓔ
5. Ⓐ Ⓑ Ⓒ Ⓓ Ⓔ
6. Ⓐ Ⓑ Ⓒ Ⓓ Ⓔ
7. Ⓐ Ⓑ Ⓒ Ⓓ Ⓔ
8. Ⓐ Ⓑ Ⓒ Ⓓ Ⓔ
9. Ⓐ Ⓑ Ⓒ Ⓓ Ⓔ
10. Ⓐ Ⓑ Ⓒ Ⓓ Ⓔ
11. Ⓐ Ⓑ Ⓒ Ⓓ Ⓔ
12. Ⓐ Ⓑ Ⓒ Ⓓ Ⓔ
13. Ⓐ Ⓑ Ⓒ Ⓓ Ⓔ
14. Ⓐ Ⓑ Ⓒ Ⓓ Ⓔ
15. Ⓐ Ⓑ Ⓒ Ⓓ Ⓔ

Section 6

1. Ⓐ Ⓑ Ⓒ Ⓓ Ⓔ
2. Ⓐ Ⓑ Ⓒ Ⓓ Ⓔ
3. Ⓐ Ⓑ Ⓒ Ⓓ Ⓔ
4. Ⓐ Ⓑ Ⓒ Ⓓ Ⓔ
5. Ⓐ Ⓑ Ⓒ Ⓓ Ⓔ
6. Ⓐ Ⓑ Ⓒ Ⓓ Ⓔ
7. Ⓐ Ⓑ Ⓒ Ⓓ Ⓔ
8. Ⓐ Ⓑ Ⓒ Ⓓ Ⓔ
9. Ⓐ Ⓑ Ⓒ Ⓓ Ⓔ
10. Ⓐ Ⓑ Ⓒ Ⓓ Ⓔ
11. Ⓐ Ⓑ Ⓒ Ⓓ Ⓔ
12. Ⓐ Ⓑ Ⓒ Ⓓ Ⓔ
13. Ⓐ Ⓑ Ⓒ Ⓓ Ⓔ
14. Ⓐ Ⓑ Ⓒ Ⓓ Ⓔ
15. Ⓐ Ⓑ Ⓒ Ⓓ Ⓔ

Final Practice Examination

SECTION 1

25 Questions • Time—30 Minutes

Directions: Solve the following problems using any available space on the page for scratchwork. On your answer sheet fill in the choice which best corresponds to the correct answer.

Notes: The figures accompanying the problems are drawn as accurately as possible unless otherwise stated in specific problems. Again, unless otherwise stated, all figures lie in the same plane. All numbers used in these problems are real numbers. Calculators are permitted for this test.

Reference Information

Circle: $C = 2\pi r$, $A = \pi r^2$
Rectangle: $A = lw$
Rectangular Solid: $V = lwh$
Cylinder: $V = \pi r^2 h$
Triangle: $A = \tfrac{1}{2}bh$
$a^2 + b^2 = c^2$

Special triangles: 45°–45°–90° with sides $x, x, x\sqrt{2}$; 30°–60°–90° with sides $x, x\sqrt{3}, 2x$.

The number of degrees of arc in a circle is 360.
The measure in degrees of a straight angle is 180.
The sum of the measures in degrees of the angles of a triangle is 180.

---

1. $.2 \times .02 \times .002 =$

    (A) .000008
    (B) .00008
    (C) .0008
    (D) .008
    (E) .08

2. If $\dfrac{p}{q} = 6$ and $q = -3$, then $\dfrac{p+q}{q} =$

    (A) −21
    (B) −14
    (C) −7
    (D) 1
    (E) 7

3. If s, t, and u are different positive integers and $\dfrac{s}{t}$ and $\dfrac{t}{u}$ are also positive integers, which of the following cannot be a positive integer?

    (A) $\dfrac{s}{u}$
    (B) $s \cdot t$
    (C) $\dfrac{u}{s}$
    (D) $(s+t)u$
    (E) $(s-u)t$

GO ON TO THE NEXT PAGE

4. Of the people attending a concert, $\frac{3}{4}$ are seated in the auditorium and the remaining $\frac{1}{4}$ are in the lobby. If $\frac{1}{2}$ of those in the lobby move to seats in the auditorium, then what is the ratio of those seated in the auditorium to those in the lobby?

   (A) 16:1
   (B) 12:1
   (C) 9:1
   (D) 7:1
   (E) 6:1

5. If the perimeter of the rectangle below is 42, then what is the area of the rectangle?

   (A) 21
   (B) 42
   (C) 84
   (D) 108
   (E) 216

   Rectangle ABCD with AB = 4m and AD = 3m.

6. $390 is 13% of the total sum of money in a bank account. How much money is in the bank account?

   (A) $6,000
   (B) $3,000
   (C) $1,057
   (D) $557
   (E) $50.70

7. If $n(q + 5) = s$ and $q(n + 4) = s$, and $n, q,$ and s are positive integers, then which of the following statements must be true?

   I. $n(q + 5) = q(n + 4)$
   II. $\dfrac{n(q+5)}{q(n+4)} = 1$
   III. $q > n$

   (A) I only
   (B) II only
   (C) III only
   (D) I and III only
   (E) I, II, and III

8. $\dfrac{\frac{2}{3}(x^2 y^3)^4}{\frac{3}{4}(x^4 y^3)^2} =$

   (A) $\dfrac{8y^6}{9}$
   (B) $\dfrac{9y^6}{8}$
   (C) $\dfrac{3}{4}xy$
   (D) $\dfrac{2y^6}{3}$
   (E) $\dfrac{8}{9y^6}$

9. Jane has walked m miles. After a rest she walks n miles. If Jane always walked s steps per mile, then how many steps did Jane take?

   (A) $s + m + n$
   (B) $\dfrac{sm}{n}$
   (C) $\dfrac{m}{sn}$
   (D) $(s + m)n$
   (E) $s(m + n)$

10. Tim can fold a certain number of brochures in 20 minutes. John can fold the same number in 15 minutes. If Tim and John work together for 3 hours and during that time John folds x brochures, how many brochures will Tim fold?

    (A) $\dfrac{4x}{3}$
    (B) $\dfrac{5x}{4}$
    (C) $\dfrac{3x}{4}$
    (D) $\dfrac{2x}{3}$
    (E) $\dfrac{x}{2}$

Questions 11 and 12 refer to the table below.

SCORE DISTRIBUTION

MATHEMATICS TEST

Score	No. of students
40–52	5
53–64	11
65–76	7
77–88	32
89–100	40

11. If the lowest passing score is 65, then, to the nearest percent, what percent of the students failed the test?

    (A) 5%
    (B) 7%
    (C) 11%
    (D) 17%
    (E) 52%

12. If 9 students scored 100, how many scored from 77 to 99?

    (A) 72
    (B) 63
    (C) 51
    (D) 40
    (E) 31

13. In the figure below, which of the following is x necessarily equal to?

    Note: Figure not drawn to scale.

    (A) $180 - 5y$
    (B) $180 + 5y$
    (C) $90 - 5y$
    (D) $190 + 5y$
    (E) $5y$

14. For which values of x will $x(x + 2)(x - 3)(x + 4)$ be equal to 0?

    (A) 0
    (B) 2, –3, and 4
    (C) 0 and –2
    (D) –2, 3, and –4
    (E) 0, –2, 3, and –4

For questions 15 and 16 let $a \square b = a^b + b^a$

15. What is the value of $2 \square 3$?

    (A) 5
    (B) 6
    (C) 13
    (D) 17
    (E) 19

16. If a and b are different positive integers, then which of the following statements must be false?

    (A) The smallest value for $a \square b$ is 3.
    (B) $a^b \cdot b^a = b^a \cdot a^b$
    (C) a^b is never equal to b^a
    (D) $a \square b$ can equal 0
    (E) $a \square b = b \square a$

17. A pool is filled to $\frac{3}{4}$ of its capacity. $\frac{1}{9}$ of the water in the pool evaporates. If the pool can hold 24,000 gallons when it is full, how many gallons of water will have to be added in order to fill the pool?

    (A) 6,000
    (B) 8,000
    (C) 12,000
    (D) 16,000
    (E) 18,000

GO ON TO THE NEXT PAGE

18. If $\frac{12m}{7}$ is an integer, m could be any of the following *except*

   (A) 63
   (B) 49
   (C) 21
   (D) 15
   (E) 7

19. What is side AD + side DC ?

   (A) $18\sqrt{2}$
   (B) $8\sqrt{2}$
   (C) $10\sqrt{2}$
   (D) 10
   (E) $6\sqrt{2}$

   Note: Figure not drawn to scale.

20. Four "*ABCD*" equals three "*EFGH*." Four "*EFGH*" equals five "*IJKL*." How many "*ABCD*" are equal to fifteen "*IJKL*"?

   (A) 4
   (B) 8
   (C) 12
   (D) 16
   (E) 20

21.

j	k
1	$\frac{2}{3}$
2	$\frac{4}{3}$
3	2
4	$\frac{8}{3}$

   According to the above chart, $k =$

   (A) $\frac{2}{3}j$
   (B) $j - \frac{1}{3}$
   (C) $\frac{3}{2}j$
   (D) $\frac{j}{2}$
   (E) $\frac{j}{3}$

22. In the figure, what is the sum of the six angles divided by the average of the six angles?

   (A) 72
   (B) 36
   (C) 12
   (D) 6
   (E) It cannot be determined from the information given.

23. An investor bought 1,200 shares of stock at $22\frac{5}{8}$ and sold the same 1,200 shares at $23\frac{1}{2}$. What is the profit not counting commissions or taxes?

   (A) $4,050
   (B) $3,050
   (C) $2,050
   (D) $1,050
   (E) $550

24. A certain neon sign flashes every 2 seconds, another sign flashes every 3 seconds, and a third flashes every 5 seconds. If they all start flashing together, how many seconds will pass before they all flash simultaneously again?

   (A) 45 seconds
   (B) 30 seconds
   (C) 20 seconds
   (D) 15 seconds
   (E) 10 seconds

25. Marianne can read at a rate of 300 words per minute. While taking a speed reading course, Marianne increases her speed by $\frac{1}{3}$. After finishing the course, Marianne's speed drops by 100 words per minute. What percent of her original speed is her current speed?

   (A) 200%
   (B) 100%
   (C) 50%
   (D) 20%
   (E) 0%

STOP

END OF SECTION 1. IF YOU HAVE ANY TIME LEFT, GO OVER YOUR WORK IN THIS SECTION ONLY. DO NOT WORK IN ANY OTHER SECTION OF THE TEST.

SECTION 2

31 Questions • Time—30 Minutes

Directions: Each of the following questions consists of an incomplete sentence followed by five words or pairs of words. Choose that word or pair of words which, when substituted for the blank space or spaces, best completes the meaning of the sentence, and mark the letter of your choice on your answer sheet.

Example:

In view of the extenuating circumstances and the defendant's youth, the judge recommended ----.

(A) conviction
(B) a defense
(C) a mistrial
(D) leniency
(E) life imprisonment

Ⓐ Ⓑ Ⓒ ● Ⓔ

1. Because he had faith in the student's integrity, the teacher offered to ---- with the principal on her behalf.

   (A) interpolate
   (B) reminisce
   (C) intercede
   (D) deprecate
   (E) repudiate

2. The new contract ---- all previous agreements between the two parties.

   (A) subdues
   (B) supersedes
   (C) precedes
   (D) relegates
   (E) warrants

3. As volcanic activity ----, the scientist was able to return to the area to ---- her studies.

   (A) commenced..augment
   (B) intervened..rescind
   (C) retreated..revert
   (D) encroached..design
   (E) abated..resume

4. Some observers believe that an emphasis on ---- has damaged the traditional spirit of societal unity and harmony.

   (A) individualism
   (B) exercise
   (C) tranquillity
   (D) syllogisms
   (E) fraternity

5. The conspirators met ---- in order to plot a(n) ---- against the oppressive regime.

   (A) reclusively..schism
   (B) clandestinely..insurrection
   (C) vicariously..invocation
   (D) imperviously..embargo
   (E) insidiously..referendum

6. His ---- of practical experience and his psychological acuity more than ---- his lack of formal academic training.

   (A) claims..compromise
   (B) background..repay
   (C) breadth..account for
   (D) wealth..compensate for
   (E) fund..elucidate

7. The merchant ---- a small neighborhood business into a city-wide chain of stores.

   (A) appraised
   (B) transferred
   (C) parlayed
   (D) redeemed
   (E) instilled

8. It is not always easy to ---- one's mistakes, but it is inevitably more ---- to try to hide them.

   (A) cover..suspect
   (B) confess..difficult
   (C) cancel..attractive
   (D) solve..satisfying
   (E) anticipate..circumspect

9. A professional journalist will attempt to ---- the facts learned in an interview by independent ----.

   (A) endorse..question
   (B) query..situation
   (C) garnish..sources
   (D) verify..investigation
   (E) embellish..scrutiny

Directions: Each of the following questions consists of a capitalized pair of words followed by five pairs of words lettered A to E. The capitalized words bear some meaningful relationship to each other. Choose the lettered pair of words whose relationship is most similar to that expressed by the capitalized pair and mark its letter on your answer sheet.

Example:

DAY : SUN : :

(A) sunlight : daylight (B) ray : sun
(C) night : moon (D) heat : cold
(E) moon : star

Ⓐ Ⓑ ● Ⓓ Ⓔ

10. PEAR : FRUIT : :

    (A) flower : seed
    (B) baseball : sport
    (C) building : windows
    (D) street : pavement
    (E) youth : juvenile

11. DISCIPLINARIAN : OBEDIENCE : :

    (A) principal : school
    (B) fireman : hose
    (C) parent : children
    (D) perfectionist : flawlessness
    (E) picture : colors

12. DECIBEL : LOUDNESS : :

    (A) gram : ounce
    (B) meter : yard
    (C) length : width
    (D) carat : weight
    (E) gallon : mile

13. WOOD : CARVE : :

    (A) paper : burn
    (B) pipe : blow
    (C) clay : mold
    (D) tree : grow
    (E) brick : build

14. GALLERY : ARTWORK : :

    (A) museum : children
    (B) zoo : animals
    (C) theater : exhibits
    (D) stadium : field
    (E) forest : park

15. FADE : VANISH : :

    (A) abate : diminish
    (B) meander : wander
    (C) chide : reprimand
    (D) deplete : replenish
    (E) infer : imply

Questions 16–24 are based on the following passage.

The Federalist Papers were written to convince readers to adopt the Constitution in place of the Articles of Confederation, in order to maintain authority with a central, federal government. This particular paper was written in 1788 by John Jay, later to become first Chief Justice of the Supreme Court.

It is not a new observation that the people of any country (if, like the Americans, intelligent and well-informed) seldom adopt and steadily persevere for many years in an erroneous opinion respecting their
(5) interests. That consideration naturally tends to create great respect for the high opinion which the people of America have so long and uniformly entertained of the importance of their continuing firmly united under one federal government, vested with sufficient powers
(10) for all general and national purposes.

The more attentively I consider and investigate the reasons which appear to have given birth to this opinion, the more I become convinced that they are cogent and conclusive.

(15) Among the many objects to which a wise and free people find it necessary to direct their attention, that of providing for their *safety* seems to be the first. The *safety* of the people doubtless has relation to a great variety of circumstances and considerations, and con-
(20) sequently affords great latitude to those who wish to define it precisely and comprehensively.

At present I mean only to consider it as it respects security for the preservation of peace and tranquillity, as well as against dangers from *foreign arms and*
(25) *influence,* as from dangers of the *like kind* arising from domestic causes. As the former of these comes first in order, it is proper it should be the first discussed. Let us therefore proceed to examine whether the people are not right in their opinion that a cordial Union,
(30) under an efficient national government, affords them the best security that can be devised against *hostilities* from abroad.

The number of wars which have happened or will happen in the world will always be found to be in
(35) proportion to the number and weight of the causes, whether *real or pretended,* which *provoke* or *invite* them. If this remark be just, it becomes useful to inquire whether so many *just* causes of war are likely to be given by *United America* as by *disunited* America;
(40) for if it should turn out that United America will probably give up the fewest, then it will follow that in this respect the Union tends most to preserve the people in a state of peace with other nations.

The *just* causes of war, for the most part, arise either
(45) from violations of treaties or from direct violence. America has already formed treaties with no less than six foreign nations, and all of them, except Prussia, are maritime, and therefore able to annoy and injure us. She has also extensive commerce with Portugal, Spain,
(50) and Britain, and, with respect to the two latter, has, in addition, the circumstance of neighborhood to attend to.

It is of high importance to the peace of America that she observe the laws of nations towards all these
(55) powers, and to me it appears evident that this will be more perfectly and punctually done by one national government than it could be either by thirteen separate States or by three or four distinct confederacies.

16. Jay opens with the observation that
 (A) Americans are right in wanting a united government
 (B) people often harbor wrong ideas about their welfare
 (C) all Americans are vested with specific powers
 (D) Americans are more intelligent than foreigners
 (E) people in America respect each other's opinions

GO ON TO THE NEXT PAGE

17. How does Jay narrowly define "safety"?

    (A) Sanctuary in a storm
    (B) Protection from foreign and domestic arms
    (C) Economic security
    (D) Certainty
    (E) Defense against the world's unrest

18. When Jay refers to a "cordial Union" (line 29), he means one that is

    (A) friendly to other nations
    (B) harmonious
    (C) warm
    (D) complimentary
    (E) spirited

19. Does Jay believe that a war can be just?

    (A) No, not if it leads to suffering.
    (B) Yes, if it can be proved in court.
    (C) Yes, if it is due to broken treaties or invasion.
    (D) No, unless it is in defense of the flag.
    (E) Yes, if it is caused by disunity.

20. Why does Jay bother to point out that five lands with which America has treaties are maritime (lines 46–48)?

    (A) They have the advantage over land-locked America.
    (B) America's cannons do not work over water.
    (C) The treaties affect ocean commerce.
    (D) They can attack America with powerful navies.
    (E) The sixth nation is the most powerful of all.

21. What does *punctually* mean in line 56?

    (A) seasonably
    (B) early
    (C) belligerently
    (D) timelessly
    (E) efficiently

22. From Jay's arguments, you can assume that the Constitution provides for

    (A) treaties with maritime nations only
    (B) guidelines to help America observe international law
    (C) procedures to decide if a war is just
    (D) a stronger central government than existed under the Articles of Confederation
    (E) thirteen separate states and three distinct confederacies

23. Based on the passage, Jay would most likely support a war to

    (A) conquer additional territory for America
    (B) expel Native Americans from the thirteen states
    (C) defend America against hostilities from Spain
    (D) extend the range of American commerce
    (E) liberate a colony of Portugal

24. What would you expect Jay to discuss after he finishes talking about foreign hostilities?

    (A) Foreign peace initiatives
    (B) Hostilities that do not affect America
    (C) Effective governments
    (D) The role of the militia
    (E) Domestic disturbances

Questions 25–31 are based on the following passage.

In between life as a printer and life as a writer, Mark Twain (Samuel Clemens) worked as a pilot aboard a Mississippi steamboat. This piece is from Old Times on the Mississippi *(1875), a collection of reminiscences first published in the* Atlantic Monthly.

At the end of what seemed a tedious while, I had managed to pack my head full of islands, towns, bars, "points," and bends; and a curiously inanimate mass of lumber it was, too. However, inasmuch as I could
(5) shut my eyes and reel off a good long string of these names without leaving out more than ten miles of river in every fifty, I began to feel that I could make her skip those little gaps. But of course my complacency could hardly get start enough to lift my nose a trifle into the
(10) air, before Mr. Bixby would think of something to fetch it down again. One day he turned on me suddenly with this settler:—

"What is the shape of Walnut Bend?"

He might as well have asked me my grandmother's
(15) opinion of protoplasm. I reflected respectfully, and
then said I didn't know it had any particular shape. My
gunpowdery chief went off with a bang, of course, and
then went on loading and firing until he was out of
adjectives.

(20) I had learned long ago that he only carried just
so many rounds of ammunition, and was sure to
subside into a very placable and even remorseful old
smoothbore as soon as they were all gone. That word
"old" is merely affectionate; he was not more than
(25) thirty-four. I waited. By and by he said:—

"My boy, you've got to know the *shape* of the river
perfectly. It is all there is left to steer by on a very dark
night. Everything else is blotted out and gone. But
mind you, it hasn't the same shape in the night that it
(30) has in the daytime."

"How on earth am I ever going to learn it, then?"

"How do you follow a hall at home in the dark?
Because you know the shape of it. You can't see it."

"Do you mean to say that I've got to know all the
(35) million trifling variations of shape in the banks of this
interminable river as well as I know the shape of the
front hall at home?"

"On my honor, you've got to know them *better* than
any man ever did know the shapes of the halls in his
(40) own house."

"I wish I was dead!"

"Now I don't want to discourage you, but"—

"Well, pile it on me; I might as well have it now as
another time."

(45) "You see, this has got to be learned; there isn't any
getting around it. A clear starlight night throws such
heavy shadows that, if you didn't know the shape of a
shore perfectly, you would claw away from every
bunch of timber, because you would take the black
(50) shadow of it for a solid cape; and you see you would
be getting scared to death every fifteen minutes by the
watch. You would be fifty yards from shore all the
time when you ought to be within fifty feet of it. You
can't see a snag in one of those shadows, but you know
(55) exactly where it is, and the shape of the river tells you
when you are coming to it. Then there's your pitch-
dark night; the river is a very different shape on a pitch-
dark night from what it is on a starlight night. All

shores seem to be straight lines, then, and mighty dim
(60) ones, too; and you'd *run* them for straight lines, only
you know better. You boldly drive your boat right into
what seems to be a solid straight wall (you knowing
very well that in reality there is a curve there), and that
wall falls back and makes way for you. Then there's
(65) your gray mist. You take a night when there's one of
these grisly, drizzly, gray mists, and then there isn't
any particular shape to a shore. A gray mist would
tangle the head of the oldest man that ever lived. Well,
then different kinds of *moonlight* change the shape of
(70) the river in different ways.

25. In line 12, Twain uses the word *settler* to mean

   (A) pioneer
   (B) perch on the railing
   (C) remark that decides the issue
   (D) problem that humbles him
   (E) questions about his origins

26. When Twain compares a question to asking his "grandmother's opinion of protoplasm" (lines 14–15), he means that

   (A) the question is inane
   (B) the speaker is very old
   (C) he does not know the answer
   (D) his grandmother would be able to respond
   (E) the words are meaningless

27. Twain compares his chief to a gun to point out the chief's

   (A) accuracy
   (B) splendid posture
   (C) peppery temper
   (D) love of hunting
   (E) violent past

28. When Twain writes that Mr. Bixby "carried just so many rounds of ammunition," he means that

   (A) Bixby used a pistol to settle arguments
   (B) Bixby loaded and fired his gun at random
   (C) Bixby was impossible to work for
   (D) Bixby's gun was out of bullets
   (E) Bixby's hot temper would soon subside

GO ON TO THE NEXT PAGE

29. Twain's reaction to Mr. Bixby's insistence on the need to know the river at night is

    (A) despair
    (B) elation
    (C) puzzlement
    (D) anger
    (E) humility

30. The word *cape* (line 50) means

    (A) cloak
    (B) robe
    (C) woodpile
    (D) peninsula
    (E) waterway

31. Mr. Bixby is shown to be extremely

    (A) knowledgeable
    (B) rude
    (C) condescending
    (D) fearful
    (E) negative

STOP

END OF SECTION 2. IF YOU HAVE ANY TIME LEFT, GO OVER YOUR WORK IN THIS SECTION ONLY. DO NOT WORK IN ANY OTHER SECTION OF THE TEST.

SECTION 3

25 Questions • Time—30 Minutes

Directions: Solve the following problems using any available space on the page for scratchwork. On your answer sheet fill in the choice which best corresponds to the correct answer.

Notes: The figures accompanying the problems are drawn as accurately as possible unless otherwise stated in specific problems. Again, unless otherwise stated, all figures lie in the same plane. All numbers used in these problems are real numbers. Calculators are permitted for this test.

Reference Information

Circle: $C = 2\pi r$, $A = \pi r^2$

Rectangle: $A = lw$

Rectangular Solid: $V = lwh$

Cylinder: $V = \pi r^2 h$

Triangle: $A = \tfrac{1}{2}bh$

$a^2 + b^2 = c^2$

45°-45°-90° triangle: sides x, x, $x\sqrt{2}$

30°-60°-90° triangle: sides x, $x\sqrt{3}$, $2x$

The number of degrees of arc in a circle is 360.
The measure in degrees of a straight angle is 180.
The sum of the measures in degrees of the angles of a triangle is 180.

Part 1: Quantitative Comparison Questions

Directions: For each of the following questions, two quantities are given—one in Column A, the other in Column B. Compare the two quantities and mark your answer sheet as follows:

(A) if the quantity in Column A is greater
(B) if the quantity in Column B is greater
(C) if the quantities are equal
(D) if the relationship cannot be determined from the information given

Notes:

(1) Information concerning one or both of the compared quantities will be centered above the two columns for some items.
(2) Symbols that appear in both columns represent the same thing in Column A as in Column B.
(3) Letters such as x, n, and k are symbols for real numbers.

Examples

	Column A	Column B	Answers
		$a > 0$	
		$x > 0$	
E1.	$a - x$	$a + x$	(A) ● (C) (D)
E2.	The average of 17, 19, 21, 23	The average of 16, 18, 20, 22	● (B) (C) (D)

DO NOT MARK CHOICE (E) FOR THESE QUESTIONS. THERE ARE ONLY FOUR ANSWER CHOICES.

GO ON TO THE NEXT PAGE

	Column A	Column B		Column A	Column B
1.	$(\sqrt{12})(27)(\frac{1}{2})$	$(29)(\sqrt{3})$	7.	$y^2 - 1$	$y^3 + 1$

Questions 8–9 refer to the figure below.

$a \| b$

2.	$z + y - x$	z			

$a > b$
$a > c$

3.	$(\sqrt{x})^2$	$\dfrac{1}{x^2}$	8.	side AC	side AB
			9.	side AB	side CB

Note: Figure not drawn to scale.

4.	a	b			
			10.	The area of a triangle with base of 6 and height of 8	The area of a rectangle with sides of 7 and 4

$x = -3$

5.	$2x^3 + 6x^2 - 2$	$5x^2 + 3x - 7$

6.	Twice the sum of the interior angles of a triangle	One-half the sum of the interior angles of a square

Column A	Column B		Column A	Column B

$t, u,$ and v are positive integers

11. $\dfrac{t+u+v}{3}$ | The average of $t, u,$ and v

Note: Both figures are rectangles.

14. Area of shaded area | Area of unshaded area

$m\ 2$

12. $\dfrac{m^2 - 2m}{\frac{1}{2}(m-2)}$ | $2m + 1$

$m < n$

13. $n - m$ | $m - n$

15. segment AB | segment CD

Points: $A(-6,-1)$, $B(-2,5)$, $C(3,0)$, $D(0,7)$

Part 2: Student-Produced Response Questions

Directions: Solve each of these problems. Write the answer in the corresponding grid on the answer sheet and fill in the ovals beneath each answer you write. Here are some examples.

Answer: $\dfrac{3}{4}$ (= .75; show answer either way)

Answer: 325

Note: A mixed number such as $3\frac{1}{2}$ must be gridded as 7/2 or as 3.5. If gridded as "3 1/2" it will be read as "thirty-one halves."

Note: Either position is correct.

GO ON TO THE NEXT PAGE

16. What is the value of $(2a^2 - a^3)^2$ when $a = -1$?

17. A jar contains 2 red marbles, 3 green marbles, and 4 orange marbles. If a marble is picked at random, what is the probability that the marble is not orange?

18. In the country of Glup, 1 glop is 3 glips and 4 glips are 5 globs. How many globs are 2 glops?

19. Solve for k: $\frac{k}{3} + \frac{k}{4} = 1$

20. If the area of a square of side x is 5, what is the area of a square of side $3x$?

21. In the diagram below, $\triangle ABC$ is *similar* to $\triangle DBF$. If $DF = 3$, $BD = BF = 6$ and $AC = 4$, what is the perimeter of $\triangle ABC$?

22. In quadrilateral *ABCD* below, the measure of $\angle A = 120°$, the measure of $\angle B = 82°$, and the measure of $\angle D = 93°$. What is the value of x?

23. If $2x + 2y = 6$ and $3x - 3y = 9$, what is the value of $x^2 - y^2$?

24. If $\frac{4}{5}$ is subtracted from its reciprocal, the result is

25. If the ratio of $a:b$ is 1:5 and the ratio of $b:c$ is 3:2, then the ratio of $(a + c):c$ is

STOP

END OF SECTION 3. IF YOU HAVE ANY TIME LEFT, GO OVER YOUR WORK IN THIS SECTION ONLY. DO NOT WORK IN ANY OTHER SECTION OF THE TEST.

SECTION 4

35 Questions • Time—30 Minutes

Directions: Each of the following questions consists of an incomplete sentence followed by five words or pairs of words. Choose that word or pair of words which, when substituted for the blank space or spaces, best completes the meaning of the sentence, and mark the letter of your choice on your answer sheet.

Example:

In view of the extenuating circumstances and the defendant's youth, the judge recommended ----.

(A) conviction   (B) a defense
(C) a mistrial   (D) leniency
(E) life imprisonment   Ⓐ Ⓑ Ⓒ ● Ⓔ

1. The meeting yielded ---- results, yet all participants were convinced that a solution was ----.

   (A) negligible..imminent
   (B) small..hurried
   (C) detrimental..as bad
   (D) fleeting..short
   (E) guarded..despicable

2. Only 25 years ago a space launching produced widespread interest; it is hard to believe trips into space are now considered ---- events.

   (A) demeaning
   (B) furtive
   (C) comely
   (D) commonplace
   (E) surly

3. The football team was once ---- by injuries; of the 20 members only 10 were fit to play.

   (A) truncated
   (B) decimated
   (C) invaded
   (D) ostracized
   (E) reviled

4. Since the city cannot ticket their cars, the diplomats can park anywhere with ----.

   (A) penury
   (B) impunity
   (C) precision
   (D) languor
   (E) ignominy

5. If you ---- the charges instead of ---- them, people may conclude that you are guilty.

   (A) delegate..enumerating
   (B) preempt..disclaiming
   (C) efface..disavowing
   (D) reduce..mitigating
   (E) ignore..rebutting

6. On the narrow and ---- mountain road, the truck skidded when it rounded a curve.

   (A) pejorative
   (B) salutary
   (C) propitious
   (D) sedulous
   (E) tortuous

7. Although her acting was ----, she looked so good on stage that the audience applauded anyway.

   (A) dynamic
   (B) laudable
   (C) implacable
   (D) execrable
   (E) intrepid

GO ON TO THE NEXT PAGE

8. Because of her unpopular opinions, she was unable to ---- broad support among the voters; however, those who did support her were exceptionally ----.

   (A) alienate..many
   (B) survey..divided
   (C) cut across..quiet
   (D) amass..loyal
   (E) evoke..languid

9. Philosophical differences ---- the unification of the two parties into one.

   (A) delegated
   (B) legislated
   (C) impeded
   (D) enacted
   (E) entrusted

10. When a job becomes too ----, workers get ----, their attention wanders, and they start to make careless errors.

    (A) diverse..busy
    (B) hectic..lazy
    (C) tedious..bored
    (D) fascinating..interested
    (E) rewarding..sloppy

Directions: Each of the following questions consists of a capitalized pair of words followed by five pairs of words lettered A to E. The capitalized words bear some meaningful relationship to each other. Choose the lettered pair of words whose relationship is most similar to that expressed by the capitalized pair and mark its letter on your answer sheet.

Example:

DAY : SUN : :

(A) sunlight : daylight
(B) ray : sun
(C) night : moon
(D) heat : cold
(E) moon : star

Ⓐ Ⓑ ● Ⓓ Ⓔ

11. SCRIBBLING : WRITING : :

    (A) pen : pencil
    (B) sound : vibration
    (C) walking : jogging
    (D) mumbling : speaking
    (E) seeing : vision

12. URGE : INSIST : :

    (A) refuse : deny
    (B) request : demand
    (C) deserve : receive
    (D) infer : imply
    (E) inspire : revoke

13. SCREAM : FRIGHT : :

    (A) moan : loudness
    (B) sweat : drops
    (C) groan : pain
    (D) fly : plane
    (E) cry : tears

14. HYPOCRITE : DUPLICITOUS : :

    (A) partisan : impartial
    (B) traitor : disloyal
    (C) soldier : tough
    (D) tailor : prosperous
    (E) prisoner : repentant

15. SOAR : HOVER : :

    (A) trail : hike
    (B) sing : harmonize
    (C) fall : trip
    (D) help : aid
    (E) swim : float

16. CARPENTER : CABINET : :

    (A) gardener : tree
    (B) musician : clarinet
    (C) cobbler : boot
    (D) banker : deposit
    (E) potter : kiln

17. BICEPS : MUSCLE : :

    (A) cobra : snake
    (B) pump : heart
    (C) bat : bird
    (D) cup : mug
    (E) ball : rubber

18. POVERTY : MONEY : :

    (A) elation : joy
    (B) despair : remorse
    (C) veracity : honesty
    (D) erudition : learning
    (E) darkness : light

19. ENGAGEMENT : MARRIAGE : :

    (A) overture : opera
    (B) night : darkness
    (C) failure : success
    (D) demands : destitution
    (E) ballgame : umpire

20. IMPORTANT : PIVOTAL : :

    (A) major : minimal
    (B) robust : strong
    (C) stern : draconian
    (D) salient : compulsory
    (E) impetuous : perfect

21. EVANESCENT : VANISH : :

    (A) effervescent : corrode
    (B) iridescent : shine
    (C) expressive : admonish
    (D) fluorescent : disappear
    (E) vacuous : expedite

GO ON TO THE NEXT PAGE

22. BOOK : CHAPTER : :

   (A) film : projector
   (B) thesis : doctorate
   (C) prelude : piano
   (D) sculpture : chisel
   (E) symphony : movement

23. ROOTS : TREE : :

   (A) foundation : building
   (B) chimney : smoke
   (C) exit : entrance
   (D) engine : automobile
   (E) sleeve : shirt

Directions: The reading passage below is followed by a set of questions. Read the passage and answer the accompanying questions, basing your answers on what is stated or implied in the passage. Mark the letter of your choice on your answer sheet.

Questions 24–35 are based on the following passage.

Jane Austen (1775–1817) had an unremarkable life but a keen eye for details even in the most mundane of situations. This excerpt from Mansfield Park *shows how sharply satiric her wit could be.*

Tom Bertram had of late spent so little of his time at home, that he could be only nominally missed; and Lady Bertram was soon astonished to find how very well they did even without his father, how well Edmund
(5) could supply his place in carving, talking to the steward, writing to the attorney, settling with the servants, and equally saving her from all possible fatigue or exertion in every particular, but that of directing her letters.
(10) The earliest intelligence of the travellers' safe arrival in Antigua after a favorable voyage, was received; though not before Mrs. Norris had been indulging in very dreadful fears, and trying to make Edmund participate in them whenever she could get
(15) him alone; and as she depended on being the first person made acquainted with any fatal catastrophe, she had already arranged the manner of breaking it to all the others, when Sir Thomas's assurances of their both being alive and well, made it necessary to lay by
(20) her agitation and affectionate preparatory speeches for a while.

The winter came and passed without their being called for; the accounts continued perfectly good;— and Mrs. Norris in promoting gaieties for her nieces,
(25) assisting their toilettes, displaying their accomplishments, and looking for their future husbands, had so much to do as, in addition to all her own household cares, some interference in those of her sister, and Mrs. Grant's wasteful doings to overlook, left her very little
(30) occasion to be occupied even in fears for the absent.

The Miss Bertrams were now fully established among the belles of the neighborhood; and as they joined to beauty and brilliant acquirements, a manner naturally easy, and carefully formed to general civility
(35) and obligingness, they possessed its favor as well as its admiration. Their vanity was in such good order, that they seemed to be quite free from it, and gave themselves no airs; while the praises attending such behavior, secured, and brought round by their aunt, served to
(40) strengthen them in believing they had no faults.

Lady Bertram did not go into public with her daughters. She was too indolent even to accept a mother's gratification in witnessing their success and enjoyment at the expense of any personal trouble, and
(45) the charge was made over to her sister, who desired nothing better than a post of such honorable representation, and very thoroughly relished the means it afforded her of mixing in society without having horses to hire.

24. In line 5, the word "supply" most nearly means.

   (A) provision
   (B) item
   (C) demand
   (D) assume
   (E) lose

25. Why does Mrs. Norris have to "lay by" her speeches (line 19)?

   (A) She is forced to defend herself against the others.
   (B) Since no disaster has occurred, she must postpone her grief.
   (C) Her work with her nieces comes first.
   (D) Her audience has left for Antigua.
   (E) The Miss Bertrams are as yet too young to be formally presented.

26. The travellers mentioned in line 10 are

   (A) Lady Bertram and Mrs. Grant
   (B) Sir Thomas Bertram and Tom Bertram
   (C) the two Miss Bertrams
   (D) Edmund and Mrs. Norris
   (E) the steward and the attorney

27. Austen's description of Mrs. Norris's many occupations (paragraph 3) depicts her as a

    (A) drudge
    (B) busybody
    (C) beauty
    (D) prankster
    (E) sinner

28. Austen undercuts her description of the lovely Miss Bertrams by pointing out that they

    (A) believed themselves faultless
    (B) gave themselves no airs
    (C) were frequently praised
    (D) had easy manners
    (E) were beautiful and brilliant

29. In line 42, the word *indolent* most nearly means

    (A) selfish
    (B) lazy
    (C) indifferent
    (D) enthusiastic
    (E) busy

30. In line 45, what does *charge* mean?

    (A) fee
    (B) attack
    (C) duty
    (D) accusation
    (E) demand

31. The last line of this passage reveals Mrs. Norris as

    (A) honorable
    (B) clumsy
    (C) delightful
    (D) cheap
    (E) fussy

32. The chief characteristic of Lady Bertram exposed in this excerpt is her

    (A) concern for her children
    (B) love of country
    (C) shyness
    (D) incredible vanity
    (E) laziness

33. Austen seems to feel that Mrs. Norris is

    (A) ludicrous
    (B) poignant
    (C) charming
    (D) forceful
    (E) uninteresting

34. Which of the following is an example of Austen's satiric wit?

    (A) Tom Bertram had of late spent so little time at home.
    (B) Sir Thomas writes that he is alive and well.
    (C) Lady Bertram is too indolent to witness her daughters' social success.
    (D) The Miss Bertrams were established as belles of the neighborhood.
    (E) Edmund carves, talks to the steward, and writes to the attorney.

35. The best description of this excerpt is that it is

    (A) coldly unsympathetic
    (B) libelous
    (C) tongue-in-cheek
    (D) tactless and coarse
    (E) lovingly tender

STOP

END OF SECTION 4. IF YOU HAVE ANY TIME LEFT, GO OVER YOUR WORK IN THIS SECTION ONLY. DO NOT WORK IN ANY OTHER SECTION OF THE TEST.

SECTION 5

10 Questions • Time—15 Minutes

Directions: Solve the following problems using any available space on the page for scratchwork. On your answer sheet fill in the choice which best corresponds to the correct answer.

Notes: The figures accompanying the problems are drawn as accurately as possible unless otherwise stated in specific problems. Again, unless otherwise stated, all figures lie in the same plane. All numbers used in these problems are real numbers. Calculators are permitted for this test.

Reference Information

Circle: $C = 2\pi r$, $A = \pi r^2$
Rectangle: $A = lw$
Rectangular Solid: $V = lwh$
Cylinder: $V = \pi r^2 h$
Triangle: $A = \frac{1}{2}bh$
$a^2 + b^2 = c^2$

Special right triangles: 45°-45°-90° ($x, x, x\sqrt{2}$); 30°-60°-90° ($x, x\sqrt{3}, 2x$)

The number of degrees of arc in a circle is 360.
The measure in degrees of a straight angle is 180.
The sum of the measures in degrees of the angles of a triangle is 180.

---

1. Which of the following is less than $\frac{1}{2}$?

   (A) $\frac{9}{16}$

   (B) $\frac{11}{21}$

   (C) $\frac{8}{17}$

   (D) $\frac{14}{27}$

   (E) $\frac{6}{11}$

2. Rectangle R has sides of x and y. Rectangle S has sides of $3x$ and $2y$. What is the area of S minus the area of R?

   (A) $12xy$

   (B) $9xy$

   (C) $6xy$

   (D) $5xy$

   (E) $4xy$

3. If the triangle below is distorted so that angle y is doubled and angle z is tripled, then angle x will become a right angle. Which of the following is a possible value for angle y?

   (A) 90
   (B) 75
   (C) 60
   (D) 45
   (E) 30

   Note: Figure not drawn to scale.

4. If $3x + 3$ is 6 more than $3y + 3$, then $x - y =$

   (A) 0
   (B) 2
   (C) 4
   (D) 6
   (E) 9

GO ON TO THE NEXT PAGE

5. Jim's average score for three bowling games was 162. In the second game, Jim scored 10 less than in the first game. In the third game, he scored 13 less than in the second game. What was his score in the first game?

   (A) 189
   (B) 179
   (C) 173
   (D) 171
   (E) 168

6. $3 \times 10^3 \times 2 \times 10^2 =$

   (A) 6,000,000
   (B) 600,000
   (C) 60,000
   (D) 6,000
   (E) 600

7. A certain machine makes a widget every 2.5 seconds. How many widgets does the machine make in 40 minutes?

   (A) 12,600
   (B) 9,600
   (C) 4,800
   (D) 1,200
   (E) 960

8. A cassette tape has two sides and each side can record for 45 minutes. A student brings 3 tapes in order to record a three-hour lecture. If the time spent loading and unloading the tapes is negligible, what percent of the total available tape will not be used to record the lecture?

   (A) 75%
   (B) 50%
   (C) $33\frac{1}{3}\%$
   (D) 25%
   (E) 20%

9. If $\frac{(a+b)}{(c+d)} = 5$ and $\frac{(e+f)}{(g+h)} = 6$, then what is the value of $\frac{(a+b)}{(g+h)} \cdot \frac{(e+f)}{(c+d)}$?

   (A) 0
   (B) 1
   (C) 11
   (D) 30
   (E) It cannot be determined from the information given.

10. The fraction $\frac{2}{7}$ is represented by the decimal .285714 repeated. $\frac{2}{7} = .285714\ 285714\ 285714\ldots$. What is the 753rd decimal digit?

    (A) 2
    (B) 8
    (C) 5
    (D) 7
    (E) 1

STOP

END OF SECTION 5. IF YOU HAVE ANY TIME LEFT, GO OVER YOUR WORK IN THIS SECTION ONLY. DO NOT WORK IN ANY OTHER SECTION OF THE TEST.

SECTION 6

12 Questions • Time—15 Minutes

Directions: The two passages given below deal with related topics. Following the passages are questions about the content of each passage or about the relationship between the two passages. Answer the questions based upon what is stated or implied in the passages and in any introductory material provided. Mark the letter of your choice on your answer sheet.

Questions 1–12 are based on the following passages.

The crafts of calligraphy and stenciling have a long history, during which each fell out of favor. Today both calli-graphy and stenciling are experiencing a comeback. The two passages present an explanation of how these art forms are practiced.

Passage 1—The Art of Calligraphy

Calligraphy, or lettering, is an art form with an ancient heritage dating back to the time of the Romans, whose capital letters are still in use today. For particu-
(5) larly important documents, the Romans carved written letters into stone surfaces. Other writings were painted on walls with brushes or charcoal. Consequently, Roman letters evolved as a combination of paintbrush and chisel styles. During medieval times, the basic Roman capital letter forms were enhanced
(10) with decoration as scribes used pen and ink on fine parchment. With the advent of the printing press and moveable type, hand lettering became a thing of the past, not to be rediscovered until it became part of the modern crafts movement. Today with the abundance
(15) of various pens and fine papers, many people can practice this art form.

There are several basic styles of letters used by calligraphers. The Roman style is a simple style, noted for its clarity. Used originally for issuing reports
(20) to the whole of the Roman Empire, these letter forms had to be simple and legible. Calligraphy in the Roman style is easy to read and write.

Celtic letters, in contrast to Roman letters, are more rounded. While using the Roman style as a basis, the
(25) Irish, who created the Celtic alphabet, added a rounded quality to Roman letters so as to incorporate Celtic circle motifs. Additionally, Celtic letters are heavier than Roman letters, and unlike the Roman style, which is extremely uniform, the Celtic style is highly indi-
(30) vidual. That is, there may be several versions of the same letter for the calligrapher to choose from.

A third style of alphabet is the Gothic letter. Its chief characteristic is uniformity, with many of the letters strongly resembling one another. Since letter
(35) space and word space are nearly identical, this makes the Gothic letter less legible; however, this alphabet has a smooth texture. It is strong and angular and hard to read.

Bookhand, modeled after Roman letters by scribes
(40) during the Renaissance, is a fourth alphabet style, specially designed for book writing. Bookhand has few alternate forms so is therefore much less expressive than Celtic. It does, however, have a subtle texture.

(45) The Italic style, which flourished in the early years of the Renaissance, is another style of calligraphy, or handwriting. Named for its country of origin, Italy, this style of writing became widespread and remains a favorite of calligraphers today.

(50) Today, calligraphers have many styles to choose from, ranging from the highly legible Roman style to the more expressive Celtic, as they create their very distinct form of visual art.

Passage 2—The Craft of Stenciling

Stenciling as an art form was common among the
(55) Egyptians and Romans. Early Japanese and Chinese cultures also used stenciling as a form of decorative art for public architecture and home furnishings.

Brought to America by Europeans during the Colonial period, stenciling on walls, floors, and furniture

GO ON TO THE NEXT PAGE

(60) became quite common. Most of the stencil designs at this time came from nature—flowers, vines, leaves, and fruits, for example.

Before the invention of cutting tools, stenciling was a laborious process. Ancient stencilers created (65) their stencil outlines by using pins to prick holes in paper in a design or pattern. They then used charcoal to fill in the dots. When the paper was lifted, the dots were connected with lines. Of course, when cutting tools became available, cut-out designs became preva- (70) lent and color was applied through the cut-out openings. Today a stencil design is drawn on a piece of durable paper, called the stencil plate; then pieces of that design are cut away with a stencil knife. Color is applied through the openings.

(75) There are two types of stencils—positive and negative. A positive stencil is one in which the design is stenciled, that is, color is applied to the area that has been cut away. In a negative stencil, the background is colored, while the cut-out remains uncolored.

(80) There are several ways to apply color to stencil designs. The first is called stippling, the most common method used in stenciling. This method requires a special brush to apply paint. The pressure exerted on the brush will determine how the color appears—light (85) pressure will allow some grain or fabric lines to appear, heavier pressure, of course, will assure more coverage. Sponging is also a common method used in stenciling. Instead of using a brush, stencilers use a sponge to apply color. The type of sponge chosen (90) determines the texture of the application. Another method is spraying, which, of course, is the easiest method. Spraying will produce a delicate texture and is well suited to stenciling on fabric.

Although there are many patterns that can be used (95) for stenciling, perhaps the easiest pattern is the border pattern. Borders can be continuous, that is, repeated bands of designs that decorate floors, walls, or fabrics. A fret border is a border that uses basically interlocking geometric shapes to form its design. Interrupted (100) borders are borders whose repeated design is regularly interrupted by a design element. Such borders lend definition to a room or floor area.

The ancient art of stenciling is practiced today by those who wish to add decoration, definition, and a (105) design element to their homes or to the fabrics that are used in their homes.

1. According to Passage 1, calligraphy as an art form dates back to the time of the

   (A) Egyptians
   (B) Greeks
   (C) Chinese
   (D) Romans
   (E) Persians

2. Most ancient calligraphy was

   (A) drawn on fine parchment
   (B) carved in stone
   (C) painted on canvas
   (D) produced with type
   (E) drawn on large screens

3. The word *advent* (line 11) means

   (A) invention
   (B) use
   (C) destruction
   (D) celebration
   (E) arrival

4. In comparison with Roman letters, the Celtic alphabet is more

   (A) simple
   (B) rounded
   (C) legible
   (D) uniform
   (E) outdated

5. The creators of the Celtic alphabet were

   (A) the Romans
   (B) the Italians
   (C) the Irish
   (D) Renaissance artists
   (E) medieval scribes

6. The letter forms that are the most difficult to read are

   (A) Roman
   (B) Italic
   (C) Celtic
   (D) Bookhand
   (E) Gothic

7. In Passage 2, the author mentions that all of the following ancient cultures used stenciling as an art form EXCEPT

   (A) German
   (B) Egyptian
   (C) Japanese
   (D) Chinese
   (E) Roman

8. The invention of which of the following made stenciling less laborious?

   (A) stencil plate
   (B) cutting tools
   (C) durable paper
   (D) charcoal
   (E) spray paint

9. Two types of stenciling are

   (A) fret and repeated
   (B) sponge and watercolor
   (C) Japanese and Burmese
   (D) negative and positive
   (E) none of the above

10. According to the passage, which of the following techniques produces the most delicate texture?

    (A) spraying
    (B) sponging
    (C) waxing
    (D) stippling
    (E) watercoloring

11. In comparison with the art of calligraphy, the craft of stenciling

    (A) has a more legalistic background
    (B) involves more chiselling
    (C) is less visually appealing
    (D) is more modern
    (E) has its roots in nature

12. The authors of these two passages would most likely agree that

    (A) calligraphy far surpasses stenciling as an art form
    (B) both art forms are relatively new
    (C) stenciling is a far superior art form to calligraphy
    (D) these two ancient art forms were rediscovered by modern crafters
    (E) the visual impact of calligraphy is more dramatic than that of stenciling

STOP

END OF SECTION 6. IF YOU HAVE ANY TIME LEFT, GO OVER YOUR WORK IN THIS SECTION ONLY. DO NOT WORK IN ANY OTHER SECTION OF THE TEST.

FINAL PRACTICE EXAMINATION
Answer Key

Section 1: Math

1. A	6. B	11. D	16. D	21. A
2. E	7. E	12. B	17. B	22. D
3. C	8. A	13. A	18. D	23. D
4. D	9. E	14. E	19. C	24. B
5. D	10. C	15. D	20. D	25. B

Section 2: Verbal

1. C	8. B	14. B	20. D	26. C
2. B	9. D	15. C	21. E	27. C
3. E	10. B	16. A	22. D	28. E
4. A	11. D	17. B	23. C	29. A
5. B	12. D	18. B	24. E	30. D
6. D	13. C	19. C	25. D	31. A
7. C				

Section 3: Math

Part 1

1. B	4. A	7. D	10. B	13. A
2. C	5. B	8. D	11. C	14. A
3. D	6. A	9. B	12. B	15. B

Part 2

16. 9	18. $7.5 = \frac{15}{2}$	20. 45	22. 65	24. $\frac{9}{20} = .45$
17. $\frac{5}{9} = .556$	19. $\frac{12}{7} = 1.71$	21. 20	23. 9	25. 1.3

Section 4: Verbal

1. A	8. D	15. E	22. E	29. B
2. D	9. C	16. C	23. A	30. C
3. B	10. C	17. A	24. D	31. D
4. B	11. D	18. E	25. B	32. E
5. E	12. B	19. A	26. B	33. A
6. E	13. C	20. C	27. B	34. C
7. D	14. B	21. B	28. A	35. C

Section 5: Math

1. C
2. D
3. E
4. B
5. C
6. B
7. E
8. C
9. D
10. C

Section 6: Verbal

1. D
2. B
3. E
4. B
5. C
6. E
7. A
8. B
9. D
10. A
11. E
12. D

FINAL PRACTICE EXAMINATION
Explanatory Answers

Note: A 🖩 following a math answer explanation indicates that a calculator could be helpful in solving that particular problem.

Section 1

1. **(A)** $2 \times 2 \times 2 = 8$. There are 6 decimal places in the factors; therefore, there must be 5 zeros in front of the 8. 🖩

2. **(E)** If $q = -3$, then p must equal -18. Plug these numbers into the problem:

   $$\frac{-18 + (-3)}{-3} = \frac{-21}{-3} = 7$$ 🖩

3. **(C)** Since $\frac{s}{t}$ is an integer, s must be greater than t. Since $\frac{t}{u}$ is an integer, t must be greater than u. The relationship among the three variables can be written as $s > t > u$. Thus $\frac{u}{s}$ cannot be an integer because the denominator is bigger than the numerator.

4. **(D)** $\frac{1}{2}$ of the $\frac{1}{4}$ go from the lobby into the auditorium. Therefore, multiplying the two fractions, this means that $\frac{1}{8}$ of the total audience returns to the auditorium. The next step would be to add $\frac{1}{8}$ and $\frac{3}{4}$.

   $$\frac{1}{8} + \frac{3}{4} = \frac{1}{8} + \frac{6}{8} = \frac{7}{8}$$

   Since $\frac{7}{8}$ of the people are in the auditorium, the ratio would be 7:1. 🖩

5. **(D)**

   $$2(3m + 4m) = 42$$
   $$6m + 8m = 42$$
   $$14m = 42$$
   $$m = 3$$
   $$\text{Area} = 3m \times 4m = 3(3) \times 4(3) = 9 \times 12 = 108$$ 🖩

6. **(B)** $390 = 13\%$ of the total $= .13x$

   $x = 3,000$

   $3,000 = $ total 🖩

7. **(E)** I. Since both of the expressions equal s, they must equal each other.

   II. Any fraction that has the same value in the numerator and denominator is equal to 1.

   III. $n(q+5) = q(n+4)$
   $$nq + 5n = nq + 4q$$
   $$5n = 4q$$

   Therefore, q is greater than n.

8. **(A)**

   $$\frac{\frac{2}{3}(x^2y^3)^4}{\frac{3}{4}(x^4y^3)^2} = \frac{\frac{2}{3}(x^8y^{12})}{\frac{3}{4}(x^8y^6)} = \frac{2}{3} \cdot \frac{4}{3} \cdot \frac{x^8y^{12}}{x^8y^6} = \frac{8y^6}{9}$$

9. **(E)** We need to know how many miles Jane walked. We find this by adding m and n. Jane walked s steps in every mile. We would find her total steps by multiplying the steps per mile by the total miles.

10. **(C)** Since Tim works slower than John, choices (A) and (B) must be wrong. A good way to solve this is to act as if Tim folds 1 brochure in 20 minutes, and John folds 1 in 15 minutes. In an hour, John will fold 4 brochures while Tim folds 3. Tim folds $\frac{3}{4}$ as many as John.

11. **(D)** There are 95 students and 16 failed the test. $\frac{16}{95}$ is close to $\frac{16}{100}$. The correct answer must be slightly bigger than 16%, so 17% is correct. 🖩

12. **(B)** 72 students scored from 77 to 100. If 9 scored 100, then 72 − 9, or 63, must be the number of students who scored from 77 to 99.

13. **(A)** $180 = x + 3y + 2y$. Subtract $5y$ from both sides. $180 − 5y = x$.

14. **(E)** If x is 0, then the entire statement must equal 0. To find the other values for x, set each factor equal to 0.
    $x + 2 = 0 \quad x − 3 = 0 \quad x + 4 = 0$
    $\qquad x = −2 \qquad x = 3 \qquad x = −4$

15. **(D)** $2 \square 3 = 2^3 + 3^2 = 8 + 9 = 17$.

16. **(D)** Since a and b are positive, there is no way that the operation can equal 0.

17. **(B)** If $\frac{1}{9}$ evaporates, then $\frac{8}{9}$ remains. Since the pool is only $\frac{3}{4}$ full, then $\frac{8}{9} \times \frac{3}{4} = \frac{24}{36} = \frac{2}{3}$. Therefore, the pool is $\frac{1}{3}$ empty. To fill the pool, it is necessary to add $\frac{1}{3}$ of 24,000 gallons, or 8,000 gallons.

18. **(D)** The question is made simpler if you realize that $\frac{m}{7}$ has to be an integer, so m must be divisible by 7. 7 does not go evenly into 15.

19. **(C)** You can use the Pythagorean Theorem to solve for side AC.
    $6^2 + 8^2 = AC^2$
    $36 + 64 = AC^2$
    $100 = AC^2$
    $10 = AC$

    Since side AD equals side DC, $\triangle ADC$ is a 45°–45°–90° triangle with legs AD and DC and hypotenuse AC. But we know that side $AC = 10$. Therefore, side AD equals $\frac{1}{2} AC \cdot \sqrt{2} = \frac{1}{2}(10)\sqrt{2} = 5\sqrt{2}$.
    $AD + DC = 2(5\sqrt{2}) = 10\sqrt{2}$.

20. **(D)** Two ratios are given, and "EFGH" is the common link between them.
    $4 \text{ "}ABCD\text{"} = 3 \text{ "}EFGH\text{"}$
    $\qquad 4 \text{ "}EFGH\text{"} = 5 \text{ "}IJKL\text{"}$

    Multiply the top equation by 4 and the second equation by 3 in order to make "EFGH" the same.
    $16 \text{ "}ABCD\text{"} = 12 \text{ "}EFGH\text{"} = 15 \text{ "}IJKL\text{"}$

21. **(A)** Plug the values of j into the answer choices in order to see which one consistently gives k as its answer.

22. **(D)** The figure has six sides, so it contains 720 degrees. The average of the six angles, therefore, would be 720 divided by 6, which is equal to 120. Now divide the sum of the angles by the average. 720 divided by 120 equals 6. (When you divide the sum of some numbers by the average of those numbers you *always* obtain the number of numbers.)

23. **(D)** Estimation works well in this problem. We know that the stock went up by almost 1 dollar. Therefore, the profit must be almost 1,200 dollars.

24. **(B)** The question might be phrased, "What is the lowest common denominator for 2, 3, and 5?" $2 \times 3 \times 5 = 30$.

25. **(B)** $300 \times \frac{1}{3} = 100$. Marianne increased her speed by 100 words. When her speed drops by 100 words, she will be back at 300, which is 100% of her original speed.

Section 2

1. **(C)** A teacher who believed in a student's integrity might be expected to *intercede* (intervene with a good word) on her behalf.

2. **(B)** Of the choices, only (B) makes sense; a new contract could *supersede* (replace) all previous agreements.

3. **(E)** The scientist could return to the area only if volcanic activity *abated* (subsided). She could then *resume* her studies.

4. **(A)** The choice must contrast with *unity* and *harmony*.

5. **(B)** Conspirators might meet *reclusively* (in solitude) or *insidiously* (treacherously), but they would be most likely to do so *clandestinely* (in secret). And faced with an oppressive regime, their aim would most likely be to plot an *insurrection* (rebellion).

6. **(D)** If you lack formal training, you can *compensate for* it with a *wealth* of practical experience.

7. **(C)** A small neighborhood business could likely be *parlayed* (exploited for further gain) into a chain of stores.

8. **(B)** The other choices do not produce a reasonable sentence.

9. **(D)** Journalists routinely *verify* (check) their facts before publishing them. They do so by research and independent *investigation*.

10. **(B)** A *pear* is a kind of *fruit*, and *baseball* is a kind of *sport*.

11. **(D)** A *disciplinarian* demands *obedience*, and a *perfectionist* demands *flawlessness*.

12. **(D)** A *decibel* is a measure of the *loudness* of sound, just as a *carat* is a measure of the *weight* of a precious stone.

13. **(C)** To *carve wood* is to form it into a desired shape. Likewise, to *mold clay* is to form it into a desired shape.

14. **(B)** A *gallery* is a place for *artwork*, and a *zoo* is a place for *animals*.

15. **(C)** To *fade* is to disappear partially; to *vanish* is to disappear completely. To *chide* is to reprove mildly; to *reprimand* is to reprove severely.

16. **(A)** Paragraph 1 concerns Americans' opinion that they should continue "firmly united" (line 8) and Jay's contention that this opinion could never be considered "erroneous."

17. **(B)** This definition comes at the beginning of paragraph 4.

18. **(B)** Jay is primarily concerned here with the smooth-working efficiency that a harmonious unity can provide.

19. **(C)** Lines 44–45 confirm Jay's opinion that the "just causes of war arise . . . from violations of treaties or from direct violence."

20. **(D)** Jay remarks that the maritime nations are "able to annoy and injure us" (line 48).

21. **(E)** This is the only response that makes sense in context. Jay speaks earlier (line 29–30) of "an efficient national government"; it is one of his key themes.

22. **(D)** According to the introduction, Jay is attempting to convince readers to adopt the Constitution in place of the Articles of Confederation. The reason he offers here is that America needs firm unity under a national government "vested with sufficient powers" for all purposes. Presumably, the Constitution would do a better job of providing such government than would the Articles of Confederation.

23. **(C)** Since Jay believes that wars are just if they are undertaken in response to treaty violations or invasions, he would likely support a war to defend America against hostilities from Spain. None of the other answer choices describes a situation in which Jay would believe that war is justified.

24. **(E)** Paragraph 4 names the two dangers that face the nation and states that Jay will deal with the two in order, beginning with foreign arms.

25. **(D)** The line before refers to Mr. Bixby's ability to "fetch down" Twain's nose when he gets a bit complacent; the *settler* in this case is another question that "settles," or "fetches down," Twain's nose.

26. **(C)** The comparison is comic in intent. Twain knows as much about the shape of Walnut Bend as he does about his grandmother's opinion of protoplasm, which is to say, nothing at all.

27. **(C)** This comparison starts on line 17 with the sobriquet "gunpowdery chief." Twain is describing his chief's tendency to blow up at the slightest provocation.

28. **(E)** There is no mention of a real gun in the selection. Twain is describing his boss's temper, which was quick to explode but subsided just as rapidly.

29. **(A)** Twain's despair is shown in the line "I wish I was dead!" (line 41).

30. **(D)** Mr. Bixby says that Twain might mistake the black shadow of a woodpile for a "solid cape," or peninsula of land.

31. **(A)** The entire passage contrasts Mr. Bixby's knowledge of the river with Twain's ignorance.

Section 3

Part 1

1. **(B)** In Column A,
   $\sqrt{12} = \sqrt{4 \times 3} = \sqrt{4} \times \sqrt{3} = 2\sqrt{3}$; so
   $(\sqrt{12})(27)(\frac{1}{2}) = (27)(\sqrt{3})$. Column B is
   $(29)(\sqrt{3})$ and thus is larger than Column A.

2. **(C)** Since x and y are corresponding angles, $x = y$. Therefore, $z + y - x = z$. Column A and Column B are equal.

3. **(D)** $(\sqrt{x})^2 = x$. When x is greater than 1, A is larger than B. But if x is a fraction, A is smaller than B. Plug in 2 for x; then plug in $\frac{1}{2}$.

4. **(A)** Since the sum of all the interior angles of a triangle is 180°, angle $b = 180° - (68° + 40°) = 72°$. Angle a is a supplementary angle to 40°, so $a = 180° - 40° = 140°$. Column A is the larger.

5. **(B)** Substituting -3 for x in Column A gives the value of -2. Substituting in Column B gives the value of 29. Therefore, Column B is larger than Column A.

6. **(A)** Twice the sum of the interior angles of a triangle is $2(180°) = 360°$. One-half the sum of the interior angles of a square is $\frac{1}{2}(360°) = 180°$. Therefore, Column A is greater than Column B ($360° > 180°$).

7. **(D)** If $y > 0$, $y^3 + 1 > y^2 - 1$. But if $y < 0$, y^3 will be negative and $y^3 + 1 < y^2 - 1$.

8. **(D)** Since we don't know the relationship of angles b and c, we cannot determine anything about the relationship between sides AC and AB.

9. **(B)** Angle a is the largest of the angles. Therefore, side CB is the largest side of the triangle and thus greater than side AB.

10. **(B)** The area of a triangle having a base of 6 and a height of 8 is $\frac{1}{2}(6)(8) = 24$. The area of a rectangle with sides of 7 and 4 is $(7)(4) = 28$. Therefore, the area of the rectangle—Column B—is larger.

11. **(C)** To figure out the average of three numbers we add them and divide by three. Columns A and B will therefore give the same answer.

12. **(B)** Column A can be simplified:
    $\frac{m^2 - 2m}{\frac{1}{2}(m-2)} = \frac{m(m-2)}{\frac{1}{2}(m-2)} = \frac{m}{\frac{1}{2}} = 2m$. Column B is $2m + 1$ and is larger than Column A by 1.

13. **(A)** Subtracting the smaller of two numbers from the larger will always be greater than subtracting the larger from the smaller, regardless of what the numbers are.

14. **(A)** The area of the larger square is $6 \times 12 = 72$. The area of the smaller square (the unshaded area) is $5 \times 7 = 35$. The shaded area is $72 - 35 = 37$. Therefore, the shaded area is larger than the unshaded area.

15. **(B)** The length of segment AB is
    $\sqrt{[-2-(-6)]^2 + [5-(-1)]^2} =$
    $\sqrt{(4)^2 + (6)^2} = \sqrt{16 + 36} = \sqrt{52}$. The length
    of segment CD is $\sqrt{(0-3)^2 + (7-0)^2} =$
    $\sqrt{(-3)^2 + (7)^2} = \sqrt{9 + 49} = \sqrt{58}$
    Segment CD is the larger of the two segments.

Part 2

16. $(2a^2 - a^3)^2$ when $a = -1$
    $(2(-1)^2 - (-1)^3)^2 = (2(1) - (-1))^2$
    $= (2 + 1)^2$
    $= 3^2$
    $= 9$

17. Probability of not orange =
    $\frac{\text{Number of ways not to pick an orange}}{\text{Number of ways to pick a marble}} = \frac{2 \text{ red} + 3 \text{ green}}{9 \text{ marbles}} = \frac{5}{9}$

18. (1 glop = 3 glips) 4   multiply by 4
    (4 glips = 5 globs) 3   multiply by 3
    4 glops = 12 glips
    12 glips = 15 globs
    ∴ 4 glops = 15 globs
    2 glops = $\frac{15}{2} = 7\frac{1}{2}$ globs = 7.5

19. Multiply by 12: $4k + 3k = 12$
$$7k = 12$$
$$k = \tfrac{12}{7} = 1.71$$

20. If the sides have a ratio 1:3, the areas have a ratio 1:9. Therefore, the area of the large square is 9(5), or 45.

21.

Establish the line ratio between $\triangle DBF$ and $\triangle ABC$.

$$\frac{\text{side of } \triangle DBF}{\text{corresponding side of } \triangle ABC} = \frac{\text{perimeter of } \triangle DBF}{\text{perimeter of } \triangle ABC}$$

$$\frac{3}{4} = \frac{(3+6+6)}{x}$$
$$\frac{3}{4} = \frac{15}{x}$$
$$3x = 60$$
$$x = 20$$

22. The sum of the measures of the four angles of a quadrilateral is 360°.

$$m\angle A + m\angle B + m\angle C + m\angle D = 360°$$
$$120 + 82 + x + 93 = 360°$$
$$295 + x = 360°$$
$$x = 65°$$

23. $2x + 2y = 6$ $\qquad 3x - 3y = 9$
$\therefore x + y = 3$ $\qquad \therefore x - y = 3$

$$(x+y)(x-y) = 3(3) = 9$$
$$x^2 - y^2 = 9$$

24. The reciprocal of $\tfrac{4}{5}$ is $\tfrac{5}{4}$.

$$\frac{5}{4} - \frac{4}{5} = \frac{25-16}{20} = \frac{9}{20}$$

25. $\dfrac{a}{b} = \dfrac{1}{5}, \dfrac{b}{c} = \dfrac{3}{2}, \dfrac{a}{c} = \dfrac{a}{b}\left(\dfrac{b}{c}\right) = \dfrac{1}{5}\left(\dfrac{3}{2}\right) = \dfrac{3}{10}$

$$\dfrac{a+c}{c} = \dfrac{a}{c} + \dfrac{c}{c} = \dfrac{3}{10} + \dfrac{10}{10} = \dfrac{13}{10} = 1.3$$

Section 4

1. **(A)** The two clauses are connected with the word *yet*. This indicates that the two clauses represent conflicting ideas. If a negative idea is first presented, a positive one must follow to counteract it.

2. **(D)** The trips into space formerly generated attention; now they are an everyday event.

3. **(B)** A team with so many injured players is said to be *decimated* (in large part destroyed).

4. **(B)** Diplomats who can't be ticketed can park anywhere with *impunity* (freedom from punishment).

5. **(E)** Of the choices, only (E) makes sense. The words "instead of" signal the need for opposing ideas, and only (E) satisfies this condition.

6. **(E)** A *tortuous* road is twisted and winding; therefore, it is likely that a truck could skid while rounding a curve.

7. **(D)** The word *although* indicates that the blank should be filled by a negative word, something not usually applauded. The best choice is *execrable*, meaning "very inferior."

8. **(D)** The candidate was not able to *amass* (gather) support from a majority of the voters; however, those who backed her were *loyal* (devoted).

9. **(C)** Differences would normally *impede*, or block, the unification of two parties.

10. **(C)** Workers' attention is likely to wander if a job is *tedious*; they become *bored*.

11. **(D)** *Scribbling* is unreadable or messy *writing*. *Mumbling* is inaudible *speaking*.

12. **(B)** *Urge* is a somewhat weaker form of *insist*; the difference is one of degree. Likewise, *request* is a somewhat weaker form of *demand*.

13. **(C)** You *scream* from *fright* and *groan* from *pain*.

14. **(B)** A *hypocrite* is by definition *duplicitous*, and a *traitor* is by definition *disloyal*. The analogy is based on defining characteristics.

15. **(E)** To *soar* is to move through the air, while to *hover* is to remain in one place. To *swim* is to move through water. To *float* is to stay in one place.

16. **(C)** A *carpenter* creates a *cabinet* just as a *cobbler* creates a *boot*.

17. **(A)** A *biceps* is a type of *muscle*: a *cobra* is a type of *snake*.

18. **(E)** *Poverty* is characrerized by a lack of *money*, and *darkness* is characterized by a lack of *light*.

19. **(A)** An *engagement* occurs before a *marriage*, and the *overture* occurs before the *opera*.

20. **(C)** *Pivotal* means extremely *important*, just as *draconian* means extremely *stern*.

21. **(B)** *Evanescent* means "tending to *vanish*"; likewise, *iridescent* means "tending to *shine*."

22. **(E)** A *book* normally is comprised of *chapters*, and a *symphony* normally is comprised of *movements*.

23. **(A)** The *roots* support a *tree*, and the *foundation* supports a *building*.

24. **(D)** The main idea of the first paragraph is that because Tom Bertram has been away so often, he is not missed at home. As a matter of fact, his son has assumed his old roles quite well—settling affairs, managing the house and taking care of his mother.

25. **(B)** Sir Thomas is fine, and all goes well, so Mrs. Norris has no need for her speeches.

26. **(B)** The first paragraph mentions that both Tom Bertram and his father are away from home. The second paragraph says that Sir Thomas has sent assurances that both travellers are alive and well. (You may infer that Sir Thomas is Tom's father and Lady Bertram's husband.)

27. **(B)** Mrs. Norris takes over her nieces' lives and interferes with her sister's household.

28. **(A)** Austen begins with a litany of qualities that the Miss Bertrams are supposed to have, but says that their constantly being praised has made them believe "they had no faults" (line 40).

29. **(B)** Lady Bertram doesn't accompany her daughters into public—an act most women would enjoy—only because she is lazy.

30. **(C)** Since Lady Bertram is so lazy, she gives the job of going into public with the Miss Bertrams to Mrs. Norris.

31. **(D)** Horses cost money; Mrs. Norris's occupation with her nieces' affairs means she can attend society functions without hiring any.

32. **(E)** Lines 3–9 and 41–49 illustrate Lady Bertram's indolence.

33. **(A)** Mrs. Norris is revealed to be cheap, histrionic, and nosy in this excerpt.

34. **(C)** Satire is defined as holding up a person's follies to ridicule; Austen's depiction of Lady Bertram's laziness is a perfect example.

35. **(C)** Austen's wit is dry, but she reveals the silliness of each character through her careful choice of words.

Section 5

1. **(C)** If $\frac{9}{18}$ is equal to $\frac{1}{2}$, then $\frac{9}{16}$ must be bigger than $\frac{1}{2}$. If two fractions contain the same numerator, the one with the smaller denominator is larger. If $\frac{8}{16}$ is equal to $\frac{1}{2}$, then $\frac{8}{17}$ must be smaller.

2. **(D)** R has an area of xy and S has an area of 6xy.

    $6xy - xy = 5xy$

3. **(E)** Since angle *y* is doubled and angle *x* is a right angle, the answer must be (E). The other answer choices are too big. If you double 45, that would be 90. This is impossible as 90 + 90 = 180, and you haven't yet added in angle *z*.

4. **(B)**

$3x + 3 = 3y + 3 + 6$

$3x + 3 = 3y + 9$

$3x - 3y = 6$ (Subtract $3y$ and 3 from both sides.)

$x - y = 2$ (Divide both sides by 3.)

5. **(C)** If the average for the three games was 162, then the total was 3×162 or 486. Let x represent the first game.

$x + (x - 10) + (x - 10 - 13) = 486$

$3x - 33 = 486$

$3x = 519$

$x = 173$

6. **(B)** $3 \times 10^3 = 3 \times 1000 = 3000$

$2 \times 10^2 = 2 \times 100 = 200$

$200 \times 3000 = 600,000$

7. **(E)** There are 60 seconds in a minute, $60 \times 40 = 2,400$. To find the number of widgets made, divide 2,400 by 2.5. This is equal to 960.

8. **(C)** Each cassette has a total of 90 minutes on it; three cassettes contain 270 minutes total. A lecture that is 3 hours long would be 180 minutes. The tape will then have $270 - 180 = 90$ minutes left. $\frac{90}{270} = \frac{1}{3} = 33\frac{1}{3}\%$.

9. **(D)** Since we are given the values of the fractions, we can simply multiply 5 times 6.

10. **(C)** There are 6 numbers in the repeated pattern: $6\overline{)753}$ = 125 r 3. The pattern repeats 125 complete times and goes 3 digits into the next pattern. The 753rd decimal digit is the same as the 3rd digit. The answer is 5.

Section 6

1. **(D)** The first sentence of Passage 1 specifically states that this art form originated with the Romans.

2. **(B)** In ancient times calligraphy was either chiseled in stone (B) or painted on walls.

3. **(E)** From the context of the sentence, it is obvious that "coming" is the correct answer.

4. **(B)** It is explicitly stated in lines 25–27 that Celtic letters are more rounded than their Roman counterparts.

5. **(C)** Paragraph 3 indicates that the Irish created the Celtic alphabet, using the Roman alphabet as a basis.

6. **(E)** Gothic letters are hardest to read because their letter and word space is almost identical.

7. **(A)** The German culture is not mentioned in the passage.

8. **(B)** Prior to the invention of cutting tools, stencilers had to use pins to prick holes in the paper.

9. **(D)** Paragraph 4 discusses the two types of stenciling.

10. **(A)** Paragraph 5 indicates that spraying will result in the most delicate texture.

11. **(E)** Stencil designs originally came from patterns found in nature among flowers, vines, leaves, and fruits (lines 60–62).

12. **(D)** The only statement that the two authors could agree on is choice (D). The other choices are not logical extensions of the material presented in the passages.

COMPUTING YOUR SCORES ON FINAL PRACTICE EXAMINATION

Congratulations! You've completed the final practice examination and are now ready to evaluate your preparedness for the real exam. To get a sense of where you would have scored had this been a real SAT, you first need to compute individual verbal and mathematical raw scores. Once you have computed these, use the conversion scales in the section that follows to compute your SAT scaled scores (200–800). Keep in mind that these formulas have been simplified to give you a "quick and dirty" sense of where you are scoring, not a perfectly precise score.

To Compute Your Raw Scores:

1. Enter the number of correct answers for each verbal and mathematical reasoning section into the boxes marked "Number of Questions Correct."
2. Enter the number of incorrect answers (not blanks) for each verbal and mathematical reasoning section into the boxes marked "Number of Questions Incorrect."
3. Total the number correct and number incorrect.
4. Follow this formula: Take the total correct and minus one-quarter of the total incorrect. Round up in your favor to compute your Raw Score.

Verbal Section	Total Number of Questions	Number of Questions Correct	Number of Questions Incorrect
2	31		
4	35		
6	12		
Totals	78	Total Correct:	Total Incorrect:

Verbal Raw Score = Total Correct − ($\frac{1}{4}$ × Total Incorrect) = _____

Math Section	Total Number of Questions	Number of Questions Correct	Number of Questions Incorrect
1	25		
3	25		
5	10		
Totals	60	Total Correct:	Total Incorrect:

Math Raw Score = Total Correct − ($\frac{1}{4}$ × Total Incorrect) = _____

CONVERSION SCALES FOR FINAL PRACTICE EXAMINATION

VERBAL REASONING

Raw Score	Scaled Score	Raw Score	Scaled Score
75	800	35	520
70	800	30	480
65	760	25	440
60	710	20	410
55	670	15	370
50	620	10	340
45	590	5	290
40	550	0	230

MATHEMATICAL REASONING

Raw Score	Scaled Score	Raw Score	Scaled Score
60	800	25	510
55	760	20	480
50	690	15	440
45	650	10	410
40	610	5	340
35	580	0	200
30	550		

Although you now have some idea of what your scores would look like had they been scaled according to unofficial ETS standards, you will probably want to know how to interpret your Raw Scores in more familiar terms. If so, use the following Self-Evaluation Charts to see what your Raw Scores actually mean.

SELF-EVALUATION CHARTS

VERBAL REASONING: Raw Score

Excellent	60 – 75
Good	50 – 60
Average	30 – 50
Fair	20 – 30
Poor	0 – 20

MATHEMATICAL REASONING: Raw Score

Excellent	50 – 60
Good	40 – 50
Average	20 – 40
Fair	10 – 20
Poor	0 – 10

PART 8

The PSAT/ NMSQT

PREVIEW

CHAPTER 18 — *All About the PSAT/NMSQT*

CHAPTER 19 — *The PSAT/NMSQT Diagnostic Examination*

Chapter **18**

All About the PSAT/NMSQT

The Preliminary SAT (PSAT) is a test that is designed to help students practice for the SAT. The exam is also called the National Merit Scholarship Qualifying Test (NMSQT) because students who do well on it are eligible for scholarships awarded by the National Merit Scholarship Corporation. The test is cosponsored by the College Board and the National Merit Scholarship Corporation. In this chapter, you learn about the PSAT content and format, how this exam differs from the SAT, and what role the PSAT plays in your bid for National Merit Scholarships. You will also learn how to make sure that you're registered for the PSAT, how to interpret your scores, and how to use your scores as a tool for SAT preparation.

HOW TO REGISTER FOR THE PSAT/NMSQT

The PSAT/NMSQT is offered on two days in October of every year (but only on one day at any single location). You'll probably take this test in October of your junior year in high school. It is usually given on a Tuesday or a Saturday, depending upon your school's testing policy. Some schools have students take the exam in tenth grade for extra practice. But only when you take the exam during your junior year do you become eligible to compete for National Merit Scholarships.

Most high school guidance departments automatically register juniors to take the PSAT. This means no fees and no hassles. But to be safe and certain, check with your guidance counselor or contact:

PSAT/NMSQT
P.O. Box 6720
Princeton, NJ 08541-6720
www.collegeboard.org

WHY THE STUDENT SEARCH SURVEY IS IMPORTANT

The answer sheet for the PSAT/NMSQT includes a "student search" survey where you provide information about your possible college major and your career interests. This information is then sent to colleges and universities, which will contact you with admission information. When you receive your

ROAD MAP

- *Find out how to register for the PSAT/NMSQT*
- *Learn why the student search survey is important*
- *Understand how the PSAT differs from the SAT*
- *Get to know the PSAT format*
- *Make sense of your PSAT scores*
- *Know how your selection index can qualify you for National Merit*

> **CAUTION**
>
> At the end of your sophomore year or immediately when you begin your junior year of high school, be sure to ask your guidance counselor or grade advisor when your school is offering the test. You should be registered automatically, but it's better not to assume anything.

score report, it will include information about the courses and skills you need to follow the academic major you've chosen. The report also lists information about career opportunities for graduates.

Make sure that you also complete the Scholarship Programs sections, if you are interested in participating. One of the sections covers general eligibility, and two other sections ask about your qualifications to enter the National Achievement Scholarship Program for Outstanding Negro Students or the National Hispanic Scholar Recognition Program.

HOW THE PSAT DIFFERS FROM THE SAT

Some of you may have heard that the PSAT is easier than the SAT. Others may have heard the opposite. Neither assessment is accurate. The substance of the PSAT is virtually identical to that of the SAT—no easier, no harder. The PSAT has fewer sections than the SAT, but you'll find the same types of questions: analogies, critical reading, sentence completions, multiple-choice math, quantitative comparisons, and grid-ins. After you have taken the sample PSAT/NMSQT, evaluate which types of questions give you the most trouble. To review different areas, see earlier chapters of this book.

A big difference between the tests is that the PSAT has recently added a 30-minute section that tests writing skills. *This section is not on the SAT*. The writing section includes questions that ask you to identify errors in sentences, rephrase sentences to make the meaning clearer, and revise paragraphs to improve sentence structure and organization. If you are shooting for National Merit recognition, then improving your score on this section is important. And if you plan to take the SAT II Writing Test, then this score is an early indicator of how you would do. But if the SAT is your main concern, you shouldn't spend too much time worrying about your performance on this section.

Probably the biggest difference between the PSAT and SAT is that PSAT scores do not "count" in terms of your bid for college admission. Colleges do not use PSAT scores when they make admissions decisions. On the other hand, every SAT score you earn throughout high school shows up on your testing transcript, so your performance on every SAT you take is critical.

GET TO KNOW THE PSAT FORMAT

As we said earlier in this chapter, the PSAT has fewer sections than the SAT, but the PSAT questions are just like those on the SAT. As you'll note in the following table, the PSAT contains analogies, critical reading, sentence completions, multiple-choice math, quantitative comparisons, and student-produced responses. The writing skills section of the PSAT, however, may represent new territory for you—the SAT doesn't have such a section. But don't worry—you get a chance to preview this portion of the PSAT in the practice examination in this book.

Format of a Typical PSAT/NMSQT

Section	Number of Questions	Time Allowed
Section 1: Verbal	26	25 min.
Sentence Completions	6	
Analogies	7	
Critical Reading	13	
Section 2: Mathematics	20	25 min.
Multiple-Choice Math	20	
Section 3: Verbal	26	25 min.
Analogies	6	
Sentence Completions	7	
Critical Reading	13	
Section 4: Mathematics	20	25 min.
Quantitative Comparisons	12	
Student-Produced Responses	8	
Section 5: Writing Skills	39	30 min.
Identifying Sentence Errors	19	
Improving Sentences	14	
Improving Paragraphs	6	

NOTE
If you're a home-schooled student, you should make arrangements to register for the PSAT/NMSQT well before the test dates in mid-October. The preceding June, contact the principal or a guidance counselor at a local public or private high school to arrange your test registration. Your scores will be sent directly to your home. When you take the test, you will fill out some basic information; be sure to enter your state's home school code in the "school code" section. The test supervisor will give you this code.

HOW TO INTERPRET AND USE YOUR PSAT SCORES

This is what you really want to know, isn't it? You'll have to wait about six weeks, but then your school will give you your score report and original test book. This will make it easy for you to review your results and identify your weaknesses.

Here's a breakdown of how the PSAT/NMSQT is scored:

Each correct answer	1 point
Each unanswered question	0 points
Each incorrect answer to a 4-choice multiple-choice question	minus $\frac{1}{3}$ point
Each incorrect answer to a 5-choice multiple-choice question	minus $\frac{1}{4}$ point
Each incorrect answer to a Student-Produced Response question	0 points

    Your score report will include separate scores for verbal, math, and writing skills, each reported on a scale of 20 to 80. This scale corresponds perfectly to the SAT scoring scale of 200 to 800. So to translate a PSAT score into an SAT score, just add a "0" to the end of each math and verbal score. (Remember: The writing section is not on the actual SAT so such a translation is unnecessary.) For example, if Jane received a 49 on verbal, 56 on math, and 44 on writing, that would correspond to a 490 on the SAT verbal and 560 on the SAT math. To get a sense of what these individual scores mean, you will receive three separate percentiles for each of your three separate scores. These percentiles tell you how your scores compare with those of everyone else who took the test.

The report will also indicate your estimated verbal and math scores for the SAT I and your estimated score on the SAT II writing test. But if you prepare thoroughly before the SAT, you should be able to surpass ETS' predictions!

The score report gives you some valuable information that will help you prepare for the SAT. It tells you the correct answer for every question that you missed and it indicates the difficulty level of those questions. With this information, you can review the questions that you answered incorrectly (or didn't answer at all), and then use the skills and strategies you've learned in this book to find the best ways to overcome the problems that contributed to your mistakes. When you review your PSAT/NMSQT answers, ask yourself if incorrect answers or omissions were the result of time pressures. Maybe a few hard questions took up too much of your time, and as a result, you omitted some easy questions that could have added to your score. Maybe you could have eliminated some of the answer choices on a few of the hard questions that you passed over. Use this analysis of your PSAT performance to focus your SAT preparation, and you'll get the most from *both* test experiences.

HOW YOUR SELECTION INDEX CAN QUALIFY YOU FOR NATIONAL MERIT

If you score well on the PSAT and want to shoot for National Merit recognition, you should be more concerned with your "selection index" than with your three individual scores. Your selection index is the sum of your three separate scores. So if we revisit Jane's performance, her selection index would be 149 (49 + 56 + 44). The National Merit Scholarship Corporation (NMSC) takes this index and compares it with those of every other high school junior in her state. The NMSC identifies the highest selection indices and awards these students with some form of National Merit recognition. Unfortunately, many students are not usually alerted of their National Merit status until fall of senior year.

BECOMING A COMMENDED SCHOLAR

If your selection index places you in roughly the top 5 percent in your state, you will receive a National Merit Letter of Commendation and become a "commended scholar." This is an impressive academic honor that you should indicate on your college applications. In 1997, a selection index of

TIP
If you haven't decided what you want to major in, just choose something general from the list. No one will hold you to this choice if you want to change your mind in a year.

199 was required to become a commended scholar in New York state. Keep in mind that these cutoffs vary from state to state and year to year, depending upon the strength of the competition. So if you earn a selection index of 199 on your PSAT, be proud but don't celebrate prematurely.

BECOMING A SEMI-FINALIST AND APPLYING FOR SCHOLARSHIPS

If your selection index places you in roughly the top 1 percent in your state, you will become a National Merit Semi-Finalist, an even more impressive feat. In 1997, you needed a selection index of 220 or higher in New York state to qualify. If you become a semi-finalist, you have to submit an application to the NMSC to qualify to become a finalist and receive scholarships. Ultimately, candidates are awarded scholarships by the NMSC, colleges, and universities based on scores, academic records, and other criteria.

NOTE
Over 2 million students took the PSAT/NMSQT in 1998—44% of high school juniors and 22% of sophomores.

Summary: What You Need to Know About the PSAT/NMSQT

- The PSAT/NMSQT is designed to help students practice for the SAT. It's also used to determine the test-taker's eligibility for scholarships awarded by the National Merit Scholarship Corporation.
- The PSAT/NMSQT is offered on one of two days in October at individual sites across the nation. Most students take this test in their junior year of high school.
- Colleges don't use the results of this test to determine your eligibility for admission.
- The exam answer sheet contains a "student search" survey; the information you enter on this survey is sent to colleges and universities, which then can send appropriate course and majors information to you.
- The PSAT offers the same format and question types that you find on the SAT. The PSAT differs from the SAT in that it now contains a 30-minute writing skills section. Your results on this section can help you in your bid for National Merit Recognition and it can help you prepare for the SAT II writing exam (if you're planning on taking that exam).
- Your PSAT scores are computed to form a selection index; your final selection index is compared to that of every other junior test-taker in the state to determine your eligibility for National Merit Recognition.

PSAT/NMSQT DIAGNOSTIC EXAMINATION
Answer Sheet

Section 1—Verbal
25 minutes

1. Ⓐ Ⓑ Ⓒ Ⓓ Ⓔ
2. Ⓐ Ⓑ Ⓒ Ⓓ Ⓔ
3. Ⓐ Ⓑ Ⓒ Ⓓ Ⓔ
4. Ⓐ Ⓑ Ⓒ Ⓓ Ⓔ
5. Ⓐ Ⓑ Ⓒ Ⓓ Ⓔ
6. Ⓐ Ⓑ Ⓒ Ⓓ Ⓔ
7. Ⓐ Ⓑ Ⓒ Ⓓ Ⓔ
8. Ⓐ Ⓑ Ⓒ Ⓓ Ⓔ
9. Ⓐ Ⓑ Ⓒ Ⓓ Ⓔ
10. Ⓐ Ⓑ Ⓒ Ⓓ Ⓔ
11. Ⓐ Ⓑ Ⓒ Ⓓ Ⓔ
12. Ⓐ Ⓑ Ⓒ Ⓓ Ⓔ
13. Ⓐ Ⓑ Ⓒ Ⓓ Ⓔ
14. Ⓐ Ⓑ Ⓒ Ⓓ Ⓔ
15. Ⓐ Ⓑ Ⓒ Ⓓ Ⓔ
16. Ⓐ Ⓑ Ⓒ Ⓓ Ⓔ
17. Ⓐ Ⓑ Ⓒ Ⓓ Ⓔ
18. Ⓐ Ⓑ Ⓒ Ⓓ Ⓔ
19. Ⓐ Ⓑ Ⓒ Ⓓ Ⓔ
20. Ⓐ Ⓑ Ⓒ Ⓓ Ⓔ
21. Ⓐ Ⓑ Ⓒ Ⓓ Ⓔ
22. Ⓐ Ⓑ Ⓒ Ⓓ Ⓔ
23. Ⓐ Ⓑ Ⓒ Ⓓ Ⓔ
24. Ⓐ Ⓑ Ⓒ Ⓓ Ⓔ
25. Ⓐ Ⓑ Ⓒ Ⓓ Ⓔ
26. Ⓐ Ⓑ Ⓒ Ⓓ Ⓔ

Section 2—Math
25 minutes

1. Ⓐ Ⓑ Ⓒ Ⓓ Ⓔ
2. Ⓐ Ⓑ Ⓒ Ⓓ Ⓔ
3. Ⓐ Ⓑ Ⓒ Ⓓ Ⓔ
4. Ⓐ Ⓑ Ⓒ Ⓓ Ⓔ
5. Ⓐ Ⓑ Ⓒ Ⓓ Ⓔ
6. Ⓐ Ⓑ Ⓒ Ⓓ Ⓔ
7. Ⓐ Ⓑ Ⓒ Ⓓ Ⓔ
8. Ⓐ Ⓑ Ⓒ Ⓓ Ⓔ
9. Ⓐ Ⓑ Ⓒ Ⓓ Ⓔ
10. Ⓐ Ⓑ Ⓒ Ⓓ Ⓔ
11. Ⓐ Ⓑ Ⓒ Ⓓ Ⓔ
12. Ⓐ Ⓑ Ⓒ Ⓓ Ⓔ
13. Ⓐ Ⓑ Ⓒ Ⓓ Ⓔ
14. Ⓐ Ⓑ Ⓒ Ⓓ Ⓔ
15. Ⓐ Ⓑ Ⓒ Ⓓ Ⓔ
16. Ⓐ Ⓑ Ⓒ Ⓓ Ⓔ
17. Ⓐ Ⓑ Ⓒ Ⓓ Ⓔ
18. Ⓐ Ⓑ Ⓒ Ⓓ Ⓔ
19. Ⓐ Ⓑ Ⓒ Ⓓ Ⓔ
20. Ⓐ Ⓑ Ⓒ Ⓓ Ⓔ

Section 3—Verbal
25 minutes

27. Ⓐ Ⓑ Ⓒ Ⓓ Ⓔ
28. Ⓐ Ⓑ Ⓒ Ⓓ Ⓔ
29. Ⓐ Ⓑ Ⓒ Ⓓ Ⓔ
30. Ⓐ Ⓑ Ⓒ Ⓓ Ⓔ
31. Ⓐ Ⓑ Ⓒ Ⓓ Ⓔ
32. Ⓐ Ⓑ Ⓒ Ⓓ Ⓔ
33. Ⓐ Ⓑ Ⓒ Ⓓ Ⓔ
34. Ⓐ Ⓑ Ⓒ Ⓓ Ⓔ
35. Ⓐ Ⓑ Ⓒ Ⓓ Ⓔ
36. Ⓐ Ⓑ Ⓒ Ⓓ Ⓔ
37. Ⓐ Ⓑ Ⓒ Ⓓ Ⓔ
38. Ⓐ Ⓑ Ⓒ Ⓓ Ⓔ
39. Ⓐ Ⓑ Ⓒ Ⓓ Ⓔ
40. Ⓐ Ⓑ Ⓒ Ⓓ Ⓔ
41. Ⓐ Ⓑ Ⓒ Ⓓ Ⓔ
42. Ⓐ Ⓑ Ⓒ Ⓓ Ⓔ
43. Ⓐ Ⓑ Ⓒ Ⓓ Ⓔ
44. Ⓐ Ⓑ Ⓒ Ⓓ Ⓔ
45. Ⓐ Ⓑ Ⓒ Ⓓ Ⓔ
46. Ⓐ Ⓑ Ⓒ Ⓓ Ⓔ
47. Ⓐ Ⓑ Ⓒ Ⓓ Ⓔ
48. Ⓐ Ⓑ Ⓒ Ⓓ Ⓔ
49. Ⓐ Ⓑ Ⓒ Ⓓ Ⓔ
50. Ⓐ Ⓑ Ⓒ Ⓓ Ⓔ
51. Ⓐ Ⓑ Ⓒ Ⓓ Ⓔ
52. Ⓐ Ⓑ Ⓒ Ⓓ Ⓔ

Section 4—Math
25 minutes

21. Ⓐ Ⓑ Ⓒ Ⓓ Ⓔ
22. Ⓐ Ⓑ Ⓒ Ⓓ Ⓔ
23. Ⓐ Ⓑ Ⓒ Ⓓ Ⓔ
24. Ⓐ Ⓑ Ⓒ Ⓓ Ⓔ
25. Ⓐ Ⓑ Ⓒ Ⓓ Ⓔ
26. Ⓐ Ⓑ Ⓒ Ⓓ Ⓔ
27. Ⓐ Ⓑ Ⓒ Ⓓ Ⓔ
28. Ⓐ Ⓑ Ⓒ Ⓓ Ⓔ
29. Ⓐ Ⓑ Ⓒ Ⓓ Ⓔ
30. Ⓐ Ⓑ Ⓒ Ⓓ Ⓔ
31. Ⓐ Ⓑ Ⓒ Ⓓ Ⓔ
32. Ⓐ Ⓑ Ⓒ Ⓓ Ⓔ

33. [grid-in]
34. [grid-in]
35. [grid-in]
36. [grid-in]
37. [grid-in]
38. [grid-in]
39. [grid-in]
40. [grid-in]

Section 5—Writing Skills
30 minutes

1. Ⓐ Ⓑ Ⓒ Ⓓ Ⓔ
2. Ⓐ Ⓑ Ⓒ Ⓓ Ⓔ
3. Ⓐ Ⓑ Ⓒ Ⓓ Ⓔ
4. Ⓐ Ⓑ Ⓒ Ⓓ Ⓔ
5. Ⓐ Ⓑ Ⓒ Ⓓ Ⓔ
6. Ⓐ Ⓑ Ⓒ Ⓓ Ⓔ
7. Ⓐ Ⓑ Ⓒ Ⓓ Ⓔ
8. Ⓐ Ⓑ Ⓒ Ⓓ Ⓔ
9. Ⓐ Ⓑ Ⓒ Ⓓ Ⓔ
10. Ⓐ Ⓑ Ⓒ Ⓓ Ⓔ
11. Ⓐ Ⓑ Ⓒ Ⓓ Ⓔ
12. Ⓐ Ⓑ Ⓒ Ⓓ Ⓔ
13. Ⓐ Ⓑ Ⓒ Ⓓ Ⓔ
14. Ⓐ Ⓑ Ⓒ Ⓓ Ⓔ
15. Ⓐ Ⓑ Ⓒ Ⓓ Ⓔ
16. Ⓐ Ⓑ Ⓒ Ⓓ Ⓔ
17. Ⓐ Ⓑ Ⓒ Ⓓ Ⓔ
18. Ⓐ Ⓑ Ⓒ Ⓓ Ⓔ
19. Ⓐ Ⓑ Ⓒ Ⓓ Ⓔ
20. Ⓐ Ⓑ Ⓒ Ⓓ Ⓔ
21. Ⓐ Ⓑ Ⓒ Ⓓ Ⓔ
22. Ⓐ Ⓑ Ⓒ Ⓓ Ⓔ
23. Ⓐ Ⓑ Ⓒ Ⓓ Ⓔ
24. Ⓐ Ⓑ Ⓒ Ⓓ Ⓔ
25. Ⓐ Ⓑ Ⓒ Ⓓ Ⓔ
26. Ⓐ Ⓑ Ⓒ Ⓓ Ⓔ
27. Ⓐ Ⓑ Ⓒ Ⓓ Ⓔ
28. Ⓐ Ⓑ Ⓒ Ⓓ Ⓔ
29. Ⓐ Ⓑ Ⓒ Ⓓ Ⓔ
30. Ⓐ Ⓑ Ⓒ Ⓓ Ⓔ
31. Ⓐ Ⓑ Ⓒ Ⓓ Ⓔ
32. Ⓐ Ⓑ Ⓒ Ⓓ Ⓔ
33. Ⓐ Ⓑ Ⓒ Ⓓ Ⓔ
34. Ⓐ Ⓑ Ⓒ Ⓓ Ⓔ
35. Ⓐ Ⓑ Ⓒ Ⓓ Ⓔ
36. Ⓐ Ⓑ Ⓒ Ⓓ Ⓔ
37. Ⓐ Ⓑ Ⓒ Ⓓ Ⓔ
38. Ⓐ Ⓑ Ⓒ Ⓓ Ⓔ
39. Ⓐ Ⓑ Ⓒ Ⓓ Ⓔ

PSAT/NMSQT Diagnostic Examination

SECTION 1

26 Questions (1–26) • Time: 25 Minutes

Directions: Each of the following questions consists of an incomplete sentence followed by five words or pairs of words. Choose that word or pair of words which, when substituted for the blank space or spaces, *best* completes the meaning of the sentence and mark the letter of your choice on your answer sheet.

Example:

In view of the extenuating circumstances and the defendant's youth, the judge recommended ----.

(A) conviction
(B) a defense
(C) a mistrial
(D) leniency
(E) life imprisonment

Ⓐ Ⓑ Ⓒ ● Ⓔ

1. The speaker fascinated us with his knowledge, but his ---- toward the end onto other topics confused us.

    (A) digression
    (B) removal
    (C) preoccupation
    (D) tipoff
    (E) apprehension

2. My accountant suggested that I should organize my ---- more carefully.

    (A) regulations
    (B) annals
    (C) profits
    (D) remainders
    (E) receipts

3. He swept into the room like a ----, blowing papers and journals off the desk.

    (A) tyrant
    (B) zephyr
    (C) cyclone
    (D) viper
    (E) satyr

4. If you make a ---- movement, you might ---- the bear.

    (A) vast..disturb
    (B) sudden..startle
    (C) graceful..perturb
    (D) slow..aggrieve
    (E) rash..promote

5. Because the motorist had been unable to control his car, the police officer questioned his ----.

    (A) sobriety
    (B) fecundity
    (C) passivity
    (D) frailty
    (E) virility

6. After the recital we all ---- to the salon for tea and cakes.

    (A) retired
    (B) restored
    (C) retorted
    (D) reviewed
    (E) remanded

GO ON TO THE NEXT PAGE →

Directions: Each of the following questions consists of a capitalized pair of words followed by five pairs of words lettered A to E. The capitalized words bear some meaningful relationship to each other. Choose the lettered pair of words whose relationship is most similar to that expressed by the capitalized pair and mark its letter on your answer sheet.

Example:

DAY : SUN : :

(A) sunlight : daylight
(B) heat : cold
(C) ray : sun
(D) moon : star
(E) night : moon

Ⓐ Ⓑ Ⓒ Ⓓ ●

7. COLLAR : NECK : :

   (A) hat : head
   (B) mitten : hand
   (C) lapel : jacket
   (D) cuff : wrist
   (E) sock : ankle

8. MASTER : CHESS : :

   (A) prodigy : game
   (B) genius : contest
   (C) acme : skill
   (D) slave : fashion
   (E) virtuoso : music

9. SNOW : BLIZZARD : :

   (A) rain : fog
   (B) hail : tornado
   (C) story : building
   (D) English : French
   (E) scale : music

10. SONG : LYRICIST : :

    (A) tune : musician
    (B) play : dramatist
    (C) poet : author
    (D) show : cast
    (E) book : publisher

11. GEOMETRY : MATHEMATICS : :

    (A) painting : calculation
    (B) astronomy : accounting
    (C) hygiene : health care
    (D) art : arithmetic
    (E) botany : science

12. DOLLAR : DIME : :

    (A) decade : year
    (B) century : time
    (C) nickel : quarter
    (D) metal : paper
    (E) value : cost

13. GRAMMAR : LANGUAGE : :

    (A) training : puppy
    (B) hanger : clothing
    (C) story : building
    (D) English : French
    (E) scale : music

Questions 14–26 are based on the following passages.

In 1891 in China, a collection of descriptive essays on other countries was compiled by a native of Kiangsu named Wang Hsi-ch'i. This excerpt is from an essay entitled "Europe to a Chinese Observer."

Europe's people are all tall and white. Only those who live in the northeast where it is very cold are short, and dwarfish. They have big noses and deep eyes. But their eyes are not of the same color, with brown, green, (5) and black being most frequent. They have heavy beards that go up to their temples, or are wound around their jaws. Some of their beards are straight like those of the Chinese. Some are crooked and twisted like curly hairs. Some shave them all off. Some leave them (10) all on. Some cut their beards but leave their mustaches. Some cut off their mustaches and leave their beards. They do what they wish. Whether old or young, all have beards. They let their hair grow to two or three inches. But if it gets longer they cut it. The women (15) leave on all of their hair. The women dress their hair somewhat like Chinese women, but gather it together in a net. The color of their whiskers and hair is different. They have yellow, red, mottled, or black, all kinds. The men wear flat-topped, tubelike, (20) narrow-brimmed hats of different heights ranging from four inches to over one foot. They are made of felt or silk. When they meet people, they lift their hats as a sign of respect. Their clothes are narrow and their sleeves are tight. The length only goes down to their (25) bellies. Their trousers are bound tightly around their waists. But their outer garments are loose and long, and reach as far down as their knees. They wear collars in front and back. Their inner garments are of cotton, but their outer garments are of wool. They often wear (30) boots which are made of leather.

Women's clothes are also tight and their sleeves stick to their bodies. They wear skirts which are long and brush the ground. This is how they generally dress. For their ceremonial hats, ceremonial clothes, (35) their military helmets and garments, they have different practices.

For their eating and drinking utensils they use gold, silver, and ceramics. When they eat they use knife and fork, and they do not use chopsticks. They eat mainly (40) bread. Potatoes are staple. They mostly roast or broil fowl and game. They usually season it with preserves or olive oil. They drink spirits and soda water, as well as coffee in which they mix sugar. Its fragrance enlivens teeth and jaws, and makes the spirit fresh and (45) clear.

14. When Wang Hsi-ch'i says that European people's "eyes are not of the same color" (line 4), he means that

   (A) they often have two eyes that do not match in color
   (B) their eyes are different from Chinese people's eyes
   (C) different Europeans have different-colored eyes
   (D) their eyes are a different color from their hair
   (E) northern Europeans have eyes that are a different color from those of southern Europeans

15. The word *dress* (line 15) is used to mean

   (A) clothe
   (B) attire
   (C) style
   (D) bandage
   (E) decorate

16. How does paragraph 3 differ from paragraphs 1 and 2?

   (A) It does not refer to personal appearance.
   (B) It compares European ways to Chinese ways.
   (C) It does not discuss European customs.
   (D) Both A and B
   (E) Both B and C

GO ON TO THE NEXT PAGE

17. This passage was intended primarily as

    (A) entertainment and amusement
    (B) digression and exchange
    (C) persuasion and argument
    (D) narration and diversion
    (E) description and instruction

18. How does Wang Hsi-ch'i feel about European customs?

    (A) They are not to be trusted.
    (B) They are unusual but interesting.
    (C) They are bizarre and hilarious.
    (D) They are pathetic.
    (E) They are preferable to Chinese customs.

Charles Darwin (1809–1882) was best known for his own observational studies, which led to his theory of natural selection, but he was quite capable of using other people's observations to support his theories, as shown in this excerpt from The Descent of Man.

Birds sometimes exhibit benevolent feelings; they will feed the deserted young ones even of distinct species, but this perhaps ought to be considered as a mistaken instinct. They will feed, as shown in an
(5) earlier part of this work, adult birds of their own species which have become blind. Mr. Buxton gives a curious account of a parrot which took care of a frost-bitten and crippled bird of a distinct species, cleansed her feathers and defended her from the at-
(10) tacks of the other parrots which roamed freely about his garden. It is a still more curious fact that these birds apparently evince some sympathy for the pleasures of their fellows. When a pair of cockatoos made a nest in an acacia tree "it was ridiculous to see the extravagant
(15) interest taken in the matter by the others of the same species." These parrots also evinced unbounded curiosity and clearly had "the idea of property and possession." They have good memories, for in the Zoological Gardens they have plainly recognized their former
(20) masters after an interval of some months.

Birds possess acute powers of observation. Every mated bird, of course, recognizes its fellow. Audubon states that a certain number of mating thrushes (Mimus polyglottus) remain all the year round in Louisiana,
(25) while others migrate to the Eastern States; these latter on their return are instantly recognized and always attacked by their southern brethren. Birds under confinement distinguish different persons, as is proved by the strong and permanent antipathy or affection which
(30) they show without any apparent cause toward certain individuals. I have heard of numerous instances with jays, partridges, canaries, and especially bullfinches. Mr. Hussey has described in how extraordinary a manner a tamed partridge recognized everybody; and
(35) its likes and dislikes were very strong. This bird seemed "fond of gay colors, and no new gown or cap could be put on without catching his attention." Mr. Hewitt has described the habits of some ducks (recently descended from wild birds) which at the ap-
(40) proach of a strange dog or cat would rush headlong into the water and exhaust themselves in their attempts to escape; but they knew Mr. Hewitt's own dogs and cats so well that they would lie down and bask in the sun close to them. They always moved away from a
(45) strange man, and so they would from the lady who attended them if she made any great change in her dress. Audubon relates that he reared and tamed a wild turkey which always ran away from any strange dog; this bird escaped into the woods, and some days
(50) afterward Audubon saw, as he thought, a wild turkey and made his dog chase it; but to his astonishment the bird did not run away, and the dog when he came up did not attack the bird, for they mutually recognized each other as old friends.

(55) Mr. Jenner Weir is convinced that birds pay particular attention to the colors of other birds, sometimes out of jealousy and sometimes as a sign of kinship. Thus he turned a reed-bunting (Emberiza schoeniculus), which had acquired its black headdress, into his avi-
(60) ary, and the newcomer was not noticed by any bird except by a bullfinch, which is likewise black-headed. This bullfinch was a very quiet bird, and had never before quarreled with any of its comrades, including another reed-bunting, which had not as yet become
(65) black-headed; but the reed-bunting with a black head was so unmercifully treated that it had to be removed.

19. Why does Darwin cite Mr. Buxton?

    (A) To support his theory about birds' powers of observation
    (B) To support his statement about birds' benevolence
    (C) To contrast with his own observations of birds
    (D) Both A and B
    (E) Both B and C

20. The word *distinct* (line 8) is used to mean

    (A) special
    (B) apparent
    (C) intelligible
    (D) definite
    (E) different

21. The word *antipathy* (line 29) means

    (A) dislike
    (B) remedy
    (C) disappointment
    (D) amusement
    (E) argument

22. Why does Darwin mention jays, partridges, canaries, and bullfinches?

    (A) To explain why some birds cannot be trained
    (B) To educate his reader on types of local birds
    (C) To contrast with a later discussion of shore birds
    (D) To support his discussion of birds' memories
    (E) To show the variety of birds in England

23. The word *reared* (line 47) is used to mean

    (A) backed
    (B) raised
    (C) leaped
    (D) ended
    (E) constructed

24. What does Darwin mean by "a sign of kinship" (line 57)?

    (A) Mark of common parentage
    (B) Premonition of future union
    (C) Symbol of compatibility
    (D) Evidence of family relationship
    (E) Indication of mutual interest

25. A good title for paragraph 3 might be

    (A) "Different-Colored Birds"
    (B) "Bullfinches and Their Colors"
    (C) "An Example of Color Recognition in Birds"
    (D) "Captive Birds"
    (E) "Birds in Peace and War"

26. The main purpose of this passage is to

    (A) contrast birds with humans
    (B) compare three species of birds
    (C) review current studies of birds
    (D) compare wild birds to confined birds
    (E) discuss some traits of birds

STOP

END OF SECTION 1. IF YOU HAVE ANY TIME LEFT, GO OVER YOUR WORK IN THIS SECTION ONLY. DO NOT WORK IN ANY OTHER SECTION OF THE TEST.

...ions (1–20) • Time: 25 Minutes

Directions: Solve the following problems using any available space on the page for scratchwork. On your answer sheet fill in the choice which best corresponds to the correct answer.

Notes: The figures accompanying the problems are drawn as accurately as possible, unless otherwise stated in specific problems. Again, unless otherwise stated, all figures lie in the same plane. All numbers used in these problems are real numbers. Calculators are permitted for this test.

Reference Information

Circle: $C = 2\pi r$, $A = \pi r^2$

Rectangle: $A = lw$

Rectangular Solid: $V = lwh$

Cylinder: $V = \pi r^2 h$

Triangle: $A = \tfrac{1}{2} bh$

$a^2 + b^2 = c^2$

Special right triangles: 45°–45°–90° with sides x, x, $x\sqrt{2}$; 30°–60°–90° with sides x, $x\sqrt{3}$, $2x$.

The number of degrees of arc in a circle is 360.
The measure in degrees of a straight angle is 180.
The sum of the measures in degrees of the angles of a triangle is 180.

---

1. $0.1 \times 0.01 \times 0.001 =$

    (A) .01
    (B) .03
    (C) .003
    (D) .0001
    (E) .000001

2. The average height of the four-member gymnastics squad is 5 feet. Three of the girls are 4 feet 10 inches tall. How tall is the fourth member?

    (A) 5 feet
    (B) 5 feet 2 inches
    (C) 5 feet 4 inches
    (D) 5 feet 6 inches
    (E) It cannot be determined from the information given.

3. $\tfrac{1}{5}$ times its reciprocal is

    (A) $\dfrac{2}{5}$
    (B) $\dfrac{1}{25}$
    (C) 1
    (D) 5
    (E) 25

4. How many sixteenths are in $5\tfrac{1}{4}$?

    (A) 17
    (B) 20
    (C) 80
    (D) 81
    (E) 84

5. Whenever a particular organism reproduces, it doubles in number each hour. If you start with one organism at 3:00, how many will you have by 6:00?

   (A) 4
   (B) 6
   (C) 8
   (D) 24
   (E) 120

6. If $x = \frac{1}{4}y$, what is the value of $\frac{x}{4}$?

   (A) 16
   (B) $\frac{y}{16}$
   (C) $\frac{y}{4}$
   (D) y
   (E) $4y$

7. If the sides of a square are tripled, what always happens to its perimeter?

   (A) It remains the same.
   (B) It is cubed.
   (C) It increases by 100%.
   (D) It is tripled.
   (E) It increases by 900%.

8. If ABC is an isosceles triangle, what is the value of z?

   (A) 60
   (B) 90
   (C) $2y$
   (D) 100
   (E) 105

9. Leo is 67. His son Robert is 29. In how many years will Robert be exactly half his father's age?

   (A) 2
   (B) 5
   (C) 7
   (D) 9
   (E) 12

10. When the numbers $\frac{1}{4}$, $\frac{3}{10}$, 0.23, and $\frac{4}{15}$ are arranged in ascending order of size, the result is

    (A) 0.23, $\frac{3}{10}$, $\frac{1}{4}$, $\frac{4}{15}$
    (B) $\frac{1}{4}$, 0.23, $\frac{3}{10}$, $\frac{4}{15}$
    (C) 0.23, $\frac{1}{4}$, $\frac{3}{10}$, $\frac{4}{15}$
    (D) $\frac{4}{15}$, $\frac{3}{10}$, $\frac{1}{4}$, 0.23
    (E) 0.23, $\frac{1}{4}$, $\frac{4}{15}$, $\frac{3}{10}$

11. If $a + b = 12$ and $\frac{b}{a} = 3$, then

    (A) $a = 9$
    (B) $b = \frac{a}{3}$
    (C) $12 = 3b$
    (D) $b - a = 9$
    (E) $ab = 27$

12. The side of a square forms the radius of a circle with a circumference of 10. What is the perimeter of the square?

    (A) $\frac{5}{\pi}$
    (B) $\frac{10}{\pi}$
    (C) $\frac{20}{\pi}$
    (D) 4π
    (E) 100π

GO ON TO THE NEXT PAGE

...AZ is on the air 24 hours a day. ... it sold ads and took in money at this ... ...% from drive-time ads at $20/minute, ... from daytime ads at $10/minute, and 30% ...m nighttime ads at $5/minute. If the station made $500 yesterday, how much air time was dedicated to ads?

(A) 30 minutes
(B) 1 hour
(C) 2 hours
(D) 3 hours
(E) 3 hours, 30 minutes

14. In the figure below, the area of the circle is equivalent to

(A) $\dfrac{AB}{\pi}$

(B) AB

(C) πAB

(D) $\pi \left(\dfrac{AC}{2}\right)^2$

(E) πAC^2

15. A motorist drives 90 miles at an average speed of 50 miles per hour and returns at an average speed of 60 miles per hour. What is her average speed in miles per hour for the entire trip?

(A) 53
(B) 54.5
(C) 56.5
(D) 58
(E) It cannot be determined from the information given.

16. If $17x - 32 = 308$, what is $\dfrac{x}{4}$?

(A) 5
(B) 10
(C) 20
(D) 50
(E) 85

17. In the square below, $\triangle UQR$ and $\triangle RST$ are equal in area. If $QR = 2$, what is the area of triangle RUT?

(A) 2
(B) 4
(C) 8
(D) 12
(E) 16

18. If the radius of a circle is increased by 10%, the area of the circle is increased by

(A) 10%
(B) 21%
(C) 100%
(D) 110%
(E) 121%

19. If 2! means 2 × 3 and 3! means 3 × 4, what does 7! + 8! mean?

    (A) 56
    (B) 128
    (C) 392
    (D) 448
    (E) 4,032

20. If one faucet fills the sink in 3 minutes and the other fills it in 2 minutes, how long will it take both faucets to fill the sink if both are turned on together?

    (A) .5 minute
    (B) 1 minute
    (C) 1.2 minutes
    (D) 1.5 minutes
    (E) 1.8 minutes

STOP

END OF SECTION 2. IF YOU HAVE ANY TIME LEFT, GO OVER YOUR WORK IN THIS SECTION ONLY. DO NOT WORK IN ANY OTHER SECTION OF THE TEST.

tions (27–52) • Time: 25 Minutes

Directions: Each of the following questions consists of an incomplete sentence followed by five words or pairs of words. Choose that word or pair of words which, when substituted for the blank space or spaces, *best* completes the meaning of the sentence and mark the letter of your choice on your answer sheet.

Example:

In view of the extenuating circumstances and the defendant's youth, the judge recommended ----.

(A) conviction
(B) a defense
(C) a mistrial
(D) leniency
(E) life imprisonment

Ⓐ Ⓑ Ⓒ ● Ⓔ

27. He soon ---- that she was making fun of him; with that ---- came a feeling of intense shame.

    (A) forgot..withdrawal
    (B) apprised..wisdom
    (C) realized..contentment
    (D) recognized..awareness
    (E) believed..contrivance

28. Her easy win in the cross-country ski race gained her much ---- from skiers in her northern community.

    (A) condemnation
    (B) consternation
    (C) tribulation
    (D) demarcation
    (E) approbation

29. The house looked ---- situated on the crumbling cliff.

    (A) prudently
    (B) precariously
    (C) predominantly
    (D) vicariously
    (E) aimlessly

30. Should we allow Paul to ---- his brother's time at the computer?

    (A) usurp
    (B) renege
    (C) depict
    (D) marshal
    (E) entail

31. The treaty was ---- almost as soon as the signatures were ----.

    (A) broken..revamped
    (B) abrogated..affixed
    (C) signed..appended
    (D) funded..initialed
    (E) prepared..fulfilled

32. The stark trees were ---- against the gray sky.

    (A) silhouetted
    (B) shackled
    (C) established
    (D) conflicted
    (E) oscillated

33. It makes no difference what we ----; her opinion is ----.

    (A) understand..reflective
    (B) assert..unwavering
    (C) opine..shifting
    (D) modify..subversive
    (E) delineate..volatile

Directions: Each of the following questions consists of a capitalized pair of words followed by five pairs of words lettered A to E. The capitalized words bear some meaningful relationship to each other. Choose the lettered pair of words whose relationship is most similar to that expressed by the capitalized pair and mark its letter on your answer sheet.

Example:

DAY : SUN : :

(A) sunlight : daylight
(B) heat : cold
(C) ray : sun
(D) moon : star
(E) night : moon

Ⓐ Ⓑ Ⓒ Ⓓ ●

34. WHEEL : WAGON : :

(A) runner : sled
(B) circle : square
(C) fin : fish
(D) engine : automobile
(E) skate : blade

35. DEFEND : PROSECUTE : :

(A) protect : serve
(B) allay : berate
(C) fortify : assail
(D) liberate : free
(E) deliberate : judge

36. SAPPHIRE : BLUE : :

(A) ruby : red
(B) tree : green
(C) silver : tarnished
(D) gem : polished
(E) jewelry : ornate

37. CASTOFFS : CLOTHING : :

(A) closet : coat
(B) castaway : ship
(C) rummage : sale
(D) trash : garbage
(E) scrap : metal

38. FOX : KIT : :

(A) pup : seal
(B) manx : cat
(C) male : female
(D) lion : cub
(E) wolf : pack

39. SHARECROPPER : PLANTATION

(A) renter : apartment
(B) farmer : crop
(C) worker : job
(D) assembly line : factory
(E) potato : root

GO ON TO THE NEXT PAGE

Questions 40–44 are based on the following passage.

Kate Chopin wrote a number of short stories about the Louisiana Creoles, but she is famous for her novel of a woman trapped in a stifling marriage. The Awakening *is a strange, moody book, basing much of its appeal on a strong sense of character and setting. In this excerpt from the beginning of the novel, we meet the main characters.*

Mr. Pontellier finally lit a cigar and began to smoke, letting the paper drag idly from his hand. He fixed his gaze upon a white sunshade that was advancing at snail's pace from the beach. He could see it plainly
(5) between the gaunt trunks of the water-oaks and across the stretch of yellow camomile. The gulf looked far away, melting hazily into the blue of the horizon. The sunshade continued to approach slowly. Beneath its pink-lined shelter were his wife, Mrs. Pontellier, and
(10) young Robert Lebrun. When they reached the cottage, the two seated themselves with some appearance of fatigue upon the upper step of the porch, facing each other, each leaning against a supporting post.

"What folly! to bathe at such an hour in such heat!"
(15) exclaimed Mr. Pontellier. He himself had taken a plunge at daylight. That was why the morning seemed long to him.

"You are burnt beyond recognition," he added, looking at his wife as one looks at a valuable piece of
(20) personal property which has suffered some damage. She held up her hands, strong, shapely hands, and surveyed them critically, drawing up her lawn sleeves above the wrists. Looking at them reminded her of her rings, which she had given to her husband before
(25) leaving for the beach. She silently reached out to him, and he, understanding, took the rings from his vest pocket and dropped them into her open palm. She slipped them upon her fingers; then clasping her knees, she looked across at Robert and began to laugh.
(30) He sent back an answering smile.

"What is it?" asked Pontellier, looking lazily and amused from one to the other. It was some utter nonsense; some adventure out there in the water, and they both tried to relate it at once. It did not seem half
(35) so amusing when told. They realized this, and so did Mr. Pontellier. He yawned and stretched himself. Then he got up, saying he had half a mind to go over to Klein's hotel and play a game of billiards.

"Come go along, Lebrun," he proposed to Robert.
(40) But Robert admitted quite frankly that he preferred to stay where he was and talk to Mrs. Pontellier.

"Well, send him about his business when he bores you, Edna," instructed her husband as he prepared to leave.

(45) "Here, take the umbrella," she exclaimed, holding it out to him. He accepted the sunshade, and lifting it over his head descended the steps and walked away.

40. The word *folly* (line 14) is used to mean

   (A) temerity
   (B) gaiety
   (C) clumsiness
   (D) tactlessness
   (E) foolishness

41. The narrator refers to "a valuable piece of personal property" (lines 19–20) to

   (A) show how very much her husband values Mrs. Pontellier
   (B) imply that Mr. Pontellier considers his wife to be his possession
   (C) remind the reader of Mr. Pontellier's great wealth
   (D) show how much the author values Mrs. Pontellier
   (E) contrast Mrs. Pontellier with her beach property

42. The incident with Mrs. Pontellier's rings symbolizes

   (A) her bondage
   (B) her love for Lebrun
   (C) her traditional values
   (D) her desire to grow
   (E) her bravery

43. The word *relate* (line 34) is used to mean

    (A) unite
    (B) recount
    (C) integrate
    (D) involve
    (E) compare

44. How does the narrator feel about Mr. Pontellier?

    (A) He is mischievous.
    (B) He is dull.
    (C) He is rude.
    (D) He is vain.
    (E) He is fiendish.

Directions: The two passages given below deal with a related topic. Following the passages are questions about the content of each passage or about the relationship between the two passages. Answer the questions based upon what is stated or implied in the passages and in any introductory material provided. Mark the letter of your choice on your answer sheet.

Questions 45–52 are based on the following passages.

As many in pre-Revolutionary Virginia cried for conciliation with Britain, Patrick Henry advocated preparing for war in a speech to the delegates to the Continental Congress. A year later, a group of writers who signed themselves Hutchinson, Cooper, Cato, & c. submitted a stinging article to the Pennsylvania Evening Post.

Passage 1—Patrick Henry to the Virginia Delegation, March 23, 1775

No man thinks more highly than I do of the patriotism, as well as abilities, of the very worthy gentlemen who have just addressed the House. But different men often see the same subject in different lights; and, (5) therefore, I hope it will not be thought disrespectful to those gentlemen, if, entertaining as I do opinions of a character very opposite to theirs, I shall speak forth my sentiments freely and without reserve. This is no time for ceremony. The question before the House is one of (10) awful moment to this country. For my own part, I consider it as nothing less than a question of freedom or slavery. . . .

Mr. President, it is natural to man to indulge in the illusions of hope. We are apt to shut our eyes against (15) a painful truth, and listen to the song of that siren till she transforms us into beasts. Is this the part of wise men, engaged in a great and arduous struggle for liberty? Are we disposed to be of the number of those who, having eyes, see not, and, having ears, hear not, (20) the things which so nearly concern their temporal salvation? For my part, whatever anguish of spirit it may cost, I am willing to know the whole truth; to know the worst, and to provide for it.

I have but one lamp by which my feet are guided, (25) and that is the lamp of experience. I know of no way of judging the future but by the past. And judging by the past, I wish to know what there has been in the conduct of the British ministry for the last ten years to justify those hopes with which gentlemen have been (30) pleased to solace themselves and the House.

Passage 2—In the *Pennsylvania Evening Post,* June 1, 1776

Notwithstanding the savage treatment we have met with from the King of Britain, and the impossibility of the colonies ever being happy under his government again, according to the usual operation of natural and (35) moral causes, yet we still find some people wishing to be dependent once more upon the crown of Britain. I have too good an opinion of the human understanding, to suppose that there is a man in America who believes that we ever shall be happy again in our old connection (40) with that crown. I, therefore, beg leave to oblige the advocates for dependence to speak for themselves in the following order:—

1. I shall lose my office. 2. I shall lose the honor of being related to men in office. 3. I shall lose the rent of (45) my houses for a year or two. 4. We shall have no more rum, sugar, tea nor coffee, in this country, except at a most exorbitant price. 5. We shall have no more gauze or fine muslins imported among us. 6. The New England men will turn Goths and Vandals, and over- (50) run all the Southern Colonies. N.B.—It is the fashion with the people who make this objection to independence, to despise the courage and discipline of the New England troops, and to complain that they are unwilling to fight out of their own colonies. 7. The (55) church will have no king for a head. 8. The Presbyterians will have a share of power in this country. N.B.— These people have been remarked, ever since the commencement of our disputes with Great Britain, to prefer a Quaker or an Episcopalian, to one of their own

was equally hearty in the cause of
...se my chance of a large tract of land
... 10. I shall want the support of the first
...els of government, to protect me in my insolence,
injustice, and villany. 11. The common people will have
(65) too much power in their hands. N.B.—The common
people are composed of tradesmen and farmers, and
include nine-tenths of the people of America.

Finally.—Sooner than submit to the chance of these
probable evils, we will have our towns burnt, our
(70) country desolated, and our fathers, brothers, and children butchered by English, Scotch, and Irishmen. . . .
And, after all, such of us as survive these calamities,
will submit to such terms of slavery as King George
and his Parliament may impose upon us.

45. The phrase "awful moment" (line 10) is used by Henry to mean

   (A) terrible time
   (B) unpleasant point
   (C) dreadful value
   (D) great importance
   (E) sudden amazement

46. Why does Henry refer to the myth about the siren?

   (A) To remind us that sweet sounds may lull us falsely
   (B) To advise us to prepare for war as the Greeks once did
   (C) To compare our democracy with that of the Greeks
   (D) To persuade us to heed the song as it is sung
   (E) To stress the need for alarm

47. The numbered list in Passage 2 contains

   (A) articles of confederation
   (B) arguments in favor of independence from Britain
   (C) moral causes
   (D) the author's opinions about independence
   (E) supposed excuses for remaining dependent on Britain

48. "Goths and Vandals" (line 49) are used as examples of

   (A) haphazard events
   (B) tribal rites
   (C) games
   (D) barbaric peoples
   (E) famous cowards

49. The word *want* (line 62) is used in Passage 2 to mean

   (A) covet
   (B) need
   (C) lack
   (D) crave
   (E) prefer

50. How does the author of Passage 2 feel about commoners?

   (A) They must be tolerated.
   (B) They have too much power.
   (C) They are in the majority.
   (D) Both A and B
   (E) Both B and C

51. Passage 1 differs from Passage 2 in its

   (A) politics
   (B) tone
   (C) attitude toward the British
   (D) both A and B
   (E) both B and C

52. With which of the following would both authors agree?

   (A) The question is one of freedom or slavery.
   (B) Men indulge in illusions of hope.
   (C) The British have done nothing to inspire hope.
   (D) All of the above
   (E) None of the above

STOP

END OF SECTION 3. IF YOU HAVE ANY TIME LEFT, GO OVER YOUR WORK IN THIS SECTION ONLY. DO NOT WORK IN ANY OTHER SECTION OF THE TEST.

PSAT/NMSQT Diagnostic Examination

SECTION 4

20 Questions (21–40) • Time: 25 Minutes

Directions: Solve the following problems using any available space on the page for scratchwork. On your answer sheet fill in the choice which best corresponds to the correct answer.

Notes: The figures accompanying the problems are drawn as accurately as possible unless otherwise stated in specific problems. Again, unless otherwise stated, all figures lie in the same plane. All numbers used in these problems are real numbers. Calculators are permitted for this test.

Reference Information

Circle: $C = 2\pi r$, $A = \pi r^2$

Rectangle: $A = lw$

Rectangular Solid: $V = lwh$

Cylinder: $V = \pi r^2 h$

Triangle: $A = \frac{1}{2}bh$

$a^2 + b^2 = c^2$

Special right triangles: 45°-45°-90° with sides x, x, $x\sqrt{2}$; 30°-60°-90° with sides x, $x\sqrt{3}$, $2x$.

The number of degrees of arc in a circle is 360.
The measure in degrees of a straight angle is 180.
The sum of the measures in degrees of the angles of a triangle is 180.

PART 1: Quantitative Comparison Questions

Directions: Questions 21–32 each consist of two quantities—one in Column A, the other in Column B. Compare the two quantities and mark your answer sheet as follows:

(A) if the quantity in Column A is greater
(B) if the quantity in Column B is greater
(C) if the quantities are equal
(D) if the relationship cannot be determined from the information given

Notes:

(1) Information concerning one or both of the compared quantities will be centered above the two columns for some items.
(2) Symbols that appear in both columns represent the same thing in Column A as in Column B.
(3) Letters such as x, n, and k are symbols for real numbers.

Examples

	Column A	Column B	Answers
E1.	$a - x$	$a + x$	(A) ● (C) (D)

$a > 0$
$x > 0$

	Column A	Column B	Answers
E2.	The average of 17, 19, 21, 23	The average of 16, 18, 20, 22	● (B) (C) (D)

DO NOT MARK CHOICE (E) FOR THESE QUESTIONS. THERE ARE ONLY FOUR ANSWER CHOICES.

GO ON TO THE NEXT PAGE →

	Column A	Column B			Column A	Column B
	...ircle with a radius of z	Area of a square with sides measuring z			two dice packed exactly into a box	
			27.	The volume of the box	The volumes of the dice added together

$$\frac{a}{2} = -b$$

	Column A	Column B
22.	ab	$\frac{a}{b}$

	Column A	Column B
28.	The perimeter of the triangle	The circumference of the circle

	Column A	Column B
23.	The number of odd numbers greater than 3 and less than or equal to 13.	4

	Column A	Column B
29.	5% of 7	7% of 5

$$x^2 = 144$$
$$2y - 18 = 32$$

	Column A	Column B
24.	$2x$	y

a and *b* are positive integers

	Column A	Column B
30.	$(a+b) - a$	$(b+a) - b$

$$m < n$$

	Column A	Column B
25.	$\frac{m}{n}$	$\frac{n}{m}$

	Column A	Column B
31.	$(x+2)(x-2)$	$x^2 - 4$

	Column A	Column B
26.	$\frac{1}{3}(c+d)$	$\frac{c}{3} + \frac{d}{3}$

	Column A	Column B
32.	The average of the even numbers greater than 2 and less than 12	The average of the odd numbers greater than 3 and less than 13

Part 2: Student-Produced Response Questions

Directions: Solve each of these problems. Write the answer in the corresponding grid on the answer sheet and fill in the ovals beneath each answer you write. Here are some examples.

Answer: $\frac{3}{4}$ (= .75; show answer either way)

Answer: 325

Note: A mixed number such as $3\frac{1}{2}$ must be gridded as 7/2 or as 3.5. If gridded as "31/2," it will be read as "thirty-one halves."

Note: Either position is correct

33. If $4x - 9 = 27$, what is x^3?

34. One-half of the contents of a container evaporates in one week, and three-fourths of the remainder evaporates in the following week. At the end of two weeks, what fractional part of the original contents remains? Express your answer in lowest terms.

35. The distance from the center of a circle to the midpoint of a chord is 3. If the length of the chord is 8, what is the length of the radius of the circle?

36. Three friends decide to split the cost of a pizza, with each chipping in $3.25. If two more friends join them, and each pays an equal share, how much less will each of the three friends have to pay?

GO ON TO THE NEXT PAGE

... of the baseball team weigh 130, 115, ... 5 pounds. If the average weight of ... team is 130 pounds, what is the average weight in pounds of the remaining four players?

38. In the figure below, what is the measure in degrees of angle n?

39. If $a + b = -4$ and $b^2 = 49$, what positive whole number can a be?

40. Danielle ate $\frac{1}{4}$ of a bag of popcorn and gave $\frac{1}{6}$ of the remainder to Phil. How much of the original container was left? Express your answer in lowest terms.

STOP

END OF SECTION 4. IF YOU HAVE ANY TIME LEFT, GO OVER YOUR WORK IN THIS SECTION ONLY. DO NOT WORK IN ANY OTHER SECTION OF THE TEST.

SECTION 5

39 Questions (1–39) • Time: 30 minutes

Directions: The sentences below contain errors in grammar, usage, word choice, and idiom. Parts of each sentence are underlined and lettered. Decide which underlined part contains the error and mark its letter on your answer sheet. If the sentence is correct as it stands, mark (E) on your answer sheet. No sentence contains more than one error.

1. <u>Not wanting</u> them to be <u>unnecessary</u> <u>distressed,</u>
    A   B   C
   I didn't tell them about our <u>mishap</u> with the car.
                                  D
   <u>No error</u>.
    E

2. By the time he <u>reached</u> the cabin, the <u>mercury</u>
                    A   B
   had dropped and his hands were <u>nearly</u> <u>froze</u>.
                                    C   D
   <u>No error</u>.
    E

3. We <u>ought to</u> <u>set</u> our prejudices aside and <u>except</u>
        A   B   C
   each other as <u>equals</u>. <u>No error</u>.
                   D   E

4. Every <u>athlete</u> has <u>their</u> own <u>way</u> of <u>preparing</u> for
          A   B   C   D
   a game. <u>No error</u>.
            E

5. As a <u>documentary</u> photographer for the Farm
         A
   Security Administration during the <u>Depression,</u>
                                        B
   Dorothea Lange <u>recorded</u> the hardships and des-
                    C
   peration of America's <u>dispossessed</u>. <u>No error</u>.
                          D   E

6. The Piltdown man, one of the most extraordinary
   scientific <u>hoax</u> of all time, was <u>accepted</u> by
               A   B
   <u>anthropologists</u> as the "<u>missing link</u>" between
    C   D
   man and the apes. <u>No error</u>.
                      E

7. Lifeguards <u>have been known</u> to <u>effect</u> rescues
               A   B
   even <u>during</u> tumultuous storms. <u>No error</u>.
   C   D   E

8. The <u>mayor</u> <u>expressed</u> concern about the large
        A   B
   <u>amount</u> of people injured at street <u>crossings</u>.
    C   D
   <u>No error</u>.
    E

9. "<u>Leave</u> us <u>face</u> the fact that <u>we're</u> in <u>trouble!</u>" he
     A   B   C   D
   shouted. <u>No error</u>.
             E

10. Jones seems <u>slow</u> on the track, but you will find
                  A
    few boys <u>quicker</u> <u>than</u> <u>him</u> on the basketball
              B   C   D
    court. <u>No error</u>.
            E

11. We had <u>swam</u> <u>across</u> the lake <u>before</u> the sun
            A   B   C
    <u>rose</u>. <u>No error</u>.
     D   E

12. The <u>loud noise</u> of the cars and trucks <u>annoys</u>
         A   B
    those <u>who</u> live <u>near the road</u>. <u>No error</u>.
           C   D   E

13. I know that you <u>will enjoy</u> <u>receiving</u> flowers
                     A   B
    that <u>smell</u> so <u>sweetly</u>. <u>No error</u>.
          C   D   E

14. He is <u>at least</u> ten years <u>older</u> <u>then</u> <u>she</u> is.
    　　　A　　　　　　　　B　　C　　D
    <u>No error</u>.
    E

15. To go out <u>dancing</u>, to have a couple of beers, and
    　　　　　A
    <u>staying</u> out late <u>is</u> <u>my idea</u> of relaxation.
    　B　　　　　　C　　D
    <u>No error</u>.
    E

16. All of the children <u>have</u> grown <u>considerable</u> since
    　　　　　　　　　A　　　　　　B
    the last time <u>their</u> uncle <u>visited</u>. <u>No error</u>.
    　　　　　　C　　　　　　D　　　E

17. What <u>does</u> <u>either</u> Rick or Alice <u>know</u> about dis-
    　　　　A　　　B　　　　　　　　　C
    ease, hunger, or <u>being poor</u>? <u>No error</u>.
    　　　　　　　　D　　　　　　　E

18. A bad <u>conscious</u> made him give <u>himself</u> up,
    　　　　　A　　　　　　　　　　　B
    though no one had suspected him <u>of</u> the crime.
    　　C　　　　　　　　　　　　　　D
    <u>No error</u>.
    E

19. <u>In his effort</u> to reach a wise decision about these
    　　A
    truants, the attendance officer <u>conferred</u> many
    　B　　　　　　　　　　　　　　　　C
    times with the dean and <u>I</u>. <u>No error</u>.
    　　　　　　　　　　　　D　　　E

Directions: The sentences below contain problems in grammar, sentence construction, word choice, and punctuation. Part or all of each sentence is underlined. Select the lettered answer that contains the best version of the underlined section. Answer (A) always repeats the original underlined section exactly. If the sentence is correct as it stands, select (A).

20. The hunter stalked the tiger slowly, cautiously, <u>and in a silent manner</u>.

    (A) and in a silent manner
    (B) and silently
    (C) and by acting silently
    (D) and also used silence
    (E) and in silence

21. The doctor believed that exercise and a hot bath were <u>equally as effective as, and less addictive than</u>, a sedative for relieving anxiety.

    (A) equally as effective as, and less addictive than
    (B) equally as affective as, and less addictive than
    (C) as effective as, and less addictive than
    (D) equally as effective, and less addictive than
    (E) equally as effective as, while being less addictive than

22. <u>When describing</u> the accident, a tone of self-justification creeps into his voice.

    (A) When describing
    (B) In describing
    (C) When there is a description of
    (D) When describing about
    (E) When he describes

23. <u>Expressing a radically different idea is Dorothy Sayers, who believes</u> that women all through history have been oppressed by men.

    (A) Expressing a radically different idea is Dorothy Sayers, who believes
    (B) Dorothy Sayers expresses a radically different idea—
    (C) Expressing a radically different idea is Dorothy Sayers, believing
    (D) Dorothy Sayers, expressing a radically different idea believes
    (E) Dorothy Sayers is expressing a radically different idea

24. How much has fuel costs raised during the past year?
    (A) has fuel costs raised
    (B) have fuel costs raised
    (C) has fuel costs risen
    (D) have fuel costs risen
    (E) has fuel costs rose

25. Being that it was raining, we decided to postpone the hike.
    (A) Being that
    (B) Being as how
    (C) In view of the fact that
    (D) Considering the fact that
    (E) Because

26. Many critics consider James Joyce's Ulysses, a novel once banned as obscene, to be the greatest novel of the twentieth century.
    (A) Ulysses, a novel once banned as obscene, to be
    (B) Ulysses, a novel once banned as obscene to be
    (C) Ulysses, which is a novel that was once banned as obscene, to be
    (D) Ulysses, a once banned as obscene novel, to be
    (E) Ulysses, a novel once banned as obscene, being

27. About three hundred people gathered, they were there protesting the construction of a nuclear power plant.
    (A) gathered, they were there protesting
    (B) gathered—they were there protesting
    (C) gathered, they were there protesting against
    (D) gathered to protest
    (E) gathered for the purpose of protesting

28. I think they, as a rule, are much more conniving than us.
    (A) as a rule, are much more conniving than us
    (B) as a rule are much more conniving than us
    (C) as a rule, are much more conniving than we
    (D) as a rule; are much more conniving than us
    (E) are, as a rule, much more conniving than us

29. The public health officer warned his audience about the danger of mixing alcohol and pills and driving after drinking also.
    (A) about the danger of mixing alcohol and pills and driving after drinking also
    (B) about the danger both of mixing alcohol and pills and of driving after drinking
    (C) about the dangerous nature of mixing alcohol and pills and driving after drinking also
    (D) about the danger of mixing alcohol and pills, and driving after drinking also
    (E) about the danger both of mixing alcohol and pills and driving after drinking

30. If you disobey traffic regulations, you will loose your driver's license.
    (A) you will loose your driver's license
    (B) you'll loose your driver's license
    (C) you will lose your driver's license
    (D) you will loose your drivers' license
    (E) your driver's license will be lost

31. "When my husband will come home, I'll tell him you called," the housewife sighed into the phone.
    (A) will come home,
    (B) will come home
    (C) will have come home
    (D) comes home,
    (E) has come home,

32. Robert did not want to set the table because <u>he did not know what time they were coming home</u>.

   (A) he did not know what time they were coming home
   (B) he did not know what time they were coming home at
   (C) he did not know what time it would be when they came home
   (D) he did not know at what time they were coming home at
   (E) he did not know what the time was that they were coming home

33. Neither Marty <u>or Christine knows</u> how to speak French.

   (A) or Christine knows
   (B) or Christine knew
   (C) nor Christine knows
   (D) nor Christine know
   (E) or Christine know

Directions: Questions 34–39 are based on a passage that might be an early draft of a student's essay. Some sentences in this draft need to be revised or rewritten to make them both clear and correct. Read the passage carefully; then answer the questions that follow it. Some questions require decisions about diction, usage, tone, or sentence structure in particular sentences or parts of sentences. Other questions require decisions about organization, development, or appropriateness of language in the essay as a whole. For each question, choose the answer that makes the intended meaning clearer and more precise and that follows the conventions of standard written English.

(1) When my family came to the United States to live, we spoke no English. (2) My parents luckily got a job and my sister and I were very young and we did what many other immigrant children did. (3) We learned English in public school and learned our native language and culture at home with our family. (4) It was not long before we all realized that success in the United States would depend on our ability to be fluent in English.

(5) Because of my own case I think that bilingual education is not as good as English in school, native language at home. (6) But I know of other people who found a bilingual education to be just what they needed, in fact it was essential to their progress since their English was so limited. (7) However, some people I knew did drop out of school later on. (8) Some of them had been labeled learning-disabled. (9) It was really just a language problem. (10) And some of my friends' parents felt that their children's bilingual education was ineffective or harmful, while others felt it was very good for them.

(11) As a result, I cannot decide for certain whether English is being taught better to foreigners today than it was in the past. (12) But I think that I would like to see small groups of non-native speakers taught in English by caring, well-trained professionals. (13) Then I would like them to be moved into regular classrooms as soon as possible. (14) In that way, I think they would be best served by a school system that has not always done justice to their needs. (15) Perhaps that would be one way to solve the problem of how to help them to succeed in school and in their life in the United States.

34. Which of the following is the best way to revise sentence (2)?

   (A) My parents luckily got a job. My sister and I were young. We did what many other immigrated children did.
   (B) My parents luckily got a job and my sister and I were very young so we did what many other immigrants did.
   (C) My parents got jobs, luckily; my very young sister and I did what many others did.
   (D) Luckily, my parents got jobs. My sister and I, who were very young, did what many other immigrant children did.
   (E) Luckily, my parents got jobs and my sister and I were very young. We did what many other immigrant children did.

35. Which of the following is the best way to revise sentence (5)?

    (A) Because of my own experience, I think that a bilingual education is not so good as learning English in school and the family's native language at home.
    (B) In my own case, bilingual education is not so good as English in school and native language at home.
    (C) I think that because of my own experience, English in school, native language at home is better than bilingual education.
    (D) As a result of my own case, I think that bilingual education is not as good as students who learn English in school and their native language at home.
    (E) Because of my own case, I consider bilingual education less effective than learning English in school and their native language at home.

36. Which of the following is the best revision of the underlined portion of sentence (6) below?

    But I know of other people who found a bilingual education to be just what they <u>needed, in fact it was essential</u> to their progress since their English was so limited.

    (A) needed; in fact it being essential
    (B) needed, being that it was essential
    (C) needed; in fact it was essential
    (D) needed; essential as it was in fact
    (E) needed. In fact essential

37. Which of the following is the best way to combine sentences (8) and (9)?

    (A) Although it was really just a language problem; some had been labeled learning-disabled.
    (B) Some of them were labeled learning-disabled, it was really just a language problem
    (C) Some of them has been labeled learning-disabled, even though what they really had was a language problem.
    (D) Some of them were learning-disabled with a language problem.
    (E) Some of them had a language problem that made them learning-disabled.

38. Which of the following is the best revision of sentence (10)?

    (A) Some of my friends' parents felt that their children's bilingual education was ineffective or harmful, while others felt it was very good for them.
    (B) Some felt that their child's bilingual education was ineffective or harmful, but other of my friends' parents felt it was very good for them.
    (C) Though some of my friends' parents felt it was very good for them, some felt that bilingual education was ineffective or harmful.
    (D) Although some of my friends' parents felt it was very good, some felt that their children's bilingual education was ineffective or harmful.
    (E) Ineffective or harmful though it may have been to some, others of my friends' parents felt that their children's bilingual education has been very good.

39. Which of the following would be the best way to improve the last paragraph?

    (A) To incorporate transitional words or phrases
    (B) To eliminate the specious argument presented
    (C) To present a more personal point of view
    (D) To adopt a less sympathetic tone
    (E) To be more exact and concise in wording

STOP

END OF SECTION 5. IF YOU HAVE ANY TIME LEFT, GO OVER YOUR WORK IN THIS SECTION ONLY. DO NOT WORK IN ANY OTHER SECTION OF THE TEST.

PSAT/NMSQT DIAGNOSTIC EXAMINATION

Answer Key

Section 1: Verbal

1. A	7. D	13. E	19. B	25. C
2. E	8. E	14. C	20. E	26. E
3. C	9. A	15. C	21. A	
4. B	10. B	16. A	22. D	
5. A	11. E	17. E	23. B	
6. A	12. A	18. B	24. D	

Section 2: Math (Code: A = Arithmetic; AL = Algebra; G = Geometry; O = Other)

1. E (A)	5. C (A)	9. D (AL)	13. B (A)	17. C (G)
2. D (A)	6. B (AL)	10. E (AL)	14. D (G)	18. B (G)
3. C (A)	7. D (G)	11. E (AL)	15. B (A)	19. B (O)
4. E (A)	8. E (G)	12. C (G)	16. A (AL)	20. C (O)

Section 3: Verbal

27. D	33. B	39. A	45. D	51. B
28. E	34. A	40. E	46. A	52. D
29. B	35. C	41. B	47. E	
30. A	36. A	42. A	48. D	
31. B	37. E	43. B	49. C	
32. A	38. D	44. B	50. C	

Section 4: Math

Part 1

21. A	25. D	29. C
22. B	26. C	30. D
23. A	27. C	31. C
24. B	28. A	32. B

Part 2

33. 729	37. 130
34. $\frac{1}{8}$	38. 45
35. 5	39. 3
36. 1.30	40. $\frac{5}{8}$

Section 5: Writing Skills

1. B	7. E	13. D	19. D	25. E	31. D	37. C
2. D	8. C	14. C	20. B	26. A	32. A	38. D
3. C	9. A	15. B	21. C	27. D	33. C	39. E
4. B	10. D	16. B	22. E	28. C	34. D	
5. E	11. A	17. D	23. B	29. B	35. A	
6. A	12. E	18. A	24. D	30. C	36. C	

PSAT/NMSQT DIAGNOSTIC EXAMINATION
Explanatory Answers

Section 1

1. **(A)** The word *confused* is your clue. The speaker has made a *digression*, or departure from the topic.

2. **(E)** What might concern an accountant? *Profits* (C) are one possibility, but they could not be *organized*, as the sentence indicates. *Receipts*, on the other hand, might be.

3. **(C)** The words *swept* and *blowing* indicate a windlike movement. A *zephyr* (B) is a kind of wind, but it is very gentle. Only *cyclone*, of the choices given, names a big, blustery wind.

4. **(B)** Both words must fit the context here. In choice (A), only the second word fits; the first makes no sense. In choices (C) and (D), if the first is true, the second is not; and choice (E) makes no sense at all.

5. **(A)** A motorist who cannot control a car may be intoxicated; in other words, lacking in *sobriety*.

6. **(A)** *Retired* has many meanings, and the one that means "retreated" or "withdrew" is the one used here.

7. **(D)** A *collar* fastens around the *neck* just as a *cuff* fastens around a *wrist*.

8. **(E)** A very great chess player is a *master*, and a very great musician is a *virtuoso*.

9. **(A)** A *blizzard* is a storm characterized by heavy, blowing snow, and a *typhoon* is a storm characterized by strong *wind*.

10. **(B)** The writer of a *song* is called a *lyricist*, and the writer of a *play* is called a *dramatist*. A musician may write a tune (A), but the more accurate word is *composer*. In addition, both lyricists and dramatists deal in words.

11. **(E)** As *geometry* is a branch of *mathematics*, so *botany* is a branch of *science*.

12. **(A)** Think of relative values here. A *dollar* equals 10 *dimes*, and a *decade* equals 10 *years*.

13. **(E)** *Grammar* is the structure on which *language* is built. In a similar way, *scales* are used to structure *music*.

14. **(C)** Return to the cited line, and you will see that the only eyes referred to are those of the Europeans, which come in brown, green, and black.

15. **(C)** Any of these might be a synonym for *dress*, but only *style* fits the context of fixing hair.

16. **(A)** Paragraph 3 *does* compare European ways to Chinese ways and discuss European customs. However, it deals with eating habits rather than with personal appearance.

17. **(E)** Looking at the passage as a whole, you can see that it primarily describes the people and customs of Europe, all with an instructive tone.

18. **(B)** The author rarely inserts himself into the passage, and he certainly says nothing negative, as choices (A), (C), and (D) would suggest. Nor does he ever imply that European customs are better than Chinese customs. He focuses on the strangeness of what he observes, stressing what his reader might find most interesting.

19. **(B)** Mr. Buxton is cited in paragraph 1. His account of a parrot who took care of a crippled bird is clearly included to support the discussion of benevolent behavior in birds.

20. **(E)** *Distinct* has several meanings, but in this case, the bird is of a *different* species from the parrot.

21. **(A)** The birds show "antipathy or affection," two opposite reactions.

22. **(D)** The list of birds appears in paragraph 2 as supporting evidence for Darwin's discussion of birds' powers of observation and recall.

23. **(B)** Returning to the cited phrase, you will see that only *raised* fits the context.

24. **(D)** Test the choices in context, and you will find that, while (A) and (C) are close, (D) is the best choice.

25. **(C)** Choice (A) is too broad, and choice (B) is too narrow. Choices (D) and (E) are off the mark. Only choice (C) is an accurate summary of the author's intent.

26. **(E)** You might be fooled into choosing choice (C), but Darwin really only cites studies to support his own observations, and there is no indication whether they are "current studies," unscientific observations by friends, or writings from long ago. Only choice (E) is accurate.

Section 2

1. **(E)** You can solve simply by counting decimal places to the right of the decimal and recognizing that the answer will have six (1 + 2 + 3).

   (This sign will appear whenever it is easy or preferable to use a calculator to solve the problem.)

2. **(D)** Convert first to inches. The average height is 60 inches. Three girls are 58 inches tall. The fourth is x.

   $(58 + 58 + 58 + x) \div 4 = 60$
   $(174 + x) = 240$
   $x = 66$ inches, or 5 feet 6 inches

3. **(C)** Any number times its reciprocal is 1.

4. **(E)** Think: $5\dfrac{1}{4} = \dfrac{x}{16}$
   $\dfrac{21}{4} = \dfrac{84}{16}$

5. **(C)** This lends itself to a draw-a-picture strategy.

   3:00
   4:00
   5:00
   6:00

   The answer is 8.

6. **(B)** You know that $x = \dfrac{y}{4}$. Therefore, stated in terms of y, $\dfrac{x}{4} = \dfrac{y}{4} \div 4$, or $\dfrac{y}{4} \times \dfrac{1}{4}$, or $\dfrac{y}{16}$.

7. **(D)** If you have any doubts, simply plug in a few numbers to test your ideas. If the side of a square = 2, the perimeter = 4 × 2, or 8. If the side is tripled to 6, the perimeter = 4 × 6, or 24. The perimeter is tripled.

8. **(E)**
   1. The sum of the angles of a triangle = 180°
      Because ABC is an isosceles trinagle, $x = y$
      $30° + x + y = 180°$
      $x + y = 150°$
      $2x = 150°$
      $x = 75°$
      $y = 75°$
      Line AC is a straight line.
   2. The sum of the angles of a straight line = 180°
      $y + z = 180°$
      $75° + z = 180°$
      $z = 180° - 75°$
      $z = 105°$

9. **(D)** The easiest way to solve is to determine the age Leo was when Robert was born: 67 − 29 = 38. Then you know that when Robert reaches age 38, he will be half his father's age. That will occur in x years, where $29 + x = 38$ years. In 9 years, Robert will be 38, and his father will be 67 + 9 = 76 years old—twice Robert's age.

10. **(E)** You can convert all the numbers to fractions with the same denominator and compare them:

    $\dfrac{75}{300}, \dfrac{90}{300}, \dfrac{69}{300}, \dfrac{80}{300}.$

    Alternatively, you can use a calculator to do the division and compare the numbers in decimal form.

11. **(E)** You know that $\dfrac{b}{a} = 3$, so you can refer to b as $3a$. Plugging that into the first number sentence, you get

    $a + 3a = 12$, so $4a = 12$, so $a = 3$
    Since $b = 3a$, $b = 9$.
    Therefore, $ab = 27$.

12. **(C)** First, draw the picture.

The reference information tells you that the circumference, 10, equals $2\pi r$.
Therefore, $\pi r = 5$.
Since $r = \frac{5}{\pi}$, the perimeter of the square $= 4 \times \frac{5}{\pi}$, or $\frac{20}{\pi}$.

13. **(B)** The station got $500 in all. Of this, 20%, or $100, was from drive-time ads at $20/minute—5 minutes of ads. 50%, or $250, was from daytime ads at $10/minute—25 minutes of ads. Finally, 30%, or $150, was from nighttime ads at $5/minute—30 minutes of ads. Add the numbers of minutes: $5 + 25 + 30 = 60$ minutes, or 1 hour.

14. **(D)** You should not need to do any calculating here. You know that the area of any circle is equal to πr^2. The radius of the circle pictured is equal to $\frac{AC}{2}$.

Therefore, the circle's area is $\pi \left(\frac{AC}{2}\right)^2$.

15. **(B)** On the first leg of the trip, the motorist drives 90 miles per hour.
Time $= \frac{\text{Distance}}{\text{Rate}}$
Time $= \frac{90}{50} = 1.8$
On the return trip, the motorist drives the 90 miles at 60 miles per hour.
Time $= \frac{\text{Distance}}{\text{Rate}}$
Time $= \frac{90}{60} = 1.5$
The total time for the trip is
1.5
1.8

3.3 hours

Rate $= \frac{\text{Distance}}{\text{Time}}$
Rate $= \frac{180}{3.3} = 54.5$ miles per hour

16. **(A)** Solve for x:
$$17x - 32 = 308$$
$$17x = 340$$
$$x = 20$$

Knowing the value of x, you can see that $\frac{x}{4} = 5$.

17. **(C)** The area of any triangle is $\frac{1}{2}$ base $\times$ height. Since $\triangle UQR$ and $\triangle RST$ are equal in area and have equal heights, they must also have equal bases. In other words $QR = RS$, and each equals 2. That means that $QS = 4$, so each side of the square $= 4$.

Now, to find the area of $\triangle RUT$,
$$\frac{1}{2}UT \times ST = \frac{1}{2}(4 \times 4) = 8.$$

18. **(B)** This is trickier than it looks. Express the increase in the radius as $r + .1r$. Then the area, which before was πr^2, now is $\pi(r + .1r)^2$, or $\pi(1.1r)^2$. $(1.1)^2 = 1.21$, so the new area is 21% greater than the old.

19. **(B)** The sign ! appears to mean "multiply the number by the next greater whole number." Therefore, $7! = 7 \times 8$, and $8! = 8 \times 9$. Solving for $7! + 8!$, you add $56 + 72$ for a sum of 128.

20. **(C)** In one minute, the faucets working together will fill $\frac{1}{3} + \frac{1}{2}$ of the sink. In two minutes, they will fill $\frac{2}{3} + \frac{2}{2}$—overflowing the sink. Returning to the first set of numbers, you can see that the faucets will fill $\frac{2}{6} + \frac{3}{6}$, or $\frac{5}{6}$ of the sink in one minute. If $\frac{5}{6}x = 1$, then $x = \frac{6}{5}$, $1\frac{1}{5}$, or 1.2 minutes.

Section 3

27. **(D)** A parallelism is set up in this sentence; the second word will be an extension of the first. Once you recognize that, you will see that only choice (D) works.

28. **(E)** She would not be *condemned* (A) or "criticized" for her win; nor would other skiers be *consternated* (B) or "alarmed." *Tribulation* (C) means "hardship," and *demarcation* (D) means "limitation." Only *approbation*, meaning "congratulations" or "praise," has the proper meaning.

29. **(B)** If the house is on a crumbling cliff, it does not look *prudently* or "carefully" situated (A). It looks *precariously* or "shakily" positioned.

30. **(A)** The words *allow* and *time* are your clues here. If Paul *usurped*, or "took over," his brother's computer time, that might be a questionable offense.

31. **(B)** Both words must fit in order for your choice to be correct. In choice (A), the first word fits, but signatures cannot be *revamped*. Choice (C) is absurd—the treaty would be signed at exactly the same time as the signatures were appended. Choice (D) makes no sense, because a treaty would not be *funded*, and choice (E) makes no sense, because signatures cannot be *fulfilled*. The answer is choice (B)—the treaty was *abrogated*, or "broken," almost as soon as the signatures were *affixed*, or "added."

32. **(A)** The sentence has to do with appearance. The trees were *silhouetted*—only their outlines were apparent.

33. **(B)** Try filling in the second word first. That means choices (B), (C), and (D) are possibilities. Now add the first word, and you will see that only choice (B) is logical.

34. **(A)** The *wheel* helps propel the *wagon* in the same way that the *runner* helps propel the *sled*. A fin might help propel a fish (C), but it works more like a rudder than like a wheel. An engine might help propel an automobile (D), but it does not do it in the same way that a wheel does.

35. **(C)** These words are used in their antithetical meanings. Of the answer choices, the only one that is a pair of opposites is (C), *fortify* and *assail*.

36. **(A)** A *sapphire* is a *blue* gem, and a *ruby* is a *red* gem. A tree may be green (B), but it is not a gem.

37. **(E)** We call discarded *clothing* "*castoffs*," and we call discarded *metal* "*scrap*."

38. **(D)** A *kit* is a baby *fox*, and a *cub* is a baby *lion*.

39. **(A)** A *sharecropper* has a relationship to a *plantation* much as a *renter* does to an *apartment*—neither has ownership; both lease the space.

40. **(E)** Mr. Pontellier regards much of his wife's actions as *folly*, by which he means "foolishness" rather than the more negative connotations.

41. **(B)** If you read the introduction, you know that this is the story of a woman "trapped in a stifling marriage." Even if you didn't know this, you could infer from Mr. Pontellier's amused and patronizing attitude toward his wife that (B) is the correct answer.

42. **(A)** Mrs. Pontellier has removed her rings, including, presumably, her wedding ring, and has left them in the care of her husband while she set off for a morning of freedom. The scene in question makes it seem as though Mrs. Pontellier is putting out her arms to be handcuffed once more.

43. **(B)** Of all of these synonyms, only *recount*, meaning "retell," has the meaning that fits the context.

44. **(B)** We see Mr. Pontellier moving ponderously about, mystified by the laughter of others, and confined to a routine. There is no support for any of the other choices, but the author plainly feels he is dull.

45. **(D)** This is *awful* as meaning "full of awe" and *moment* as the root of *momentous*. Henry means that this is a time of great importance.

46. **(A)** Rereading the entire sentence in which the reference is found will help you recognize that this myth is referred to as a parallel for those men who cling to false hope.

47. **(E)** If you understand the passage at all, you will see that the list is one of excuses those who advocate dependence use to explain why America should remain connected to Britain.

48. **(D)** The clues in the sentence are *men* and *overrun*. The author suggests that people fear that New

Englanders will take over the South, much as the barbarian Goths and Vandals took over Europe long ago.

49. **(C)** One fear cited is that the independent Americans will *want*, or "lack," protection.

50. **(C)** This is delineated in one of the N.B. asides. The author does not believe (B); he believes that those in favor of dependence believe it.

51. **(B)** The passages share the same political bent and attitude toward the British, but whereas Passage 1 is heartfelt and solemn, Passage 2 is tongue-in-cheek and ironic.

52. **(D)** Both authors refer to slavery—in line 12 in Passage 1, and in line 73 in Passage 2. Both remark on the fact that some people have deluded themselves with vain hopes about the British, despite the fact that the British have done nothing to inspire such hope. Since (A), (B), and (C) are correct, the answer is (D).

Section 4
Part 1

21. **(A)** Draw a picture to help you solve this problem. Just looking at the picture will convince you that the area of the circle will be greater than that of the square.

22. **(B)** Try plugging in some numbers. Suppose a is a positive number such as 4.

$$\frac{4}{2} = -(-2)$$

In that case, ab, $4(-2)$, equals -8.

$$\frac{a}{b}, \frac{4}{-2}, \text{ equals } -2.$$

Now suppose a is a negative number such as -4.

$$\frac{-4}{2} = -2$$

In that case, ab, $-4(2)$, equals -8 again.

$$\frac{a}{b}, \frac{-4}{2}, \text{ equals } -2.$$

23. **(A)** There are five odd numbers greater than 3 and less than or equal to 13: 5, 7, 9, 11, and 13.

24. **(B)** If $x^2 = 144$, $x = 12$, and $2x = 24$.

If $2y - 18 = 32$, $2y = 50$, and $y = 25$.

25. **(D)** There is not enough information to solve this. If m and n are positive whole numbers, then $\frac{n}{m}$ is greater, but if n is positive and m negative, then $\frac{m}{n}$ is greater.

26. **(C)** One glance should tell you that these numbers are equivalent, but if you wish, try some numbers in place of c and d. If $c = 1$ and $d = 2$, $\frac{1}{3}(c + d) = 1$. $\frac{c}{3} + \frac{d}{3} = \frac{1}{3} + \frac{2}{3} = 1$.

27. **(C)** You may wish to draw a picture to check this.

The volume of the large box = $2 \times 4 \times 2 = 16$.
The volume of each of the dice = $2 \times 2 \times 2 = 8$.
$8 + 8 = 16$

28. **(A)** Draw a picture, ascribe values, and solve.

The perimeter of the triangle = $2 + 2 + \sqrt{8}$.
The circumference of the circle = $2\pi r$, and since $r = 1$, you can restate that as 2π.
$\pi \approx 3.14$, so $2\pi \approx 6.28$.
$\sqrt{8}$ lies between 2.8 and 2.9, so $2 + 2 + \sqrt{8} \approx 6.8$ or 6.9.

29. **(C)** If you do not recognize the equivalence immediately, use your calculator to solve.

5% of 7 = .35
7% of 5 = .35

30. **(D)** Unless you know which is greater, a or b, you cannot answer this question.

31. **(C)** $(x + 2)(x - 2) = x^2 + 2x - 2x - 4$, or $x^2 - 4$.

32. **(B)** The even numbers greater than 2 and less than 12 are 4, 6, 8, and 10. Their average is 5. The odd numbers greater than 3 and less than 13 are 5, 7, 9, and 11. Their average is 8.

Part 2

33. **(729)** $4x - 9 = 27$, so $4x = 36$. $9^3 = 729$

34. **($\frac{1}{8}$)** At the end of week 2, you have the following:

$$1 - \left[\frac{1}{2} + \left(\frac{1}{2} \times \frac{3}{4}\right)\right] =$$

$$1 - \left(\frac{4}{8} + \frac{3}{8}\right) =$$

$$\frac{1}{8}$$

35. **(5)** If the chord is 8, half of it is 4, which sets you up with a nice 3-4-5 right triangle, as here:

36. **(1.30)** The pizza costs $3 \times \$3.25$, or \$9.75. If that is now divided by 5, each person pays $\$9.75 \div 5$, or \$1.95. That is \$1.30 less for each of the original friends. (Although you will not record a dollar sign, do not forget the final 0.)

37. **(130)** This is less difficult than it may at first seem. Average the five players you know:

$(130 + 115 + 120 + 140 + 145) \div 5 = 130$

In order to maintain the 130 average, the average weight of the remaining players must be 130 as well.

38. **(45)** You can solve this if you recall that the sum of the measures of the angles of a quadrilateral will equal 360. Redraw the picture, writing in all the measures you know or can calculate:

$360 - (150 + 25 + 140) = 45$

39. **(3)** The key to this is the phrase "positive whole number." If a is positive, b must be negative, and the only negative number whose square is 49 is -7. If $a + (-7) = -4$, $a = 3$.

40. **($\frac{5}{8}$)** Express the consumed popcorn this way:

$$1 - \left[\frac{1}{4} + \left(\frac{3}{4} \times \frac{1}{6}\right)\right] =$$

$$1 - \left(\frac{1}{4} + \frac{3}{24}\right) =$$

$$1 - \left(\frac{2}{8} + \frac{1}{8}\right) =$$

$$\frac{5}{8}$$

Section 5

1. **(B)** The adverbial form *unnecessarily* is required to modify an adjective, *distressed*.

2. **(D)** The past participle of *freeze* is *frozen*.

3. **(C)** The verb meaning "receive willingly" or "agree to" is *accept*, not *except*.

4. **(B)** The pronoun should be singular (either *his* or *his or her*) to agree with the singular subject.

5. **(E)** This sentence is correct.

6. **(A)** The plural of *hoax* is *hoaxes*.

7. **(E)** This sentence is correct.
8. **(C)** Use *number* for a quantity thought of as a collection of individual things or people.
9. **(A)** The use of *leave* to mean "allow" is nonstandard; use *let*.
10. **(D)** The complete comparison would be *quicker than he is*; the shortened form is *quicker than he*.
11. **(A)** The past participle of *swim* is *swum*.
12. **(E)** This sentence is correct.
13. **(D)** The verb *smell* takes a predicate adjective, *sweet*.
14. **(C)** The word used in comparisons is *than*.
15. **(B)** Parallel structure requires a third infinitive, *to stay*.
16. **(B)** The adverbial form *considerably* is required.
17. **(D)** Items in a series should be grammatically parallel. A third noun, *poverty*, is needed to balance the nouns *disease* and *hunger*.
18. **(A)** The word for a sense of right and wrong is *conscience*. *Conscious* is an adjective meaning "awake" or "aware."
19. **(D)** The object of a preposition (*with*) should be in the objective case (*me*).
20. **(B)** Items in a series should be parallel in form. In this case, a third adverb, *silently*, is required.
21. **(C)** The construction *or . . . as* expresses the notion of equality. The use of *equally* is therefore redundant.
22. **(E)** The original makes it seem as if the tone is describing the accident. The dangling phrase may be replaced by a dependent clause containing its own subject, *he*.
23. **(B)** The original sentence is awkward.
24. **(D)** The correct verb form is *have risen*, plural to agree with the plural subject *costs*. Risen is the past participle of the intransitive verb *to rise*.
25. **(E)** The use of *being that* to mean "because" or "since" is nonstandard.
26. **(A)** The sentence is correct.
27. **(D)** The original version is a run-on sentence.
28. **(C)** In a comparison introduced by *than* or *as*, use the case of the pronoun that you would use if you were completing the comparison. The complete version here would be *they are more conniving than we are conniving*, so the shortened form is *they are more conniving than we*.
29. **(B)** The awkwardness of the original sentence is removed by the construction *both of . . . and of . . .* used with parallel verbs.
30. **(C)** As a verb, *to loose* means "to set free."
31. **(D)** The present tense is used to express future time in subordinate clauses beginning with *if, when, after, before, until*, and *as soon as*.
32. **(A)** This sentence is correct.
33. **(C)** Use *neither* with *nor* and *either* with *or*.
34. **(D)** What is required is a grammatically sound and precisely worded revision. The adverb *luckily* is best placed at the beginning of the sentence. Choice (D) is best.
35. **(A)** The only choice that is not awkward and does not misrepresent the material given is choice (A).
36. **(C)** A comma cannot join two independent clauses as in sentence (6). Choice (C) corrects this error by replacing the comma with a semicolon. In choices (A) and (D), the words following the semicolon do not form an independent clause. The use of *being that* in choice (B) is incorrect. Choice (E) creates a fragment.
37. **(C)** The word *it* in sentence (9) has no clear reference. Choices (A) and (B) have the same problem. In addition, choice (A) has a fragment, and choice (B) has a comma splice error. Choices (D) and (E) change the intended meaning. Choice (C) correctly eliminates the vague *it* and makes it clear that these students had a language problem.
38. **(D)** Choices (A), (B), and (C) are poor since the antecedent of the pronoun *them* is not clear. Choice (E) is wrong since the sentence is awkwardly phrased. Choice (D) is best.
39. **(E)** The use of the pronouns *they* and *them* in sentences (13), (14), and (15) is not always clear. One is not certain to whom the pronoun refers. Often, a precise noun would be a better choice.

COMPUTING YOUR SCORES ON PSAT/NMSQT DIAGNOSTIC

To get a sense of how your performance on this diagnostic exam would be scored on a "real" PSAT/NMSQT, you first need to compute individual verbal, mathematical, and writing raw scores. Once you have computed these, use the conversion scales in the section that follows to compute your PSAT scaled scores (20–80). Keep in mind that these formulas have been simplified to give you a "quick and dirty" sense of where you are scoring, not a perfectly precise score.

To Compute Your Raw Scores:

1. Enter the number of correct answers for each verbal and mathematical reasoning section into the boxes marked "Number of Questions Correct."
2. Enter the number of incorrect answers (not blanks) for each verbal and mathematical reasoning section into the boxes marked "Number of Questions Incorrect."
3. Total the number correct and number incorrect.
4. Follow this formula: Take the total correct and minus one-quarter of the total incorrect. Round up in your favor to compute your Raw Score.

Verbal Section	Total Number of Questions	Number of Questions Correct	Number of Questions Incorrect
1	26		
3	26		
Totals	52	Total Correct:	Total Incorrect:

Verbal Raw Score = Total Correct − ($\frac{1}{4}$ × Total Incorrect) = _____

Math Section	Total Number of Questions	Number of Questions Correct	Number of Questions Incorrect
2	20		
4	20		
Totals	40	Total Correct:	Total Incorrect:

Math Raw Score = Total Correct − ($\frac{1}{4}$ × Total Incorrect) = _____

Writing Section	Total Number of Questions	Number of Questions Correct	Number of Questions Incorrect
5	39		
Totals	40	Total Correct:	Total Incorrect:

Writing Raw Score = Total Correct − ($\frac{1}{4}$ × Total Incorrect) = _____

To Compute Your Scaled SAT Score:

1. Add a "0" to the end of your mathematical and verbal scaled scores.

PINPOINTING RELATIVE STRENGTHS AND WEAKNESSES ON THE PSAT/NMSQT

VERBAL QUESTION TYPES

Sentence Completions

1. Count up the number of sentence completions you answered correctly (Section 1: 1–6 and Section 3: 27–33).
2. Write that number in the box marked "Number of Questions Correct."
3. Divide that number by the "Total Number of Questions" and write down your percentage in the shaded box.

Analogies

1. Count up the number of analogies you answered correctly (Section 1: 7–13 and Section 3: 34–39).
2. Write that number in the box marked "Number of Questions Correct."
3. Divide that number by the "Total Number of Questions" and write down your percentage in the shaded box.

Critical Reading

1. Go back through the exam's passages and count up the number of questions that you answered correctly.
2. Write that number in the box marked "Number of Questions Correct."
3. Divide that number by the "Total Number of Questions" and write down your percentage in the shaded box.

Type of Verbal Question	Number of Questions Correct	Total Number of Questions	Percent Correct (number correct/total)
Sentence Completions		13	
Analogies		13	
Critical Reading		26	

Compare these three percentages to assess your relative strengths and weaknesses within the subtopic areas of the PSAT verbal tests. If any individual percentage was considerably lower than others, you've found an area upon which you need to focus further study. To work on that area, read the appropriate strategy chapter in Part 3 and do the exercises.

If sentence completions and/or analogies gave you difficulty, you should work through Part 5 to upgrade your vocabulary. Learning vocabulary words is a critical step to improving on these sections of the PSAT.

MATH QUESTION TYPES

Multiple-Choice Math

1. Count up the number of multiple-choice questions you answered correctly (Section 2).
2. Write that number in the box marked "Number of Questions Correct."
3. Divide that number by the "Total Number of Questions" and write down your percentage in the shaded box.

Quantitative Comparisons

1. Count up the number of quantitative comparisons you answered correctly (Section 4: 21–32).
2. Write that number in the box marked "Number of Questions Correct."
3. Divide that number by the "Total Number of Questions" and write down your percentage in the shaded box.

Grid-Ins

1. Count up the number of grid-ins that you answered correctly (Section 4: 33–40).
2. Write that number in the box marked "Number of Questions Correct."
3. Divide that number by the "Total Number of Questions" and write down your percentage in the shaded box.

Type of Math Question	Number of Questions Correct	Total Number of Questions	Percent Correct (number correct/total)
Multiple Choice		20	
Quantitative Comparison		12	
Grid-In		8	

Compare these three percentages to assess your relative strengths and weaknesses within the math subject areas of the PSAT. If any individual section produced a percentage that is considerably lower than others, that question type deserves more of your preparation study and attention. To work on PSAT math subject areas, read the appropriate strategy chapter in Part 4 and do the exercises.

MATH SUBTOPICS

To get an even more in-depth look at your performance, look back at the answer key to the multiple-choice math questions (Section 2). You'll notice that each question has been subdivided into one of four categories—arithmetic, algebra, geometry, and other.

Arithmetic

1. Count up the number of arithmetic multiple-choice questions you answered correctly.
2. Write that number in the box marked "Number of Questions Correct."
3. Divide that number by the "Total Number of Questions" and write down your percentage in the shaded box.

Algebra

1. Count up the number of algebra multiple-choice questions you answered correctly.
2. Write that number in the box marked "Number of Questions Correct."
3. Divide that number by the "Total Number of Questions" and write down your percentage in the shaded box.

Geometry

1. Count up the number of geometry multiple-choice questions you answered correctly.
2. Write that number in the box marked "Number of Questions Correct."
3. Divide that number by the "Total Number of Questions" and write down your percentage in the shaded box.

Type of Math Subtopic	Number of Questions Correct	Total Number of Questions	Percent Correct (number correct/total)
Arithmetic		8	
Algebra		4	
Geometry		6	

Compare these three percentages to assess your relative strengths and weaknesses by mathematical subcategory. If an individual percentage is considerably lower than others, you've found an SAT math subtopic in which you need to concentrate further study. Read the appropriate math chapter in Part 6 and do the exercises.

WRITING SKILLS
Error Identifications

1. Count up the number of error identifications you answered correctly (Section 5: 1–19).
2. Write that number in the box marked "Number of Questions Correct."
3. Divide that number by the "Total Number of Questions" and write down your percentage in the shaded box.

Improving Sentences

1. Count up the number of sentence corrections you answered correctly (Section 5: 20–33).
2. Write that number in the box marked "Number of Questions Correct."
3. Divide that number by the "Total Number of Questions" and write down your percentage in the shaded box.

Improving Paragraphs

1. Count up the number of questions you answered correctly (Section 5: 34–39).
2. Write that number in the box marked "Number of Questions Correct."
3. Divide that number by the "Total Number of Questions" and write down your percentage in the shaded box.

Type of Writing Question	Number of Questions Correct	Total Number of Questions	Percent Correct (number correct/total)
Error Identifications		19	
Improving Sentences		14	
Improving Paragraphs		6	

Compare these three percentages to assess your relative strengths and weaknesses. If any individual percentage was considerably lower than others, you need to concentrate further study in that area.

MEASURING YOUR PROGRESS

As you visit chapters and do exercises, don't forget to compare your performance on those exercises with the verbal and mathematical percentages you calculated here. Down the road, you can also measure your progress very easily by comparing how did on this PSAT test with how you do on other practice SAT examinations. Remember: The difficulty levels of the PSAT and SAT are comparable.

Take note of whether you had difficulty finishing any particular part of the test. It might be that you are spending too long on certain questions and not allotting enough time for others. This should improve as you work through the strategy sections of this book and increase your familiarity with the test and question format. If you are worried about spending too long on particular question types, see Chapter 16 for a discussion of timing drills.

PART 9

The SAT and Beyond

PREVIEW

APPENDIX A	*Choosing the Right College*
APPENDIX B	*Applying to the College of Your Choice*
APPENDIX C	*Finding Financial Aid*
APPENDIX D	*Using Other Study Aids*

Appendix

Choosing the Right College

WHICH COLLEGE IS RIGHT FOR YOU?

Choosing a college is a long and arduous process—but it can also be a lot of fun.

You know that this will be one of the most important decisions you'll ever make. You're choosing where you're going to spend the next four (or more!) years of your immediate life, where you're going to learn the skills you'll need for your adult life, and where you'll meet friends you will cherish for *all* of your life. You don't want to make the wrong choice, but you still have to make *a* choice—and probably sooner than you'd like!

So, how do you determine which is the right college for you?

First, make sure you choose the college that offers the best mix of academics, environment, and extracurricular activities for your particular needs and wants. Don't choose a school just on its academic merits; remember, you'll be spending the next four years of your life there, so you better make sure you enjoy the non-academic life on campus, too!

You also have to take into account *where* the college is (how far away from your parents do you *really* want to be?) and *how much* it costs to attend. Your dream school might be too far away or simply cost too much to make it practical. (Although even if a college appears out of reach monetarily, you should always evaluate the potential for financial aid at that institution.)

If you have an idea of what career you wish to pursue after graduation, you should look for universities that are known for their excellence in the field that interests you. When comparing the merits of different schools, be sure to examine the caliber of the faculty, average class size in upper division courses, its academic reputation, and finally, the facilities. Visiting the prospective campus can be the most decisive factor in your choice of a school.

Even if a school meets *your* requirements, though, you might not meet *theirs*. You should examine the admissions requirements of each school that you are interested in very carefully to determine which ones offer the most

ROAD MAP

- *Find the college that's right for you*
- *Tips for campus visits— what to do and how to get the most from your trip*
- *Learn how to get student-views of the campus, online*
- *Use our college search sites list to find college home and information Web sites*

realistic opportunities for gaining admission. Consider the school's SAT and ACT standards, whether or not they require an interview, that sort of thing. Don't waste your time, money, or hope applying to schools that you have little, if any, chance of getting into.

In a nutshell, then, here are some of the key points to consider when choosing a college:

- **Size.** Are you more comfortable at a college (1,000–2,500 population), a small university (2,500–6,000), or a big university (7,000 and up)? Colleges and small universities might offer a more comfortable environment with more extracurricular comradery, while big universities offer more extracurricular activities, period—and more class and subject selection.
- **Location.** Do you prefer a school situated in a rural setting, a town, a small city, or a megalopolis. Does the location of the school in any way enhance the curriculum? How far away from home do you want to be—one hour, one gas tank, or one airplane ticket? How much will it cost you to travel home—and how often will you be making the trip? What are the local transportation options? Can you park a car on campus—or do you have to take the bus?
- **Curriculum.** Which is most important to you, a liberal arts, professional, or technical degree? What is the school known for? What are its academic strengths and weaknesses? Do they offer the courses and the degree track that you really want?
- **Faculty.** What percentage of the faculty has attained the terminal degree (Ph.D., masters, etc.) in their field? Are professors available to meet with students outside of their classrooms? How many classes will actually be taught by a professor, vs. a teaching assistant? Is there an academic advising program? What about tutoring?
- **Job placement.** What percentage of students have job offers when they graduate? What percentage of alums continue on to graduate school? How strong is the alumni network?
- **Admissions requirements.** Are they academically rigorous? Too much so? Can you pass muster—or can *too many others* pass muster?
- **Costs and financial aid.** Can you afford this particular institution? What financial aid can you obtain to help you afford it? Are there any "hidden" costs of living on this campus?
- **Housing/food.** Are there different types of on-campus housing options? Do you *have* to live in a dorm? With how many roommates? What off-campus housing is available? What about fraternities and sororities? What are your dining options? Just how bad is the dorm food? Where is the closest pizza place—and do they deliver?
- **Extracurricular activities.** What do you like to do *outside* of class? What sports activities are available for non-athletic majors? What about music, theater, and clubs? Where are the closest nightspots? What is the legal drinking age in that state?

- **Social atmosphere/student body.** Is this a fun place to live? Too much fun? Is the school known as a "party" campus? Is it elitist or populist? Are the students there people you'd choose to hang out with, given the choice?

How do find the answers to all these questions? There are numerous sources of information available to you, from official university brochures to comprehensive college selection Web sites. However, the best sources of information are often the college's students—and you can meet them either on campus or online.

TIPS ON VISITING CAMPUSES

You should try to visit as many schools as possible before deciding where to apply. This is helpful in many ways, especially if you get accepted into more than one school and have to choose between them. A campus visit is even more important if you're applying under an Early Decision Plan and must commit to that school if you're accepted. Remember, the school you choose is going to be your home for the next four to five years; make sure it's a place you really want to live.

Walking and talking, observing and interacting are things you can *only* do in person. Here are some things to look for when you visit a school:

- **Walk around.** By all means, check out the campus. Walk around, take in the sights. Does it seem cold and impersonal, or warm and friendly? Is this a campus you'll remember 20 years from now? Visit the student center, and find out what activities the university has to offer—free movies, games, lectures, etc. See whether or not the classrooms and lecture halls are relatively close together. Will you have to do a great deal of walking? What is the campus transportation like? How do you get to your favorite *off-campus* places for shopping, eating, drinking, and socializing?
- **Check out the weather.** What's the weather like? Learn the weather patterns of the area. What are the winters like? How cold does it get—and how much snow will you have to hike through between classes? How much rain can you expect? When does it start warming up—and how hot does it get? What about the humidity? Make sure that, weather-wise, this can be a comfortable place for you to live.
- **Visit the dorms.** Take a look at everything—the bathrooms, bedrooms, lounges, you name it. Are the rooms big enough? Are they clean? Quiet enough for studying? If possible, stay the night and take a trip to the dining hall and try the food. Can you keep it down? If there is more than one dorm or dining area, then check out several, and determine your preferences.
- **Visit the classrooms.** Stop by the departments that you might be majoring in, and pick up their course lists. Take the time to ask questions of the people working in each department. Find out a little about the first-year professors you might have.

TIP
Don't forget that you can get a lot of information about a college by checking out its campus newspaper. Almost every college journalism department produces a campus "rag." The school's Web site may have contact information for the campus newspaper, or you can ask the Admissions Office for information on how you can get a copy. While you're at it, find out the name of the local city newspaper and get a copy of it, too. You'll learn a lot from these papers about the cultural climate, the cost of living, and other critical aspects of the school's locale.

> **TIP**
>
> Whenever possible, contact the college admission's office a week or two ahead of time to arrange some portions of your on-campus visit. They'll send you a campus map, and they can help you set up meetings with faculty, give you directions to specific classrooms, or arrange for sleeping accommodations in a dorm. Don't worry—you don't have to turn over control of your visit to the admissions office. But their assistance can help make your visit more productive.

- **Talk to people!** Most importantly, stop and strike up conversations with some of the students. Ask them what they think about the school, their coursework, the social scene, the Greek system, the dorms, the dorm food, or anything else that you were wondering about. Find out from the students what are the best dorms, which places have the best pizza, where are the best parties, who are the best professors. Maybe you'll even make a few new friends and exchange phone numbers or e-mail addresses. Students are your best resource—use them!

When you do visit, visit during the school year, not during spring, summer, or Christmas break. You should also try to avoid making visits during midterms and finals, or during the first few weeks of a new school year, before students are truly settled in. Also, it's probably better to visit during the week, if you can; a lot of students go home on weekends, and the atmosphere isn't quite the same.

HANGING OUT WITH OTHER STUDENTS ONLINE

If you can't hang out with college students in person, you can do so online, in *Usenet newsgroups* and in *e-mail mailing lists*. Newsgroups and mailing lists are like topic-specific discussion groups where you post messages (called *articles*) and read articles posted by similarly-interested users; they're a great way to interact with others electronically.

USENET NEWSGROUPS

Usenet newsgroups are the easiest discussion forums to find and to use. Since Usenet is part of the Internet, you need a computer and Internet access to visit them. You'll also need a *newsreader* software program. Two of the most popular newsreader programs are **Microsoft Outlook Express** (included free with both Windows 98 and Microsoft Internet Explorer) and **Netscape Messenger** (included free with the Netscape Communicator suite, which also includes the Netscape Navigator Web browser). If you access the Internet via America Online, just go to the keyword **newsgroups** to use AOL's built-in newsreader.

Newsgroups are arranged in hierarchies, so that all "alternative" newsgroups start with **alt.**, and alternative newsgroups related to colleges start with **alt.college.**, and on down the hierarchy. Here are some of the better newsgroups to peruse:

- alt.college
- alt.college.food
- alt.college.fraternities
- alt.college.greek.organizations
- alt.college.sororities

- alt.college.us
- alt.education.higher.stu-affairs
- alt.penpals.college
- alt.student.affairs.net
- soc.college
- soc.college.admissions
- soc.college.financial-aid

E-MAIL MAILING LISTS

You can also communicate with college students through e-mail mailing lists. Mailing lists are like newsgroups, except you do all your message posting and reading via normal e-mail, and the lists are typically moderated (resulting in less unwanted "noise" and spam).

You can find a master list of all available mailing lists at the **Liszt** Web site (http://www.liszt.com); some of the more appropriate mailing lists for your needs include:

- **college_tips,** for students who want to share ideas that have improved their college life. For more information to *http://www.geocities.com/ CollegePark/Lab/1616/*.
- **fresch,** the weekly newsletter of scholarship and financial aid information. Go to http://users.plinet.com/~reisa/index.htm for more information.
- **noirsurblanc,** a list about higher education, universities, and students. For more information, send an e-mail to *noirsurblanc@sorengo.com* with the word **info** in the subject line of the message.
- **oncourse,** presenting innovative strategies for helping college students achieve their potential. For more information, send an e-mail to *majordomo@ari.net* with the phrase **info oncourse** in the subject line of the message.
- **studentactivism,** for students who want to become more active in issues affecting the world. For more information, go to *http://www.onelist.com/subscribe.cgi/studentactivism*.
- **student-parents,** for parents who are also students. Go to their Web site at *http://www.eGroups.com/list/student-parents/* for more information.
- **Students-Online,** for students and others interested in a variety of educational topics. To get more information, send an e-mail to *listcaster@listserv.rogersu.edu* with the phrase **info Students-Online** in the subject line of the message.

CHECK OUT COLLEGE AND STUDENT WEB PAGES

Almost every college has its own Web site. These sites often include a lot of good information about the school, the faculty, the classes, and the

> **TIP**
>
> Here's a quick way to find most schools' Web sites: In your browser, type *http:// www.college.edu/*, where *college* is the college's name or initials. For example, type *http:// www.duke.edu/* to connect to Duke University's Web site, or enter *http:// www.ucla.edu/* to go to UCLA's home page.

campus. In many cases you'll also be able to access individual student Web pages directly from the main college Web site.

To search for college Web sites, go to **Yahoo! College Search,** at *http:// features.yahoo.com/college.search.html*. Enter the name of the college you're looking for and click the **Find Colleges** button. You can also search for search for schools by major, location, enrollment, and "wiredness" (level of PC use on campus).

In addition to the official college Web sites, it's also fun and informative to check out the Web pages created by students of a particular college. While you can access some student pages from some college Web sites, you can also find listings of student pages at the following independent sites:

- **Personal Page Direct** *(http://www.student.com/feature/ppd/)*, from Student.com, listing more than 200,000 student Web pages.
- **Personal Pages Worldwide** *(http://www.utexas.edu/world/personal/ index.html)*, which links to collections of personal pages at colleges and universities worldwide.
- **Student Homepages** *(http://www.westegg.com/students/)*, listing student pages from more than 300 different colleges.

COLLEGE SEARCH SITES ON THE INTERNET

You'll also find dozens, if not hundreds, of sites on the Web devoted to helping you learn more about and choose a college. Here's just a small list of the best and/or most popular of these college selection sites.

- **Admissions Offices** *(http://www.yahoo.com/Education/ Higher_Education/College_Entrance/Admissions_Offices/)*, Yahoo's comprehensive list of links to college admissions offices across the U.S.
- **All About College** *(http://www.allaboutcollege.com)*, compiling thousands of links to college and university Web sites around the world. Includes admissions office e-mail addresses for most schools.
- **American College Entrance Directory** *(http://www.aaced.com)*, a site that lists and categorizes the most essential college entrance sites on the Internet.
- **Campus Tours** *(http://www.campustours.com)*, online virtual tours of thousands of college campuses, complete with interactive maps, college webcams, QuickTime VR tours, campus movies, and pictures. A great way to "tour" a school without actually being there!
- **College Base** *(http://library.advanced.org/17038)*, a site (created by two high school students!) that offers help for the SAT/ACT, a collection of college stories written by college students, and an appraisal section that evaluates colleges from the students' perspective.
- **College Board Online** *(http://www.collegeboard.org)*, the official Web site of the non-profit college organization that sponsors the SAT. Includes a College Search database of more than 3,200 two- and four-

year colleges, a Scholarship Search service, a Career Search service, and online prep for the SAT.

- **College Bound.net** *(http://www.cbnet.com)*, a resource that bills itself as "a student's interactive guide to college life," with sections like Money, College Profiles, Sports, and Food.
- **College E-Mail Addresses** *(http://www.qucis.queensu.ca/FAQs/college-e-mail/college.html)*, an extremely useful site that explains how to find e-mail addresses for undergraduate and graduate students, faculty, and staff at various colleges and universities.
- **The College Guide** *(http://www.pathfinder.com/money/colleges/)*, *Money* magazine's annual guide to the best buys in college educations.
- **College Is Possible** *(http://www.collegeispossible.org)*, a resource guide for parents, students, and education professionals, prepared by the Coalition of America's Colleges and Universities. A good reference for preparing for, choosing, and paying for college.
- **College Spot** *(http://www.collegespot.com)*, dedicated to helping high school students through the college selection and application process. Includes a college search engine, admissions info, scholarship info, and financial aid info.
- **College411** *(http://www.college411.org)*, a collection of links to other college-oriented Web sites.
- **CollegeDegree.com** *(http://www.collegedegree.com)*, which lists all available distance learning courses available at major colleges and universities.
- **CollegeEdge** *(http://www.collegeedge.com)*, with college planning advice, a campus tour, a scholarship search, a financial calculator, and an extensive careers and majors section. This site offers one of the most comprehensive college search databases with 5,850 two- and four-year colleges (plus vocational/technical schools) generating extensive (30+ pages) profiles of admissions, tuition, financial aid, curriculum, minority enrollment, and campus life. Make sure you check out the Pack and Go section, with advice on how to pack for school, what to do your first semester, and how to get along with your roommate.
- **CollegeNET** *(http://www.collegenet.com)*, offering school searches by major, location, and tuition. You can also search by state for four-year colleges and community, technical, and junior colleges. Includes virtual tours of selected colleges, complete with live "campus cams."
- **Colleges & Careers Center** *(http://www.usnews.com/usnews/edu/)*, from U.S. News Online. Includes a full-color Class Scheduler, a sophisticated College Planner to help you find the right college for you, a Find a Scholarship service, and the ability to compare up to four schools on features such as admissions, demographics, and financial aid. Most important, this is the source of the famous (or infamous) yearly College Rankings.
- **Colleges.com** *(http://www.colleges.com)*, a "virtual campus" that provides an online community for college students across the country. Sections include Entertainment, Academics, Sports, Music, Books, Games, Research, and Search Engines.

> **TIP**
> A warning about Web site addresses: They change. The Internet is a very active place, and Web page addresses can be ephemeral things. That's why it's important to familiarize yourself with general Internet search engines (such as Yahoo!, at *http://www.yahoo.com*) so that you can always find the information you want without the hassles of following a rabbit trail in cyberspace.

- **CollegeView** *(http://www.collegeview.com)*, with sections on financial aid, careers, resume writing, and interviewing, as well as a searchable database of all accredited colleges and universities in the U.S. and Canada. Includes an online self-assessment test to help you determine your best career options, as well as virtual tours of hundreds of schools.
- **CollegeXpress** *(http://www.collegexpress.com)*, profiling private and independent institutions (no state universities or community colleges). You can search for schools by location or programs offered, get an overview of financial aid and scholarships, and read about the admissions process. Includes a section for parents.
- **Critical Comparisons of American Colleges and Universities** *(http://www.memex-press.com/cc/)*, incorporating data from the U.S. Department of Education's IPEDS database, studies conducted by the National Research Council, and assorted crime statistics. Offers interactive graphs and statistical analyses to help you compare and contrast various schools.
- **The Education Network** *(http://www.ccounsel.com)*, offering general tips on applying and preparing for college. You can select colleges by state for a brief overview of a school's student body, favorite majors, basic admissions requirements, and tuition costs.
- **Educational Resources Information Center** *(http://www.accesseric.org)*, the site of the National Library of Education. Includes the ERIC Database, the world's largest source of education information, with more than 950,000 abstracts of documents and journal articles. This site also lets you access a large inventory of brochures for parents.
- **ETS Net** *(http://www.ets.org)*, the official site of the Educational Testing Service. Includes information on colleges and universities, careers and jobs, and disabilities and testing, as well as a variety of articles about colleges, college preparation, and college life.
- **Getting Ready for College Early** *(http://www.ed.gov/pubs/GettingReadyCollegeEarly/)*, an online handbook for parents of students in the middle and junior high school years, from the U.S. Government.
- **GoCollege** *(http://www.gocollege.com)*, offering a college search based on your desired major, test scores, class rank, location, and tuition. Includes free online SAT/ACT practice tests, and the capability to apply to 850 colleges directly online.
- **Kaplan** *(http://www.kaplan.com/precoll/)*, from the giant test prep company, with a site packed with free information, including several free newsletters, financial aid information, and a college search engine.
- **Mapping Your Future** *(http://mapping-your-future.org)*, which guides you from paying for school, selecting a school, and planning a career. Includes guided tours for middle and high school students, nontraditional students, and parents.
- **National Association for College Admission Counseling** *(http://www.nacac.com)*, a site created by the education association of secondary school counselors, college and university admission officers, and